W9-CCY-863

American Higher
Education in the
Twenty-First Century

American Higher Education in the Twenty-First Century

Social, Political, and Economic Challenges

SECOND EDITION

EDITED BY

Philip G. Altbach, Robert O. Berdahl, and Patricia J. Gumport

The Johns Hopkins University Press ❧ *Baltimore and London*

60.00

The Johns Hopkins University Press
2715 North Charles Street
Baltimore, Maryland 21218-4363
www.press.jhu.edu

Library of Congress Cataloging-in-Publication Data

American higher education in the twenty-first century : social, political, and
economic challenges / edited by Philip G. Altbach, Robert O. Berdahl, and
Patricia J. Gumport.— 2nd ed.
p. cm.
Includes bibliographical references and index.
ISBN 0-8018-8034-3 (hardcover : alk. paper) —
ISBN 0-8018-8035-1 (pbk. : alk. paper)
1. Education, Higher—Aims and objectives—United States. 2. Education,
Higher—Social aspects—United States. 3. Education, Higher—Political
aspects—United States. I. Altbach, Philip G. II. Berdahl, Robert Oliver.
III. Gumport, Patricia J.
LA227.4.A45 2005
378.73—dc22   2004013766

A catalog record for this book is available from the British Library.

➣ Contents

Part Two   External Forces

Part Three   The Academic Community

Part Four
Central Issues for the Twenty-First Century

American Higher
Education in the
Twenty-First Century

The Contexts of American Higher Education

*Robert O. Berdahl, Philip G. Altbach, and
Patricia J. Gumport*

This volume seeks to capture several critical dynamics in the higher-education/society nexus. Many aspects of the relationship between colleges and universities and their external environments have recently gained increased visibility in the media. Today one is surrounded by messages about the values of the free market. From society and the broader economy in general to the halls of academe in particular, we are assured that the correct path to improvement and prosperity is that of deregulation, decentralization, privatization, globalization, information technology (IT), reinventing government, total quality improvement (TQI), and the list goes on. We are forcefully told that getting power as close to the operational level as possible is the wisest mode of its application. We have also seen the emergence of for-profit providers, in part due to technological capabilities for distance education. Participants in these new ventures and even some observers advocate such new organizational forms that prioritize efficiency and expanded revenue-generating capacities. One consequence is that traditional institutional and state boundaries can no longer be presumed and may, according to these arguments, be rendered moot in discussions about designing alternative futures.[1] Clearly, American higher education is in a state of ferment! But, of course, this is nothing new. The list of issues above contrasts interestingly with those identified in the previous edition of this book:

multiculturalism in the curriculum, racially based admissions procedures, violence and hate crimes on campus, grade strikes waged by graduate student teaching assistants, accountability to the state, assessment of student learning, monitoring of faculty productivity, scientific misconduct and fraud, university/industry partnerships, technology transfer, university mismanagement of indirect cost funds, and most recently, budget cuts and downsizing mandates from state legislatures.

These issues, in turn, were built on earlier critiques of American higher education such as those of Allan Bloom's *The Closing of the American Mind* (1987) and Dinesh D'Souza's *Illiberal Education* (1991).[2] While the co-editors of this volume agree that no social institution should be considered above criticism, they should perhaps inform the readers that they do not perceive the recent broadsides to be balanced. Therefore, two of the co-editors (Altbach and Gumport) have edited another volume, *In Defense of American Higher Education* (2001), and the third co-editor (Berdahl) often cites two relevant publications: Robert Birnbaum's *Management Fads in Higher Education* (1999) and a paper he co-authored, "The 'Crisis' Crisis in Higher Education" (2001).[3] Birnbaum argues that movements such as PPBS, TQI, and Re-inventing Government have been tried in the broader society and have sometimes done some good but ultimately collapsed of their own shortcomings at about the time they were tried in higher education, with an equal lack of success. And in his "Crisis" piece, he sharply points out that persons of good will have been predicting higher education's decline and fall, not just for decades but also for centuries! American higher education certainly has its faults, but by any world or historical perspective, it has overall been doing a pretty good job under difficult circumstances.

This does not mean that persons should not continue to criticize American higher education but, rather, that such efforts should be carefully evaluated for what improvements they can offer and then carefully rebutted when they have overstepped the boundaries of accurate criticism. We hope that this volume will help readers make their own judgments about the present and future state of American higher education.

In a system of higher education as large and decentralized as that in the United States, it is difficult to analyze the cumulative record of twentieth-century strains and transitions comprehensively, much less reassess priorities so that higher education will survive and prosper. However, there is analytical utility in examining the affairs of colleges and universities within their changing social, political, and economic contexts. Accordingly, the editors of this volume and its contributors share a common view of colleges and universities as social institutions embedded in the wider society and subject to society's constraining forces.

In trying to assess the validity of criticisms of American higher education, it is helpful to bring a broader perspective to the process, and that is why this volume begins in Part One with chapters on American higher education in comparative world comparisons (which helps to show that other countries are also wrestling with at least some of our current problems) and on American higher education in historical dimensions (which helps to show that our universities and colleges have long been in some degree of tension with their surrounding societies). Part One also includes chapters on such fundamental issues as autonomy and accountability, academic freedom, and concludes with an overview chapter on the emerging issues facing higher education in the new century.

Part Two, "External Forces," includes chapters analyzing the roles of the major external constituencies: the federal government, the state governments, the court system, and the nongovernmental elements.

Part Three, "The Academic Community," provides coverage of the internal constituencies: the faculty, the students, and the presidency.

Part Four, "Central Issues for the Twenty-First Century," offers more detailed analysis of several key issues: finance, technology, graduate education, the curriculum, race, and what Derek Bok has recently termed the *commercialization of higher education*.[4]

We have, in effect, posed macro questions like the following to ourselves and our contributors: Given our casting of universities and colleges as social institutions, what are they like today? What forces, either unique to our era or continuing from the past, are shaping higher education? What is the future of higher education, in the context of twenty-first-century America?

Universities as Social Institutions

Universities—and by extension many four-year and two-year postsecondary institutions—have generally had ambivalent relations with their surrounding societies—both involved and withdrawn, both servicing and criticizing, both needing and being needed. Eric Ashby identifies the central dilemma of this ambivalence: a university "must be sufficiently stable to sustain the ideal which gave it birth and sufficiently responsive to remain relevant to the society which supports it."[5]

The medieval universities of Europe developed as supranational institutions under the jurisdiction of a distant pope and operating in a uniform cultural milieu, which allowed them to combine practical learning for the "higher" vocations or professions with a search for universal truths. Later, when nation-states replaced the Catholic Church as the dominant authority over universities, the latter were often able to retain significant autonomy. Clark Kerr noted how remarkably stable many of these medieval universities have proven: "About eighty-five institutions in the Western World established by 1520 still exist in recognizable forms, with similar functions and with unbroken histories, including the Catholic Church, the Parliaments of the Isle of Man, of Iceland and of Great Britain, several Swiss Cantons and seventy universities."[6]

Of course, it was easier for a nation to grant its universities autonomy when only a small proportion of its youth were attending, when students were not going much beyond the trivium and the quadrivium in their curriculum, and when few, if any, state funds were involved. In the nineteenth century, however, three developments were to occur that would increase tension between autonomy and accountability. First, beginning in German universities and spreading to universities in other Western countries was the notion of the importance of science and research in higher education. Governments began to see the links among universities, economic growth, and military strength. Second, the Morrill Land-Grant Act of 1862 in the United States broadened the curriculum to include the agricultural and mechanical arts. This led to the diversification of higher education institutions, a larger and more heterogeneous student body, higher state costs, and the notion of university public service. The American pattern, like the German, eventually spread to other countries. Third, the public and governments grew reluctant to increase public spending, which led to increased accountability on the part of higher education institutions and to a constraint on their growth.

Martin Trow shows how the autonomy/accountability dichotomy has changed as higher education has moved from an "elite" system to a "mass" system—that is, from educating less than 15 percent of the college-age cohort to educating between 15 and 50 percent of it.[7] Trow also examines the probable consequences of another transition, to "universal access," which has been tried in only a few states.[8]

In the present era, questions have arisen about the usefulness of mass access and about whether higher education is a public good, which primarily benefits society and which, therefore, merits public expenditure, or whether it is a private good, which directly benefits the individual, who should therefore bear the cost.[9] Some have come to see higher education as a "mature industry," in which expansion will be slow; basic assumptions about the nature of the academic enterprise will focus on stability rather than on growth.[10]

A Matter of Definitions

The terms *autonomy* and *accountability* at first glance do not seem to present semantic problems. Taken most simply, *autonomy* means the power to govern without outside controls, and *accountability* means the requirement to demonstrate responsible actions to external constituencies. In theory, there is not necessarily incompatibility between being both highly autonomous and rigorously accountable. However, in practice, in cases in which more accountability is required, less autonomy remains. The ideal would seem to be a balance of both. Too much autonomy might render universities unresponsive to society, while too much accountability might destroy the academic ethos.

The dilemma, however, is more complicated. For example, given academic complaints about "intrusions" into institutional autonomy, one would like to know what the action in question is; academic freedom and institutional autonomy are not the same, and the academy's reactions should reflect this distinction. We need to distinguish among three concepts of autonomy:

—*Academic freedom* is the freedom of the individual scholar to pursue truth wherever it leads, without fear of punishment or of termination of employment for having offended some political, methodological, religious, or social orthodoxy.
—*Substantive autonomy* is the power of the university or college in its corporate form to determine its own goals and programs (the *what* of academe).

—*Procedural autonomy* is the power of the university or college in its corporate form to determine the means by which its goals and programs will be pursued (the *how* of academe).

These three concepts are obviously interrelated; for example, a college enjoying substantive and procedural autonomy would normally be better able to protect the academic freedom of its faculty (although autonomous Oxford and Cambridge in the early nineteenth century denied academic freedom to their faculty, whereas nonautonomous Berlin University became known for its *Lehrfreiheit,* or academic freedom). Along another dimension, onerous procedural government controls would seriously hinder a college's ability to achieve its chosen goals. Notwithstanding such blurring of categories in real life, an examination of relations between higher education and government will be helped by distinguishing these three concepts.

Ashby envisions academic freedom as an "internationally recognized and unambiguous privilege of university teachers, which must be protected whenever and however challenged," even though "the question as to what constitutes autonomy in universities is anything but unambiguous, and the patterns of autonomy which satisfy academics in different countries are very diverse."[11] Therefore, in exploring autonomy issues it is helpful to clarify whether the intervention is in *procedural* or *substantive* matters. Intervention in procedural matters (preaudits and controls over purchasing, personnel, and some aspects of capital construction) can be an enormous bother to academe and often even counter to efficiency, but it does not usually prevent colleges or universities from achieving their goals. In contrast, governmental actions that affect substantive goals compromise the very essence of academe. What is needed in this sensitive area is negotiation of the roles of government and universities, leading to a division of powers and a decision on which one will make which decisions relating to academe. For Ashby, the real safeguard for autonomy lies in ensuring that the "essential ingredients" of autonomy "are widely understood among the public, politicians, and civil servants":[12]

— The freedom of universities to select staff and students and to determine the conditions under which they remain in the university.
— The freedom of universities to determine curriculum content and degree standards.
— The freedom of universities to allocate funds (within the amounts available) across different categories of expenditures.

The definition of *accountability* must also be examined. To speak of demonstrating "responsible actions" begs the following questions: What constitutes such actions? Who determines the form and content of the reporting process? What are the sanctions for inadequate performance? In addition to furnishing information on planning, programs, and budgets to justify public tax funds before the fact, colleges and universities are also held accountable after the fact. There are at least three ways in which postaudits can be conducted (for legality, for efficiency, and for effectiveness), with varying consequences. Traditionally, governmental postaudits have focused on legality and efficiency and, through such concerns, have exerted considerable pressure on colleges and universities to tighten their operational procedures. Normally, such pressures have not forced institutions to alter their substantive goals; however, a performance audit aspect of the accountability movement has arisen at the state level that focuses on the effectiveness of the policy area being examined. If extended more deeply into academe, this development could greatly affect its substantive dimensions.[13]

Three lessons arise from this discussion. First, governments ought to stay away from issues that threaten the academic freedom of persons undertaking teaching and research at colleges and universities. Second, governmental procedural controls are probably counterproductive and certainly irritating but do not justify the same academic outrage as legitimate threats to academic freedom. Third, in the crucial domain of substantive autonomy, government and universities must form a partnership wherein—while force majeure obviously lies with the former—sensitive mechanisms reconcile state concerns with accountability and academic concerns with autonomy. In the U.S. federal system, the primary governmental interface for most public sector institutions—and some private sector ones as well—lies at the level of state government.

Cooperation, Coordination, and Consolidation

At least three major modes of resolution can be envisaged: bottom-up voluntary cooperation, top-down consolidated governance, or an intermediate form of statutory coordination that goes beyond cooperation but stops short of consolidated governance.

Comparative experience suggests that voluntary cooperation is normally unable to make tough decisions because the voluntary association usually operates on a principle of near unanimity, and objection from a threatened party usually halts the association's progress. Fred Harcleroad's chapter illustrates the many valuable ends that may be accomplished when universities and colleges cooperate, but such collaborative ventures have not usually included making difficult decisions. The consortium movement in the United States and the history of the British Committee of Vice-Chancellors and Principals (now Universities UK) bear witness to the limits of interinstitutional cooperation. Certain goals can be accomplished, but disagreements over serious issues cannot usually be overcome.

While authority to resolve differences between academic and governmental perspectives could be obtained through a political decision to merge all universities into one consolidated university, again, comparative perspectives suggest that this response could lead to too much accountability and too little autonomy. Those states in which such consolidation has occurred do exhibit top-down retrenchment, and this retrenchment often appeals to those who yearn for a simple method of accountability. But these states also often exhibit excessive centralization of power and a preoccupation with details of governance at the expense of careful planning and coordination.

Having revealed both voluntary cooperation and consolidated governance as ineffective in taking into account the legitimate perspectives of both academe and government in the area of substantive autonomy, we are left with coordination as the most desirable (or least undesirable) means of accomplishing this vital process.

Coordination: Political, Bureaucratic, Academic, and Market

A state that honors academic freedom and resists inappropriate procedural controls may nevertheless harm its system of higher education by intervening in substantive matters. The structure, function, membership, and staffing of the mediating agency thus become crucial. In discussing the role of such an agency as potentially a "suitably sensitive mechanism" in its responsibilities for coordination, we must heed Burton Clark's warning against treating the coordination process too narrowly, as only a function of a bilateral government/institutional relationship. In an insightful article entitled, "The Many Pathways of Academic Coordination," Burton Clark urges that, to the traditional political and bureaucratic modes of coordination, we add those modes emanating from the academic profession and the market. After being ignored by political analysts as major factors in the development of U.S. universities and colleges, the market and privatization are now being so aggressively pushed that excessive claims are being advanced on their behalf. What may be desirable for the economies of Central and Eastern European countries after decades of communist control may not be desirable for U.S. universities and colleges, which operate in a very different social, political, and economic context:

> The special function of political coordination is to articulate a variety of public interests . . . as these are defined by prevailing groups within and outside of government. The special function of bureaucratic coordination is to compose a formal system out of fragmented parts and to provide fair administration. The function of academic oligarchy is to protect professional self-rule, to lodge the control of academic work, including its standards, in the hands of those permanently involved and most intimately connected with it. And the special function of the market is to enhance and protect freedom of choice, for personnel, clientele, and institutions and thereby indirectly promote system flexibility and adaptability.[14]

The proportions of each mode of coordination vary markedly from one system to another. For example, earlier in Britain, British academics had a pervasive role in making the system function behind the formal facade of the secretary of state for the Department of Education and Science, the civil servants in that department, and the University Grants Committee. Similarly, in the United States, a fundamental role was played by market forces based on student choice and fortified by institutional, state, and national student financial aid programs.

The simplified arguments connected with each of these modes of coordination run as follows:

—Political and bureaucratic coordination tends to overdo accountability and to be insensitive to academe's needs for flexibility and creativity.
—Collegial or academic coordination may be preoccupied with the protection of autonomy and unresponsive to the public interest.
—Coordination by market forces may promote responsiveness to social demand while relieving public authority of the burden and blame for deciding which programs and which institutions may

survive during a period of retrenchment, but it may compromise the integrity of the university as the purveyor of truth and knowledge.

Thus, one is left with Clark's observation that most systems partake of varying degrees of the elements of coordination. What may be a correct balance for one system may not be appropriate for another system; and indeed, what may be correct for one system at one stage in its development may not be correct for that same system at another stage. There is no theoretical model for the correct balance at a given time, so we are left with making subjective judgments based upon common sense and upon both conscious and unconscious biases.

We are concerned in this book not only with how specific governmental actions affect the administration of postsecondary education but also with how broader societal forces impact the entire academic community. Unraveling the web of relationships between higher education and society is paramount to understanding the academic enterprise and all that goes on within it. We hope that the following chapters will help readers make up their own minds about many of the pressing issues covered.

NOTES

1. A key voice arguing the merits of the market approach is Robert Zemsky. Co-authoring with Susan Shaman and Daniel Shapiro, he published *Higher Education as a Competitive Enterprise,* New Directions for Institutional Research, no. 111 (San Francisco: Jossey-Bass, 2001). D. T. Seymour was one of many voices urging higher education to discover the merits of the total quality process: *On Q: Causing Quality in Higher Education* (New York: American Council on Education/Macmillan, 1992).

2. Allan Bloom, *The Closing of the American Mind* (New York: Simon and Schuster, 1987); Dinesh D'Souza, *Illiberal Education* (New York: Free Press, 1991).

3. Philip G. Altbach, Patricia J. Gumport, and D. Bruce Johnstone, eds., *In Defense of American Higher Education* (Baltimore: Johns Hopkins University Press, 2001). Robert Birnbaum, *Management Fads in Higher Education* (San Francisco: Jossey-Bass, 1999); Robert Birnbaum and Frank Shushok, Jr., "The 'Crisis' Crisis in Higher Education," in *In Defense of American Higher Education,* eds. Philip G. Altbach, Patricia Gumport, and D. Bruce Johnstone.

4. Derek Bok, *Universities in the Marketplace: The Commercialization of Higher Education* (Princeton: Princeton University Press, 2003).

5. Eric Ashby, *Universities: British, Indian, African* (Cambridge: Harvard University Press, 1966), 3.

6. Clark Kerr, *The Uses of the University* (Cambridge: Harvard University Press, 1982), 152.

7. Martin Trow, "Problems in the Transition from Elite to Mass Higher Education," in *Policies for Higher Education* (Paris: Organization for Economic Co-operation and Development, 1974).

8. Universal access means that no one is prevented from going to college for lack of resources or institutions; in some states, more than 50 percent of high school graduates go on to postsecondary institutions.

9. David W. Breneman, "The 'Privatization' of Public Universities: A Mistake or a Model for the Future?" *Chronicle of Higher Education,* Mar. 7, 1997.

10. Arthur Levine, "Higher Education's New Status as a Mature Industry," *Chronicle of Higher Education,* Jan. 31, 1997.

11. Ashby, *Universities,* 292.

12. Ibid., 296.

13. J. Folger and R. Berdahl, *Patterns in Evaluating Systems of Higher Education: Making a Virtue out of Necessity* (College Park, Md.: National Center for Postsecondary Governance and Finance, 1987).

14. Burton Clark, "The Many Pathways of Academic Coordination," *Higher Education* 8 (1979): 251–68.

 **Part One**

The Setting

Chapter One

Patterns in Higher Education Development

Philip G. Altbach

Universities áre singular institutions. They have common historical roots yet are deeply embedded in their societies. Established in the medieval period to transmit knowledge and provide training for a few key professions, in the nineteenth century universities became creators of new knowledge through basic research.[1] The contemporary university is the most important institution in the complex process of knowledge creation and distribution, serving as home not only to most of the basic sciences but also to the complex system of journals, books, and databases that communicate knowledge worldwide.[2] Universities are key providers of training in an ever growing number of specializations. Universities have also taken on a political and cultural function in society, serving as centers for the civil society. At the same time, academe is faced with unprecedented challenges, stemming in large part from a decline in resources. After almost a half century of dramatic expansion worldwide, universities in many countries are being forced to cut back on expenditures and, in some cases, to downsize. The unwritten pact between society and higher education that provided expanding resources in return for greater access for students as well as research and service to society has broken down, with significant implications for both higher education and society.

This chapter is concerned with the patterns of higher education development evident in the post–World War II period throughout the world, analyzing some of the reasons for these trends and pointing to likely directions for universities in the coming decades. Issues such as autonomy and accountability, research and teaching, reform and the curriculum, and the implications of the massive expansion of universities in most countries are of primary concern.

A Common Heritage

There is only one common academic model worldwide. The basic European university model, established first in Italy and France at the end of the twelfth century, has been significantly modified but remains the universal pattern of higher education. The Paris model placed the professor at the center of the institution and enshrined autonomy as an important part of the academic ethos. It is significant that the major competing idea of the period, the student-dominated University of Bologna, did not gain a major foothold in Europe, although it had some impact in Spain and later in Latin America.[3] The university rapidly expanded to other parts of Europe—Oxford and Cambridge in England, Salamanca in Spain, Prague and Krakow in Central Europe—and a variety of institutions in the German states were established in the following century.

Later, the European imperialist nations brought universities to their colonies, along with other accoutrements of colonialism. The British, for example, exported academic models first to the American colonies and later to India, Africa, and Southeast Asia.[4] The French in Vietnam and West Africa, the Spanish and the Portuguese throughout Latin America, the Dutch in Indonesia, the Americans in the Philippines, and other colonial powers also exported academic institutions.[5] Colonial universities were patterned directly on institutions in the metropole but often without the traditions of autonomy and academic freedom in the mother country.[6]

The university has by no means been a static institution but has changed and adapted to new circumstances. With the rise of nationalism and the Protestant Reformation in Europe, the universal language of higher education, Latin, was replaced by national languages. Academic institutions became less international and more local in their student bodies and orientations and were affected by their national circumstances, Protestant Amsterdam differing, for example, from Catholic Salamanca. Harvard University, although patterned on British models, slowly developed its own traditions and orientations, reflecting the realities of colonial North America. Academic institutions have not always flourished. Oxford and Cambridge, strongly linked to the Church of England and the aristocracy, played only a minor role in the industrial revolution and the tremendous scientific expansion of the late eighteenth and nineteenth centuries.[7] In France, universities were abolished after the revolution, in 1793; gradually, they were reestablished, and the Napoleonic model became a powerful force not only in France but also in Spain and Latin America.[8] German universities, which were severely damaged during the Nazi period by the destruction of autonomy and the departure of many professors, lost their scientific preeminence.[9]

For the purposes of this chapter, two more recent modifications of the Western academic model are relevant. In the mid-nineteenth century, a newly united Germany harnessed the university for nation building. Under the leadership of Wilhelm von Humboldt, German higher education was given significant resources by the state, took on the responsibility for research aimed at national development and industrialization, and played a key role in defining the ideology of the new German nation.[10] German universities also established graduate education and the doctoral degree. For the first time, research became an integral function of the university, and the university was reorganized as a hierarchy based on the newly emerging scientific disciplines. American reformers further transformed higher education by stressing the relationship between the university and society through the concept of service and direct links with industry and agriculture. They also democratized the German chair system, through the establishment of academic departments, and developed the land-grant concept for both research and expanded access to higher education.[11] Thus, even institutions that seem deeply embedded in national soil have in fact been influenced by international ideas and models.

Virtually without exception, the institutional pattern followed by the world's universities derives from these Western models. Significantly, in one of the few remaining fully non-Western institutions, Al-Azhar University in Cairo, which focuses mainly on traditional Islamic law and theology, science faculties are now organized along European lines.[12] There are many variations of the Western model —open universities, two-year vocational institutions, teacher training colleges, polytechnics—but while the functions of these institutions differ from those of traditional universities, their basic organization, pattern of governance, and ethos remain remarkably close to the Western academic ideal.[13]

Networks of Knowledge and Higher Education

There are many explanations for the dominance of the Western academic model. The institutionalization of the study of science and, later, scientific research are central elements. The link between universities and the dominant world economic systems no doubt is an important reason for Western hegemony. In many parts of the world, academic institutions were imposed by colonizers, and there were few possibilities to develop independent alternatives. Indigenous institutional forms were destroyed, as in nineteenth-century India with the British imposition of European patterns.[14] None of the formerly colonized nations have shifted from their basically European academic model; the contemporary Indian university, for example, resembles its preindependence predecessor.

Japan, which was never colonized, recognized after 1868 that it had to develop scientific and industrial capacity and jettisoned its traditional academic institutions in favor of Western university traditions, importing ideas and models from Germany, the United States, and other countries. Other noncolonized nations, such as China and Thailand, also imported Western models and adapted them to local needs and conditions.[15]

The harnessing of higher education to the broader needs of national economic and social development was perhaps the most important innovation of this era. Western universities were seen as successful in providing advanced education, fostering research and scientific development, and assisting their societies in the increasingly complex task of development. Universities in both the United States and Germany fostered industrial and agricultural development. The idea that higher education should be supported by public funds, that the university should participate in the creation as well as the transmission of knowledge, and that academic institutions should at the same time be permitted a degree of autonomy was behind much of the growth of universities in the nineteenth century. Further, Western universities were at the center of a knowledge network that included research institutions, the means of knowledge dissemination such as journals and scientific publishers, and an "invisible college" of scientists. As science became more international, a common scientific language emerged, first German, and since the mid-twentieth century, English. Even scholars in such industrialized nations as Sweden and the Netherlands often communicate their research findings in English. The large Dutch multinational publishers Elsevier and Kluwer publish virtually all of their scholarly and scientific books and journals in English.

The circulation of scholars and students worldwide—even the so-called brain drain—is an element of the international knowledge system, helping to circulate ideas and also maintaining the research hegemony of the major host countries. More than one and one-half million students study outside their home countries, the large majority of them from Third World nations and the newly industrializing countries of the Pacific rim. They are studying in the industrialized nations, especially the United States, Britain, France, and Germany. Japan is both a major sending and major receiving country.[16]

As a result of their sojourns abroad, students gain expertise in their studies but also learn the norms and values of the Western academic system, often returning home with a zeal to reform their local universities. Frequently, foreign graduates have difficulty readjusting to their home countries, in part because the advanced training they acquire abroad may not be easily assimilated into less industrialized economies. Such frustrations, along with significantly better remuneration in industrialized countries, lead to the brain drain. However, in the contemporary world, brain drain is often not permanent. Members of the Third World scientific diaspora maintain contact with their colleagues at home, contributing advanced knowledge and ideas.[17] They often return home for periods of time to work with local academics and, increasingly, return home permanently, when conditions are favorable. These returning students bring with them to their native countries considerable expertise and often assume leadership positions in the local scientific and academic communities. With few exceptions, knowledge and institutional patterns are transferred from the major industrialized nations to the Third World —or even to more peripheral industrial countries—with very little traffic in the other direction.[18]

The knowledge network is complex and multifaceted; while its centers remain extraordinarily powerful, there is a movement toward greater equalization of research production and use. Japan, for example, already has a powerful and increasingly research-oriented uni-

versity system, and some of the newly industrializing countries of
East and Southeast Asia are building research capacity in their universities, with China playing a particularly important role.[19] But while
hegemony may be slowly dissipating, inequality remains endemic in
the world knowledge system.

Expansion: Hallmark of the Postwar Era

Postsecondary education has expanded since World War II in virtually
every country in the world. This growth has, in proportional terms,
been more dramatic than that of primary and secondary education.
Writing in 1975, Martin Trow spoke of the transition from *elite* to
mass and then to *universal* higher education in the context of the industrialized nations.[20] The United States enrolled some 30 percent of
the relevant age cohort (eighteen- to twenty-two-year-olds) in higher
education in the immediate postwar period, while European nations
generally maintained an elite higher education system, with fewer
than 5 percent attending postsecondary institutions. By the 1960s,
many European nations were educating 15 percent or more of the age
group; in 1970, Sweden enrolled 24 percent, France 17 percent. That
year, the United States increased its proportion to more than 50 percent and was approaching universal access. By the end of the twentieth century, most Western European countries had increased their
enrollment rates to about half, thus reaching close to "universal" access. Thus, while American patterns of access have stabilized, Europe
and many newly industrializing countries continue to expand.

In the Third World, expansion has been even more dramatic. Building on tiny and extraordinarily elitist universities, Third World higher
education expanded rapidly in the immediate postindependence period. In India, enrollment grew from approximately 100,000 at the
time of independence, in 1947, to more than 4 million in the 1990s.
Expansion in sub-Saharan Africa has also been rapid, with the postsecondary student population growing from 181,000 in 1975 to more
than 1.7 million two decades later. Expansion continues despite economic crisis and the AIDS epidemic. There has been a decline in per
capita student expenditure and this has contributed to a decline in
academic standards.[21]

Similar trends can be seen among other non-Western countries. In
a few instances, such as the Philippines, where more than one-third

of the age cohort enters postsecondary education, enrollment ratios have reached those of industrialized nations, although in general the Third World lags far behind in terms of proportion of the population attending higher education institutions. Even China, with more than 14 million students in postsecondary education (approximately the same number as the United States) enrolls only 15 percent of the age group. Expansion in the Third World has, in general, exceeded that in the industrialized nations, at least in proportional terms. Among the highest rates of expansion and participation are in Asian newly industrializing countries, such as South Korea and Taiwan, and recently in Latin America as well.

Regardless of political system, level of economic development, or educational ideology, the expansion of higher education has been the single, most important trend worldwide. About 7 percent of the relevant age cohort attends postsecondary educational institutions, a statistic that has increased each decade since World War II. Higher education expanded first in the United States, then in Europe, and later in the Third World and the newly industrializing countries. Women now constitute approximately 40 percent of university enrollment, with considerable variation by country. The industrialized nations, with a few exceptions, have a higher proportion of the age cohort in postsecondary education than Third World countries. Generalized statistics concerning enrollments in postsecondary education mask many key differences. For example, industrialized nations have, in general, a higher proportion of students in technological and scientific fields than in liberal arts, which tend to predominate in the developing nations—although even here there are exceptions, such as China.

There are many reasons for the expansion of higher education, a central one being the increasing complexity of modern societies and economies, which demands a more highly trained workforce. Almost without exception, postsecondary institutions have been called upon to provide the required training. Indeed, training in many fields that was once imparted on the job has become formalized in institutions of higher education. Whole new fields, such as computer science, have come into existence and rely on universities as a source of research and training. Nations now developing scientific and industrial capacity, such as South Korea and Taiwan, as well as emerging agents China and India, depend on academic institutions to provide high-level training as well as research expertise.[22]

Not only do academic institutions provide training, they also test and provide certification for many occupations in contemporary society. These roles have been central to universities since the medieval period but have been vastly expanded in recent years. A university degree is a prerequisite for an increasing number of occupations in most societies. Indeed, academic certification is necessary for most positions of power, authority, and prestige in modern societies, which places immense power in the hands of universities. Tests to gain admission to higher education are rites of passage in many societies and are important determinants of future success.[23] Competition within academe varies from country to country, but in most cases stress is also placed on high academic performance and tests. There are often further examinations to permit entry into specific professions.

The role of the university as an examining body has grown for a number of reasons. As industrial and economic expansion has taken place, more sorting mechanisms have been needed. The older, more informal, and often more ascriptive means of controlling access to prestigious occupations no longer provide the controls needed, nor are they perceived as fair. Universities are seen as meritocratic institutions, which can be trusted to provide impartial tests to measure accomplishment and, therefore, to determine access. When such mechanisms break down—as they did in China during the Cultural Revolution—or when they are perceived as subject to corrupt influences—as in India—universities are significantly weakened. Furthermore, entirely new fields have developed for which no sorting mechanisms exist, and academic institutions are frequently called upon to provide not only training but also examination and certification.

Expansion has also occurred because the growing segments of the population of modern societies demand it. The middle classes, seeing that academic qualifications are necessary for success, demand access to higher education, and governments generally respond by increasing enrollment.[24] When governments do not move quickly enough, private initiative frequently establishes academic institutions to meet the demand. In countries like India, the Philippines, and Bangladesh, as well as in many Latin American nations, a majority of the students are educated in private colleges and universities.[25] At present, there are powerful worldwide trends toward imposing user fees in the form of higher tuition charges, increasing the stress on private higher education, and in general considering higher education as a private good, in economic terms. These changes are intended to reduce the cost of postsecondary education for governments while maintaining access, although the long-term implications for the quality of, access to, and control over higher education remain unclear.

In most societies, higher education is heavily subsidized by the government, and most, if not all, academic institutions are in the public sector. While there is a growing trend toward private initiative and management sharing responsibility with public institutions, governments will likely continue to be a central source of funding for postsecondary education. The dramatic expansion of academic institutions in the postwar period has proved very expensive for governments. Nonetheless, the demand for access has been extraordinarily powerful.[26]

Many analysts writing in the 1960s assumed that the world, and particularly Western industrialized nations, would move from elite to mass and finally to universal access to higher education, generally following the American pattern. But the path to universal access has proved to be circuitous.[27] For a period in the 1970s, expansion slowed, only picking up again in the late 1980s. The nations of the European Union are in general moving toward U.S. levels of access. The causes for the slowdowns were in part economic, given the problems in the Western economies that followed the oil shocks of the 1970s; in part demographic, resulting from a significant drop in the birth rate and a smaller cohort of young people; and in part philosophical, as countries became less sympathetic to the growth of public institutions, including universities. Generally, the proportion of the age cohort going on to higher education in Western Europe stabilized at under 20 percent in the 1970s; it began to increase again in the late 1980s and continues to expand.[28] This expansion has taken place in a context of steady population trends and has been impelled by changes in European economies, which have moved to the postindustrial stage. By 2003, most Western European countries were sending half of their age group on to postsecondary education.

In sharp contrast to Western industrialized countries, Third World universities have, in general, continued to expand without interruption. With only a very few exceptions, such as the Philippines, Third World enrollment ratios remain significantly lower than those in the industrialized nations, but there continues to be a strong commitment to continued expansion and access. This is the case even in countries like India, where there is severe unemployment of graduates and a brain drain of university graduates. In many Third World countries, it remains impossible for local universities to absorb all of those qualified to attend, creating an exodus of students abroad. This is the case in, for example, Malaysia.[29] As in the industrialized nations, there is a notable trend toward shifting the burden of funding for higher education from the state to the individual.

The Third World presents a special set of circumstances. Unmet demand, an expanding middle class, and continuing population growth in many countries mean that the bulk of the world's higher education growth in the coming decades will be in developing countries. Many of these countries are building more complex economies that require more skilled workers, and this too contributes to expansion. Even if political authorities wanted to slow expansion, they would find it impossible to do.

General agreement that postindustrial economies need large numbers of university graduates means that participation rates in the industrialized world will continue to expand. At the same time, the retirement of the large cohort of people hired in the 1960s will open additional highly skilled jobs. At the same time, demographic trends will limit the need for more university places.[30]

Change and Reform: The Legacy of the Sixties

The demands placed on institutions of higher education to accommodate larger numbers of students and to expand their functions resulted in reforms in higher education in many countries. Much debate has taken place concerning higher education reform in the 1960s, and a significant amount of change did take place.[31] Without question, the student unrest of the period contributed to disarray in higher education. This unrest was in part precipitated by deteriorating academic conditions, which were the result of rapid expansion. In a few instances, students demanded far-reaching reforms in higher education, especially an end to the rigid, hierarchical organization of the traditional European university.[32] The chair system was modified or eliminated, and the responsibility for academic decision making, formerly a monopoly of full professors, was expanded—in some countries, to include students. At the same time, the walls of the traditional academic disciplines were broken down by interdisciplinary teaching and research.

Reform was greatest in several traditional Western European academic systems. Sweden's universities were completely transformed:

decision making was democratized, universities were decentralized, educational access was expanded to previously underserved parts of the country, interdisciplinary teaching and research was instituted, and the curriculum was expanded to include vocational courses.[33] Reforms also took place in France and the Netherlands, where reformers stressed interdisciplinary studies and the democratization of academic decision making. In Germany, the universities in states dominated by the Social Democratic Party were also reformed, with the traditional structures of the university giving way to more democratic governance patterns.

In the 1990s, the major trend in restructuring European universities has been improving administrative efficiency and accountability. Many of the reforms of the 1960s were modified or even eliminated. Students, for example, have less power now. In the Netherlands, national restructuring increased the power of administrators. Similar trends can be seen in Germany, Sweden, and other countries.

In many industrialized nations, structural change was modest. In the United States, for example, despite considerable debate during the 1960s, there was very limited change in the structure or governance of higher education.[34] Japan, where unrest disrupted higher education and spawned a number of reports on university reform, experienced virtually no basic change in its higher education system, although several "new model" interdisciplinary institutions were established, such as the science-oriented Tsukuba University near Tokyo. Britain, less affected by student protest and with a plan for expansion in operation, also experienced few reforms during the 1960s.[35] Some of the changes implemented at that time have been abandoned. In Germany, reforms in governance that gave students and junior staff a dominant position in some university functions were ruled unconstitutional by German courts.[36]

Many of the structural reforms of the 1960s were abandoned after a decade of experimentation or were replaced by administrative arrangements that emphasized accountability and efficiency. Outside authorities, such as government—but also including business, industry, and labor organizations—came to play a more important role in academic governance. Curricular innovations have proved more durable; interdisciplinary programs and initiatives and the introduction of new fields such as gender studies remain.

At the end of the twentieth century, there was a second wave of reforms evident worldwide. These reforms can be characterized as a "managerial revolution" in higher education, where the overall goal was to ensure more accountability and efficiency in the management of academic institutions. These reforms generally increased the power of administrators and reduced faculty authority and, in the public sector, provided for more supervision by government authorities. These changes were stimulated both by the growing size and complexity of many academic institutions and systems and by a desire to rein in expenditures. Efforts were made to privatize elements of public institutions and, in some countries, to stimulate the private sector in higher education.

Vocationalization has been an important trend in the past two decades. Throughout the world, there is a conviction that the university curriculum must provide relevant training for a variety of increasingly complex jobs. Students, worried about obtaining remunerative employment, have pressed universities to focus more on job preparation. Employers have also demanded that the curriculum become more relevant to their needs. Enrollment in the social sciences and humanities, at least in industrialized nations, has declined.

Curricular vocationalism is linked to another worldwide trend in higher education: the increasingly close relationship between universities and industry.[37] Industrial firms have sought to ensure that the skills they need are incorporated into the curriculum. This trend also has implications for academic research, since many university/industry relations are focused largely on research. Industries have established formal linkages and research partnerships with universities to obtain help with research of interest to them. In countries such as Sweden, representatives from industry have been added to the governing councils of higher education institutions. In the United States, formal contractual arrangements have been made between universities and major corporations to share research results. In many industrialized nations, corporations provide educational programs for their employees, sometimes with the assistance of universities.

Technical arrangements with regard to patents, confidentiality of research findings, and other fiscal matters have assumed importance as university/industry relations have become crucial. Critics also point out that the nature of research in higher education may be altered by this relationship, as industrial firms are not usually interested in basic research. University-based research, which has traditionally been oriented toward basic research, may be increasingly skewed to applied and profit-making topics. There has also been some discussion of research orientation in fields like biotechnology, in which broader public policy matters may conflict with the needs of corporations. Specific funding arrangements have also been questioned. Pressure to serve the training and research requirements of industry has implications for the organization of the curriculum, the nature and scope of research, and the traditional relationship between the university and society.[38]

The traditional idea of academic governance stresses autonomy, and universities have tried to insulate themselves from the direct control of external agencies. However, as universities expand and become more expensive, there is immense pressure by those providing funds for higher education—mainly governments—to expect accountability. The conflict between autonomy and accountability has been a flashpoint for controversy in recent years. Without exception, university autonomy has shrunk, and administrative structures have been put into place in such countries as Britain and the Netherlands to ensure greater accountability.[39] The issue takes on different implications in different parts of the world. In the Third World, traditions of autonomy have not been strong, and demands for accountability, both political and economic, sometimes mean government domination of academe.[40] In the industrialized nations, accountability pressures are usually more fiscal in nature.

Despite the varied pressures on higher educational institutions for change and the significant reforms that have taken place in the past two decades, there have been few structural alterations in universities. One of the few places where this has occurred is Sweden. Elsewhere, curricula have been altered, expansion has taken place, and there have been continuing debates concerning accountability and autonomy, but universities as institutions have not changed significantly. As Edward Shils has argued, the "academic ethos" has been under strain, and while in some ways it has been weakened, it has so far survived.[41]

The Millennium

The university is a durable institution. The modern university retains key elements of the historical models from which it sprang even while evolving to serve the needs of societies during a period of tremendous change.[42] There has been a convergence of ideas and institutional pat-

terns and practices in higher education, due in part to the implan-
tation of European-style universities in developing areas during and
after the colonial era and in part to universities' having been crucial
to the development and internationalization of science and scholarship. Many of the changes discussed here are the result of great external pressure and were instituted despite opposition from within the
institution. Some scholars argue that the university has lost its soul.[43]
Others claim that the university is irresponsible because it uses public
funds without meeting the needs of industry and government. Pressure from governmental authorities, militant students, and external
constituencies have all placed great strains on academic institutions.

The period since World War II has been one of unprecedented
growth in universities, and higher education has assumed an increasingly central role in virtually all modern societies. While growth may
continue, the dramatic expansion of recent decades is at an end, at
least in the industrialized countries. It is unlikely that the position of
the university as the most important institution for training in virtually all of the top-level occupations in modern society will be weakened, although other institutions have become involved in training.
The university's research role is more problematical because of the
fiscal pressures of recent years. There is no other institution that
can undertake basic research, but the consensus that has supported
university-based basic research has weakened.[44]

The challenges facing universities are, nonetheless, significant.
The following issues are among those that will be of concern in the
coming decade and beyond.

Access

Access remains a controversial issue in most countries. Worldwide,
higher education is more readily available to wealthier segments of
the population. With expansion, the demand has broadened, and providing access to lower-income groups is a challenge, especially in the
context of fiscal constraints in higher education. Even in the United
States, where access is relatively open regardless of social class because of a highly differentiated higher education system and govern-
ment-sponsored loan and grant programs, some racial and ethnic minorities remain underrepresented in the student population. There
is greater inequality of access in Western Europe, although there is
widespread commitment to broaden participation. In much of the rest

of the world, the lack of participation of those with low incomes, rural youths, and in some countries, women remains a central issue. Access remains a challenge of both concern and controversy.

Administration, Accountability, and Governance

As academic institutions become larger and more complex, there is increasing pressure for professional administration, as in the United States. At the same time, the traditional forms of academic governance are increasingly criticized for being unwieldy and, in large and bureaucratic institutions, inefficient. As the administration of higher education increasingly becomes a profession, an "administrative estate" will be established. Growing demands for accountability will cause academic institutions considerable difficulty. And as academic budgets expand, there will be inevitable demands to monitor and control expenditures. At present, no general agreement exists concerning the appropriate level of governmental involvement in higher education. The challenge will be to ensure that the traditional—and valuable—patterns of faculty control over governance and basic academic decisions are maintained in a complex and bureaucratic environment. Worldwide, the rise of "managerialism" and ever more complex bureaucratic arrangements is part of the academic landscape. So far, the trend is for traditional governance to lose authority and power.

Knowledge Creation and Dissemination

Research is a central part of the mission of many universities and of the academic system generally. Decisions that will be in contention in the future will concern the control and funding of research, the relationship of research to the broader curriculum and teaching, the uses made of university-based research, and related issues. Further, the system of knowledge dissemination, including journals and books and computer-based data systems, is rapidly changing. Who should control the new data networks? How will traditional means of communication, such as journals, survive in this new climate? How will the scientific system avoid being overwhelmed by the proliferation of data?[45] Who will pay for the costs of knowledge dissemination? The needs of peripheral scientific systems, including both the Third World and smaller academic systems in the industrialized world, have been largely ignored but are, nonetheless, important.[46]

Information technology (IT) has become a central element of the knowledge distribution network. Individual scientists and scholars use the Internet for direct communication. Databases accessible on the World Wide Web are increasingly important. Libraries use a greater number of electronic resources to access journals and other kinds of information and data. Issues such as the ownership of knowledge, the cost of access to electronic networks, and the influence of new electronic journals and other publications, among others, remain to be determined. At present, publishers and other data providers in the United States and other English-speaking countries stand to gain most from the new technologies. The effect on academic institutions, especially in developing countries, remains unclear in terms of access and cost.

Major Western knowledge producers currently constitute a kind of cartel of information, dominating not only the creation of knowledge but also most of the major channels of distribution. Simply increasing the amount of research and creating new databases will not ensure a more equal and accessible knowledge system. Academic institutions are at the center, but publishers, copyright authorities, funders of research, and others are also necessarily involved.

The Academic Profession

In most countries, the professoriate has been under great pressure in recent years. Demands for accountability, the increased bureaucratization of institutions, fiscal constraints in many countries, and an increasingly diverse student body have all challenged the professoriate. In most industrialized nations, a combination of fiscal problems and demographic factors led to a stagnating profession.[47]

Circumstances vary by region, but some factors are evident worldwide. Fiscal problems create multiple difficulties. Remuneration has not kept up with either cost of living or salaries offered elsewhere in the economy, and it is now difficult to lure the "best and brightest" to academe. The terms of academic appointments have deteriorated in many places—tenure has been abolished, for example, in Britain, and in many countries, a larger proportion of the profession is part time. Traditional career ladders have been modified. Class sizes have increased and academic autonomy has been limited. Pressures on the professoriate, not only to teach and do research but also to attract external grants, do consulting, and earn additional income for themselves and for their universities have grown. The difficulties faced by the academic profession in developing countries are perhaps the greatest—to maintain a viable academic culture under deteriorating conditions and without the protection of established norms.

Private Resources and Public Responsibility

In almost all countries there has been a growing emphasis on increasing the role of the private sector in higher education. One of the most direct manifestations of this trend is the role of the private sector in funding and directing university research. In many countries, private academic institutions have expanded or new ones have been established. Students are paying an increasing share of the cost of their education as a result of tuition and fee increases and through loan programs. Governments try to limit their expenditures on postsecondary education. Privatization has been the means of achieving this broad policy goal.[48] Inevitably, decisions concerning academic developments will move increasingly to the private sector, with the possibility that broader public goals may be ignored. Whether private interests will support the traditional functions of universities—including academic freedom, basic research, and a pattern of governance that leaves the professoriate in control—is unclear. Some of the most interesting developments in private higher education can be found in such countries as Vietnam, China, and Hungary, where private institutions have recently been established. Private initiatives in higher education will bring a change in values and orientation, but it is not clear that these values will be in the long-term best interests of the university. At the beginning of the twenty-first century, the major expansion of higher education worldwide is taking place in the private sector.

Diversification and Stratification

While diversification—the establishing of new postsecondary institutions to meet diverse needs—is not new, it is of primary importance and will continue to reshape the academic system. In recent years, the establishment of research institutions, community colleges, polytechnics, and other academic institutions designed to meet specialized needs and to serve specific populations has been a primary characteristic of growth. At the same time, the academic system has become

more stratified—individuals in one sector of the system find it difficult to move to a different sector. There is often a high correlation between social class (and other variables) and participation in a particular sector. To some extent, the reluctance of traditional universities
to change is responsible for some of the diversification. Perhaps more
important is the belief that limited-function institutions are more efficient and less expensive. An element of diversification is the inclusion
of larger numbers of women and other previously disenfranchised
segments of the population. Women now constitute 40 percent of the
student population worldwide and more than half in many industrialized countries.[49] In many countries, students from lower socioeconomic groups and racial and ethnic minorities have entered postsecondary institutions in significant numbers.

Economic Disparities

The substantial inequalities among the world's universities and academic systems are likely to grow. Major universities of the industrialized nations generally have the resources to play a leading role in
scientific research, in a context in which it is increasingly expensive
to keep up with the expansion of knowledge.[50] Universities in much of
the Third World, however, simply cannot cope with the increased enrollments, budgetary constraints, and in some cases, fiscal disasters.
Universities in much of sub-Saharan Africa, for example, have experienced dramatic budget cuts and find it difficult to function, not to
mention to improve quality and compete in the international knowledge system.[51] Academic institutions in the Asian newly industrializing countries, where significant academic progress has taken place,
will continue to improve. Thus, the economic prospects for postsecondary education worldwide are mixed.

Conclusion

Universities share a common culture and a common reality: in many
basic ways, there is a convergence of institutional models and norms.
At the same time, there are significant national differences that will
continue to affect the development of academic systems and institutions. It is unlikely that the basic structures of academic institutions
will change dramatically: the Humboldtian academic model will sur-

vive, although administrative structures will grow stronger and the traditional power and autonomy of the faculty will diminish. Open universities and other distance education institutions may provide new institutional arrangements, and efforts to save money may yield further organizational changes. Unanticipated change is also possible; while the emergence of significant student movements, at least in industrialized nations, do not seem likely, circumstances may change.[52] The situation for universities in the first part of the twenty-first century are not, in general, favorable. The realities of higher education as a "mature industry" in industrialized countries, with stable rather than growing resources, will affect not only the funds available for postsecondary education but also academic practices. Accountability, the impact of technologies, and the other forces discussed in this chapter will all affect colleges and universities, although patterns will vary. Some academic systems, especially those in the newly industrializing countries, will continue to grow. In parts of the world affected by significant political and economic change, the coming decades will be ones of reconstruction. Worldwide, the coming period is one of major challenge for higher education.

NOTES

I am indebted to Robert Arnove, the late Gail P. Kelly, and Lionel Lewis for their comments on an early version of this chapter and to Lalita Subramanyan and Patricia Murphy for their help with editing.

1. For a historical perspective, see Charles Haskins, *The Rise of Universities* (Ithaca: Cornell University Press, 1957).

2. Philip G. Altbach, *The Knowledge Context: Comparative Perspectives on the Distribution of Knowledge* (Albany: State University of New York Press, 1987).

3. For further discussion of this point, see A. B. Cobban, *The Medieval Universities: Their Development and Organization* (London: Methuen, 1975).

4. The history of British higher education expansion in India and Africa is described in Eric Ashby, *Universities: British, Indian, African* (Cambridge: Harvard University Press, 1976).

5. See Philip G. Altbach and Viswanathan Selvaratnam, eds., *From Dependence to Autonomy: The Development of Asian Universities* (Dordrecht, Netherlands: Kluwer, 1989).

6. Irene Gilbert, "The Indian Academic Profession: The Origins of a Tradition of Subordination," *Minerva* 10 (1972): 384–411.

7. For a broader consideration of these themes, see Lawrence Stone, ed., *The University in Society,* 2 vols. (Princeton: Princeton University Press, 1974).

8. Joseph Ben-David, *Centers of Learning: Britain, France, Germany, the United States* (New York: McGraw-Hill, 1977), 16–17.

9. Friedrich Lilge, *The Abuse of Learning: The Failure of the German University* (New York: Macmillan, 1948).

10. Charles E. McClelland, *State, Society, and University in Germany, 1700–1914* (Cambridge: Cambridge University Press, 1980). See also Joseph Ben-David and Awraham Zloczower, "Universities and Academic Systems in Modern Societies," *European Journal of Sociology* 3 (1962): 45–84.

11. In the German system, a full professor was appointed as head (chair) of each discipline, and all other academic staff served under his direction; the position was permanent. Many other countries, including Japan, Russia, and most of Eastern Europe, adopted this system. On developments in America, see Laurence Veysey, *The Emergence of the American University* (Chicago: University of Chicago Press, 1965); E. T. Silva and S. A. Slaughter, *Serving Power: The Making of the Academic Social Science Expert* (Westport, Conn.: Greenwood, 1984).

12. For a discussion of the contemporary Islamic university, see H. H. Bilgrami and S. A. Ashraf, *The Concept of an Islamic University* (London: Hodder and Stoughton, 1985).

13. Philip G. Altbach, "The American Academic Model in Comparative Perspective," in *Comparative Higher Education,* ed. Philip G. Altbach (Greenwich, Conn.: Ablex, 1998), 55–74.

14. See David Lelyveld, *Aligarh's First Generation: Muslim Solidarity in British India* (Princeton: Princeton University Press, 1978).

15. Michio Nagai, *Higher Education in Japan: Its Take-off and Crash* (Tokyo: University of Tokyo Press, 1971). See Altbach and Selvaratnam, *From Dependence to Autonomy,* for case studies of Asian universities.

16. See Philip G. Altbach, David Kelly, and Y. Lulat, *Research on Foreign Students and International Study: Bibliography and Analysis* (New York: Praeger, 1985).

17. Hyaeweol Choi, *An International Scientific Community: Asian Scholars in the United States* (Westport, Conn.: Praeger, 1995).

18. The number of American students studying abroad is only a small proportion of the number of foreign students studying in the United States, and the large majority of Americans who do study in other countries go to Canada and Western Europe. See also Robert Arnove, "Foundations and the Transfer of Knowledge," in *Philanthropy and Cultural Imperialism,* ed. Robert Arnove (Boston: Hall, 1980).

19. For a discussion of higher education development in the newly industrializing countries, see Philip G. Altbach et al., *Scientific Development and*

Higher Education: The Case of Newly Industrializing Countries (New York: Praeger, 1989).

20. Martin Trow, "Problems in the Transition from Elite to Mass Higher Education," paper prepared for a conference on mass higher education held by the Organization for Economic Cooperation and Development, 1975.

21. See Task Force on Higher Education and Society, *Higher Education in Developing Countries: Peril and Promise* (Washington, D.C.: World Bank, 2000).

22. Altbach et al., *Scientific Development and Higher Education.*

23. Max A. Eckstein and Harold J. Noah, "Forms and Functions of Secondary School Leaving Examinations," *Comparative Education Review* 33 (1989): 295–316.

24. Academic institutions serve as important sorting institutions, sometimes diverting students from highly competitive fields. See, for example, Steven Brint and Jerome Karabel, *The Diverted Dream: Community Colleges and the Promise of Educational Opportunity in America, 1900–1985* (New York: Oxford University Press, 1989).

25. Roger L. Geiger, *Private Sectors in Higher Education: Structure, Function, and Change in Eight Countries* (Ann Arbor: University of Michigan Press, 1986). For a focus on Latin America, see Daniel C. Levy, *Higher Education and the State in Latin America: Private Challenges to Public Dominance* (Chicago: University of Chicago Press, 1986). See also Philip G. Altbach, ed. *Private Prometheus: Private Higher Education and Development in the 21st Century* (Westport, Conn.: Greenwood, 2000).

26. World Bank, *Education in Sub-Saharan Africa* (Washington, D.C.: 1988), strongly argues against continued expansion of higher education, believing that scarce educational expenditures could be much more effectively spent on primary and secondary education. See also D. Bruce Johnstone, *Sharing the Costs of Higher Education: Student Financial Assistance in the United Kingdom, the Federal Republic of Germany, France, Sweden and the United States* (Washington, D.C.: College Board, 1986).

27. Trow, "Problems in Transition."

28. See Ladislav Cerych and Paul Sabatier, *Great Expectations and Mixed Performance: The Implementation of Higher Education Reforms in Europe* (Trentham, England: Trentham Books, 1986), pt. 2.

29. Jasbir Sarjit Singh, "Malaysia," in *International Higher Education: An Encyclopedia,* ed. Philip G. Altbach (New York: Garland, 1991).

30. There are also significant national variations. For example, Britain under Margaret Thatcher's leadership consistently reduced expenditures for postsecondary education, with significant negative consequences for higher education. See, for example, Sir Claus Moser, "The Robbins Report 25 Years After: And the Future of the Universities," *Oxford Journal of Education* 14 (1988): 5–20.

31. For broader considerations of the reforms of the 1960s, see Cerych and Sabatier, *Great Expectations*; Ulrich Teichler, *Changing Patterns of the Higher Education System* (London: Kingsley, 1989); Philip G. Altbach, ed., *University Reform: Comparative Perspectives for the Seventies* (Cambridge, Mass.: Schenkman, 1974).

32. For an example of an influential student proposal for higher education reform, see Wolfgang Nitsch et al., *Hochschule in der Demokratie* (Berlin: Luchterhand, 1965).

33. Jan Erik Lane and Mac Murray, "The Significance of Decentralization in Swedish Education," *European Journal of Education* 20 (1985): 163–72.

34. See Alexander W. Astin et al., *The Power of Protest* (San Francisco: Jossey-Bass, 1975), for an overview of the results of the ferment of the 1960s on American higher education.

35. "The Legacy of Robbins," *European Journal of Education* 14 (1988): 3–112.

36. For a critical viewpoint, see Hans Daalder and Edward Shils, eds., *Universities, Politicians, and Bureaucrats: Europe and the United States* (Cambridge: Cambridge University Press, 1982).

37. See, for example, "Universities and Industry," *European Journal of Education* 20 (1985): 5–66.

38. Of course, this is not a new concern for higher education. See Thorstein Veblen, *The Higher Learning in America: A Memorandum on the Conduct of Universities by Business Men* (New York: Viking, 1918).

39. See Klaus Hufner, "Accountability," in *International Higher Education: An Encyclopedia,* ed. Philip G. Altbach (New York: Garland, 1991).

40. Philip G. Altbach, "Academic Freedom in Asia: Learning the Limitations," *Far Eastern Economic Review,* June 16, 1988.

41. Edward Shils, *The Academic Ethic* (Chicago: University of Chicago Press, 1983).

42. See Ben-David and Zloczower, "Universities and Academic Systems."

43. See, for example, Robert Nisbet, *The Degradation of the Academic Dogma: The University in America, 1945–1970* (New York: Basic Books, 1971). Allan Bloom, in his *The Closing of the American Mind: How Higher Education has Failed Democracy and Impoverished the Souls of Today's Students* (New York: Simon and Schuster, 1987), echoes many of Nisbet's sentiments.

44. In those countries that have located much of their research in nonuniversity institutions, such as the academies of sciences in Russia and some Central and Eastern European nations, there has been some rethinking of this organizational model, a sense that universities may be more effective locations for major research. Since the collapse of the Soviet Union, there have been some moves to abolish the academy model. See Alexander Vuci-

nich, *Empire of Knowledge: The Academy of Sciences of the USSR (1917–1970)* (Berkeley: University of California Press, 1984).

45. See Thomas W. Shaughnessy et al., "Scholarly Communication: The Need for an Agenda for Action—A Symposium," *Journal of Academic Librarianship* 15 (1989): 68–78. See also *Scholarly Communication: The Report of the National Commission* (Baltimore: Johns Hopkins University Press, 1979).

46. These issues are discussed in Altbach, *The Knowledge Context.* For a different perspective, see Irving Louis Horowitz, *Communicating Ideas: The Crisis of Publishing in a Post-Industrial Society* (New York: Oxford University Press, 1986).

47. For an American perspective, see Martin Finkelstein, Robert Seal, and Jack H. Schuster, *The New Academic Generation: A Profession in Transformation* (Baltimore: Johns Hopkins University Press, 1998).

48. Levy, *Higher Education.* See also Geiger, *Private Sectors in Higher Education.*

49. Gail P. Kelly, "Women in Higher Education," in *International Higher Education: An Encyclopedia,* ed. Philip G. Altbach (New York: Garland, 1991).

50. A possible exception to this situation are universities in Britain, where a decade of financial cuts by the Thatcher government sapped the morale of the universities and made it difficult for even such distinguished institutions as Oxford and Cambridge to continue top-quality research. See Geoffrey Walford, "The Privatization of British Higher Education," *European Journal of Education* 23 (1988): 47–64.

51. World Bank, *Education in Sub-Saharan Africa* (Washington, D.C.: World Bank, 1988), 68–81.

52. For a survey of student movements, see Philip G. Altbach, ed., *Student Political Activism: An International Reference Handbook* (Westport, Conn.: Greenwood, 1989).

Chapter Two

The Ten Generations of American Higher Education

Roger L. Geiger

We study the history of higher education because things change and because some things do not change. Continuity is evident in individual institutions in which circumstances or self-images of origin and development continue to influence current conditions. Basic forms persist as well, perhaps most notably in the intractable centrality of the American college. Issues also recur, particularly those concerned with curriculum, institutional mission, and student development. But change also is an irreducible reality and must, by its nature, be analyzed in a temporal dimension. The key elements here are understanding the processes of change and aggregating such changes to discern fundamental transformations in the entire system of higher education. This last element forms the premise of the analysis that follows: that the character of American higher education has perceptibly shifted in each generation, or approximately every thirty years. The exploration of these successive generations is intended to illuminate these historical dynamics as well as the underlying processes of which they are composed.

The ten generations of American higher education, from the founding of Harvard to the current era, are characterized here in terms of what was taught, the experience of students, and the array of institutions. Extant knowledge is screened by institutions and their faculty for certified acceptance into the curriculum. That curriculum, in turn, has an implied relationship with subsequent uses. The place of higher education in the lives of students can be captured in the phrase "origins and destinations." The expansive nature of American higher education has meant that student origins have tended to be broad and diverse. Yet, expectations about ultimate destinations have largely motivated college attendance, and these same expectations have inspired crucial interventions by third parties—whether governments, churches, foundations, or individuals. Between origins and destinations lies the college experience itself, certainly one of the most critical variables. Finally, there is the institutional order—all the institutions offering higher education and their internal makeup. This scheme is intended to be heuristic, highlighting central features for monitoring change over time without excluding any factors impinging on higher education.

Generation 1: Reformation Beginnings, 1636–1740s

Each of the first three colleges in the British colonies of America was unique, but all may be described as "schools of the Reformation."[1] Harvard, William and Mary, and Yale were established as adjuncts of their respective churches, which in turn were integrally related to their respective civil governments. The long head start enjoyed by Harvard gave it a special, settled character. A true product of the Wars of Religion when it was chartered in 1636, it evolved in the eighteenth century into a more cosmopolitan and tolerant institution. This evolution away from strict Calvinism reflected the spreading heterodoxy of Puritan society and the support of the more secular and mercantile elements in that community. William and Mary was formally linked with the Church of England. Its founder, James Blair, and his successors were titular heads of the church in Virginia. William and Mary did not offer regular collegiate instruction until the 1740s. It then embodied the relative tolerance of official Anglicanism, a stance congenial to the planter families who governed the colony.[2] Only Yale preserved and cultivated the sectarian zeal of the Reformation era into the middle of the eighteenth century.

Some original features persisted long after the Reformation era. External governance was a natural outgrowth of viewing the colleges as an emanation of the polity. Both Harvard and William and Mary had dual structures, consisting of corporations and boards of overseers or visitors. Yale was guided by a single board, originally consisting of ten Congregational ministers, but it looked to the General Assembly of Connecticut for financial support and legal backing.[3] This combination of provincial authority external to the college and the clerical authority lodged within it generated recurring conflicts. Control of Harvard was contested among old-line Puritans and more liberal Congregationalists. Yale's minister-trustees, left to themselves, could not agree where to locate the college. And at William and Mary, the inability of the board of visitors to control the faculty was a perpetual problem. All three colleges nevertheless received financial support from their respective colonies.

A relatively powerful college president eventually emerged as the natural complement to lay authority. A circumscribed role remained to be played by the faculty of tutors, who were usually recent graduates preparing for the ministry. The curriculum of the colleges in this era was little changed from that of the Middle Ages. Its aim was to provide students with a liberal education, which meant facility with classical languages, grounding in the three basic philosophies of Aristotle—ethics, metaphysics, and natural philosophy or science—and a smattering of general worldly knowledge. In order to be admitted, students had to show some knowledge of Latin, a bit of Greek, and arithmetic. The first two years were spent for the most part mastering the classical languages and, particularly, achieving a working knowledge of Latin. Philosophy, general subjects, and divinity were taught in the final two years. Although these colleges lagged well behind Europe, the education offered was a practical one for the seventeenth and early eighteenth centuries, when most learned texts were in Latin. The process of education was undoubtedly as valuable as the content. The collegiate way of living and the constant presence of tutors gave students complete immersion in a learning environment. Composing declamations and engaging in disputations inculcated a facility with language that was indispensable to the oral public culture they would enter.

The founding documents of all three schools speak to the aim of educating ministers. Indeed, except at William and Mary, this was the chief expectation associated with college matriculation. Actual ministerial training, nevertheless, followed upon a liberal education. Nearly two-thirds of the graduates of seventeenth-century Harvard entered the ministry. But nonministerial students were both welcomed and expected. William and Mary sought to make youths "piously educated in good Letters and Manners"; and the founders of

Yale intended to provide education "for Publick employment both in Church & Civil State."[4]

The nexus between college and the ministry would erode slowly during the eighteenth century. Under John Leverett (1708–24), Harvard already possessed a clientele of young gentlemen who took scant interest in studies or piety. At William and Mary, where a ministerial career required a journey to England for ordination, most sons of the Virginia gentry sought only a patina of liberal education, and almost none graduated.

Harvard surmounted the narrow role of a Reformation college in another way by the third decade of the eighteenth century. Gifts from Thomas Hollis created two professorships, in divinity (1721) and in mathematics and natural philosophy (1727). The hiring of individuals who could specialize over the years in a single field of knowledge overcame an important curricular limitation. By the next generation, learned professors in addition to young tutors would be sought by the colonial colleges.[5]

Generation 2: Colonial Colleges, 1745–1775

The mold of Reformation colleges was broken with the founding of the College of New Jersey in 1746. A compromise between Presbyterians and the colony of New Jersey produced a board of trustees having twelve ministers, ten laymen, and the governor of the colony as ex officio presiding officer. The college was rooted in the colony yet served a far wider constituency of Presbyterians; it was denominational in nature yet tolerant of other Protestant sects. The next four colleges to be founded followed this same pattern of "toleration with preferment," although for somewhat different reasons. King's College (1754), as an Anglican founding, had to assuage fears of institutionalizing a state religion. The College of Philadelphia (1755), successor to the academy that Benjamin Franklin had helped to found, continued the tradition of toleration in a context of considerable religious diversity. Baptists, too, believed in toleration, even while insisting upon control over the College of Rhode Island (1765). New Hampshire's eagerness to have a provincial college, above all, prompted it to entice Eleazer Wheelock to found Dartmouth (1769). Only the creation of Queen's College (1771), by and for the Dutch Reformed community, introduced an exclusive (and unsuccessful) model at the end of this period.[6]

Harvard and William and Mary also conformed to the new model of provincial colleges. Yale under Thomas Clap (1740–66), however, resisted this form in the name of doctrinal purity but, in doing so, demonstrated that the theocratic ideal of the Reformation was no longer tenable. Clap's rearguard action to defend Yale against the doctrines of the Great Awakening, against an Anglican presence in Connecticut, and finally against the Connecticut General Assembly ended, ironically, when he lost control of the college to rebellious students.

On the eve of the Revolution, the colonial colleges enrolled nearly 750 students, but three-quarters of them attended the four oldest colleges.[7] The latter, in particular, exemplified instruction that had become more secular in curriculum and purpose. Fewer than half of the graduates of Princeton pursued careers in the ministry. In the small but vital urban centers of the colonies, a sizable class of gentlemen now existed, consisting of professional men and successful merchants. At King's College perhaps 40 percent of the students originated from that milieu, and the proportion at Harvard may well have been higher. Still, many students clearly came from more humble circumstances, chiefly sons of farmers. They no doubt were more likely to be destined for the ministry, while gentlemen's sons more typically followed the path that led to law and public life.[8]

At the outset of this period, the curriculum was an incoherent amalgam of works predicated on both the old, theocentric universe and the new, enlightened views reflecting the writings of John Locke and Sir Isaac Newton. The doctrines of the "Moderate Enlightenment" gradually prevailed.[9] The enlightened spirit also included a more thorough teaching and appreciation of the classical authors. Latin and Greek thus remained at the heart of the curriculum, but Latin ceased to be a language of instruction. Classical authors introduced the generation of the Founding Fathers to the political forms and lessons of the ancient world. Scottish "common-sense philosophy," as taught by John Witherspoon (1768–95) at Princeton, reconciled Christian doctrines and the new knowledge. Students also received more competent instruction in these decades as college teaching became a settled occupation, attracting men of genuine learning.[10]

In sum, during the colonial generation the colleges balanced duties to both church and province, offered a richer and more secular intellectual fare, and served, among others, a constituency of aspiring gentlemen. The new nation soon called upon them to make a still larger contribution.

Generation 3: Republican Education, 1776–1800

The revolution against England was clearly a spark for igniting political feelings in the colleges. However, college life was disrupted for much of the War for Independence and then developed slowly before the nation was united under the Constitution in 1788. Despite this triumph of federalism, political passions rose to a crescendo at the end of the century.

The ideal for collegiate education in this period sought a harmonious joining of disparate elements. First was the notion of republican education—instilling selflessness, patriotism, and virtue in the citizens and leaders of the new republic. Such an outlook was conveyed through the choice of texts, topics for student oratory, and the widely touted (though unsuccessful) introduction of the study of law. Second, Enlightenment learning was welcomed as never before, although the fiscal limitations of colleges made realization fall far short of aspirations. Indeed, these years mark the zenith of Enlightenment influence in American colleges, a time in which theology sought to accommodate the truths of science and reason. Samuel Stanhope Smith (1795–1812), who succeeded Witherspoon at Princeton, epitomized both the ascendancy and the fragility of this "republican Christian Enlightenment": learning was valued in the colleges, and higher education was valued in the polity.[11]

After independence, the newly sovereign states made provision for collegiate education for their citizens. States that had no colleges chartered new institutions—Maryland (1782 and 1784), Georgia (1785), South Carolina (1785), North Carolina (1789), and Vermont (1791)—although some years passed before most of these institutions were able to open. Elsewhere, this same impulse sometimes became entwined with controversial changes in existing colleges. The board of visitors of William and Mary imposed a reorganization of the faculty in 1779. The same year, Pennsylvania supplanted the College of Philadelphia with a "public" institution (the two were merged in 1791 to form the University of Pennsylvania). The superstructure of the University of the State of New York was erected in the 1780s to counter the conservative influence of Columbia. Where continuity was the rule, state officials were made ex officio trustees of colleges (Massachusetts, Connecticut, New Hampshire, and New Jersey), and financial support was sporadically provided. Denominationally sponsored colleges found few students and little influence in these years. The new colleges founded near the frontier often reflected close-knit denominational communities, but they too assumed a public outlook.

The vision of republican higher education was undermined considerably by the material weaknesses of the colleges. The nation's most solid institution, Harvard University, had just three professors at the turn of the century, but that was two more than Yale or Princeton could manage. Collegiate enrollments for the last quarter of the century did not keep pace with population growth, despite the proliferation of new institutions. Where roughly 1 percent of a four-year male cohort attended college in 1775, the corresponding figure for 1800 was 0.75 percent. In some new colleges, like North Carolina, the absence of experienced teachers for a time fomented chaotic conditions. Student unruliness was a particular blight at institutions associated with Jeffersonian republicanism, like William and Mary and Dickinson. Public subsidies for state-sponsored colleges were soon terminated, leaving these institutions in an exceedingly weak state. At the end of the eighteenth century, there was no functioning model of a state college.[12]

Ironically, popular sentiment now began to turn decisively in support of religion, but the religion of the heart, not the head. In this respect, as in others, the consequences of the dissolution of republican education were realized after 1800.

Generation 4: The Passing of Republican Education, 1800–1820s

The first generation of the nineteenth century is perhaps the least understood in American history. It has largely been associated with negative developments. Indeed, the most widely known historiographical treatment interprets it as the beginning of a "great retrogression."[13] Signs of trouble are not hard to find. The underpinnings of republican education were dislodged by the election of Thomas Jefferson, to the horror of Federalists, who dominated most colleges, and by the upsurge of religious spirit known as the Second Great

Awakening, to the detriment of denominations with learned ministers. In addition, many institutions were in a parlous state. In a plea some other colleges might have echoed, Columbia trustees described the college's sorry state as "mortifying to its friends, [and] humiliating to the city."[14] The Universities of Maryland and North Carolina lost their state support; and such major institutions as Princeton and William and Mary began prolonged declines.

Such a picture, however, portrays only misfortunes. Harvard, Yale, Brown, and Union all strengthened notably, and even Columbia was much improved by the 1820s. Moreover, an important group of institutions opened their doors shortly after 1800 — Transylvania, Bowdoin, and the state colleges of Georgia and South Carolina. College enrollments outpaced the rapid population growth, except during the depression caused by the War of 1812, bringing male participation back to 1 percent by the end of the 1820s. Underlying the fortunes of individual institutions, nevertheless, lay fundamental questions stemming in large measure from the obsolescence of the putative republican model: Who owned the colleges? What was their mission? What should students be taught? And how could they be controlled?

In the first three decades of the century, colleges experienced the worst student violence of their histories. Unruliness had long been endemic in all-male residential colleges, but these years were distinguished by episodes of collective resistance to college authority.[15] They invariably began with some minor or major transgression of college rules, but what followed was the key. In certain cases, students deemed disciplinary action, based upon measured degrees of public disgrace, to be unjustly severe. Believing their rights and dignity to have been violated, they would either remonstrate or commit further acts of insubordination. The colleges invariably won these contests of will, but at considerable cost. Numerous unrepentant students were expelled, and the college's reputation was besmirched. Such riots at Princeton and William and Mary were factors in precipitating their declines; Harvard endured its periodic riots more stoically; North Carolina forfeited public support.

Steven Novak interpreted student riots as the stimulus for college leaders to shift the emphasis of the curriculum back toward the ancient languages. Latin and Greek were considered safe, and their difficult study promoted behavioral as well as mental discipline. However, "having embraced [this] curriculum for the wrong reasons— as a bulwark against dangerous ideas—academics were never able to bring it to life."[16] Other factors played a role here as well. Most conspicuous was the collapse of efforts to construct a republican curriculum of scientific and professional subjects due to lack of suitable teachers or interested students. Moreover, attempts to deemphasize classical languages threatened to undermine the entire enterprise. At Transylvania University the college course without Latin and Greek lasted just two years; and Dickinson students in 1800 demanded and were granted a reduction of the course to a single year. Socially, some knowledge of the classical languages was a badge of cultural distinction appropriate to gentlemen. As a practical matter, lax entrance requirements brought immature and poorly prepared students to campus. Most established colleges thus made concerted efforts to raise their entrance requirements, impose a minimum age, and strengthen instruction in Latin and Greek.

This restandardization of the classical curriculum corresponded to a refocusing of institutions on their collegiate missions. In a reciprocal development, the links between professional education and the colleges were dissolving. This trend has seldom been noted. Yale and other colleges sprouted professional schools during these years and appeared to become fledgling universities. Few institutions followed this path, however, and in those that did professional schools were largely proprietary undertakings with little organic connection to the parent college. They resembled, in fact, the independent professional schools that began to flourish in this era.

The most vigorous law school after 1800 operated independently—in Litchfield, Connecticut. Unlike earlier attempts to teach law in the colleges, which were intended for civic education, Litchfield prepared students for professional practice. In medicine, the dominant institution was the University of Pennsylvania. With enrollments exceeding four hundred, this medical school was the largest higher education unit in the country. But its students paid the professors directly for lectures, making the school virtually independent of the university. Other medical schools either sought similar arrangements or else they collapsed. The Columbia medical school faltered and was absorbed by another school; Harvard's medical school achieved greater autonomy by moving to Boston; and Brown's medical school folded when the college sought to control its faculty.[17] The most consequential change for the colleges, nevertheless, concerned the training of ministers.

The preparation of ministers was an integral mission of the colleges, even though ministerial training per se fell outside the undergraduate course. When New England Congregationalists reacted to the Unitarian capture of Harvard by establishing Andover Theological Seminary (1808), a new alternative became available. During the next two decades, more schools for ministerial training were opened than new colleges. These institutions were in a sense alternatives to collegiate education and, as in the case of the Princeton Theological Seminary (1812), were votes of no confidence in the colleges. Seminaries became the locus for serious scholars of language and philology (and hence, German learning); and they attracted substantial gifts that might have gone to colleges.[18] Most seriously, they distanced colleges from the function of ministerial preparation because, like future lawyers and medical doctors, aspiring ministers increasingly dispensed with collegiate degrees.

The final issue hanging over the colleges was the ambiguous mix of public function and private control. Controversies arising from this situation had plagued the colleges since the Revolution. What proved to be a definitive resolution had to await the justly celebrated Dartmouth College case (1819). When the Supreme Court ruled that New Hampshire could not without cause alter the charter of an "eleemosynary corporation" like Dartmouth College, it effectively provided colleges with a shield against unwanted intrusions of democratic legislatures. More significantly, it resolved an implicit question of ownership that had plagued virtually every college. In Massachusetts, for example, the composition of the board of overseers had been altered by the legislature three times in the 1810s. Justice Joseph Story, a member of that board, was undoubtedly as concerned with the autonomy of Harvard as with that of Dartmouth when he voted on the case. Years passed before the import of the Dartmouth College case became fully apparent; the colleges continued to present both public and private personae, but an agenda of privatization clearly triumphed. Not only did the eastern provincial colleges become fully private institutions, but the way was cleared for the establishment of a new type of unambiguously private denominational college.[19]

Generation 5: The Classical, Denominational Colleges, 1820s–1850s

Generation 5 began in the 1820s, with widespread challenge to the classical college, and was superseded in the 1850s by new waves of re-

form. The first efforts largely failed, but the second produced permanent change. In between, the private, denominational college emerged
as the characteristic institution of American higher education. Its
success drove a rapid expansion in both the number of colleges and
total enrollments. At the same time, sectional differences created distinctive patterns for higher education in the Northeast, the South,
and the trans-Appalachian West.[20]

Criticism of the classical college in the 1820s in part reflected the
success of efforts to bolster the curriculum. Now colleges were attacked for their obsession with dead languages, for neglecting practical subjects and science, and for the continued unruliness of apparently disgruntled students. A flurry of specific reforms occurred in
the middle of the decade.[21] George Ticknor, after a student insurrection at Harvard, managed to reform his own modern languages department, offering advanced courses outside the rigid boundaries of
the separate classes. Thomas Jefferson's University of Virginia (1824)
provided an entirely new departure, aimed at achieving the nation's
first true university. And Eliphalet Nott created a parallel course for
a bachelor of science degree at Union College (1827). Little lasting
change resulted from this ferment of reform. The efforts of Ticknor
and Nott remained isolated achievements, and the University of Virginia proved an incongruous setting for the sons of southern planters.
Instead, the reforms provoked a magisterial defense of the classical
college—the Yale Report of 1828.

In defending the classical curriculum, the report defined the purpose of college as "to lay the foundation of a superior education."[22]
The object, above all, was to discipline the mind and only secondarily to provide content, or "furniture." The classical languages were
championed as the ideal vehicle for instilling mental discipline as well
as culture and "balance." From these premises, the report could argue that all other forms of education—for practical training or advanced learning—should be relegated to other kinds of institutions.
This position rationalized the de facto undergraduate focus of the colleges. The cogency of the Yale Report, moreover, seemed to grow over
time and became the principal defense of the classical course for the
next sixty years.

The classical college drew upon deeper strengths than the arguments of the Yale Report. Furthermore, it had rather different histories on the eastern and western sides of the Appalachians. In the
Northeast, generally, the colleges preserved their narrow focus on

preprofessional, liberal education and were content to serve the relatively limited clientele who valued such an expensive badge of cultural distinction. Student life in these institutions changed profoundly during this era and served to fortify this sense of distinction. As the colleges relaxed their oppressive discipline, the students themselves developed a rich extracurriculum of their own. Student life was transformed into a self-contained world of activities and social ceremony that engendered deep loyalties instead of intense hostility.[23] In the West, the most salient development of this era was the proliferation of denominational colleges in territories that had, only short years before, been considered the frontier.

The prototypical denominational college nevertheless emerged in the East in the 1820s. The definition given by the Lutherans of Pennsylvania College (Gettysburg, 1832) cut to the heart of the matter: noting that its students, teachers, trustees, and benefactors all were church members, they concluded that the college "may then with truth be said to belong to that Church." The denominational college was thus consciously established as an alternative to the mixed ownership of "provincial colleges." These colleges were established by religious minorities (some of whom had previously disdained advanced education for their ministers) so that they might have educational institutions that fully belonged to their church. Regional church organizations generally played an important role in their founding as well as in their governance. Thus, Baptists established Waterville College (Colby, 1820) and Columbian College (George Washington, 1821). Episcopalians finally broke the Yale monopoly in Connecticut in 1826 (Trinity). And Methodists joined the collegiate movement by founding Randolph-Macon (1830) and Wesleyan (1831). State legislators required that the charters of these colleges impose no religious tests. The conditions described by the Gettysburg Lutherans nevertheless defined the foremost reality of the denominational colleges.

On the western side of the Appalachians, where colleges were virtually nonexistent in 1820, denominational colleges soon proliferated. The earliest exemplars were founded by Congregational or Presbyterian missionaries almost as soon as the frontiers were settled. Later foundings tended to be sponsored by regional church organizations. In both cases, a crucial role was played by local boosters, who believed that a college would enhance the cultural and economic standing of their towns.[24] The western colleges were capable of notable experi-

ments, especially where student access was concerned. Manual labor
schemes were tried repeatedly in the 1830s and 1840s, and Oberlin became the first college to admit women. Pedagogically, though,
they initially replicated the classical curriculum. Given denominational sponsorship and clerical leadership (often from graduates of
Yale or Princeton), this path was a natural course to follow. Colin
Burke argues that these institutions need to be viewed in a different
framework from the established colleges of the East: they served the
basic need for educational upgrading for their localities. Nearly all
found it necessary to establish preparatory departments, for example.
Over time, they tended to add diverse educational programs to the
classical core in spite of limited means. The average size of western
colleges in 1860 was about 56 students (compared with 174 in New England), and costs were kept low for their far-from-wealthy students.
By 1860, the Southwest and Midwest contained 59 percent of colleges
and 43 percent of students.[25]

A somewhat different institutional pattern, characterized by dominant state universities, emerged in the South during this era. The
College of South Carolina (1803) and the University of Virginia (1824)
were the region's strongest institutions and the only universities in
the country to receive regular state appropriations before the Civil
War. Both institutions catered to sons of the planter aristocracy,
which dominated their states politically and socially. Such students,
with exaggerated notions of personal honor, made student unrest
endemic in southern universities. Denominational colleges in such
milieus developed later and attracted a more humble clientele. The
pattern of strong state universities spread throughout the Cotton
Belt but conspicuously failed in states like Kentucky and Tennessee,
where social and religious fragmentation favored denominational colleges.

The 1820s and 1830s were two of the most expansive decades for
higher education. Enrollments jumped by roughly 80 percent in each
decade, fueled by the establishment of denominational colleges. The
1840s, however, were years of comparative stagnation: they were no
doubt hampered by the severe economic downturn that followed the
crash of 1837 and by the limited appeal of the classical college. Ex-
asperation with these conditions prompted one last spasm of reform.
Brown president Francis Wayland (1827–56) diagnosed the weakness of the eastern colleges: they catered solely to the professional
class and furnished students with only a preprofessional education

—precisely the narrow focus advocated in the Yale Report. Entirely neglected were practitioners of industry and commerce, who were responsible for the transformation taking place in the American economy.[26] However, these were the polemics of the 1820s in more sophisticated guise. Wayland's attempt to restructure Brown in order to appeal to this new class proved disastrous. Ironically, his failure occurred at the opening of one of the most dynamic eras of American higher education. The ensuing generation, rather than displacing the classical college, created new institutions and studies to complement it.

Generation 6: New Departures, 1850s–1890

The Civil War has long been the conventional dividing line for the history of American higher education. However, most of the new departures associated with the postbellum years emerged in preliminary form in the 1850s, if not earlier. German-style universities, offering graduate education, are associated with the opening of Johns Hopkins in 1876, but Henry Tappan (1853–63) transformed the University of Michigan in these same directions. The Morrill Land-Grant Act of 1862 can lay exclusive claim to neither "schools of science" nor agricultural colleges. Daniel Coit Gilman estimates that twenty such institutions existed before 1860, including Yale's Sheffield Scientific School, which had evolved from a few extracurricular courses into a department in which both practical and advanced subjects could be studied.[27] In addition, at least four agricultural colleges were chartered in the 1850s, in Pennsylvania, Michigan, Maryland, and Ohio.

In the same decade, collegiate education was broadened to include other than white males. More than forty women's institutions were chartered to offer collegiate degrees before Matthew Vassar presumed to give women "a college in the proper sense of the word."[28] Ashmun Institute (Lincoln University, 1854) in Pennsylvania and Wilberforce University (1856) in Ohio provided college education for free African Americans.

Perhaps the greatest continuity from antebellum to postbellum years existed for denominational colleges. They began a second period of proliferation in the 1850s, which carried through to the early 1870s. The dynamics of this expansion derived from a dual process of extension and elaboration. Through extension, colleges followed close be-

hind the ever moving frontier into the trans-Mississippi West. Once
again, the agents of these initial foundings were largely missionaries from the principal denominations. In the wake of this movement,
and indeed throughout the Midwest, a second process of elaboration
occurred as denominations without colleges made provision for the
education of their church members. These colleges differed from their
earlier counterparts in being multipurpose in nature. They still preserved the classical core but added degree courses in English and science as well as practical courses in business and teaching. In keeping with this impulse to serve their denominations broadly, these
multipurpose colleges were usually coeducational, except for denominations opposed in principle (Roman Catholics, Presbyterians, German Lutherans). This great expansion of denominational colleges
proceeded unfazed by the dawning age of the university, until conditions changed radically after 1890.[29]

The Morrill Land-Grant Act still largely determined the character of the new utilitarian education. Enthusiasm among the industrial classes for education in agriculture or the mechanical arts turned
out to be sparse. True, well-publicized Cornell attracted the nation's
largest entering class in 1868, but these initial students were mixed in
aspirations and qualifications. Only 10 percent eventually graduated.
Outside of New England, preparatory departments overshadowed collegiate ones in the new land-grant colleges. After a slow start, enrollment in the mechanical arts (engineering) grew in the 1880s and
then accelerated after 1890. Matriculants in agriculture, however, remained few and far between. Reformers simply misjudged the nexus
between farming and advanced education.

Contrary to the conventional view, land-grant colleges did not meet
an exigent popular demand, nor did they appreciably democratize
higher education. Had they been dependent on enrollment, many
undoubtedly would have failed. However, the circumstances of their
beginnings gave them an assured, if meager, income as well as an implicit relationship with their respective states. They were thus sustained long enough through their sickly infancy for social and economic conditions to catch up to the expectations that had prompted
their somewhat premature founding. In 1890, after intensive lobbying by land-grant presidents, the Second Morrill Act gave them direct
annual infusions of federal funds, a crucial advantage at a time when
universities were entering their most dynamic era of growth.[30]

The first Morrill Act nevertheless set the most important precondition for utilitarian education when it stipulated the establishment of "at least one *college*" in which these subjects would be taught, "without excluding other scientific and classical studies."[31] Unlike continental Europe, where modern languages and useful subjects were taught in less prestigious institutions than those offering classical and theoretical studies, in the United States the progeny of the industrial classes would eventually study in the same institutions as those from the professional classes.

Despite the salience of the Morrill Act, these years were characterized far more by private initiatives and, particularly, single acts of philanthropy. Gifts of hitherto unprecedented size sought to fill lacunae in American higher education. Matthew Vassar, Henry Wells, Sophia Smith, and Henry Durant created colleges for women between 1861 and 1875 that were intended to equal the best men's colleges.[32] Ezra Cornell and John Purdue enhanced the effectiveness of land-grant colleges. Trustees of estates were responsible for establishing the Stevens Institute of Technology and the Johns Hopkins University. The end of this era was marked by the most spectacular new institutions (after Hopkins)—Clark and Stanford Universities and the University of Chicago.

The American university is the most enduring legacy of these developments, even though its ascendancy over American higher education would have to await the next generation. Charles Eliot said in 1869 that no university yet existed in the United States, and prior to 1890 it was uncertain what form an American university would assume. Indeed, Daniel Coit Gilman, G. Stanley Hall, David Starr Jordan, and William Rainey Harper each independently attempted to invent such an institution (at Hopkins, Clark, Stanford, and Chicago, respectively). The chief conundrum was the relationship between advanced learning, or graduate education, and the American college.

The true paradigm of the American university evolved instead at the country's paramount institution. Charles W. Eliot assumed the presidency of Harvard in 1869 with a clear sense of the changes that were needed in both college and professional schools. For the college, he sought to replace recitations and the classical curriculum with an elective system that could accommodate true learning. This reform took a decade and a half, but by then the old regime was vanquished at Harvard and in retreat at other eastern colleges. Eliot also attacked the decadence of the professional schools at the outset of his presidency. A learned, full-time faculty replaced practitioner-teachers; a

mandatory curriculum was put in place; and professional education
was eventually defined as requiring a bachelor's degree. Eliot's in-
stincts were by no means as sure when it came to graduate education.
But as the elective system allowed him to appoint many more learned
professors, a distinguished faculty emerged, capable of scholarship,
research, and advanced instruction. In 1890 the scientific school and
the college faculty were merged into the faculty of arts and sciences.
The Graduate School of Arts and Sciences was its other face. Finally,
Eliot felt that Harvard was "now well on the way to the complete
organization of a university in a true sense." The American university would be an institution in which the instruction of large numbers of undergraduates would support a numerous, specialized faculty, who would also teach graduate students. Not even the ingenious
William Rainey Harper could devise anything better. Moreover, this
model was a natural one for the more vigorous state universities,
whose growth was about to explode. The next generation of American
higher education would see the efflorescence of this powerful combination of mixed purposes.[33]

Generation 7: Growth and Standardization, 1890 to World War I

The character of growth in American higher education changed profoundly around 1890. During the previous generation, enrollment
growth had been absorbed into an increasing number of institutions,
but during generation 7 the net number of institutions remained
fairly stable while enrollments swelled. The average institution in
1870 had 10 faculty and 98 students; in 1890, these figures had grown
to just 16 faculty and 157 students; but in 1910, they were up to 38
faculty and 374 students. Moreover, the largest institutions led this
growth: in 1895 the ten largest universities averaged nearly 2,000 students; in 1910 they approximated 4,000 and in 1915, 5,000.[34] At the
other end of the spectrum, colleges that failed to grow were threatened with extinction. The institutional order was anything but stable;
the founding of new colleges continued unabated into the 1890s, but
many institutions expired during these years.

One important source of growth was the assimilation of women
into higher education. In 1890 the majority of female students were
found in single-sex colleges, most of which were regarded by contem-

poraries as inferior. This situation changed abruptly with the opening of the elective curriculum and the expansion of universities. The proportion of women students grew slowly, from 32 to 37 percent (1890–1913), but the proportion of women in coeducational institutions nearly doubled, to 68 percent. The gulf between the educational experiences of women and men narrowed much further in the next generation.[35]

The standardization of the universities after 1890 is the central theme of Laurence Veysey's classic study. His deliberate emphasis on the cerebral aspects of this subject, however, may slight some of the more mundane features, largely caused by similar adaptations to a common environment. The rapid growth of universities resulted from the growth of their several parts. Most added units in engineering, business, education, plus different combinations of other smaller specialties (e.g., mining, forestry, dentistry, pharmacy, veterinary medicine, art, architecture, and music), in addition to schools for graduate study, medicine, and law. Universities became compartmentalized institutions, whose parts shared little common intellectual ground. Administrative structures were necessary to serve these autonomous compartments and especially to secure ever more resources to fulfill their needs.[36]

By 1908 it was possible to define the standard American university. It admitted only bona fide high school graduates. It provided them with two years of general education followed by two years of advanced or specialized courses. It offered doctoral training in at least five departments, appropriately led by Ph.D.s, and had at least one professional school. A sizable list of desirable options might be added: summer sessions, extension work, correspondence courses, a university press, and the publication of learned journals. Idiosyncrasies faded away in this environment: Eliot's unconstrained elective system and proposed three-year bachelor's degree. Outliers moved closer to the norm: Johns Hopkins enrolled more undergraduates and lengthened the bachelor of arts course to four years; the Massachusetts Institute of Technology established units for research and graduate education.

The universities, in turn, were the most powerful force in generating standards for the rest of higher education, chiefly by defining academic knowledge and the academic profession. From about 1890 to 1905 all of the major disciplinary associations assumed their modern form. In a parallel development, the departmental structure of colleges and universities replicated these contours. Academic disciplines henceforth possessed a dual structure, whereby scientific recognition was embodied in disciplinary organizations while the most consequential positions, those commanding the means to advance these fields, were in university departments. As teaching positions were increasingly reserved for faculty who contributed to the knowledge base of disciplines, the universities imposed a definition on the academic profession. University faculty then took this definition a step further by organizing the American Association of University Professors (1915) to champion their professional rights, particularly academic freedom.[37]

Probably much more apparent to contemporaries was the spread of a set of practices that can best be called the collegiate ideal. Church ties were weak threads for sustaining liberal arts colleges. An alternative emerged from younger alumni with business careers in urban centers. They appreciated the social qualities that were instilled by extracurricular activities, including athletics. Their ability to contribute badly needed funds gave their wishes weight among college trustees and eventually influenced the selection of modernizing presidents. Denominational doctrines were soon deemphasized in favor of broad, middle-of-the-road Protestantism. New kinds of students began to matriculate, eager to throw themselves into campus activities and consciously destined for careers in the business world. Intercollegiate athletics tended to be the catalyst in this process, galvanizing the enthusiasm of students and the loyalties of alumni.[38]

The collegiate ideal developed first out of the unique traditions of the Ivy League schools, especially Harvard and Yale. It quickly captured the principal eastern colleges and spread to include state universities. The older generation of university leaders, like Charles Eliot, had scant regard for such activities, but the next generation —Eliot's successor Abbott Lawrence Lowell (1909–33) and above all Woodrow Wilson (1902–10) at Princeton—sought to amalgamate the collegiate ideal with their own solicitude for undergraduate learning. The collegiate ideal projected clear normative standards about the nature of the college experience, while another form of standardization found champions after 1900.

In 1905 the Carnegie Foundation for the Advancement of Teaching was chartered to provide pensions for college teachers. The same year, the General Education Board reoriented its activities toward promoting "a comprehensive system of higher education in the United States." Both foundations sought to alleviate the "chaos" and "confusion" they perceived in American higher education. The former promulgated stringent criteria of eligibility for its pensions, and institutions scrambled to conform. The latter worked more subtly by providing matching endowment grants that forced colleges to turn to their alumni.[39] Neither required an institution to have a football team, but they validated the types of schools that did: residential colleges with strong alumni support.

Following the model of the Land-Grant College Association (1887), successive associations were formed in this era, and their efforts also furthered standardization. The National Association of State Universities formulated the definition of the "standard American university." The Association of American Universities, formed to set standards for graduate education, soon became, in effect, an accrediting agency for colleges.[40]

A generation of standardizing activities gave much greater definition to the American system of higher education, even if it left the system still highly diverse and decentralized. By World War I, American colleges and universities by and large conformed to a single pattern in terms of admissions, credit hours, offerings, majors, and so on. The large difference among institutions pertained chiefly to the level of resources each commanded for the fulfillment of this pattern. Differences in resources would henceforth produce an increasingly steeper hierarchy among American institutions of higher education.

Generation 8: Hierarchical Differentiation between the Wars

Enrollments in higher education approximately doubled during the 1920s, and this expansion triggered qualitative changes analogous to what Martin Trow would later identify as the transition from elite to mass higher education.[41] Elite patterns are characterized by full-time, residential students, by cultural ideals of liberal learning and character formation, and by destinations in high-status professions. In contrast, mass forms of higher education cater to part-time or commuting students, convey applicable knowledge, and prepare students for employment in technical or semiprofessional positions. American higher education had always been somewhat hierarchical in terms of resource levels and admissions requirements. Between the two world wars, however, it became much more explicitly so. Emergent forms of higher education fulfilled "mass" roles, and educational leaders directly addressed the issue of offering qualitatively different kinds of instruction for different levels of student.

The growth of a mass sector in American higher education was apparent in the burgeoning junior colleges, teachers colleges, and urban, service-oriented universities.[42] Teachers colleges resulted from the process of continuously upgrading normal schools. This process began in the 1900s, although the majority of normal schools converted in the 1920s. Many teachers colleges remained for years confined to education degrees. In addition, they faced competition in this sphere from traditional universities. But as heirs to the normal schools they provided access to higher education for a broad segment of the population, especially women.

The expansion of higher education to serve city dwellers included both new and existing institutions. The free municipal university established in Akron (1913) exemplified the former. Typically with programs in engineering, home economics, commerce, and teaching, it aimed to produce employable graduates for the region. The College of the City of New York was perhaps the most spectacular exemplar of this phenomenon, growing to more than 24,000 students during the 1920s. Private municipal universities shared in this growth, largely by creating special programs for part-time students. In 1930, for example, part-time and summer students exceeded full-time students at New York, Northwestern, Southern California, Boston, and Western Reserve universities. By that date, the biggest American institutions were no longer research universities but municipal universities with large irregular enrollments.

True junior colleges first appeared in the decade of the 1900s but multiplied in the 1920s. They provided local access to higher education for both sparsely populated areas of the West and cities. By 1940, 11 percent of college students were enrolled in junior colleges, many of which were still attached to local high schools. The emergence of junior colleges nevertheless profoundly affected thinking about the structure and purpose of American higher education.

The waves of mass higher education lapping the shores of traditional institutions produced largely defensive reactions. President Ernest Hopkins of Dartmouth caused a stir by declaring that "too many young men are going to college." Probably the most vehement critic was Abraham Flexner, who charged that universities had become " 'service' stations for the general public."[43] A number of educators took inspiration from the apparent success of junior colleges and concluded that democratic access should extend through the sophomore year of college. The University of Minnesota created a two-year General College for students deemed unfit for its regular programs. Another clear rationalization of hierarchical differentiation was the Carnegie Foundation's 1932 report, *State Higher Education in California,* which defined separate roles for the university in Berkeley, regional state colleges, and largely vocational junior colleges. This document was representative of a crystallization of opinion that sought to redefine the most open sector of higher education—the junior colleges—as terminal programs.

Determined efforts by the leaders of higher education had the effect of hardening the outlines of the mass sector of higher education, which had emerged almost spontaneously. Similarly, purposeful actions were required to define the upper reaches of American higher education. As with the mass sector, this was a matter at once of social origins and destinations, manner or style of attendance, and links with higher learning.

Three general criteria could be used to claim elite status. The *collegiate ideal,* especially popular in the 1920s, was determined by the peer society of students, by extracurricular activities, and by expectations of subsequent careers in the business world. *Quality of undergraduate learning* was a persistent concern, and not only did colleges attempt to raise their standards but also many educators sought to recreate the elusive ideal of liberal education. In universities, the imperative of *advancing knowledge* was an end in itself, the touchstone of research and graduate education but also a distinguishing feature of only a handful of institutions.

At the leading private institutions, financial constraints and rising applications prompted limits on the number of students after World War I. At the same time, these institutions became more sensitive to the social composition of their students and to the implications it had for their collegiate image. Columbia pioneered a form of selective admissions in which social criteria were used to limit the proportion of Jewish students, and the same discriminatory procedures were soon copied by Princeton, Yale, and Harvard.[44] Selective admissions was part of a larger pattern of fashioning elite status. These institutions shaped the peer society and collegiate environment not only by excluding supposedly nonconforming social types but also by widening their recruitment pool to encompass the entire country. They simul-

taneously became national rather than regional institutions, culling
the weakest academic performers from among their traditional clientele and raising the level of study, at least slightly. As these institutions prospered in the 1920s, they vastly increased educational spending on each student. When Yale launched the largest endowment drive
in university history in 1927, it promised "to make a finer, not a big-
ger Yale." [45]

For elite universities, additional wealth was invested in more and
better faculty—in scientists and scholars actively engaged in the advancement of knowledge. This phase of development was strongly
assisted by philanthropic foundations, particularly the Rockefeller
trusts. Participation in research also conferred prestige and elite
status. Recognition in this dimension lay outside of universities, in
international communities of scholars. It thus created an altogether
different set of imperatives, which universities could scarcely ignore.
It was no paradox, then, that a Jew could be a physics professor at
Princeton but not an undergraduate: universalism prevailed in the
former sphere but not in the latter.

Probably the most difficult course for sculpting an elite status was
to excel in only undergraduate education. However, Swarthmore under president Frank Aydelotte (1921–39) was a notable success in
this regard. Inspired by his Oxford experience as a Rhodes scholar,
Aydelotte established an honors program to provide a rigorous course
of study for able and motivated students. At the same time, he pro-
gressively deemphasized the underpinnings of the collegiate ideal—
sororities, fraternities, and big-time football. The honors program
was used to attract academically ambitious students and soon made
Swarthmore one of the most selective colleges in the country. The
high cost of this education was met with help from supporters of elitism, Abraham Flexner and the General Education Board. [46]

The hierarchical differentiation of the institutional order between
the wars moved American higher education simultaneously in several
different directions with respect to elite and mass sectors, access, and
curriculum. American higher education became open to virtually all
high school graduates, a category that grew from 9 to 51 percent of
age cohorts between 1910 and 1940. Yet, social exclusiveness among
many elite institutions increased, too, as nativist prejudice strengthened. The system was only weakly meritocratic and largely mirrored
the social biases prevailing in the workplace. In curricular matters,
the expanding mass sector was dominated by vocationally oriented

programs, including attempts to define terminal tracks. A preoccupation of the era was nevertheless the persistent desire to fashion a true
liberal education. At the same time, the implacable advancement of
the academic disciplines weighed ever more heavily on the structure
of college courses. Which trends predominated? The answer would become apparent during the next generation of American higher education: democratic access triumphed over social exclusiveness; academic
development raised the stature of mass institutions, even as elite ones
became strongly meritocratic; and an academic revolution confirmed
the ascendancy of the academic curriculum.

Generation 9: The Academic Revolution, 1945–1975

The thirty years following the end of World War II were possibly the
most tumultuous in the history of American higher education. Two
fundamental movements nevertheless underlie these myriad developments: expansion and academic standardization. Beginning with the
flood of returning soldiers, supported by the Servicemen's Readjustment Act of 1944 (the GI Bill), and concluding with the tidal wave
of community college students of the early 1970s, this period was the
most expansive in the American experience. The proportion of young
people attending college tripled from 15 to 45 percent; undergraduates grew almost fivefold, graduate students almost ninefold (1940–
70); the 1960s alone registered the largest percentage growth of any
decade.[47]
     While previous growth spurts, like the 1920s, were associated with
new types of institutions reaching new clienteles, the postwar period
was characterized by an implacable movement toward common academic standards. Not only did institutions become more alike in terms
of curricular offerings, faculty training, and administrative practices,
but students migrated toward studies in the arts and sciences. The
principal dynamics of this era fortified these developments.
     Most generally, an excess demand for college places existed through
most of the era. This phenomenon arose when returning veterans
took advantage of the GI Bill in unprecedented and unanticipated
numbers. In 1947, 1.1 million ex-GIs were enrolled, compared with
1.5 million total students before the war. This surge did little to raise
standards, though, as overcrowded institutions were forced to run
year-round, to shorten courses, and to curtail requirements. This in-

terlude nevertheless rebuilt depleted institutional treasuries and boosted morale as well. In the wake of this experience, most institutions sought to consolidate and bolster their programs.

Enrollment backtracked only slightly in the early 1950s, before larger cohorts began coming of age and seeking college places. Student numbers grew by approximately 50 percent in the 1950s. By the end of the decade, however, the baby-boom generation had already filled the high schools. The 1960s experienced a double effect: participation rates increased by half (from 30% to 45%), and the eighteen-to-twenty-one-year-old age cohort grew even more (from 9 million to 15 million). This flood of students flowed into flagship state universities, which expanded to their limits and then became increasingly selective. Private institutions, without generous appropriations to fund expansion, largely sought to optimize their efforts by building stronger academic programs for a more select student body. A large portion of the new students found places at burgeoning regional state institutions. Formerly teachers colleges, they eagerly expanded academic programs, ventured into graduate education, and became regional universities. The final component of this growth came from new public community colleges, which from 1965 to 1972 were opened at a rate exceeding one per week.

The idealism suffusing higher education after the war lent support for the basic arts and sciences. Institutions emphasizing these subjects had assumed preponderant prestige in the interwar years. Now, a consensus formed endorsing the *Harvard Report on General Education,* which pronounced that a judicious sampling of the basic disciplines would compose the foundation for a liberal education.[48] The pattern of institutional expansion also supported this trend toward arts and sciences. Service institutions that had embraced vocational/professional programs (or were confined to teacher education) in the interwar years gradually fortified disciplinary departments. A shift in student majors ensued in the 1960s, when bachelor's degrees awarded in the arts and sciences rose to a peak of 47 percent.[49]

These trends were powerfully fortified by a prodigious expansion of research and graduate education, largely due to federal support.[50] Federal sponsorship of research initially extended, under different organizational headings, the channels established for the wartime emergency. For more than a decade after World War II, the bulk of the increased funding for academic research came from the defense establishment and was skewed toward the physical sciences. However, a new federal relationship with higher education emerged from the Sputnik crisis of 1957. For about a decade after Sputnik, funding growth for academic science came from the civilian side of the federal government: the National Science Foundation, the National Aeronautical and Space Administration, and most prolifically, the National Institutes of Health. Moreover, this bounteous support was accompanied by assistance for universities to support graduate students, build laboratories, and develop new science programs. Sputnik also provoked Washington to support higher education directly, first through the National Defense Education Act and later through direct aid for buildings and students. The federal largess, superimposed on mushrooming enrollments and state support, produced an ephemeral golden age in American higher education.

Christopher Jencks and David Riesman characterized the transformation that occurred during this era as "the academic revolution."[51] They meant the process by which the theoretical and specialized academic outlook of graduate schools was conveyed throughout the institutional order. It was a process that transcended the sciences, ultimately affecting virtually every school and department. The agents were the new Ph.D.s, trained in burgeoning graduate programs, who staffed the expanding universities. Their teaching and their writings brought the most current and specialized academic knowledge into the classrooms of all types of institutions. Ultimately, however, the expectations and idealism of the academic revolution set the stage for a backlash that arose in the late 1960s. Its chief manifestation was the great student rebellion.

The student movement crystallized from the Free Speech Movement at Berkeley and Students for a Democratic Society. The national issues of the war in Vietnam and racial injustice largely propelled its evolution toward increasing radicalism and militancy. Although the major campuses suffered their greatest disruption from 1967 to 1969, the enduring impact was to alter the prevailing atmosphere of higher education. The momentum of the academic revolution was checked. The university's relation to its students was profoundly altered, from paternalism to exaggerated permissiveness. And universities retreated for a time to a heightened aloofness. The student rebellion was the crescendo to the tumultuous postwar generation, but it only partially foreshadowed the dawning new era.

Generation 10: Regulation, Relevance, and
the Steady State

To extend historical analysis beyond the point in which documentation is available and ensuing consequences can be known is perilous.
But even if the ultimate shape and meaning of generation 10 of American higher education is as yet unfathomable, important features may
still be identified. It is now apparent in retrospect that in the first half
of the 1970s significant discontinuities occurred in the demographics,
the politics, and the social relations of American higher education.

In 1975, enrollments in higher education topped 11 million for the
first time, but then an unprecedented change occurred: student numbers for the first time ceased to grow. In the ensuing years there was
an upward creep, but twenty years later the number of full-time students had grown by just 20 percent. Never before had enrollments
been so stagnant for so long. One important dynamic was nevertheless at work: whereas 55 percent of students were male in 1975, 55
percent were female in 1995.

Higher education's relationship with the federal government
changed in these years. Support for academic research was essentially
capped in 1968, and aid for infrastructure and graduate education was
largely phased out. However, direct support for research remained at
high levels and, eventually, expanded once more in the 1980s. Still,
the federal investment in higher education increased significantly in
the 1970s, with the new funds being used to support student access.
The 1972 amendments to the Higher Education Act were a watershed
in two respects. First, they formalized a major commitment to provide aid to students on the basis of financial need. The centerpiece of
this commitment was what are now called Federal Pell Grants, which
provide direct support for the neediest low-income students. During
the 1980s, however, the bulk of federal student aid shifted from Pell
grants to guaranteed student loans. Nevertheless, the emergence of
financial need as the dominant rationale for student support, by institutions as well as government, has been a distinguishing feature of
generation 10.

The 1972 amendments also extended the government's regulatory
control over higher education. The student rebellion of the 1960s had,
in effect, staked the claim for a greater presence in higher education
for minorities and women. Title IX now provided the means for legal

enforcement. It was perhaps the most significant of a number of measures by which federal regulation became an inescapable presence in higher education.

One clarion call of the student rebellion was for relevance in university studies. Relevance indeed became a hallmark of the new era but in ways not anticipated by student activists. They had advocated a tendentious relevance predicated on the university's role as an aloof critic of society. Thus, they urged universities to study and seek to ameliorate problems stemming from the Vietnam War, racial inequality, poverty, and the environment. These topics long remained preoccupations on campuses, but more powerful trends toward relevance were welling up. Students sought a more tangible form of relevance by turning away from the arts and sciences and toward more vocational or professional majors. Bachelor's degrees in arts and sciences plummeted to just over one quarter of the total, barely more than the number awarded in business alone. Elsewhere, the conviction that academic knowledge should remain in the ivory tower slowly ebbed in the 1970s. A decisive change of attitude occurred in the early 1980s, when universities embraced the notion of economic relevance, specifically furthering economic development through technology transfer and closer involvement with the productive economy.

In the closing decade of the twentieth century, American higher education endured another storm of public criticism. Yet, from the perspective of this historical analysis, the contemporary vista appears unusually clear. Although the value of a college education was called into question frequently in the 1970s, higher education has become increasingly recognized since then as essential for acquiring the skills and adaptability needed in the modern workplace. The middle-class social destinations made possible by higher education are now so widely recognized that they are undoubtedly the principal force behind rising participation rates. The contributions of academic knowledge were similarly disparaged at the beginning of generation 10. However, the economic relevance of at least some academic research has become widely accepted as a major factor in the strong performance of the U.S. economy. The advancement of basic knowledge, the special province of universities, should now be recognized as a national asset of inestimable value.[52] The institutional order, finally, has remained stable throughout generation 10. Despite recurrent financial pressures and demographic pressures looming in the next century, the immeasurable contribution of colleges and universities to American life should sustain them through the inevitable challenges lying ahead.

NOTES

This chapter is a substantially revised version of "The Historical Matrix of American Higher Education," *History of Higher Education Annual* 12 (1992): 7–28, which benefited from the comments of E. D. Duryea, Jurgen Herbst, and W. Bruce Leslie published in the same volume. Additional material has been drawn from Roger L. Geiger, ed., *The American College in the Nineteenth Century* (Nashville: Vanderbilt University Press, 2000). Comments from Karen Paulson and Roger Williams were greatly appreciated. References have been reduced to principal secondary works and quotation sources.

1. Jurgen Herbst, *From Crisis to Crisis: American College Government, 1636–1819* (Cambridge: Harvard University Press, 1982), 1–61.

2. Samuel Eliot Morison, *Three Centuries of Harvard, 1636–1936* (Cambridge: Harvard University Press, 1936), 53–82; Richard Hofstadter, *Academic Freedom in the Age of the College* (New Brunswick, NJ: Transaction, 1996 [1955]), 98–113; Susan H. Godson et al., *The College of William and Mary: A History,* 2 vols. (Williamsburg, Va.: King and Queen Press, 1993), 3–80.

3. Herbst, *From Crisis to Crisis,* 38–47; Richard Warch, *School of the Prophets: Yale College, 1701–1740* (New Haven: Yale University Press, 1973).

4. Bruce A. Kimball, *The "True Professional Ideal" in America: A History* (Cambridge, Mass.: Blackwell, 1992), 75–84; Herbst, *From Crisis to Crisis,* 1.

5. William D. Carrell, "American College Professors: 1750–1800," *History of Education Quarterly* 8 (1968): 289–305.

6. Herbst, *From Crisis to Crisis,* 82–137; Howard Miller, *The Revolutionary College: American Presbyterian Higher Education, 1707–1837* (New York: New York University Press, 1976), 65–75. J. David Hoeveler, *Creating the American Mind: Intellect and Politics in the Colonial Colleges* (Lanham, Md.: Rowman and Littlefield, 2002).

7. Beverly McAnear, "College Founding in the American Colonies: 1745–1775," *Mississippi Valley Historical Review* 42 (1952): 24–44.

8. David C. Humphrey, *From King's College to Columbia, 1746–1800* (New York: Columbia University Press, 1976), 199; Robert McCaughey, *Stand Columbia: A History of Columbia University* (New York: Columbia University Press, 2003); Morison, *Three Centuries,* 102–3; James McLachlan, introduction to *The Princetonians, 1748–1768: A Biographical Dictionary* (Princeton: Princeton University Press, 1977).

9. Edmund S. Morgan, *The Gentle Puritan: A Life of Ezra Styles, 1727–*

1795 (Chapel Hill: University of North Carolina Press, 1962), 47–57; Henry F. May, *The Enlightenment in America* (New York: Oxford University Press, 1976).

10. Mark A. Noll, *Princeton and the Republic, 1768–1822: The Search for a Christian Enlightenment in the Era of Samuel Stanhope Smith* (Princeton: Princeton University Press, 1989), 16–98; Miller, *Revolutionary College,* 82–94.

11. Noll, *Princeton and the Republic,* 185–213, 297–99; David W. Robson, *Educating Republicans: The Colleges in the Era of the American Revolution, 1750–1800* (Westport, Conn.: Greenwood, 1985), 143–77.

12. Robson, *Educating Republicans,* 247.

13. Hofstadter, *Academic Freedom,* 209–53. However, see Roger L. Geiger, "The Reformation of the Colleges in the Early Republic," *History of Universities,* 16, no. 2 (2000): 129–81.

14. *A History of Columbia University, 1754–1904* (New York: Columbia University Press, 1904), 100. See McCaughey, *Stand Columbia.*

15. Steven J. Novak, *The Rights of Youth: American Colleges and Student Revolt, 1798–1815* (Cambridge: Harvard University Press, 1977); Leon Jackson, "The Rights of Man and the Rites of Youth: Fraternity and Riot at Eighteenth-Century Harvard," *American College,* 46–79.

16. Novak, *Rights of Youth,* 166. However, see Caroline Winterer, *The Culture of Classicism: Ancient Greece and Rome in American Intellectual Life, 1780–1910* (Baltimore: Johns Hopkins University Press, 2002).

17. Alfred Z. Reed, *Training for the Public Profession of the Law* (New York: Scribner, 1921), 116–60; William F. Norwood, *Medical Education in the United States before the Civil War* (Philadelphia: University of Pennsylvania Press, 1944).

18. Natalie A. Naylor, "The Theological Seminary in the Configuration of American Higher Education: The Ante-Bellum Years," *History of Education Quarterly* 17 (1977): 17–30; Glenn T. Miller, *Piety and Intellect: The Aims and Purposes of Ante-Bellum Theological Education* (Atlanta: Scholar's Press, 1990).

19. Herbst, *From Crisis to Crisis,* 232–43; Leon Burr Richardson, *History of Dartmouth College* (Hanover, NH: 1932), 287–346; John S. Whitehead and Jurgen Herbst, "How to Think about the Dartmouth College Case," *History of Education Quarterly* 26 (1986): 333–50.

20. Roger L. Geiger, "Introduction: New Themes in the History of Nineteenth-Century Colleges," *American College,* 1–36, esp. 16–24.

21. Stanley M. Guralnik, *Science and the Ante-Bellum American College* (Philadelphia: American Philosophical Society, 1975), 18–46.

22. *Reports on the Course of Instruction in Yale College; by a Committee of the Corporation and the Academical Faculty* (New Haven, 1828).

23. Frederick Rudolph, *Mark Hopkins and the Log: Williams College,*

1836–1872 (New Haven: Yale University Press, 1956); Roger L. Geiger with Julie Ann Bubolz, "College as It Was in the Mid-Nineteenth Century," *American College,* 80–90.

24. Charles H. Glatfelter, *A Salutary Influence: Gettysberg College, 1832–1985,* 2 vols. (Gettysburg, Pa.: Gettysburg College, 1987), 175; David B. Potts, " 'College Enthusiasm' as Public Response: 1800–1860," *Harvard Education Review* 47 (1977): 28–42.

25. Colin Burke, *American Collegiate Populations: A Test of the Traditional View* (New York: New York University Press, 1982).

26. Francis Wayland, *Report to the Corporation of Brown University on Changes in the System of Collegiate Education* (Providence, 1850).

27. Daniel Coit Gilman, "Our National Schools of Science," *North American Review* (Oct. 1867): 495–520. Richard J. Storr, *The Beginnings of Graduate Education in America* (Chicago: University of Chicago Press, 1953), 60–65, 112–17.

28. Thomas Woody, *A History of Women's Education in the United States,* 2 vols. (New York, 1929), 145–47; Christie Anne Farnham, *The Education of the Southern Belle: Higher Education and Student Socialization in the Antebellum South* (New York: New York University Press, 1994); Sidney Sherwood, *The University of the State of New York* (Washington, D.C., 1900), quotation on 447.

29. Roger L. Geiger, "The Era of Multipurpose Colleges in American Higher Education, 1850–1890" in *American College,* 127–52.

30. Roger L. Geiger, "The Rise and Fall of Useful Knowledge" in *American College,* 153–68; Roger L. Williams, *The Origins of Federal Support for Higher Education: George W. Atherton and the Land-Grant College Movement* (University Park: Pennsylvania State University Press, 1991).

31. Richard Hofstadter and Wilson Smith, eds., "The Morrill Act, 1862," in *Higher Education: A Documentary History,* vol. 2 (Chicago: University of Chicago Press, 1961).

32. Helen Lefkowitz Horowitz, *Alma Mater: Design and Experience in the Women's Colleges from Their Nineteenth Century Origins to the 1930s* (Boston: Beacon, 1984).

33. Hugh Hawkins, *Between Harvard and America: The Educational Leadership of Charles W. Eliot* (New York: Oxford University Press, 1972); Morison, *Three Centuries,* 323–99, quotation on 361; Laurence Veysey, *The Emergence of the American University* (Chicago: University of Chicago Press, 1965).

34. Roger L. Geiger, *To Advance Knowledge: The Growth of American Research Universities, 1900–1940* (New York: Oxford University Press, 1986), 270–71.

35. Roger L. Geiger, "The 'Superior Instruction of Women,' 1836–1890" in *American College,* 183–95; Barbara Miller Solomon, *In the Company of Edu-*

cated Women: A History of Women and Higher Education in America (New Haven: Yale University Press, 1985); Lynn D. Gordon, *Gender and Higher Education in the Progressive Era* (New Haven: Yale University Press, 1990).

36. Veysey, *Emergence;* Geiger, *To Advance Knowledge,* 14–19; enrollments by professional school or department are given in Edwin E. Slosson, *Great American Universities* (New York: Macmillan, 1910).

37. Geiger, *To Advance Knowledge,* 30–39; Walter P. Metzger, "Origins of the Association," *AAUP Bulletin* 51 (1965): 229–37.

38. W. Bruce Leslie, *Gentlemen and Scholars: College and Community in the "Age of the University," 1865–1917* (University Park: Pennsylvania State University Press, 1992); Ronald A. Smith, *Sports and Freedom: The Rise of Big-Time College Athletics* (New York: Oxford University Press, 1988).

39. Geiger, *To Advance Knowledge,* 45–47; Ellen Condliffe Lagemann, *Private Power for the Public Good: A History of the Carnegie Foundation for the Advancement of Teaching* (Middletown: Wesleyan University Press, 1983), 3–53.

40. Hugh Hawkins, *Banding Together: The Rise of the National Associations in American Higher Education, 1887–1950* (Baltimore: Johns Hopkins University Press, 1992), 107–10.

41. Martin Trow, *The Transition from Elite to Mass Higher Education* (Paris: OECD, 1974).

42. The following draws on David O. Levine, *The American College and the Culture of Aspiration, 1915–1940* (Ithaca: Cornell University Press, 1986).

43. Geiger, *To Advance Knowledge;* Abraham Flexner, *Universities: American, English, German* (New Brunswick, NJ: Transaction, 1994 [1930]).

44. Harold Wechsler, *The Qualified Student: A History of Selective Admissions in America* (New York: Wiley, 1977); Marcia G. Synnott, *The Half-Opened Door: Discrimination in Admissions to Harvard, Yale, and Princeton, 1900–1970* (Westport, Conn.: Greenwood, 1977); Geiger, *To Advance Knowledge,* 129–39.

45. Geiger, *To Advance Knowledge,* 206; see appendixes for institutional finances.

46. Burton R. Clark, *The Distinctive College* (New Brunswick, NJ: Transaction, 1992 [1970]), 184–232.

47. Enrollment data are from the *Digest of Education Statistics.* For postwar academic development, see Richard M. Freeland, *Academia's Golden Age: Universities in Massachusetts, 1945–1970* (New York: Oxford University Press, 1992); Roger L. Geiger, *Research and Relevant Knowledge: American Research Universities since World War II* (New York: Oxford University Press, 1993).

48. Harvard University, *General Education in a Free Society* (Cambridge: Harvard University Press, 1945).

49. Sarah E. Turner and William Bowen, "The Flight from the Arts and

Sciences: Trends in Degrees Conferred," *Science* 250 (1990): 517–21; Roger L. Geiger, "The College Curriculum and the Marketplace: What Place for Disciplines in the Trend Toward Vocationalism?" *Change,* Nov. 1980.

50. The following draws on Geiger, *Research and Relevant Knowledge.*

51. Christopher Jencks and David Riesman, *The Academic Revolution* (Chicago: University of Chicago Press, 1968); Geiger, *Research and Relevant Knowledge,* 198–203.

52. Roger L. Geiger, *Knowledge and Money: Research Universities and the Paradox of the Marketplace* (Stanford: Stanford University Press, 2004).

Chapter Three

Autonomy and Accountability

Who Controls Academe?

Frank A. Schmidtlein and Robert O. Berdahl

If a college or university is effectively to define its purposes and select or invent the means of attaining them, it must have a high degree of autonomy. Howard Bowen observed that the "production process" in higher education is far more intricate and complicated than that in any industrial enterprise.[1] Turning resources into human values defies standardization. Students vary enormously in academic aptitude, in interests, in intellectual dispositions, in social and cultural characteristics, in educational and vocational objectives, and in many other ways. Furthermore, the disciplines and professions with which institutions of higher learning are concerned require diverse methods of investigation, intellectual structures, means of relating methods of inquiry and ideas to personal and social values, and processes of relating knowledge to human experience. Learning, consequently, is a subtle process, the nature of which may vary from student to student, from institution to institution, from discipline to discipline, from one scholar or teacher to another, and from one level of student development to another. The intricacy and unpredictability of both learning and investigation require a high degree of freedom from intellectually limiting external intervention and control if an institution of higher education is to perform effectively.

These characteristics of colleges and universities have led Etzioni[2] to make a distinction between "administrative" and "professional" authority. This distinction has important implications for the tensions between the concepts of autonomy and accountability in higher education. Unfortunately, this distinction commonly is not understood nor, perhaps, appreciated by public officials who are more familiar with the "administrative" concept of organizational coordination and control and who believe that direct bureaucratic intervention can, or should be able to, effectively alter academic practices in institutions. Etzioni contrasts decision-making authority in organizations whose workforce is primarily composed of professionals with those where the primary workforces possess less complex skills: "Administration assumes a power hierarchy. Without a clear ordering of higher and lower in rank, in which the higher in rank have more power than the lower ones and hence can control and coordinate the latter's activities, the basic principle of administration is violated; the organization ceases to be a coordinated tool. However, knowledge is largely an individual property; unlike other organization means, it cannot be transferred from one person to another by decree. Creativity is basically individual and can only to a very limited degree be ordered and coordinated by the superior in rank." He then concludes that, in organizations made up of professionals, "the surgeon has to decide whether or not to operate. Students of the professions have pointed out that the autonomy granted to professionals who are basically responsible to their consciences (though they may be censured by their peers and in extreme cases by the courts) is necessary for effective professional work. . . . It is this highly individualized principle which is diametrically opposed to the very essence of the organizational principle of control and coordination by superiors—i.e., the principle of administrative authority."

Autonomy and Academic Freedom

On first thought, one might identify academic freedom with autonomy. Certainly, a high degree of intellectual independence is necessary for faculty and students in choosing the subjects of study and investigation, in searching for the truth without unreasonable or arbitrary restrictions, and in expressing scholarly conclusions without censorship. Some forms of external control or even subtle efforts to influence teaching, learning, or research may endanger intellectual freedom. However, academic freedom and university autonomy, though related, are not synonymous. Academic freedom as a concept is universal and absolute, whereas autonomy is of necessity parochial and relative.

Presumably, state boards of higher education designating the missions of sectors or particular institutions after appropriate studies and consultation would not be an unwarranted invasion of autonomy. But specifying the content of academic programs, academic organization, curriculum, and methods of teaching for the attainment of designated missions is likely to be considered unjustified intervention. A coordinating or governing board might phase out a doctoral program at a particular campus (after appropriate study and consultation) without unwarranted invasion of institutional autonomy or violation of academic freedom. The federal government might impose antidiscrimination procedures in admitting students or in appointing and promoting faculty members without interfering unjustifiably in academic affairs, provided the means do not make unreasonable demands on the institutions or violate necessary confidentiality of records. If appropriate safeguards are followed, no invasion of academic freedom need be suffered.

Requirements for accountability may impose onerous procedures on an institution, but even these restraints may not endanger academic freedom. Whether restrictions on DNA research put an undesirable limit on choice of problems for investigation remains a controversial issue. In this case, public protection may justify some interventions that seem to infringe on academic freedom. One may agree that the absence of external controls does not guarantee academic freedom and that certain elements of external control do not endanger intellectual independence, but an institution's right to mobilize its intellectual resources—and within reasonable limits, even its financial resources—toward the attainment of its agreed-upon purposes is at least strongly fortified by a relatively high degree of autonomy.[3]

The Nature of Accountability

Zumeta,[4] in an excellent review of accountability in higher education, notes that institutions historically were viewed "as necessarily freewheeling and unconstrained." He quotes Trow, saying they "were treated with unusual deference by their state sponsors, who were often content to 'leave the money on the stump' with few questions asked." Today, however, Zumeta observes that colleges and universities face unprecedented external demands and "this shift in states' expectations and relations with colleges and universities is significant not only for academe's own interests but . . . for important societal values."

Growing external demands on institutions have produced conflicting concepts of how to maintain institutional accountability. Some states have reduced some substantive and procedural controls on institutions, usually to encourage market forces that are expected to promote consumer interests and innovation, while some have strengthened administrative controls. In some cases, states have reduced financial, personnel, procurement, and other procedural controls while imposing less direct substantive and procedural controls by mandating accountability, quality assessment, and performance budgeting processes. There is a vigorous debate over what mix of market incentives and administrative controls are appropriate and effective to assure that institutions meet their public responsibilities. Both administrative controls and marketplace pressures can restrict institutions' autonomy, but they generally prefer accommodating the more diverse pressures of the marketplace over the centralized imposition of administrative controls. A delicate balance is required between an unregulated marketplace and expensive and stultifying government-imposed administrative controls.

Shulock[5] observes that "the meaning of accountability has evolved as new models of public management have emerged in the last 15 years. The older view emphasizes accountability for sound fiscal management and following rules. The newer view emphasizes outcomes and argues that public managers should be given flexibility to produce the desired outcomes with minimal oversight of how funds were allocated or what methods were used—a kind of oversight viewed as micromanagement." She also points out that accountability and assessment of student learning are not the same: "State-level accountability is about the effectiveness of our institutions and public policies, *collectively,* in meeting the educational needs of the citizens of the state; it is not about assessing the effectiveness of each institution or providing consumer information to support the private choices of citizens" (emphasis in original).

Financial austerity causes legislatures, state coordinating boards, and even consolidated governing boards to look more critically at institutional roles, at the availability and distribution of functions and programs, at effectiveness, and at educational and operational costs. As the federal government extends support for higher education, it prohibits discrimination in the admission of students and in the appointment and promotion of faculty members. The public at large has become more conscious of its institutions of higher education. States and localities are more demanding of education and service, more critical of what they perceive institutions to be doing, and more vocal in expressing their criticisms and desires. Public institutions, always answerable to the general interest, can no longer avoid defending what they do or do not do. They increasingly have to explain themselves, defend their essential character, and demonstrate that their service is worth the cost. They will become increasingly answerable (i.e., accountable) to numerous constituencies for the range of their services and the effectiveness of their performance.

Accountability is not confined to an institution's external relationships. Internally, a college or university is a complex of mutual responsibilities and reciprocal pressures for accountability with a wide variety of ongoing and periodic performance assessments. As Etizioni[6] pointed out, professionals have a primary accountability to their peers for the quality and integrity of their efforts. These include not only the peers at their institutions but also those in their disciplines and professional fields nationally and, increasingly, internationally. External accountability to peers is accomplished largely through processes such as accreditation, peer review of manuscripts for publication, and peer review of research proposals. Important as these bases of accountability are, this chapter is devoted to a discussion of accountability to external agencies.

In this environment of increasing demands for accountability, intellectual freedom in colleges and universities generally has maintained widespread public and governmental support, although occasionally governmental officials attempt to sanction academics who express unpopular views or criticize government policies. Also some institutions have abolished tenure, thus potentially inhibiting faculty expression of unpopular views.

Accountability to the Public

Ultimately, public institutions of higher education are broadly answerable to the people who support them. After California voters earlier failed to approve a state bond issue providing large sums for the construction of medical school facilities and gave other evidences of disaffection, the then president of the University of California recognized the ultimate public accountability of the university: "Make no mistake," he said to the Assembly of the Academic Senate, "the university is a public institution, supported by the people through the actions of their elected representatives and executives. They will not allow it to be operated in ways which are excessively at variance with the general public will. By various pressures and devices, the university will be forced to yield and to conform if it gets too far away from what the public expects and wants."[7]

At one time, the people were relatively remote from their public institutions, but citizens now find their future economic, social, and cultural lives increasingly influenced, in some cases virtually determined, by their colleges and universities. Consequently, public institutions have had to become responsive to a wider range of economic interests and to a more diverse pattern of ethnic and cultural backgrounds and aspirations. Minority groups are pressing for financial assistance, for remedial programs when necessary for admission or attainment of academic standards, and for academic programs that will meet their interests and perceived needs. As special interest groups have pressed the university to provide the services they believe they need, students have organized to promote their interests. With the prospect of declining enrollments in the 1980s, many colleges and universities responded to that student market by establishing new vocational and professional programs of study, and most institutions are struggling to redistribute faculty, equipment, and resources as students shift from liberal arts courses to vocational and professional curricula.

Serving the public interest is a complicated process; not all institutions will undertake the same missions or serve common purposes. Accountability is further complicated by a question of what special interests should be served and what should be put aside.

The interests to be served by an institution are determined through both external and internal political processes resulting in complex compromises and the accommodation of many, often conflicting, objectives. As a consequence, accountability, which implies agreed upon purposes and objectives, has significant political as well as technical dimensions. Many attempts to institute accountability processes have failed because they were based on an inaccurate assumption that substantial agreement was possible on a stable set of measurable institutional goals and objectives. The directions institutions take result from a constantly evolving complex set of compromises among a variety of contending internal and external interests and from the accommodation of resource and time constraints.

Conflicts over the appropriate locations for making various kinds of decisions have occurred since tribal times. They typically involve balancing collective and private interests. Schmidtlein describes a number of factors that influence where decisions are located. He observes that persons at various locations in governance structures have ready access to differing kinds of information. Those in state government are in a better position to observe the relationships among colleges and universities and typically have a more holistic sense of public sentiment. Consequently, they are likely to be more sensitive than institutions to the appropriateness of the entire pattern of institutions and their missions, the relationships among institutions, and priorities across the entire state system of higher education.

In contrast, those located in institutions possess more information about local circumstances and the trade-offs involved in making decisions affecting local issues. When decisions involve internal institutional issues, central officials are likely to have oversimplified views of the factors involved and make inappropriate decisions. Many highly relevant kinds of information are hard to quantify and communicate effectively to those in government and difficult for them to evaluate. Consequently, they are likely to delay decisions by requesting increasing numbers of costly reports and data to assure themselves that their decisions are correct because often they are aware of their relative ignorance of local complexities. Lacking intimate knowledge of local complexities, they also are more susceptible to simplistic solutions to issues, more likely to embrace management fads, and tend to focus more on information collection and decision-making processes than on the substance of the decisions.

In practice, higher education's systems need to achieve a balance between the benefits and costs of central and local decision making. Government oversight and steering are needed to assure, for example, that a set of institutions exist whose missions serve the diverse needs of the public and to counter occasional attempts of two-year colleges to become four-year institutions and four-year teaching institutions to become graduate/research universities.[8] Changes in institutional missions should serve the public interest; not be based primarily on institutional ambitions to move up the prestige ladder. Government oversignt also is needed to assure that a diverse set of academic programs exists that meets the legitimate needs of the public while avoiding unnecessary duplication. Institutions, however, should have the freedom to design the content of their academic programs and courses and their research initiatives. They also should have the procedural freedom needed to pursue their programs in an efficient manner. As Berdahl notes,[9] governments need to retain authority over substantive issues related to the character of higher education systems while institutions should be given a very large measure of freedom over procedural aspects of their programs. Unstructured competition reduces diversity and increases costs through program duplication, while excessive regulation restricts the ability of competent institutional leaders to take expeditious advantage of new opportunities and adjust to new circumstances. Government controls seldom remedy the errors of those lacking competence. Thus, accountability is both general (responding to definitions of the broad public interest) and particular (responding to more limited constituencies).

Later chapters in this book will elaborate on the tensions between autonomy and accountability in higher education for state governments, the federal government, and the courts. Here, we merely provide brief overviews.

Governmental Intervention

The State Government

Accountability to the public is mediated by the operation of several governance layers between it and the institutions in question. Colleges and universities are answerable most immediately to their governing boards. Most public boards have statutory status: they were created by legislatures and are in nearly all respects under legislative control. Seven or eight states have given constitutional status to their public universities: "The idea was to remove questions of management, control, and the supervision of the universities from the reach of politicians in state legislatures and governors' offices. The universities were to be a fourth branch of government, functioning co-authoritatively with the legislature, the judiciary, and the executive."[10]

The purpose for creating universities' constitutional status was to give them a much greater degree of autonomy and self-direction than statutory status would provide. Their autonomy, however, has been materially eroded over the years. A study of statutory and constitutional boards in 1973 showed that the supposedly constitutionally autonomous university "is losing a good deal of its ability to exercise final judgment on the use not only of its state funds but also of those derived from other sources. It now undergoes intensive reviews of budgets and programs by several different state agencies, by special commissions, and by legislative committees, all of which look for ways to control."[11] Whether an institution has statutory or constitutional status, or even whether it is public or private, it is moving into the governmental orbit.

Most students of university governance believe that government officials should not serve on governing boards, since this identifies the institution too closely with political and governmental agencies. In California the governor, the lieutenant governor, the superintendent of public instruction, the president of the state board of agriculture, and the speaker of the legislative assembly are among the ex officio voting members of the board of regents of the University of California. Governors may also use their appointive power to attempt to influence governing boards, although most boards have staggered terms that prevent governors from appointing a majority of members until they have served several years in office.

However, sometimes governors can accomplish through other means what they lack the power to do through direct appointment of trustees or regents. For example, when Ronald Reagan was governor of California, he heartily disapproved of the way President Clark Kerr was handling the mid-1960s student uprisings. A minority of university regents agreed with Governor Reagan; to them he added a few appointments to seats that had fallen vacant. He still lacked a majority who agreed with him, however, until he emphatically noted that the university's budget did not have constitutional autonomy and that he would not look kindly at continued resistance to his point of view. Consequently, Clark Kerr, as he later commented, left the university as he had come to it, "fired with enthusiasm!" Enough additional regents had been intimidated by the governor's statements to swing opinions over to his side.

Although governors may thus influence institutions via their governing boards, they make their greatest impact "through the executive budget process." [12] The state finance or budget officer, who is ordinarily responsible to the governor, may also exercise an important element of authority by controlling shifts or changes in line-item budgets. Some state finance departments conduct preaudits of expenditures that not only pass on the legality of the use of itemized funds but also give the state officer the opportunity to rule on the substance or purpose of the expenditures.

But important as the executive officers of state government may be to public colleges and universities, state legislatures are more so. The institutions are dependent on the legislature's understanding of their broad missions and programs, its financial support, and its judgment of the institutions' educational effectiveness. Even a constitutionally autonomous public university is ultimately accountable to the legislature for the ways in which it uses its state-appropriated funds and for the effectiveness of its educational services. Legislators have become increasingly restless in the face of what some regard as the continuing neglect of undergraduate teaching and the overemphasis on research at graduate/research universities. Studies of faculty workload are common, with some legislatures considering mandated faculty teaching loads. At times the long arms of state finance officers have reached into academic affairs by conducting program audits or even program evaluations. [13]

> Issues raised in program evaluation include the consistency of the program with the assigned institutional role and function; the adequacy of planning in regard to the objectives, program structure, processes, implementation, and evaluation of outcomes; the adherence of program operation to the objectives, structural features, processes, sequence, and outcome appraisal originally specified or the presentation of a sound rationale for any deviations from the original prescription; an evaluation of planning and operation and use of feedback for alteration and improvement; and provision for cost benefit analyses. [14]

State governments determine eligibility for state aid to both public and private postsecondary institutions. Most states charter and license degree-granting institutions, but some observers believe that in most instances the standards specified are insufficient to ensure quality. The Education Commission of the States has urged that the states establish minimum quality standards for all postsecondary institutions.

Student Assessment

As reported in chapter 7, states are seeking to hold institutions answerable for the attainment of their professed goals in the form of demonstrable changes in students. Historically, there appeared to be an implicit assumption that responsibility for learning outcomes should be placed primarily on students. However, over the past three or four decades, institutions increasingly have been viewed as having a major portion of this responsibility. Today, institutional demonstration of student learning outcomes is commonly viewed as part of their responsibility for public accountability and states are seeking evidence they are meeting this challenge. However, as noted earlier, Shulock asserts that demonstration of learning outcomes is *assessment* and is an internal institutional responsibility. Complex learning outcomes are extremely difficult to identify, to agree on and assign priorities, and to communicate to government officials and the public. This view may be simple in conception, but it is extremely difficult in implementation. First, it is essential to translate goals into relevant and agreed upon outcomes. An even more complicated task is to devise means of determining the extent to which students have attained these outcomes. The first question to be asked is, How has the student changed at a given point in relation to this characteristic at entrance? This requires information on how students vary at the starting point not only in previous academic achievement but also in general and special academic aptitude; information on students' intellectual dispositions, such as a theoretical or pragmatic orientation; and information on students' interests, attitudes, values, and motivations, to mention only some of the dimensions relevant to the educational process. These attributes establish baselines for estimating the amount of change over stated periods, and some are indicative of students' educability.

Studies of the influence of institutions on student development also require means of measuring or describing college characteristics, "the prevailing atmosphere, the social and intellectual climate, the style of a campus," as well as "educational treatments."[15] One of the complications involved in describing college environments is that student characteristics and institutional qualities are by no means unrelated. Furthermore, most institutions are not all of a piece and the total environment may have less influence on particular students than the suborganizations or subcultures of which they are members.

It is even more difficult to determine the impact of the environment on students. First, environmental variables probably do not act singly but in combination. Second, changes that occur in students may not be attributable to the effect of the college environment itself. Developmental processes established early in the individual's experience may continue through the college years; some of these processes take place normally within a wide range of environmental conditions, and in order to alter the course and extent of development, it would be necessary to introduce fairly great changes in environmental stimulation. Third, changes that occur during the college years may be less the effect of college experience as such than of the general social environment in which the college exists and the students live.[16]

For these and many other reasons it is extremely difficult to relate changes in behavior to specific characteristics of the college or to particular patterns of educational activity. Studies of change in students' characteristics reveal wide differences from person to person and detectable differences from institution to institution. Bowen summarizes the evidence on change in students in both cognitive and noncognitive outcomes and also differences in the effects of different institutions: "On the whole, the evidence supports the hypothesis that the differences in impact are relatively small—when impact is defined as value added in the form of change in students during the college years."[17]

Given these complexities, the assessment of student learning outcomes and their implications for academic programs appear best accomplished within institutions by faculty who are the ones with detailed knowledge of the students and their academic progress and accomplishments. The appropriate role of state government and accrediting agencies should be to assure that institutions have appropriate policies and procedures for assessing student learning outcomes and to review the effectiveness of their academic programs.

Notwithstanding the complexity of the processes described above, a number of states have established policies seeking to assess student learning. But in most states, policy makers were persuaded to place the responsibility for developing the assessment program on each public institution, allowing each one to develop a program appropriate to its particular role and mission. Only by allowing for such diversity is it likely that any institution will gain a sense of ownership of the process and be encouraged to use the results for self-improvement.

The Federal Government

Autonomy/accountability issues of American higher education vis-à-vis the federal government primarily involve three major relevant federal policies areas: federal support for research, federal support for student aid, and federal interventions to support social justice. While later chapters in this volume will discuss both the federal policies and the role of the courts in much greater detail, here we present a brief overview of our perspectives on those key issues relating to autonomy and accountability. Issues in the research domain include the following:

— Are internal research priorities among major research universities unnaturally distorted by federal priorities?
— Does the peer review process for awarding federal research grants allow enough recognition to women and minority scientists at so-called second-level research institutions?
— Has the right balance been struck between the need for federal accounting requirements and the setting of indirect research costs and the need for research institutions to have both flexibility and sufficient research funds to cover their internal related costs?
— Are the costs and limitations of federal requirements for human subjects' protection and avoidance of fraud excessive?

Our response to the first research issue is not only to acknowledge that federal policies have obviously tilted research universities' priorities in ways that they might not have chosen, absent the federal funds, but also to point out that the bottom line has been to aid a small, but substantial, number of public and private research institutions to become world class, as noted by their international achievements. Thus, on balance, we regard this federal role as somewhat mixed but, overall, a very positive influence.

Similarly, on the criticisms of peer review as too elite oriented, while we welcome the broadening of most panels of peer review to reflect a greater diversity of institutions, we defend the basic principle of concentrating most of the federal research funds at a limited number of institutions and with a limited number of scientists widely recognized as constituting "the best." Obviously, the persons judging "the best" must be drawn from a fair cross section of qualified scientists.

The federal government's accounting requirements for institutions to justify their "overhead" costs are expensive, but they are designed to ensure that cost calculations are accurate and comparable across institutions. The federal government needs to work closely with institutions to minimize this burden, to avoid the impression of being driven by overzealous attempts primarily aimed at reducing federal costs, and to recognize and support the infrastructure costs associated with the research projects or programs.

The federal government has instituted extensive requirements to help ensure that researchers at colleges and universities do not engage in practices that harm research subjects and to reduce incidences of academic fraud. The principal issue is whether these requirements have become overly restrictive and so rigidly applied that they hamper legitimate research and add to its costs. There appears to be a tendency for the federal government to react strongly to individual cases of misconduct by imposing burdensome requirements on all receiving federal support. Reaching an appropriate balance between reducing misconduct through regulation, on the one hand, and the hampering of legitimate research practices and increasing the costs of research, on the other, is a difficult task that merits further attention.

Issues in the area of student aid policies relate to federal efforts to tighten up on student loan defaults, and more recent proposals from a few in Congress and in the U.S. Department of Education consider linking eligibility for federal funds to student attrition/graduation rates and even, possibly, to student grades and quality dimensions. Here we recognize that loan default rates have declined markedly in the face of reform efforts and then warn that proposed federal moves to link student aid to assessments of student quality outcomes may be no more successful than our earlier analysis of the shortcomings of state efforts along the same dimensions.

Issues concerning the federal role in promoting social justice pertain to the effects of executive orders and court rulings on such institutional policies as student admissions, faculty hiring and promotion, and composition of governing boards. We recognize that federal activities in these areas have obviously lessened the former autonomy of most public and private institutions but are justified to many observers, including us, in the name of broader social values. We realize that some aspects of this set of issues are still controversial and that people of good will can disagree. Chapter 8 will examine the role of the courts in this area in greater detail.

Judicial Intervention

The increasingly intimate relationship between government and higher education means that colleges and universities are in and of the world, not removed and protected from it. Toward the end of the earlier period of student disruption on college campuses it was observed that "judicial decisions and the presence on campus of the community police, the highway patrol, and the National Guard symbolize the fact that colleges and universities have increasingly lost the privilege of self-regulation to the external authority of the police and the courts. . . . It is apparent that colleges and universities have become increasingly accountable to the judicial system of the community, the state, and the national government."[18]

William Kaplin's book on higher education and the law summarizes legal conditions bearing on higher education institutions and gives numerous examples of court decisions involving trustees, administrators, faculty members, and students, as well as cases involving relationships between institutions and both state and federal governments.[19] Recourse to the courts to settle disputes has increased greatly during the past four decades. Faculty members may sue over dismissal, appointment, tenure, and accessibility to personnel records. Students may sue to secure access to their records, over discrimination in admissions and over failure by an institution to deliver what it promised from the classroom and other academic resources. Institutions may take governments to court for the purpose of protecting their constitutional status and, as we illustrate above, in contention over the enforcement of federal regulations.

The traditional aloofness of the campus has been shattered. Kaplin pointed out that "higher education was often viewed as a unique enterprise, which could regulate itself through reliance on tradition and consensual agreement. It operated best by operating autonomously, and it thrived on the privacy which autonomy afforded."[20] The idea of the college or university as a sanctuary was once considered necessary to protect the institution and its constituencies from repressive external control and invasions upon intellectual freedom. Now, other means must be devised to protect an institution's essential spirit while it bows to the world of law and tribunal.

Accrediting Agencies

Accreditation is a process for holding postsecondary institutions accountable to voluntary nongovernmental agencies for meeting certain minimum educational standards. Institutional reviews are conducted by representatives from institutions according to standards derived by member institutions.

Institutional and program accreditation are the two types usually noted. Six regional agencies are responsible for accrediting entire institutions' schools, departments, academic programs, and related activities. Program accreditation, extended by professional societies or other groups of specialists or vocational associations, is extended to a specific school, department, or academic program in such fields as medicine, law, social work, chemistry, engineering, and business administration. A variation is an agency for accrediting single-purpose institutions, such as trade and technical schools.

If the institutions or program being accredited fails to meet minimum standards, the obvious sanction is withdrawal of approval (or rejection for a first-time candidate). Since accreditation is, in theory, voluntary and nongovernmental, an institution or program judged inadequate will suffer loss of prestige but could presumably survive without it. However, in practice, since the federal government requires accreditation by some federally recognized accrediting association for the institution to be eligible for federal research and student aid funds, the process has in effect become much less "voluntary."

The issue then shifts to the federal government's decision to approve a given accrediting association for inclusion on the Department of Education's list. For these decisions the department is presumably influenced by the recognition status accorded the association in question by the recently formed (1996) Council for Higher Education Accreditation (CHEA). CHEA functions as an umbrella national group for accreditation activities and works actively with the federal government on matters of quality assurance, student outcomes, and internationalizing higher education.

Accreditation issues and the particular role of CHEA are discussed at greater length in chapter 9.

Educational Costs

Although "a tidy dollar comparison of costs and benefits is conspicuously absent," Bowen goes on to list the financial value of higher education.[21] First, the monetary returns from higher education alone are probably sufficient to offset all the costs. Second, the nonmonetary returns are several times as valuable as the monetary returns. And third, the total returns from higher education in all its aspects exceed the cost by several times.

It is usually said that institutions should be accountable for both effectiveness and efficiency, the latter having to do with the cost of the outcomes attained. But costs are extremely difficult to compute in analyzing differences in student change, both within and among institutions. And, as pointed out above, it is extremely difficult to relate changes to significant features of educational environments. Bowen and others have made a significant contribution to the analysis of institutional costs, including expenditures per student, cost differences among institutions, and the implications of cost data for administrative policies and decisions.[22] But we have a long way to go before sound means of determining cost effectiveness are developed.

Conclusion

Although autonomy cannot be absolute, only a high degree of independence will permit colleges and universities to devise and choose effective academic means of realizing their professed goals. First of all, institutions must ensure academic freedom to faculty and students. Autonomy does not guarantee intellectual independence, but some forms of external intervention, overt or covert, may undermine such freedom.

While intellectual fetters must be opposed, institutions may legitimately be expected to be held accountable to their constituencies for the integrity of their operations and, as far as possible, for the efficiency of their operations. Colleges and universities are answerable to the general public, which supports them and needs their services. Responding to the public interest, federal and state governments intervene in institutional affairs. At times, government pressure may induce an institution to offer appropriate services; at other times, government agencies may attempt to turn an institution, or even a system, in inappropriate directions. Only constructive consultation and requirements for accountability that recognize the fundamental characteristics of academe will effectively serve the public interest and give vitality to the educational enterprise.

Most institutions, including those supported by legislatures, are not immediately controlled by the general public. Public accountability is mediated by several layers of representation. Institutions are directly answerable to their governing boards. They may be responsible to a consolidated governing board. They may be first responsible to institutional or systemwide governing boards, and these in turn may be under the surveillance of statewide coordinating boards. They also must respond to the requirements of accrediting agencies. Institutions thus may be controlled by a hierarchy of agencies, an arrangement that may complicate their procedures for accountability but that may provide a measure of protection from unwise or unnecessary external intervention.

Colleges and universities are in a period when they are being asked to provide not only data on the attainment of defined outcomes, including changes in students during undergraduate, graduate, and professional education, but also evidence that results have been gained at "reasonable" cost. They are confronted with the difficult challenge of resisting inappropriate government accountability processes, with their added costs and damages to the academic enterprise, while recognizing legitimate state interests and avoiding the appearance of self-interest and resisting sincere efforts to improve their performance. Institutions need to communicate clearly the accountability and assessment practices they currently employ and take the lead in designing processes that are compatible with the character of colleges and universities and with the complex political and professional judgments faculty and institutional administrators must make to maintain and achieve a quality academic program.

NOTES

This chapter is a revision of a previously published chapter by T. R. McConnell, now deceased. It is dedicated to his memory.

1. Howard R. Bowen, *Investment in Learning* (San Francisco: Jossey-Bass, 1977), 12.

2. Amitai Etzioni, *Modern Organizations* (Englewood Cliffs, NJ: Prentice-Hall, 1964), 75–84.

3. Eric Ashby discusses the relationship between academic freedom and autonomy in *Universities: British, Indian, African* (Cambridge, Mass.: Harvard University Press, 1976), chap. 10.

4. William Zumeta, "Public Policy and Accountability in Higher Education: Lessons for the Past and Present for the New Millennium," in *States and Public Higher Education Policy: Affordability, Access, and Accountability*, ed. Donald E. Heller (Baltimore: Johns Hopkins University Press, 2001), 155–97.

5. Nancy Shulock, "An Accountability Framework for California Higher Education: Informing Public Policy and Improving Outcomes" (Sacramento: Institute for Higher Education Leadership & Policy, California State University, November 2002).

6. Etzioni, *Modern Organizations.*

7. C. J. Hitch, "Remarks of the President," address delivered to the Assembly of the California Academic Senate, June 15, 1970.

8. Frank Schmidtlein, "Assumptions Commonly Underlying Governmental Quality Assessment Practices" (paper presented at the 25th EAIR Forum, Limerick, Ireland, August 25, 2003).

9. Robert O. Berdahl, "Universities and Governments in the 21st Century: Possible Relevance of U.S. Experience to Other Parts of the World," in *Toward a New Model of Governance for Universities?* eds. Dietmar Braun and Francois-Xavier Merrien (London: Jessica Kingsley, 1999).

10. Lyman A. Glenny and Thomas K. Dalglish, *Public Universities, State Agencies, and the Law: Constitutional Autonomy in Decline* (Berkeley: University of California, Center for Research and Development in Higher Education, 1973), 42.

11. Ibid., 43.

12. John W. Lederle, "Governors and Higher Education," in *State Politics and Higher Education,* ed. Leonard E. Goodall (Dearborn: University of Michigan Press, 1976), 43–50.

13. Robert O. Berdahl, "Legislative Program Evaluation," in *Increasing the Public Accountability of Higher Education,* ed. John K. Folger (San Francisco: Jossey-Bass, 1977), 35–65.

14. Paul L. Dressel, ed., *The Autonomy of Public Colleges* (San Francisco: Jossey-Bass, 1980), 43.

15. C. R. Pace, "When Students Judge Their College," *College Board Review* 58 (Spring 1960): 26–28.

16. T. R. McConnell, "Accountability and Autonomy," *Journal of Higher Education* 42 (1971): 446–63.

17. Bowen, *Investment in Learning,* 257. Other evidence on changes in students over the college years is presented in Alexander W. Astin, *Four Criti-*

cal Years (San Francisco: Jossey-Bass, 1977); Patrick Terenzini and Ernest Pascarella, *How College Affects Students* (San Francisco: Jossey-Bass, 1991).

18. McConnell, "Accountability and Autonomy."

19. William A. Kaplin, *The Law of Higher Education* (San Francisco: Jossey-Bass, 1983).

20. Ibid., 4.

21. Bowen, *Investment in Learning*, 447–48.

22. Howard R. Bowen, *The Cost of Higher Education* (San Francisco: Jossey-Bass, 1980).

Chapter Four

Academic Freedom

Past, Present, and Future beyond September 11

Robert M. O'Neil

The subject of academic freedom has been a central theme throughout the recent history of American higher education. Within the collegiate community, there have been widely differing perspectives on certain key issues—for example, whether academic freedom applies as fully to students as to professors, how far beyond the classroom and laboratory such protection extends, and what circumstances might warrant the curtailment of academic freedom to serve broader societal interests. This chapter explores the meaning and scope of academic freedom in four phases: its origins and early historical development, its current status in the courts and in institutional policy, challenges that are certain to arise as teaching and learning occur increasingly in an electronic environment, and the fate of academic freedom in the aftermath of September 11, 2001.

Academic Freedom's Roots and Legacy

The origins of the concept of academic freedom lie deep in the history of teaching and scholarly inquiry.[1] German universities long recognized the concept of *Lehrfreiheit,* or freedom of professors to teach, with a corollary *Lernfreiheit,* or freedom of students to learn. Other countries recognized in different ways the distinctive status of university teachers and students, though in widely varying degrees. What is most striking about the importation of these concepts to the United States is the recency of any systematic protection for academic freedom in a currently recognizable form. As late as the second decade of the twentieth century, some of our most eminent universities could discharge—or refuse even to hire—professors solely because their views on economic or social issues were deemed radical or subversive. While many within the academic community found such actions abhorrent, and many governing boards took a more tolerant view of outspoken scholars, the establishment of clear principles protecting the expression of unpopular views within or outside the classroom occurred surprisingly late in our history.

The formal origins of academic freedom in this country almost certainly lie in the issuance in 1915 of a "declaration of principles" by a committee of senior scholars who had been convened by the fledgling American Association of University Professors (AAUP). That declaration, some twenty pages in length, canvassed a wide range of issues. Professor Walter Metzger, the preeminent historian of academic freedom, describes the declaration in this way: "Utilitarian in temper and conviction, the theorists of 1915 did not view the expressional freedoms of academics as a bundle of abstract rights. They regarded them as corollaries of the contemporary public need for universities that would increase the sum of human knowledge and furnish experts for public service—new functions that had been added to the time-honored one of qualifying students for degrees."[2] The drafters of the declaration thus characterized the emerging university of their time as an "intellectual experiment station, where new ideas may germinate and where the fruit, though still distasteful to the community as a whole, may be allowed to ripen until finally, perchance, it may become part of the accepted intellectual food of the nation and the world."[3]

Such an institution must, the declaration went on to insist, be prepared to tolerate a range of views on controversial issues. It must also tolerate those members of its faculty who expressed such aberrant views. Academic institutions that sought to repress or silence such views simply did not deserve the respect of the higher education community. Thus, concluded the declaration, any university that places restrictions on the intellectual and expressive freedom of its professors effectively proclaims itself a proprietary institution and should be so described in making any appeal for funds, and the general public should be advised that the institution has no claim to general support or esteem.

The reception of these views was not entirely harmonious, even in intellectual circles. The *New York Times,* in an editorial fairly representative of the more conservative media of the time, scoffed at the newly declared principles: " 'Academic freedom,' that is, the inalienable right of every college instructor to make a fool of himself and his college by . . . intemperate, sensational prattle about every subject under heaven . . . and still keep on the payroll or be reft therefrom only by an elaborate process, is cried to the winds by the organized dons."[4] The reference to "an elaborate process" was not entirely unfair, since a major element of the declaration was a cornerstone of what would become the concept of academic tenure—the precept that academic freedom entailed procedural due process for the dismissal of faculty as much as a limitation on the reasons for which such dismissal might occur.[5]

Thus by the time the United States entered World War I (an event that would create new tensions between professors and society), three vital elements were already in place. There was a rather elaborate and forceful declaration of the basic principles of academic freedom. There was the nucleus of a guarantee of tenure, in the form of procedures that should be followed in the event an institution wished to remove or terminate a professor. And there was an organization, created by and for the benefit of university faculty, committed not only to promulgating and publicizing the new principles but also to enforcing those principles by investigating egregious departures from them and disseminating the results of such inquiries in a form that would eventually become known as *censure.*

The next major milestone along the route to broader recognition of academic freedom was a statement adopted in 1940 as a joint effort between AAUP and the Association of American Colleges (now Association of American Colleges and Universities), a longtime partner in this enterprise. The 1940 "Statement of Principles of Academic Freedom and Tenure" soon drew the support and adherence of many learned societies and academic organizations. By the time of its sixtieth anniversary at the turn of a new century, the Statement had the formal endorsement of more than 150 such groups, representing virtually every facet of academic life and every scholarly discipline, as well as the endorsement of the great majority of research universities and liberal arts colleges.[6]

The 1940 Statement remains almost as nearly inviolate as the U.S. Constitution. There have been a few "interpretive comments" added over the years and codified in 1970, and the gender-based language of the original document was modified to achieve neutrality in 1990. The core of the Statement is a declaration, remarkably brief, that university professors are entitled to academic freedom in three vital dimensions—freedom in research and in the publication of the results of research, freedom in the classroom in discussing the subject matter of the course and when speaking or writing as citizens, and freedom from institutional censorship or unwarranted sanction. Each of these freedoms entails corollary responsibilities and limitations; with regard to research, for example, the Statement cautions that, "research for pecuniary return should be based upon an understanding with the authorities of the institution." In the classroom, college professors "should be careful not to introduce . . . controversial matter which has no relation to their subject." Teachers, when speaking or writing as citizens, "should at all times be accurate, should exercise appropriate restraint, should show respect for the opinions of others, and should make every effort to indicate that they are not speaking for the institution."

The balance of the 1940 Statement defines the basic elements of faculty tenure, including the need for every institution to adopt a clear statement of the terms and conditions of appointment, a finite probationary period (recommended but not mandated of seven years), during which a nontenured teacher on the tenure track fully enjoys academic freedom, and rigorous procedures for the handling of charges that might lead to dismissal for cause. The Statement also envisions that tenured and continuing appointments might be terminated for demonstrated "financial exigency," or when a program or department is eliminated for sound academic reasons, or on the basis of a proven medical disability.

Over the years since 1940, AAUP has adopted many Statements and Policies, most of which appear today both in the *Redbook* (most recently revised in 2000) and on the Association's Web site, www.aaup.org. Especially meaningful to the evolution of professorial interests is a 1994 "Statement on the Relationship of Faculty Governance to Academic Freedom." This statement notes the vital link between meaningful faculty participation in the governance of a university and the probable condition of academic freedom on that campus. Central to such freedom is the right of a faculty member, without fear of reprisal or loss of influence, to criticize the administration and the governing board on matters of faculty concern. Thus the nexus between governance and academic freedom is vital, as this recent statement serves to remind those on both sides of this relationship.

It is not only the endorsement of virtually all learned societies and so many universities that has given the 1940 Statement such stature as a source of academic common law. The U.S. Supreme Court in one major case, and the lower federal and state courts on numerous occasions, have cited the Statement as an exemplar, guide, and template of academic freedom principles.[7] "Probably because it was formulated by both administrators and professors," observed a federal appeals court in a 1978 case, "all of the secondary authorities seem to agree [that the 1940 Statement] is the 'most widely accepted academic definition of tenure.'" Another federal court of appeals approvingly cited the AAUP policy on nonrenewal of continuing appointments, noting that its language "strikes an appropriate balance between academic freedom and educational excellence on the one hand and individual rights to fair consideration on the other." Judges have also recurrently invoked AAUP standards for determining financial exigency as a prelude to the dismissal of tenured faculty. On most issues of that sort, there simply are few if any other credible and widely accepted sources to guide lawyers and judges. Moreover, AAUP standards tend to emerge from practical experience at the campus level and have often been revised in light of further and constantly changing experience in the field. Thus it is not surprising to discover the degree of judicial reliance and respect they have received.

The actions and practices to which these standards are addressed have of course changed substantially over time as well. In the early years, those faculty members at greatest risk were economists and others in the social sciences who had spoken and written unpopular views about the nation's foreign policy or its domestic economic system, making the business and government leaders who comprised the typical board of trustees and alumni officers acutely uncomfortable. The pressures that such leaders brought to bear on the administration led even so illustrious an institution as the University of Pennsylvania to discharge from the faculty of its Wharton School the nonrevolutionary Marxist Scott Nearing; for the next several years, Nearing was an unemployable pariah in higher education, until finally the University of Toledo offered him a teaching position.[8] There were other egregious cases of outspoken critics of capitalism who were either not hired at all or, if their controversial views became known after they began teaching, were summarily dismissed, even by the most prestigious universities.

Of course there were also striking cases to the contrary. Some universities fought to keep, and to protect, "radical" or "subversive" professors, even without the full force of academic freedom and tenure—much less at this early stage the prospect of an AAUP investigation that might result in censure. Harvard's example was notable in this regard; President A. Lawrence Lowell refused in 1916 to discipline a prominent professor for his avowedly pro-German statements and outspoken opposition to U.S. entry into World War I. Lowell wisely observed that a university that officially condemns faculty views it dislikes would quickly find attributed to it—simply by the absence of such condemnation—a host of professorial utterances from which it had not formally distanced itself.

Though there were a few serious breaches during the 1920s and 1930s, the gravest challenges to academic freedom and tenure occurred during the McCarthy era of the late 1940s and early 1950s. Many professors (as well as screenwriters, actors, and others) were summoned before federal and state antisubversive legislative hearings. Often, there was no evidence that the target of such inquiry had personally done anything remotely "subversive" or "anti-American" much less actually joined the Communist Party. Rather, the witness had often befriended, collaborated, or simply met casually one or more suspected Communists or front-group members. Many professors summoned under such conditions either declined to appear at all, fearing that their mere presence would place them at risk, or appeared and (while sometimes candidly describing their own activities and associations) refused to identify suspected colleagues, describe political gatherings they had attended, or in other ways jeopardize long-standing relationships of trust within the academic community.

Recalcitrance led in many such cases to demands for reprisal. Few administrations and governing boards, especially at public institutions, were able to resist such pressures completely. The stakes were too high, the publicity too intense, and the forces too powerful, to avoid taking some action against faculty members who invoked constitutional claims to avoid compelled testimony, even when many had nothing of their own to hide. Professor Ellen Schrecker, the preeminent chronicler of faculty fates in those unhappy times, has reported that nearly 170 tenured or tenure-track professors were dismissed during the McCarthy era, mostly for suspected disloyalty never convincingly documented.[9] The most reputable (and normally most protective) institutions were among the most culpable—Harvard, Michigan, Rutgers, the University of Washington, and other top research institutions.

Much of the damage to faculty freedoms came not through outright dismissals, but in subtler (if no less insidious) forms such as the exaction of disclaimer-type loyalty oaths. When all University of California professors were required in the early 1950s to sign such oaths, some principled nonsigners simply left the faculty as a matter of conscience, though they had nothing to hide or conceal. Others brought a lawsuit in state court, which yielded a classically Pyrrhic victory. The California Supreme Court agreed with the professors that, given the constitutional autonomy of the university and its regents, they could not be made to take an oath prescribed by the legislature for all state employees. Instead, in a bitter irony, they were left subject to the even more intrusive and distrustful loyalty oath devised by the regents exclusively for University of California faculty and staff. It was not until 1967, long after the political climate had changed, that the California courts finally invalidated all loyalty oaths, following the lead that the U.S. Supreme Court had set several years earlier.

Since the McCarthy era happened just a decade after the issuance of the AAUP's 1940 Statement, and after most of the academic community had signed on, it is fair to ask whether academic freedom and tenure failed their first critical test. This is a difficult and complex question to which at least two contrasting views are responsive. One view is that the academic community, which is especially vulnerable at all times and unusually suspect during this perilous time, would have fared even worse had not such safeguards existed—that many careers were in fact saved because protective administrators and trustees could tell livid legislators and angry alumni that "our hands are tied since he/she has tenure." Some evidence supports that hypothesis; for example, the fact that no faculty were fired at institutions like Indiana University (despite pressure from an extremely conservative congressional delegation) because the insiders gave the outsiders an unwelcome but irrefutable account of the legal protections that professors enjoyed. The contrary view takes to task not only those eminent universities that caved under anti-Communist pressure but also notes that the AAUP as well as organizations like the American Civil Liberties Union were slow to respond. During the later stages of the McCarthy period, these groups did become active both on campus and in court in ways that undoubtedly afforded some protection, if arguably it was too little and too late. Thus the jury remains out on the question of whether the 1940 Statement failed its inaugural test; surely a less auspicious time for a debut could hardly be imagined.

The end of the McCarthy era brought a period of relative calm to the academic world. The 1960s launched a massive expansion of higher education during which the demand for young scholars grew geometrically and strongly diminished the likelihood of reprisals against those with unconventional views. Besides, this was a time when young people were expected to have and to express unconventional views, with college professors likely to be leading the pack. The later years of the Vietnam War did bring some institutional pressures to bear on outspoken faculty, both for publicly expressed attacks on U.S. policy in Southeast Asia, and for such collateral actions as "reconstituting" courses to focus on the rising disenchantment with Vietnam policy, as well as on poverty, racism, and the environment. But the sanctions were few and relatively mild and dismissals (at least by major institutions) almost unknown. The AAUP's investigative caseload, which certainly did not diminish during these years, consisted disproportionately of mishandled personnel actions at smaller and less sophisticated institutions, relating more to strained finances or lack of experience than to aberrant faculty voices.

The recent history of academic freedom contains one other promising feature. While those who teach in private colleges and universities cannot claim (against their institutions) the protection of the First Amendment—which applies only to government action—state university professors enjoy not only the speech rights of citizens but also a special sensitivity that courts have shown for the academic setting. Starting with a 1950s case that barred a government demand for a teacher's lecture notes, through several key rulings in the next decade that struck down loyalty oaths, to later judgments invalidating laws of other sorts that repressed campus speech, the courts consistently recognized a special role for academic freedom. Perhaps the clearest statement is that of Justice William J. Brennan, Jr., in sounding the death knell for New York State's loyalty oath in 1967:

> Academic freedom . . . is of transcendent value to all of us and not merely to the teachers concerned. That freedom is therefore a special

concern of the First Amendment, which does not tolerate laws that cast
a pall of orthodoxy over the classroom. . . . The classroom is peculiarly a
marketplace of ideas. The Nation's future depends upon leaders trained
through wide exposure to its robust exchange of ideas which discovers
truth out of a multitude of tongues, [rather] than through any kind of
authoritative selection.[10]

Although the Supreme Court has never retreated from that view
of academic freedom—indeed, has amplified it in such varied contexts as race-sensitive admission policies of state universities—there
has been some recent erosion in lower federal courts. In cases during
the late 1990s and the first years of the new century, several appeals
courts effectively created a new tension between individual and institutional academic freedom. When a faculty member challenges on
First Amendment grounds a government policy by which the institution is bound, several recent cases seem to favor the institutional
interest to the detriment of the individual professor's interest. Most
dramatically, when the Fourth Circuit Court of Appeals sustained a
1996 Virginia law that bars the use by state employees of state-owned
or state-leased computers to access sexually explicit material, save
with official approval for "bona fide research projects," the majority
expressly rejected a professorial academic freedom claim, recognizing
only an institutional interest.[11] Scholars and chroniclers of academic
freedom have written critically of that and several other recent rulings that similarly disparage individual academic freedom claims.

Despite occasional setbacks, and despite important differences between court-declared and institutionally shaped academic freedom
precepts, these two sources have interacted and blended throughout
the twentieth century in ways that, as Professor William Van Alstyne
notes, constantly reinforce one another. Although the First Amendment does not bind them, most major private universities pride themselves on voluntary adherence to standards (typically those crafted by
AAUP) that are at least as rigorous as the standards legally imposed
on their state-supported counterparts. The historic development of
academic freedom, covering as it does most of the twentieth century,
reflects gradual and at times checkered progress toward enhanced
security for professorial speech and political activity. Along the way
there have been (and continue even now, as we shall see in the review
of post–September 11 developments) some truly chilling casualties.
Yet that history suggests, in the main, how much less well the Ameri-

can professoriate would have fared had there not emerged early in the last century a set of widely accepted principles, and a nearly universal commitment to fair procedures for the termination of faculty appointments.

Academic Freedom Faces New Tests and Challenges

University professors have not for many years been forced to sign loyalty oaths, or to demonstrate their loyalty in other ways. Rarely these days—even in the perilous times since September 11, 2001, to which we turn a bit later—are lecture notes or laboratory files subpoenaed by legislative committees or law enforcement officials seeking to prove that college campuses are enclaves for radical or subversive activity. Save for an occasional professor who may still become embroiled in a political controversy, as indeed several have since September 11, most of today's academic freedom issues are subtler, if no less urgent for those whose careers may be at risk.

The emergence of sexual harassment as a campus concern illustrates the change. Disparaging and insensitive remarks by male professors to and about female colleagues and students were surely prevalent a half century ago—indeed, probably far more so than they are today. Yet such transgressions went largely unredressed in the absence of specific policies and procedures designed to target and prevent such harassment. Only within the past two decades has the academic community given adequate attention to such abuses and their corrosive effect on the collegial and learning environments. The implications both for gender equity and for academic freedom are profound.

A major court case illustrates how different are the current challenges. Dean Cohen had for some years been an English teacher at a California community college. He used a teaching style that he conceded to be at times "abrasive" and "confrontational." He also read to his classes occasional excerpts from sources such as Penthouse and Hustler, and used vulgarity, profanity, and sexual themes to "enliven" class discussion. Many students and colleagues lauded Cohen's ability to reach and excite slower learners and students whose spontaneous interest was minimal. But in 1993, one female student formally charged Cohen with sexual harassment. A campus committee agreed with the charges and ordered Cohen to "become sensitive to the needs of his students" and to "modify his teaching strategy when it becomes apparent that his techniques create a climate which impedes the students' ability to learn."

Cohen went to federal court and filed suit against the college, claiming that his freedom of speech and his academic freedom had been abridged. The trial judge disagreed, though recognizing that the college's harassment policy was hardly a model of clarity, and that the policy might give a veto over course content and class discussion to "the most sensitive and easily affected students." The appeals court, finding greater merit in Cohen's claims, reversed the trial judge.[12] To the higher court, the sexual harassment policy created a "legal ambush" because the terms were too vague to afford adequate guidance, especially to a teacher whose classroom style had for many years "been considered pedagogically sound and within the bounds of teaching methodology permitted at the College." Thus Cohen prevailed on all counts, and the college suffered a humiliating setback in the pursuit of its laudable concern to spare its students from sexually hostile learning experiences.

The Cohen case was the first judgment directly addressing the growing tension between academic freedom and sexual harassment. The Cohen court did not say that the use of vulgarity or sexual themes are categorically within the scope of a professor's free speech; indeed, some years later a federal appeals court in Michigan would take a much less tolerant view of similar classroom speech in a strikingly similar case that involved a Detroit-area community college teacher.[13] That very same federal appeals court had earlier reviewed the case of a basketball coach who had been fired for using racial slurs to motivate a mostly minority group of athletes; the court split the difference there, striking down on First Amendment grounds the university's speech code but upholding the coach's dismissal on the basis of singularly poor judgment in guiding a racially mixed team.[14] Several other harassment cases since Cohen have reached conflicting results, though more often than not faulting vague standards or summary procedures while stopping short of any ringing declarations about academic freedom.

The AAUP felt called on to enter the fray as dissonance between its policies on harassment and on academic freedom became increasingly apparent and troubling. Thus at its annual meeting in 1995, the Association approved a policy that defines as forbidden harassment such relatively readily identifiable (and intolerable) verbal abuses as offering a student a higher grade in exchange for sexual favors or targeting an individual student with persistent gender-demeaning epithets and insults. The policy also addresses the much harder and subtler issues of nontargeted but offensive speech posed by cases like Cohen's. Before it may be punished as harassment, "speech . . . of a sexual nature . . . directed against another" must be shown to be "abusive" or "severely humiliating" or to "persist . . . despite objection," or alternatively that it be "reasonably regarded as offensive and substantially impair the academic work opportunity of students." That last option carries an essential corollary: "If [speech] takes place in the teaching context, it must also be persistent, pervasive, and not germane to the subject matter."

Would such a policy help in cases like Professor Cohen's? It almost certainly would help in two very distinct ways. For one, such a policy would provide precision that should cure the vagueness and lack of fair warning that so troubled the Cohen court. It would also enable institutions to distinguish between the merely salty teaching style, on the one hand—even if it is occasionally offensive to a few students— and the unacceptable classroom infliction of persistent and pervasive sexism, on the other. A single example should make the point: If a professor begins every other class with a round of sexist jokes, the conditions of the AAUP policy would seem to be met (unless they were made in the rare course on "Modern American Humor"). Assuming the jokes offended some students enough to provoke a formal harassment complaint, such material could be found to be "persistent, pervasive and not germane to the subject matter."

The AAUP policy also addresses one other important element— procedure. Many institutions, including most of those that have been taken to court over such issues, relied on special or ad hoc procedures to handle harassment claims. Where any other serious charge of faculty misconduct that could lead to dismissal—plagiarism, for example —would involve a committee of faculty peers, strict secrecy, and full due process, the separate harassment procedures often dispense with such safeguards and entrust the fate of a senior professor to a panel that may include nonfaculty members and may follow casual or informal rules on evidence, confidentiality, and the like. Such processes would be unacceptable for any other charge that might place a professor's status at risk. The federal court that ruled in Professor Silva's favor, ordering his reinstatement at the University of New Hampshire, faulted on many grounds the informal, ad hoc procedure for handling harassment claims.[15] However appealing the case for informality and flexibility may seem in the investigative stages, dispensing with or bypassing the guarantees of due process in the trial of such charges seems (as several courts have made clear) unacceptable. The concern of academic freedom is as much a concern for process as it is for substantive standards and policies.

If sexual harassment has been the most visible and contentious academic freedom area in recent years, several other catalysts have evoked major concern from the professorial community. Faculty expression and political activity have been notably less free in certain types of institutions, mainly those with weak or even nonexistent traditions of shared academic governance and at certain church-related institutions where curbs on faculty speech not only serve theological needs, but may go well beyond theology in ways that have no secular counterpart. Yet there is no monopoly on academic freedom violations at small and untutored campuses; in recent years the AAUP's list of censured administrations has included such eminent institutions as New York University and the University of Southern California (both now having taken corrective action that brought about their removal from the censure list).

The censure list increasingly involves procedural violations rather than (as was more common in earlier times) direct reprisals for expression of professorial views or activities. Moreover, termination of continuing academic appointments for reasons of financial exigency continues to draw AAUP scrutiny and, on occasion, litigation. Association policies and court decisions define a clear and acceptable path by which to declare financial exigency and, if necessary, to reduce the faculty size in a way that does not reflect strict seniority. Often it is done by the book, as when seventy tenured faculty at several University of Wisconsin campuses were laid off in the 1970s. However, investigations at Bennington and St. Bonaventure showed the darker side of the process—not because the latter institutions clearly lacked adequate financial reasons for cutting back the number of teaching personnel but because the determination of such "exigency" and the way in which that judgment was applied fell far short of prescribed standards and procedures. Here, as with terminations for "cause" or because of the "bona fide elimination of a program or department," the way in which it is done may be far greater cause for concern and scrutiny—including the potential for censure—than that action itself.

These discussions raise an issue that deserves closer attention:

Does academic freedom require, or does it depend on, the existence of tenure? The pros and cons of academic freedom have been vigorously debated at least for the past three or four decades since the founding of several institutions (notably Hampshire College) that did not offer tenure but promised their faculties academic freedom. Of the small number of such institutions that began without a tenure track, several (for example, Evergreen State College in Oregon and the University of Texas–Permian Basin) have since adopted at least de facto, if not de jure, tenure.

Even so, nothing in AAUP policy requires a tenure system. Hampshire College, for example, would never risk censure by declining to offer tenure to a new teacher or by refusing to renew a contract of a person who had served well beyond seven years—so long as the scrupulous procedures that Hampshire has adopted were faithfully followed and the nonrenewal was not premised on an invalid premise, such as reprisal for an unpopular statement or activity or affiliation. Rather, the AAUP position is that tenure best serves the interests of both individuals and institutions. It is not only the likeliest guarantor of academic freedom but offers other benefits. Tenure provides continuity and stability of employment in a profession whose members often engage in long-term research and where institutions need the capacity to project curricular needs and staffing well into the future. A tenure system also forces (toward the close of the probationary period) a critical review and assessment of the potential of every junior faculty member. In the absence of tenure, there is no such imperative.

Despite these virtues, even the strongest champions of tenure would concede some reservations. First, the current system is far from perfect. More rigorous review of the performance of those seeking tenure would benefit them and their careers as well as their students and the institution. Those who have achieved tenure are not, and should not be, immune from continuing scrutiny despite the greater security they enjoy. Nothing in the principles of academic freedom converts senior faculty status to a sinecure. Second, alternative safeguards for academic freedom may exist and should be carefully considered. The fact that almost all universities and baccalaureate colleges do confer tenure does not settle the matter, as Hampshire's experience and that of a few other nontenure track institutions suggests. Finally, among the flaws, there is no doubt that tenure creates the risk of an exaggerated hierarchy within the academic profession. There have surely been abuses by senior faculty of junior colleagues who should be their protégés. It is hardly surprising that some younger faculty, with or without tenure, view the current system with ambivalence or even resentment. For some, the trade off between greater protection for those who survive the system and the hardships for those who do not may appear an excessive cost. The quest for alternatives should thus continue, and even the most securely tenured professors should bear some responsibility to improve the current system.

Academic Freedom in the Digital Age

As new technologies convey an ever-growing share of intellectual exchanges, academic freedom must adapt to cyberspace, however uncomfortably.[16] An initial question is whether expressive freedoms even apply to digital or electronic communications. There seems no good reason why such media should not be fully protected; after all, the focus of the Constitution's framers on printed and spoken words has never allowed courts to draw a line between traditional and nontraditional or unfamiliar formats. Thus "speech" and "press" have come to encompass motion pictures, broadcasting and cable, fax machines, and other new media. Thus it was no surprise when, in the spring of 1997, the Supreme Court unanimously declared that communication on the Internet was as fully protected as was communication through more traditional and familiar means. That view remains central, even though later cases have brought some qualifications; the high court upheld in the summer of 2003, for example, Congress's requirement that public libraries filter Internet access as a condition of continued eligibility for federal funding. At the same time, the justices struck down, in 2002, a federal law that would have criminalized "virtual child pornography," wherein the majority found that such a ban would severely constrain artistic expression for a purpose that could not be directly linked to the clearly valid interest in protecting real children from abuse and exploitation.

Academic freedom issues are bound to be somewhat different in cyberspace. The sanctity of the classroom, and of the speech that takes place there, is at the core of academic freedom. Yet when an instructor creates a course home page, and when much communication between teacher and student occurs through e-mail, it is fair to ask whether such media are an extension of the physical classroom or whether they evoke a completely different analysis. Distinctions that have existed since time immemorial between "on campus" and "off campus" activity obviously break down in an electronic environment. Other familiar tests blur on the Internet. For example, professors are constrained by the 1940 Statement to avoid any implication they speak for their institutions when they are not authorized to do so. The force of that rule is clear when letters are written on either institutional or personal stationery. But when many communications are exchanged via e-mail, with an address or heading that may or may not appear to implicate the server, the lines become far less distinct.

During the 1990s, there were several early skirmishes over these issues. When a University of Oklahoma journalism professor challenged his institution's refusal to make available to the faculty a full array of alt.sex newsgroups, he sued in federal court. The judge found the case an easy one to dismiss when the plaintiff conceded he could obtain the same material through a commercial Internet service provider. The university, meanwhile, adopted a two-tiered Internet access system, with a broader menu for faculty and advanced graduate students than for undergraduates. On the other hand, when a student at California State University, Northridge, posted on his Web site, through the university server, a hideous image of a state senator morphing into a skull, the administration felt it had no choice but to remove the offending image when the senator's staff complained. But the student went to court, claiming his free speech had been abridged, and a state trial judge agreed, noting that political expression enjoyed the highest level of protection.

The judge ordered the university to restore the Web page, which posed an impossible dilemma for the administration until another judge upheld new university policies adopted during the litigation that regulated political expression on the university's media. When four male freshmen at Cornell University sent rampantly sexist e-mails to a group of female classmates and when a homophobic student at Virginia Tech invaded and upended a chat room for gay and lesbian students, both institutions discovered, as had Oklahoma and Northridge, the limitations of print-era law in the age of cyberspace and the difficulty of anticipating a host of new challenges with a still largely unfamiliar technology. Most recently, demands (and actual subpoenas) from the recording industry have forced many colleges and universities to consider whether to "unmask" students who have "borrowed" excessive amounts of protected music or to risk harsh sanctions for violating a clear mandate of federal law.

Another acute dilemma has been that suggested by the Oklahoma case—what restrictions, if any, universities should impose on Internet access through the campus server. Ironically, the issue first surfaced in the mid-1990s at Carnegie Mellon University, the nation's first fully wired campus. The administration announced severe restrictions on such access, after revelations (which turned out to be highly exaggerated) of the range of salacious material that students could easily download. The administration's initial concern was that providing unrestricted access could make the university complicit in violating state obscenity and child pornography laws. After an outcry that went well beyond Pittsburgh, the policy was substantially modified and seems to have invited no followers elsewhere. Meanwhile, the futility of such efforts became increasingly obvious because students at Carnegie Mellon, or elsewhere, who wished to access material they could not obtain through the campus server had many alternative channels.

One other issue of academic freedom in cyberspace, still largely unresolved despite extensive analysis, is the status of faculty e-mail. It would be quite naïve to suppose that a message sent electronically from one person to another through a university network is truly "private." Every server has monitors, both human and electronic, and randomly backs up some portion of all messages passing over the system. Short of using highly sophisticated encryption, which few academics would even consider doing for routine messages, the prospect of genuine privacy is quite remote. Yet there are reasonable expectations that one's chairman or dean (or information technology center) will not randomly read one's e-mail without permission (or without a subpoena). When a University of California, Irvine, librarian found on returning from a prolonged illness that her mailbox had in fact been diverted to her supervisor without her knowledge or consent, the need for a more protective policy became apparent. The University of California system has since adopted a policy that presumes privacy of e-mail, subject only to exigent needs (serious threats, for example) that might warrant unauthorized invasion or diversion, and even then only after first seeking the subscriber's consent.

A host of other issues await resolution, in addition to litigation. When Northwestern University professor Arthur Butz published a book in which he effectively denied the existence of the Holocaust, the institution could and did distance itself from such abhorrent views, as long as he never imposed them on his students or used campus facilities to disseminate his thesis. But when the very same message appeared on Butz's home page, accessible through the university server, the process of distancing Northwestern from Holocaust denial became vastly more difficult.[17] Similar issues arise when students conduct highly critical course surveys and post the results on campus-based Web pages; here too, the disavowals and disclaimers that were routine when "confidential guides" were published and distributed entirely off campus become much more difficult. The making of policy has been, remains, and is likely to continue to lag behind the creativity of campus Internet users and their capacity and inclination to test the system.

Academic Freedom after September 11

For most American professors, even those who taught during the Vietnam era, relative peace and stability have been a major premise of academic life. The events of September 11 dramatically altered such placid assumptions. The attacks on the World Trade Center made almost inevitable substantial changes in the relationship between government and the academy and certainly posed the threat of challenges to academic freedom comparable to those of the McCarthy era. From the perspective of two years later, the worst fears seem not to have materialized. Conditions have worsened in certain respects, and some dimensions of academic freedom have suffered but in ways quite different from expectations in the days that immediately followed the terrorist attacks.[18]

To look first at the undeniably darker side of the ledger, freedom of university research has suffered in important respects. Reliance on the heretofore unused concept of "sensitive but unclassified" research has undoubtedly slowed the release and publication of some important studies and may have discouraged some investigators from even seeking federal support because of growing uncertainty about the degree to which the sharing of data might be inhibited. The handling of certain research materials has been restricted; the availability of important data on government (and even nongovernmental) Web sites, and in libraries, has also been affected by post–September 11 policies.

Scientists from certain parts of the world have been barred from some research activity within the United States, and those who seek entry from "sensitive" countries—by no means all of them in the Middle East—have found the journey tortuous and, at times, impossible.

The effect on access and entry of foreign graduate students has been especially severe. A monitoring system that was supposed to be in full operation by late 2002 or 2003 languished for many months, with growing doubt that it would ever be fully operational and effective. Monitoring of graduate students already here has included bizarre incidents, such as the group of Saudi Arabians in Colorado who were summarily arrested for having (quite innocently, as it turned out) underregistered by one credit hour for the coming semester and were thus deemed to have forfeited their visa status. There is at least reliably anecdotal evidence that an appreciable number of foreign students who would ordinarily have studied here have gone instead to England, Germany, or Japan simply because the burdens and risks of coming to the United States seemed, for the first time in history, to outweigh the obvious benefits.

Access to information seems to have suffered in ways other than removal or classification of research data. Prominent in the U.S.A. Patriot Act is a "business records" provision that empowers federal law enforcement officials to obtain, through subpoenas issued by a secret court, sensitive materials chosen by library borrowers or bookstore purchasers. The problem is compounded by a clause that prevents a librarian or bookseller served with such an order from disclosing that fact to anyone, including the person whose records have been sought and obtained. Thus it had been impossible to estimate the probable volume of such activity until, in late September 2003, Attorney General John Ashcroft revealed the Justice Department had made no use of the business records provision. Such news brought small comfort to the academic community because the prospect of future use remained likely without any public knowledge of its extent and focus. Indeed, throughout the post–September 11 response to terrorism, a major concern has been the growing difficulty of determining the extent to which special government powers have been invoked.

Finally and perhaps most germane to a study of academic freedom are the effects of September 11 on academic personnel. Initial (and quite plausible) fears of a resurgence of McCarthyism in the wake of the terrorist attacks proved to be unfounded. With one notable exception, the fate of professors who made unpopular, even outrageous, statements during the tensest time in recent history was surprisingly moderate. On the very afternoon of September 11, University of New Mexico history professor Richard Berthold said to his freshman class, "anyone who bombs the Pentagon gets my vote." Despite intense pressure for Berthold's dismissal from legislators and irate citizens, the administration suspended him, conducted a careful semester-long investigation, and eventually sent him a letter of reprimand. A week or so after the attacks, Muslim students charged a California community college professor named Hearlson of calling them "terrorists" and "Nazis" and of leveling such accusations as, "You drove two planes into the World Trade Center." A suspension and thorough investigation followed. The inquiry concluded that, although Hearlson may have been insensitive toward his Islamic students, the specific accusations could not be substantiated.[19]

At the end of September, a teach-in took place at the City College of New York. Several faculty members expressed views strongly critical of U.S. foreign policy, specifically blaming "American colonialism" for the attacks. Despite intense dismay within and beyond the university, and administration conjecture about possible sanctions, CUNY Board Vice Chairman Benno Schmidt (formerly president of Yale and a lifelong First Amendment scholar) enlightened his fellow trustees on basic principles of academic freedom, and the issue entirely disappeared from the board's agenda. Across town a year and a half later, a similar event occurred at Columbia University. At the height of the war in Iraq, anthropology professor Nicholas De Genova said at a teach-in that he wished for "a million Mogadishus"—a reference that recalled the tragic ambush of U.S. troops portrayed in the film *Blackhawk Down*. Demands for De Genova's dismissal extended far beyond angry Columbia alumni and other irate New Yorkers. Over a hundred members of Congress signed a petition calling for his resignation, insisting that the issue was not "whether De Genova has the right to make idiotic comments . . . but whether he has the right to a job teaching at Columbia University after making such comments." Once again cooler heads prevailed. Columbia's new president, Lee Bollinger (also a First Amendment expert), expressed his own "shock" at De Genova's statements, which in his view "crossed the line," but insisted throughout the spring that no sanctions would be taken, and none was ever imposed. Such a response and the Columbia community's eventual acceptance of it suggest that understanding academic freedom may be clearer in the aftermath of September 11, contrary to what many feared on the day of the attacks.

The one notable exception was the case of Palestinian-born computer science professor Sami Al-Arian, a longtime U.S. citizen and faculty member at the University of South Florida. Soon after September 11, Al-Arian appeared on Fox News's *The O'Reilly Factor.* Identified to viewers as a University of South Florida professor, he acknowledged on the air that he had made comments such as "death to Israel" and had led a university-affiliated institute with a strongly pro-Palestinian bias. When the university was flooded with calls from angry alumni, anxious parents, and irate citizens, the administration placed Al-Arian on paid leave, followed by a suspension and, in December, by a board of trustees' directive to seek his removal from the faculty. Several months later, a federal judge dismissed the university's suit that sought a ruling that Al-Arian's tenured appointment could be terminated with impunity. That sent the personnel dispute back into campus channels. About this time, a federal grand jury indicted Al-Arian and several others on charges of raising funds and providing material support to terrorist organizations. The university then summarily dismissed Al-Arian from his faculty position, citing both the indictment and related criminal charges not invoked by the grand jury.

The meaning of Al-Arian's case for academic freedom is deeply troubling, as an AAUP investigation made clear.[20] The administration's initial declaration of its intent to dismiss a tenured professor reflected institutional interests no stronger than parental anxiety, alumni anger, and community concern. The conundrum here was the degree to which later developments (specifically the federal indictment) buttressed a case that was so insubstantial from its inception. Yet even if it were beyond dispute that proof of such charges would justify the forfeiture of a faculty position—constituting proof of unfitness to continue teaching—so dire a conclusion could not be inferred simply from a grand jury's accusation but must be demonstrated at an adversary hearing, the administration bearing the burden of proof, in ways that South Florida has yet to pursue.

One other action suggests the degree to which the Al-Arian case may have been the exception and not the rule. When Mark Yudof (yet another seasoned First Amendment scholar) returned to Texas as chancellor of the University of Texas system, the first issue awaiting him was a proposal that extensive criminal background checks be required of all new employees. Such a burden would of course include all new faculty. In rejecting the proposal for all but highly sensitive police, child-care, and hazardous material–handling positions, Yudof expressed concern for academic freedom, noting wryly that "faculty would wince if they thought that every Chaucer scholar was being vetted." The contrast between this recent outcome and treatment of outspoken Texas professors several decades ago tends to confirm the more hopeful view of the post–September 11 period.

Several other events not directly involving faculty personnel actions tend to support this more sanguine view. In the fall of 2002, conferences on Middle East tensions were scheduled on several campuses. The prospect of speakers with strongly pro-Palestinian views (including Professor Al-Arian in one instance) led opposing groups to seek the cancellation of these events and to file lawsuits designed to bar conferences at the University of Michigan and the University of North Carolina at Chapel Hill. Both administrations and their university attorneys stood firm, refusing to alter the schedule and resisting the lawsuits. Both cases were dismissed by trial judges, both conferences went on as planned, and a different dimension of academic freedom prevailed.

Much the same has been true of controversial visiting speakers. Despite strong legislative pressure, several Colorado campuses refused to cancel appearances by Palestinian spokesperson Hanan Ashrawi. Harvard initially wavered on the appearance of Irish poet Tom Paulin after faculty learned of his open and virulently anti-Semitic views, but the invitation was soon renewed. A controversial British cleric, Rev. Michael Prior, was able to speak on Middle Eastern issues at Harvard, Notre Dame, Boston University, and was barred only at Holy Cross after his faculty sponsors acceded to pleas from colleagues newly aware of Prior's anti-Semitic statements. Only two commencement speakers seem to have been prevented from completing their planned addresses—*Sacramento Bee* publisher Janis Heaphy in December 2001 and Pulitzer Prize–winning *New York Times* reporter Chris Hedge in May 2003; both were shouted down by audience members (not graduating students in either case) who found statements in their brief addresses to be unacceptably unpatriotic.

It is still much too soon to draw conclusions with any confidence about the effect on academic freedom of September 11 and the nation's response. Even early returns are quite mixed. The situation differs dramatically from World War I or the McCarthy era in terms of faculty personnel consequences. There are, however, deeply troubling signs elsewhere, such as using "sensitive but unclassified" research designations, curtailing and withdrawing vital government information from the research community, raising new barriers to the flow of foreign scholars and students, and heightening surveillance through the Patriot Act and other security-prompted measures. As the new millennium evolves, and basic principles of academic freedom mature, we remain alert and justifiably concerned.

NOTES

1. See Walter Metzger, "The 1940 Statement of Principles on Academic Freedom and Tenure," in *Freedom and Tenure in the Academy,* ed. William W. Van Alstyne (Durham: Duke University Press, 1993).
2. Ibid., 13.
3. "General Report of the Committee on Academic Freedom and Academic Tenure," *AAUP Bulletin* 17 (1915): 1.
4. Quoted in "The Professors Union," *School and Society* 175 (1916): 3.
5. See Metzger, "The 1940 Statement," 9.
6. See American Association of University Professors, *Policy Documents and Reports* (Washington, D.C.: AAUP, 2000), 3–10.
7. See *Tilton v. Richardson,* 403 U.S. 672, 681–2 (1971); *Jiminez v. Almodovar,* 650 F.2d 363, 369 (1st Cir. 1981); *Krotkoff v. Goucher College,* 585 F.2d 675, 679 (4th Cir. 1978); *Gray v. Board of Higher Education,* 692 F.2d 901, 907 (2d Cir. 1982); *Levitt v. Board of Trustees,* 376 F. Supp. 945, 950 (D. Neb. 1974). See also Matthew W. Finkin, ed., *The Case for Tenure* (Ithaca: Cornell University Press, 1966); Ralph S. Brown, Jr., and Matthew W. Finkin, "The Usefulness of AAUP Statements," *Educational Record* 59 (1978): 30–44.
8. See "Report of the Committee of Inquiry on the Case of Professor Scott Nearing of the University of Pennsylvania," *AAUP Bulletin* 127 (1916): 2.
9. Ellen Schrecker, *No Ivory Towers: McCarthyism and the Universities* (New York: Oxford University Press).
10. *Keyishian v. Board of Regents,* 385 U.S. 589, 603 (1967).
11. *Urofsky v. Gilmore,* 216 F.3d 401 (4th Cir. 2001).
12. *Cohen v. San Bernardino Valley College,* 92 F.3d 968 (9th Cir. 1996).
13. *Bonnell v. Lorenzo,* 241 F.3d 800 (6th Cir. 201).
14. *Dambrodt v. Central Michigan University,* 55 F.3d 1177 (6th Cir. 1995).
15. *Silva v. University of New Hampshire,* 888 F. Supp. 293 (D.N.H. 1994).
16. See generally for discussion of such issues of academic freedom in cyberspace Robert M. O'Neil, *Free Speech in the College Community* (Bloomington: Indiana University Press, 1997), 52–76.

17. See ibid., 74.

18. See generally Special Committee of the American Association of University Professors, "Academic Freedom and National Security in a Time of Crisis," *Academe,* Nov.–Dec. 2003.

19. For discussion of both the Berthold and Hearlson cases, see Robin Wilson and Scott Smallwood, "One Professor Cleared, Another Disciplined Over September 11 Remarks," *Chronicle of Higher Education,* Jan. 11, 2002, A12.

20. For the final AAUP report on the Al-Arian case, see "Academic Freedom and Tenure: The University of South Florida," *Academe,* May–June 2003, 49–73. Delegates to the Association's June 2003 annual meeting voted to condemn the University of South Florida administration for its "grave departures" from AAUP-supported standards of due process.

Chapter Five

Challenges Facing Higher Education in the Twenty-First Century

Ami Zusman

The twenty-first century has brought with it profound challenges to the nature, values, and control of higher education in the United States. Societal expectations and public resources for higher education are undergoing fundamental shifts. Changes both within and outside the academy are altering its character—its students, faculty, governance, curriculum, functions, and very place in society. As Clark Kerr and Marian Gade noted nearly twenty years ago, crisis and change in higher education "have been the rule, not the exception."[1] Nevertheless, current changes are transforming higher education to an extent not seen since the end of World War II.

This chapter focuses on the effect of major external influences on U.S. higher education, particularly government and market pressures, and in turn, the effect of resulting institutional decisions in program choices, tuition charges, and research conducted on the outcomes of higher education for society at large. The five issues addressed here discuss changing answers by the public, policy makers, and higher education to central questions about the value, the role, and the control of higher education: Who pays for higher education? Who benefits? Who decides who should benefit, what should be offered, and what the outcomes should be?[2] By necessity, of course, other significant issues are omitted from this discussion. While each

of the five issues raises all three questions, for this discussion, they
are organized as follows:

Who Pays?　　—Growing privatization of public colleges and univer-
　　　　　　　　sities
　　　　　　　—A more commercialized and politicized research sys-
　　　　　　　　tem?
Who Benefits?—Who will attend college? Challenges to access
　　　　　　　—The changing and uncertain job market for Ph.D.s
Who Decides? —Accountability, governance, and coordination

　　A common thread connects these issues: challenges to the content
of colleges' and universities' "social contract." These challenges are
apparent in ongoing conflicts over public and private benefits of
higher education, equity and merit, undergraduate and graduate education, "basic" and commercially oriented research, or institutional
autonomy and public control.

The Growing Privatization of Public
Colleges and Universities

States today have become "minority partners" in the colleges and
universities that typically bear their names. On average, states now
supply only a little more than one-third of public colleges' revenues.
Yet because these funds generally pay most basic instructional costs,
such as faculty and staff salaries, state support remains critical to
public institutions. Over the next decade, a combination of acute state
revenue constraints, competing demands for state resources, and ongoing changes in public attitudes toward higher education will likely
result in continued shrinking and unpredictable state support for
higher education. Although many private colleges are also facing serious budget difficulties due to rising costs, market limits on tuition
increases, reduced private giving, and declining endowment income,
public institutions, which generally have less ability to tap private
sources, will be hit harder. This section addresses the far-reaching
effects of declining state support for public institutions in the United
States, which enroll three-quarters of all college students and two-
thirds of all students in four-year colleges.[3]

Shrinking State Funding for Higher Education

Because higher education is the largest discretionary item in states' budgets, state funding for higher education tends to rise when the economy and resulting state revenues are good and to drop during recessions. Even during boom times, funding may be less than it appears once inflation and rising enrollments are taken into account. During the U.S. economic recession of the early 1990s, states cut higher education appropriations by amounts unequaled in constant dollars since at least World War II, despite enrollment growth. In the late 1990s, state funding per student finally began returning to pre-1990 levels—only to be cut almost immediately during the recession early in the new century. As a result, state dollars per student in public institutions were 12 percent lower in fiscal year 2004 than they were 15 years earlier, as figure 5.1 shows, despite an improving revenue picture in many states. Although state funding patterns varied widely, twenty-three states allocated less money in 2004 than in 2003, even without considering inflation or enrollment growth, with nine states reporting cuts of 5 percent or more.[4]

Long-term prospects for state higher education funding are not favorable. Many experts believe that states' revenue problems will persist even after the economy improves because state tax systems are obsolete—for example, a growing percentage of economic activity is in nontaxed services and Internet sales—and because voter-imposed limits have made raising revenues more difficult. At the same time, an estimated 40–50 percent of state expenditures are locked up in mandated program costs, particularly for K–12 education and Medicaid. These mandated costs are expected to increase, especially for Medicaid, which already consumes about 20 percent of state budgets, as the rising numbers of the elderly require more health services. Also, state actions taken during economic boom times, such as tax cuts or implementation of popular new programs, are hard to eliminate when the economy weakens.[5] In this environment of restricted revenues and mandated expenditures, higher education funding is a tempting target to cut, not only because it is discretionary but also because colleges, unlike many other state programs, can tap other revenue sources, and because a growing proportion of the public believes that students should pay more of their college costs.[6]

Unpredictable state funding is equally problematic. In fiscal year

Ami Zusman

Enrollments
in thousands $ per FTE

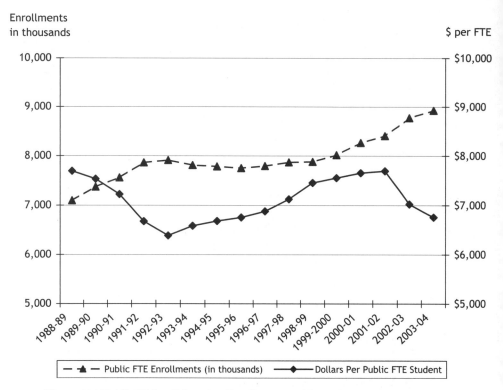

Figure 5.1 Public Higher Education Enrollments and State Appropriations to Higher Education Per Student, 1988–89 to 2003–04 (in constant 2003 dollars)

Source: (1) Funding: "Appropriations of State Tax Funds for Higher Education Operating Expenses—50 States," *Grapevine* (Normal: Illinois State University, Center for the Study of Education Policy, 2004), and State Higher Education Executive Officers (SHEEO), 2003: www.sheeo.org/finance/fiscalres.htm; (2) Students: National Center for Education Statistics, *Projections of Education Statistics to 2013* (Washington, D.C.: U.S. Department of Education, 2003), table 22.

Note: Enrollment data for 2001–02 to 2003–04 are projected.

2003, twenty-seven states imposed midyear reductions in their higher education allocations, including a 16 percent midyear cut in Colorado and cuts of 5 percent or more in eleven other states. Unexpected cuts made during the academic year, after faculty have been hired, programs put in place, and student fees set, leave institutions with difficult choices.

Declining capital dollars for funding to construct, to renovate, and to maintain classroom or research buildings and campus infrastructure may be as big a constraint on institutions' ability to accommodate enrollment growth, recruit faculty, and conduct research as are state appropriations for operating expenses. A 1995 survey (the most recent available) by the Association of Higher Education Facilities Officers and the National Association of College and University Business Officers estimated that higher education institutions had a $26 billion backlog in deferred maintenance of existing facilities. A new survey, to be conducted in late 2003, was expected to show that this estimate had increased by at least 25 percent.[7] Ultimately, these repairs will cost more than if maintenance and replacement had been made on schedule. In addition, fewer state bonds for capital construction at public colleges may be placed on the ballot in the next decade if they are seen as lowering a state's credit rating or as competing with bonds for other purposes, including covering state deficits. Although many policy makers are looking to distance education and computer-based technologies to reduce space needs, technology costs remain high, and computers will not supplant the need for teaching and research laboratories.

Privatization

As institutions seek to offset declining state dollars, public colleges and universities are becoming increasingly "privatized." For the nine-campus University of California, for example, state funds dropped from 37 percent of the total operating budget in fiscal year 1990 to 23 percent in 2004. At Pennsylvania State University, state appropriations declined from 21 percent in 1990 to just 13 percent in 2002.[8] Nor are these declines occurring only at research universities. Nationally, state funds for all public institutions dropped from 46 percent of current fund revenues in 1981 to 36 percent in 2000. While the declining proportion of state funding at some institutions is due in part to success in obtaining more extramural grants and private donations as well as growth in auxiliary enterprises, nationally two-thirds of the change reflects the substitution of tuition and fee income for state support. In 1980, tuition and fees constituted 13 percent of public institutions' current-fund revenues; by 2000, they constituted about 19 percent of revenues for all public colleges and nearly one-third of that for public nondoctoral baccalaureate institutions.[9] Although these trends have been going on for at least 20 years, the extraordinary pressures being placed on state revenues and expenditures for competing services today are likely to accelerate the move toward more reliance on private funding for "public" higher education—unless there is a paradigm shift in public support or unless state or federal policy makers impose mandatory tuition limitations.

Many public institutions are themselves pursuing privatization as a means to raise revenues or reallocate scarce state dollars. Some institutions are requiring that certain academic programs, especially high-demand, high-return professional programs like law or business, become fully or nearly fully funded by clients (students), business, or other private sources. The University of Virginia's law and business schools became fully self-supporting by 2004, and many other public research universities have been exploring similar moves; most already charged business, law, and medical students much higher fees than those charged other students. Even teacher or school administrator training programs (which generally are not high return) have been privatized in some cases. While institutions often want to use the state dollars "saved" for programs less able to charge high fees, the result in some cases may be a further decrease in state funds. Institutions are pursuing other strategies as well. Many are expanding self-supporting part-time degree programs geared to working professionals. Community colleges and other institutions are expanding contract education programs with specific businesses or industries. Both public and private universities have adopted commercial technology transfer and other for-profit collaborations with industry. Colleges and universities are "outsourcing" many institutional functions to private vendors or other education institutions, including operation of residential dorms, employment training, and even academic functions such as remedial education and beginning language instruction. University hospitals have formed partnerships with both nonprofit and for-profit health organizations. Other institutions have established shared-use facilities with private enterprise.

Consequences of State Funding Declines and Privatization

State funding declines and resulting institutional strategies raise many questions:

Access, Success, and Diversity

How will further tuition increases affect student access to and success in higher education? Unless sufficient need-based financial aid is provided, low-income students and historically underrepresented ethnic groups may be excluded. Even if students and their parents are able and willing to pay higher tuition, some institutions and state policy makers facing fiscal pressures are preparing to cap or even to reduce enrollments, despite growing enrollment demands. If so, what will happen to students unable to get in? These issues will be examined further in a subsequent section.

Effects on Faculty

Over the next decade, many new faculty will be needed, both to replace the large numbers of expected retirements and to teach the growing numbers of students. How will conflicting forces of budget constraints and the need for new faculty affect how many faculty will be hired and for what types of positions? Although student/faculty ratios could rise—indeed, many faculty positions were eliminated during the recession of the early 2000s, primarily by not replacing tenured faculty and not renewing contracts for non-tenure-track faculty —new faculty will nevertheless be needed. In this environment, both public and private institutions may hire an increasing proportion of faculty who are ineligible for tenure, generally at lower salaries than tenure-track faculty. In 1998, about 55 percent of all instructional faculty and over a quarter of full-time faculty at four-year institutions were ineligible for tenure.[10] Budgetary problems and enrollment growth may well accentuate this trend. Growing use of temporary faculty presents both advantages and problems. On the one hand, it increases institutions' ability to respond to changing student demand and reduces institutional costs. On the other hand, it creates a two-tier academic labor force. According to the American Association of University Professors, the increasing reliance on part-time, temporary, and adjunct faculty threatens the tenure system and may harm the quality of higher education.[11]

Program Reallocations

In a more market-driven environment, will institutions (private as well as public) respond by shifting program resources toward fields that promise tuition-paying students high-paying jobs or that bring in more external research grants? To date, the effect of budget cuts on programs appears largely unplanned. In some cases, disproportionate numbers of faculty positions in certain fields have been left vacant, leaving an imbalance between faculty expertise and institutional needs. In terminating non-tenure-track faculty, institutions have indirectly made decisions to reduce or eliminate programs such as remedial education, beginning language courses, and teacher education, which often heavily depend on non-tenure-track faculty. Repetitive across-the-board cuts have gradually weakened once viable programs until they become obvious candidates for termination. However, as fiscal constraints continue, more institutions are intentionally reducing, consolidating, or eliminating specific programs. State policy makers have at times been the driving force behind program reallocations. In the 1990s, statewide coordinating agencies in Ohio, Virginia, and Illinois, in response to pressures from governors or legislators, encouraged or required institutions to eliminate scores of programs, especially doctoral programs, or to reduce graduate enrollments sharply. By contrast, governors in California, Oregon, Washington, and other states in recent years have pushed institutions to *expand* enrollments in high-tech fields perceived as bringing economic growth to the state.

Often the programs cut have been identified as academically weak, high cost, duplicative, having low market demand, or less central to institutional mission or state need. Deciding what programs are low quality or less important may be subjective, however. Based on faculty retrenchment cases in the 1980s, Sheila Slaughter suggested that departments serving primarily women or fields unable to tie themselves to market needs may be disproportionately cut.[12] Over the next decade, humanities and social science programs may be at risk if institutions implement budget systems that require departments to generate income equal to their costs. Or to generate revenues, these departments may increase both enrollments and teaching loads and reduce teaching costs by using more adjunct faculty. If so, this would exacerbate the difference, especially within universities, between a relatively low teaching load and highly research-oriented science and engineering sector and a relatively high teaching load and less research-oriented humanities and social sciences sector. If institutions are to prevent such imbalances from growing, they may need to consider reallocating scarce dollars to support important areas unlikely to be sustained by extramural dollars or high tuition. Where programs are being eliminated, students should be given adequate resources or alternatives to complete their degrees.

Narrowing of Institutional Missions

Will budget cuts result in a contraction of institutional missions? In California, after several years of increased state funding for college "outreach" programs to improve the academic preparation of public school students, especially in schools with low-income and limited-English students, the state slashed these funds in 2002 and 2003, undermining efforts to increase college preparation, enrollment, and graduation of disadvantaged students. The state similarly cut university funds for other K–12 and public service programs, as well as for state-funded research centers.

Conflicting Pressures on Governance and Control

Within the institution, budget constraints may lead to both greater centralization and greater decentralization of authority. Slaughter concluded that retrenchment "generally undermined faculty participation in governance and faculty authority over the direction of the curriculum."[13] At the same time, institutional decisions to require academic units, especially professional schools like business and law, to become self-supporting through tuition revenues or private gifts and contracts tend to shift control from central administration to more autonomous units and to diminish adherence to institution-wide missions. At the state level, many states are demanding greater and more detailed accountability of diminishing state revenues, for example, over faculty workload, even as other states are considering reducing controls in exchange for reduced state appropriations.

Effects on the Higher Education System as a Whole

Will declining state funding, along with government or market limits on tuition, widen the gaps between the "haves" and the "have-nots" in the U.S. higher education system overall—between faculty and student resources at most public institutions and those at well-endowed private institutions, between elite and less elite institutions within the public sector, between tenure-track and non-tenure-track faculty, or between science and nonscience fields? The answer in many cases appears to be "yes." Over the past decade, the gaps have grown between public and private institutions on a number of measures generally considered quality indicators, such as faculty salaries and student/faculty ratio, leading to questions about whether public institutions can retain past levels of instructional and research quality.[14] This problem may be particularly severe at public two-year or four-year comprehensive institutions, which have fewer opportunities to offset declining state dollars with federal grants or private gifts. Another issue is the distribution of students among institutions. If tuition at public institutions continues to rise, will enrollments shift from public to private higher education or from four-year to less expensive two-year institutions? In recent years, some small shifts in these directions occurred. However, enrollment shifts to public two-year colleges assume that two-year colleges will have the resources to enroll more students and that students can afford their rising fees. If insufficient resources force institutions and students to make choices, nontraditional students, including returning adults and those whose initial preparation precludes admission at other institutions, may well be shut out of traditionally open-door community colleges.

A More Commercialized and Politicized Research System?

In the past 25 years, significant changes in the nature of scientific research have occurred. These include the development of fields and techniques not even imagined a quarter century ago, growing university/industry collaboration in the commercial marketing of research discoveries, increased targeting of federal research funding for specific projects, more political involvement in funding—and in prohibiting funding—of research in politically charged areas, and a movement toward "big science" projects involving hundreds of researchers and billions of dollars.

University/Industry Collaboration

Between 1980 and 2000, industry funding for university research and development (R&D) in science and engineering grew much more rapidly than any other funding source, nearly doubling as a percentage of total university research dollars, from 4 to almost 8 percent.[15] Although this is a small percentage of total dollars, industry support plays a much larger role in certain fields, such as biotechnology and civil engineering. For example, a mid-1990s survey found that 79 percent of university faculty in engineering received at least some industry funding.[16] During the 1990s, pharmaceutical funding for university biomedical research shot up. At a time when there are concerns that the growing national deficit together with increased expenditures for federal defense and security may lead to reduced federal research funding, researchers may seek industrial sponsorship much more aggressively.

University/industry partnerships, where researchers in both sectors are jointly involved in research activities, have also grown dramatically over the past two decades. This trend reflects the increasing permeability of boundaries between the two sectors, as universities engage in more commercial marketing and as more new Ph.D.s take jobs in industry but maintain ties with their former faculty advisers. One indicator of this is the growth in the number of university-based research centers with close ties to industry, which increased nearly two and one-half times between 1980 and 1990.[17] Another indicator is the increasing proportion of articles co-authored by academic and industry researchers in fields such as engineering (now more than 15%), as well as physics and clinical medicine. Federal and state agencies have further stimulated these partnerships by linking research funding to industry participation; as a result, even public funding takes on characteristics of industry sponsorship.

University/industry collaboration can provide additional sources of support for university research, access to a broader range of talent, and more rapid development and transfer of useful products like vaccines. However, such collaboration is also subject to potential problems, such as hindering the flow of research information and of graduate students' degree completion when industrial sponsors require researchers to delay release of potentially marketable results; suppressing undesirable results (for example, in drug tests); and skewing research agendas toward corporate interests. Nor are these effects limited to the hard sciences and engineering. In its battle to overturn jury damage awards in the 1989 Exxon Valdez oil tanker spill, for example, Exxon funded psychologists, economists, and law and business faculty to research the competence of juries to set punitive damages. High-profile cases where corporations have provided millions of dollars to universities in return for prior review of and right to delay presentation or publication of results or for influence in

setting the research agenda have raised concerns about bias and in-
hibition of research, as well as the use of universities' credibility to
legitimize industry goals.[18]

Commercialization

A still more problematic trend is the growing involvement of university researchers and of universities themselves in the commercial marketing of scientific and technological discoveries, a trend
stimulated by the 1980 passage of the Bayh-Dole Act, which allowed universities to patent inventions developed with federal research funding. During the 1980s, leading university researchers
established or became associated with for-profit biotechnology and
other "high-tech" companies based on their federally funded university research, a development that prompted Congress to enact
conflict-of-interest regulations. Nevertheless, this trend continued
throughout the 1990s. Many universities have established for-profit
technology-transfer units designed to speed the flow of scientific discoveries and products to the private sector and bring dollars to the
institution. They have also encouraged spin-off companies based on
faculty research and have acquired equity in the spin-off firms they
generated. Universities have moved aggressively into securing commercial patents, especially in drug and other biomedical areas, as well
as negotiating royalty and licensing arrangements with private companies. Between 1993 and 2002, the number of patents issued to academic institutions increased almost two and one-half times, although
two-thirds of these went to just thirteen universities or university
systems.[19] As the National Science Board notes, these trends reflect
"the confluence of two developments: a growing eagerness of universities to exploit the economic potential of research activities conducted under their auspices and the readiness of entrepreneurs and
companies to recognize and invest in the market potential of this research."[20]

Many of these efforts suffered a setback when the high-tech "bub-
ble" burst in the economic recession at the start of the twenty-first
century. Nevertheless, despite strong faculty opposition in some cases,
as well as the limited success of these initiatives at most universities,[21]
they are likely to grow, especially during a period of limited state
and federal funding because they promise universities increased revenues. Like industry sponsorship, commercial marketing of university

research also poses threats to the research system, among them the possibility that it will create conflicts of interest for individuals and institutions, restrict the flow of information, increase the university's fragmentation into entrepreneurial fiefdoms, and shift power to non-academic personnel who typically control for-profit enterprises within the university.[22] Critics also charge that commercialization may further shift research priorities toward more marketable areas in science and technology fields, distort traditional academic missions, and replace science dedicated to the public good with the "privatization of knowledge."[23]

Political Involvement in Science

Political involvement in universities' scientific research is not new. Federal and state policy makers have long set aside research dollars for projects intended to stimulate economic development in particular business sectors or to cure specific health problems. But two recent trends highlight how political intervention may subvert the research process to serve partisan or ideological ends. First, Congress increasingly "earmarks" research monies for universities in the home districts or states of powerful legislators. In 2003, these noncompetitive earmarks, which bypass the academic peer review system intended to ensure that funding is based on merit, totaled more than $2 billion —more than six times the amount earmarked in 1996 and equal to about 10 percent of federal research dollars to universities.[24] Although there have been calls to reduce such earmarks, pressures on legislators to benefit their constituents may ensure that they continue. Second, ideology, in some cases, guides what and who are studied. In line with views of some religious groups, for instance, President Bush in 2001 banned federal funding of research using human embryonic stem cells except in limited cases, and Bush administration staff reportedly warned researchers that grant proposals on AIDS research that contained such terms as "men who have sex with men" and "needle exchange" would receive extra scrutiny.[25]

In sum, these changes in how scientific research is funded, conducted, and used provide opportunities for universities to develop new revenue streams and to serve economic and other public needs more effectively and for government to help meet important policy goals. However, they also pose threats to university missions and priorities, academic integrity, and faculty control. The challenge for research universities and for government and private funders of university research will be to address more fully the public's legitimate needs, while implementing policies and decisions to maintain university support for core academic areas; to enforce policies and accountability mechanisms designed to prevent conflicts of interest or acquiescence to external pressures; and to take a more active role in informing and shaping public discussion about national priorities.

Who Will Attend College? Challenges to Access

The United States truly has a system of "mass higher education." In 2003, more than 60 percent of recent high school graduates and more than one-third of the traditional college-age population (eighteen to twenty-four year olds) were enrolled in postsecondary education institutions. Total enrollments have increased dramatically, rising nearly 50 percent over the past 25 years, to more than 16 million students in 2003. Participation in college remains uneven, however. Moreover, shifting demographic, political, and economic forces are challenging past assumptions about who will—and even who should—enroll in our colleges and universities.

A Changing Student Pool and
Rising Enrollment Demand

Students in U.S. colleges and universities today are very different from those of even twenty years ago.[26] A much larger proportion than in the past are older, part-time, and from ethnic minority groups. In 2000, students aged 25 years and older composed about 40 percent of total college enrollments and nearly one-quarter of full-time enrollments. Over one-quarter of all college students were ethnic minorities, up from 16 percent in 1980, with the greatest increases among Latino students, who are likely to surpass African American enrollments in the next few years.

However, college participation, especially in four-year colleges and universities, remains unequal. Despite growth in numbers, African American and Latino students remain significantly underrepresented in higher education, as Table 5.1 shows, as are Native American students. Fewer minority students complete high school, although in recent decades the gaps in high school dropout rates among ethnic

Table 5.1

High School Drop-Out and College Enrollment Rates, by Race/Ethnicity, Income, and Parents' Education, Selected Years

Year	Total	Race/Ethnicity				Family Income		Parents' Education	
		African American[a]	Latino U.S.-born	All	White[a]	Lowest 20%	Highest 20%	High School Gradua-tion	Bachelor's Degree
High school drop-out rates of 16- to 19-year-olds									
1990	11	14	15	22	10	n.a.	n.a.	n.a.	n.a.
2000	10	12	14	21	8	n.a.	n.a.	n.a.	n.a.
College enrollment rates of recent high school graduates[b]									
1981	54	43		52	55	34	68	n.a.	n.a.
1991	63	46		57	65	40	78	51	87
2001	62	55		52	64	44	80	52	81

Sources: Richard Fry, *Hispanic Youth Dropping Out of U.S. Schools: Measuring the Challenge* (Washington, D.C.: Pew Hispanic Center, *2003*); National Center for Education Statistics (NCES), *Digest of Education Statistics, 2002* (Washington, D.C.: U.S. Department of Education, 2003), table 183; NCES, *Condition of Education,* 2003 (Washington, D.C.: U.S. Department of Education, 2003), tables 18-1, 18-3.

a. Drop-out rates include Latino whites; college enrollment rates exclude them.

b. Rates are for individuals aged 16–24 who graduated from high school during the preceding twelve months. Data for African Americans and Latinos are subject to relatively large sampling errors, due to small sample size.

groups educated in the United States are narrowing.[27] Once they graduate high school, however, only a little over half of African American and Latino graduates enter college, compared with nearly two-thirds of white high school graduates. Close to half of underrepresented students who do attend college enroll in two-year institutions. Because most of these students do not transfer to baccalaureate-granting institutions, an even smaller proportion receive bachelor's or higher degrees, although these numbers are slowing rising. In 2000–2001, African Americans received fewer than 9 percent of all bachelor's degrees, and Latinos received only 6 percent, even though together these two groups constitute one-quarter of high school graduates and one-third of the college-age population.

Poverty is the biggest barrier to college attendance. Students from poor families of all ethnic backgrounds and those whose parents did not have a college education are even less likely than underrepresented minorities as a whole to enroll in college or even to complete high school, as a result of what some critics argue is "an elaborate, self-perpetuating system of social and economic class that systematically grants advantages to those of privilege."[28] Among those who do enter college, perhaps a third or less enroll in four-year colleges, and very few enroll in the nation's elite institutions. Young adults from families in the bottom income bracket are eight times less likely than others in their age group to complete a bachelor's degree. Financial burden, lower levels of academic preparation, and lower expectations —all of which correlate with poverty and parental education—contribute to these negative outcomes.[29]

Demand for college will continue to grow in the next decade. The National Center for Education Statistics projects that college enrollments will increase 11 percent nationally between 2003 and 2013, even though high school graduation rates are expected to level off or decline by the end of the decade. Enrollment demand will be fueled especially by high growth in the numbers of high school graduates in such large Sunbelt states as Florida, California, and Texas, as well as in other large states such as Michigan and New Jersey. (By contrast, some states, mainly more rural ones, may see declines.) By the end of the decade, students of color will constitute close to 40 percent of the college-age population nationally. Demographic changes will be dramatic in some states, especially the growth of Latino populations in the Southwest and Asian populations in the West. By 2010, for example, California projects that more than 40 percent of public high school graduates will be of Latino background, while just over one-third will be white.[30] In some states, many immigrant students may have limited English proficiency, which will restrict their college options.[31] In 2002–2003, for example, 16 percent of California's public high school students were identified as "English Learners."[32]

Access Implications

These changes will have important implications for higher education and especially for college access and completion. First, the growing demand for higher education will collide with forces limiting enrollment: budgetary demands on governments that already have limited revenues to meet other social needs, greater public readiness to consider higher education a private good, and consequent reduction in public funding for higher education. Public institutions will face pressures to enroll more students with less funding and to shift admission priorities—to reduce the number of graduate students and deny admission to students needing remedial assistance, for example. Many private institutions and some public ones will have a seller's market, allowing them to become more selective. More institutions may "leverage" financial aid funds by directing more of their limited dollars to relatively well-off, tuition-paying students. Enrollment caps, increased selectivity, and targeted admissions may create what has been described as a "cascading" effect, where higher-income or better-prepared students take the place of students who otherwise would have been admitted, who in turn enroll in those institutions one step "down" in selectivity, until those at the bottom have no place to enroll.

Second, rising tuition costs, if not coupled with adequate financial support, may keep low-income students from entering or from completing college. For example, for students from the bottom 25 percent of family income, total costs at four-year public colleges equaled more than 70 percent of family income in 2003. Although financial aid reduces these charges substantially (and costs vary greatly among states and institutions), the "net price" for college (tuition and fees less average grant aid per student) has increased at both public and private institutions. Moreover, over the past 25 years, federal, state, and institutional financial aid programs have increasingly shifted away from both grants and need-based support. Federal financial aid has moved overwhelmingly toward loans, rising from about half to about 70 percent of all federal aid, and aid eligibility has been expanded to include more middle-class students. At the state level, non-need-based "merit" aid, which disproportionately aids middle- and upper-income students, rose from 10 percent of state grant dollars in the early 1990s to nearly one-quarter in 2002.[33] Low-income students are most affected by these changes because they are less willing to incur large amounts of debt to finance college and may not be eligible for "merit" aid, and grant programs have not increased enough to cover the expanded pool.

Third, financial support alone will not ensure access and success in college. Low-income, underrepresented ethnic minorities—and first-generation students often come from schools with fewer academic resources—have less academic preparation and may have lower expectations. In Jonathan Kozol's view, the differences in the resources available to rich and poor school districts have created "savage in-equalities" in the education their pupils receive.[34] Unless higher edu-cation institutions work with low-wealth schools and communities to advocate for increased resources and to improve their students' college readiness, U.S. society will lose the talents of a growing seg-ment of the population. In addition, relatively few such students will attend four-year colleges and universities without active interven-tion. Finally, the increasingly diverse student body will continue to change the face of the campus. Colleges will need to develop ways to respond effectively, especially to those low-income, first-generation African American and Latino students who do make it to college but who tend to drop out at higher rates than do middle-class white stu-dents. This may mean more academic support—including remedial education where necessary—and more support for English as a sec-ond language, as more non-native-English speakers enter college. It will also require college climates and curricula that welcome students' differing backgrounds and perspectives as opportunities to enlarge the range of voices and experiences and to build upon students' di-verse language and cultural backgrounds in preparing them for a more interdependent global society.

Changing Public Expectations

Both policy makers and the general public increasingly view higher education as primarily a private benefit rather than a broader so-cial good. More than 90 percent of U.S. adults believe that every high school student who wants a four-year college education should have the opportunity to gain one, according to a 2003 survey, and two-thirds believe state and federal governments should invest more money in higher education. But nearly two-thirds believe that stu-dents and their families should pay the largest share of the cost of a college education.[35] Given ongoing access barriers, these perceptions may make it more difficult than in the past for historically under-served groups to enroll in college, at a time when they are becoming a larger proportion of the college-age pool.

Ironically, these changed perceptions come at a time when high school students of all ethnic backgrounds are completing substan-tially more college preparatory and advanced coursework in science and mathematics than previous generations as a result of higher state graduation and college admission requirements.[36] Having achieved higher levels of academic preparation, however, students may find themselves shut out of four-year colleges if these institutions reduce enrollments or raise admissions standards further.

The ongoing backlash against affirmative action is occurring in this context of changed perceptions and scarce resources. Although the 2003 U.S. Supreme Court decision on the University of Michigan's admissions practices reaffirmed the legality of including race or ethnicity as one of multiple admissions criteria,[37] many institutions are still prevented from considering race, ethnicity, or gender in admissions or financial aid. In California and Washington, for instance, the electorate has outlawed such considerations; elsewhere, governors or governing boards have disallowed or discouraged their use. As a result, increasing the numbers of underrepresented students will remain more difficult. Moreover, the continuing opposition to affirmative action or to admissions criteria that go beyond standardized tests and grades has radically changed the debate over equity and access.[38] While supporters see these practices as a means to "level the playing field" for underserved students, to recognize a broader range of qualities for admission, and to enhance valued diversity, critics portray these practices as creating new inequities that grant access to unqualified individuals who must compete with academically better prepared students. In turn, the latter view is creating a more hostile campus climate for minorities, which could discourage some from even applying to many colleges and universities. In this environment, how colleges identify ways to maintain and increase access by all segments of the population will be a critical test.

As powerful as the anti-affirmative action backlash has been in altering past consensus on access and equity, reduced public funding and changing public expectations pose even more serious threats to higher education participation. If policy makers and higher education leaders in effect "change the rules" just when a new generation of students—less white, less middle class—prepares to enter college, questions about equity in a democratic society and risks to social stability are raised. Reducing access to higher education also raises concerns about meeting society's economic and civic needs at a time of increasing technological, economic, social, and political complexity and interdependence. Slowing or even reversing the country's historic movement toward universal access to higher education is especially problematic because it is being driven largely by governmental and institutional decisions made on financial grounds, rather than by explicit policy decisions on higher education access and participation.

The Changing and Uncertain Job Market for Ph.D.s

Projecting the labor market for new Ph.D.s has perhaps never been more difficult than it is in the current fluid economic, political, and demographic environment. There is ongoing debate over whether U.S. universities are training too many or too few doctorates. Among the questions being raised are these: Is the U.S. training more Ph.D.s than the labor market can absorb, leading to declining prospects for permanent employment for new doctorate recipients, especially in academe? Are we producing Ph.D.s at the expense of undergraduate access? Or is the United States preparing too few doctoral scientists and engineers, particularly in high-tech–oriented fields, to meet economic and technology needs? Are universities enrolling too few U.S. citizens in doctoral programs, especially too few minorities, to advance the nation's educational, economic, and social well-being and to improve individuals' income levels? Should those who want to pursue the life of the mind have opportunities to pursue doctorates, without regard to the job market?

Current Realities

The job market for new Ph.D.s appears less secure today than it was twenty or thirty years ago. One measure of this is the percentage of Ph.D.s who have obtained jobs by the time they have completed their doctoral studies. As Figure 5.2 shows, in most fields a lower percentage of new Ph.D.s had jobs in 2002 than in the early 1970s or 1980s, although the situation was better than in the early 1990s, a low point in the Ph.D. market. Although this is a flawed measure—it does not show the much higher percentage of jobs obtained within six months of the degree, according to professional association surveys, and, conversely, it excludes the rising proportion of those accepting postdoctoral study rather than employment—it still provides a general picture of employment trends for new Ph.D.s. The growing proportion of new Ph.D.s in postdoctoral positions is another measure of this softer job market, especially in the sciences. Nearly three-quarters of

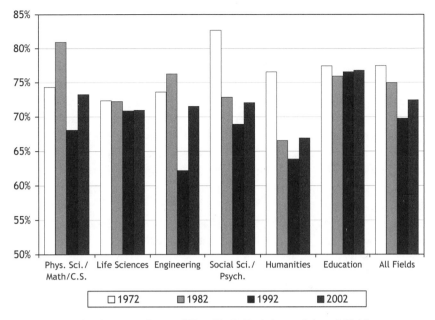

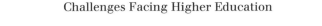

Figure 5.2 Job Placement Rates of New Ph.D. Recipients, Selected Fields

Source: Derived from National Research Council, "Surveys of Earned Doctorates," in *Summary Report: Doctoral Recipients from United States Universities* (Washington, D.C.: National Academy Press, 1974–94).

Note: Numbers exclude those planning postdoctoral study.

new biochemistry Ph.D.s, over half of physicists, and nearly a third of psychologists sought postdoctoral study positions in 2002, and the number of years spent in postdoctoral positions appears to be lengthening.[39] While the rise in "postdocs" reflects a dramatic change in expectations about how scientists are prepared, it is also a response to a weaker job market.

The types of jobs that doctoral recipients take has undergone significant changes as well. Most U.S. science and engineering doctorates and more than one-third of all social science Ph.D.s no longer work in four-year colleges or universities, once the traditional employer of most Ph.D.s. Rather, by 1991 business and industry had become the largest single employment sector for both engineering and physical science Ph.D.s, employing about 60 percent of engineers, nearly half of physical scientists, and a growing proportion of those in other fields. By contrast, only a quarter of doctoral engineers and a third of physical scientists work in four-year institutions, including those in postdoctoral positions. Even in history, a placement survey of recent Ph.D.s suggested that about half would find jobs outside academe.[40]

In recent years, these shifts have been accelerating. Moreover, as noted earlier, the nature of academic employment is also changing. A growing proportion of faculty are in non-tenure-track adjunct or temporary positions, and increasing numbers of other Ph.D.s are in postdoctoral or other non-faculty research positions. Larger numbers of Ph.D.s are also taking positions in community colleges, which traditionally have not required the doctorate to teach. As a 1995 national study concluded, "Ph.D.s are increasingly finding employment outside universities and more and more are in types of positions that they had not expected to occupy."[41]

These and other trends raise several concerns. According to some studies, a majority of doctoral students in most arts and science fields continue to want faculty careers, despite the fact that the percentage of new Ph.D.s obtaining the kind of faculty position that most seek—permanent tenure-track positions in four-year institutions—has declined. Compared with 20 years ago, Ph.D.s take longer to graduate and longer to enter permanent career positions. In most science fields, a lower percentage of full-time faculty in the late 1990s than in the late 1980s received federal research funding, typically deemed necessary for success in these fields. In addition, for the growing number of women in the doctoral workforce, conflicts between professional demands and family responsibilities may limit career options. Perhaps not surprisingly, a 1997 National Science Foundation survey found a relatively high level of dissatisfaction among science and engineering doctorates who had graduated one to five years earlier; for example, 24 percent of physicists, 18 percent of biologists, 16 percent of sociologists, and 15 percent of engineers reported they would be "not at all likely" to choose the same field of study again.[42]

Nevertheless, many signs remain positive. Unemployment among science, social science, and engineering Ph.D.s remains quite low—under 2 percent in most fields in 2001. The percentage of those involuntarily employed part time or outside their academic fields in 2001 was also relatively low, although some disciplines, such as physics and political science, had higher rates of 5 to 9 percent.[43] Conditions fluctuate with the state of the economy, however, and individual subfields may have very different trajectories from the overall discipline.

Future Ph.D. Supply and Demand

While trends are visible in hindsight, projecting future doctorate workforce needs is a risky endeavor. Over the past two decades, labor economists, governmental agencies, and professional associations have presented analyses that disagreed not only about the scope and nature of future Ph.D. workforce needs but whether there would be shortages or surpluses. Most have turned out to be wrong, projecting shortages—or, alternatively, gloomy unemployment levels—that did not materialize. Their conclusions were influenced by their assumptions and methodologies as well as by economic conditions at the time in which they were developed.[44] In the late 1980s, for example, several influential studies predicted critical shortages of higher education faculty and other Ph.D.-trained scientists and engineers by 1997 or earlier, but by the mid-1990s, an economic downturn, the end of the cold war, and higher production of Ph.D.s than projected dissolved the predicted shortages.[45] Similarly, econometric model simulations of Ph.D. supply and demand based on conditions prevailing in the early 1990s predicted that about 22 percent of U.S. science and engineering Ph.D.s could fail to find suitable employment—a prediction that also has not occurred.[46]

The future Ph.D. labor market is difficult to predict for many reasons. Demand will heavily depend on the state of the economy and, for faculty positions, on state budgets for higher education. Within academe, new faculty will be needed to teach growing numbers of students, but how many faculty and in which fields will depend on what disciplines students major in, the types of institutions they enroll in, and the student/faculty ratio. Unexpected external events—wars, new breakthrough technologies, or changes in national and state priorities, for example—could have major impacts on increasing or decreasing demand in certain fields. On the supply side, the number of doctorates in the U.S. workforce will depend on how many new Ph.D.s are produced, retirement ages of those now in the workforce, and employment of foreign doctorate recipients, which are all uncertain.[47]

In addition, workforce projections themselves influence decisions by individuals, institutions, and government, thereby altering the future demand/supply ratio. In the 1970s, Richard Freeman concluded that a "boom and bust" cycle exists in the academic labor market. When Ph.D. jobs appear plentiful, growing numbers of individuals apply to graduate programs, but fewer apply when Ph.D. jobs are in short supply. Because a lag exists between job market needs and Ph.D. production, job shortages are inevitably followed by surpluses and surpluses by shortages.[48] Responses by universities and departments to these trends also vary. Some departments reduce graduate admissions if applicant quality declines or if they cannot provide students full financial support, but other departments dig more deeply into applicant pools or increase foreign admissions to maintain enrollments.

Given these uncertainties, perhaps the best that can be done is to note trends that suggest a stronger Ph.D. job market and those that portend a weaker one, as of late 2003. A number of factors do indeed suggest improved job opportunities for Ph.D.s over the next decade, especially to meet replacement and growth needs. Large numbers of faculty and other doctorate holders in the workforce will retire in the next decade and need to be replaced. In 1999, about a quarter to a third of doctoral-level engineers, scientists, and social scientists in the workforce were age fifty-five or older, depending on the field. Nearly one-third of full-time faculty were age fifty-five or older in 1998. Although Ph.D.s, especially faculty, tend to retire later than labor force participants, they do retire—just two years or so later than those with bachelor's or master's degrees. Additional faculty will be needed to teach the growing numbers of students expected to enter college.[49] Outside academe, many experts believe that demand will be high in computer-related, biotechnology, and other high-tech fields, despite what is considered a temporary economic slowdown.[50] If historical patterns hold, the economy—and with it, college hires and industry positions—will improve within a couple of years.

Other factors are less promising with regard to improved Ph.D. labor market opportunities. Even when the economy improves, colleges and universities, especially public institutions, may not hire new faculty in the numbers once expected. Rather, in the face of continuing public funding constraints and limits on tuition increases, institutions may continue to raise the student/faculty ratio, rely more heavily on instructional technology, and hire more temporary and part-time faculty at lower salary levels. In addition, if college access and affordability decline as the proportion of the college-age population from poor families and underrepresented minority groups increases, college participation rates could drop. In the nonacademic labor market, prospects remain uncertain as well, given new threats of "outsourcing" of high-skilled jobs to cheaper labor markets abroad and downsizing in private-sector R&D.[51] On the supply side, first-year graduate enrollments have begun increasing in some fields—most often due to additional foreign student enrollments—after declining for several years. Although these increases may be temporary if state policy makers refuse to support expensive doctoral enrollments, they may translate into higher numbers of Ph.D.s entering the labor market in six to ten years, unless most foreign students return to their home countries. In addition, there will be fewer openings for new doctorates from U.S. institutions if more scientists and engineers with foreign doctorates (now perhaps a quarter to a third of the total U.S. science and engineering doctoral workforce) come to the United States.[52]

But a list of positive and not-so-positive trends does not give the whole picture. There is not one labor market for doctorates but many hundreds. Whether the outlook is strong or weak depends on very particular subfields and differs by type of position and institution and region of the country. In many fields, employment opportunities outside academe appear stronger than academic ones. Within higher education, faculty employment prospects are better in faster-growing comprehensive colleges than in research universities. *Better* or *worse* are also relative terms. Individuals' (or their faculty advisers') expectations of what is an appropriate job for a Ph.D. also determines how "good" the job market is and how satisfied the individual is. In this regard, it is important to note that Ph.D.s not only fill existing workforce needs but also shape them, creating new labor market demands and new opportunities, as well as effecting economic, social, and cultural development. Ph.D. recipients in careers that might once have been considered "out of field" or inappropriate have transformed those positions by bringing skills and knowledge to bear on their work, so that holding an advanced degree becomes a job requirement.

Policy Options

The uncertain job market outlook for Ph.D.s, combined with competing demands for scarce public dollars, has prompted widespread demands for changes in graduate training, ranging from radical restructuring of the doctoral curriculum to sizable reductions in doctoral programs and enrollments. A number of different responses have been proposed, including the following:

Broaden the Doctoral Curriculum to Prepare
Students for Alternative Careers

Many reports have recommended that universities prepare Ph.D.s for nonacademic (as well as academic) careers—in applied R&D positions in industry, in the nonprofit sector, or in K–12 teaching or science writing. To support this option, the Woodrow Wilson Foundation has provided awards to departments, students, and postdoctorates to encourage humanists to pursue careers outside the university, and the Council of Graduate Schools has initiated a "Preparing Future Professionals" project. Many faculty now appear more open to such alternatives. How many additional openings there will be in such "nontraditional" positions remains uncertain, however.

Shift the Graduate Balance toward Master's Programs

Others urge that we "reinvent" the master's degree in the sciences so that it serves as a gateway to science careers, rather than as a consolation prize for failed Ph.D.s. Professionally oriented master's programs, these advocates argue, hold the most promise.[53] The Alfred P. Sloan Foundation has supported start-up costs for universities to create new two-year professional science master's degree programs, although their total enrollments so far are small.

Impose Academic "Birth Control"

A more radical solution is "zero population growth" in doctoral enrollments and, in fields with an oversupply of Ph.D.s, a moratorium on admissions, at least until the reserve pool of unemployed or underemployed Ph.D.s is significantly reduced. Critics, both within and outside higher education, argue that unrestrained growth of doctoral enrollments and programs has been a major cause of the Ph.D. surplus. These critics argue that doctoral enrollments are driven less by workforce needs than by internal university interests in obtaining graduate students to teach introductory undergraduate courses, help faculty do their research, attract top faculty eager to work with talented professionals-in-training, and raise institutions' standing in prestige rankings. Critics also charge that some government or industry leaders want to increase Ph.D. supply in order to hold down salaries.[54] Foreign students, who in 2002 constituted more than half of new engineering doctorates in the United States, and from a quarter to nearly half of new Ph.D.s in life sciences, business, physics, and mathematics, are a particular target of those who would reduce graduate enrollments because they are seen as artificially propping up graduate programs and worsening the job market for U.S. citizens.

Make Doctoral Studies in Engineering and the Natural Sciences More Attainable and Attractive to U.S. Citizens

If there are shortages of U.S. citizens in some fields, many policy experts argue that the United States must better prepare public school and undergraduate students to pursue science and engineering careers. Others argue that the main problem is not preparation but disincentives to pursue lengthy doctoral studies with vacillating career prospects. These critics argue that, among other things, foregone earnings must be lessened by reducing time-to-degree and postdoctoral periods.

Eliminate Weaker Doctoral Programs

Many favor this solution—for universities other than their own. Few institutions voluntarily close doctoral programs. Still, in the face of budgetary constraints, some universities are cutting weaker programs on their own campuses, and some state agencies have forced the termination of doctoral programs judged weak or duplicative.

Retain the Current System

Many scholars favor retaining the current system, which has served the United States well, while providing students with better information and holding programs more accountable. Other scholars urge caution. Unemployment rates among Ph.D.s remain low. Moreover, students entering doctoral programs now will graduate in six to ten years, when employment needs may be far different. If market difficulties are temporary and institutions turn away promising individuals, the ability of academia, industry, and government to conduct essential teaching, research, and other services could be impaired. These analysts urge that institutions take much more aggressive steps to advise students about current and prospective market conditions, provide data on completion rates and times, and hold departments accountable if student attrition, time-to-degree, or financial support is deemed unacceptable.

Restructure Demand and Expand Understanding of the Value of the Ph.D.

Finally, many in the research community argue that higher education and its allies not only must identify new roles that Ph.D.s can and should play to enhance society but also must make a strong public case for the value of Ph.D.-trained professionals in contributing to national goals. Scholars advocate as well that the higher education community explain why doctoral education, like education in general, is important, not only because it serves utilitarian job market or economic development needs but also because it has intrinsic value to the individual and, because it trains individuals to think and create, to society.

Who Decides? Accountability, Governance, and Coordination

All of the previously discussed issues have significant implications for the relationship between higher education, the public, and government authorities. Higher education is costly to taxpayers and individuals, and it is important to both individuals and the broader society—for economic mobility, preparation of an educated workforce and citizenry, transmission and creation of culture, economic growth, and public health and social welfare. A college education may be a path to social and economic mobility, but college can also represent a barrier to mobility for those unable to gain entrance to the elite institutions that are closely tied to social class. University research provides technological advances and a better understanding of society, but some research may be seen as contrary to certain religious values, pose potential health hazards, or advance private interests at public expense.

Institutional Autonomy and Accountability

Given the costs and value of higher education it should come as no surprise that, as state budgets have become tighter and student fees have risen, governors and legislators have sought to ensure attention to state priorities, to control institutional costs by regulating academic matters such as faculty workloads, and to demand evidence of "accountability" regarding student outcomes such as graduation rates. The kinds of accountability that institutions must meet and the enforcement mechanisms imposed have both changed. Policy makers now demand that institutions not only demonstrate fiscal responsibility but also achieve explicit governmental performance standards such as minimum faculty contact hours and specified student outcomes, and some states have tied institutional funding to performance indicators, which tend to measure only what is readily quantified, and these may not be the essential goals of higher education.[55]

State governments will remain the dominant players in higher education in the foreseeable future because states continue to fund most of public colleges' basic instructional costs, and public institutions enroll most U.S. college students. In addition, states retain extensive regulatory authority over most public colleges, ranging from authority over institutional missions and degrees to regulation of purchasing procedures. Legislative term limits, now in place in sixteen states, also pressure legislators to make their marks quickly before many can develop in-depth expertise or experienced staff. In recent years, governors and legislators have been key catalysts in the revision and restructuring of higher education in a number of states, where they implemented statewide review of degree programs, created—or abolished—statewide boards, or pushed institutions to redirect enrollments and research programs toward engineering, teacher preparation, or other state priorities. In some states, legislatures have enacted requirements that once would have been considered inappropriate political intrusions into academic affairs, such as requirements for student learning assessment, increased faculty teaching workloads, and standards for English-language competence for teaching assistants. Legislative regulation of faculty workloads is a case in point. By 1995, twenty-three states had mandated some kind of action regarding faculty workloads. In most states, these mandates simply required institutions to report on their faculty workload policies and practices, but ten states imposed more substantive requirements. In Ohio, for instance, the legislature mandated that the Board of Regents increase undergraduate teaching by 10 percent.[56]

The most frequent and probably most effective state approach to compel or to induce institutions to pursue desired actions is through the budgetary process. Performance funding, which directly links state funding to institutions' performance on specified indicators, is one tool. Others are performance budgeting, which lets policy makers consider institutions' achievement on specified indicators as one factor in determining allocations, and performance reporting, which seeks to use the power of information to stimulate change but is not linked to institutional funding.[57] However, the amount of state dollars set aside for these strategies is very small. Much more important is the ongoing negotiation—usually invisible to the public—between state officials and institutional leaders in the development of budget requests. The extensive compromises and agreements between the parties on what will be expected is typically not written into the formal budget document.

In addition to elected state officials, the state's electorate may directly regulate higher education matters, bypassing the legislative process. In a number of states, the electorate has imposed requirements regarding academic governance, admissions, or curriculum through ballot initiatives, including prohibiting affirmative action for student admission and faculty employment in California, as part of a broader initiative against public-sector affirmative action, and reinstituting a university governance system in Florida. Some electoral initiatives would intrude into core academic decisions about what is taught, for example, the failed initiative in Oregon in 2000 that, by banning instruction that "encourages . . . homosexual behavior" in public schools and community colleges, would have prohibited faculty from discussing gay or lesbian issues or AIDS education.

Federal officials, too, are using their funding power to regulate institutional actions in admissions and other areas under the aegis of accountability. The federal government will continue to have a major effect in shaping higher education through regulations placed on federal student financial aid (essential to virtually all institutions) and research funding (critical to research universities). This involvement may expand. During the debate leading up to the reauthorization of the omnibus Higher Education Act, expected to be enacted in 2005, influential members of Congress threatened to punish institutions that raised student tuition above certain levels. Arguing that college fee increases were "pricing students and families out of the college market, and forcing prospective students to 'trade down' in their postsecondary educational choices"—and rejecting arguments that a main reason for fee increases was the decline in public funding—these Congress members threatened to withdraw institutions' eligibility to participate in federal student aid if fees to "consumers of higher education" were raised too high.[58] Regional accreditation associations have also played an increasingly important role in influencing colleges and universities, especially because of state and federal requirements that institutions be accredited to receive public dollars.

Nevertheless, the threat of governmental or electoral intervention into core academic affairs should not be overstated. To date, most policy makers' demands for evidence of student learning, increased faculty workload, and institutional performance on state-determined criteria have left much discretion to institutions to determine appropriate responses, though sometimes after extended negotiations and discussion. Moreover, higher education institutions, especially universities with strong alumni support, alternative revenue sources, and complex, loosely coupled structures, have considerable ability to adopt strategies to help retain institutional autonomy.[59] Indeed, from the state perspective, research suggests that strategies such as faculty workload requirements or performance funding may not be effective.[60] Of course, when institutions "voluntarily" adopt actions desired by policy makers under threat of regulatory or budgetary action, it is difficult to say whether political authorities are wielding inappropriate influence. Three points should be noted here. First, governmental regulation and centralization of decision making in higher education tend to wax and wane over time in response to budgetary crises, salience of higher education vis-à-vis other social needs, and particular incidents or situations.[61] Second, each of the fifty states will follow its own path based on its particular conditions and history. Some states may give institutions greater autonomy in return for reduced state funding, as Maryland and Oregon granted to selected institutions in the 1990s—or may even allow public colleges to become autonomous private institutions if they agree to forego state dollars, as South Carolina's governor proposed in 2003. Third, institutional autonomy and public accountability need not be in conflict, if accountability is broadly and appropriately defined.[62] Given higher education's important role in U.S. society, there are legitimate public demands for institutional accountability. The challenge for higher education is a long-standing one: to respond forthrightly to public needs while establishing with political authorities appropriate expectations for institutional accountability and autonomy.

Changing Approaches to Higher Education Governance and Coordination

The governance and coordination of higher education in the United States differs enormously by public versus private control, type of institution, and state, and it differs within each of these categories as well. Historically, most higher education institutions had their own governing boards, although their powers and those of different campus constituencies varied widely. While most institutions and almost all private ones still have individual campus governing boards, most students and faculty in the United States now study and teach in institutions that are part of multicampus systems, a few with hundreds of thousands of students. In addition, all but a handful of states have a statewide coordinating or governing board with some degree of authority or responsibility for all public (or at least all public four-year) postsecondary institutions in the state and sometimes for the state's private institutions as well. During the 1980s and 1990s, significant and sometimes unpredicted shifts in the powers and structures of governance or coordination at each of these levels—campus, multicampus, and statewide—occurred. Political and budgetary forces make it likely that additional changes will occur in the next decade. The question is, what will those changes be and how might they affect the functions and control of higher education in American society?

At the campus level, the past two decades have seen contrary movements toward more centralization and more decentralization of authority. College and university presidents and other top administrators have gained more authority to deal with budget pressures and external demands for accountability, and continuing pressures make it likely that this trend will continue. Simultaneously, a number of institutions have decentralized substantial control to individual schools and departments as a means to center accountability in the units directly responsible for instruction and research, and more institutions are exploring this option. Some units, especially professional schools, have in effect been spun off from the larger university. Decentralization and "responsibility-centered budgeting," which rewards entrepreneurship and priority setting, are creating new approaches intended to increase flexibility at lower institutional levels and, in some cases, enable resource reallocation to other institutional functions or units. These approaches, however, also raise questions as to whether university-wide missions and values (for example, commitment to access) will be maintained and whether departments that typically have not had the slack that comes with large amounts of external funding will retain their priority. Shared governance between trustees, administration, and faculty is another ongoing campus governance issue. At some institutions, particularly elite universities with long histories of faculty influence, shared governance remains strong. At these institutions, except in extraordinary cases, faculty in departments and through academic senate committees retain authority to make faculty hiring and promotion decisions, select graduate students, determine the curriculum, and with administration set the broad outlines for campus priorities and directions. However, some scholars argue that at many institutions faculty have become "managed professionals."[63] Moreover, shared governance may be undermined in the future as the percentage of faculty who are not permanent increases.

Governance and structures of multicampus systems (where two or more campuses have a single governing board and some kind of central administration) are in considerable flux. As with campus governance, there are conflicting trends, and generalizations are difficult because the functions, powers, and integration of these systems vary substantially. In some cases, they are loose collections of very different types of institutions. In other cases, such as the University of California system, they are a set of relatively similar campuses (here, research institutions) with common admissions and faculty promotion standards, under a relatively strong systemwide board and administration. During budget crises, systemwide administrations have often been cut more extensively than those on the campuses. Some multicampus systems have been broken up; in Illinois, for example, two multicampus governing boards were abolished in 1995 and replaced with seven local boards of trustees. In other states, multicampus boards have been strengthened and their administrations expanded in the face of external demands and environmental uncertainties. In yet other states, most notably Florida beginning in 2000, multicampus systems and boards have become political footballs— abolished, re-established, and bypassed in quick succession. Although budgetary problems and "bureaucratic bloat" are often given as rationales for changing multicampus or statewide governance structures, Michael McLendon concluded that political agendas unrelated to higher education were often the primary motive.[64]

Depending on their powers and traditions, systemwide governing boards and administrations have the potential to exercise broad leverage over their campuses through budget and program review powers. Systems may act as buffers against political intervention or as channels for it. On the one hand, system boards and administrations may reduce campus autonomy and flexibility if they impose inappropriately standardized priorities or expectations. Systems also increase bureaucratization and make shared governance more difficult to achieve. On the other hand, systemwide leaders can bring to bear broader perspectives on the overall educational needs of the campuses and the state. System leadership—boards, administrators, and systemwide faculty committees—may be especially important in matters that have relatively weak campus constituencies but are important to the system or to the state, such as undergraduate general education, teacher education, or improvement of K–12 education. They may also ensure that a last surviving program in a particular field is not eliminated through uncoordinated actions by individual institutions. Especially during tight budget periods or under political pressure, system administrations may provide incentives for intercampus collaborations that individual campuses are unable to mount —for example, for programs in less studied languages. How well these collaborations survive when budgets improve is uncertain, however. Moreover, where a system office does not exercise adequate quality control, other more political actors, such as the state's executive branch, may step into the vacuum.[65]

Statewide coordinating agencies or consolidated governing boards[66] are even more buffeted by changing political and budgetary winds and whims than are multicampus systems. This is especially true for coordinating agencies, which can claim no students, faculty, or alumni. Following a period of generally increased budgetary and program review authority to statewide boards, state governors and legislators in a number of states beginning in the 1990s have weakened or even eliminated statewide coordination functions, most notably in New Jersey, where the governor abolished the once powerful coordinating board in 1994 and replaced it with a much weaker agency. In other states, such as California, even where the coordinating structure was left intact, severe budget cuts in 2003 left the agency unable to carry out many of its responsibilities. However, elsewhere, as in South Carolina, state officials continued to pursue reorganizations that would substantially increase statewide control over public higher education. Another potential reorganization of great importance to higher education is the effort in several states, including Florida, to place higher education coordination under the purview of the state's elementary/secondary board of education. Such efforts reflect the failure of higher education institutions to persuade state policy makers that there is effective articulation between the public schools and higher education institutions, so that students can move smoothly from high school into college. Unless broadly conceived, however, creating a single system for all of education risks submerging higher education's unique purposes into those of the much larger K–12 system and of holding higher education to the much more prescriptive and uniform standards applied to the public schools. Even without changes in coordination, policy makers appear more willing to apply K–12 approaches to higher education.

Although in many cases these reorganizations have sought to use structural changes to solve what in fact were budgetary or political problems rather than governance or coordination ones, structure nevertheless makes a difference. James Hearn and Carolyn Griswold found that, independent of other social, educational, and economic factors, states with relatively centralized higher education structures (whether governing boards or strong coordinating boards) were more likely to adopt certain academic policy changes, such as mandatory student assessment, than were states with more decentralized structures.[67] Like multicampus systems, statewide boards may be buffers or conduits for state influence. They may also provide leadership to ensure that the overall higher education system maintains an appropriate balance and range of programs and flexibility to respond to new needs. In any case, given external pressures and political agendas, additional structural and governance changes seem likely in the next decade, but the individual state context will largely determine whether these moves will be toward more centralization, more decentralization, or a mix of centralization and decentralization at different levels. Change itself has costs, however. Structural reorganizations disrupt settled processes and relationships and create greater uncertainty, as new players establish their authority, priorities, and rules of interaction.

Conclusion: Revisiting the Social Contract
for Higher Education

More than thirty years ago, the Carnegie Commission on Higher Education asserted that "benefits from higher education flow to all, or nearly all, persons in the United States directly or indirectly, and the costs of higher education are assessed against all, or nearly all, adults directly or indirectly," although benefits and costs are assigned in "quite unequal amounts."[68] Today higher education continues to confer both public and private benefits. Higher education provides high economic returns to individuals, and it develops a skilled workforce and an educated citizenry, among other public benefits.

Since the Carnegie report, however, as this chapter has discussed, there has been a marked transfer of higher education's costs from public sources to individual students and parents, as well as increased payments from commercial sources. These changes reflect the growing perception by policy makers and the general public that higher education is largely a private benefit, rather than a public good. In turn, this perception risks creating the reality of a private-oriented, market-driven system "disengaged from the public interest."[69] Policy makers who focus on higher education's benefits to individual "consumers" and "clients" have been more willing to reduce general government support for higher education or make it contingent on loans and specific outcomes. In part to make up for declining government support, in part to take advantage of what Derek Bok has argued is the enormous growth in opportunities in recent years to market higher education, institutions have raised tuition and have turned to commercial ventures that benefit private firms or narrow and short-term institutional interests. Bok has concluded that the rapid commercialization of American colleges and universities—where everything may be up for sale—threatens to undermine academic values and standards, impair the university's reputation for the kind of objective teaching and research essential for a democratic society, reduce public trust, and increase government intervention.[70] Robert Zemsky has argued that when institutions become market driven, "their role as public agencies significantly diminishes—as does their capacity to provide venues for the testing of new ideas and agendas for public action."[71]

This chapter has sought to highlight a set of challenges regarding the purposes and outcomes of higher education, each of which is affected by the intertwined pressures of market and government. There is much to applaud in the record of what has been accomplished in these areas, even as concerns remain. Among the accomplishments and concerns are these:

Privatization of Funding

In absolute dollars, more public monies (federal and state) are being allocated for postsecondary education than ever, but more of the costs are being paid by individual students and parents. This is true for both public and private colleges and universities.

Research Mission

The university research enterprise, by any number of measures, is extraordinarily strong, but growing incentives for market and commercial orientation, as well as political intervention and demands for quick, practical products from basic research, risks undermining research integrity and long-term advances in knowledge.

Access

A larger proportion of the population than ever before are participating in some form of postsecondary education, but college access and completion remain inadequate for traditionally underserved groups, especially the poor, ethnic minorities, and older students. The increased share of college costs being borne by individuals, so far without a similar increase in financial aid for underserved groups or improved public school preparation for them, continues this disparity.

Ph.D. Job Market

U.S. doctoral education remains widely admired around the world, and U.S. doctoral students develop the skills and habits of mind to enter many different careers, but most new Ph.D.s are not getting the kinds of academic positions that in many fields most still say they desire. Here, too, market pressures as well as internal priorities may influence how many students universities admit and what careers Ph.D.s expect to obtain.

Accountability and Governance

Because higher education is both costly and important, there are legitimate public policy reasons to hold colleges and universities accountable for using funds appropriately and for serving broad public interests—but if political authorities or the electorate intrude into academic functions, they may undermine higher education's critical function of providing open and objective discussion of ideas and reduce institutions' capability to respond to long-term social objectives.

These challenges raise questions about the implied social contract between the public, elected officials, and institutions of higher education. Some critics suggest that this contract has been broken by public officials who are not providing funding sufficient to ensure access, for example, or by institutions that have retreated from academic values and from the public realm. Yet, the public and elected officials continue to value higher education greatly and, despite the emphasis on private returns and economic benefits, continue to voice support for access, basic research, and other broader institutional missions. For their part, college and university faculty, students, and staff continue to engage in the public realm, by working with the public schools, staffing community health clinics, and providing expertise on important policy issues, for example, and, despite some egregious exceptions, academic integrity remains high. The open question is whether, in the face of market forces and limited public resources, higher education institutions, elected officials, and the public can nevertheless commit to a revised social contract that would acknowledge higher education's role in and responsibilities for achieving broader societal goals, government's responsibility to provide institutions and individuals the resources, autonomy, and flexibility necessary to realize these goals, and the public's willingness to endorse and support these agreements and to pay higher education's costs individually and collectively.

NOTES

1. Clark Kerr and Marian L. Gade, "Current and Emerging Issues Facing American Higher Education," in *Higher Education in American Society,* ed. Philip G. Altbach and Robert O. Berdahl, rev. ed. (Buffalo, NY: Prometheus Books, 1987), 129.

2. These questions build on those posed by the classic 1973 report of the

Carnegie Commission on Higher Education, *Higher Education: Who Pays? Who Benefits? Who Should Pay?* (New York: McGraw-Hill, 1973).

3. Federal funding, the other major source of public support, provides half as much funding, primarily through student financial aid and university research grants and contracts.

4. "Appropriations of State Tax Funds for Operating Expenses of Higher Education in the 50 States," *Grapevine,* current and historical state allocations (Normal: Illinois State University, Center for the Study of Education Policy, 2004), data accessed from *Grapevine* Web site (www.coe.ilstu.edu/grapevine/50state.htm) and State Higher Education Executive Officers Web site (www.sheeo.org/finance/fiscalres.htm), January 2004; National Center for Education Statistics, *Projections of Education Statistics to 2013* (Washington, D.C.: U.S. Department of Education, 2003, table 22). Appropriations data are for higher education operating expenses in the fifty states; a relatively small amount of funds go directly to students through financial aid (about 6% in 2003) or to private institutions. Enrollment data include District of Columbia and U.S. territories (about 2% of total).

5. *A Brief Overview of State Fiscal Conditions and the Effects of Federal Policies on State Budgets* (Washington, D.C.: Center on Budget and Policy Priorities, October 2003); Raymond C. Scheppach, *Update on the State Fiscal Crisis* (Washington, D.C.: National Governors Association, November 2003); Dennis Jones, *State Shortfalls Projected Throughout the Decade: Higher Ed Budgets Likely to Feel Continued Squeeze* (San Jose, CA: Center for Public Policy and Higher Education, February 2003); Steven D. Gold, ed., *The Fiscal Crisis of the States: Lessons for the Future* (Washington, D.C.: Georgetown University Press, 1995).

6. "*Chronicle* Survey of Public Opinion on Higher Education" (conducted February 15–March 17, 2003, with a representative sample of adults aged twenty-five to sixty-five), *Chronicle of Higher Education,* May 2, 2003.

7. Association of Higher Education Facilities Officers and National Association of College and University Business Officers, *A Foundation to Uphold* (Washington, D.C.: APPA Publications, 1996); Audrey Williams June, "More Than Just Maintenance: Repairs Delayed to Save Dollars Yesterday Have Become a Costly Problem for Colleges Today," *Chronicle of Higher Education,* October 10, 2003, A27.

8. University of California, Office of the President, 1990–91 and 2004–5 *Budget for Current Operations* (Oakland: University of California, 1989 and 2003), excludes the system's three federally funded Department of Energy laboratories; Jeffrey Selingo, "The Disappearing State in Public Higher Education," *Chronicle of Higher Education,* February 28, 2003, A22.

9. National Center for Education Statistics, *Digest of Education Statistics, 2002* (Washington, D.C.: U.S. Department of Education Statistics, 2003). See also College Entrance Examination Board, *Trends in College Pricing*

2003 (New York: College Board, 2003), which discusses the relationship between shrinking state appropriations and rising public sector fees and tuition.

10. National Center for Education Statistics, *Tenure Status of Postsecondary Instructional Faculty and Staff: 1992–98* (Washington, D.C.: U.S. Department of Education, 2002). Some non-tenure-track faculty in universities are clinical faculty in medical schools.

11. American Association of University Professors, "The Status of Non-Tenure-Track Faculty," *Academe* 79 (July/August 1993): 39–46.

12. Sheila Slaughter, "Retrenchment in the 1980s: The Politics of Prestige and Gender," *Journal of Higher Education* 64 (May/June 1993): 250–82.

13. Ibid., 276.

14. F. King Alexander, "The Relative Fiscal Capacity of Public Universities to Compete for Faculty," *Review of Higher Education* 24 (Winter 2001): 113–29; Ronald Ehrenberg, "Financing Higher Education Institutions in the 21st Century" (invited address prepared for the 2003 annual meeting of the American Educational Finance Association, St. Louis, March 29, 2003).

15. Data on research trends in this section draw heavily on the National Science Board, *Science and Engineering Indicators—2002* (Arlington, VA: National Science Foundation, 2002).

16. National Science Board, *Science and Engineering Indicators—1996* (Washington, D.C.: U.S. Government Printing Office, 1996).

17. Harvey Brooks, "Current Criticisms of Research Universities," in *The Research University in a Time of Discontent,* ed. Jonathan R. Cole, Elinor G. Barber, and Stephen R. Graubard (Baltimore: Johns Hopkins University Press, 1994), 231–52.

18. D. Blumenthal, E. G. Campbell, M. S. Anderson, N. Causino, and K. S. Louis, "Withholding Research Results in Academic Life Science: Evidence from a National Survey of Faculty," *Journal of the American Medical Association 277* (1997): 1224–28; Alan Zarembo, "Funding Studies to Suit Need," *Los Angeles Times,* December 3, 2003. Examples of high-profile collaborations that have sparked much debate include the five-year, $25 million agreement between the University of California at Berkeley and Novartis in 1998 and the ten-year agreement of up to $225 million between Stanford, Exxon Mobil, and three other firms in 2003. It should be noted that the worst fears regarding these collaborations have not always been borne out. See, for example, Goldie Blumenstyk, "A Vilified Corporate Partnership Produces Little Change (Except Better Facilities)," *Chronicle of Higher Education,* June 22, 2001, A24, and Goldie Blumenstyk, "Greening the World or 'Greenwashing' a Reputation?" *Chronicle of Higher Education,* January 10, 2003, A22.

19. Association of University Technology Managers, *AUTM Licensing Survey, FY 2002 Survey Summary* (Northbrook, IL: AUTM, 2003); Goldie Blumenstyk, "Inventions Produced Almost $1 Billion for Universities in 2002," *Chronicle of Higher Education,* December 19, 2003, A28.

20. National Science Board, *Science and Engineering Indicators—2002*, 5–56.

21. Joshua B. Powers, "Commercializing Academic Research: Resource Effects on Performance of University Technology Transfer, *Journal of Higher Education* 74 (January/February 2003): 26–50.

22. Roger L. Geiger, "Research Universities in a New Era: From the 1980s to the 1990s," in *Higher Learning in America, 1980–2000,* ed. Arthur Levine (Baltimore: Johns Hopkins University Press, 1993), 67–85; Sheila Slaughter and Larry L. Leslie, *Academic Capitalism: Politics, Policies, and the Entrepreneurial University* (Baltimore: Johns Hopkins University Press, 1997).

23. Sheldon Krimsky, *Science in the Private Interest: Has the Lure of Profits Corrupted Biomedical Research?* (Lanham, MD: Rowman and Littlefield, 2003).

24. Jeffrey Brainard and Anne Marie Borrego, "Academic Pork Barrel Tops $2 Billion for the First Time," *Chronicle of Higher Education,* September 26, 2003, A18.

25. Jocelyn Kaiser, "Studies of Gay Men, Prostitutes Come under Scrutiny," *Science* 300 (April 18, 2003): 403.

26. Much of the data in this section is drawn from the National Center for Education Statistics, including *Digest of Education Statistics 2002, Projections of Education Statistics to 2013,* and *Condition of Education 2003* (Washington, D.C.: U.S. Department of Education, 2003).

27. For the Latino population, it is important to distinguish between those educated in the United States and those who immigrated to the United States, often as adults coming to seek work. Ninety percent of Latino immigrants who were educated outside the United States did not complete high school. Addressing the needs of these individuals is important, but including them in statistics on U.S. educational attainment (as national data typically do) gives a misleading image of dropout rates for Latino students educated in U.S. schools. See Richard Fry, *Hispanic Youth Dropping Out of U.S. Schools: Measuring the Challenge* (Washington, D.C.: Pew Hispanic Center, 2003).

28. Peter Sacks, "Class Rules: The Fiction of Egalitarian Higher Education," *Chronicle of Higher Education,* July 25, 2003, B7.

29. Susan Choy, *Students Whose Parents Did Not Go to College: Postsecondary Access, Persistence, and Attainment* (Washington, D.C.: U.S. Department of Education, National Center for Education Statistics, 2001); Douglas S. Massey, Camille Z. Charles, Garvey F. Lundy, and Mary J. Fischer, *The Source of the River: The Social Origins of Freshmen at America's Selective Colleges and Universities* (Princeton, NJ: Princeton University Press, 2003); Arthur Levine and Jana Nidiffer, *Beating the Odds: How the Poor Get to College* (San Francisco: Jossey-Bass, 1995).

30. California Department of Finance, *California Public K–12 Enrollment Projections by Ethnicity, 2003 Series* (Sacramento: State of California, 2003).

31. Adalberto Aguirre, "Ethnolinguistic Populations in California: A Focus on LEP Students and Public Education," *Journal of Educational Issues of Language Minority Students,* 15 (Winter 1995).

32. California Department of Education, Educational Demographics Office, "DataQuest" Web site (data1.cde.ca.gov/dataquest/).

33. College Entrance Examination Board, *Trends in College Pricing 2003* (New York: College Board, 2003); College Entrance Examination Board, *Trends in Student Aid 2003* (New York: College Board, 2003). For further discussion of the intertwined effects of tuition and financial aid on access and affordability, see also Donald E. Heller, "Trends in the Affordability of Public Colleges and Universities: The Contradiction of Increasing Prices and Increasing Enrollment," in *The States and Public Higher Education Policy: Affordability, Access, and Accountability,* ed. Donald E. Heller (Baltimore: Johns Hopkins University Press, 2001), 11–38.

34. Jonathan Kozol, *Savage Inequalities: Children in America's Schools* (New York: Crown, 1991).

35. *"Chronicle* Survey of Public Opinion on Higher Education."

36. National Center for Education Statistics, *Condition of Education 2002* (Washington, D.C.: U.S. Department of Education, 2002), indicator 26.

37. *Grutter v. Bollinger,* 539 U.S. 306 (2003).

38. William G. Bowen and Derek Bok, *The Shape of the River: Long-Term Consequences of Considering Race in College and University Admissions* (Princeton, NJ: Princeton University Press, 1998).

39. National Science Foundation, Annual Survey of Earned Doctorates, caspar.nsf.gov/ (accessed from NSF WebCASPAR database system).

40. National Science Foundation, *Characteristics of Doctoral Scientists and Engineers in the United States: 2001* (Arlington, VA, 2003); Robert B. Townsend, "History Jobs Take a Tumble, but the Number of PhDs also Falls," *Perspectives* (newsletter of the American Historical Association), December 2003. Unfortunately, data on employment of doctorate recipients in humanities, arts, or professional fields are limited, since the National Science Foundation no longer funds most such data collection.

41. Committee on Science, Engineering, and Public Policy (COSEPUP) of the National Academy of Sciences, the National Academy of Engineering, and the Institute of Medicine, *Reshaping the Graduate Education of Scientists and Engineers* (Washington, D.C.: National Academy Press, 1995): 2–3.

42. Chris M. Golde and Timothy M. Dore, *At Cross Purposes: What the Experiences of Today's Doctoral Students Reveal About Doctoral Education* (Madison: Wisconsin Center for Education Research, University of Wisconsin–Madison, 2001); Renate Sadrozinski, Maresi Nerad, and Joseph Cerny, *PhDs in Art History—Over a Decade Later: A National Career Path Study of Art Historians* (Seattle: University of Washington, 2003); Mary Ann Mason and Marc Goulden, "Do Babies Matter? The Effect of Family Formation on

the Lifelong Careers of Academic Men and Women," *Communicator* (newsletter of the Council of Graduate Schools), April 2003; National Science Foundation, *Characteristics of Doctoral Scientists and Engineers in the United States: 2001;* National Science Board, *Science and Engineering Indicators—2002.*

43. National Science Foundation, *Characteristics of Doctoral Scientists and Engineers in the United States: 2001.*

44. For a critique of current projection models, see National Research Council, *Forecasting Demand and Supply of Doctoral Scientists and Engineers: Report of a Workshop on Methodology* (Washington, D.C.: National Academy of Sciences, 2000).

45. William G. Bowen and Julie Ann Sosa, *Prospects for Faculty in the Arts and Sciences: A Study of Factors Affecting Demand and Supply, 1987 to 2012* (Princeton, NJ: Princeton University Press, 1989); Richard Atkinson, "Supply and Demand for Scientists and Engineers: A National Crisis in the Making," *Science* 248 (April 27, 1990): 425–32; William G. Bowen and Neil L. Rudenstine, *In Pursuit of the Ph.D.* (Princeton, NJ: Princeton University Press, 1992).

46. Charles A. Goldman and William F. Massy, *The Ph.D. Factory: Training and Employment of Science and Engineering Doctorates in the United States* (Bolton, MA: Anker Publishing, 2000), first released as a draft report in 1995.

47. For further discussion of academic supply and demand factors, see Ronald G. Ehrenberg, "Studying Ourselves: The Academic Labor Market," *Journal of Labor Economics* 21 (2003): 267–87.

48. Richard Freeman, *The Overeducated American* (New York: Academic Press, 1976).

49. National Science Board, *Science and Engineering Indicators—2002;* National Center for Education Statistics, *Digest of Education Statistics* 2002, table 233; National Center for Education Statistics, *Projections of Education Statistics to 2013.*

50. National Research Council, Committee on Workforce Needs in Information Technology, *Building a Workforce for the Information Economy* (Washington, D.C.: National Academy Press, 2002); National Science Board, *The Science and Engineering Workforce: Realizing America's Potential* (Arlington, VA: National Science Foundation, 2003).

51. Dan McGraw, "My Job Lies Over the Ocean," *Prism* (newsletter of the American Society for Engineering Education), December 2003; Michael S. Teitelbaum, "Do We Need More Scientists?" *The Public Interest* 153 (Fall 2003): 40–53.

52. Given the current set of factors, a 2000 report from the National Research Council recommended that overall Ph.D. production in the basic biomedical sciences and in the behavioral and social sciences not be increased,

although it suggested growth in certain subfields. In reaching its assessment
of supply and demand, the report excluded positions that in the past had been
filled by non-Ph.D. researchers. See National Research Council, Committee
on National Needs for Biomedical and Behavioral Scientists, *Addressing the
Nation's Changing Needs for Biomedical and Behavioral Scientists* (Washington, D.C.: National Academy Press, 2000).

53. Sheila Tobias, Daryl E. Chubin, and Kevin D. Aylesworth, *Rethinking Science as a Career: Perceptions and Realities in the Physical Sciences*
(Tucson, AZ: Research Corporation, 1995).

54. See, for example, David Goodstein, "Scientific Ph.D. Problems," *The
American Scholar* 62 (Spring 1993): 215–20; Cary Nelson, "Lessons from the
Job Wars: What Is to Be Done?" *Academe* 81 (November/December 1995): 18–
25; or Teitelbaum, "Do We Need More Scientists?" Goodstein calculated that,
in physics, each research university professor on average produces about fifteen new Ph.D.s in a career, an exponential growth rate that cannot continue
indefinitely. (However, physics is a field where Ph.D. production and new enrollments have declined over the past decade.)

55. William Zumeta, "Public Policy and Accountability in Higher Education: Lessons from the Past and Present for the New Millennium," in *The
States and Public Higher Education Policy: Affordability, Access, and Accountability,* ed. Donald E. Heller (Baltimore: Johns Hopkins University
Press, 2001), 155–97. Zumeta notes that improved capacity for data collection
and analysis has increased the ability of policy makers to demand and get detailed information on such quantifiable measures of performance.

56. Edward R. Hines and J. Russell Higham III, *State Policy and Faculty
Workload* (Normal: Center for Higher Education and Educational Finance,
Illinois State University, 1996).

57. Joseph C. Burke and Henrik Minassians, "Performance Reporting:
'Real' Accountability or Accountability 'Lite'—Seventh Annual Survey 2003"
(Albany: Nelson A. Rockefeller Institute of Government, State University of
New York, Albany, 2003).

58. House Committee on Education and the Workforce, Subcommittee on
21st Century Competitiveness, *The College Cost Crisis: A Congressional
Analysis of College Costs and Implications for America's Higher Education
System,* prepared by Rep. John A. Boehner (R-OH) and Rep. Howard P.
"Buck" McKeon (R-CA) (Washington, D.C.: U.S. House of Representatives,
2003): 2. In response, some House Democrats proposed penalizing states that
cut higher education appropriations below a certain level.

59. Ami Zusman, "Legislature and University Conflict: The Case of California," *Review of Higher Education* 9 (Summer 1986): 397–418.

60. James S. Fairweather and Andrea L. Beach, "Variations in Faculty
Work at Research Universities: Implications for State and Institutional Pol-

icy," *Review of Higher Education* 26 (Fall 2002): 97–115; Burke and Minas-sians, "Performance Reporting."

61. Lois Fisher, "State Legislatures and the Autonomy of Colleges and Universities: A Comparative Study of Legislatures in Four States, 1900–1979," *Journal of Higher Education* 59 (March/April 1988): 133–62; Carol Everly Floyd, "Centralization and Decentralization of State Decision Making for Public Universities: Illinois 1960–1990," *History of Higher Education Annual 1992* 12 (1992): 101–18.

62. See Frank Newman, *Choosing Quality: Reducing Conflict between the State and the University* (Denver, CO: Education Commission of the States, 1987) for a discussion of what constitutes appropriate public policy versus in-appropriate governmental intrusion.

63. Gary L. Rhoades, *Managed Professionals: Unionized Faculty and Restructuring Academic Labor* (Albany: State University of New York Press, 1998).

64. Michael K. McLendon, "Setting the Governmental Agenda for State Decentralization of Higher Education," *Journal of Higher Education* 74 (September/October 2003): 479–515.

65. Clark Kerr and Marian L. Gade, *The Guardians: Boards of Trustees of American Colleges and Universities* (Washington, D.C.: Association of Governing Boards of Universities and Colleges, 1989); Marian L. Gade, *Four Multicampus Systems: Some Policies and Practices That Work* (Washington, D.C.: Association of Governing Boards of Universities and Colleges, 1993); Ami Zusman, "Multicampus University Systems: How System Offices Coordinate Undergraduate and K–12 Education" (paper presented at the annual meeting of the Association for the Study of Higher Education, Minneapolis, October 1992); Patricia J. Gumport, "Built to Serve: The Enduring Legacy of Public Higher Education," in *In Defense of American Higher Education,* ed. Philip G. Altbach, Patricia J. Gumport, and D. Bruce Johnstone (Baltimore: Johns Hopkins University Press, 2001), 85–109.

66. Multicampus systems that include all public or all public four-year in-stitutions in a state also may carry out statewide governance and coordina-tion functions for the state. Coordinating agencies have more limited powers but often broader scope.

67. James C. Hearn and Carolyn P. Griswold, "State-Level Centraliza-tion and Policy Innovation in U.S. Postsecondary Education," *Educational Evaluation and Policy Analysis* 16 (Summer 1994): 161–90.

68. Carnegie Commission on Higher Education, *Higher Education: Who Pays? Who Benefits? Who Should Pay?* vii.

69. James J. Duderstadt and Farris W. Womack, *The Future of the Public University in America: Beyond the Crossroads* (Baltimore: Johns Hopkins University Press, 2003), 6.

70. Derek Bok, *Universities in the Marketplace: The Commercialization of Higher Education* (Princeton, NJ: Princeton University Press, 2003). See also David Kirp, *Shakespeare, Einstein, and the Bottom Line: The Marketing of Higher Education* (Cambridge, MA: Harvard University Press, 2003).

71. Robert Zemsky, "Have We Lost the 'Public' in Higher Education?" *Chronicle of Higher Education,* May 30, 2003, B7.

 **Part Two**

External Forces

Chapter Six

The Federal Government and Higher Education

Lawrence E. Gladieux, Jacqueline E. King, and Melanie E. Corrigan

The framers of the U.S. Constitution lodged no specific responsibility for education with the national government; yet, the federal influence on American colleges and universities has been enduring and pervasive. From sponsorship of land-grant colleges in the nineteenth century to the underwriting of student loans and university-based research and development in the twentieth century, the federal government has actively and extensively supported higher education to serve a variety of national purposes.

Today, the federal government provides less than 15 percent of all college and university revenues. But in two types of spending, direct aid to students and funds for research and development (R&D), federal outlays far exceed those of the states, industry, and other donors. Higher education is also affected by federal tax policies, both in the financing of institutions and in family and student financing of the costs of attendance. Moreover, as a condition of federal spending and tax support, Congress and executive agencies of the government impose a variety of rules and mandates on postsecondary institutions and students. Finally, the federal government has primary responsibility for setting, interpreting, and enforcing civil rights legislation that affects colleges and universities. Such policies may affect higher education in much the same way as other institutions (as in equal opportunity procedures for hiring employees) or may be tailored to address specific issues in higher education (such as gender equity in sports or affirmative action in admissions). Federal policy in civil rights is covered by Michael Olivas in his chapter on the legal environment.

The effect of the federal government on campuses and on students is substantial, diverse, and constantly changing. It is the product of deeply rooted traditions but also short-term decisions. This chapter analyzes the federal government's relationship to higher education, beginning with the historical underpinnings and current means and dimensions of support. It then discusses issues in research support, student aid, tax policy, and regulation, and concludes with thoughts on federal policy directions into the future.

The Responsibility for Higher Education in the American System

That the states have the basic responsibility for education at all levels is an American tradition. The Tenth Amendment, reserving powers not delegated to the central government to the states, coupled with the fact that "education" is nowhere mentioned in the Constitution, pointed toward a secondary role for the federal government in this field. While some of the founding fathers urged a national system of education run by the federal government, the majority favored state, local, and private control, perhaps with a national university to cap the system. All proposals to establish such a university in the capital city failed, despite the fervent support of George Washington and several of his successors in the presidency. To this day, the federal government does not directly sponsor institutions of higher learning, apart from the military academies and a few institutions serving special populations. Still, early federal policy was crucial in promoting higher education as an adjunct of western migration and public land development in the late eighteenth and nineteenth centuries. The Morrill Land-Grant College Act of 1862 fostered the creation and development of what are now some of the nation's great public and private universities.[1]

Federal investment in university-based R&D and in student aid via the GI Bill soared following World War II. Beginning with the Soviet challenge of Sputnik, Congress created a variety of aid-to-education programs in the late 1950s and 1960s, and by the 1970s, the federal government had become the largest source of direct assistance to individual students for financing their college expenses. Fundamentally, however, federal expenditures have remained supplementary to state subsidies and private support of higher learning. Terry Sanford, former governor of North Carolina, U.S. senator, and president of Duke University, once put it this way: "The money for the extras came from the national funds. . . . This is the glamour money. . . . It is needed, it has improved the quality. . . . It is proper to remember, however, for all the advantages brought by the extras, the train was put on the track in the first place by the states, and continues to be moved by state fuel and engineers."[2]

Over the past two centuries, the states have moved with varying speed to create and expand public systems of higher education and, more recently, to assist private colleges and universities or to purchase educational services from them. Although state funding as a percentage of total higher education revenues has declined since 1980, the lion's share of *government* support for postsecondary institutions continues to come from the states.

The traditional division of responsibilities between the federal and state governments was reaffirmed in the early 1970s when Congress debated and ultimately rejected proposals for general purpose federal institutional aid. In passing the 1972 amendments to the Higher Education Act, "Congress pulled up short of a plan that amounted to federal revenue sharing with institutions of higher education— across-the-board general operating support distributed on the basis of enrollments. It was unwilling to underwrite the entire system without reference to any national objective other than preserving and strengthening educational institutions. The responsibility for general support of institutions, it was decided, should continue to rest with the states.[3]

This is not to say that the federal government has been unconcerned about the health and capacity of institutions. Certain types of institutions have received special federal attention because of their particular contributions to the national interest. Major research and graduate-oriented universities, particularly their medical schools, are one such category. They are supported by grants and contracts from multiple federal agencies. The historically black colleges and Hispanic-serving institutions are also beneficiaries of federal institution-based support, primarily through programs authorized under Title III (Institutional Aid) and Title V (Developing Institutions) of the Higher Education Act.

In addition, a few federal programs address institutional capacity for research. These include the National Institutes of Health's Biomedical Research Support Grants and the National Science Foundation's Institutional Development Program. Other federal funding goes to support the arts and humanities, occupational and vocational education, international exchanges and studies, the provision of military training, and other purposes. Although the amounts are relatively small, they are significant for some institutions and certain parts of the education community.

Meanwhile, student aid represents at least an indirect subsidy of consequence to nearly every institution in the country.[4] About 40 percent of the 19 million students who attend postsecondary education each year are estimated to receive some federal aid, in the form of grants, loans, or work/study programs.[5] The aid programs benefit all sectors of postsecondary education, but the rate of participation is by far the highest in proprietary schools (79%), followed by private nonprofit colleges (51%), public four-year institutions (43%), and public two-year institutions (23%). Whenever the Higher Education Act comes up for reauthorization in Congress, the stakes are high for institutions. Representatives of all the postsecondary sectors—two-year, four-year, public, private, proprietary—struggle over scores of amendments that determine who gets what under Title IV of the statute, which authorizes the federal student aid programs. Likewise, when federal budget cutbacks threaten, the higher education community tends to close ranks to defend the programs.

In sum, while federal education monies are much sought after, the historical parameters of the federal role continue to prevail. The states retain the fundamental responsibility for higher education, primarily through provision of operating support for public systems of colleges and universities. The federal role is to provide particular kinds of support to meet perceived national objectives, generally without distinguishing between public and nonpublic higher education. The federal government:

— purchases R&D services and thereby supports the research capacity as well as graduate-level training programs of universities;

—fills gaps and meets special needs, such as college library support, foreign language and area studies, and health professions development, to name just a few;

—directs almost half its aid to students and families rather than institutions, with the aims of removing barriers facing individuals who aspire to postsecondary education and relieving the financial burden on middle-class families of paying for college.

Overview: Mechanisms and Dimensions of Federal Support

In the nineteenth century, states served as intermediaries in federal patronage of higher education. Proceeds from the sale of public lands provided endowments that helped the states establish and finance the early land-grant institutions, agricultural extension programs, and other forerunners of today's public colleges and universities. These federal grants to the states were broad and carried few restrictions.

Toward the beginning of the twentieth century, however, the pattern began to change. Federal support became piecemeal and started going directly to institutions themselves, bypassing state governments. In recent decades, nearly all federal monies have been channeled to institutions (or to departments, schools, and faculty members within institutions) or to individual students. For this reason, a federal-state "partnership" in supporting higher education is meaningful only in a general sense. In fact, there is virtually no conscious meshing of funding purposes and patterns between the two levels of government. By and large, the federal activity proceeds independently. One observer concluded that "with a few modest exceptions, federal postsecondary spending arrangements make no attempt to stimulate state spending, to compensate for differences in state wealth or effort, or to give state governments money to allot as they see fit."[6] Nor, it might be added, would it be easy to implement a program or funding formula that would effectively achieve any combination of such objectives. Likewise, most analysts agree that state policy takes little cognizance of federal spending patterns or policy decisions.

The federal government's activities affecting higher education are so decentralized and so intermixed with other policy objectives that

simply trying to enumerate the programs and tally the total investment is problematic. Creation of the U.S. Department of Education in
1979 consolidated only about a fourth of the more than 400 programs
that existed then and less than a third of total federal expenditures
for higher education—not substantially more than were encompassed
by the old Office of Education in the U.S. Department of Health, Education, and Welfare. The remaining programs and funds are still scat-
tered across a number of federal agencies, from the Departments of
Defense, Labor, Agriculture, Transportation, and Health and Human
Services to the Veterans Administration, Agency for International
Development, National Aeronautics and Space Administration, and
Smithsonian Institution. This diffuse pattern within the executive
branch is mirrored in Congress, where committee responsibilities
tend to follow agency structures. Thus the fragmentary nature of federal influence and support for higher education seems likely to persist.

Table 6.1 provides an overview of federal support for higher education. In fiscal year 2001, federal spending totaled $52 billion, with
44 percent of this amount for university-based R&D, 23 percent for
the net cost of providing student aid, 18 percent for tax programs
benefiting students and their families, 8 percent for tax benefits affecting nonprofit institutions of higher education, and the balance
for assorted categorical assistance and payments to colleges and universities. The more than $11 billion spent on student aid programs
is considerably less than the $62 billion in federal aid actually made
available to students through these programs because the federal government guarantees and subsidizes private loans, requires nonfederal
matching in certain programs, and recoups some of the cost of student aid expenditures through interest payments on federal education loans.[7]

Research Support

Federal spending on R&D and other aspects of science at colleges and
universities predates the federal commitment to student aid, going
back to an 1883 law to support agricultural experiment stations. But
the investment in academic science was fairly small until the needs
of World War II caused federal spending for campus-based research
to skyrocket. The boom in federally sponsored research continued

Table 6.1

Net Federal Financial Assistance to Higher Education, by Type and Source, Fiscal Year 2001

Type and Source	Millions of Dollars	Percentage
Student aid	11,726	22.5
Department of Education	7,776	
Department of Veterans Affairs	1,679	
ROTC scholarships and other military assistance	968	
Health professions scholarships/fellowships	1,173	
Programs for Native Americans	122	
Other scholarship/fellowship programs	8	
Tax benefits for students and families	9,600	18.4
HOPE and Lifetime Learning tax credits	6,500	
Exclusion of scholarship and fellowship income	1,210	
Parental exemption for students age 19 or older	1,010	
Other tax benefits	880	
Research and development	22,781	43.7
Tax benefits for institutions	4,370	8.4
Other institutional support	3,584	6.9
Department of Education	1,877	
Special institutions	425	
Military academies	307	
National Science Foundation	478	
International education/cultural exchange	321	
Other	176	
Total federal aid	52,091	99.9

Sources: U.S. Department of Education, National Center for Education Statistics, *Digest of Education Statistics 2001* (Washington, D.C.: U.S. Department of Education, 2001), table 364. Office of Management and Budget, Fiscal Year 2003.

Notes: Some student aid amounts differ from those in figure 6.1. Figure 6.1 describes total aid available to students for academic year 2001–02, including the volume of borrowing generated by federal loan guarantees and subsidies, as well as amounts contributed by states and institutions. Military training assistance is included here but not in figure 6.1. The figure here for student assistance from the Department of Education reflects receipts from the federal student loan programs totaling $2.2 billion as well as expenditures of $10 billion.

The research and development figure includes federal obligations for research and development centers administered by colleges and universities, unlike federal R&D figures in table 6.2.

Other tax benefits for students and families include the following: education individual retirement accounts, deductibility of student loan interest, state prepaid tuition plans, exclusion of interest on savings bonds used for educational expenses, and exclusion of employer-provided educational assistance. Tax benefits for institutions include the deductibility of charitable contributions and exclusion of interest on bonds for nonprofit educational facilities. Some portion of these benefits actually went to private nonprofit elementary and secondary schools.

through the 1950s and early 1960s. The federal government remains the largest source of financing for campus-based research, supplying more than $22 billion in 2001.

Unlike student aid, federal research funding is highly concentrated on a relatively small number of institutions, most of them major research universities. According to the National Science Foundation (NSF), one hundred doctorate-granting institutions receive more than 80 percent of all federal science and engineering obligations to academia, a proportion that has remained quite stable over the years.[8] This support flows from multiple federal agencies and policy objectives. When NSF was created in 1950, presidential science adviser Vannevar Bush envisioned a single agency having broad purview over federal funding of research in the physical sciences, medicine, and defense with a separate science advisory board to evaluate and integrate technical research sponsored by other government departments.[9] This vision is far from today's diffuse reality, with more than a dozen mission-oriented agencies funding academic science for a variety of purposes.

The federal investment in scientific research has allowed a relatively small cadre of American research universities to attain global preeminence in many fields, and the diffusion of funds in various agencies has prevented any single set of federal bureaucrats from setting the entire research agenda. However, the growth of federally funded research has clearly influenced the priorities of research universities and, according to many observers, created imbalances, leading the universities to emphasize research over teaching, graduate work over undergraduate education, and the sciences over social science and the humanities.[10]

R&D expenditures at colleges and universities are summarized in table 6.2. In constant dollars, the federal contribution increased by almost 90 percent between 1980 and 2000. Contributions from industry, institutional funds, and other sources also grew faster than inflation. Overall, this has been an extraordinary period for investment in university-based science.

This growth curve continued despite the end of the cold war and the dissolution of the former Soviet Union, which diminished public interest in military research and the "big science" projects that were a hallmark of competition between the superpowers. In large part, this growth was fueled by the commitment of congressional leaders to double spending on medical research funded through the National

Table 6.2

R&D Expenditures at Universities and Colleges, by Source of Funds, Fiscal
Years 1980 and 2000

	Constant 2002 Dollars (millions)		
Source	1980	2000	Increase (%)
Federal government	9,746	18,408	88.9
State and local governments	1,167	2,314	98.3
Industry	594	2,433	310.0
Institutional funds	2,068	6,288	204.0
All other sources	942	2,321	146.4
Total	14,517	31,764	118.8

Source: National Science Board, *Science and Engineering Indicators, 2002* (Arlington,
Va.: National Science Board, 2002).

Note: Federal government dollars do not include amounts for federally funded research
and development centers.

Institutes of Health (NIH). Can such spending persist? What priorities will the federal government set for its research investment? How will it award and what constraints will it impose on this money?

For most of the past fifty years, America invested disproportionate resources and dedicated many of its best minds to defense-related science and technology. During the 1990s, federal appropriators reoriented their priorities toward investments that promised benefits to the American economy and quality of life. Hence, their commitment to double funding for NIH. The fastest-growing area of federal research funding is biomedical research, a field in which breakthroughs yield economic and "quality of life" returns. Federal policy makers also assign high priority to projects with clear potential for "technology transfer," commercial applications, and job creation. In the wake of September 11, there is renewed interest in defense and homeland security-related research projects as well.

Meanwhile, federal policy makers are divided over how federal dollars for academic science should be awarded. In 1980, Congress earmarked a total of roughly $10 million for specific projects and institutions, bypassing formal competition and merit review. By 2002 such earmarking had ballooned to more than $1.8 billion, sparking intense debate between congressional critics of "pork barrel science" and appropriators grown accustomed to awarding research grants to campuses in their home districts.[11]

Traditionally, federal campus-based research funds have been distributed on the basis of competition, with experts evaluating grant proposals in their field. Peer reviews, along with considerations of cost effectiveness, largely determine which proposals receive funding. Proponents of the peer review system argue it ensures that the best research is supported. Opponents argue it is a vintage old boys network that precludes many worthwhile projects because the researchers are not tied into the network, and discriminates against younger faculty members, women, and minorities.[12]

In part, congressional earmarking is a reaction to the heavy concentration of federal R&D spending on a relatively few institutions. Institutions outside this group go to their elected representatives and plead their case, often hiring expensive lobbyists. Earmarking is also a response to a long-term problem affecting virtually all research universities—the deterioration and obsolescence of scientific equipment and facilities. Only a small proportion of federal research funds support renovation, new construction, or the purchase of equipment. In the 1950s and 1960s, separate appropriations were made for such things, but in recent decades, the federal government has persisted in a policy of procuring R&D from universities and leaving the institutions to their own devices for maintaining the necessary infrastructure. In reaction, some institutions have gone directly to the congressional appropriations committees to fund construction or renovation of particular facilities.

Budget constraints, however, may limit the federal contribution to both competitively based research and "pork barrel science" for the foreseeable future. Virtually all R&D funding for universities comes from the shrinking portion of the federal budget that is discretionary, which means what's left after mandatory (entitlement) spending and interest on the national debt. Excluding defense as well, this share of the budget is now down to 19 percent. The country's investment in science and technology will compete with interstate highways, national parks, environmental protection, housing, and a host of other domestic needs—all vying for a smaller and smaller piece of the federal pie. On the bright side, academic science, especially biomedical research, continues to enjoy broad bipartisan support.

Not only will budgets be tight but also questions surrounding the management and conduct of university research may have weakened the case for academic science support. The nation's investment in science during the past half century has been repaid many times over in the form of path-breaking discoveries and practical applications. The computer, radar, polio vaccine, America's world leadership in agriculture—these can all be traced to academic science. Yet, controversy and skepticism have beset the university research establishment in recent years. Publicized cases of research fraud and other ethical breaches by federally sponsored researchers, including violations of protocols for the use of human subjects and treatment of laboratory animals, have triggered investigations and doubts about the integrity of scientific research.

In the late 1980s and early 1990s, indirect-cost recovery on government grants and contracts also clouded the outlook for federal support of campus research. Stanford University became the lightning rod for public and legislative concern when it was revealed that expenses for a number of questionable items had been charged to the government over the years as part of Stanford's indirect costs of federally sponsored research.[13] Adverse publicity and congressional hearings led to investigations of other research universities. Several institutions were required to return millions of dollars in questionable billings.

The existing system of indirect-cost recovery, developed by the Office of Management and Budget (OMB) more than thirty years ago, is based on the principle that an institution's indirect-cost recovery should be tied to the share of research-related costs in an institution's total budget. Such a system gives institutions great incentive to categorize as much of their spending as possible as research related. Several reforms in the OMB regulations were instituted in the wake of the problems at Stanford and elsewhere, but indirect-cost recovery remains an arena of ongoing negotiation. On the one hand, the government always wants to pay as low a price as possible for the research it supports. On the other hand, faculty are interested in diverting as many funds as possible from indirect to direct costs, and there is always a risk that one or more universities will stretch the rules too far or fail to abide by them.

All these issues take on particular significance in light of the dependence of universities on federal research dollars. While federal grants and contracts constitute less than 10 percent of total revenues to higher education, at some major research institutions, federal dollars represent 25 percent or more of revenues, and indirect-cost reimbursements have in some cases exceeded 10 percent of a university's budget.

In sum, tight federal budgets and questions about academic research practices will stir continued debate on the federal responsibility for R&D. Universities will be challenged to do more with less, to identify their comparative advantages, to consolidate efforts with other research institutions, and to articulate more clearly how research contributes to societal goals.

Student Aid

While the national investment in science helped establish the world preeminence of U.S. research universities, the federal government's investment in student aid has helped extend college opportunities to a larger segment of the population than any other system of higher education in the world. Starting with the Servicemen's Readjustment Act of 1944, or GI Bill, federal student assistance has helped transform attending college in America from an elite to a mass activity. Congress passed the GI Bill to reward veterans who had served their country during wartime and to help them catch up with their peers whose lives had not been interrupted by military service. During the 1940s and 1950s, the GI Bill sent thousands of men and women to college who otherwise would not have had the opportunity.

The GI Bill was so successful that it inspired broader proposals for scholarship assistance unrelated to military service. But federal aid-to-education proposals of all kinds faced an uphill struggle in the early postwar years, blocked in Congress by civil rights and church-state controversies, fear of federal control of education, and (in the case of college scholarships) resistance from those who believed students should not get "a free ride." Many members of Congress of that era had worked their way through college.

The Soviet launch of Sputnik—the first unmanned space satellite —gave Congress the occasion to justify a limited form of student assistance in the name of national security and cold war competitiveness. The National Defense Education Act of 1958 provided low-interest loans for college students, with debt cancellation for those who became teachers after graduation.

The big breakthrough, however, came during the crest of the civil rights movement and War on Poverty of the mid-1960s. As part of President Lyndon Johnson's Great Society, the Higher Education Act of 1965 embodied, for the first time, an explicit federal commitment to equalizing college opportunities for needy students. Programs were designed to identify the college-eligible poor and to facilitate their access with grants, replacing contributions their families could not afford to make. Colleges and universities that wanted to participate in the new Educational Opportunity Grant program were required to make "vigorous" efforts to identify and recruit students with "exceptional financial need." The legislation also authorized Federal Work-Study to subsidize the employment of needy college students and the federally guaranteed student loan program to ease the cash-flow problems of middle-income college students and their families. Federal Pell Grants and State Student Incentive Grants were enacted in the early 1970s, rounding out the principal student aid programs under Title IV of the Higher Education Act.

Thus began more than a quarter century of dramatic growth in federal financial aid for students enrolled in postsecondary education and training. In 1963, the federal government invested a total of approximately $200 million in a handful of graduate student fellowships and the newly established National Defense Student Loan program. Forty years later, the federal government generates more than $94 billion in student assistance annually, either through direct appropriations, loan guarantees and subsidies, or tax benefits. Figure 6.1 summarizes the types and amounts of aid to postsecondary students from federal as well as nonfederal sources in academic year 2001–02.

For most of this period, the federal commitment to direct student financial aid has had wide bipartisan support. This commitment was tested following President Reagan's election; in the budget retrenchment of the early 1980s, grant support dropped, as did the overall purchasing power of student aid, before gradually resuming upward growth (see figure 6.2). It was also tested in the late 1980s when student loan defaults and widespread abuse by for-profit vocational trade schools put the federal student aid programs on political trial; legislative and regulatory reforms helped address these problems, and the programs survived. The commitment to student aid was tested again in the mid-1990s when Republican leaders of Congress advanced their Contract with America. And it surely will be tested in the years ahead as federal policy makers struggle to contain the growing budget deficit. The federal grant and work/study programs will be vying for the same shrinking discretionary portion of the federal budget for which university-based research must also compete. Most federal student loans, however, operate as entitlements in the federal budget and are

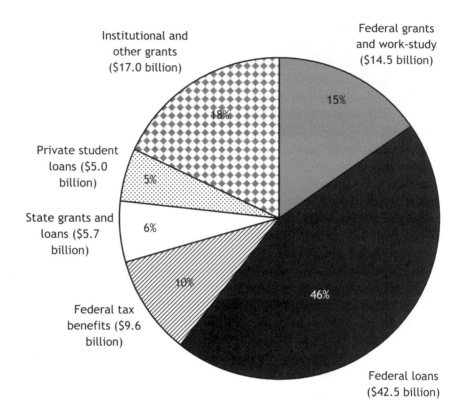

Figure 6.1 Aid to Postsecondary Students, by Type, 2001–02 (total = $94.2 billion)

Source: College Board, *Trends in Student Aid: 2002* (Washington, D.C.: College Board, 2002). Office of Management and Budget, *Fiscal Year 2003 Analytical Perspectives* (Washington, D.C.: Government Printing Office, 2002).

thereby less subject to the vagaries of annual budgeting and appropriations. The most durable programs are probably the higher education tax credits and tax-advantaged savings programs created under Presidents Clinton and George W. Bush, because any cuts would constitute a tax increase and therefore be politically unpalatable.

Trends in Aid, Affordability, and Access

Although there may be little room to maneuver in the federal budget, policy makers are nonetheless clamoring to address the public's anxieties about financing higher education. What has pushed the issue of college affordability so high on the national policy agenda? Alarmist coverage by the media has been a factor. The media tend to focus on

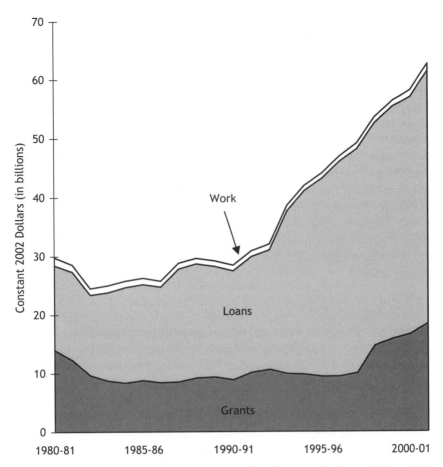

Figure 6.2 Federal Aid Awarded to Postsecondary Students, by Type, 1980 to 2001 (constant 2002 dollars)

Source: College Board, *Trends in Student Aid: 2002* (Washington, D.C.: The College Board, 2002).

the most expensive institutions in the country, obscuring the fact that college remains highly affordable for many Americans at a range of institutions. But the public alarm is also rooted in real economic trends of the past twenty years. Adjusted for inflation, average tuition has risen almost 145 percent at private and public four-year institutions between 1980–81 and 2002–03. And what has happened to the principal resources available to pay these rising prices? Median family income has grown a comparatively small amount (23% between 1980 and 2001).[14] At the same time, income disparities have widened since

1980, which means that the share of family income required to pay rising college costs has gone up the most for those on the bottom rungs of the economic ladder. Student aid, meanwhile, has increased in real value, but not enough to keep pace with growth in tuition levels or in the eligible student population, and most of the growth in aid has come in the form of loans.

By contrast, during the 1970s, tuition rose roughly in step with the Consumer Price Index, income inequality was less, increases in federal aid outstripped growth in tuition and growth in the eligible student population, and grant aid was more common than borrowing. After 1980, all these trend lines shifted for the worse from the standpoint of keeping college affordable.

Yet, overall, college participation rates have risen since 1980. The potential investment returns to the individual are high, demand has been robust, and more people have been going to college. The problem is that enrollment growth is not spread evenly across society by income and race. Wide gaps persist in who benefits from higher education in America. Students from families of low and moderate income attend and graduate from college at much lower rates than middle- and upper-income students. The goal of equalizing college opportunities emblazoned in national policy forty years ago has proved elusive.

Policy Drift

One must look well beyond economics to explain the continuing gaps in opportunity. Enrollment and success in higher education are determined by many factors—differences in prior schooling and aptitude, family and community attitudes, student motivation and awareness of opportunities, campus environment and support. However, the underpinnings of federal aid policy have clearly shifted over the past quarter century.

Erosion of Need-Based Standards

In its conception, federal student aid primarily was about helping those who otherwise might not be able to attend college. In their evolution, federal policies have become as much (or more) about relieving the cost burden for those who probably would go without such aid.

This development has been double-edged. On the one hand, the broadening of eligibility has popularized student financial aid with the middle class and thus strengthened the programs' political base. The Middle Income Student Assistance Act of 1978 probably helped to protect these programs from what could have been worse cutbacks in the early 1980s. On the other hand, the shift has diluted the federal emphasis on assuring postsecondary access for low-income students.

The movement of federal policy away from need-based principles is reflected most dramatically in the tuition tax breaks enacted as part of the Taxpayer Relief Act of 1997 and expanded in the Economic Growth and Tax Relief Reconciliation Act of 2001 (EGTRRA). The so-called Hope Scholarships and Lifetime Learning Tax Credits primarily benefit middle- and upper-middle-income taxpayers who incur tuition expenses for postsecondary education. Along with education IRAs and related provisions of the federal tax code, these benefits are estimated to cost the U.S. Treasury $60 billion in lost revenue over the five-year period, 2004–08 (see later in this chapter for further discussion of tax policies affecting higher education).

Like the federal government, many state governments are legislating tuition tax credits and deductions and are investing more heavily in non-need-based merit scholarships as well as college savings and prepaid plans oriented to middle- and upper-income families. And the colleges themselves have increasingly turned to merit-based aid and preferential packaging not necessarily based on need.

Various forces have contributed to the erosion of need-based policies in the higher education community. In 1986 and 1992, Congress wrote a "federal methodology" of need analysis into law to govern the award of student aid under Title IV of the Higher Education Act. Legislating the methodology has had the effect of freezing ability-to-pay rules over time. Rather than an evolving set of standards examined and adjusted from year to year by economists and experts in the education community, federal need analysis has become nearly static, prompting institutions to adopt divergent standards for awarding their own aid.

Another catalyst in the erosion of need-based standards has been the lingering effects of the Justice Department's antitrust investigation in the early 1990s that targeted the so-called Overlap Group, 30 or so elite and expensive private colleges that collectively considered aid applications and determined how much aid should be awarded in individual cases. While the purported aim of the investigation was to protect the right of consumers (students and their families) to get the best financial aid deal they could from institutions, the Justice Department seems to have acted on the basis of an overwrought market-place ideology that was not in the best interests of low- and moderate-income students. The Overlap Group's cooperative arrangement had the objective of focusing aid on those with the greatest need. In effect, the antitrust action undermined sound social policy, with repercussions far beyond the Overlap Group. It contributed to the splintering of consensus on need-based policies in the higher education community at large.

Toward a Loan-Centered Aid System

At the same time, student aid has evolved from a grant-based to a loan-based system. The original Higher Education Act called for need-based grants for the disadvantaged, while helping middle-class families with government-guaranteed but minimally subsidized bank loans. Figure 6.3 shows how the balance of loan and grant aid has shifted over time. Loans accounted for 20 percent of federal aid in 1975–76 and 69 percent in 2001–02, while grants and work/study dropped from 80 percent to 23 percent over the same period. Today, loans are far and away the largest source of aid. Federal student and parent loans totaled more than $42 billion in 2001–02, three times more than the Pell grant program that was meant to be the system's foundation. Even those most at risk—low-income students, students in remediation, students taking short-term training with uncertain returns—increasingly must borrow to gain postsecondary access.

The loan trend dates back to 1978 when Congress passed the Middle Income Student Assistance Act, which modestly expanded eligibility for Pell grants but, more significantly, made subsidized guaranteed loans available to any student regardless of income or need (the major subsidy to the borrower being government payment of interest during the period of enrollment). A year later Congress assured banks a favorable rate of return on guaranteed student loans by tying their subsidies to changes in Treasury bill rates. With the economy moving into a period of double-digit inflation and interest rates, student loan volume and associated federal costs mushroomed. During the retrenchment of the early Reagan years, loan eligibility and subsidies were scaled back, but as an entitlement that had become popular with the middle class, guaranteed student loans proved the most resilient form of aid. Loan volume continued to grow, although at rates slower than between 1978 and 1981.

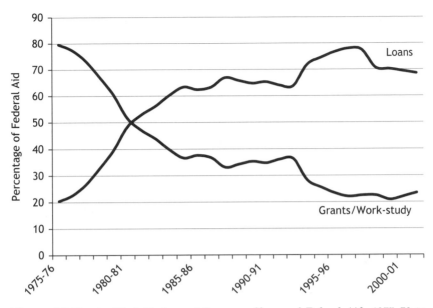

Figure 6.3 Grants, Work-Study, and Loans as Shares of Federal Aid, 1975–76 to 2001–02

Source: See figure 6.2.

When Congress reauthorized the student aid programs in both 1986 and 1992, the borrowing trend was a major focus of concern. Congressional leaders said they wanted to restore a better balance between grants and loans, but the legislative outcome in both years continued the policy drift in the opposite direction. In 1992, the prospect of a post–cold war peace dividend had fueled hopes that Pell grants might be turned into an entitlement or mandated spending program with automatic annual increases for inflation. But the peace dividend never materialized, leaving no room under the budget rules for such an expansion. After the Pell entitlement failed, Congress followed a path of less resistance in boosting the dollar ceilings in the existing loan programs. The 1992 reauthorization bill also established an unsubsidized loan option not restricted by need, intended to make loans available to middle-income students who had been squeezed out of eligibility for the regular subsidized loan (unsubsidized meaning that the government does not pay interest costs while the borrower is in school). All told, the principal effect of the 1992 legislation is clear: far from correcting the grant-loan imbalance, it expanded borrowing capacity for students and parents at all income levels, spurring a 70 percent increase in borrowing through the main federal loan programs in the three years after the law took effect.

Reforming the Delivery of Student Aid

The 1992 reauthorization law, along with legislation the Clinton administration proposed and Congress passed in 1993, changed the way student need is calculated, mandated a stand-alone federal application form for determining eligibility and called for major changes in the way student loans are financed, originated, serviced, and repaid. In the 1990s, policy makers and aid administrators were preoccupied with implementing these major legislative changes and making the new delivery systems work for students.

In the years following the 1992 reauthorization, one of the most daunting challenges for the government and the student aid community was the creation of a system of direct federal lending through institutions to compete with traditional bank-based, government-guaranteed student loans. The promise of the Clinton reform program was a streamlined loan system that serves students better, promotes improvements in the bank-based system through competition, and, in the long run, saves tax dollars by reducing subsidies to private lenders and guarantee agencies. Despite general agreement among student aid administrators that—while no panacea—direct lending has improved service to students and schools, Republicans remain skeptical that an entirely government-run student loan program is necessary, and the Bush administration has suggested that it may not be willing to sustain the direct loan program created by President Clinton.

As loans have come to predominate in the student aid system, policy makers have attempted to mitigate the potentially adverse effects of debt financing on students' career choices and on equity of access to higher education by providing greater flexibility in repayment. Under the federal loan programs, borrowers are offered graduated and extended repayment terms and may also repay loans as a percentage of future income. For borrowers who know in advance that they want to pursue relatively low-paying service occupations, as well as those who later fall on hard times, alternative repayment methods can be helpful. The vast majority of borrowers, however, continue to choose the traditional fixed-payment, ten-year schedule for discharging their loan obligations.

In 1998, Congress turned its attention to streamlining and modernizing the overall delivery of student aid. Under the reauthorization law of that year, the paper-based application system feeding into a multitude of computer systems was to be overhauled with the creation of a Performance Based Organization (PBO) within the Department of Education. An idea born of Vice President Gore's Reinventing Government initiative, the PBO aims to improve service to students and the postsecondary institutions they attend by changing the fundamental processes of management, procurement, and accountability at the Department of Education. The PBO created a new management structure and established incentives for high performance and accountability for results, in exchange for more flexibility to promote innovation and increased efficiency on the part of institutions, lenders, and other players in the student aid system. The PBO objectives included cost-effective services responsive to the rapid rate of technological change in the financial services industry, implementation of a common integrated system across student aid programs, and the provision of complete, timely, and accurate data to all constituencies. In addition, the modernization effort focused on the development of streamlined systems to help reduce student loan defaults, increase the use of the Internet and electronic applications for student aid, and better integrate the computer systems required to administer student aid.

However, the effect as well as the future of the PBO is uncertain. The Department of Education's 2002 Strategic plan identified improvements in the management of federal student aid as a priority goal of the Bush administration. However, little attention has been given to the role that the PBO will play in this endeavor.

Special Initiatives and Populations

Community Service

The Bush administration is committed to expanding opportunities established during the Clinton administration for students to pay for their education by serving the nation or community. Legislation passed in 1993 established the AmeriCorps program to enable individuals to earn postsecondary education or training benefits by serving in areas of public need for up to two years. The benefits could be used either to pay postservice educational expenses or to repay educational debts already incurred. The Clinton service initiative has many historical antecedents, including the Civilian Conservation Corps of the 1930s, the Peace Corps, VISTA, the National Health Service Corps, and a number of loan forgiveness and deferment provisions written into the student aid legislation over the past forty years. In addition, the 1993 legislation modified the Federal Work-Study program to require institutions to direct 5 percent of their work-study allocation to fund employment in community service. In 1998, that set-aside was increased to 7 percent with an additional requirement to support literacy programs.

Counseling and Outreach

Policy makers also recognize that student aid dollars alone are not sufficient to assure greater access to higher education by underrepresented groups. Earlier, larger, and sustained interventions in the education pipeline are necessary. Historically, this need has been addressed through the so-called TRIO programs of counseling, outreach, and special support services for the disadvantaged, created as a complement to the student aid programs in the original Higher Education Act. Congressional appropriations for the TRIO programs have grown steadily over the years, but funding of these efforts still falls far short of the need. The 1998 reauthorization called for a new initiative inspired by Eugene Lang's "I Have a Dream" movement in cities around the country, which seeks to mentor disadvantaged junior high students, widen their horizons, and see them through to high school graduation and postsecondary opportunities. The Gaining Early Awareness and Readiness for Undergraduate Programs (GEAR UP) program provides five-year grants to states and partnerships to provide services to an entire cohort of students, beginning no later than the seventh grade and following the cohort through high school. GEAR UP funds are also used to provide college scholarships to low-income students. Some tension has emerged between TRIO and GEAR UP supporters as these programs compete for resources and as some policy makers question the potential redundancy of multiple federal early intervention programs.

Graduate Student Assistance

The bulk of federal student aid goes to undergraduates, and the policy debates in Washington focus largely on issues of educational access and choice at the undergraduate level. Yet a portion of the aid available through the loan and work/study programs goes to graduate and professional students. Federal support for graduate students also comes in the form of research assistantships, fellowships, and traineeships, and much of this support is built into the funding of R&D administered by institutions.

Overall, fellowship and other grant money for graduate students has declined since the 1960s, and universities have looked to alternative sources. The Federal Work-Study program, for example, requires only 20 percent matching by institutions and has been increasingly used to fund teaching assistants. But the most common recourse for filling the gap has been student borrowing. Federal student loans have become an integral part of financing graduate and professional education, and many privately sponsored supplemental loan programs have been created to serve students in high-cost fields such as the health professions. It is at this level that concerns about mounting student indebtedness can become acute, especially among students who have already accumulated substantial loan obligations as undergraduates.

Traditionally, graduate institutions and departments have awarded aid primarily on the basis of academic merit. But recent financing trends indicate a dual system. Research assistantships and what remains of fellowship support from federal and private sources continue to be awarded on competitive academic criteria, whereas the great proportion of subsidized work, loan, and other aid to graduate and professional students is directed to students according to their financial need.

Distance Education

One of the more vexing problems facing federal policy makers has been how to provide aid to the growing number of students taking their classes via some form of distance education. The issues regarding distance education fall into two major types: resolving administrative problems that arise when students at traditional institutions take distance education courses and whether to allow institutions that only operate via distance education to participate in the Title IV program. While the unique nature of distance education (nonstandard terms, enrollment at more than one institution simultaneously, etc.) presents important administrative challenges for financial aid administrators, the higher-stake issues revolve around eligibility for all-distance institutions. These institutions are currently blocked from participation by a rule instituted in 1992 to bar correspondence schools from receiving student aid funds. The Bush administration and its Republican colleagues in Congress have expressed a strong desire to loosen these restrictions, but Democrats and advocates for traditional institutions fear that such a change might lead to increased fraud and abuse in the student aid programs.

Access to What?

For most of the past forty years, federal policy under Title IV of the Higher Education Act has consistently emphasized access. But policy makers today also want assurances that they are supporting access to *quality* academic and vocational programs. Are dollars being directed effectively to those who really need help and have a reasonable chance of benefiting from the education and training that is being subsidized? Are the programs aid recipients attend of reasonable quality? Do federal aid recipients complete their programs? Do they secure jobs in the fields for which they have prepared? In short, are students and taxpayers getting their money's worth?

A principal though not exclusive object of concern regarding quality and standards has been the proprietary trade schools. In the 1970s, Congress substituted the term *postsecondary* for *higher* in the student aid statutes, and eligibility was broadened to include short-term vocational training provided by for-profit schools, as well as the traditional programs of public and private nonprofit institutions. Congress embraced a marketplace philosophy: students would "vote with their feet," taking their federal aid to institutions that met their needs. But the marketplace rationale begged important questions of institutional effectiveness and accountability. Few foresaw the burgeoning of the trade school industry that would be stimulated by the new federal incentives. Many for-profit programs came to be subsidized almost entirely by tax dollars, setting their prices based on the aid package available to students from the federal government.

For quality control, the federal student aid programs have traditionally relied on a so-called triad of institutional accreditation, state review, and federal oversight. The federal responsibility, as carried out by the Department of Education, has included certifying accreditation agencies as well as ultimately approving institutions to participate in the federal aid programs. Over time, however, the triad arrangement has proven inadequate to the task.

Restoring "integrity" to the student aid process was a principal theme of the 1992 reauthorization of the Higher Education Act, and the principal new thrust was to rely more on state agencies to help determine which postsecondary institutions should be eligible to participate in the federal Title IV programs. Ultimately, however, the higher education community balked at the authority that the 1992 law vested with so-called state postsecondary review entities (SPREs), and states themselves proved to be reluctant partners in such an endeavor. The SPRE initiative was short lived, abandoned within a year or two of its enactment.

Meanwhile, the Department of Education has tried to crack down on institutions with excessively high student loan default rates, and this effort *has* helped to reduce the overall level of defaults and eliminate schools that were clearly abusing the system. Some of the worst problems have been remedied. As a result of these remedies (and a generally prosperous economy), the national default rate has dropped from a high of 22 percent in 1990 to less than 6 percent in 2001.

As Congress and the Bush administration prepare for the 2004 reauthorization of the Higher Education Act, policy makers are again talking about accountability and are focusing particular attention on student retention and graduation rates. Access has been the touchstone of federal student aid policy for many decades, but some policy leaders argue that the government needs to do a better job of ensuring that more students stay in school and get their degrees. And to do that, the Bush administration and others have floated proposals that would reward or punish institutions based on the completion rates of their students. The potential intrusiveness and complexity of implementing such proposals are likely to stymie their enactment, but a new debate over institutional performance and graduation rates has begun in the nation's capital.

The Cost Side of the Equation

Finally, questions about quality ultimately are linked to concerns about cost and price. Policy makers along with the general public worry about the tuition spiral, where it will lead, and whether it will ever end. Federal student aid seems unlikely to catch up any time soon. Might the government at some point try to intervene on the other side of the affordability equation, namely, try to curb growth in the price of a college education?

In 1997, Congress established a National Commission on the Cost of Higher Education, which issued a report less than a year later saying there was no single, tidy explanation for the tuition spiral. The commission examined factors that may be driving up institutional budgets and the underlying costs of providing instruction—everything from faculty salaries and facilities to technology, curriculum, government regulation, and expectations of students (and parents) about quality and amenities on campus. It concluded that "the available data on higher education expenditures and revenues make it difficult to ascertain direct relationships among the cost drivers and increases in the price of higher education. Institutions of higher education, even to most people in the academy, are financially opaque."[15]

A part of the equation that the commission did not address directly was demand for the service. In some measure colleges and universities charge what they do because they can. No nonprofit institution sets tuition to recover the full costs of instruction, but many colleges could no doubt charge considerably higher tuition than they already do and still fill their classes (in some cases, several times over). This is true of prestigious private institutions, which surely underprice their services in the pure economic sense of supply and demand. The same holds for flagship public institutions.

If the commission came short of pinpointing causes of the tuition spiral, the hottest political question it considered was whether the federal government should try to contain college costs and prices. This was an especially sensitive issue at the time because Congress was about to review and reauthorize the Higher Education Act in 1998, and college leaders were worried that if the commission recommended some kind of cost controls, it might lead to a contentious debate in Congress, if not intrusive federal regulation.

In the end, the commission said it was up to institutions to contain costs and to do a better job of explaining their finances to students and families. The commission admonished the colleges to intensify their efforts to increase institutional productivity and organize an awareness campaign to inform the public about the actual price of postsecondary education, the returns on investment, and preparation for college. As for the federal role, the commission called on the government to do a better job of collecting and reporting standardized data on costs, prices, and subsidies in higher education and analyzing the relationship between tuition and institutional expenditures—but not to try to impose cost or price controls.

The essentially status quo outcome of the 1998 national commission study was neither surprising nor unreasonable. It is far from clear that the federal government has sufficient mandate (including constitutional authority) or political leverage to intervene constructively in tuition pricing by public or independent nonprofit institutions of higher education. While the federal government contributes the lion's share of direct student aid, overall it provides less than 15 percent of revenues of colleges and universities. In the final analysis, federal officials are too far from the action and ought to leave cost containment and price setting to state and local authorities and market forces.

It does not appear, however, that the 1998 cost commission put this issue to rest, not for good anyway. In 2003, Congressman Howard "Buck" McKeon, a conservative Republican and chairman of the House subcommittee in charge of reauthorizing the Higher Education Act in 2004, introduced the first legislation to impose federal price controls on colleges and universities. His proposal would potentially impose sanctions—including withholding federal student aid money—on institutions that increased tuition at more than twice the Consumer Price Index. While debate about the effectiveness and unintended consequences of price controls will continue, the proposition of such an extreme measure reflects the public concern and outcry on college prices.

Tax Policies

In addition to direct funding of students and institutions, the government assists college students and their families as well as colleges and universities through a variety of tax policies. A number of exclusions, exemptions, credits, and deductions added to the federal tax code over the years have benefited education at all levels. Some of these provisions—for example, the personal exemptions parents may claim for dependent students aged nineteen to twenty-four, tax-advantaged savings plans, and tuition tax credits—affect individual and family ability to save for and pay college costs. Other provisions affect the revenue and financing arrangements of colleges and universities; for example, their charitable 501(c)3 status allows them to receive tax-deductible contributions. The monetary benefits to institutions and students of these tax provisions—so-called tax expenditures in federal budgetary parlance—are measured by the estimated amount of federal revenue that would be collected in the absence of such provisions. Estimated annual "tax expenditures" for higher education totaled $14 billion in 2001 (see table 6.1).

Institutional tax-exempt status and the deduction of contributions from the taxable income of donors are the crucial tax policies benefiting higher education institutions. The tax exemption predates most of the nation's colleges and universities and the federal tax code. This long-standing precedent and the political implications of change have preserved institutions' tax-exempt status. However, the federal unrelated business income tax (UBIT) is required of institutions for all activities unrelated to their charitable purpose.

Corporate investment in university-based research was promoted by the tax legislation of 1981, which gave tax credits to industry for investment in cooperative, applied research projects with universities and permitted enhanced deductions for gifts of research and research training equipment. The 1986 tax bill amended these provisions to balance the tax incentives for corporate investment in basic and applied research. But overall, the reform legislation of 1986, a watershed in federal tax policy, had adverse implications for higher education. For colleges and universities, particularly private nonprofit institutions, the principal setback came in the form of limitations on charitable giving. The Omnibus Budget Reconciliation Act of 1990 further limited the deductibility of charitable contributions. Despite repeated efforts to gain more favorable treatment of charitable contributions, higher education institutions have regained little ground in this area.

Major new tax breaks for students and families were enacted in 1997. Individual tax-based relief from the growing cost of education has become an important and expanding tool for students and families. The challenge to federal policy makers is to find ways to promote affordability for middle-income families—the primary beneficiaries of most tax policies—without detracting from efforts to assure postsecondary access for those with the greatest need.

On two previous occasions, the federal government came close to enacting tuition tax benefits. In 1965, there was a groundswell of congressional support for tuition tax deductions to help the middle class, but they were countered by the Johnson administration when it added the guaranteed student loan program to the Higher Education Act. Tuition tax bills built another head of steam in the mid-1970s, but President Carter agreed to the Middle Income Student Assistance Act to head them off. On both occasions, instead of trying to deliver educational assistance through the tax code, the response was to expand eligibility and expenditures on direct student aid.

During his 1996 reelection campaign, President Clinton countered Senator Bob Dole's across-the-board tax cut proposal with his plan of "targeted" tax relief, including credits and deductions for families paying college tuition that would cost the federal government an estimated $36 billion in lost revenue over six years. President Clinton was the first president to actively support the enactment of tuition tax breaks. The resulting Taxpayer Relief Act of 1997 was a watershed in the use of tax policy to address the burden of rising college prices for middle and upper income families.

The Hope and Lifetime Learning tax credits were the largest of the tuition tax benefits incorporated into the 1997 law. The Hope tax credit provides a $1,500 tax credit per student per year for tuition expenses during the first two years of postsecondary education. The Hope credit is not refundable; it can only be claimed up to the amount of the taxpayer's tax liability, effectively eliminating many low-income families from eligibility.

The Lifetime Learning tax credit provides one credit per household up to $2,000 for up to 20 percent of tuition and related expenses. This is in contrast with the Hope credit, which may be claimed for each eligible student in the household. One cannot use the Hope Scholarship with the Lifetime Learning tax credit for the same student in the same year, but they can be used for different students' educational expenses in the same year. These credits represent a major shift in federal higher education policy away from targeted aid for low- and moderate-income families to cost relief primarily benefiting middle- and upper-income families.

The 1997 tax law also created several new vehicles for tax-advantaged savings for higher education expenses. Education IRAs (now Coverdell Education Savings Accounts), State Prepaid Tuition Plans and College Savings Plans (529 Plans, named after the provision in the tax code), and Roth IRAs expanded and complicated the landscape for families saving for future education expenses. In addition, Congress reestablished the deductibility of student loan interest, which had been eliminated along with consumer loan interest by the 1986 tax reform law.

The scope of the 1997 Taxpayer Relief Act was dramatic and a significant political victory for President Clinton. And its political significance was not lost on the Bush administration when it drafted new tax legislation just a few years later.

In 2001, President Bush signed the Economic Growth and Tax Reconciliation Act of 2001 (EGTRA), which built on the 1997 tuition tax provisions. The Bush tax cut raised the applicable income limits for Hope and Lifetime Learning tax credits, increased annual limits on contributions to Educational IRAs, and eliminated taxes on interest earned under state prepaid-tuition programs and college-savings plans. Other provisions of the 2001 tax legislation included:

— A new deduction for taxpayers earning too much to qualify for the Lifetime Learning or Hope tax credits. This provision allows a deduction from taxable income of $3,000 per year for college tuition in 2002 and 2003 and $4,000 per year in 2004 and 2005. This provision is scheduled to expire in 2005. Taxpayers will only be allowed to use one of these three tax breaks at a time.
— Elimination of the sixty-month limit on the amount of time student borrowers can deduct student-loan interest payments and higher annual income limits for claiming the interest deduction.
— A permanent tax deduction for employer-paid tuition assistance (Section 127) and expansion to cover graduate and professional courses.

The cost of the 2001 tax bill was enormous and required unprecedented budgeting compromises. Except for the tuition tax deduction described above that "sunsets" in 2005, each of the higher education tax provisions is slated to expire in 2010. However, no one expects this to happen, as political pressure is likely to build relentlessly in the intervening years to extend these tax benefits. For example, assets in state sponsored savings plans more than doubled in 2002, from $8.5 billion in 2001 to $18.5 billion by the end of 2002. With more than three million accounts open in 2002 and continued growth in asset investment, it is likely there will be considerable pressure on Congress to make these tax provisions permanent.[16]

Federal Regulation and Its Impact

Federal regulation of higher education derives from two principal sources: (1) the requirements of accountability that accompany the receipt of federal funds and (2) the dictates of social legislation, as well as executive orders and judicial decisions, stemming from such legislation.[17] To the degree that government officials insist on accountability, and congressional mandates addressing a range of social problems remain in force, there will be complexity and strain in the relationship of government and higher education. Tensions are inherent, given the traditions of academic autonomy, the mandates of Congress, the missions of federal agencies, and the responsibilities of those agencies for the stewardship of taxpayer dollars.

The academic community has long been wary of entanglement with government, but only a few—mainly independent, religiously affiliated—institutions have consistently refused funds from Washington. The great majority of colleges have accepted federal patronage even though it exacts a price in the expenses of compliance and in the distraction and intrusion of external controls. The federal government influences higher education through scores of statutes and regulations administered by diverse federal agencies. Some mandates, such as the Americans with Disabilities Act or regulations of the Environmental Protection Agency and the Occupational Safety and Health Administration, affect all types of organizations equally. Others, such as the Buckley Amendment on privacy rights of students and Title IX of the Education Amendments of 1972 barring gender bias, are specific to educational institutions. Colleges have long argued that such regulatory burdens contribute to their spiraling costs. But there is no documentation of the extent to which higher education is disproportionately affected by federal requirements, thereby justifying the more rapid increases in college charges during the past decade and a half relative to prices of other goods and services in the economy.

During the 1980s, higher education's concerns on this front receded to some degree. The Reagan administration's widely publicized support for regulatory relief altered the climate of regulation. Enforcement eased in some areas, and over the years, colleges learned to accommodate the bureaucratic requirements of the government, tempering previous conflicts. Some institutions actually bargained with the federal government to lessen their regulatory burden. Before the highly publicized controversy over indirect costs in the early 1990s, for example, Yale and Stanford had accepted lowered indirect cost reimbursement on research contracts in exchange for reduced federal reporting requirements. But in many respects, regulatory burdens have mounted, not only for colleges but also for all sectors of society in recent years. Higher education, along with other constituencies, has complained about the proliferation of "unfunded mandates" from Washington — legislative and regulatory requirements imposed by the federal government without federal funding to help pay the costs of compliance.

In the student aid arena, the unique regulatory dilemma is the sheer number and diversity of schools and kinds of training supported by programs under Title IV of the Higher Education Act. Applying the same rules and simultaneously regulating the use of student aid subsidies by eight thousand–plus proprietary and collegiate institutions strains the capacity of the Department of Education and imposes undue burdens on schools that do a good job of administering federal programs.

The 1998 reauthorization of the Higher Education Act resulted in a number of new rules addressing special issues in higher education, outside of student aid. In the absence of specific legal remedies for perceived problems, the legislation introduced complex new reporting requirements on the success of teacher preparation programs, campus crime, and equity in athletics. The burden on institutions and commensurate costs have not gone unnoticed. In 2001, some members of Congress sought input from colleges and universities through the Fed Up Initiative to identify unnecessary or burdensome regulations. Despite these efforts, it remains difficult to fend off new requirements, especially those based on a tragic event and advanced by a single-interest group. More recently, concerns about homeland security have resulted in increased scrutiny of international students who are enrolled at colleges and universities. New policies have required institutions to assume greater responsibility for tracking the visa status of international students through the Student and Exchange Visitor Information System (SEVIS).

Prospects for the Federal Role in Higher Education

In summary, here are some of the issues that will influence the federal role in higher education in the early twenty-first century:

— Clouding the generally positive outlook for federal patronage of university-based research are persistent concerns about research practices in academia and pressure to reduce federal budget deficits. Some policy makers are calling for science and technology investments that are more sharply focused on areas of national need. Universities will be challenged to articulate more clearly how research contributes to societal goals. Debate will also focus on the balance of funding between research and commercial applications, the need to upgrade the physical infrastructure of scientific research, and the adequacy of government support to train the country's next generation of top-flight scientists and engineers.

— Policy makers will continue to worry about the consequences of growing student indebtedness for individuals and society, and there will be efforts to restore the purchasing power of federal grant aid. But the policy drift toward a loan-based system seems likely to continue. Issues of quality control, the costs of education, and consumer protection will also continue to concern federal policy makers.

— Sweeping tax legislation during the late 1990s and early part of the twenty-first century have resulted in a complex web of tax benefits for families and institutions. At least in the near term, tax policy debates will center on the relative equity and effectiveness of these programs in creating access, spurring savings, and promoting workforce development.

— The federal government now has two ways of delivering college financial assistance: (1) through the tax code and (2) through ordinary spending programs authorized under Title IV of the Higher Education Act. These two sets of benefits operate on different principles and serve different, though overlapping, populations. Over the long haul, how will they interact? Which will predominate? Will the federal government sustain its traditional commitment to equalizing opportunities for higher education? This will not be a zero-sum game, but these parallel systems are likely to compete for resources over time.

— Higher education will continue to petition federal agencies for regulatory relief. But as long as government officials insist on accountability for taxpayer dollars and legislative mandates addressing a range of educational and social problems remain in force, the burden of rules and regulations will be the price universities must pay for federal assistance.

From the Morrill Land-Grant Act to the GI Bill and the Higher Education Act, the federal government has played a pivotal role in extending opportunities for higher education to a wider segment of our society. As we enter the twenty-first century, the number of students coming of college age is growing rapidly, and the new cohort is more diverse than ever. Will the federal government sustain its historic commitment to assuring a fair chance of a college education for all citizens?

The federal government will undoubtedly continue to make important contributions to enhancing the academic enterprise and equalizing educational opportunities in America. As in the past, federal support will supplement the basic funding provided from state and private sources, and it will spring from objectives such as economic competitiveness, health, and quality of life rather than from an interest in education for its own sake. And funds, along with regulations, will continue to flow from a variety of agencies in Washington. Such support is untidy, piecemeal, and not without headaches for institutions, students, and states. But the pattern serves a variety of national purposes and, in fact, ultimately may better serve to protect institutional diversity, students' freedom of choice, and independent thought in American education than would an overarching federal policy.

NOTES

1. For the historical development of the federal role in higher education, see George N. Rainsford, *Congress and Higher Education in the Nineteenth Century* (Knoxville: University of Tennessee Press, 1972). The two private universities benefiting from the Morrill Land-Grant College Act are the Massachusetts Institute of Technology (established in 1861) and Cornell University (1865).

2. Terry Sanford, *Storm Over the States* (New York: McGraw Hill, 1967), 63.

3. Lawrence E. Gladieux and Thomas R. Wolanin, *Congress and the Colleges: The National Politics of Higher Education* (Lexington, MA: Lexington Books, 1976), 226.

4. For an approach to assessing the indirect effects of student aid, see Michael S. McPherson, "Silver Linings: Student Aid's Unintended Good Deeds" (paper presented at the annual meeting of the American Educational Research Association, April 1987).

5. Analysis by authors of the *National Postsecondary Student Aid Study (NPSAS), 1999–2000.*

6. Chester E. Finn, Jr., "A Federal Policy for Higher Education?" *Alternative* (May 1975): 18–19.

7. College Board, *Trends in Student Aid: 2002* (Washington, D.C.: College Entrance Examination Board, 2002).

8. National Science Foundation, Division of Science Resources Statistics, *Federal Science and Engineering Support to Universities, Colleges, and Nonprofit Institutions: Fiscal Year 2000,* NSF 02-319 (Arlington, VA: National Science Foundation, 2002).

9. Deborah H. Shapley and Roy Rustum, *Lost at the Frontier* (Philadelphia: Institute for Scientific Information Press, 1985), 39.

10. For a thorough discussion of this topic, see Clark Kerr, *The Uses of the University,* 5th ed. (Cambridge, MA: Harvard University Press, 2001).

11. Jeffrey Brainard, "Another Record Year for Academic Pork," *Chronicle of Higher Education,* September 27, 2002.

12. U.S. General Accounting Office, *Peer Review: Reforms Needed to Ensure Fairness in Federal Agency Grant Selection,* GAO/PEMD-94-1 (Washington, D.C.: U.S. General Accounting Office, 1994).

13. Stanford was later exonerated on charges of mishandling federal funds.

14. U.S. Census Bureau, historical tabulations. See www.census.gov/hhes/income/histinc/f11.html. Figures based on median total money income for families in which the householder is age forty-five to fifty-four.

15. National Commission on the Cost of Higher Education, *Straight Talk about College Costs and Prices* (Phoenix: Oryx Press, 1998), 12.

16. Investment Company Institute, *Mutual Fund Fact Book,* 43rd ed. (Washington, D.C.: Investment Company Institute, 2003), 57–58.

17. John T. Wilson, *Academic Science, Higher Education, and the Federal Government: 1950–1983* (Chicago: University of Chicago Press, 1983), 104–6.

Chapter Seven

The States and Higher Education

Aims C. McGuinness, Jr.

The period of the early years of the twenty-first century is likely to be one of the most troubling in the history of the nation's higher education enterprise. Relations between state government and higher education are likely to be especially strained because of four broad trends:

— Escalating demands: These are driven not only by numbers but also by higher expectations for what an increasingly diverse student population should know and be able to do as the result of a college education. The demands extend to virtually every dimension of higher education, including research and service.

— Severe economic constraints: Even with gradual economic recovery, it is unlikely that higher education will see significant improvements in funding, at least on a per student basis, within the next decade. The federal deficit, competing priorities for public funds, public anger about rising student costs, and severe competition for limited corporate and philanthropic funds will all contribute to the continuing financial constraints.

— The academy's inherent resistance to change: As demands increase and resources dwindle, institutions are slowly recognizing that, if they continue to do business as usual, their ability to educate students and continue their research and service missions will be seriously compromised. But translating this slow awareness into changes at the institutional core—in curriculum, in modes of

teaching and learning, and in faculty governance—will be a long-term, incremental process. The resulting public frustration with the academy's inability to respond to major societal needs only intensifies the danger of blunt governmental intervention.
—Instability of state political leadership: The trend toward term limitations and the demands of political office are contributing to major changes in the state leadership. This is especially pronounced in state legislatures. As each legislative session begins, the proportion of new members increases. The relative stability provided by the memory about state higher education policies of long-term legislative leaders is being lost. Other issues are dominating the agendas. The twenty-year trend toward larger and more dominant legislative staffs is accelerating.[1]

These conditions are certain to exacerbate already frayed state relationships with higher education. Constructive resolution of these conflicts is essential both to the continued strength of American higher education and to its capacity to respond to major societal priorities. The purpose of this chapter is to present a framework and basic information about the state role as a beginning point for further reading and study.

Relationships between State Government and Higher Education

For some within higher education even the mention of state government conjures up negative images. There continues to be a widespread sense within the academy that virtually any state involvement, other than providing funding with no strings attached, is an infringement on legitimate institutional autonomy. The relationships are viewed along a continuum: at one end, complete institutional autonomy is good; at the other end, state involvement is seen as bad. Frank Newman suggests a different, more constructive view. The point is that both institutional autonomy and state involvement are important. Governments have a legitimate interest in the responsiveness of the academy to major societal needs. At the same time, it is important for both society and the academy that higher education be able to pursue values and purposes that are different from and, in some cases, may conflict with the prevailing values and priorities of the state. "What becomes clear," Newman states, "is that the real need is not simply for more autonomy but for a relationship between the university and the state that is constructive for both, built up over a long period of time by careful attention on the part of all parties."[2]

Robert Berdahl makes a similar distinction between the concept of academic freedom, which is universal and absolute, and autonomy, which is "of necessity parochial and relative." He continues by emphasizing that "the real issue with respect to autonomy . . . is not whether there will be interference by the state but whether the inevitable interference will be confined to the proper topics and expressed through a suitably sensitive mechanism."[3] The key is for the higher education community to recognize that it has a stake, if not responsibility, to engage actively with state political leaders in defining the nature of the relationship. This includes defining the major societal ends toward which the academy should direct its energies and shaping the policies and other "suitably sensitive" mechanisms that will govern the relationships.

State governments play a central, if not a dominant role, in American higher education. Historically, states have always provided the legal framework within which both public and private institutions operated. The state role differs distinctly from that of the federal government. Since the historic decision in the Education Amendments of 1972 to reject direct general purpose aid to institutions, the federal government has emphasized aid to students, not to institutions. Federal funding to institutions is either through students in the form of student financial assistance or restricted funding for research and other purposes. The federal government is generally impartial about a particular provider's ownership and control (public, private, or proprietary), assuming other conditions for receiving subsidy are met. The federal government thus tends to emphasize a strict separation between the government's role as "overseer" of the "public interest" and the institutional role of providing services.

In contrast to the federal government, states primarily finance higher education through direct subsidy of public institutions. In this respect, states play a dual role of "overseer" of the "public interest" and "provider of higher education services." States also provide aid to students, ranging from large programs in states such as New York to small programs in states such as Alabama.[4] But only a few states (for example, Illinois, Maryland, Michigan, New Jersey, New York, and

Pennsylvania) provide grants to private not-for-profit institutions for the purposes of general institutional subsidy.[5]

From a comparative perspective, American higher education remains perhaps the most diverse, decentralized, private, market-driven system (if it can even be called a *system*) in the world. Yet state governments have gradually come to play a more central role than is often conveyed in international comparisons. In fact, there appears to be a worldwide convergence toward the kind of mixed public-private system that has evolved in the United States. As Clark Kerr observed in 1985, the decade of the mid-1980s to mid-1990s (and perhaps beyond) would be a decade of state and private leadership in higher education. He pointed out that this has been the dominant pattern in U.S. history. Periods of federal leadership have been relatively brief: 1860–1890 and 1955–1985. He further observed that as the effect of higher education on states' economies has become more politically important, state governors have emerged as the most important political figures.[6]

Enrollments and Financing

With the dramatic expansion of the public sector since the 1950s and 1960s, states became dominant forces in terms of enrollments in public institutions and financing policy. From the 1950s to the end of the 1980s, the share of total enrollments in public institutions (including many community colleges partially funded from local revenue) increased from about 60 percent to 76 percent.[7] The private sector continued to grow but this was outstripped by increases of one and a half times in public four-year enrollments and five times in public two-year institutional enrollments. The proportion of institutions in the private sector dropped from 65 percent to 59 percent.[8]

In 1995–96, state and local governments provided approximately 35 percent of the current revenue for higher education, both public and private, excluding sales and services (for example, hospitals, dormitories, restaurants). This compared with 16 percent from the federal government, 38 percent from student tuition and fees, and 11 percent from other sources (including endowments, private gifts, and grants).

State financing of higher education has followed a rollercoaster pattern over the decades, with periods of significant increases in state appropriations when economic times are good followed by dramatic decreases in periods of economic downturn or recession. From 1980 to 1998, higher education appropriations as a percentage of total state funding decreased. But in the same period, state appropriations to public colleges and universities actually *increased* 13% (in constant dollars per student) even as enrollment increased. Nationwide, state higher education appropriations *increased,* but this was a decreasing share of an expanding pie. In other words, overall state funding increased at a rate faster than increases in state appropriations to higher education.

The reality is that, even as state appropriations increased, state funding did not increase at a rate that could keep pace with escalating college and university costs. From 1980 to 1998, total institutional revenues (in constant dollars per student) rose 41 percent, from $10,265 to $14,502. The principal revenue source fueling this increase was tuition. From 1980 to 1998, tuition revenues at public institutions increased by 107 percent, from $1,696 to $3,512 (in constant dollars per student).[9]

Because governors and state legislatures recognize that higher education has a revenue source (tuition and fees) in contrast to most other governmental services, higher education tends to be the "budget balancer." Consequently, in each period of economic downturn, tuition and fees have increased dramatically.[10]

The long-term direction of state policy is away from institutional subsidies and low tuition to higher tuition and greater institutional reliance on tuition and other nonstate revenue sources. State funding for student aid (student subsidies) to offset tuition increases is increasing, but the trend is for this aid to be awarded largely on the basis of merit (academic performance/qualifications) rather than need. The shift from institutional subsidy to greater reliance on tuition is taking place on a largely ad hoc basis, primarily without coordination with student aid policy and attention to the long-term implications for student access and opportunity.[11]

The dramatic cuts in state funding for higher education in the state fiscal crisis of the early 2000s were raising fundamental questions about the states' commitment to higher education as a public good and their future role in oversight and funding of public higher education.[12] The crisis reflected a long-term trend toward a decreasing share of revenue for higher education from public sources. For example, in 1969–70, revenues for all institutions of higher education in the United States were roughly half from governmental sources (federal, state, and local) and half from nonpublic sources (student tuition and fees, private grants and contracts, sales of services, endowments, etc.). Beginning in the late 1970s and early 1980s, the percentage of revenue from students and nonpublic sources began to increase steadily to the point that by 1995–96, 62 percent of the revenue was from students and nonpublic sources and only 38 percent from government.[13] This trend is continuing as economic conditions have worsened.

Even when the economy recovers, higher education is likely to feel a continued squeeze in state funding.[14] The reasons are more structural than the result of deliberate decisions about higher education per se. In many states, the demand for higher education is far outstripping the states' fiscal capacity—a consequence of conditions such as the faltering economy, mandated increases in funding for health care and K–12 education, and deliberate tax reductions.[15]

Accountability and Performance Funding

During the 1980s, the states led a fundamental change in the definition of accountability, and these changes continue to underlie many of the state policy initiatives. Up to the 1980s, states had primarily focused on issues of resource allocation and utilization and rarely became involved in basic questions about the outcomes of a college or university education. By the end of the 1980s, questions about outcomes—especially student outcomes—dominated states' agendas. More than any other force, it was state policies' requiring institutions to assess student learning and to provide information to the states and the public that stimulated higher education's attention to these issues. Many colleges and universities now report that they have active efforts to assess student learning. Although state mandates initially stimulated this attention, voluntary accreditation and other forces sustain that attention.

The states also led during the 1980s in developing new funding systems, such as competitive, incentive, and performance funding. Use of funding "on the margin" to support centers of excellence in research and technology and to stimulate improvement in undergraduate education was widespread.[16] Relating this to the earlier discussion of autonomy, since the early 1980s, states had been much more willing to enter into the area Berdahl defines as "substantive autonomy."

These developments continued through the 1990s. Joseph C. Burke and associates at the Rockefeller Institute of Government began tracking state policies linking accountability with funding in 1997 and have continued these annual surveys ever since. The initial surveys tracked two kinds of policies: performance funding and performance budgeting. The Seventh Annual Survey added an additional but closely related policy—performance reporting.[17] The survey uses several definitions. Performance funding ties specified state funding *directly* and *tightly* to the performance of public campuses on individual indicators. Performance funding focuses on the distribution phase of the budget process. Performance budgeting allows governors, legislators, and coordinating or system boards to *consider* campus achievement on performance indicators as *one factor* in determining allocations for public campuses. Performance budgeting concentrates on budget preparation and presentation and often neglects or even ignores the distribution phase of budgeting. In performance funding, the relationship between funding and performance is tight, automatic, and formulaic. If a public college or university achieves a prescribed target or an improvement level on defined indicators, it receives a designated amount or percent of state funding. In performance budgeting, the possibility of additional funding due to good or improved performance solely depends on the judgment and discretion of state, coordinating, or system officials. And finally, performance reporting recounts statewide results and often the institutional results mostly of public higher education on priority indicators, similar to those found in performance funding and budgeting. However, since they have no formal link to allocations, performance reports can have a much longer list of indicators than performance budgeting and especially performance funding. The reports are usually sent to governors, legislators, and campus leaders and increasingly appear on the Web sites of coordinating or system boards and of individual institutions.[18]

The number of states using performance funding and performance budgeting increased significantly during the late 1990s. The number peaked in 2000 at a time when state budgets were still robust. In 2000, eighteen states had performance funding and twenty-eight states had performance budgeting. The number of states with these policies dropped as the state fiscal crisis developed. In the 2003 survey, fifteen states indicated that they were using performance funding and twenty-one indicated that they were using performance budgeting. At the same time, the number of states indicating that they had policies of performance reporting increased significantly. Burke and associates attribute the upswing in performance reporting both to the reality that this form of accountability is both less costly and less controversial than the other two forms and to the effect of the national state-by-state report card on higher education, *Measuring Up 2000* and *Measuring Up 2002*.[19] The number of states with performance reporting increased from thirty-nine in 2001 to forty-six in 2003.

The findings of the Seventh Annual Survey were that performance reporting—which now covers all but four states—was by far the preferred approach to accountability for higher education. However, bad budgets for states and higher education continued to erode support for performance funding and budgeting. More policy makers in state government and higher education agencies seemed to see performance reporting as a "no cost" alternative to performance funding and budgeting. Some policy makers still viewed performance reporting as an informal form of performance budgeting. *Measuring Up 2002* continued to spur interest in statewide performance reporting, but only a limited number of states were revising their reports to link them with those reports cards. State governments were making only modest, and coordinating and system boards only moderate, use of performance reports in planning and policy making. None of the three programs demonstrated the desirable effect on the improving performance, but performance funding showed more effect than budgeting or reporting.[20]

Differences among States

In addition to the obvious differences in size, population, and enrollments, the fifty states differ significantly in history, culture, and political and economic dynamics. These differences are further reflected in overall performance of their higher education systems, financing policies, governance, and in state regulatory culture related to higher education. A particularly informative, yet controversial, way of thinking about state variations is presented by the political science literature on state political "cultures." Daniel Elazar, for example, sets forth a theory of political subcultures and classifies states according to whether they are moralistic, individualistic, traditionalistic; their culture and ethnicity; and whether their "ethos" is "public-regarding" or "private-regarding."[21]

The following are several of the more important differences among states in terms of higher education.[22]

Differences in Overall Performance of State Higher Education Systems

Measuring Up, the state-by-state report card on state performance in higher education published every other year by the National Center for Public Policy and Higher Education, assigns grades to states based on their performance compared with the best-performing states. The report card grades each state on the performance of the higher education system as a whole in terms of its effect on the state's population and economy. The report card does not grade institutions, but the grades reflect indirectly each state's combined institutional capacity and the alignment of that capacity with state priorities. The important point is that differences in state performance are related to differences in *state policies* (financing, regulation, accountability, and structure/governance).[23] States are graded on five measures. Preparation: How well are students in each state prepared to take advantage of college? Participation: Do state residents have sufficient opportunities to enroll in college-level programs? Affordability: How affordable is higher education for students and families in each state? Completion: Do those who enroll make progress toward and complete their certificates and degrees in a timely manner? Benefits: What economic and civic benefits does each state receive from the education of its residents? In future report cards, states will be graded on a sixth measure: Learning: What do we know about student learning as a result of education and training beyond high school? The national report card grades states on the performance of the higher education system as a whole in terms of its effect on the state's population and economy.

Differences in Financing Policy

States differ significantly in their capacity and effort to finance higher education. State funding ranges from a high of more than $325 per capita to a low of less than $100 per capita.[24] States differ significantly in the shares of funding of public institutions borne by state and local governments, students, and other sources. States range from those that provide more than 65 percent of the core funding for public institutions from state and local appropriations (for example, Alaska,

Florida, North Carolina, and Mississippi), to those that provide less than 40 percent of the funding from these sources (for example, Montana, Colorado, Pennsylvania, Delaware, New Hampshire, and Vermont). The extent to which states supplement state appropriations with revenue from tuition and other sources also varies greatly. North Carolina, for example, has historically maintained comparatively low public tuition, while Vermont has deliberately relied on high tuition offset by state student financial aid.[25]

States differ in the extent to which they fund need-based financial aid for low-income students. A measure of the level of this funding is the state funding as a percent of Federal Pell Grant aid to low-income families in the state. Four states (Illinois, Pennsylvania, Minnesota, and New Jersey) provide state need-based aid at a level of more than 100 percent of Pell grant aid; sixteen states, however, provide less than 10 percent of Pell grants.[26] States with limited need-based student financial aid may provide access through low tuition and may also have other non-need-based student financial aid programs.

Differences in State Structures

The general pattern, as well as tradition, in the United States is that state governments (meaning the governor, executive branch, administrative and fiscal agencies, and the state legislature) treat public higher education differently from other state agencies, such as state transportation departments.

Each state has a unique state structure and relationship between government and higher education. The differences among states reflect, among other points, the differences in the general governmental structure (for example, different legal responsibilities of the executive and legislative branches), political culture, and history. Most states have established an entity (for example, state board of higher education, state board of regents, or higher education commission) explicitly charged with statewide policy for higher education.

Despite the complexity of the differences, the approaches taken by states can be understood in terms of the variations in the authority and responsibility of state higher education entities for key policy tools and processes such as budget review and approval, review and approval of academic programs, public accountability, and the extent to which these entities are directly involved in institutional operations (governance). The following is an overview of these variations.[27]

The distinction between *governance* and *coordination* is fundamental for understanding state higher education structures and the assignment of responsibility for budget/financing decision making and for institutional financial management. Some structures are established to *govern institutions* while others are established to *coordinate the state postsecondary education system or sectors* (for example, a system of locally governed community colleges).

The term *governance* has a particular meaning when applied to the authority and responsibility of governing public boards of colleges and universities. There is a strong historical and legal tradition in American postsecondary education of institutional autonomy—a high degree of freedom from external intervention and control. Institutional autonomy is a *relative,* not an *absolute,* concept to be tempered by the broader interests of the public and society.[28] A basic responsibility of governing boards is to oversee the delicate balance between institutional autonomy and public accountability.

All states assign responsibility for governing public colleges and universities to one or more boards, most often composed of a majority of lay citizens representing the public interest. The names of these boards vary, but "board of trustees" and "board of regents" are the most common. The responsibilities of these boards are similar to those of boards of directors for nonprofit corporations. Public institution governing boards were modeled after the lay boards of private colleges and universities. Private college boards usually govern a single institution. In contrast, public institution boards most often govern several public institutions. In fact, 65 percent of the students in American public postsecondary education attend institutions whose governing boards cover multiple campuses.[29]

Common responsibilities of public governing boards include governing a single corporate entity, including all the rights and responsibilities of that corporation as defined by state law and, if a system board, encompassing all institutions within a system. Individual institutions within the board's jurisdiction usually do not have separate corporate status, although governing boards may have subsidiary corporations for hospitals, foundations, or other purposes. Other responsibilities include appointing, setting the compensation for, and evaluating both system and institutional chief executives; strategic planning, budgeting (operating and capital), and allocating resources between and among the institutions within the board's jurisdiction; ensuring public accountability for effective and efficient use of resources to achieve institutional missions; maintaining the institution's assets (human, programmatic, and physical), and ensuring alignment of these assets with institutional mission; developing and implementing policy on a wide range of institutional concerns (for example, academic and student affairs policies) without approval of external agencies or authorities; awarding academic degrees; advocating for the needs of the institutions under the board's jurisdiction to the legislature and governor; and establishing faculty and other personnel policies, including approving awarding of tenure and serving as the final point of appeal on personnel grievances.

There are a number of ways to categorize public governing boards, but the approach suggested by Clark Kerr and Marian Gade in *The Guardians: Boards of Trustees of American Colleges and Universities* is particularly useful.[30] They categorize public governing boards in three ways. First, consolidated governance systems in which one board governs all public two- and four-year institutions or one board covers all four-year campuses with separate arrangements for two-year institutions. Second, segmental systems in which separate boards govern distinct types of campuses (for example, research universities, comprehensive colleges and universities, community colleges; this may include separate boards for postsecondary technical institutes or colleges and adult education, as well); and campus-level boards in which governing boards have full, "autonomous" authority over a single campus that is not part of a consolidated governing board or multicampus system. Several states combine consolidated governance and campus-level boards. For example, in North Carolina and Utah, campus-level boards have authority delegated by the central board and can make some decisions on their own. The State University of New York, the University of Maine System, and the University System of Maryland also have campus boards, though they are largely advisory.

A number of states have established *coordinating* boards responsible for key aspects of the state's role in postsecondary education. Some coordinating boards have the responsibility for the statewide coordination of many policy tools or functions (for example, planning and policy leadership, institutional missions, program review and approval, and budget development and resource allocation). Other coordinating boards are responsible for only a single sector such as community colleges.

The important point is that coordinating boards do *not* govern institutions, in the sense defined above (for example, appoint institutional chief executives or set faculty personnel policies). Specifically, coordinating boards appoint, set compensation for, and evaluate only the agency executive officer and staff but not the institutional chief executives. In several states, the governor is the final appointing authority for the agency executive, but usually with recommendations from the coordinating board. Coordinating boards do not generally have corporate status independent of state government; they focus more on state and system needs and priorities than on advocating the interests of a particular institution or system of institutions, and they plan primarily for the state postsecondary education system as a whole. In most coordinating board states, this planning includes both public and private institutions and in some states, for-profit institutions. Coordinating boards may or may not review and make recommendations on budgets for the state system as a whole rather than only for one part of that system. A few coordinating agencies recommend consolidated budgets for the whole public system. Others simply make recommendations to the governor or legislature on individual institutional or segmental budgets. Most coordinating boards have responsibility to implement budget policy only for funds appropriated specifically to the agency for operations, special initiatives, or reallocation to the institutions for performance, incentives, or other purposes; they may or may not review or approve proposals for new academic programs and may or may not have authority to require institutions to review existing programs. They are not involved directly in setting or carrying out human resource or personnel policies, except to carry out legislative mandates for studies of issues such as faculty workload and productivity or tenure policy.

Twenty-three states plus the District of Columbia and Puerto Rico are consolidated governing board states. These states organize all public higher education under one or two statewide governing boards. None of these states has established a statewide coordinating agency with significant academic policy or budgetary authority between the governing board and state government. Nine of these states organize all public higher education under a single governing board. The other fourteen states have two boards: most often a board for universities and a board for community colleges and/or technical colleges. In several of these states, the second board is a coordinating board for community and/or technical colleges. Twenty-four states are coordinating board states. Twenty-two of these states have regulatory coordinating boards with academic program approval authority. Fifteen of these boards have significant budgetary authority, six have limited budget authority, and one has no role in the budgetary process. Two states have advisory boards with no program approval authority and only authority to review and recommend budgets. One consolidated governing board state (Alaska) also has an advisory board with limited authority to review and make recommendations on budgets. Three states (Delaware, Michigan, and Pennsylvania) have planning/service agencies but no other boards between the governing boards for public institutions and state government. In addition, three other states (Minnesota, New Hampshire, and Oregon) plus the District of Columbia and Puerto Rico have planning/service agencies between their consolidated governing boards and state government. These agencies perform functions such as administration of student aid and institutional licensure and authorization. In Vermont, the Higher Education Council is a nonstatutory voluntary planning entity. Five states (Florida, Idaho, Michigan, New York, and Pennsylvania) have state boards with formal legal authority for all levels of education (early childhood education through higher education). Nevertheless, the formal authority of these boards for higher education varies significantly. Only in Idaho and New York does the state board have significant program and/or budgetary authority related to all higher education. A constitutional amendment approved by Florida voters in November 2002 removes the responsibility for universities from the previous P–20 (early childhood through graduate education) State Board of Education and creates a new Board of Governors with governing responsibility for the state universities. The state universities continue to have local boards. The State Board of Education continues to have responsibility for coordinating the locally governed community colleges.

Differences in Budgeting and Financing Relationships between States and Institutions

Within the broad categories of states with coordinating or governing boards, states differ fundamentally in the legal status accorded to public colleges and universities and, as a consequence, in the nature of the budgeting and financing relationships. The four levels of state control of institutions can be represented on a continuum from high to low (table 7.1).

Table 7.1
State Control of Institutions

Level of Control	Type of Institution	Legal Status
High	A. Institution as state agency	Higher education institutions are treated in a manner similar to other state agencies such as the transportation/highway department.
	B. State-controlled institution	The distinctiveness of higher education institutions from other state agencies is recognized, but most of the budget and financing policies applied to other state agencies are also applied to higher education.
	C. State-aided institution	Higher education institutions have a legal status according them substantial autonomy from state government. State provides base, categorical, and capital funding but with expectation of substantial non-state funding (tuition, private giving, etc.).
Low	D. Corporate model for institutional governance	As in model C, institutions have a legal status (e.g., public corporation) according them substantial autonomy. The expectation of state funding is less certain and may be allocated not in grants to the institution but in the form of vouchers or grants to students to offset tuition charges.

The four categories of institutional legal status represent theoretical types. In practice, no state currently treats all of its public institutions as if they were in either of the two extremes: institution as state agency or institution as an independent corporation.[31] There are three common patterns:

— Pattern A: Different sectors are accorded different levels of independence from state procedural controls. For example, both the University of California and the California State University System are treated as "state-aided" institutions, although each is subject to specific regulations that treat the institutions as "state-controlled." The University of California is established in the state constitution and has a higher level of independence from state procedural controls than the California State University, which is established in state statutes and until the early 1990s was closely linked to state budget, personnel, and purchasing requirements. In contrast to the two university systems, the California Community Colleges are governed by extensive state statutory and regulatory policies and in many respects are treated as state-controlled institutions.

— Pattern B: All public universities are established as public corporations (state-aided) but are subject to detailed state oversight in specific areas such as capital construction or personnel. The two cases included in this chapter, North Dakota and Kentucky, are examples of this pattern—the North Dakota University System (NDUS) as a single university system and Kentucky, with each university as a separate public corporation. In both cases, the institutions are subject to specific state procedural controls related to capital construction and other areas. As another example, the University of Wisconsin System is organized as a public corporation but is subject to detailed oversight by the Wisconsin State Department of Administration on all capital projects and all classified (nonprofessional) personnel are included in the state civil service system.

— Pattern C: Most public institutions are established as public corporations (state aided), but specific institutions are accorded greater independence from state procedural controls as the result of deliberate state actions to decentralize governance and diversify revenue sources. The University System of Maryland, for example, is accorded a degree of independence as a public corporation (state aided), but St. Mary's College of Maryland was granted increased autonomy in return for meeting specific accountability requirements. The State of Colorado has implemented a similar policy through which institutions may enter into "compacts" with the state in return for increased autonomy.[32]

In the United States, universities are often accorded "substantive" autonomy within the bounds of state-defined missions and account-ability requirements; but at the same time, they are required to con-form to state regulatory/procedural requirements. As state funding is becoming a smaller share of these institutions' revenues, some are urging that the institutions be given "corporate" status as reflected in the "low control" end of the continuum.[33]

Forces Leading to Changes

The basic patterns of state-level organization across the nation today were in place in the early 1970s. The year 1972 marked the culmina-tion of more than a decade of development of state higher education agencies formed to coordinate the massive expansion in the late 1950s and 1960s. By that year, forty-seven states had established either con-solidated governing boards responsible for all senior institutions (and, in some cases, community colleges also) or coordinating boards re-sponsible for statewide planning and coordination of two or more gov-erning boards. Three small states with a limited number of institu-tions did not form a special statutory agency but continued to handle statewide higher education issues through existing governing boards, informal coordination, and direct involvement of the governor and state legislature.

Despite the apparent continuity in state structures over time, sig-nificant changes have taken place and continue to take place in the form and substance of state coordination and governance.[34] Changes in political leadership (for example, newly elected governors or changes in party control of the state legislature) are often the occa-sions for restructuring. The forces behind the changes can be grouped in two broad categories: first, "perennial" issues that throughout the past have consistently spurred governors and legislators to make higher education reorganization proposals and, second, broader changes in state expectations and roles.

Perennial issues tend to be long-standing problems that may fester for years but then, especially at points of changes in political leader-ship or severe economic downturns, they trigger debates, lead to spe-cial study commissions, and often eventually result in full-scale re-organization. Examples of several of the most common issues are

—Access to high-cost graduate and professional programs: In most
states, regional economic, political, and cultural differences present serious challenges to state policy makers. These regional
stresses are amplified and played out in conflicts within the states'
postsecondary education systems. A common scenario begins with
pressure from a growing urban area to have accessible graduate
and professional programs. Subsequent local campaigns and state
lobbying efforts to expand these initiatives from a few courses
to full-scale programs and then new campuses lead to opposition
from existing universities and other regions. The same scenario
often plays out when isolated rural areas struggle to gain access
to programs for place-bound adults. Local and regional end runs
to the governor or legislature to get special attention either to
advance or block such initiatives usually spark political struggles
that inevitably lead to major restructuring proposals.

—Conflict between the aspirations of two institutions (often under
separate governing boards) in the same geographic area: Again,
conflicts tend to be over which institution should offer high-cost
graduate and professional programs. Major reorganization proposals, usually mergers or consolidations, frequently occur after
years of other efforts to achieve improved cooperation and coordination.

—Political reaction to institutional lobbying: As governors and legislators face politically difficult and unattractive choices to curtail
rather than expand programs, intense lobbying by narrow, competing institutional interests can spark demands for restructuring. Political leaders seek to push such battles away from the immediate political process by increasing the authority of a state
board, with the hope that the board will be able to resolve the conflicts before they get to the legislature. The reverse situation also
occurs frequently. A state board will act to curtail an institutional
end run and then face a legislative proposal, frequently stimulated by the offending institution, to abolish the board. Short-
term victories gained through end running the established coordinating structures usually lead to greater centralization.

—Frustrations with barriers to student transfer and articulation: Cumulative evidence that student transfer between institutions is
difficult, or the number of credits limited, often leads to proposals
to create a "seamless" system. Before the mid-1990s, most of the

reorganization proposals were limited to postsecondary education (for example, consolidating institutions under a single governing board), but an increasing number of states are debating proposals to create P–16 (primary through postsecondary education) structures.

—Concerns about too many institutions with ill-defined or overlapping missions: At issue may be small, isolated rural institutions or institutions with similar missions in close proximity to one another. The governance debates often emerge from proposals to merge, consolidate, or close institutions or to make radical changes in institutional missions. The intense lobbying and publicity by persons who oppose the changes often lead to proposals for governance changes. In some cases, the proposals are to abolish the board that proposed the changes. In other cases, just the opposite is proposed—to increase the board's authority out of frustration with its inability to carry out a recommended closure or merger.

—Lack of regional coordination among institutions (for example, community colleges, technical colleges, branch campuses) offering one- and two-year vocational, technical, occupational, and transfer programs: Many states have regions or communities where two or more public institutions, each responsible to a different state board or agency, are competing to offer similar one- and two-year programs. In the worst situations, this may involve a postsecondary technical institute, a community college, and two-year lower-division university branches competing for an overlapping market in the same region.

—Concerns about the current state board's effectiveness or continuing relevance to state priorities: Reorganizations often result from efforts to change leaders or leadership styles. As illustrated by the brief summary of changes over the past 25 years, state leaders tend to see the importance of statewide coordination in times of severe fiscal constraints, but when the economy is strong and these leaders face fewer difficult choices among competing priorities, the relevance of state agencies is less evident. Common triggers for change include a sense that a board, or its staff, is ineffective or lacks the political influence or judgment to address critical issues facing the state, which are often one or more of the other perennial issues. They may be perceived as unable to resolve problems before they become major political controversies, or they may have handled difficult issues poorly in the past. Another trigger is often a desire to change leadership style or underlying philosophy of the state role. This may be a reaction to aggressive, centralized leadership and an effort to shift to a more passive, consultative leadership approach—or the reverse. The change may be to move from a focus on administrative, regulatory or management issues internal to postsecondary education to a focus on policy leadership relative to a broader public agenda. Finally, state leaders also may propose reorganization not because the structure has problems but simply to change the leadership or personalities involved in the process.

Other governance changes result from changing state expectations and roles. Even in a period of constrained resources, many state leaders—as well as governmental leaders throughout the world—increasingly recognize that higher education is the key to the future of the quality of life of the state population and the ability of the state to compete in the global knowledge economy. The disjuncture between higher education and state leaders is not that states don't care; it is that they care about agendas different from those that drive institutional behaviors. This divergence is calling into question the role of government and related policy goals.

Rather than emphasize state support for higher education per se, the new leaders are increasingly emphasizing a broader "public agenda." [35] A public agenda defines long-term goals to address a state's major social, economic, and educational challenges and sets forth strategies to link higher education to the achievement of these goals. An example of a long-term goal would be to raise a state's per capita income to the national average or above. Strategies would link higher education to that strategy through raising the state's education attainment, contributing to economic development through research and technology transfer, and other educational initiatives. In contrast to the traditional state master plan for higher education, a public agenda focuses not on "higher education" issues per se, but on issues concerning the status and performance of the state's population and education system as a whole. These issues are distinctly different from issues that concern institutional leaders: issues about institutional mission and the basic capacity to accomplish that mission (faculty resources, programs, facilities and other assets). A public agenda also sets forth strategies that cut across higher education sectors, all education levels, and other public policy domains such as economic development and health.

The issues raised by the national report card, *Measuring Up 2002,* illustrate the kinds of issues addressed by a public agenda. The scores on *Preparation* raise questions about the effectiveness of preschool/kindergarten through high school (P/K–12) reform: standards, assessment, curriculum, and course-taking patterns; secondary school retention and completion; and alignment of K–12 standards with requirements for college-level work or employment in a twenty-first-century workforce. The scores on *Participation* raise questions about differences in college-going rates among different groups (for example, race, ethnicity, gender, and income) and the state's regions, about relationships between the adequacy of preparation and affordability, and about the nature of provision (for example, the regional availability of community college services). The scores on *Affordability* raise questions about the overall relationship of student financing policy (tuition and student aid) to incomes of the state's families and students and about the interrelationship between tuition policy, student aid policy, and state appropriations for higher education. The scores on *Completion* raise questions related to the adequacy of preparation and affordability as well as incentives and accountability requirements for institutional performance. Initiatives to improve retention and completion and the proportion of a state's population completing a degree require articulation and coordination between education levels and an environment that focuses on student success rather than institutional status. The scores on *Benefits* raise questions related to state strategies to raise education attainment, to improve the quality of the state's workforce, and to improve the civic participation and quality of life of the state's population. The new emphasis on a public agenda suggests that the case for future state support for higher education will be made in fundamentally different terms than in the past.

Accompanying the changes in state expectations is a subtle yet fundamental shift in the basic assumptions about the role of government in higher education. These changes are summarized as shifts in policy assumptions (table 7.2).[36]

As described by Dennis Jones, the focus of state financing policy is shifting from a traditional emphasis on institutional viability—on *building and maintaining institutional capacity*—to a focus on targeted funding policies to *utilize institutional capacity* to achieve state

Table 7.2
The Changing Role of Government in Higher Education

A shift from:	To:
Focus primarily on providers and serving as "owner-operators" of public institutions as the principal means of serving public purposes	Focus on clients (students/learners, employers, and governments) and utilization of the capacity of multiple providers to serve public purposes
Financing policies focused primarily on institutional subsidy and on the adequacy of institutional financing	Financing policies designed to "enter the market on behalf of the public" and to channel competitive forces toward public purposes
Accountability focused on institutional performance	Accountability focused on public priorities: the impact of higher education on the education attainment and performance of the state's population and the competitiveness of the state's economy

purposes. Institutional viability remains an important state funding priority—not as an end in itself but as a means for maintaining the capacity to address state priorities. State financing policies have traditionally emphasized primarily creating and maintaining institutional capacity. The principal approaches to budgeting and resource allocation have been either "base-plus" funding (taking the previous year's funding and adjusting it for increased costs and other variables) or formulas based on a combination of costs and a measure of workload such as enrollment or credit hours. Policies regarding student financing have traditionally focused on establishing tuition and student aid policies designed to maximize institutional revenues.

In the new environment, states continue to be concerned with the objective of *capacity building,* but they are increasingly concerned also with *capacity utilization,* that is, on investment or performance funding of institutions or targeted aid to students.[37]

These changes in expectations and state roles have far-reaching implications for the state leadership or "governance" structures. Structures and policies established when states were primarily "owner-operators" and the principal revenue sources for public institutions are no longer appropriate. The alternatives are likely to be found not in the traditional modes of governance but in new structures for policy leadership and alignment of finance and other policies with a clearly defined public agenda.

Reality of Change in the States

Despite the need for new approaches to state policy leadership, the reality of change varies dramatically across the states. In the 1990s, several states led the nation in implementing new approaches not only to state leadership but also to related policies of finance and accountability. These included changes within their existing structures (Georgia, Illinois, Missouri, Oklahoma, and Texas) as well as major restructuring initiated by the governor and/or state legislature (Kentucky, North Dakota, and West Virginia). Each of these states had three characteristics. First, they focused on a long-term public agenda linking higher education to the future of the state's quality of life and economy; second, they linked financing policy and accountability to the public agenda; and finally, they pursued balanced strategies emphasizing both *capacity building* and *capacity utilization*.

In most states, however, the trends were far less certain. State decision-making structures were seemingly unable to make the transition to new missions and modes of operation. Governors focused on short-term agendas or immediate budget crises. Legislatures increasingly were unable to sustain attention to long-term change agendas because of legislative turnover, short-term agendas, intensified interest-group pressures, and lack of core staff capability focused on the "public interest" perspective on higher education. There is no venue within most legislative processes to link a strategic agenda with strategic financing policy.

State-level governing boards (consolidated systems as well as multi-campus universities) continued to focus primarily on *internal* institutional concerns. They often functioned as vertically organized, closed systems designed to protect the institutions from competition for students and resources from other providers and continued to emphasize one-size-fits-all policies that ran counter to strategies to address the unique needs of each state's regions. Their effectiveness was increasingly challenged by weaknesses in the quality of board and system leadership.

State coordinating boards remained mired in regulatory practices shaped by the statutory mandates of the 1970s and 1980s. They continued to focus primarily on *coordinating public institutions* and not on leading a public agenda and were increasingly politicized through appointments of both board members and staff and were experiencing an accelerating turnover of senior staff leadership. These agencies had significant deficits in terms of core information and analytic capabilities (especially those necessary for leading a public agenda as summarized above).

State structures and politics continued to create barriers to collaboration between and among sectors to address common, crosscutting issues (for example, "picket-fence" relationships among the three California segments resulting in competing, uncoordinated services within each of the state's regions). Many higher education and other state policies were *not* aligned with a public agenda—in fact, were not aligned with any long-term agenda. The structures resulted in splintered decision making organized around specific programs or sectors. Financing policy was characterized by short-term agendas and was driven by the most immediate fiscal crisis. States continued to make decisions separately on the interrelated areas of state appropriations, student aid, and tuition policy. Financing policies provided few incentives for performance and collaboration. State regulatory policies in areas such as human resources, purchasing, and capital financing were often mired in state bureaucratic processes and did little to achieve efficiencies and often hindered the capacity of the higher education system to respond to public priorities

In summary, despite growing concerns about the public or societal purposes of higher education and the need for new approaches to policy leadership and related policies, the reality is that few states have the capacity to pursue a long-term agenda focused on public purposes. In blunt terms, there is "no one at home" when it comes to the responsibility to articulate and defend basic public purposes. State leaders are preoccupied with the fiscal crisis and short-term political agendas. Higher education leaders appear far more concerned about the future of their own institutions in turbulent fiscal and competitive times than about the need for policy leadership structures and policies essential to ensure that higher education responds to public priorities.

Conclusion

Sustaining attention to the public/societal purposes of higher education in the turbulent times of the next decade and beyond will require fundamental improvements in the state-level capacity to lead change in the public interest. As summarized above, few states now can meet the fundamental prerequisites for that leadership. Many of the state structures formed for other purposes in an earlier time cannot be expected to make the transition to new missions and modes of leadership. New thinking is needed about the ways states can shape decision-making structures and policies designed explicitly for new missions and functions. Shaping new alternatives must be a shared responsibility of both higher education and state leaders.

NOTES

1. See Sandra S. Rupert, *Where We Go From Here: State Legislative Views on Higher Education in the New Millennium* (Washington, D.C.: National Education Association, 2001), for the results of a survey of state legislative views.

2. Frank Newman, *Choosing Quality* (Denver: Education Commission of the States, 1987), xiii.

3. Robert O. Berdahl, *Statewide Coordination of Higher Education* (Washington, D.C.: American Council on Education, 1971), 9.

4. See annual survey of student financial aid programs published by the National Association of State Student Aid Grant Programs (NASSGAP). *NASSGAP 32nd Annual Survey Report* (New York: New York State Higher Education Corporation, 2002).

5. Education Commission of the States. *The Preservation of Excellence in American Higher Education* (Denver: Education Commission of the States, 1990).

6. Clark Kerr, "The States and Higher Education: Changes Ahead," *State Government*, 58, no. 2 (1990) 45–50.

7. The following statistics are from National Center for Education Statistics, *Digest of Education Statistics, 2002* (Washington, D.C.: U.S. Department of Education, 2002), tables 172 and 243.

8. Ibid., table 333.

9. National Center for Public Policy and Higher Education (2002); *Losing Ground: A National Status Report on Affordability in American Higher Education* (San Jose: NCPPHE), chap. 1.

10. American Association of State Colleges and Universities (AACU) and the National Association of State Universities and Land-Grant Colleges (NASULGC); *Student Charges and Financial Aid, 2002* (Washington, D.C.: AASCU and NASULGC, 2002).

11. Institute for Higher Education Policy, *Accounting for State Student Aid: How State Policy and Student Aid Connect* (Washington, D.C.: Institute for Higher Education Policy, 2002).

12. See Jeffrey Selingo, "The Disappearing State in Public Higher Education," *Chronicle of Higher Education,* February 28, 2003, A22.

13. National Center for Education Statistics, *Digest of Education Statistics, 2001,* table 334.

14. Dennis Jones, "State Shortfalls Projected Throughout the Decade," in *Policy Alert* (San Jose: National Center for Public Policy and Higher Education, 2003).

15. Don Boyd, *State Spending for Higher Education in the Coming Decade,* A Report of the Nelson A. Rockefeller Institute of Government (Boulder: National Center for Higher Education Management Systems, 2002). For further reading on state policy and higher education finance, see Patrick M. Callan and Joni E. Finney, eds., *Public and Private Financing of Higher Education: Shaping Public Policy for the Future* (Washington, D.C.: American Council on Education and Oryx Press, 1997); and Donald E. Heller, ed., *The States and Public Higher Education Policy: Affordability, Access, and Accountability* (Baltimore: Johns Hopkins University Press, 2001).

16. For greater analysis of these developments, see Newman, *Choosing Quality;* Robert O. Berdahl and Barbara Holland, eds., *Developing State Fiscal Incentives to Improve Higher Education: Proceedings from a National Invitational Conference* (College Park: National Center for Postsecondary Governance and Finance, University of Maryland, 1990); Peter T. Ewell and Dennis Jones, *Assessing and Reporting Student Progress: A Response to the "New Accountability"* (Denver: State Higher Education Executive Officers, 1991); and James R. Mingle, *State Policy and Productivity in Higher Education* (Denver: State Higher Education Executive Officers, 1992).

17. Joseph C. Burke and Henrik Minassians, *Performance Reporting: "Real" Accountability or Accountability "Lite,"* Seventh Annual Survey (Albany, NY: Rockefeller Institute of Government, 2003).

18. Ibid., 3.

19. National Center for Public Policy and Higher Education, *Measuring Up 2000* and *Measuring Up 2002* (San Jose: National Center for Public Policy and Higher Education, 2000 and 2002).

20. Burke and Minassions, *Performance Reporting,* 21.

21. Daniel Elazar, *American Federalism: A View from the States* (New York: Thomas Y. Crowell, 1966), chap. 4.

22. See the Web site for the National Information Center for Higher Education Policy Making and Analysis, www.higheredinfo.org, for comparison of states and analysis of differences within states on a wide range of variables.

23. National Center for Public Policy and Higher Education, *Measuring Up 2002: The State-by-State Report Card for Higher Education* (San Jose: NCPPHE, 2002), www.highereducation.org/.

24. Center for Higher Education and Finance, *Grapevine: A National Database for Tax Support for Higher Education* (Normal: Illinois State University), www.coe.ilstu.edu/grapevine/table10.htm.

25. National Center for Education Statistics, IPEDS, NCHEMS Finance Data Set.

26. National Center for Public Policy and Higher Education, *Measuring Up 2002*, based on data from Office of Postsecondary Education. Title IV/Pell Grant End of Year Report, 2000–2001 (Washington, D.C.: U.S. Department of Education, 2002), table 21; and Kristen DeSalvatore, *National Association of State Student Grant and Aid Programs 32nd Annual Survey, 2000–2001*, Academic Survey Report (Albany, NY: National Association of State Student Grant and Aid Programs, 2002), table 1.

27. The following section on state structures is drawn from A. C. McGuinness, Jr., State Postsecondary Education Governance Database, www.ecs.org/clearinghouse/31/02/3102.htm (Education Commission of the States, 2002).

28. Berdahl, *Statewide Coordination of Higher Education,* 9.

29. For further reading on the subject of multicampus systems, see Gerald Gaither, ed., *The MultiCampus System: Perspectives and Prospects* (Sterling, Va.: Stylus, 1999); E. K. Fretwell, *More Than Management: Guidelines for System Governing Boards and Their Chief Executive* (Washington, D.C.: Association of Governing Boards of Universities and Colleges, 2000); Marian L. Gade, *Four Multicampus Systems: Some Policies and Practices That Work,* AGB Special Report (Washington, D.C.: Association of Governing Boards of Universities and Colleges, 1993); and Aims C. McGuinness, Jr., "Perspectives on the Current Status of and Emerging Policy Issues for Public Multicampus Higher Education Systems," AGB Occasional Paper No. 3 (Washington, D.C.: Association of Governing Boards of Universities and Colleges, 1991).

30. C. Kerr and M. Gade, *The Guardians: Boards of Trustees of American Colleges and Universities: What They Do and How Well They Do It.* (Washington, D.C.: Association of Governing Boards of Universities and Colleges [AGB], 1989), 116, 128–29.

31. Robert Berdahl makes an important distinction between "substantive" autonomy, meaning autonomy on matters of standards, curriculum, faculty appointments, and similar matters, and "procedural" autonomy, meaning autonomy from state procedural controls.

32. See Robert O. Berdahl, "Balancing Self-Interest and Accountability: St. Mary's College of Maryland," and other chapters, in *Seeking Excellence Through Independence,* eds. T. J. MacTaggart and Associates (San Francisco: Jossey-Bass, 1998).

33. Berdahl, *Statewide Coordination of Higher Education,* 11. Discussion of procedural and substantive autonomy, pp. 10–12.

34. For historical perspectives on statewide coordination, see Ernest Boyer, *Control of the Campus* (Princeton: Carnegie Foundation for the Advancement of Teaching, 1982); Berdahl, *Statewide Coordination of Higher Education;* Carnegie Commission on Higher Education, *The Capitol and the Campus: State Responsibility for Postsecondary Education* (New York: Mc-

Graw-Hill, 1971); Carnegie Foundation for the Advancement of Teaching, *States and Higher Education: A Proud Past and a Vital Future* (San Francisco: Jossey-Bass, 1976); Education Commission of the States, *Challenge: Coordination and Governance in the 1980s* (Denver: ECS, 1980); Lyman A. Glenny, *Autonomy of Public Colleges* (New York: McGraw-Hill, 1959); Glenny and others, *Coordinating Higher Education for the '70s* (Berkeley: Center for Research and Development in Higher Education, University of California, 1971); John D. Millet, *Conflict in Higher Education: State Government versus Institutional Independence* (San Francisco: Jossey-Bass, 1982). For more recent commentaries on statewide coordination, see Paul E. Lingenfelter, *State Policy for Higher Education: The 21st Century Challenge* (Denver: State Higher Education Executive Officers, 2003); Richard C. Richardson et al., *Designing State Higher Education Systems for a New Century* (Washington, D.C.: American Council on Education and Oryx Press, 1999); James R. Mingle and Rhonda Martin Epper, "State Coordination and Planning in an Age of Entrepreneurship," *Planning and Management for a Changing Environment* (San Francisco: Jossey-Bass, 1997), 45–65; Terrence J. MacTaggart, ed., *Restructuring Higher Education* (San Francisco: Jossey-Bass, 1996).

35. This section draws on Aims C. McGuinness, Jr., "State Policy Leadership in the Public Interest: Is Anyone At Home?" (paper prepared for the Macalester Forum on Higher Education, Macalester College, St. Paul, Minn., June 10–11, 2003). See Terrence J. MacTaggart and James R. Mingle, *Pursuing the Public Agenda* (Washington, D.C.: Association of Governing Boards of Universities and Colleges, 2002).

36. Aims C. McGuinness, Jr., *Reflections on Postsecondary Education Governance Changes* (Denver: Education Commission of the States, July 2002), www.ecs.org/clearinghouse/31/02/3102.htm.

37. Dennis P. Jones, *Financing in Sync* (paper prepared for the Western Interstate Commission on Higher Education, February 2003).

Chapter Eight

The Legal Environment
The Implementation of Legal Change on Campus

Michael A. Olivas

In modern higher education, few major decisions are made without considering the legal consequences, and though the core functions of higher education—instruction and scholarship—are remarkably free from external legal influences, no one would plausibly deny the increase of legalization on campus. We know surprisingly little about the law's effect upon higher education, but virtually no one in the enterprise is untouched by statutes, regulations, case law, or institutional rules promulgated to implement legal regimes.

Lewis Thomas, perhaps our most thoughtful commentator on medicine and science in society, ascribes organic qualities to the university, and his view of a college as a "community of scholars" is grounded in an appreciation of the history of education. Paul Goodman and John Millett also exemplify this perspective. Like a prism refracting light differently depending upon how you hold it up for viewing, higher education can appear differently. For Herbert Stroup and many other sociologists, colleges are essentially bureaucracies, and no student confronting course registration today is likely to be dissuaded from this view. To Victor Baldridge, universities are indisputably political organizations, as they also appear to Clark Kerr and Burton Clark. To critics, higher education is stratified by class (Randall Collins), resistant to legal change (Harry Edwards), and in need of fundamental restructuring (Paolo Freire).[1] As many observers would insist, all are equally close to the truth or truths, depending upon which truth is being refracted. The cases in this chapter reveal many truths and, often frustratingly, few answers. As the following cases reveal, legal considerations can pare governance issues down to the essential question, What is a college?

Legal Governance

Despite the seeming obviousness of the question posed above, a variety of cases probe the fundamental definitional issue. In *Coffee v. Rice University,* the issues were whether the 1891 trust charter founding Rice University (then Rice Institute), which restricted admissions to "white inhabitants" and required that no tuition be charged, could be maintained in 1966.[2] The court held that an "institute" was a postsecondary institution by any other name, and its postcompulsory, collegiate nature rendered it a college. On the issue of whether the trust could be maintained with its racial restrictions and tuition prohibition, the court applied the doctrine of cy pres, which theory allowed the trustees to reformulate the provisions and admit minorities and charge tuition, for to continue the practices would have been impracticable; if the trust provisions can no longer be realistically carried out, a court can reconstitute the trust to make it conform to the changed circumstances.

A court is not always so disposed as the *Coffee* court was. In *Shapiro v. Columbia University National Bank and Trust Co.,* the court allowed a trust reserved only for male students to remain male only, refusing to apply cy pres.[3] My personal favorite is *U.S. on Behalf of U.S. Coast Guard v. Cerio,* in which a judge allowed the Coast Guard Academy to reformulate a major student prize when the endowment's interest had grown to more than $100,000.[4] The judge began, "This is essentially a case of looking a gift horse in the mouth and finding it too good to accept as is" and allowed the academy to use some of the prize interest for other support services.

Sometimes a zoning ordinance raises the issue of what constitutes a college. In *Fountain Gate Ministries v. City of Plano,* a city wished to keep colleges from locating in residentially zoned housing areas.[5] The church argued that its activities were those of a church rather than those of a college. However, the court took notice of the educational instruction, faculty, degree activities, and other collegelike activities and determined that these constituted a college, protestations to the contrary notwithstanding. In the opposite direction, a court held that a consultant firm's use of the term "Quality College" to describe its activities did not make it a college or subject it to state regulation. In wry fashion, the court noted that to make use of the word *college* in an organization's title would make a college bookstore or the Catholic College of Cardinals into institutions!

Sometimes the definition drives a divorce decree. In *Hacker v. Hacker,* a father who had agreed to pay for his daughter's college tuition did so while she was a theater major at the University of California but refused to do so when she moved to Manhattan and enrolled in the Neighborhood Playhouse (TNP), a renowned acting school; that it was not degree-granting persuaded the judge that TNP failed to meet the definition of a college.[6] Occasionally, the definition turns on accreditation language (*Beth Rochel Seminary v. Bennett*), while at other times it turns on taxation issues (*City of Morgantown v. West Virginia Board of Regents*).[7]

Due to the different constitutional considerations between public and private colleges, such as free speech and due process not applying to private colleges, it is important to distinguish between the two forms in order to understand the full panoply of rights and duties owed to institutional community members. Consider the public/private distinction as a continuum, with *Trustees of Dartmouth College v. Woodward* at the purely private end and *Krynicky v. University of Pittsburgh* at the other end, that of purely public colleges.[8] In *Dartmouth,* the first higher education case considered by the U.S. Supreme Court, the State of New Hampshire had attempted to rescind the private charter of Dartmouth College, which was incorporated in the state nearly fifty years earlier, and to make it a public college with legislatively appointed trustees to replace the college's private trustees. The Supreme Court held that the college, once chartered, was private and not subject to the legislature's actions, unless the trustees wished to reconstitute themselves as a public institution. At the other end of the spectrum, *Krynicky* held that Temple University and the University of Pittsburgh were public colleges, due to the amount of money given by the state, the reconstitution of the board to include publicly appointed trustees (including ex officio elected officials), state reporting requirements, and other characteristics that injected state action into the act of reconstituting the institutions into the state system of higher education.

Complex issues arise in public institutions, such as the reach of sovereign immunity. A state's sovereign immunity is often referred to as its Eleventh Amendment immunity, although this nomenclature is somewhat of a misnomer. The Eleventh Amendment provides "the Judicial power of the United States shall not be construed to extend to any suit in law or equity, commenced or prosecuted against one of the United States by Citizens of another State, or by Citizens or Subjects of any Foreign State." While the Eleventh Amendment grants a state immunity from suit in federal court by its citizens and citizens of other states, sovereign immunity is much more.

When the United States was formed, the Constitution created a system of government consisting of two sovereigns—one national and one state. Although the states did concede some of their sovereign powers to the national government, the states did retain substantial sovereign powers under the constitutional scheme. On this relationship, the U.S. Supreme Court has observed: "The sovereign immunity of the States neither derives from, nor is limited by, the terms of the Eleventh Amendment. Rather, as the Constitution's structure, its history, and the authoritative interpretations by this Court make clear, the States' immunity from suit is a fundamental aspect of the sovereignty which the States enjoyed before the ratification of the Constitution, and which they retain today . . . except as altered by the plan of the Convention or certain constitutional Amendments." Although a state's sovereign immunity is significant, it is not absolute.

Of course, if there are pure archetypes such as Dartmouth and the University of Pittsburgh, there must be intermediate forms, such as Alfred University, where several students were arrested, the court holding in *Powe v. Miles* that regular students were entitled to no elaborate due process, as the institution was private.[9] However, the ceramics engineering students were entitled to hearings before dismissal, as the Ceramics College in which they were enrolled was a state-supported entity; New York contracted with the private college to provide this program rather than establish such a program in a state school. Other hybrid examples of a state-contracted unit within a private school include Cornell University's agricultural sciences program and Baylor's College of Medicine, both of which operate as if they were state institutions.

Other important foundational issues have also resulted in litigation, resulting in a complex definitional process. For example, in *Cahn and Cahn v. Antioch University,* trustees of the institution were sued by co-deans of the law school to determine who had authority for governance decisions; the court ruled that trustees have the ultimate authority and fiduciary duty.[10] In contrast to *Dartmouth,* where there was a "hostile takeover" of the institution by the state, private trustees can close a college or surrender its assets, such as its accreditation (*Fenn College v. Nance* and *Nasson College v. New England Association of Schools and Colleges*).[11] Another important issue involving the definition and legal governance of colleges turns on consortial or collective behavior of institutions: Does their mutual recognition in athletics accreditation and information sharing subject them to state action? In *NCAA v. University of Oklahoma,* the U.S. Supreme Court held that the NCAA was a "classic cartel" engaged in restraint of trade by its negotiated television contract; another court held that the activities of the Overlap Group—a group of elite institutions that share information on financial aid offers with other colleges admitting the same students so as to "coordinate" the awards —similarly violated antitrust law (*U.S. v. Brown University*).[12] However, in accreditation activities, mutual-recognition agreements have been allowed by courts, as not constituting a restraint of trade, as in *Marjorie Webster Jr. College v. Middle States Association* and *Beth Rochel Seminary v. Bennett,* in which an institution that was not yet accredited failed to negotiate the complex exceptions to the accreditation requirement for financial aid eligibility.[13]

In sum, despite the seeming simplicity of legally defining a college, it is not always easy. Cases were cited on which entities not labeled colleges were found to be colleges, while some that resembled colleges were held not to be, including a commercial program ("Quality College") that was held not to be an institution of higher education. For some technical, eligibility-driven issues—such as child support or taxation—the definition was extremely important. The bottom line appears, from these cases, to be that a college is an entity with instructional programs and degree-granting authority. In addition, the definitional issue is raised in the context of who is responsible for governance of the institution. The answer is ultimately the trustees, although the *Yeshiva* case, discussed in the following section, appears to hold the opposite.[14] With this foundational layer in place, we turn to the two major campus actors: faculty and students.

Faculty and the Law

Although there have not been many studies of patterns in postsecondary law, the few that have been undertaken show that faculty bring many of the suits in higher education. A 1987 study of Iowa case law shows that litigation against colleges brought by students totaled 11 percent, while faculty brought 31 percent; a 1988 study of Texas litigation shows that faculty brought 35 percent of all college cases in that state.[15] These numbers are surprising for two reasons. First, higher education has traditionally been a "gentlemen's club," to use William Kaplin's apt term.[16] This meant that if faculty members did not receive tenure, or were forced to move for another reason, they would simply find another position or fall upon their sword. To do otherwise would brand them as troublemakers or contentious colleagues. Second, there were no civil rights laws or widespread collective bargaining until the 1960s and 1970s, so faculty had fewer opportunities to bring suit or engage in collective protection, such as that afforded by security provisions in collective bargaining agreements.

Tenure

The two leading U.S. Supreme Court tenure cases were decided the same day in 1972, and both *Perry v. Sinderman* and *Board of Regents v. Roth* turn on what process is due to faculty, should institutions wish to remove them.[17] In *Perry,* a community college instructor who had been a thorn in the side of college administrators was fired for "insubordination," without a hearing or official reasons. The college had no tenure policy, except one that said, "the Administration of the College wishes the faculty member to feel that he has permanent tenure as long as his teaching services are satisfactory and as long as he displays a cooperative attitude toward his coworkers and his supervisors, and as long as he is happy in his work." The court held that the instructor thus had a property interest in his continued employment and ordered the lower court to determine whether he had been fired for his protected speech or for cause. In short, the administrators were required to give him notice of the reasons for his firing and an opportunity to explain his side of the matter. This is what tenure grants: a presumption of continued employment, absent certain circumstances

(financial exigency, etc.). In *Roth,* the Court held that an untenured professor had no constitutional right to continued employment, beyond the contractual period for which he was hired.

These two cases, together with several others fleshing out the terms of faculty employment, delineate the contours of tenure. For example, in *Wellner v. Minnesota State Junior College Board,* an untenured teacher was removed from his position for allegedly making racist remarks; he was sanctioned without a hearing or an opportunity to explain his behavior.[18] The appeals court ordered that he be accorded a hearing, as his liberty interest had been infringed. That is, his record was stigmatized and his reputation was at stake, so the court ordered a hearing to allow him to clear his name.

In addition to contract and liberty interests, faculty may have property interests as well, as in *State ex rel. McLendon v. Clarksville School of Theology,* in which the court held that Professor McLendon had a property interest in being considered for tenure, since she ostensibly qualified by being in rank the requisite period of time.[19] Although many cases, including *Roth,* have held that no reasons need be given for denying tenure, McLendon had, on the surface, appeared to earn tenure by default, and a hearing was required to show why she was not entitled to tenure. These cases are very grounded in fact and case specific, due to individual institutional policies and each state's contract or employment law.

A surprising number of cases deal with the ambiguities of tenure rights, as in whether or not American Association of University Professors (AAUP) guidelines apply (*Hill v. Talladega College*), exactly when the tenure clock applies (*Honore v. Douglas*), if financial reasons apply once a candidate has been evaluated in the tenure review process (*Spuler v. Pickar*), and whether institutional error can be sufficient grounds for overturning a tenure denial (*Lewis v. Loyola University of Chicago*).[20]

As for discrimination in the tenure process, hundreds of cases have been reported, most of which defer to institutional judgments about the candidates. Most find that the plaintiff, whether a person of color or an Anglo woman, did not prove that the institution acted in an unfair or discriminatory fashion. In *Scott v. University of Delaware,* the court held that, "while some of this evidence is indicative of racial prejudice on the University campus, it does not suggest to me that Scott was a victim of racial discrimination by the University in its renewal process, or that he was treated differently than non-black faculty by the University."[21] That this is so is particularly due to the extraordinary deference accorded academic judgments, as in *Faro v. NYU:* "Of all fields, which the federal courts should hesitate to invade and take over, education and faculty appointments at a University level are probably the least suited for federal court supervision."[22]

Even so, occasionally an institution goes too far, as the Claremont Graduate School (CGS) did in the 1992 case of *Clark v. Claremont Graduate School.*[23] In this case, a black professor chanced upon the meeting in which his tenure consideration was being reviewed. From the room, whose door was apparently left ajar, he overheard the committee making racist remarks, such as "us white folks have rights, too" and "I couldn't work on a permanent basis with a black man." When the court and jury reviewed his entire record, compared it with others who had recently been considered for (and received) tenure, and noted that no other minority professor had ever received tenure at CGS, it was determined that Professor Clark had been discriminated against due to his race, and he was awarded $1 million in compensatory damages as well as punitive damages and lawyers' fees.

Women have won several cases in which it was held that they were treated discriminatorily, as in *Sweeney v. Board of Trustees of Keene State College, Kunda v. Muhlenberg College, Mecklenberg v. Montana State Board of Regents,* and *Kemp v. Ervin,* among others, in which courts or juries found for women faculty plaintiffs.[24] Professor Jan Kemp particularly prevailed, winning six years on the tenure clock and more than $2.5 million in compensatory and punitive damages from the University of Georgia. She left the University without being awarded tenure.

Recent developments in employment law have made it more difficult for faculty to prevail in state and federal courts, particularly by extending cases outside higher education to the college enterprise. Thus, *Hazelwood School District v. Kuhlmeier,* a U.S. Supreme Court decision about school boards' right to control editorial content in a public K–12 school setting, has been cited in college faculty cases such as *Bishop v. Aranov* and *Scallet v. Rosenblum,* while *Waters v. Churchill,* a public hospital case that held that public employees whose speech was "disruptive" could be removed for cause, was cited in *Jeffries v. Harleston.*[25] Professor Leonard Jeffries, removed from his department chair position for his offensive and anti-Semitic speech, had won at trial and upon appeal, but the Supreme Court remanded and ordered the appeals court to review his case in light of *Waters.*

After this review, the appeals court overturned and vacated its earlier opinion.

Collective Bargaining

Since the first college faculties were unionized in the 1960s and 1970s, collective bargaining has become widespread in higher education. Union data indicate that 830 of the 3,284 institutions in the United States (25%) were covered by faculty collective bargaining agreements; figures for nonfaculty college employees were even higher.[26] By 1984, nearly 200,000 faculty (27% of all faculty) were unionized, 83 percent of them in public colleges and 17 percent in private institutions. Unionized public senior colleges totaled 220, private four-year colleges 69, public two-year colleges 524, and private two-year colleges 13. In the last two decades, there were 138 full-time college faculty strikes (or work stoppages), averaging almost 15 days; the longest, 150 days, was at St. John's University in 1966.

Collective bargaining is governed by federal and state laws, although several states also authorize local boards of junior colleges (hence, local laws) to govern labor. Twenty-six states and the District of Columbia have such authorizing legislation. While state or local laws, if they exist, govern the respective state or local institutions, the National Labor Relations Act (NLRA) governs faculty collective bargaining in private institutions. In 1951, the National Labor Relations Board (NLRB) decided that colleges would not fall under NLRB jurisdiction if their mission was "noncommercial in nature and intimately connected with the charitable purposes and education activities."[27] This refusal to assert jurisdiction remained in force until 1970, when the NLRB reversed itself.[28] After reviewing labor law trends in the twenty years that had passed, the NLRB noted, "we are convinced that assertion of jurisdiction is required over those private colleges and universities whose operations have a substantial effect on commerce to insure the orderly, effective, and uniform application of the national labor policy." The board set a $1 million gross revenue test for its standard, a figure that would today cover even the very smallest colleges.

The NLRB decision to extend collective bargaining privileges to Yeshiva University faculty, however, was overruled by the U.S. Supreme Court, which held that faculty were, in effect, supervisory personnel and therefore not covered by the NLRA. This important decision, of course, reversed a decade of organizing activity and struck a heavy blow to faculty unionizing efforts. Since the decision not to entitle Yeshiva faculty to organize collectively, nearly a hundred private colleges have sought to decertify existing faculty unions or have refused to bargain with faculty on *Yeshiva* grounds. Dozens of faculty unions have been decertified, and an untold number of organizing efforts have been thwarted because of the decision or because of the absence of state enabling legislation.

The decision, which affected only private colleges, has recently been applied to public institutions, such as the University of Pittsburgh. The State of Pennsylvania has a labor law (Public Employment Relations Act) that was construed by a Pennsylvania Labor Relations Board hearing examiner to exclude faculty: "As the faculty of the University of Pittsburgh participate with regularity in the essential process which results in a policy proposal and the decision to [hold a union election] and have a responsible role in giving practical effect to insuring the actual fulfillment of policy by concrete measures, the faculty of the university are management level employees within the meaning of PERA and thereby are excluded from PERA's coverage."[29]

In some instances, a court has found that *Yeshiva* criteria were not met and that the faculty did not govern the institution, as in *NLRB v. Cooper Union* and *NLRB v. Florida Memorial College*.[30] Scholars and courts will continue to sort out the consequences of *Yeshiva* and its successors, and unless legislation is enacted at the federal level (to amend the NLRA, for instance) or in the states (to repeal "right to work" legislation), this issue will remain a major bone of contention between faculty and their institutions, both public and private. In addition, in the late 1990s, graduate students, adjunct faculty, and academic staff have successfully negotiated labor contracts, although these remain a small part of the landscape.

Students and the Law

There are many ways to approach the topic of students and the law, but the most interesting and historically based approach is to track the changes in the common law definition of the legal relationship between colleges and college students. This history, which resembles that of faculty and the colleges, began with few rights but now includes many protections. Private institutions afford students fewer rights than public institutions do, and constitutional rights extend only to students in public institutions. Moreover, there is no evidence of statutory development comparable to Title VII or the Equal Pay Act. Although since *Bakke v. Regents of University of California,*[31] students have used Title VI to gain legal standing and student athletes, especially women, have utilized Title IX to litigate for parity in intercollegiate athletic programs, the status of students is largely the province of constitutional protections.

The traditional status of students relative to their colleges was that of child to parent or ward to trustee: in loco parentis, literally, "in the place of the parent." This plenary power gave colleges virtually unfettered authority over students' lives and affairs. Thus, the hapless Miss Anthony of *Anthony v. Syracuse University* could be expelled from school for the simple offense of "not being a typical Syracuse girl," which, the record reveals, meant that she could be expelled from school for smoking a cigarette and sitting on a man's lap. An earlier case, *Gott v. Berea College,* held that colleges could regulate off-campus behavior, while more recent cases up until the 1970s still held that students were substantially under institutional control. The weakening of this doctrine began with *Dixon v. Alabama State Board of Education,* a case involving black students dismissed from a public college for engaging in civil disobedience at a lunch counter. When the court held that they were entitled to a due process hearing before expulsion, it was the first time such rights had been recognized.[32]

The age of majority changed from twenty-one to eighteen years in 1971, and since that time, student rights have either been grounded in tort law (*Tarasoff v. Regents of University of California, Mullins v. Pine Manor College*) or contract theories (*Johnson v. Lincoln Christian College, Ross v. Creighton University*).[33] An area that has developed recently accords protection to students under legislation addressing consumer fraud and deceptive trade practices. While these arguments have been used primarily for tuition refund or proprietary school (for-profit) cases, they have picked up momentum and in some states can provide for damage awards. For example, courts used the theory of fraudulent misrepresentations against a college in *Gonzalez v. North American College of Louisiana* (1988) and consumer statutes in *American Commercial Colleges, Inc. v. Davis* (1991).[34]

The case studies that follow are excellent proxies for the many cases in admissions, affirmative action, and other student issues that might be appropriate for this review. Two case studies involve subjects that are litigated often and represent important societal developments outside the academy. I situate the case studies in their legal and societal context to suggest alternative ways they could have been decided. In law, as in life, it is not always the end result that is important but the reasoning itself.

Admissions and Race

Hopwood v. State of Texas was arguably the most important postsecondary affirmative action case since the U.S. Supreme Court decision in *Bakke,* until the 2003 *University of Michigan* cases, which on balance upheld *Bakke.* The *Bakke* case struck down racial quotas in higher education but allowed race as a discretionary factor in admissions. *Hopwood* is both more and less than *Bakke.* It is more harsh and unyielding in its analysis and result than *Bakke,* but it is also less compelling and intuitive than Justice Lewis Powell's carefully crafted and nuanced plurality opinion, which struck down the use of quotas and set-asides but upheld the use of race as an acceptable criterion in admissions. While some absolutists have since lampooned Powell's balancing act, it served a great purpose in reassuring universities that they still had discretion and latitude in choosing from among their many applicants. *Hopwood,* however, is the opposite. To this panel of the Fifth Circuit, nearly all was black and white (literally, since these justices also seemed to believe that Mexican Americans in Texas never faced any state action to discriminate against them), race or merit, qualified or preferential.

In my reading of *Hopwood,* these justices got it wrong, both in legal terms and in the practicalities of the admissions process. Remarkably, two of the three judges on the Fifth Circuit's panel attempted to overturn *Bakke* or suggested that the Supreme Court abandoned *Bakke:* "The law school places much reliance upon Justice O'Connor's concurrence in *Wygant* for the proposition that Justice Powell's *Bakke* formulation is still viable."[35] They characterize Justice Powell's decision as a "lonely" opinion. Whereas Mr. Powell began his *Bakke* opinion by holding that to seek diversity was clearly "a constitutionally permissible goal for an institution of higher education," this panel opinion stated that, in *Bakke,* "any consideration of race or ethnicity by the law school for the purpose of achieving a diverse student body is not a compelling interest under the Fourteenth Amendment."[36] This opinion is unequivocally wrong.

While it is true that *Wygant, Croson,* and *Adarand* trimmed back the reach of affirmative action, striking down federal minority set-asides unless they are narrowly tailored and, in general, requiring exacting tests for enacting preference programs, *Bakke* remains the law of the land.[37] For instance, Justice O'Connor wrote in *Wygant,* "although its precise contours are uncertain, a state interest in the promotion of racial diversity has been found to be sufficiently 'compelling,' at least in the context of higher education, to support the use of racial considerations in furthering that interest."[38] In *Adarand,* the federal minority set-aside case, O'Connor wrote that, "when race-based action is necessary to further a compelling interest, such action is within the constitutional constraints if it satisfies the 'narrow tailoring' test this Court has set out in previous cases."[39] These opinions hardly sounded like the death knell of well-crafted admissions programs.

As this panel misread *Bakke,* so it misread the admissions process. The panel also did not understand that Cheryl Hopwood wanted affirmative action to apply in her case: she was a mother with a child born with cerebral palsy, and the panel found the case one of "unique background," in which Hopwood's "circumstances would bring a different perspective to the law school." But when she applied, the University of Texas (UT) law school committee did not have this information. Incredibly, Hopwood provided no letters of recommendation and no personal statement outlining her unique background.[40] Yet, she was certain she was displaced from her rightful place by lesser-qualified minorities. Another of the plaintiffs had a letter of recommendation from a professor describing the plaintiff's academic performance at his undergraduate institution as "uneven, disappointing, and mediocre."[41] That such students could score high on an index utilizing only grade point averages and LSAT (Law School Admission Test) scores indicates why law schools look to features other than mere scores. Any law school would be wary of incomplete applications or ones in which letters of recommendation singled out a student for "mediocre" academic achievement.

White beneficiaries of racial practices often assume that they have reached their station in life on their merits and that minority communities have advanced only through bending the rules. Critics of affirmative action and some federal judges believe that higher scores translate into more meritorious applications and that "objective" measures are race neutral. The evidence for this proposition is more

intuitive than verifiable; indeed, a substantial body of research literature and academic practice refutes it. Heavy reliance on test scores
and the near-magical properties accorded them inflate the narrow
use to which these scores should be put. Accepted psychometric principles, testing industry norms of good practice, and research on the
efficacy of testing all suggest more modest claims for test scores,
whether standing alone or combined with other proxy measures. Test
scores are at best imperfect measures to predict first-year grades, and
first-year grades are only a small part of the aptitude for law study.
More important, the same score means different things for different populations. For example, studies consistently show that scores
on standardized tests are less predictive of minority students' first-
year grade-point averages (both underpredicting and overpredicting)
than Anglo students' averages. This finding weakens substantially
the claim by affirmative action critics that the LSAT and other standardized tests should be given more weight in the admissions process.

The plaintiffs and the Fifth Circuit panel acted as if a massive dis-
location of deserving whites had occurred, in which a great many un-
deserving students of color have taken whites' rightful places. The
data contradict this view. The number of white law students today
is at an all-time high: more than 125,000, nearly 82 percent of the
total enrollment in the fifty states and the District Columbia. Blacks
constitute just over 6 percent, and other minorities an even smaller
percentage. For Mexican Americans and Puerto Ricans, among the
fastest growing ethnic minority groups in the country, these enrollments represent an actual numerical and percentage decline from the
early 1980s. In 2000, white students took 79 percent of all the LSAT
exams administered, and 58 percent of all the whites who applied
to law schools were admitted; of other groups, only Asians were admitted in a higher percentage (61%). There is no evidence of slippage
here and no hint of unfairness. No law school can afford to admit unqualified students, as its spaces are precious and competitive. Moreover, in the case of the University of Texas law school, more whites
were taken off the waiting list than the total number of new minorities enrolled. Virtually all the applicants in the pool could achieve at
UT law school, where there is almost no attrition. However, criticism
of affirmative action is likely to continue because the transition to a
more meritorious and heterogeneous legal profession will inevitably
lead to a loss of white privilege, particularly white male privilege.

Current admissions programs at nearly all law schools are more

thorough and better administered than at any point in legal education history. Most admissions officers and financial aid administrators
are capable and dedicated professionals who sift through thousands
of papers and files to assemble as accomplished and diverse a class
as possible. The sheer crush of applicants—Georgetown receives over
ten thousand applications per year—means that admissions officers
can choose among many exceptionally qualified persons. This is a key
point. When they can choose from thousands of applicants, most of
whom have the credentials to do the work, admissions committees are
doing exactly what they are charged to do: assembling a qualified, diverse student body. *Bakke* and *Grutter* sanction this approach, common sense dictates it, and no anecdotal horror stories or isolated allegations can change this central fact.

In June 2003, the U.S. Supreme Court decided two admissions
cases involving the University of Michigan (UM), the undergraduate
program (*Gratz v. Bollinger*), and the law school (*Grutter v. Bollinger*).[42] In *Gratz*, the Court struck down UM's use of a racial point
system in undergraduate admissions by a 6-3 majority. The Court
found the use of a points system was not sufficiently "narrowly tailored" to survive strict scrutiny. University of Michigan had awarded
twenty points (on a one hundred–point scale) to minority applicants,
and the Court ended this particular practice. However, by a 5-4 decision, the Court upheld the full-file review practice of the UM Law
School, which took racial criteria into account for reasons of diversity
(upholding the original rationale of *Bakke*) and to obtain a "critical
mass" of minority students. This opinion has become the key decision
as many schools follow the full-file review of the *Grutter* case and now
have the imprimatur of the Supreme Court to use race as allowed in
the *Bakke* decision more than twenty-five years ago.

Race is a fugue that plays throughout U.S. society, including higher
education. In the 1990s, there has been a societal backlash against
affirmative action, as evidenced by a major political party's platform
plank against the principles, California voters' ballot initiative to out-
law affirmative action in state services and employment, the University of California regents' action to overturn admissions affirmative
action, later rescinded, and congressional action to dismantle a number of federal education programs. In addition, there is a new and resurgent nativism evident, as in California Ballot Initiative 197 to deny
undocumented alien children public education (struck down by the
California courts) and in federal initiatives to deny benefits to legal

permanent residents. As society has become more conservative on affirmative action, so too have the courts and legislatures. The *Grutter* decision will likely lead to other state ballot initiatives.

Faculty Rights versus Student Rights`

In several important legal cases, faculty and student rights have come into direct conflict.[43] One involved prayer in the public college classroom, in which the court precluded the practice, finding that the Establishment Clause mandated that the college discontinue the practice. Another religion case, *Bishop v. Aranov,* pitted a public university against an exercise physiology professor who invited students in his class to judge him by Christian standards and to admonish him if he deviated from these tenets.[44] The appeals court held that colleges exercised broad authority over pedagogical issues and that "a teacher's speech can be taken as directly and deliberately representative of the school." This troubling logic, which reached the correct decision to admonish the professor, did so for the wrong reasons and rested upon the erroneous ground that faculty views are those of the institution. The court could have more parsimoniously and persuasively decided the same result by analyzing the peculiar role of religion injected into secular fields of study, especially when the teacher invites a particular religious scrutiny.

In another course, a studio art teacher was dismissed for his habit of not supervising his students; he argued that this technique taught students to act more independently. The court disagreed that his behavior was a protected form of professorial speech, as did a court that considered a professor's extensive use of profanity in the classroom. In a similar view, a basketball coach, dismissed for angrily calling his players "niggers" on the court to inspire them, found an unsympathetic court, which held that the remarks were not a matter of public concern and, therefore, not protected speech. A white professor also lost his position at a black college for making a remark that was interpreted by students as racist and for refusing to go back to teaching until the college administrators removed a student he considered disruptive.[45]

These and other cases have made it clear that students have some rights in a classroom, while well-known cases such as *Levin v. Harleston* and *Silva v. University of New Hampshire* have made it clear that courts still protect professors' ideas, however controversial (*Levin*), and teaching styles, however offensive (*Silva*).[46] A proper configuration of professorial academic freedom is resilient enough to resist extremes from without or within, to fend off the New Hampshire legislative inquiry of *Sweezy* and the proselytizing of *Bishop*.[47] In this view, professors have wide-ranging discretion to undertake their research and to formulate teaching methods in their classrooms and laboratories. However, this autonomy is, within broad limits, contingent upon traditional norms of peer review, codes of ethical behavior, and institutional standards. In the most favorable circumstances, these norms will be subject to administrative guidelines for ensuring requisite due process and fairness. Even the highly optimistic and altruistic 1915 AAUP Declaration of Principles holds that "individual teachers should [not] be exempt from all restraints as to the matter or manner of their utterances, either within or without the university."[48] In short, academic freedom does not give carte blanche to professors but, rather, vests faculty with the establishment and enforcement of standards of behavior, which are to be reasonably and appropriately applied in evaluations. Although I attempt to persuade that the academic common law is highly normative, contextual, and faculty driven, I do not lose sight of the range of acceptable practices and extraordinary heterogeneity found in classroom styles.

Additionally, persuasive research has emerged to show that persons trained in different academic disciplines view pedagogy differently. John Braxton and his colleagues summarize how these norms operate across disciplines:

> Personal controls that induce individual conformity to teaching norms are internalized to varying degrees through the graduate school socialization process. Graduate school attendance in general and doctoral study in particular are regarded as a powerful socialization experience. The potency of this process lies not only in the development of knowledge, skills, and competencies but also in the inculcation of norms, attitudes, and values. This socialization process entails the total learning situation. . . . Through these interpersonal relationships with faculty, values, knowledge, and skills are inculcated.[49]

Moreover, they are all inculcated differently. To grab a student and put my hands on his chest would be extraordinarily wrong in my immigration law class, but it could happen regularly and appropriately in a voice class, physical education course, or acting workshop. Discussing one's religious views in an exercise physiology class may be inappropriate, but certainly it is appropriate in a comparative religion course. Discussions of sexuality, which would be salacious in a legal ethics course, would be appropriately central to a seminar in human sexuality. Each academic field has evolved its own norms and conventions.

However, courts are not in the business of contextualizing pedagogical disputes, as is evident from *Mincone v. Nassau County Community College,* a case that wended its awkward way through the judicial system.[50] Although *Mincone* has forbears in other decisions, it is sufficient to make my points: if colleges do not police themselves, others will; disputes between teachers and pupils are on the rise; and poor fact patterns and sloppy practices will lead to substantial external control over the classroom. One other thread is that it arose in a two-year community college, making it likely that the results will be taken by subsequent judges as directly pertinent for higher education in a way that K–12 cases (notwithstanding *Hazelwood*'s leaching into postsecondary cases) have not been held to be controlling. Given the overlap with the mission of senior institutions and their usual transfer function, two-year colleges will not be easily distinguished. If a K–12 case is not in my favor, I can always try to convince a judge to limit it to the elementary/secondary sector; I will not be able to muster such a finely graded distinction in a postcompulsory world, even though two-year colleges are, on the average, more authoritarian and administrator driven than are four-year colleges. The widespread use of part-time and non-tenure-track faculty makes academic freedom more problematic at community colleges, where faculty do not always have the security or autonomy to develop traditional protections of tenure and academic freedom.

This is the second round of a case that began as a request for public records, in this instance, course materials for Physical Education 251 (PER 251), "Family Life and Human Sexuality." The course is taught in several sections to nearly three thousand students each year, and in *Mincone,* a senior citizen auditor (enrolled under terms of a free, noncredit program for adults over sixty-five years of age), who reviewed the course materials before he took the class (to be offered in summer 1995), sued to enjoin the course from using the materials or from using federal funds to "counsel abortion in the PER 251 course materials." Mincone, the representative of a co-plaintiff party, the Organization of Senior Citizens and Retailers (OSCAR), filed in May 1995 a lawsuit with eight causes of action: PER 251, under these theories, violates the strict religious neutrality required of public institutions by the New York State constitution; burdens and violates state law concerning the free exercise clause of the New York State constitution by "disparagement" of Judeo-Christian faiths and by promoting the religious teaching of Eastern religions with regard to sexuality; violates the federal First Amendment; violates the plaintiffs' civil rights guaranteed under Sec. 1983; teaches behavior that violates Sec. 130.00 of the New York State Penal Law (sodomy statutes); violates federal law concerning religious neutrality by singling out one "correct view of human sexuality"; disregards the duty to warn students of course content so they can decide whether or not to enroll in the course; endangers minors who may be enrolled in the course; and violates federal law enjoining abortion counseling.

This broad frontal attack on the course is virtually without precedent, as the plaintiff was not even enrolled in the course for credit and enjoined the course even before the term began and before he took the course as an auditor. But the wide-ranging claims, particularly those that allege religious bias, are so vague and poorly formulated that it is difficult to believe they will survive.

If we begin with the premise that faculty members have the absolute right, within the limits of germaneness and institutional practice, to assign whatever text they wish, subject only to the text being appropriate for the course and to academic custom, then professors can pick whichever texts seem best for their courses. Sometimes, this means a compromise, as in using a central text supplemented by the extra materials they might wish were in the basic text (not everyone can or is inclined to write their own book). Therefore, materials could be assigned that are a compromise, or materials may be not assigned because they are inappropriate. Surely, for a course known to be a lightning rod (by the earlier suit), sex education and physiology faculty carefully chose the filmstrips and materials; this is the contextual and professional judgment that my theory requires. As AAUP general counsel, I would have no qualms in defending the course materials: they were picked by professionals with considerable expertise in this field; the course is widely accepted and regularly fully enrolled; it does what it sets out to do: expose students to wide-ranging issues of sexuality; and the materials clearly put students on notice what the course covers. Except for the personal and moral objections of the plaintiffs concerning the materials, this course is generically like any course.

Context is all, as is professional authority to determine how it will be taught.

Cases like this are fraught with implications for higher education practice, especially for teacher behavior. In *Cohen v. San Bernardino Community College,* the District Court could have gone in the opposite direction, as it had for Professors Silva and Levin, by stressing their academic freedom rather than by balancing the competing interests.[51] However, by characterizing the issues as ones of classroom control and students' learning environment, Professor Cohen's interests are trumped, at least with the admonishment. (His orders were to do essentially as Professor Silva was ordered by the University of New Hampshire to do: take counseling, alter his class style, etc.) He had been admonished to stop teaching from *Hustler* and other "pornographic" materials in his remedial English class. And the court did suggest that the admonishment was mild: "A case in which a professor is terminated or directly censored presents a far different balancing question." But does it? Can there be any doubt that Cohen considers himself "directly censored" by the formal complaint of one student? Was Levin censored by City University of New York's "shadow section"? Is reading *Hustler* letters a good idea for a remedial English class?

Additionally, there is the issue of a solution to the conundrum of faculty autonomy and sexual harassment jurisprudence. The difficulty is acknowledging that a classroom can be a hostile environment in some instances. In the AAUP, we have hammered out a compromise attempt to preserve faculty autonomy and to acknowledge and deal with an environment so hostile that it can stifle learning opportunities. The AAUP Proposed Statement of Policy for Sexual Harassment[52] reads as follows:

> It is the policy of this institution that no member of the academic community may sexually harass another. Sexual advances, requests for sexual favors, and other speech or conduct of a sexual nature constitute sexual harassment when:
>
> 1. Such advances or requests are made under circumstances implying that one's response might affect academic or personnel decisions that are subject to the influence of the person making the proposal; or
>
> 2. Such speech or conduct is directed against another and is either abusive or severely humiliating, or persists despite the objection of the person targeted by the speech or conduct; or

3. Such speech or conduct is reasonably regarded as offensive and substantially impairs the academic or work opportunity of students, colleagues, or co-workers. If it takes place in the teaching context, it must also be persistent, pervasive, and not germane to the subject matter.

The academic setting is distinct from the workplace in that wide latitude is required for professional judgment in determining the appropriate content and presentation of academic material. In our search for the perfect, clarifying epiphany, this proposed policy falls short: What is "severely humiliating"? Is it more than "humiliating"? How much more? How long does harassment have to persist in order to be found "persistent"? Isn't the classroom a "workplace" for faculty?

To me, in interpreting academic standards, it is not surprising that things work so badly but, rather, that they work so well. My own experiences as a student and as a professor lead me to believe that any comprehensive theory of professorial authority to determine "how it shall be taught" must incorporate a feedback mechanism for students to take issue, voice complaints, and point out remarks or attitudes that may be insensitive or disparaging. At a minimum, faculty should encourage students to speak privately with them to identify uncomfortable situations. Professor Bishop asked his students to point out inconsistencies between his Christian perspectives and his lifestyle. This is excessive and could itself provoke anxiety on the part of both Christian and non-Christian students. But a modest attempt to avoid stigmatizing words and examples is certainly in order for teachers, and schools should have in place some mechanism to address these issues. I cringe when exams consign "Jose", "Maria," or "Rufus" to criminal questions or when in-class hypotheticals use "illegal aliens" or sexist examples and stereotypes to illustrate legal points. Such misuse may be especially prevalent in fact patterns involving criminal activities, such as rape and consent. Students have a right to expect more thoughtful pedagogical practices.

Finally, there is the issue of grading, a hotly contested arena. For years, I have told my students that no grade has ever been overturned by a court, so they should not try and overturn mine. However, that was before *Sylvester v. Texas Southern University*. *Sylvester* is, arguably, the first federal case where a grade is overturned. But the circumstances are so bizarre that no one can really insist that the grade was "properly awarded." Therein lies a very odd tale, one that demonstrates just how obstinate a faculty member can be and how badly a mistake can be compounded without proper faculty or administrative leadership.

Karen Sylvester, a 2L at Thurgood Marshall Law School (TSU) at Texas Southern University in Houston, was at the top of her class, having received almost all A's. In the spring of 1994, she completed Professor James Bullock's Wills and Trusts class and was awarded a D. This had the effect of dropping her from first in her class, whereas a C or a "pass" would have kept her in first place.

First, she protested orally to the associate dean, who did not respond. The next semester, she protested in writing and did so several times without receiving any response from the professor or the law school administration. Bullock was later asked to produce her exam book, and he said it had been lost. After a more thorough search, it was discovered. She had appealed to the law school's oversight committee, a standing committee that included faculty and student members, that reviewed such disputes. Nearly a year later, when she was scheduled to graduate, Sylvester sought to enjoin the graduation ceremony until her grade and its effect on her rank-in-class could be resolved. TSU promised the judge that if she allowed the ceremony to go forward, it would review the case and adjust her standing accordingly.

What follows is not pretty. The judge found that "Bullock was defiant." The court ordered him to meet with the student to review the grade. She returned to Houston from Dallas, where she learned that Bullock either had no answer key or had not used one, so he could not review the exam properly. Angered, the judge ordered him to pay her travel expenses and to attend all subsequent meetings scheduled on this issue. The record tersely records that "he did neither." At the next court session, the judge sent marshals to fetch the missing professor, who admitted that he had received proper notice.

The issue was punted back to the law school committee, which decided — contrary to its published regulations — that students could not serve on the committee because of privacy issues. The committee, without its student members, decided that the review had been adequate and that "no inconsistencies were found." Yet, one member told the court that the committee had been informed by Bullock that the correct answer to the essay question had been "yes." The judge, incredulous that this defiance had been ratified by the committee, threw the book at them.

He wrote in a remarkable and sweeping voice, "Governmental actions cannot be arbitrary. Having no basis for comparison is arbitrary. Changing the committee on the chairman's malicious whim is arbitrary. Once the committee had been changed from the official, university-constituted form it was nothing but a mob." He then ordered that she be given a "pass" for the course and that she be listed as covaledictorian, extraordinary actions needed to provide an "equitable adjustment." We now know the contours of bad faith in awarding a grade and the inexcusable behavior that leads critics to complain about tenured professors such as Bullock.[53]

Policy Implications and Conclusion

If events continue as in the past, there can be no doubt that higher education will become increasingly legalized, by the traditional means of legislation, regulation, and litigation as well as the growing areas of informal lawmaking, such as ballot initiatives, insurance carrier policies, and commercial or contract law in research. This cascade will shower down upon institutions, each leaving its residue in the form of administrative responsibility for acknowledging and implementing the responsibilities.

Understanding how legal initiatives become policy, particularly complex regulatory or legislative initiatives, should contribute greatly to improving administrative implementation of legal change on campus. Even with this modest review, it is clear that some legal policies will be more readily adopted than others. It is also clear that academic policy makers have substantial opportunities and resources to shape legal policy and smooth the way for legal changes on campus. Of course, no one can be expected to endorse all legal initiatives with equal enthusiasm or to administer them as if they were all high institutional priorities. Not all will be. Some will be implemented only grudgingly. However, understanding the implementation of legal change will influence the amount of policy output produced, the distribution of policy outputs, and the overall extent of compliance achieved.

The considerable autonomy and deference accorded higher education often translate into institutions designing their own compliance regimes for legislative and litigative change, and increased understanding of this complex legal phenomenon should increase this independence. As no small matter, higher education officials could begin to convince legislators that mandated legal change has a better chance of achieving the desired effects if institutions are allowed to design their own compliance and implementation strategies. This role could ease the sting so many campuses feel when another regulatory program is thrust upon them, or when they lose an important case in court, as happened at the University of Texas in *Hopwood v. State of Texas*. It could also lead higher education officials to seek reasonable compliance rather than exemption, which occurs often in practice. As higher education becomes more reliant upon government support and as colleges offer themselves for hire as participants in commercial ventures and as social change agents, legal restrictions are sure to follow. Understanding the consequences of legalization is a first step toward controlling our fate.

This and the other chapters in this book show how interdependent the higher education system is and reveal why we need to adapt to the times. Our timeless values, such as academic freedom, tenure, institutional autonomy, and due process are in danger of being legislated or litigated away, if we do not remain vigilant and alert and if we do not self-police. There are many police outside the academy all too willing to do it if we do not.

NOTES

1. Lewis Thomas, *The Youngest Science: Notes of a Medicine Watcher* (New York: Viking, 1983); Paul Goodman, *The Community of Scholars* (New York: Free Press, 1962); John Millett, *The Academic Community* (New York: McGraw-Hill, 1962); Herbert Stroup, *Bureaucracy in Higher Education* (New York: Free Press, 1966); Victor Baldridge, *Power and Conflict in the University* (New York: Wiley, 1971); Burton R. Clark, *The Higher Education System* (Berkeley: University of California Press, 1983); Clark Kerr, *The Uses of the University* (Cambridge, MA: Harvard University Press, 1982); Randall Collins, *The Credential Society* (New York: Academic, 1979); Harry T. Edwards, *Higher Education and the Unholy Crusade against Governmental Regulation* (Cambridge, Mass.: Institute for Educational Management, 1980); Paolo Freire, *Education for Critical Consciousness* (New York: Seabury, 1973).

2. *Coffee v. Rice University,* 408 S.W.2d 269 (1966).

3. *Shapiro v. Columbia Union,* 576 S.W.2d 310 (1979).

4. *U.S. on behalf of U.S. Coast Guard v. Cerio,* 831 F.Supp. 530 (E.D. Va. 1993).

5. *Fountain Gate Ministries, Inc., v. City of Plano,* 654 S.W.2d 841 (Tex. App. 5 Dist. 1983).

6. *Hacker v. Hacker,* 522 N.Y.S. 768 (Supp. 1987).

7. *Beth Rochel v. Bennett,* 825 F.2d 478 (D.C. Cir. 1987); *City of Morgantown v. West Virginia Board of Regents,* 354 S.E.2d 616 (W. Va. 1987).

8. *Trustees of Dartmouth v. Woodward,* 4 Wheaton (U.S.) 518 (1819); *Krynicky v. University of Pittsburgh,* 742 F.2d 94 (1984).

9. *Powe v. Miles,* 407 F.2d 73 (1968).

10. Three exceptions have been created by the Supreme Court to limit a state's sovereign immunity: waiver, abrogation, and the *ex parte Young* exceptions. The first exception to the doctrine of sovereign immunity occurs when a state waives its immunity. A state's waiver of sovereign immunity may subject it to suit in state court, but it is not enough, absent some other indicator of intent, to subject the state to suit in federal court. A state can also waive its Eleventh Amendment immunity against suits in federal court by other clearly stated means, such as successfully moving a federal case to state court. Congress can abrogate a state's sovereign immunity by exercising its powers under section 5 of the Fourteenth Amendment. Since the 1996 decision in *Seminole Tribe of Florida v. Florida,* the Court has begun to limit Congress's rights to abrogate a state's sovereign immunity. Thus, Congress has the power to abrogate a state's sovereign immunity when it is acting pursuant to its Fourteenth Amendment powers under section 5. However, the Court requires the Congress to act unambiguously when doing so. For an excellent summary of these issues, see Brian Snow and William Thro, "The Significance of Blackstone's Understanding of Sovereign Immunity for America's Public Institutions of Higher Education," *Journal of College and University Law,* 28 (2002): 97–128. Snow and Thro have summarized the *ex parte Young* exemption: "This doctrine holds that sovereign immunity does not bar federal court actions against individual state officers . . . seeking (1) declaratory judgment that the state officer is currently violating federal law and (2) an injunction forcing the state officer to conform his current conduct to federal law." This exception does not apply to violations that occurred in the past, rather it "applies only where there is an on-going violation of federal law, which can be cured by declaratory or injunctive relief."

11. *Fenn College v. Nance,* 210 N.E.2d 418 (1965); *Nasson College v. New England Association of Schools and Colleges,* 16 B.C.D. 1299 (1988).

12. *NCAA v. University of Oklahoma,* 488 U.S.85 (1984); *U.S. v. Brown University,* 5 F.3d 658 (3d Cir. 1993).

13. *Rochel Beth Seminary v. Bennett,* 825 F.2d 478 (D.C. Cir. 1987); *Marjorie Webster Junior College v. Middle States Association,* 139 U.S.App. D.C. 217, 432 F.2d 650 (1970).

14. *NLRB v. Yeshiva University,* 444 U.S.672 (1980).

15. Lelia Helms, "Patterns of Litigation in Postsecondary Education: A Caselaw Study," *Journal of College and University Law* 14 (1987): 99–110; Margaret Lam, *Patterns of Litigation at Institutions of Higher Education in Texas, 1878–1978* (Houston: IHELG, 1988).

16. William Kaplin and Barbara Lee, *The Law of Higher Education* (San Francisco: Jossey-Bass, 1995); Matthew Finkin, *The Case for Tenure* (Ithaca: Cornell University Press, 1996); George LaNoue and Barbara Lee, *Academics in Court* (Ann Arbor: University of Michigan Press, 1985); Patricia Spacks, ed., *Advocacy in the Classroom* (New York: St. Martin's, 1996).

17. *Perry v. Sindermann,* 408 U.S.593 (1972); *Board of Regents v. Roth,* 408 U.S.564 (1972).

18. *Wellner v. Minnesota State Junior College Board,* 487, F.2d 153 (1973).

19. *State ex rel. McLemore v. Clarksville School of Theology,* 636 S.W.2d 706 (1982).

20. *Hill v. Talladega College,* 502 So.2d 735 (Ala. 1987); *Honore v. Douglas,* 833 F.2d 565 (5th Cir. 1987); *Spuler v. Pickar,* 958 F.2d 103 (5th Cir. 1992); *Lewis v. Loyola University of Chicago,* 500 N.E.2d 47 (Ill. App. 1 Dist. 1996).

21. *Scott v. University of Delaware,* 455 F.Supp. 1102 (1978).

22. *Faro v. NYU,* 502 F.2d 1229 (1974).

23. *Clark v. Claremont Graduate Center,* 8 Cal. Rptr. 2d 151 (Cal. App. 2 Dist. 1992).

24. *Sweeney v. Board of Trustees of Keene State College,* 569 F.2d 169 (1978); *Kunda v. Muhlenberg College,* 463 F.Supp. 294 (E.D. Pa. 1978); *Mecklenberg v. Montana State Board of Regents,* 13 EPD 11, 438 (1976); *Kemp v. Irvin,* 651 F.Supp. 495 (N.D. Ga. 1986).

25. *Hazelwood School District v. Kuhlmeier,* 108 S.Ct. 562 (1988); *Bishop v. Aranov,* 926 F.2d 1066 (11th Cir. 1991); *Scallet v. Rosenblum,* unpublished opinion, U.S. Court of Appeals, 4th Cir., Jan. 29, 1997 (C.A. 94-16-c); *Waters v. Churchill,* 114 S.Ct.1878 (1994); *Jeffries v. Harleston,* 828 F.Supp. 1066 (S.D.N.Y. 1993) 21 F.3d 1238 (2d Cir. 1994), vac. and rem. 115 S.Ct.502 (1995) vac. and rev'd, 52 F.3d 9 (2d Cir. 1995), cert den. 116 S.Ct.173 (1995).

26. Data from Joel Douglas, "Professors on Strike: An Analysis of Two Decades of Faculty Work Stoppages, 1960–1985," *Labor Lawyer* 4 (1988): 87–101.

27. *Trustees of Columbia University,* 29 LRRM 1098 (1951).

28. *Cornell University,* 183 NLRB 329 (1970).

29. *United Faculty v. University of Pittsburgh,* PLRB No. PERAR-84–53W (March 11, 1987).

30. *NLRB v. Cooper Union,* 78 3 F.2d 29 (2d Cir. 1985); *NLRB v. Florida Memorial College,* 820 F.2d 1182 (11th Cir. 1987).

31. *Bakke v. Regents of University of California,* 438 U.S.265 (1978).

32. *Anthony v. Syracuse University* 231 N.Y.S.435 (1928); *Gott v. Berea,* 156 Ky.376, 161 S.W.204 (1913); *Dixon v. Alabama State Board of Education,* 294 F.2d 150 (1961).

33. *Tarasoff v. Regents of University of California,* 551 F.2d 334 (1976); *Mullins v. Pine Manor College,* 449 N.E.2d 331 (Mass. 1983); *Johnson v. Lincoln Christian College,* 501 N.E.2d 1380 (Ill. App. 4 Dist. 1986); *Ross v. Creighton,* 957 F.2d 410 (7th Cir. 1992).

34. *Gonzalez v. North American College of Louisiana,* 700 F.Supp. 362

(S.D. Tex. 1988); *American Commercial Colleges, Inc., v. Davis,* 821 S.W.2d 450 (Tex. App.-Eastland 1991).

35. *Hopwood v. State of Texas,* 78 F.3d 945 (5th Cir. 1996) (reviewing constitutional standards). For a review of this and other higher education cases, see Michael A. Olivas, *The Law and Higher Education* (Durham, NC: Carolina Academic Press, 1997) and 2003 supplement.

36. Ibid., 948.

37. *Wygant v. Jackson Board of Education,* 476 U.S.267 (1986); *City of Richmond v. Croson,* 488 U.S.469 (1989); *Adarand v. Pena,* 115 S.Ct.2097 (1995).

38. *Wygant v. Jackson Board of Education,* 476 U.S.267, 286 (1986).

39. *Adarand v. Pena,* 115 S.Ct.2097, 2117 (1995).

40. *Hopwood v. State of Texas,* 78 F.3d 946 (5th Cir. 1996).

41. *Hopwood v. State of Texas,* 861 F.Supp. 551, 566–67 (W.D. Tex. 1994).

42. *Gratz v. Bollinger,* 123 S.Ct.2411 (2003); *Grutter v. Bollinger,* 123 S.Ct. 2325 (2003).

43. Michael A. Olivas, "Professorial Academic Freedom: Second Thoughts on the 'Third Essential Freedom,' " *Stanford Law Review* 45 (1993): 1835–58.

44. *Bishop v. Aranov,* 926 F.2d 1066 (11th Cir. 1991).

45. *McConnell v. Howard University,* 818 F.2d 58 (D.C. Cir. 1987).

46. *Levin v. Harleston,* 770 F.Supp. 895 (S.D.N.Y. 1991), aff'd in relevant part, vac. on other grounds, 996 F.2d 85 (2d Cir. 1992); *Silva v. University of New Hampshire.*

47. *Sweezy v. New Hampshire,* 354 U.S.234 (1957); *Bishop v. Aranov,* 926 F.2d 1066 (11th Cir. 1991).

48. "General Report of the Committee on Academic Freedom and Academic Tenure," *AAUP Bulletin* 17 (1915): 1, reprinted in *Law and Contemporary Problems* 393 (1990): 53.

49. John M. Braxton, Alan Bayer, and Martin Finkelstein, "Teaching Performance Norms in Academia," *Research in Higher Education* 33 (1992): 533–70, quotation on 535–36.

50. *Mincone v. Nassau County Community College,* 923 F.Supp. 398 (E.D.N.Y. 1996). See also *Gheta v. NCCC,* 33 F.Supp.2nd 179 (E.D.N.Y. 1999).

51. *Cohen v. San Bernadino Valley Community College,* 883 F.Supp. 1407 (C.D. Cal. 1995), rev'd in part, 92 F.3d 968 (9th Cir. 1996).

52. American Association of University Professors, "AAUP Proposed Statement of Policy for Sexual Harassment," in *Policy Documents and Reports* (Washington, D.C.: AAUP, 1995), 171.

53. *Sylvester v. Texas Southern University,* 957 F.Supp. 944 (S.D. Tex. 1997).

Chapter Nine

The Hidden Hand

External Constituencies
and Their Impact

Fred F. Harcleroad and Judith S. Eaton

Postsecondary institutions have endured in the United States for over three and one-half centuries. All except those established recently have been modified over the years and have changed greatly in response to pressures from external forces. Particularly in the last century and a half, literally thousands of diverse institutions have opened their doors, only to close when they were no longer needed by sufficient students or the public and private constituencies that founded and supported them. Those in existence today are the survivors, the institutions that adapted to the needs of their constituencies.

The varied external forces affecting postsecondary education in the United States have grown out of our unique three-sector system of providing goods and services for both collective consumption and private use. First, the *voluntary enterprise sector,* composed of millions of independent nonprofit organizations, often has initiated efforts to provide such things as schools, hospitals, bridges, libraries, environmental controls, and public parks. They are protected by constitutional rights to peaceful assembly, free speech, and petition for redress of grievances. These formidable protections plus their record of useful service led to their being nontaxable, with contributions to them being tax free. Second, the *public enterprise group,* composed of all local, state, and federal governments, administers the laws that hold our society together. Third, the *private enterprise sector,* com-posed of profit-seeking business and commerce, provides much of the excess wealth needed to support the other two sectors. This pluralis-tic and diverse set of organizations implements the basic ideas behind our federated republic.

Our constitution provides for detailed separation of powers at the federal level between the presidency, the Congress, and the judiciary. The Tenth Amendment establishes the states as governments with "general" powers, delegating "limited" powers to the federal govern-ment. Education is not a delegated power and therefore is reserved to the states, whose constitutions often treat it almost as a fourth branch of government. In addition, the Tenth Amendment reserves "general" powers to citizens, who operate through their own vol-untary organizations, their state governments, or state-authorized private enterprise. Consequently, only a few higher education institu-tions are creations of the federal government (mostly military institu-tions, to provide for the common defense); more than 99 percent are creations of states, voluntary organizations, or profit-seeking busi-nesses.

Both of the oldest institutions in the country, Harvard (established in 1636) and the College of William and Mary (established in 1693), have closed for different reasons but opened up again when changes were made. Harvard closed for what would have been its second year (in 1639–40), after Nathaniel Eaton, its first head, was dismissed for cruelty to students and stealing college funds. After being closed for the year, government officials determined that the Massachusetts Bay Colony still needed a college to train ministers and to advance learning. A new president, Henry Dunster, reopened the college in 1640, and by changing regularly, and sometimes dramatically, the col-lege has remained in operation ever since. Two small examples illus-trate this process. As Massachusetts grew and secularized, ministerial training at Harvard became only one function, so it was placed in a separate divinity school. Also, by the late 1700s required instruction in Hebrew was replaced by student choice, a beginning of our current elective system.

William and Mary was the richest of the colonial colleges, sup-ported by the Commonwealth of Virginia, which included income from taxes on tobacco, skins, and hides. Nevertheless, the college had to make many adaptations in order to remain politically supported.

For example, after the Revolution, in 1779, it dropped its chair of divinity and established the nation's first professorship of law and police. The college closed during the 1861–65 Civil War, reopened briefly, but closed again in 1881. It eventually reopened in 1888, when the state agreed to make it a state-supported institution if it would become Virginia's main teacher education college. Thus, it changed from being essentially a private college operated by the Episcopal Church, an excellent example of a government taking over a private institution to meet the developing needs of the society as a whole. Interaction of this type between government and private constituencies is a singular characteristic of the democratic republic established in the United States, and it is important to consider in studying the relationships of colleges and universities to their external environment.

External groups, associations, and agencies from all three sectors impact on the institutions of postsecondary education. This diverse group of external organizations includes everything from athletic conferences and alumni associations to employer associations and unions (or organized faculty groups that function as unions). Of course, the corporate boards that administer all of the private colleges, universities, and institutes authorized to operate in the respective states belong in this group. Their power to determine institutional policies is clear and well known. However, many other voluntary associations can and do have significant effects on specific institutions or units of the institutions. This is particularly true in the funding of colleges and universities, since the American system is based on income from varied sources. As states have decreased the proportion coming from their budgets for both public and private institutions, other sources and ways to economize have become increasingly critical in the twenty-first century. External associations can play an important role in providing badly needed alternative funding and/or more effective operational use of existing funds. Five of these—private foundations, institutionally based and other voluntary associations, voluntary accrediting associations, voluntary consortia, and regional compacts—are described below in some detail, indicating their backgrounds, their development, and their possible impact on institutional autonomy and academic freedom.

Private Foundations

The beginnings of private foundations in the United States took place over two centuries ago.[1] Benjamin Franklin led in the establishment, in Philadelphia, of a number of voluntary sector organizations, including the American Philosophical Society in 1743, an association with many foundation characteristics. In 1800 the Magdalen Society of Philadelphia, possibly the first private foundation in the United States, was established as a perpetual trust to assist "unhappy females who had been seduced from the paths of virtue." In the 1890s and early 1900s, long before the federal income tax became legal due to the Sixteenth Amendment to the U.S. Constitution, the Carnegie foundations, followed shortly by the Rockefeller foundations, set a pattern that continues to this day. These foundations established a high standard of operations and service. Few academics realize that their current TIAA pensions were developed and are currently administered by a foundation resulting from Andrew Carnegie's feeling of public service responsibility. Decades before such "contributions" became tax deductible, he gave several million dollars to set up the first pension fund for college teachers.

Today, private foundations vary greatly in form, purpose, size, function, and constituency. Some are corporate in nature, many are trusts, and others are only associations. Many of them can affect postsecondary institutions through their choice of areas to support. They can be classified into five types as follows: (1) community foundations, often citywide or regional, which make a variety of bequests or gifts (local postsecondary institutions often can count on some support from such foundations for locally related projects), (2) family or personal foundations, often with limited purposes, (3) special purpose foundations (including such varied examples as the Harvard Glee Club and a fund set up to provide every girl at Bryn Mawr with one baked potato at each meal), (4) company foundations established to channel corporate giving through one main source, and (5) national independent foundations (including many of the large, well-known foundations, such as (Carnegie, Rockefeller, Ford, Lilly, Kellogg, Mellon, and Johnson, plus more recent ones such as Murdock, Hewlett, Packard, Lumina, and the Pew Trusts). The number of grant-making foundations, estimated at sixty thousand in 2004–05, grows constantly. Their total assets are variously estimated at 420 billion to 600 billion dollars, and their yearly awards range from 32–35 billion dollars yearly. A significant portion of these funds go regularly to higher education. A recent special report from the Foundation Center[2] stressed the wide range of their fields of interest and their increasing attraction as a valuable resource for institutions with budget problems.

This special report also stressed that the constant change in the interests of foundations reflected changing needs of the society and higher education's responses. For example, with more than three-fourths of lower division students now in community colleges, increasingly grants go to planning these colleges' programs and articulation arrangements between two- and four-year institutions. At the same time, grants continue in such diverse areas as international education, student exchange, medical education, public health, art, minority access, rural development, theater, dance, and vocational education. And the proportion of funding from these sources grows constantly as other sources diminish.

Foundations, especially those in the national independent category, by their choice of areas to finance entice supposedly autonomous colleges to do things they might not do otherwise. Institutional change continues to be a prime goal of foundations, as it has been for most of the past century. Thus, although their grants still provide a relatively small proportion of the total financing of institutions, they have had significant effects on program development and even operations. Grants from foundations have been instrumental in the establishment of new academic fields such as microbiology and anthropology and the redirection of the fields of business and the education of teachers.

An excellent, somewhat different, example of a valuable foundation-supported activity during the first decade of the twenty-first century is the National Policy Center for Public Policy and Higher Education, which was supported initially by the Pew Trusts and the Ford Foundation; it provides numerous useful studies for decision making. The National Policy Center recognizes the importance of state responsibility for chartering, regulating, and supporting higher education of most colleges and universities, and it published a "report card" on each of the states in six areas: (1) student preparation, (2) participation (opportunities to enroll), (3) affordability, (4) student completion of programs, (5) benefits to the states from an educated population, and (6) student learning. Titled *Measuring Up*, these reports for 2000, 2002, 2004, and 2006 have been funded by several additional foundations and produced vital information on which to base state efforts to improve opportunity in, and operations of, their colleges and universities. Other key publications include *Losing Ground* (in-depth data on affordability) and *State Policy and Community College-Baccalaureate Transfer.* These data, and many others from this foundation-supported center, provide useful beginnings of benchmarks, or social indicators, for improving higher education in the United States.

It is important to stress, however, that private foundations affect institutional freedom only if the institutions voluntarily accept the funds for the purposes prescribed by the foundation. The redirection of programs and even of private institutional goals is possible and has occurred on occasion. Nevertheless, the private foundation model has been so successful that government has adopted it in forming and funding such agencies as the National Science Foundation, the Fund for the Improvement of Postsecondary Education, and the National Endowments for the Arts and for the Humanities. Clearly, private foundations have been and undoubtedly will continue to be important external forces affecting postsecondary education.

Institutionally Based and Other Voluntary Associations

Voluntary membership organizations of this type are almost infinite in possible number.[3] The 2003 *Higher Education Directory* (HED), a compendium of higher education associations, institutions, and government agencies, lists 298 of these organizations. Although formed by institution officials for their own purposes, the associations often end up having indirect or direct effects on the institutions themselves. The American Council on Education, probably the major policy advocate for postsecondary education at the national level, plays a critical coordinative role as an umbrella organization, composed of a wide spectrum of institutions. Other major national institutional organizations include the Association of American Colleges and Universities, the American Association of Community Colleges, the American Association of State Colleges and Universities, the Association of American Universities, the Council of Independent Colleges, the National Association of Independent Colleges and Universities, and the National Association of State Universities and Land-Grant Colleges. The American Council on Education also coordinates a larger group, of fifty higher educational associations, known as the Washington Higher Education Secretariat; it convenes monthly to exchange information and to discuss current or projected activities, many of them national policy issues, often regarding federal financing or control. These organizations represent most of the public and private nonprofit postsecondary institutions in the United States, with some institutions belonging to two or three of them. Based for the most part in Washington, they represent the differing interests of the varied institutions. Also, especially when they work together as a united front, they can influence congressional committees and government agencies on key issues affecting higher education.

The strength of these national associations will continue to grow along with taxes, the federal budget, and federal purchase of selected services from their member institutions. Even though most postsecondary institutions are state chartered and many are basically state funded, the increasing power of the federal tax system will make such national associations even more necessary.

Many specialized voluntary membership associations contribute in diverse ways to the development and operations of functional areas within institutions. For example, the American College Testing Program and the College Entrance Examination Board (its service bureau, the Educational Testing Service, is not a membership organization) provide extensive information resources to their member institutions and program areas. These data are vital for counseling and guidance purposes, admission of students, student financial aid programs, and related activities. In addition, different administrative functions (such as graduate schools, registrars, institutional research units, and business offices) have their own, extremely useful, representative associations. Likewise, most academic fields and their constantly increasing subdivisions or spin-offs have set up specialized groups. Prime examples are engineering and the allied health professions, both with dozens of separate associations. Many of these academic organizations affect institutions and their program planning in direct ways. In particular, the associations that set up detailed criteria for membership in the association often directly influence allocation of resources. Of the several-thousand-member organizations in this category, sixty to seventy of them, from architecture to veterinary medicine, probably exert the greatest influence, since those programs or academic units admitted to membership are considered accredited.

(The following section provides more detail on this group.) A sampling of these organizations illustrates their services, emphasizes their significance, and shows in a limited way their potential impact.

The American Council on Education (ACE) includes separate institutions and other associations, with approximately 1,600 institutional members, representing more than 70 percent of all college and university enrollments in the United States. (There are an additional 200 or so noninstitutional members.)

Since the council's establishment in 1918, its work has changed from emphasis on "consensus building," its primary charge for the first fifty years, to initiating action to improve higher education. Its special offices and centers indicate its thrusts: Office of Women in Higher Education, Center for Adult Learning and Educational Credentials, Office of Minorities in Higher Education, Center for Leadership Development, International Initiatives, Division of Policy Analysis and Research, Division of Governmental Relations, Washington Higher Education Secretariat, Labor/Higher Education Council, Health Resource Center (a national clearinghouse on postsecondary education for individuals with disabilities), and numerous other special programs.

The publication program of the ACE provides major documents on the field of higher education, such as the annual editions of *American Universities and Colleges*. It also prepares and distributes such important guidebooks as the *Guide to the Evaluation of Educational Experiences in the Armed Services*. This guide is updated periodically and serves as a bible for most registrars' offices. A comparable ACE publication is *The National Guide to Credit Recommendations for Non-Collegiate Courses*. The extensive service and publications program includes reports from the policy analysis service and many special studies on current critical issues in higher education.

The Council of Independent Colleges (CIC) began in 1956, as the Council for the Advancement of Small Colleges. By 2003, it had grown to a membership of 523 college and university members, fifty-three affiliate members, and eight international members, including state associations of private colleges, regional consortia, and educational offices of religious denominations. The council, from its beginnings, has had a significant program of services to its members. In its early years, some of its member institutions operated without planned budgets or accreditation and with only limited accounting records. Many CIC institutions took advantage of its workshops, seminars, handbooks, and consultants and earned regional accreditation. CIC has secured many millions of dollars to operate programs for its constituency. Many of its special services are supported by useful publications, such as *Academic Workplace Audit, The New Liberal Learning, Technology and the Liberal Arts,* and *International Business Curricula in Independent Liberal Arts Colleges and Universities.*

The Association of Governing Boards of Universities and Colleges is a nonprofit association serving more than 34,500 trustees and officials of close to 1,800 colleges and universities or their foundations, from all types of boards—private, public, two-year, four-year, governing, coordinating, and advisory. Its mission is described as "to strengthen the practice of voluntary trusteeship as the best alternative to direct government and political control of higher education." In addition to membership fees, its support comes from several dozen national, personal, private, and corporate foundations. Its extensive program of publications, videotapes, conferences, and seminars is designed to provide trustees and institutional leaders with timely and useful resources in this specialized area. One package of materials, *Fundamentals of Trusteeship,* is designed for the orientation of new trustees. Another specialized service is its Presidential Search Consultation Service, which often serves several dozen institutions a year. Other projects include a major study of multicampus system operation, a compendium called *Strategic Indicators for Higher Education* (a selection of 150 financial and nonfinancial indicators from more than 700 colleges and universities), and the Trustee Information Center, which provides answers to queries on all aspects of lay trusteeship and governance of higher education institutions, based on the most comprehensive governance library in existence.

The American Association of State Colleges and Universities (AASCU) represents 430 public colleges and universities representing 56 percent of the enrollments in public four-year institutions. Since its beginnings in 1961, the association has been a leading stimulator of all facets of international education. Its many presidential missions to such countries as Egypt, Israel, Greece, Poland, the People's Republic of China, Cuba, Argentina, Taiwan, Malaysia, and Mexico have fostered continuing educational exchange and on-campus programs. It has taken the national leadership in developing cooperative interassociation and interinstitutional programs and networks, such as the Service Members Opportunity Colleges (with many AASCU institutions involved) and the Urban College and University Network.

Its Office of Federal Programs monitors current funding programs and priorities and has been instrumental in increasing AASCU institutions' participation in this ever increasing source of funds. Its Office of Governmental Relations and Policy Analysis analyzes pending legislation, prepares testimony on major national issues, monitors state issues affecting public higher education, conducts surveys, studies trends, and keeps institutional officials informed. The Academic Affairs Resource Center and Academic Leadership Academy serve the chief academic officers of the institutions, emphasizing planning, faculty development, opportunities for minorities and women to attain senior administrative positions, leadership training, financial management, legal matters, and innovative educational ideas for new clientele.

An extensive seminar, conference, and publication program supports this alignment of institutional services. Some examples are the annual summer council of presidents, which emphasizes current issues and presidential leadership; regular meetings of the chief academic affairs officials; the annual President's Academy for new campus chief executive officers; and the National Minority Feeder Program, sponsored jointly with the National Association of State Universities and Land-Grant Colleges. Overall, the AASCU has had a profound effect on the institutions that founded it in 1961, and their graduates represent more than one-fourth of all those earning baccalaureate degrees and one-third of those earning master's degrees in the United States.

These summaries illustrate the significance and impact of this type of voluntary association. Each contributes in varied ways to the diverse needs of their member institutions or to the program units within them. Fundamentally, the organizations are the creatures of their founding and continuing members, and they serve important functions for these institutions. When institutions need assistance in preserving such important features as autonomy of operation or academic freedom for students and faculty, these professional associations are buffers and important sources of support.

Voluntary Accrediting Associations

The voluntary membership organizations in this important group barely existed a century ago.[4] However, the end of the nineteenth century was a confused and uneasy time in higher education, and major changes were under way. Five key factors contributed to the turbulent state of affairs in the period from 1870 to 1910: (1) the final breakdown of the fixed, classical curriculum and the broad expansion of the elective system, (2) the development and legitimation of new academic fields (psychology, education, sociology, American literature), (3) the organization of new, diverse types of institutions to meet developing social needs (teachers colleges, junior colleges, land-grant colleges, research universities, specialized professional schools), (4) the expansion of both secondary and postsecondary education and the resultant overlapping, leading to the question, What is a college? and (5) a lack of commonly accepted standards for admission to college and for completing a college degree.

To work on some of these problems, the University of Michigan as early as 1871 sent out faculty members to inspect high schools and admitted graduates of the acceptable and approved high schools on the basis of their diplomas. Shortly thereafter, pressures developed for regional approaches to these problems in order to facilitate uniform college entrance requirements.

In keeping with accepted American practice and custom, groups of educators banded together in various regions to organize private, voluntary membership groups for this purpose. In New England, for example, a group of secondary schoolmasters took the initiative. In the southern states, it was Chancellor Kirkland and the faculty of Vanderbilt University. Six regional associations have developed throughout the United States, starting with the New England Association of Schools and Colleges in 1885. It was followed in 1887 by the Middle States Association of Colleges and Schools, in 1895 by the Southern Association of Colleges and Schools and the North Central Association of Colleges and Schools, in 1917 by the Northwest Association of Schools and Colleges, and in 1923 by the Western Association of Schools and Colleges. Criteria and requirements for institutional membership (which now serve as the basis for institutions being considered accredited) were formally established by these six associations at different times: in 1910 by North Central, with the first list of accredited colleges in 1913; in 1919 by Southern; in 1921 by Northwest and Middle States; in 1949 by Western; and in 1954 by New England. Thus, at the same time that the federal government instituted regulatory commissions to control similar problems (the Interstate Commerce Commission in 1887, the Federal Trade Commission in 1914, and the Federal Power Commission in 1920), these nongovernmental voluntary membership groups sprang up to provide yardsticks for student achievement, quality assurance, and institutional operations.

Regional groups dealt in the main with colleges rather than with specialized professional schools or programs. The North Central Association finally determined to admit normal schools and teachers colleges but on a separate list of acceptable institutions. Practitioners and faculty in professional associations gradually set up their own membership associations. These groups established criteria for approving schools and, based on these criteria, made lists of accredited schools and program units. In some cases, only individuals with degrees from an approved school could join the professional association. Later, some membership groups made the approved program unit or school a basis for association membership. In any case, the specialized academic program and its operational unit had to meet exacting criteria, externally imposed, to acquire and retain standing in the field.

The first of the specialized or programmatic discipline-oriented associations was the American Medical Association (AMA) in 1847. However, approving processes for medical schools did not start until the early 1900s. From 1905 to 1907 the Council on Medical Education of the AMA led a movement for rating medical schools. The first ratings in 1905 were a list based on the percentages of failures on licensing examinations by students from each school. This was followed in 1906–07 by a more sophisticated system, based on ten specific areas to be examined and inspections of each school. Of 160 schools inspected, classified, and listed, 32 were in Class C, "unapproved"; 46 were in Class B, "probation"; and 82 were in Class A, "approved." The Council on Medical Education was attacked vigorously for this listing and approving activity. The recently established Carnegie Foundation for the Advancement of Teaching (1905) provided funds for Abraham Flexner and N. P. Colwell to make their famous study (1908–10) of the 155 schools still in existence (5 already had closed). By 1915, only 95 medical schools remained, a 40 percent reduction, and they were again classified by the AMA Council on Medical Education, with 66 approved, 17 on probation, and 12 still unapproved. This voluntary effort led to the ultimate in accountability: the merger and closing of 65 medical schools. In the process, medical education was changed drastically, and the remaining schools completely revised and changed their curricula, a process still continuing to this day. This case provides an excellent example of the work of an external voluntary professional association that, with financial support from a private foundation, took the initiative to protect the public interest. Thus, in some cases intrusions into autonomy can have beneficial results.

The success of the AMA did not go unnoticed. The National Home Study Council (now the Distance Education and Training Council) started in 1926 to do for correspondence education what the AMA had done for medical education. Between 1914 and 1935 many other professional disciplinary and service associations were started in the fields of business, dentistry, law, library science, music, engineering, forestry, and dietetics, plus the medically related fields of podiatry, pharmacy, veterinary medicine, optometry, and nurse anesthesia. From 1935 to 1948 new associations starting up included architecture, art, Bible schools, chemistry, journalism, and theology, plus four more medically related fields (medical technology, medical records, occupational therapy, and physical therapy). Between 1948 and 1975 the number of specialized associations continued to expand rapidly, for programs from social service to graduate psychology and from construction education to funeral direction. Medical care subspecialties also proliferated, particularly in the allied health field, which included more than twenty-five separate groups. After 1975 the expansion slowed greatly, and only a few new specialized associations developed during the following two decades, these few being in developing allied health areas, for nontraditional types of institutions that could not obtain "listing" by recognized national associations, or to expand accreditation opportunities in fields in which existing associations were unduly restrictive. For example, the Association of Collegiate Business Schools and Programs (established in 1988 and recognized by the U.S. Department of Education in 1992) met a need for improved articulation and recognition of business programs in community colleges and teaching-oriented colleges and universities, both four-year and graduate. As of 2003, it had 430 members, about equally divided between the two types of institutions, and an established, ongoing program of accreditation with 261 members holding accredited status.

All of these external professional associations affect institutional operations directly, including curricular patterns, faculty, degrees offered, teaching methods, support staff patterns, and capital outlay decisions. In many cases, priorities in internal judgments result from the outside pressures. Local resource allocations often are heavily influenced by accreditation reports. For example, the law library, a chemistry or engineering laboratory, and teaching loads in business or social work may have been judged substandard by these external private constituents. If teaching loads in English or history also are heavy or physics laboratories are inadequate, will they get the same attention and treatment as specialized program areas with outside pressures? In such cases, these association memberships are not really voluntary, if the institution is placed on probation, is no longer an accredited member, and sanctions are actually applied. Often, students will withdraw from or not consider attending a professional school or college that is not accredited. States often limit professional licenses to practice in a field to graduates of accredited schools. Federal agencies may not allow students from unaccredited institutions to obtain scholarships, loans, or work/study funds. The leverage of a voluntary association in such cases becomes tremendous, and the pressure for accredited status can be extremely powerful.

Presidents of some of the larger institutions, starting in 1924, have attempted to limit the effects of accrediting associations. Through some of the institutionally based associations described in the previous section, they established limited sanctions and attempted to restrict the number of accrediting associations to which they would pay dues and allow on-campus site visits. These efforts to limit association membership and accreditation failed repeatedly to stem the tide. In 1949, a group of university presidents organized the National Commission on Accrediting, a separate voluntary membership association of their own, designed to cut down on the demands and influence of existing external associations and to delay or stop the development of new ones. The number of new ones dropped for a few years, but pressures of new, developing disciplines on campus led, since the 1950s, to many new organizations of this type.

In 1949, the regional associations also felt the need for a new cooperative association and set up what became the Federation of Regional Accrediting Commissions. In 1975 the two organizations, FRACHE and NCA, agreed to merge, and they became major factors in the founding of the new Council on Postsecondary Accreditation (COPA). COPA also included four national groups accrediting specialized institutions, plus seven major, institutionally based associations. They, in turn, endorsed COPA as the central, leading voluntary association for the establishment of policies and procedures in postsecondary accreditation. After a few years, the large representative board became unwieldy and was made much smaller. Also, the presidents, through their various associations, pushed vigorously for more representation. As a result, COPA reorganized further, into three assemblies: the Assembly of Institutional Accrediting Bodies (six national and eight regional), the Assembly of Specialized Accrediting Bodies (forty-two associations), and the Presidents Policy Assembly on Accreditation (seven national associations of presidents from differing types of institutions).

The system for funding COPA required the member associations, particularly the large regional associations, to collect COPA dues along with their own dues, which were tied to institutional accreditation. When in 1993 several regional associations decided not to collect the dues for COPA, it found itself without financial support and disbanded on December 31, 1993. One of COPA's major functions was the "recognition" and "listing" of approved voluntary accrediting bodies, and on January 1, 1994, the less-expensive, streamlined Commission on Recognition of Postsecondary Accreditation (CORPA) was set up by a voluntary founding commission to maintain this phase of the work. Nine organizations paid sustaining fees to keep this critical accrediting function alive. They included the American Association of Community Colleges, the American Association of Dental Schools, the American Association of State Colleges and Universities, the American Council on Education, the Association of American Universities, the Association of Collegiate Business Schools and Programs, the Association of Governing Boards of Universities and Colleges, the National Association of Independent Colleges and Universities, and the National Association of State Universities and Land-Grant Colleges. Later, a tenth was added, the Western Association of Bible Colleges and Christian Schools.

From 1994 through 1996, various alternatives were debated throughout higher education, alternatives designed to continue a more extensive national accrediting presence beyond the efforts of CORPA. Finally, a presidents work group on accreditation, consisting of twenty-five leaders from all types of institutions, developed a prospective new association to be called the Council for Higher Education Accreditation (CHEA). After a number of associations voted to approve its plan for operation, in 1995–96, a ballot was sent to 2,990 colleges and universities. Replies were received from 1,574 (52.5%); of these, 1,476 voted to support the new organization (94%).

CHEA differs from COPA and CORPA in three critical respects. First, it is an institutional membership organization led by college and university presidents. Second, this membership is available only to degree-granting (associate degree and above) institutions. Third, CHEA controls its own financial destiny by directly billing institutions for dues. By contrast, COPA collects dues through regional accrediting organizations. CHEA is the largest higher education institutional membership organization in the United States, with approximately three thousand degree-granting colleges and universities.

CHEA is the only national higher education association exclusively devoted to advocacy for quality assurance and improvement through accreditation. The organization sustains three major functions: government relations, recognition of accrediting organizations, and membership services.

Government relations involves work with the U.S. Department of Education and Congress on federal policy matters that relate to accreditation. Many of the federal policy issues with which CHEA deals stem from the 1965 Higher Education Act (HEA) as amended, Title IV (Student Assistance), Part H (Program Integrity Triad). This section of the law provides for federal scrutiny of accrediting organizations (also known as *recognition*). The federal government, since 1952, has relied on accrediting organizations for affirmation of the quality of institutions and programs for which federal funds (for example, student grants and loans and research) are made available. However, these organizations must be federally recognized. Only institutions and programs that are accredited by these federally recognized accreditors are eligible for federal funds. As of 2002, fifty-six accreditors were recognized by the Department of Education. Government relations issues before CHEA include, for example, how well accreditation addresses quality in distance learning, accreditation and student learning outcomes, and the affect on U.S. accreditation of efforts by the World Trade Organization (WTO) to address quality in higher education through the General Agreement on Trade in Services (GATS).

The CHEA recognition function began in 1999. By the end of 2003, sixty institutional and programmatic accrediting organizations have been recognized by CHEA. Many of these organizations are also recognized by the Department of Education. CHEA's membership services include conferences and meetings and an extensive publications program. CHEA conducts research and undertakes policy analysis of accreditation and makes this work available in print and electronic form.

CHEA, after six years, is emerging as a major policy forum for

U.S. accreditation through the framing of key complex topics such as accreditation and public accountability. CHEA's research and policy analysis is focused on emerging issues and enhancing accreditation's capacity to deal with the extensive changes and challenges facing higher education and quality assurance, such as the internationalization of higher education.

In the meantime, new needs lead to additional accrediting bodies developing in special areas. Three recent examples are the American Academy for Liberal Education (AALE) (1993), the Teacher Education Accreditation Council (TEAC) (1997), and the Association of Collegiate Business Schools and Programs (ACBSP) (1988). All have complete programs of accreditation and have been listed by the Department of Education as recognized accrediting bodies in their fields. The ACBSP emphasizes teaching quality in the business field, in both community colleges and baccalaureate/graduate institutions. The AALE is recognized as the first accrediting body for liberal arts institutions and programs, based on its emphasis on teaching, a commitment to undergraduate education, and a core of studies in the arts, sciences, and humanities. TEAC is devoted to the improvement of academic degree programs for professional educators. To achieve this goal, TEAC's accreditation process places primary emphasis on audit of evidence of student achievement. These three new, quite different voluntary accrediting bodies graphically illustrate the importance of the voluntary sector in our society and its constant renewal.

The relationship of voluntary accrediting associations to state and federal governments also is a major factor in current considerations of academic freedom, institutional autonomy, and institutional accountability. Of course, the states charter most of the institutions and, thus, establish their missions, general purposes, and degree levels offered. However, the states also license individuals to practice most vocations and professions. In many fields the licensing of individuals is based on graduation from accredited programs. Thus, a form of sanction has developed, and membership in the involved, specialized professional associations, supposedly voluntary, becomes almost obligatory. In the federal area, the listing of institutions by federal government agencies had little or no effect before World War II.

The entrance of the federal government into the funding of higher education on a massive basis since World War II has drastically changed the overall uses of accreditation. Reported abuses of the Servicemen's Readjustment Act of 1944 (GI Bill) led to a series of congressional hearings, which led in turn to major additions related to accreditation in Public Law 550, the Veterans Readjustment Act of 1952. Section 253 of that law empowered the commissioner of education to publish a list of accrediting agencies and associations that could be relied upon to assess the quality of training offered by educational institutions. State approving agencies then used the resulting actions of such accrediting associations or agencies as a basis for approval of the courses specifically accredited. The enormous increase in federal assistance to students attending postsecondary education since 1972 made this federal listing process extremely important. Federal efforts to exert control over institutional processes have been constant for the past thirty years, with institutional membership in a listed accrediting association almost obligatory. Default rates on student loans have been blamed on the institutions and accrediting associations, and laws have been passed making the institutions enforce the police power of the government. Since voluntary associations cannot be either forced or allowed to enforce state police powers, Congress established a new state enforcement system, in 1992, called state postsecondary review entities (SPREs). The public outcry against this law led Congress to rescind it in 1994–95 by not funding it. And in 1995 the president's budget contained no request for funds to continue SPREs, effectively eliminating them. SPREs were eliminated from the law in 1998.

Extensive legal arguments about the resulting powers of the Department of Education still continue. However, greater institutional dependence on eligibility for funding is now based on membership in much less voluntary accrediting associations. A delicate relationship exists among the federal government and eligibility for funding, the state government and its responsibilities for establishing or chartering institutions and credentialing through certification or licensure, and voluntary membership associations that require accreditation for membership.

Thus these voluntary associations have come to represent a major form of private constituency with direct impact on internal institution activities. The possible sanctions from state licensing of graduates, the loss of eligibility for funds from federal agencies, and problems caused by peer approval or disapproval enhance the importance of these sometimes overlooked educational organizations.

Voluntary Consortia

Formal arrangements for voluntary consortia based on interinstitutional cooperation among and between postsecondary institutions
have been in operation for many decades. The 2003 HED lists 106
such entities. Probably the oldest continuous consortium is the Ohio
College Association, founded in 1867, and finally incorporated in 1967
after its first century of operation. Its *Administrative Directory* is
called "the telephone book" of Ohio higher education. Its booklet for
prospective college students, *Toward College in Ohio,* has been published yearly since 1940. And its rating programs for workers' com
pensation have saved more than forty of its almost ninety current
institutions more than a million dollars yearly. Decades later, Claremont Colleges (California) started in 1925 with Pomona College and
the Claremont University Center and were joined by Scripps College
in 1926. The Atlanta University Center (Georgia), sometimes called
the Affiliation, started shortly thereafter, in 1929, and included Morehouse College, Spelman College, and Atlanta University. Over the decades, both of these groups have added additional institutions to their
cooperative arrangements and proven that voluntary consortia can be
valuable for long periods of time. Some early examples from 1927–29
illustrate the reality of the cooperation between Morehouse and Spelman. In those years, several faculty were jointly appointed to both
faculties. Upper-division students could take courses offered by the
other college. Also, they operated a joint summer school with Atlanta
University. In 1932, a new library was built, and the three libraries
were consolidated into a joint library serving all three institutions.
Thus, although they remained separate institutions, they sacrificed
some autonomy to extend academic offerings and services.

In the years since these early beginnings, hundreds of institutions
have developed informal and increasingly formal arrangements for interinstitutional cooperation. The Council for Interinstitutional Leadership, a voluntary national organization formed in 1968, was comprised of many of the consortia. It published an updated directory
regularly for more than two decades, until 1991; shortly thereafter,
it was replaced by the newly established Association for Consortium
Leadership. In 2003 the sixteenth edition of the *Consortium Directory*
was published by this organization. This directory listed data from
more than one hundred consortia of many diverse types and repre-

senting about 1,800 institutional members. A considerable number of the consortia also include business, commercial, public service non-profit, and public school district associate members. A careful reading of the directory and consortium activities clearly demonstrates the importance of consortia in the cutting-edge innovations in higher education as well as in overall operational efficiency in providing educational services.

The importance of voluntary consortia to concerns regarding institutional autonomy becomes evident with the enumeration of their activities. The recent directory listed several dozen widely differing programs and services being carried on cooperatively, in seven major areas: administrative and business services; enrollment and admissions; academic programs, including continuing education; libraries, information services, and computer services; student services; faculty; and community services, including economic development. Cross-registration between nearby institutions is quite common, as are joint library services, professional development activities, seminars, joint purchasing through group-negotiated contracts, high school and college career advising services, and new technology joint development projects. Many of the consortia have World Wide Web pages, e-mail, and fax capability and some have teleconferencing capability.

A few brief examples illustrate the diversity of services expedited by the consortium method of organizing. The Intelecom/Southern California consortium of almost 50 community colleges (started in 1970 by 18 of them) has provided course credit via television and cable for 665,000 students. The National Student Exchange (founded in 1967 and incorporated in 1974) has more than 160 members and an intra–United States exchange program with tuition reciprocity for students in the program. The International University Consortium (incorporated in 1980) has members from the United States and several other countries. It develops and acquires high-quality, mediated instructional materials for use by its members in their distance education programs. The Massachusetts Higher Education Consortium (MHEC) (1981) provides an exceptional and extensive group-purchasing service for almost one hundred institutions, including members of seven smaller consortia (with varied projects). It saves each college from developing individual contracts (MHEC has more than eighty contracts for its institutions to use), and the joint buying power saves many millions of dollars on purchases totaling more than 150 million dollars a year. The Council of Christian Colleges and Universities (founded in 1976 and incorporated in 1982) has ninety member institutions and provides internship, travel, and service learning opportunities to their students in such areas as Russia, the Middle East (particularly Egypt), and Latin America (especially Costa Rica).

One other, more extensive example illustrates the nature of the many comprehensive consortia and their program possibilities. The Virginia Tidewater Consortium (VTC) for Higher Education is one of six regional consortia covering all of Virginia. They were established in 1973 by state law to coordinate off-campus continuing education courses. The Tidewater Consortium is an example of what can happen when the leadership of institutions works cooperatively. It now offers a variety of services, including cross-registration of students, faculty exchanges, interlibrary courier services, cooperative degree programs, and faculty and administrative development programs. In addition, it operates the consortium's higher education cable channel, off-campus centers and their continuing education programs, the Equal Opportunity Center, and promotion of college courses by television.

In the years since its founding in the Hampton Roads area, it has grown from eight original institutions to fifteen, and includes four community colleges; four public colleges and universities; four private institutions; two nonresident public universities; a national defense university (the Joint Forces Staff College); an associate member, WHRO-TV; and an affiliate member, Cox Communications. This is similar to many of the comprehensive consortia that have varied memberships, such as businesses, community organizations, and multiple school districts.

The early cooperative projects have expanded and new ones have been developed. Cross-registration has expanded to the new college and university members, on both a credit and an audit basis. Articulation programs between the community college and four-year baccalaureate degree institutions have been developed so students earning associate of arts and associate of science two-year degrees have them fully recognized when transferred. The Educational Opportunity Center provides free educational, career, and financial aid counseling at nine locations. The cable channel operates full time and serves almost five hundred thousand homes, offering college courses. Study abroad programs are coordinated and offered by seven of the institutions, and an International Education Committee operates to broaden global understanding and cooperative academic efforts. For a quarter century, a Summer Institute on College Teaching has been attended by hundreds of college teachers. More recently, specialized programs on substance abuse prevention and institutional security have been developed. And yearly videoconferences on higher education issues have been held for national audiences. In addition, the consortium works closely with the military community with offices at differing military bases.

Another important service of the Virginia Tidewater Consortium is providing the National Office of the Association for Consortium Leadership. After beginning in 1968 the National Office was housed at Kansas Regional Council for Higher Education until 1991. After 1991, the Virginia Tidewater Consortium assumed this key responsibility, with great success. Nearly seventy groups of all types and with three to 1,500 members comprise the consortium. The expanded directory now includes extensive data on more than one hundred consortia.[5] The "Topic Index" lists the major activities of consortia (twenty-eight categories of service) and the individual consortium each provides one. The "Geographic Index" lists consortia by state location. Data for each individually listed consortium are name and location, governance and staffing, funding, membership, and programs and services. The association also provides mentoring services for new groups of institutions interested in consortial-type collaboration and a regular newsletter of consortia activity. A detailed book, *Leveraging Resources through Partnerships*[6] was prepared by the leaders of the VTC and published for the association in December 2002 by Jossey-Bass. A yearly conference/workshop on consortia activity and future-oriented programs round out the extensive and valuable efforts that the association has undertaken through the Tidewater leadership and is open to other groups that can profit by such cooperative ventures.

The examples above illustrate the move of consortia from being primarily private institutions to development in all three sectors. Although started essentially by the voluntary enterprise sector, the public enterprise sector has moved in, and several consortia now include the profit-seeking sector. A number of states passed laws to facilitate their start-up. The Illinois Higher Education Cooperative Act of 1972 provided some state support for voluntary combinations of private and public institutions. California, Connecticut, Massachusetts, Minnesota, Ohio, Pennsylvania, Virginia, and Texas have used the consortium approach for specific purposes. This trend toward public financing of consortia thus becomes a factor in institutional planning and even regional intrastate planning.

In the past, consortia have been developed to provide for interinstitutional needs both in times of growth and in times of decline. They are uniquely capable of handling the mutual problems of public and private institutions and thus provide a powerful deterrent to further governmental incursions into private and sometimes public institutional operation. At various levels of formality, consortia currently are being used by significant numbers of institutions of all types to adjust to changing curricular and funding necessities. As governmental controls continue to increase and to affect institutional autonomy and academic freedom, voluntary consortia provide another way to plan independently for future operations and program development.

Regional Compacts

Regional compacts, although they are nonprofit, private organizations, are quasi-governmental. Groups of states create them, provide their basic funding, and contract for services through them. They operate much like private organizations and receive considerable funding from other sources, including private foundations. Some of their studies, seminars, workshops, and policy studies directly affect the institutions in their regions.

Soon after World War II three regional interstate compacts developed to meet postsecondary education needs that crossed state lines. Originally, they concentrated on student exchange programs in the medical education field; however, in the past half-century, their areas of service and influence have expanded considerably. Although established, funded, and supported basically by state governors and legislatures, their indirect effects on institutional programs and operations can be significant. Listed in order of establishment, they are the Southern Regional Education Board (1948), the Western Interstate Commission for Higher Education (1953), the New England Board of Higher Education (1955), and the Midwestern Higher Education Commission (1991). By 2004, forty-six of the fifty states were actively involved in one of the four state compacts, and Iowa was seriously considering joining the Midwestern compact. Only New York, New Jersey, and Pennsylvania were not members or were considering joining.

The valuable and varied programs of the compacts have often expanded far beyond the four state groups. Some interesting examples are the now National Center For Higher Education Management Systems (NCHEMS), which developed out of the Western Interstate Commission and the American TelEd Communications Alliance (has developed from a Midwestern compact program with a Michigan group [MiCTA], a cooperative purchasing effort). Since 2001, all four of the compacts have combined in this nationwide low-cost telecommunications technology purchasing service. Southern Regional Education Board (SREB) developed a High Schools That Work Network that has greatly expanded into thirty states. Several other joint projects between compacts include SREB's Educational Cooperative and the Western Interstate Compact for Higher Education's (WICHE) Technology Costing Methodology. These varied projects illustrate the current and the potential value of the compacts beyond their regional borders. But each one still meets regional needs in varied ways.

The SREB includes governors, legislators, and other figures, some from higher education, from sixteen states (Alabama, Arkansas, Delaware, Florida, Georgia, Kentucky, Louisiana, Maryland, Mississippi, North Carolina, Oklahoma, South Carolina, Tennessee, Texas, Virginia, and West Virginia). SREB was formed by the political leaders of its member states, and they retain leadership in the organization. SREB has played a major part in the development of such important areas as equal opportunity for all students in higher education and expanded graduate and professional education. Its research and information program has been vital in state and institutional planning. Its regular legislative work conferences, planned by its Legislative Advisory Council, have been influential in setting policy and funding directions in the region.

Regionally, SREB has provided extensive "state services" including the State Data Exchange and its outstanding *Fact Book on Higher Education*. Its Academic Common Market and Doctoral Scholars Programs assist students to attend out-of-state colleges and provide states with cost-effective programs that do not duplicate expensive majors unnecessarily. The electronic campus uses modern technology to deliver educational opportunity throughout the region (and beyond). In 2003–04 it provided more than eight thousand courses and 325 major programs at more than three hundred institutions, for online, anytime, anyplace education. SREB's special institute designed to help minority scholars is a key part of the effort that has resulted in 90% graduation of doctoral scholars from the program to prepare college professors. The Council on Collegiate Education for Nursing keeps nurse educators informed about regional developments in their field. The Distance Learning Policy Laboratory provides key studies on all phases of distance and e-learning, regionally and nationally. Current initiatives include a leadership program for staff for state agencies in higher education and a college readiness project to better prepare prospective students for study in higher education institutions. These varied areas illustrate the breadth and positive effects of this first regional compact and its influence on collegiate institutions.

WICHE has members from fifteen states: Alaska, Arizona, California, Colorado, Hawaii, Idaho, Montana, Nevada, New Mexico, North Dakota, Oregon, South Dakota, Utah, Washington, and Wyoming. WICHE was planned originally to pool educational resources, to help the states plan jointly for the preparation of specialized skilled manpower, and to avoid, where feasible, the duplication of expensive facilities. The student exchange program has been a major effort. Originally in the fields of medicine, dentistry, and veterinary medicine, it expanded greatly to include physical therapy, occupational therapy, optometry, podiatry, osteopathic medicine, dental hygiene, nursing, mental health, physician's assistant, pharmacy, public health, architecture, and graduate library studies. Later, the Western Regional Graduate program (except for California) included specialized interdisciplinary fields not commonly available in the WICHE states, allowing nonresident students to pay in-state rates in 134 programs in thirty-seven universities. Thousands of professionals, most in health care professions, have received this support while enrolled in one of the contract programs in another WICHE state. Another special program supports efforts to recruit minority students into graduate degree programs and to assist them in becoming college and university faculty members. All told, WICHE programs of this type assist close to twenty thousand students a year, making maximum use of regional institution facilities and saving costs for the states involved and for the students who participate.

WICHE contributes by sponsoring annual legislative workshops and timely special projects. Currently, it makes policy analysis and data available, through the Internet, on higher education in North America. A comparative research series was published on major policy issues and differences in higher education in Mexico and the United States. WICHE has developed a Western Cooperative for Educational

Telecommunications which serves at least forty states and four continents in effective use of technology in higher education. Also, WICHE has produced quality standards for distance learning (Principles of Good Practice), a purchasing service for electronic equipment and services, and research on actual returns in learning from these investments, plus an attempt to meet the needs of students in rural or underserved areas. In 1996, WICHE helped design the Western Virtual University, as requested by the governors of the WICHE states.

Another unique WICHE program, with national and international impact, is the Consortium for North American Higher Education Collaboration (CONAHEC). As a founding partner, WICHE has been active in establishing a regional bank of institutions and programs available to students from participating colleges and universities in Canada, Mexico, and the United States. CONAHEC sponsors the North American Student Exchange program and higher education's role in building economic ties and development in the North American trade area. During the first decade of the twenty-first century, student exchanges from WICHE states were expected to expand from thirty-four institutions in the three countries to more than ninety institutions offering some 350 areas of study.

The enormous diversity of the WICHE programs and the ability to change to meet new needs is again indicative of the value of the regional compacts. Their diverse services provide flexibility in the states they serve, often with positive influences far beyond their immediate region.

The New England Board of Higher Education (NEBHE) serves six states: Connecticut, Maine, Massachusetts, New Hampshire, Rhode Island, and Vermont. It administers such programs as the regional student exchange program and conducts studies regarding current needs in higher education that cross state lines. Data on higher education in the New England states are collected, analyzed, and published widely for use by all interested groups in the region. Its Excellence Through Diversity Project collects data from all six states and analyzes and publishes the data for regional planning purposes in each of the states. An informed journal, *Connections,* published five times a year, provides coverage about notable higher education activities throughout the region. Also, timely special projects are coordinated through NEBHE, such as Project Photon, a funded project stressing photonics as an important educational subject in all phases of education from elementary schools through higher education. Another topic, the STEM project, emphasizes work in science, technology, engineering, and mathematics through the NEBHE Science Network and is another example of meeting a critical need in the six states. However, the major program continues to be the student exchange, with its savings for students and optimum use of facilities. In one year, 2002–03, eight thousand New England students saved more than 37 million dollars in tuition and fees.

One interesting project of NEBHE was its studies of the need for veterinary medicine in the region. Political disputes about its potential location were so great that it did not develop until Tufts University started one in 1978. In this way, an important project of a regional compact (to bring a needed academic program to its area) led to the service being established by a private university. Currently, about six hundred students from many locations apply for admission, and sixty-five to seventy are accepted in each class, for a four-year program leading to the doctoral degree in veterinary medicine. This is an excellent example of the law of unintended consequences in higher education and of the importance of the voluntary enterprise in American higher education.

The Midwestern Higher Education Commission (MHEC) serves nine states: Illinois, Indiana, Michigan, Minnesota, Missouri, Nebraska, North Dakota, Ohio, and Wisconsin. Iowa was still considering membership in 2003–04. MHEC was the last of the four regional compacts to be formed. Originally, it was formed to provide for interstate student exchanges at in-state tuition rates, similar to the other compacts. In addition, it included cooperative programs in vocational and higher education, and an areawide approach to gathering and reporting information that facilitates state educational planning. Since its beginning in 1991, the commission (now often referred to as the "compact") has sponsored twenty-five regional programs to "enhance productivity, encourage access, foster academic cooperation, facilitate educational innovation, and promote sound public policy" (from the *2002 Annual Report*). MHEC is recognized by legislation in each of its member states and governed by a fifty-member commission made up of legislators, governors' appointed representatives, and leaders in higher education appointed by the governors and legislatures.

In its first decade, MHEC productivity and cost-saving projects resulted in savings of 146 million dollars. Key initiatives came from such items as a natural gas contract system, risk management (property insurance), purchasing contracts for computer hardware and operational software, and operational maintenance. They set up the original American TelEd Communications Alliance, with a nonprofit Michigan group (MiCTA). This was so successful that SREB, WICHE, and NEBHE joined it. It provides nationwide contracts for local area networks, wide area networks, and national wireless technology systems, including local voice services.

The original student exchange program has involved thousands of students attending more than one hundred of the colleges in all ten states. The Graduate Exchange Program for Minority Scholars combined three smaller projects and has increased scholarship aid and completion by future faculty members. A recent project, funded by the Lumina Foundation, expanded the Midwestern Data Book to provide further analysis of distance learning in the Midwest, of economic growth factors and other policy priorities regarding student access, of student retention, and of adult education in the region.

The Midwest Higher Education Commission was the last of the regional compacts to develop but has clearly shown that such an organization of the states can have significant effects for colleges and universities. With the governors and key legislators an active part of the system, they can influence the operation and services of the colleges and universities.

The current four interstate compacts cover all but a few of the states of the entire country. Their diversified programs change as the needs of their regions change. The basic costs of their operations are funded by state legislatures from tax revenues, but foundation grants plus federal projects pay for several of the new thrusts of the regional commissions. This provides another excellent example of the flexible way that the mixed society of the United States operates to adapt to changing needs and emphases.

Conclusion

During the first two centuries of American higher education's existence, religious tenets and basic social agreements resulted in a relatively fixed, classically oriented program of studies. However, as the society began to open up, to industrialize and expand, it demanded change in its colleges. When this was slow to occur, new institutions met these needs, and many existing ones closed. Normal schools, engineering schools, military academies, and universities were copied from Europe and adapted to American needs between 1830 and 1900. However, even these were not sufficient to meet democracy's needs. New types of institutions were developed, unique or almost unique to America. The land-grant colleges of 1862 and 1890, the junior colleges of the early 1900s, the comprehensive state colleges of the 1960s to 1980s, and the post–World War II community colleges all represent essentially new types of institutions. Private constituency groups often pressured state or local governments to establish them. In some cases, private constituency groups pressured Congress into funding some of them, including the 1862 land-grant colleges and, particularly, the 1890 land-grant colleges. The critical point, again, is that in the United States new institutions replace existing ones that do not change.

Private constituencies such as the five types detailed here have a significant impact on institutional autonomy and academic freedom. Much of this impact is positive, supportive, and welcome. However, those that provide funds can affect institutional trends and direction by determining what types of academic programs or research efforts are supported. As federal and state funds tighten up even more in the years ahead, funds from alternate sources will become even more attractive. Acceptance of grants moves institutions in the direction dictated by fund sources, and faculties are well advised to consider this possibility as the "crunch" of the twenty-first century becomes greater.

Finally, the real benefits provided to institutions by private organizations must be mentioned again. Many membership organizations have been created to provide such benefits. In some cases, these benefits have been greater than anyone could have foreseen. Probably the most dramatic examples have come from private accrediting associations in relation to state political efforts to limit the autonomy and academic freedom of their public institutions. In 1938 the North Central Association (NCA) dropped North Dakota Agricultural College from membership because of undue political interference. The U.S. Court of Appeals upheld the action of the NCA, and the state government backed away from its prior method of political interference in internal institutional affairs. In the post–World War II period, sanctions of the Southern Association stopped legislation banning on-campus speakers in North Carolina and, after 1954, contributed strongly to the development of open campuses in other states in its region. As the nation has worked to expand higher education opportunities for minorities in the 1990s, almost every type of association has participated. And as the society has demanded that higher education become more cost-effective, many of these associations and commissions have adopted systems that have saved large amounts of money, so that academic programs may still be offered to the students they were established to serve.

Private organizations related in some way to postsecondary education clearly continue the great tradition of direct action by voluntary citizen associations. Increasingly, they stand in the middle, between control-oriented federal and state agencies and the private and public institutions. Governments have abandoned the self-denying ordinance that in recent decades kept the state at a distance from the essence of many of its institutions. The nurturance of supportive and helpful private constituencies, therefore, becomes even more critical as higher education enters the twenty-first century.

NOTES

1. For detailed information about foundations, the best overall source is the Foundation Center, 79 Fifth Avenue, New York, NY 10003. Twelve regular publications constitute its core collection. They have offices and reference collections also in Atlanta, San Francisco, Washington, D.C., and Cleveland and cooperating collection centers in numerous libraries in each state. Its two main references are its own annual, *Foundation Directory,* and the *Annual Register of Grant Support* (R. R. Bowker Co., P.O. Box 1001, Summit, NJ 07902-1001).

2. Ibid.

3. Three major references with extensive information about institutionally based associations are the *Encyclopedia of Associations,* published annually by Gale Research, 835 Penobscot, Detroit, MI 48226, the regular editions of *American Universities and Colleges,* available from the American Council on Education, One Dupont Circle, Washington, D.C. 20036, and the 2003 *Higher Education Directory,* published annually by Higher Education Publications, Inc., 6400 Arlington Blvd. Suite 648, Falls Church, VA 22042.

4. Two key sources of historical background information regarding voluntary institutional accreditation are Kenneth E. Young, Charles Chambers, H. R. Kells, and associates, *Understanding Accreditation* (San Francisco: Jossey-Bass, 1983); and Fred F. Harcleroad, *Accreditation: History, Process, and Problems* (Washington, D.C.: ERIC Clearinghouse on Higher Education, 1980). Since 1997, the Council for Higher Education Accreditation (CHEA) has published an electronic *Directory of CHEA Participating and Recognized*

Organizations (updated as changes become known) and a print *Almanac of External Quality Review* (biannual). CHEA's address is One Dupont Circle, Suite 510, Washington, D.C. 20036. Web site is www.chea.org. A somewhat different list of accrediting associations, by the U.S. Department of Education, has been available since it was required in the Veterans Readjustment Assistance Act of 1952. Inclusion on this list is one of several ways that institutions can participate in a number of federal funding programs.

5. The best source of current information on consortia is the *Consortium Directory,* published by the Association for Consortium Leadership, c/o The Virginia Tidewater Consortium, 1417 43rd. St., Norfolk, VA 23529. A current, best reference about the work of consortia is by Lawrence G. Dotolo and John B. Noftsinger, Jr., eds., *Leveraging Resources Through Partnerships* (San Francisco: Jossey-Bass, 2002).

6. Ibid.

Part Three

The Academic Community

Chapter Ten

Harsh Realities

The Professoriate Faces
a New Century

Philip G. Altbach

American higher education finds itself in a period of significant strain. Financial cutbacks, enrollment uncertainties, pressures for accountability, and confusion about academic goals are among the challenges facing American colleges and universities at the end of the twentieth century. The situation is in many ways paradoxical. The American academic model is the most successful in the world, admired internationally for providing access to higher education to a mass clientele as well as some of the best universities in the world. Yet, higher education has come under widespread criticism. Some argue that the academic system is wasteful and inefficient and place the professoriate at the heart of the problem.[1] Others urge that higher education reconsider its priorities and place more emphasis on teaching, reasoning that the core function of the university has been underemphasized as the professoriate has focused on research.[2] Again, the professoriate is central to this criticism.

A combination of the restructuring of the American economy and a popular revolt against paying for public services, including education, has contributed to the pervasive fiscal problems that colleges and universities face. Because of demands for lower taxes in the public sector and growing price resistance at private colleges and universities, most observers believe that higher education will not fully recover financially in the foreseeable future. It has been argued that higher education's golden age—the period of strong enrollment growth, increasing research budgets, and general public support—is over.[3] This means that the academic profession, as well as higher education in general, must adjust to new circumstances. This adjustment, which has already begun, would be difficult under any circumstances, but it is all the more troubling to the professoriate, coming directly after the greatest period of growth and prosperity in the history of American higher education.

The American professoriate has been shaped by the social, political, and economic context of higher education. While academe enjoys relatively strong internal autonomy and considerable academic freedom, societal trends and public policy have affected institutions of higher education as well as the national and state policies concerning academe. There are many examples. In the 1860s, the Land-Grant Acts contributed to the expansion of public higher education and an emphasis on both service and research, while after World War II the GI Bill led to the greatest and most sustained period of growth in American higher education. Court decisions on government's role in private higher education, race relations, affirmative action, the scope of unions on campus, and other issues have affected higher education policy and the professoriate. Education is a basic responsibility of the states, and the actions of the various state governments have ranged from support for the "Wisconsin idea" in the nineteenth century to the promulgation of the California "master plan" in the 1960s. In New York and Massachusetts, as elsewhere, state policies in the postwar period had a formative influence on postsecondary education and the professoriate.[4] A recurring theme in this chapter is the tension between the autonomy and internal life of the academic profession and the many external forces for accountability.

Precisely because the university is one of the central institutions of postindustrial society, the professoriate finds itself under pressure from many directions. Increasingly complicated accounting procedures attempt to measure professorial productivity as part of the effort to increase accountability. But there is so far no way to measure accurately the educational outcomes of teaching. Calls for the professoriate to provide social relevance in the 1960s were replaced in the 1980s by student demands for vocationally oriented courses. A deteriorating academic job market raised the standards for the award of tenure and increased the emphasis on research and publication. At the same time, there were demands to devote more time and attention to teaching.

A constant tension exists between the traditional autonomy of the academic profession and external pressures. The processes of academic promotion and hiring remain in professorial hands but with significant changes: affirmative action requirements, tenure quotas in some institutions, the occasional intrusion of the courts into promotion and tenure decisions. The curriculum is still largely a responsibility of the faculty, but the debates over multicultural courses or over number of vocational courses, for example, affect curricular decisions. Governmental agencies influence the curriculum through grants and awards. The states engage in program reviews and approvals and through these procedures have gained some power in areas traditionally in the hands of the faculty.

The academic profession has largely failed to explain its centrality to society and to make the case for traditional academic values. Entrenched power, a complicated governance structure, and the weight of tradition have helped protect academic perquisites in a difficult period. But the professoriate itself has not articulated its own ethos.[5] The rise of academic unions helped to increase salaries during the 1970s but contributed to an increasingly adversarial relationship between the faculty and administrators in some universities.[6]

The unions, with the partial exception of the American Association of University Professors (AAUP), have not defended or articulated the traditional professorial role. Few have effectively argued that the traditional autonomy of the faculty and faculty control over many aspects of academic governance should be maintained. We are in a period of profound change in American higher education, and it is likely that these changes will result in further weakening of the power and autonomy of the professoriate. This chapter considers the interplay of forces that have influenced the changing role of the American academic profession.

A Diverse Profession

The American professoriate is large and highly differentiated, making generalizations difficult. There are more than 1 million full- and part-time faculty members in America's 3,500 institutions of postsecondary education. Almost 1,400 of these institutions grant baccalaureate or higher degrees, and 213 give the doctoral degree. More than a quarter of the total number of institutions are community colleges. A growing number of faculty are part-time academic staff, numbering close to half nationwide. They enjoy little or no job security and only tenuous ties with their employing institutions. The proportion of part-time staff has risen in recent years, reflecting fiscal constraints. A new and growing category of faculty are full time but non-tenure-track appointees. The new group usually hold limited term jobs, and often have a major responsibility for teaching. Faculty are further divided by discipline and department. While one may speak broadly of the American professoriate, the working life and culture of most academics is encapsulated in a disciplinary and institutional framework. Variations among the different sectors within the academic system —research universities, community colleges, liberal arts institutions, and others—also shape the academic profession.[7] Vast differences exist in working styles, outlooks, remuneration, and responsibilities between a senior professor at Harvard and a beginning assistant professor at a community college. Further distinctions reflect field and discipline; the outlook of medical school professors, for example, and that of scholars of medieval philosophy are quite dissimilar. Indeed, given the changing nature of the academic workforce, it is increasingly irrelevant to speak of a unified academic profession. One must focus on the increasingly differentiated segments of the professoriate.

A half century ago, the academic profession was largely white, male, and Protestant. It has grown increasingly diverse. In recent years, the proportion of women in academe has grown steadily and is now 36 percent of the total, although women are concentrated at the lower academic ranks and suffer some salary discrimination.[8] While salary inequalities based on gender persist, women are now a majority in many humanities fields and can increasingly be found at all academic ranks. Racial and ethnic minority participation has also increased, and while Asian Americans are well represented in the academic profession, African Americans and Latinos remain proportionately few. African Americans constitute only around 5 percent of the total professoriate, and they are concentrated in the historically black colleges and universities.[9] Racial and ethnic minorities make up about 15 percent of the total academic profession. The substantial discrimination that once existed against Catholics and Jews has been largely overcome, and there has been a modest decline in the middle- and upper-middle-class domination of the academic profession.[10] Despite these demographic changes and expansion in higher education, the academic profession has retained considerable continuity in terms of its overall composition.

Any consideration of the role of the professoriate must take into account demographic, cultural, disciplinary, and other variations in the academic profession. If there ever was a sense of community among professors in the United States, it has long since disappeared. At the same time, the large majority of the professoriate retain a basic commitment to the essential values of the profession—teaching, research, and service—and they retain considerable optimism about the profession.

The Historical Context

The academic profession is conditioned by a complex historical development. Universities have a long historical tradition, dating to medieval Europe, and the professoriate is the most visible repository of this tradition.[11] While national academic systems differ, all stem from common roots in Europe. The model of professorial authority that characterized the medieval University of Paris, the power of the dons at Oxford and Cambridge, and the centrality of the "chairs" in nineteenth-century German universities all contributed to the ideal of the American academic profession. The medieval origins established the self-governing nature of the professorial community and the idea that universities are communities of scholars. The reforms in German higher education in the nineteenth century augmented the authority and prestige of the professoriate, while at the same time linking both the universities and the academic profession to the state.[12] Professors were civil servants, and the universities were expected to contribute to the development of Germany as a modern industrial nation.[13] Research, for the first time, became a key responsibility of universities. The role and status of the academic profession at Oxford and Cambridge in England also had an impact on the American professoriate, since the early American colleges were patterned on the British model, and the United States, for many years, was greatly influenced by intellectual trends from Britain.[14]

These models, plus academic realities in the United States, helped to shape the American academic profession. To understand the contemporary academic profession requires a look at the most crucial period of development, beginning with the rise of land-grant colleges following the Civil War and the establishment of the innovative, research-oriented private universities in the last decade of the nineteenth century.[15] The commitment of the university to public service and to "relevance" meant that many academics became involved with societal issues, with applied aspects of scholarship, and with training for the emerging professions and for skilled occupations involving technology. The contribution of the land-grant colleges to American agriculture was the first and best-known example. Following the German lead, the new innovative private universities (Johns Hopkins, Chicago, Stanford, and Cornell), followed a little later by such public universities as Michigan, Wisconsin, and California, emphasized research and graduate training. The doctorate soon became a requirement for entry into at least the upper reaches of the academic profession; earlier, top American professors had obtained their doctorates in Germany. The prestige of elite universities gradually came to dominate the academic system, and the ethos of research, graduate training, and professionalism spread throughout much of American academe. As these norms and values gradually permeated the American academic enterprise, they have come to form the base of professorial values.

The hallmark of the post–World War II period has been massive growth in all sectors of American higher education. The profession tripled in numbers, and student numbers expanded just as rapidly. The number of institutions also grew, and many universities added graduate programs. Expansion characterized every sector, from community colleges to research universities. Growth was especially rapid in the decade of the 1960s, a fact that has special relevance for the 1990s, for many academics hired at that time will soon be retiring, creating an unprecedented generational shift in the academic profession. Expansion became the norm, and departments, academic institutions, and individuals based their plans on expectations of continued expansion.

But expansion ended in the early 1970s, as a result of a combination of circumstances, including population shifts, inflation, and government fiscal deficits. Part of the problem in adjusting to conditions of diminished resources is the very fact that the previous period of unusual growth was a temporary phase. It can be argued that the period of postwar growth was an aberration and that the current situation is the more normal.[16] The legacy of this aberrant growth is significant for understanding how the professoriate has reacted to current realities.

Expansion shaped the vision of the academic profession for several decades, just as prolonged stagnation now affects perceptions. Postwar growth introduced other changes, which came to be seen as permanent when, in fact, they were not. The academic job market became a seller's market, in which individual professors were able to sell their services at a premium. Almost every field had a shortage of teachers and researchers.[17] Average academic salaries improved significantly, and the American professor moved from a state of semi-penury into the increasingly affluent middle class.[18] The image of Mr. Chips was replaced by the jet-set professor. University budgets increased, and research-oriented institutions at the top of the academic hierarchy enjoyed unprecedented access to research funds. The space program, the cold war, rapid advances in technology, and a fear in 1958 (after Sputnik) that the United States was "falling behind" in education contributed to greater spending by the federal government for higher education. Expanding enrollments meant that the states also invested more in higher education and that private institutions prospered.

The academic profession benefited substantially. Those obtaining their doctorates found ready employment. Rapid career advancement could be expected, and interinstitutional mobility was fairly easy. This contributed to diminished institutional loyalty and commitment. To retain faculty, colleges and universities lessened teaching loads, and average time spent in the classroom declined. Salaries and fringe benefits increased. Access to research funds from external sources increased greatly, not only in the sciences but also, to a lesser extent, in the social sciences and humanities. The availability of external research funds made academics with such access less dependent on their institutions. Those professors able to obtain significant funds were able to build institutes, centers, and in general to develop "empires" within their institutions.

Rapid expansion also meant unprecedented growth in the profession itself, and this has had lasting implications. An abnormally large cohort of young academics entered the professorial ranks in the 1960s. This large academic generation is now precipitating a variety of problems relating to its size, training, and experience. With the end of expansion, this large group, in effect, limited entry to new scholars and has created a "bulge" of tenured faculty members who will retire in massive numbers in the 1990s and beyond. Many in this cohort participated in the campus turmoil of the 1960s and were affected by it. Some graduated from universities of lower prestige that began to offer doctoral degrees during this period and may not have been fully socialized into the traditional academic values and norms. But this generation expected a continuing improvement in the working conditions of higher education.

The turmoil of the 1960s had an impact on contemporary higher education and on the consciousness of the professoriate. A number of factors in the turbulent sixties contributed to emerging problems for higher education. The very success of the universities in moving to the center of society meant that they were taken more seriously. In the heady days of expansion, many in the academic community thought that higher education could solve the nation's social problems, from providing mobility to minorities to suggesting solutions to urban blight and deteriorating standards in the public schools. It is not surprising, in this context, that the colleges and universities became involved in the most traumatic social crises of the period, the civil rights struggle and the antiwar movement triggered by the Vietnam War. The antiwar movement emerged from the campuses, where it was most powerful.[19] Student activism came to be seen by many, including government officials, as a social problem for which the universities were to be blamed. Many saw the professors as contributing to student militancy.

The campus crisis of the 1960s went deeper than the antiwar movement. The new and much larger generation of students, from more diverse backgrounds, seemed less committed to traditional academic values. The faculty turned its attention from undergraduate education, abandoned in loco parentis, and allowed the undergraduate curriculum to fall into disarray. Overcrowded facilities were common. The overwhelming malaise caused by the Vietnam War, racial unrest, and related social problems produced a powerful sense of discontent. Many faculty members, unable to deal constructively with the crisis and feeling under attack from students, the public, and government authority, became demoralized. Faculty governance structures proved unable to bring the diverse interests of the academic community together. This period was one of considerable debate and intellectual liveliness on campus, with faculty taking part in teach-ins and a small number becoming involved in the antiwar movement. However, the lasting legacy of the 1960s for the professoriate was largely one of divisiveness and the politicization of the campus.

The Sociological and Organizational Context

Academics are at the same time both professionals and employees of large bureaucratic organizations. Their self-image as independent scholars dominating their working environment is increasingly at odds with the realities of the modern American university.[20] Indeed, the conflict between the traditional autonomy of the scholar and demands for accountability to a variety of internal and external constituencies is one of the central issues of contemporary American higher education. The rules of academic institutions, from stipulations concerning teaching loads to policies on the granting of tenure, govern the working lives of the professoriate. Despite the existence in most institutions of an infrastructure of collegial self-government, academics feel increasingly alienated from their institutions. In a 1990 survey, two-thirds described faculty morale as fair or poor, and 60 percent had negative feelings about the "sense of community" at their institutions.[21] Things have not improved since then.

Academics continue to exercise considerable autonomy over their basic working conditions, although even here pressures are evident. The classroom remains largely sacrosanct and beyond bureaucratic controls, although recent debates about "political correctness" have had some impact on teaching in a few disciplines, and the emerging technologies may stimulate some changes in teaching styles. Professors retain much autonomy over the use of their time outside the classroom. They choose their own research topics and largely determine what and how much they publish, although research in some fields and on some topics requires substantial funding and therefore depends on external support. There are significant variations based on institutional type, with faculty at community colleges and at nonselective teaching-oriented institutions subject to more constraints on autonomy than professors at prestigious research universities.[22] Non-tenure-track and part-time faculty also have much less autonomy than their tenured colleagues and as noted these groups are an increasingly large part of the profession.

As colleges and universities have become increasingly bureaucratized and as demands for accountability have extended to professors, this autonomy has come under attack. The trend toward decreased teaching loads for academics during the 1960s has been reversed, and now more emphasis is placed on teaching and, to some extent, the quality of teaching. Without question, there is now tension between the norm (some would say the myth) of professional autonomy and the pressures for accountability. There is little doubt that the academic profession will be subjected to increased controls as academic institutions seek to survive in an environment of financial difficulties. Professorial myths—of collegial decision making, individual autonomy, and the disinterested pursuit of knowledge—have come into conflict with the realities of complex organizational structures and bureaucracies. Important academic decisions are reviewed by a bewildering assortment of committees and administrators. These levels of authority have become more powerful as arbiters of academic decision making.

The American academic system is enmeshed in a series of complex hierarchies. These hierarchies, framed by discipline, institution, rank, and specialty, help to determine working conditions, prestige, and in many ways, orientation to the profession. As David Riesman pointed out four decades ago, American higher education is a "meandering procession," dominated by the prestigious graduate schools and ebbing downward through other universities, four-year colleges, and finally to the community college system.[23] Most of the profession attempts to follow the norms, and the fads, of the prestigious research-oriented universities. Notable exceptions are the community colleges, which employ one-fourth of American academics, and some of the less selective four-year schools. Generally, prestige is defined by how close an institution, or an individual professor's working life, comes to the norm of publication and research, a cosmopolitan orientation to the discipline and the national profession, rather than to local teaching and institutionally focused norms.[24] Even in periods of fiscal constraint, the hold of the traditional academic models remains strong indeed. Current efforts to emphasize teaching and to ensure greater productivity from the faculty face considerable challenges from the traditional academic hierarchy.

Within institutions, academics are also part of a hierarchical system, with the distinctions between tenured and untenured staff a key to this hierarchy. The dramatic growth of part-time instructors has added another layer at the bottom of the institutional hierarchy.[25] Disciplines and departments are also ranked into hierarchies, with the traditional academic specialties in the arts and sciences along with medicine and, to some extent, law at the top. The hard sciences tend to have more prestige than the social sciences or humanities. Other applied fields, such as education and agriculture, are considerably lower on the scale. These hierarchies are very much part of the realities and perceptions of the academic profession.

Just as the realities of postwar expansion shaped academic organizations and affected salaries, prestige, and working conditions and gave more power to the professoriate over the governance of colleges and universities, current diminished circumstances also bring change. While it is unlikely that the basic structural or organizational realities of American higher education will profoundly change, there has been an increase in the authority of administrators and increased bureaucratic control over working conditions on campus. In general, professors have lost a significant part of their bargaining power, which was rooted in moral authority. As academic institutions adjust to a period of declining resources, there will be subtle organizational shifts that will inevitably work to diminish the perquisites, and the authority, of the academic profession. Universities, as organizations, adjust to changing realities, and these adjustments will work against the professoriate.

Legislation, Regulations, Guidelines, and the Courts

In a number of areas the academic profession has been directly affected by the decisions of external authorities. American higher education has always been subject to external decisions, from the Dartmouth College case in the period immediately following the American Revolution to the Land-Grant Act in the mid-nineteenth century. Actions by the courts and the legislative authority have profoundly affected higher education and the professoriate. In the contemporary period, governmental decisions continue to have an impact on American higher education and the academic profession. The fiscal crisis of higher education has already been discussed. However, academe's problems stem not only from new economic priorities but also from quite deliberate policies by government at both the federal and state levels to deemphasize higher education and research. Other pressing social needs combined with public reluctance to pay higher taxes have worked to restrict higher education budget allocations. Cuts in research funding have been felt by both public and private institutions and their faculties.

Specific governmental policies have also had an impact on the profession. One area of considerable controversy has been affirmative action, the effort to ensure that college and university faculties include women and members of underrepresented minorities, to reflect the national population.[26] A variety of specific regulations have been mandated by federal and state governments relating to hiring, promotion, and other aspects of faculty life to ensure that women and minorities have greater opportunities in the academic profession. Many professors have opposed these regulations, viewing them as an unwarranted intrusion on academic autonomy. These policies have, nonetheless, had an impact on academic life. Special admissions and remedial programs for underrepresented students have also caused considerable controversy on campus and have been opposed by many faculty. These too are programs that have been implemented by governmental intervention.

The legal system has had a significant influence on the academic profession in the past several decades. The courts have ruled on university hiring and promotion policies as well as on specific personnel cases. While the courts are generally reluctant to interfere in the internal workings of academic institutions, they have reviewed cases of gender or other discrimination, sometimes reversing academic decisions.[27] The U.S. Supreme Court decision that compulsory retirement regulations are unconstitutional has had a major impact on the academic profession and has meant that many faculty are retiring later and, as a result, fewer new positions open up.

These examples illustrate the significance and pervasiveness of governmental policies on the academic profession. In a few states, there is now legislation concerning faculty workloads. Other accountability measures have also been considered. Such laws, as well as those dealing with affirmative action, directly affect the professoriate. Shifts in public opinion are often reflected in governmental policies on higher education and the professoriate. The courts, through the cases they are called on to decide, also play a role. The cumulative impact of governmental policies, laws, and decisions of all kinds has profoundly influenced the professoriate.[28] In the post–World War II era, as higher education has become more central to society, government has involved itself to a greater extent with higher education, and this trend is likely to continue.

The Realities of the Twenty-First Century

The past decade has been, without question, one of the low points in the postwar history of the American professoriate. The immediate future does not offer the promise of any significant improvement. The demographic changes that have resulted in more retirements have resulted in a larger number of part-time and non-tenure-track full-time faculty, rather than more regular appointments. There has been deterioration, but it has been within the context of the established system. The following issues are likely to be central in the debates of the coming period.

Teaching, Research, and Service

One of the main debates, the appropriate balance between teaching and research in academe, goes to the heart of the university as an institution and is critical for the academic profession. Many outside academe, and quite a few within, have argued that there should be more emphasis on teaching in the American higher education system. It is agreed that research is overvalued and that, especially considering fiscal constraints and demands for accountability, professors should be more productive.[29] The reward system in academe has produced this imbalance. Critics charge that, outside of the hundred or so major research universities, the quality and relevance of much academic research is questionable. Some have gone further, saying that much academic research is a scam.[30]

The issue of faculty productivity has produced action in several states and on a few campuses. Massachusetts, Nevada, New York, Arizona, and Wisconsin are among the states that have been involved in workload studies. The California State University has compared the teaching loads of its faculty members with professors in other institutions. A few states require annual reports on workloads, and some have mandated minimum teaching loads; Hawaii and Florida, for example, require twelve hours of classroom instruction or the equivalent for faculty in four-year institutions.[31] Academic institutions are also studying workloads.

American professors seem to be working longer, not shorter, hours, and classroom hours have not declined in recent years. In 1992, according to a study by the Carnegie Foundation for the Advancement of Teaching, full-time American professors spent a median 18.7 hours a week in activities relating to teaching (including preparation and student advisement).[32] On average, professors spend 13.1 hours per week in direct instructional activity, with those in research universities spending 11.4 hours and those in other four-year institutions teaching 13.8 per week.[33] Not surprisingly, professors in research universities produce more publications than do their colleagues in other institutions. For example, 61 percent of faculty in research universities reported publishing six or more journal articles in the past three years, compared to 31 percent of faculty working elsewhere.[34]

With the pressure for the professoriate to focus more on teaching and, probably, to spend more time in the classroom, there is likely to be more differentiation among sectors within the academic system, so that academics at the top research universities will teach significantly less than their compeers in comprehensive colleges and universities. Greater stratification between the academic sectors and perhaps less mobility among them are probable outcomes. A shift in thinking has taken place about research and its role. External funding for research has declined in most fields, and competition for resources is intense. There is also an orientation toward more applied research, closer links between industry and universities, and more service to the private sector. These changes will affect the kind of research that is conducted. There may well be less basic research and more small-scale research linked to products.

So far, the professoriate has not fully responded to these externally initiated debates and changes. The profession has sought to adapt to changing patterns in funding and to the more competitive research climate. In the long run, however, these structural changes will transform the research culture and the organization of research. In some ways, academics have moved closer to their clientele through the emphasis on service to external constituencies. The debate about total quality management (TQM) in higher education is, in part, an effort to convince academic institutions and the professoriate to think more directly about student needs, using a model designed to focus attention on the customer.[35]

Demographic Changes and the Decline of Community

The "age bulge," discussed earlier, has meant that the large cohort of academics who entered the profession in the 1960s and 1970s takes up a disproportionate share of jobs, especially when openings are restricted. Part-time faculty make up an increasing segment of the profession, further altering the nature and orientation of the profession.[36] It is much harder for a midcareer academic to find another position if he or she becomes dissatisfied or desires a change in location. The safety valve of job mobility no longer functions as well. While the number of retirements is rising rapidly and many institutions have used early retirement incentives to meet mandated budget cuts, this has not produced significant numbers of full-time academic jobs. This remains a time of diminished expectations.

The academic job market for new entrants has dramatically deteriorated as well, although there are some variations by field and discipline. Smaller numbers of recent Ph.D.s are being hired, and as it has become clear that the academic job market has contracted, enrollments in many fields at the graduate level have declined or leveled off, especially in the traditional arts and sciences disciplines. Bright undergraduates have gravitated to law school or management studies. Perhaps the greatest long-term implication is a missing generation of younger scholars, although there is also a generation of gypsy scholars, who are relegated to part-time teaching, with little chance of a full-time tenure-track position. Further, a generation of fresh ideas has been lost. While there is currently a need for new Ph.D.s to handle growing enrollments and to take the place of retirees, there has been only a modest growth in full-time faculty positions because part-timers and non-tenure-track appointees are being hired in large numbers.[37]

The size and increased diversity of the academic profession have made a sense of community more difficult.[38] As institutions have grown to include well over a thousand academic staff, with elected senates and other, more bureaucratic, governance arrangements taking the place of the traditional general faculty meeting, a sense of shared academic purpose has become elusive. Even academic departments in larger American universities can number up to fifty. Committees have become ubiquitous, and the sense of participation in a common academic enterprise has declined. Increasing specialization in the disciplines contributed to this trend. Two-thirds of the American professoriate in the Carnegie study judged morale to be fair or poor on campus, and 60 percent felt similarly about the sense of community at their institution.[39]

Tenure, Retrenchment, and Unions

The profession has seen its economic status eroded, after a decade of significant gains in real income during the 1960s. Academic salaries began to decline in terms of purchasing power in the 1970s. There was a leveling off in the 1980s and a modest improvement in the 1990s. During the recession of the late 1970s and early 1980s, faculty members in Massachusetts and California saw actual salary cuts, while many states, including New York and Maryland, froze salaries, sometimes for more than a year. Professional prerogatives seemed less secure, and autonomy was threatened.

Perhaps most significantly, the tenure system came under attack in the 1970s and again in the 1990s. Some argued that the permanent appointments offered to professors once they had been evaluated and promoted from assistant to associate professor bred sloth among those with tenure, although there was little evidence to back up this claim.[40] Tenure was also criticized because it interfered with the institution's ability to respond to fiscal problems or changes in program needs. Professors could not easily be replaced or fired. Originally intended to protect academic freedom, the tenure system expanded into a means of evaluating assistant professors as well as offering lifetime appointments. As fiscal problems grew and the job market deteriorated, it became more difficult for young assistant professors to be promoted. Tenure quotas were imposed at some institutions, and many raised the standards for awarding tenure. These measures added to the pressures felt by junior staff. The system that was put into place to protect professors was increasingly seen as problematic.

The tenure debates of the 1970s ended without any significant changes and with tenure intact. The renewed discussion in the 1990s, stimulated by many of the same concerns as in the earlier period, also resulted in little direct change.[41] Post-tenure review and other reforms have to some extent been implemented. There are also a growing number of academics who are not part of the tenure system, and these full-time, non-tenure-track staff are likely to increase in number as institutions try to maximize their flexibility.

Retrenchment—the firing of academic staff without regard to tenure—has always been one of the major fears of the professoriate.[42] During the first wave of fiscal crises in the 1970s, a number of uni-

versities attempted to solve their financial problems by firing professors, including some with tenure, following programmatic reviews
and analyses of enrollment trends. The AAUP, several academic
unions, and a number of individual professors sued the universities
in the courts, claiming that such retrenchment was against the implied lifetime employment arrangement offered through the tenure
system. The courts consistently ruled against the professors, arguing
that tenure protects academic freedom but does not prevent firings
due to fiscal crisis. Universities that were especially hard hit, such
as the City University of New York and the State University of New
York, declared fiscal emergencies and fired academic staff, including
tenured professors, and closed departments and programs. Many institutions found that the financial savings were not worth the legal
challenges, decline in morale, and bad national publicity, and in later
crises fewer tenured faculty were terminated. The fact is that tenure
in American higher education does not fully protect lifetime employment, although, in general, commitments are honored by colleges and
universities.[43] The retrenchments, and discussions and debates about
retrenchment, left an imprint on the thinking of the academic profession, contributing to low morale and feelings of alienation.

The growth of academic unions in the 1970s was a direct reaction
to the difficulties faced by the professoriate. Most professors turned to
unions with some reluctance, and despite accelerating difficulties in
the universities, the union movement has not become dominant. Indeed, the growth of unions slowed and even stopped in the late 1980s.
In 1980, 682 campuses were represented by academic unions. Of this
number, 254 were four-year institutions. Very few research universities are unionized; only one of the members of the prestigious Association of American Universities is unionized, for example. Unions are
concentrated in the community college sector and in the public lower
and middle tiers of the system.[44] Relatively few private colleges and
universities are unionized, in part because the U.S. Supreme Court,
in the *Yeshiva* case, made unionization in private institutions quite
difficult. The Court ruled that faculty members in private institutions
were, by definition, part of "management" and could not be seen as
"workers" in the traditional sense. However, further court rulings
have made it easier for private college faculty to organize unions.

The growth of academic unions has essentially stopped in the past
decade. Legal challenges such as the *Yeshiva* decision and a realiza-

tion that academic unions were not able to solve the basic problems of higher education have been contributing factors. In addition, while unions brought significant increases in salaries in the first years of contractual arrangements, this advantage lessened in later contract periods. In normal times, many faculty see unions as opposed to the traditional values of academe, such as meritocratic evaluation. Often, unions are voted in following severe campus conflict between faculty and administration. Further, unions have been unable to save faculty from retrenchment or a deterioration in working conditions. Both public university systems in New York are unionized, but both have been hard hit by fiscal problems, and faculty unions have not shielded staff from retrenchment, salary freezes, and the like. Unions, however, were part of an effort in the 1970s to stop the erosion of faculty advantages. Unions were also an expression of the attempt by professors in institutions with only limited autonomy and weak faculty governance structures to assert faculty power. In both of these areas, unions had only limited success.

Accountability and Autonomy

The academic profession has traditionally enjoyed a high degree of autonomy, particularly in the classroom and research. While most academics are only dimly aware of it, the move toward accountability has begun to affect their professional lives. This trend will intensify, not only due to fiscal constraints but because all public institutions have come under greater scrutiny. Institutions, often impelled (in the case of public universities) by state budget offices, require an increasing amount of data concerning faculty work, research productivity, expenditure of funds for ancillary support, and other aspects of academic life. What is more, criteria for student/faculty ratios, levels of financial support for postsecondary education, and the productivity of academic staff have been established. New sources of data permit fiscal authorities to monitor how institutions meet established criteria so that adjustments in budgets can be quickly implemented. While most of these measures of accountability are only indirectly felt by most academics, they nonetheless have a considerable impact on the operation of universities and colleges, since resources are allocated on the basis of closely measured formulas. The basic outputs of academic institutions—quality of teaching and quality and impact of research—cannot be calculated through these efforts at accountability. Indeed, even the definitions of teaching quality and research productivity remain elusive.

If autonomy is the opposite side of the accountability coin, then one would expect academic autonomy to have significantly declined. But, at least on the surface, this has not occurred. Basic decisions concerning the curriculum, course and degree requirements, the process of teaching and learning, and indeed all of the matters traditionally the domain of the faculty have remained in the hands of departments and other parts of the faculty governance structure. Most academics retain the sense of autonomy that has characterized higher education for a century. This is especially the case in top-tier institutions. There have been few efforts to dismantle the basic structure of academic work in ways that would destroy the traditional arrangements.

Yet, there is change taking place at the margins that will continue to shift the balance increasingly from autonomy to accountability and erode the base of faculty power. Decisions concerning class size, the future of low-enrollment fields, the overall academic direction of the institution, and other issues have been shifted from the faculty to the administration or even to systemwide agencies. Academic planning, traditionally far removed from the individual professor and seldom impinging on the academic career, has become more of a reality as institutions seek to streamline their operations and worry more about external measures of productivity.

Academic Freedom

American professors at present enjoy a fairly high degree of academic freedom, although just half of the professoriate agrees that there are "no political or ideological restrictions on what a scholar may publish."[45] There are few demands for ensuring the political or intellectual conformity of professors, and the concept of academic freedom seems well entrenched. The AAUP has noted very few cases in which institutions have sought to violate the academic freedom of their staff. There has been virtually no governmental pressure to limit academic freedom. The tensions of the McCarthy era seem far removed from the current period.[46] The fact that the past decade or more has not experienced the major ideological and political unrest and activism that characterized some earlier periods, such as the Vietnam War era, certainly has contributed to the calm on campus; however, even during the Vietnam War, academic freedom remained relatively secure. This record was, however, not entirely spotless. A number of junior faculty were denied tenure during this period because of their political views.[47]

Nevertheless, academic freedom remains a contentious issue. One of the most visible academic debates of the 1980s and 1990s relates to political correctness, an unfortunate shorthand term for a variety of disputes concerning the nature and organization of the undergraduate curriculum, interpretations of American culture, the perspectives of some disciplines in the humanities and social sciences, and what some conservatives claim is the infusion of ideology into academe. Dinesh D'Souza, a conservative writer, argues in his 1991 book, *Illiberal Education,* that American higher education is being taken over by left-wing ideologists seeking to transform the curriculum through the infusion of multicultural approaches and the destruction of the traditional focus on Western values and civilization.[48] Conservative critics, including then Secretary of Education William Bennett, took up the call, and a major national debate ensued.[49] Some conservatives claim that the academic freedom of some conservative faculty is being violated, although there is no evidence that this is the case. The debate, however, has affected the thinking about the curriculum and the role of multiculturalism on campus. While it has not affected academic freedom directly, the politics of race, gender, and ethnicity has left a significant mark on academic life.[50] These social issues have entered into discussions of the curriculum, and some faculty have claimed that they have inappropriately influenced decision making. There have also been incidents of racial or gender-based intolerance on some campuses.

Some analysts see threats to academic freedom from more indirect but, in some ways, just as dangerous sources. The increasing links between universities and industry in terms of research and other relationships have created some tensions on campus concerning academic freedom in the view of some critics. In some cases, corporations have made agreements with universities that restrict the publication of research results, and in general, corporate influence is seen to constrain faculty members who may be in departments or schools with such corporate links. However, academic freedom is largely free of basic structural constraints. During the past few decades, while there have been occasional external pressures and issues such as "political correctness" on campuses have become controversial, academic freedom has been reasonably secure.

Students

The two central parts of any college or university are students and faculty. These two groups are not often linked in analyses of higher education, although students have profoundly affected the academic profession throughout the history of American higher education. Before the rise of the research university at the end of the nineteenth century, American higher education was student oriented and interaction between faculty and students was substantial. Even in the postwar period, most colleges remained oriented to teaching, although with the decline of in loco parentis in the 1960s, faculty became less centrally involved in the lives of students.[51] Students affect faculty in many ways. Increases in student numbers had the result of expanding the professoriate, and changes in patterns of enrollments also affected the academic profession. Student demands for relevance in the 1960s had implications for the faculty, as did the later vocationalism of student interests. American higher education has traditionally responded to changing student curricular interests by expanding fields and departments or by cutting offerings in unpopular areas. Student consumerism is a central part of the ethos of American higher education.[52]

Student interests have also had some impact on academic policy and governance. In the 1960s, students demanded participation in academic governance, and many colleges and universities opened committees and other structures to them. These changes were short-lived, but the student demands aroused considerable debate and tension on campus.[53] Recently, students have shown little interest in participating in governance and have been only minimally involved in political activism, on campus or off, although there has been a recent increase in student voluntarism for social causes. Student interests and attitudes affect the classroom and enrollments in different fields of study. Students are themselves influenced by societal trends, government policies concerning the financial aspects of higher education, perceptions of the employment market, and many other factors. These student perceptions are brought to the campus and are translated into attitudes, choices, and orientations to higher education. Student opinions about the faculty and the academic enterprise have a significant influence on institutional culture and morale.[54]

Conclusion

The analysis presented in this chapter is not optimistic. The academic profession has been under considerable pressure, and the basic conditions of academic work in America have deteriorated. Some of the gains made during the period of postwar expansion have been lost. The golden age of the American university is probably over. The basic fact is, however, that the essential structure of American higher education remains unaltered, and it is unlikely to change fundamentally. Despite the likely overall stability of the American academic system, considerable change is taking place, and much of this will adversely affect the academic profession. The professoriate stands at the center of any academic institution and is, in a way, buffered from direct interaction with many of higher education's external constituencies. Academics do not generally deal with trustees, legislators, or parents. Their concerns are with their own teaching and research and with their immediate academic surroundings, such as the department. Yet, external constituencies and realities increasingly affect academic life.

It is possible to summarize some of the basic trends that have been discussed in this analysis, factors likely to continue to affect the academic profession in the coming period.

— Increased competition for federal research funds made research funds more difficult to obtain in most fields.[55] Governmental commitment to basic research declined as well, and funding for the social sciences and humanities fell. With the end of the cold war, the emphasis on military research has somewhat diminished.

— Financial difficulties for scholarly publishers and cutbacks in budgets for academic libraries reduced opportunities for publishing scholarly work, thereby placing added stress on younger scholars, in particular, and on the entire knowledge system in academe. Library cutbacks also place restrictions on access to knowledge.

— Changes in student curricular choices have been significant: from the social sciences in the 1960s, to business, engineering, and law in the 1980s, and currently, to a limited extent, back to the social sciences but with a continuing vocational focus. Declines in enrollments in the traditional arts and sciences at the graduate level have also been notable.

— Demands for budgetary and programmatic accountability from government have affected higher education at every level.

—In this climate of increased accountability, academic administrators have gained power over their institutions and, inevitably, over the professoriate.

—Economic problems in society have caused major financial difficulties for higher education, affecting the faculty directly in terms of salaries, perquisites, and teaching loads. The financial future of higher education, regardless of broader economic trends, is not favorable in the medium term.

—A decline in public esteem and support for higher education, triggered first by the unrest of the 1960s and enhanced by widespread questioning of the academic benefits of a college degree, has caused additional stress for the professoriate. There is a tendency to see an academic degree as a private good rather than a public good, so individuals and families rather than the state should pay for higher education.

—The academic profession will become further differentiated. The full-time tenure-track professoriate is already shrinking, and the numbers of part-timers and non-tenure-track teachers are growing. In addition, terms and conditions of academic work in the different segments of the academic system will be more diverse and unequal.

—The shrinking academic employment market has meant that fewer younger scholars have been able to enter the profession and has limited the mobility of those currently in the profession. The increased use of part-time faculty has further restricted growth.

Given these factors, it is perhaps surprising that the basic working conditions of the American professoriate have remained relatively stable. The structure of postsecondary education remains essentially unchanged, but there have been important qualitative changes, generally in a negative direction from the perspective of the professoriate. Academic freedom and the tenure system remain largely intact, but there have been increased demands for accountability. Academics retain basic control over the curriculum, and most institutions continue to be based on the department, which remains strongly influenced by the professoriate. Institutional governance, although increasingly influenced by administrators, remains unchanged.

The period of expansion and professorial power of the middle years of the twentieth century will not return. How, then, can academics face the challenges of the coming period? At one level, the academic profession needs to represent itself effectively to external constituencies. If academic unions could more effectively assimilate traditional academic norms, they might have the potential of representing the academic profession. The traditional academic governance structures are the most logical agencies to take responsibility for presenting the case for the academic profession to a wider audience, both to the public and to political leaders, probably in cooperation with university administrators.

The professoriate reacted to the challenges of the postwar period. It was glad to accept more responsibilities, move into research, and seek funding from external agencies. It relinquished much of its responsibility to students. The curriculum lost its coherence in the rush toward specialization. Now, it is necessary to reestablish a sense of academic mission that emphasizes teaching and the curriculum. To a certain extent, this has occurred on many campuses, with the rebuilding of the undergraduate general education curriculum and the reestablishment of liberal education as a key curricular goal. The current emphasis on teaching is another important trend that may restore the credibility of the profession.

It is always more difficult to induce changes as a result of conscious planning and concern than it is to react to external circumstances. For much of this century, the professoriate has reacted to conditions. Now, there are signs that the crisis has stimulated the academic profession to implement positive solutions to difficult problems.

NOTES

I am indebted to Lionel S. Lewis, Patricia Gumport, Robert Berdahl, and Edith S. Hoshino for comments on this essay.

1. See Allan Bloom, *The Closing of the American Mind: How Higher Education has Failed Democracy and Impoverished the Souls of Today's Students* (New York: Simon and Schuster, 1987); Charles J. Sykes, *Profscam: Professors and the Demise of Higher Education* (Washington, D.C.: Regnery, 1988); Martin Anderson, *Imposters in the Temple* (New York: Simon and Schuster, 1992). For a more optimistic perspective, see Philip G. Altbach, Patricia J. Gumport, and D. Bruce Johnstone, eds., *In Defense of American Higher Education* (Baltimore: Johns Hopkins University Press, 2001).

2. Ernest L. Boyer, *Scholarship Reconsidered: Priorities of the Professoriate* (Princeton, NJ: Carnegie Foundation for the Advancement of Teaching, 1990).

3. Harold T. Shapiro, "The Functions and Resources of the American University of the Twenty-First Century," *Minerva* 30 (1992): 163–74.

4. Richard M. Freeland, *Academia's Golden Age: Universities in Massachusetts, 1945–1970* (New York: Oxford University Press, 1992).

5. Edward Shils, "The Academic Ethos under Strain," *Minerva* 13 (1975): 1–37. See also Henry Rosovsky, *The University: An Owner's Manual* (New York: Norton, 1990).

6. Robert Birnbaum, "Unionization and Faculty Compensation, Part II," *Educational Record* 57 (1976): 116–18.

7. Kenneth P. Ruscio, "Many Sectors, Many Professions," in *The Academic Profession: National, Disciplinary, and Institutional Settings*, ed. Burton R. Clark (Berkeley: University of California Press, 1987).

8. Mary M. Dwyer, Arlene A. Flynn, and Patricia S. Inman, "Differential Progress of Women Faculty: Status 1980–1990," in *Higher Education: Handbook of Theory and Research,* vol. 7, ed. John Smart (New York: Agathon, 1991).

9. Martin J. Finkelstein, *The American Academic Profession* (Columbus: Ohio State University Press, 1984), 187–89.

10. Jake Ryan and Charles Sackrey, *Strangers in Paradise: Academics from the Working Class* (Boston: South End, 1984).

11. Charles Homer Haskins, *The Rise of Universities* (Ithaca, NY: Cornell University Press, 1965).

12. Joseph Ben-David and Awraham Zloczower, "Universities and Academic Systems in Modern Societies," *European Journal of Sociology* 3 (1962): 45–84.

13. Fritz K. Ringer, *The Decline of the German Mandarins: The German Academic Community, 1890–1933* (Cambridge: Harvard University Press, 1969).

14. Frederick Rudolph, *The American College and University: A History* (New York: Vintage, 1965).

15. Laurence Veysey, *The Emergence of the American University* (Chicago: University of Chicago Press, 1965).

16. This theme is developed at greater length in David Henry, *Challenges Past, Challenges Present* (San Francisco: Jossey-Bass, 1975).

17. The academic job market of this period is captured in Theodore Caplow and Reece J. McGee, *The Academic Marketplace* (New York: Basic Books, 1958). Current realities are reflected in Dolores L. Burke, *A New Academic Marketplace* (Westport, CT: Greenwood, 1988), a replication of the earlier Caplow and McGee study.

18. See Logan Wilson, *American Academics: Then and Now* (New York: Oxford University Press, 1979).

19. Seymour Martin Lipset, *Rebellion in the University* (New Brunswick, NJ: Transaction, 1993).

20. Burton R. Clark, *The Academic Life* (Princeton, NJ: Carnegie Foundation for the Advancement of Teaching, 1987). For a structural discussion of American higher education, see Talcott Parsons and Gerald Platt, *The American University* (Cambridge: Harvard University Press, 1973).

21. These figures come from a survey of the views of the American academic profession undertaken by the Carnegie Foundation for the Advancement of Teaching in 1992. See J. Eugene Haas, "The American Academic Profession," in *The International Academic Profession: Portraits of Fourteen Countries,* ed. Philip G. Altbach (Princeton, NJ: Carnegie Foundation for the Advancement of Teaching, 1997).

22. See James S. Fairweather, *Faculty Work and Public Trust: Restoring the Value of Teaching and Public Service in American Academic Life* (Boston: Allyn and Bacon, 1996); Robert T. Blackburn and Janet H. Lawrence, *Faculty at Work: Motivation, Expectation, Satisfaction* (Baltimore: Johns Hopkins University Press, 1995).

23. David Riesman, *Constraint and Variety in American Education* (Garden City, NY: Doubleday, 1958), 25–65.

24. Alvin Gouldner, "Cosmopolitans and Locals: Toward an Analysis of Latent Social Roles, 1 and 2," *Administrative Science Quarterly* 2 (1957, 1958): 281–303 and 445–67.

25. Judith M. Gappa and David W. Leslie, *The Invisible Faculty: Improving the Status of Part-Timers in Higher Education* (San Francisco: Jossey-Bass, 1993).

26. See, for example, Valora Washington and William Harvey, *Affirmative Rhetoric, Negative Action: African-American and Hispanic Faculty at Predominantly White Institutions* (Washington, D.C.: George Washington University, School of Education, 1989).

27. William A. Kaplin and Barbara A. Lee, *The Law of Higher Education: A Comprehensive Guide to Legal Implications of Administrative Decision Making* (San Francisco: Jossey-Bass, 1995).

28. Edward R. Hines and L. S. Hartmark, *The Politics of Higher Education* (Washington, D.C.: American Association for Higher Education, 1980).

29. The most influential consideration of this topic is Boyer, *Scholarship Reconsidered.* See also William F. Massy and Robert Zemsky, *Faculty Discretionary Time: Departments and the Academic Ratchet* (Philadelphia: Pew Higher Education Research Program, 1992).

30. Sykes, *Profscam.* See also Page Smith, *Killing the Spirit: Higher Education in America* (New York: Viking, 1990). Both of these volumes received widespread attention in the popular media and sold well.

31. Arthur Levine and Jana Nidiffer, "Faculty Productivity: A Re-Examination of Current Attitudes and Actions," Institute of Educational Management, Harvard Graduate School of Education, 1993.

32. See Ernest L. Boyer, Philip G. Altbach, and Mary Jean Whitelaw, *The*

Academic Profession: An International Perspective (Princeton, NJ: Carnegie Foundation for the Advancement of Teaching, 1994). Academics in other countries report that they teach similar amounts: Germany, 16.4 hours per week; Japan, 19.4; Sweden, 15.9; England, 21.3.

33. Haas, "The American Academic Profession," 351.

34. Ibid.

35. D. Seymour, "TQM: Focus on Performance, Not Resources," *Educational Record* 74 (1993): 6–14. See also Robert Birnbaum, *Management Fads in Higher Education* (San Francisco: Jossey-Bass, 2000).

36. Elaine El-Khawas, *Campus Trends, 1991* (Washington, D.C.: American Council on Education, 1991), 7.

37. William G. Bowen and Julie Ann Sosa, *Prospects for Faculty in the Arts and Sciences* (Princeton: Princeton University Press, 1989). Demographic projections, however, must be carefully evaluated because they have frequently been wrong. See also Martin J. Finkelstein, Robert K. Seal, and Jack H. Schuster, *A New Academic Generation* (Baltimore: Johns Hopkins University Press, 1998).

38. Carnegie Foundation for the Advancement of Teaching, *Campus Life: In Search of Community* (Princeton, NJ: Carnegie Foundation for the Advancement of Teaching, 1990). See also Irving J. Spitzberg Jr. and Virginia V. Thorndike, *Creating Community on College Campuses* (Albany: State University of New York Press, 1992).

39. Haas, "The American Academic Profession."

40. Bardwell Smith et al., eds., *The Tenure Debate* (San Francisco: Jossey-Bass, 1973). For a more recent attack on tenure, see Anderson, *Imposters in the Temple*.

41. Matthew W. Finken, ed., *The Case for Tenure* (Ithaca: Cornell University Press, 1996). See also Cathy A. Trower, *Tenure Snapshot* (Washington, D.C.: American Association for Higher Education, 1996) and Richard P. Chait, ed., *The Questions of Tenure* (Cambridge, MA: Harvard University Press, 2002).

42. See Marjorie C. Mix, *Tenure and Termination in Financial Exigency* (Washington, D.C.: American Association for Higher Education, 1978).

43. Sheila Slaughter, "Retrenchment in the 1980s: The Politics of Prestige and Gender," *Journal of Higher Education* 64 (1993): 250–82. See also Patricia Gumport, "The Contested Terrain of Academic Program Reduction," *Journal of Higher Education* 64 (1993): 283–311.

44. For example, in the sixty-four-campus State University of New York system, which is unionized, there is a bifurcation between the four research-oriented university centers, which have been reluctant to unionize, and the fourteen four-year colleges, which favor the union. Since the four-year college faculty are in the majority, the union has prevailed.

45. Boyer, Altbach, and Whitelaw, *The International Academic Profession,*

101. The United States falls at the lower end on this question, with scholars in Russia, Sweden, Mexico, Germany, Japan, and other countries feeling more positive about the freedom to publish.

46. See Noam Chomsky et al., *The Cold War and the University* (New York: New Press, 1997), for a general discussion of the impact of the cold war period on American higher education.

47. Joseph Fashing and Stephen F. Deutsch, *Academics in Retreat* (Albuquerque: University of New Mexico Press, 1971).

48. Dinesh D'Souza, *Illiberal Education: The Politics of Race and Sex on Campus* (New York: Free Press, 1991).

49. Among the numerous books on the topic, see Paul Berman, ed., *Debating P.C.: The Controversy over Political Correctness on College Campuses* (New York: Dell, 1992); Patricia Aufderheide, ed., *Beyond PC: Towards a Politics of Understanding* (Saint Paul, MN: Graywolf, 1992); Francis J. Beckwith and Michael E. Bauman, eds., *Are You Politically Correct? Debating America's Cultural Standards* (Buffalo: Prometheus, 1993).

50. William A. Smith, Philip G. Altbach, and Kofi Lomotey, eds., *The Racial Crisis in American Higher Education* (Albany: State University of New York Press, 2002).

51. Helen Lefkowitz Horowitz, *Campus Life: Undergraduate Cultures from the End of the Eighteenth Century to the Present* (Chicago: University of Chicago Press, 1987).

52. Arthur Levine, *When Dreams and Heroes Died: A Portrait of Today's College Student* (San Francisco: Jossey-Bass, 1980).

53. Alexander W. Astin et al., *The Power of Protest* (San Francisco: Jossey-Bass, 1975).

54. Alexander W. Astin, *What Matters in College: Four Critical Years Revisited* (San Francisco: Jossey-Bass, 1993).

55. See Roger L. Geiger, *Research and Relevant Knowledge: American Research Universities since World War II* (New York: Oxford University Press, 1993).

Chapter Eleven

College Students in Changing Contexts

Eric L. Dey and Sylvia Hurtado

The student role within American higher education and society is complex and requires a new epistemology, or way of thinking about that role, which enhances our understanding. Although college students have received a tremendous amount of attention in the popular and scholarly literature, this attention has largely drawn from perspectives that tend to limit our ability to understand the important interconnections between students, colleges, and society. Over the last three decades, both our society and the nature of our institutions have undergone tremendous changes that call for an understanding of these interconnections in order to improve undergraduate education.

As social institutions, colleges and universities are one element of a larger set of social systems that compose society. Simultaneously, within colleges and universities there exist interconnected social systems composed of groups of students, faculty, and other constituents. It is convenient to think of such systems as separate and discrete entities, but it is perhaps more accurate to acknowledge that these systemic boundaries are permeable and that changes in the social system that is the student body of a college are related to changes in other aspects of the institution and the larger social context. Our goal in this chapter, then, is to review these perspectives and consider recent changes among undergraduates from a perspective that takes into ac-

count the challenges posed by recent changes in students' characteristics, attitudes and preferences, and behaviors.

We begin by explaining some of the traditional perspectives that
both administrators and researchers adopt in their approach to understanding students in college. Next, we introduce the notion of a
dynamic occurring between students, the institutions that both are
influenced by students and attempt to shape their development, and
changes in the larger social context in American society. This is accomplished through the examination of trend data on generations of
college students across four decades. In illustrating these trends, we
raise important questions about our assumptions regarding views of
college students, the extent to which institutions adapt to changes in
student characteristics and activities, and the impact of college during these eras. We conclude with a call for a more dynamic, ecological
perspective to understand the interconnections among students, institutions, and society.

Traditional Perspectives

Undergraduates have traditionally been viewed by the ways in which
their background attributes—character, preparation, gender, and
race—contribute to and help describe the culture and status of individual campuses and larger systems of higher education institutions.
Burton Clark, for example, has noted that "students are important to
the character of their institution" and that "the student body becomes
a major force in defining the institution."[1] Selective admissions policies are often used to select students not only on the basis of academic
criteria but on the basis of character and the student's potential to
contribute to the college in any number of ways. In addition, students
and their perceived academic quality are often seen as an organizational resource and as a measure of institutional quality.[2] More recently, it has become popular to think of undergraduates as the recipient of collegiate influences that produce certain psychological, social,
and economic outcomes for individuals as well as for the larger society. This perspective has been popularized by the assessment movement and scholarly interest in questions of college impact; from such
a perspective, high-quality programs and institutions are those that
bring about the largest growth in student knowledge and personal development.[3]

In addition to these main perspectives, it is also important to consider the ways in which students influence colleges and universities. This view, which acknowledges students as sources of institutional change and contributors to institutional effectiveness through peer-based learning occurring in both formal and nonformal settings, has received much less attention in the research literature.[4] The most visible source of student-led change is protest and direct action, which is reinforced by the observation that an "inactive student body is a much more curious phenomenon than one which is involved to some degree in activism."[5] Historically, student activists have tended to pursue agendas focused on broad social and political concerns, although relatively recent examples of activism include student efforts to institutionalize ethnic studies and multicultural centers, prevent tuition increases, and urge institutions to develop proactive responses to racist and sexist situations on campus.[6] Of course, not all student-led change comes about as a direct result of student protest or other forms of political action. In fact, a tremendous amount of such change develops as a result of natural institutional responses to changing student needs and preferences.

An Ecological Perspective

Although each of these three views is useful in helping us understand different aspects of the role of students within higher education, they can also serve to artificially restrict the ways in which we view students. A more complete view is one in which the relationship between students and the college environment is seen as both reciprocal and dynamic. Such an orientation has been described as an ecological perspective and portrays students as actively shaping their interpersonal environments and, by extension, their institutions and society, with these environments simultaneously providing the potential for transforming the individual.[7]

The ecological perspective is based on Urie Bronfenbrenner's observations about the limitations inherent in the study of human development using traditional perspectives. Of particular concern to Bronfenbrenner was the lack of recognition paid in the research literature to the process of "progressive accommodation between a growing human organism and its immediate environment."[8] Although the importance of the interaction between individuals and environments in fostering human development has long been recognized, psychological research has focused almost exclusively on aspects of the individual, to the neglect of the environment and its influence.

Research on students in higher education, in contrast, has long been concerned with environmental influences, yet the conception of the environment is similar to the traditional psychological perspectives described by Bronfenbrenner. In short, the environment is conceptualized as a "static structure that makes no allowance for the evolving processes of interaction."[9] Such a conception ignores the important processes of personal choice and organizational change that have been described as dynamic stability, or "the process by which the individual constructs circumstances which help maintain prior orientations and which in turn feed back on the person so as to maintain stability over time. The person is thus not only the recipient of influences from the environment; she is also an active agent in shaping that environment."[10]

To explore an ecological perspective of college students and the dynamic relationship between students and institutions, we discuss two important social and educational trends that have helped shape American higher education over the past four decades: changes in the demography of higher education and entering students' educational plans and preferences. We also consider the changes in the experiences of students during college as a third group of data-based observations. In examining these trends, we hope to show the utility of adopting an ecological perspective by highlighting patterns of institutional change related to these student trends. The interplay among students, institutions, and society is both subtle and complex, in which direct cause-and-effect relationships are difficult to detect. We hope to illustrate this perspective by linking what we believe to be interrelated trends. Although our preference would be to provide a more definitive analysis, we are unaware of data resources that would allow us to do so. Our goal here is to encourage others to consider this perspective, since it opens up new possibilities for studying students and higher education institutions and the processes that foster individual, institutional, and social change.

The data on entering college students come primarily from the Cooperative Institutional Research Program (CIRP), coordinated by the Higher Education Research Institute at the University of California, Los Angeles. The CIRP data are based on responses from an annual survey of some 250,000 students entering about six hundred colleges and universities nationwide.[11] Given the large sample sizes we are dealing with, any differences large enough to be interesting are going to be statistically significant. Since this is the case, we do not show formal statistical tests. Furthermore, the CIRP focuses primarily on what are considered traditional American students, so the patterns discussed are likely to understate the extent to which changes have occurred in the general college population. Data on the changing pattern of in-college experiences of students are based on longitudinal surveys of college students who participated in the CIRP freshman surveys and who were followed up several years later.[12]

The Changing Demography of Higher Education

Despite the many changes that have occurred in access to and enrollment in American higher education over the past several decades, we suspect that the traditional image of college students is surprisingly persistent. One reason that traditional images are common is that we often think of specific generations of college students when trying to describe their attributes. Unfortunately, truth and fiction are intertwined in the stereotypes that become attached to each generation. At the same time, some of these generational stereotypes do describe groups of students at particular institutions. To be sure, some institutions continue to seek and enroll students who fit a traditional college student image, while others have taken on more diverse clienteles in order to better serve changing state and local populations. This suggests that there have been changes not only in the type of student now attending college but in institutional mission and policy, as well, that differentiate institutions across the higher education system.

American higher education enrollments have grown considerably despite predictions to the contrary based on the declining number of college-age students during the 1980s. Between 1975 and 1994, fall enrollment in higher education institutions grew more that 25 percent, increasing from 11.2 to 14.3 million students.[13] The increase in enrollment between 1988 and 1998 was at a slightly lower rate of 11 percent, reaching nearly 15 million in 1995. The 1994 figures represent the second year of small declines in fall enrollments, dropping from an all-time high of 14.4 million in 1992. Much of the growth over the last several decades has been due to increased access by nontradi-

Table 11.1

Demographic Characteristics of Entering College Students, 1961–2001 (%)

Characteristic	1961	1974	1984	1994	2001
Gender					
Women	44	48	52	56	55
Men	56	52	48	44	45
Age distribution					
18 or younger	–	78	76	68	70
19 or older	–	22	24	32	30
Racial/ethnic background					
White/Caucasian	97	89	86	82	74
African American/black	2	7	10	10	11
American Indian	Z	1	1	2	1
Asian American/Oriental	1	1	2	4	8
Mexican American/Chicano	–	2	1	2	4
Puerto Rican	–	1	1	1	1
Other	Z	2	2	3	6

Source: Alexander W. Astin and Robert J. Panos, *Educational and Vocational Development of College Students* (Washington, D.C.: American Council on Education, 1969); Eric L. Dey, Alexander W. Astin, and William S. Korn, *The American Freshman: Twenty-five Year Trends* (Los Angeles: University of California, Los Angeles, Higher Education Research Institute, 1991); Linda J. Sax, Alexander W. Astin, William S. Korn, and Kit M. Mahoney, *The American Freshman: National Norms for Fall 1995* (Los Angeles: University of California, Los Angeles, Higher Education Research Institute, 1995).

Note: Racial/ethnic labels vary between survey years. Racial/ethnic percentages may total more than 100 after 1974 due to multiple responses given by individual students. Z indicates less than 0.5 percent; – indicates comparable data not available.

tional students. Adults over the age of twenty-five have been a fast-growing group and currently represent about 44 percent of students in higher education.[14] Although there has been a shift toward part-time enrollment in higher education since 1965, holding steady at 41 percent of all students, we will see nearly 2.6 million new students by 2015, many of whom constitute traditional-aged students or the "echo boom." It is estimated that about 80 percent of these new students will be racial/ethnic minorities.[15]

In addition to the changes brought about by increased numbers of nontraditional students, striking changes in the general composition of college entrants demand a reconception of the traditional college student. Table 11.1 shows the changing demographics of first-time,

full-time students drawn from the CIRP data. A typical American college student in the twenty-first century is likely to be female: women
constituted 55 percent of first-year students pursuing a baccalaureate degree in 2001, compared to 44 percent in 1961. The proportion
of older students attending college as first-time entering students has
also increased over time. These changes in the traditional college-
going population indicate that child care services, reentry services,
women's centers, women's studies, and the incorporation of gender-
related issues in the classroom will continue to be salient for increasing proportions of campus communities.

Table 11.1 also shows that the proportion of white students has
steadily declined, while the representation of all other ethnic minority
groups has increased among first-time entrants to four-year colleges.
Increased access, coupled with the growing representation of minorities within college-age cohorts, has changed the ethnic composition on
many campuses. As a result, campuses will need to continue restructuring to become multicultural environments. What is not evident
from table 11.1, however, is that while all racial and ethnic groups
have recorded enrollment gains, participation rates are not necessarily equitable. For example, although Hispanics posted gains in
higher education enrollments, they have experienced a decline in college participation rate. Both Native Americans (49%) and Hispanics
(56%) are also more likely to be represented in two-year colleges
than either African American or white students (41 and 36%, respectively).[16]

These changing characteristics of America's college students are
the result of a combination of demographic growth, changing social
views, government policies, and institutional initiatives to recruit students from all potential college populations. Some institutions, for
example, have altered their missions and strengthened their commitment to serve special populations. Such changes would have been impossible without the equity reform movements that brought about
changes in the nation's collective consciousness as well as tangible
federal assistance in the form of financial aid policies. We have also
witnessed the development and strengthening of types of specialized
institutions. Over the past two decades, more than two dozen tribal
colleges were established and have steadily increased their enrollments, and women's colleges and historically black institutions have
strengthened their position in terms of attaining a stable and increas-

ing student enrollment in the last ten years. In addition, an increasing number of institutions are expected to become Hispanic-serving toward the end of this decade (defined as institutions that have a minimum Hispanic enrollment of 25 percent).[17] In each case, student characteristics have given further definition to the institution's mission. Aside from these special types of institutions, traditional institutions respond to the new student populations by creating new services and incorporating new perspectives in the curriculum and extracurricular programming.[18]

While these changes may appear to have occurred rapidly, creating multicultural environments continues to come about slowly for those who confront institutional resistance. A college's historical legacy of exclusion of specific groups may, for example, continue to influence seemingly neutral institutional policies. Generating a commitment to institutional transformation among administrators and faculty who refuse to examine their own attitudes and practices that affect students remains one of the greatest challenges, made harder by political attacks on and misunderstandings of policies designed to ameliorate past injustices.[19] In short, ideologies at the individual, institutional, and social levels continue to present barriers to recognizing and meeting the needs of today's college student.

Student Values and Politics

Along with the changing demographics of higher education, there has been a shift in the values and ideologies of students compared to those held by students in the recent past. One area in which this has occurred most visibly is in student politics. Following on the heels of the volatile, activist 1960s, there is the perception that recent generations of students are more conservative, apathetic, and politically inactive. This perception is true, however, only if we think about student political preferences in traditional ways. From an institutional perspective, the sociopolitical character of students is important for several reasons. To begin with, an accumulation of research evidence concerns the influence that student peers have upon one another.[20] Thus, when the attitudes and values within college peer environments change, the impact of college *regardless of institutional intentions* is altered. In addition, the educational process requires common ground between students and faculty. If students and faculty find few points of agree-

Table 11.2

Political Self-Characterization and Attitudes of Entering College
Students (%)

	1970–72	1980–82	1990–92	2000–02
Political self-characterization				
Liberal	37	21	26	29
Middle of the road	47	60	54	51
Conservative	17	19	21	21
Conservatives/liberals	46/100	94/100	80/100	72/100
Political and social attitudes				
Federal government is not doing enough to control environmental pollution	90	79	87	
Federal military spending should be increased		39	24	45
Busing is OK if it helps to achieve racial balance in the schools		45	55	
Wealthy people should pay a larger share of taxes than they do now	73	71	72	51
A national health care plan is needed to cover everybody's medical costs		57	76	54
Abortion should be legal		54	64	
The activities of married women are best confined to the home and family	42	26	26	22
Marijuana should be legalized	41	34	21	37
Capital punishment should be abolished	57	31	21	32
There is too much concern in the courts for the rights of criminals	50	68	66	65

Source: Cooperative Institutional Research Program, Higher Education Research Institute, University of California, Los Angeles.

ment on attitudes and values, these ideological differences increase the potential for conflicts between students and faculty.

How have the political preferences of students changed? As we can see in the data from entering college students shown in table 11.2, there has been an interesting pattern of change in the way that students characterize themselves politically. For example, the percentage of students who classified themselves as liberal declined by nearly one-half between the early 1970s and the early 1980s. While the decline was sharp, it stabilized and actually rebounded somewhat during the 1980s, a time period in which we might have expected to see the strongest conservative influences, given events occurring on the national political scene.

Another interesting trend is that the declining number of student liberals seems to have been accompanied mainly by increases in the number of political moderates. Indeed, the number of students who said they were in the "middle of the road" jumped by about one-quarter in the 1970s, while the number of self-proclaimed conservatives increased a scant two percentage points. This may suggest that the issues associated with the 1960s political and social movements are now seen as relatively mainstream issues and are no longer "liberal" causes. It also seems to reflect political trends within the larger society, with politicians of nearly all ideological persuasions concertedly trying to appear moderate while simultaneously painting all others as being outside of the political mainstream.

Taken together, these trends reveal that there has been a tremendous shift in the balance of liberals and conservatives on campus: whereas there were two liberals for every conservative during the early 1970s, by the early 1980s the number of liberals and conservatives were roughly equal. Although this ratio has shifted back somewhat to favor the politically liberal, the ratio of liberals to conservatives is much closer to one-to-one than it was two decades ago. This may help explain the relatively increased effectiveness of conservative political agendas on college campuses and may portend a continuation of the polarized campus politics that have become evident in recent years.

Another way to look at the political preferences of students is to consider the changing patterns of attitudes that entering students have toward a variety of political and social values. Table 11.2 shows a complex set of trends among attitudes that would traditionally be classified as both conservative and liberal. For example, there has been a movement toward the liberal position in areas such as military spending, school busing, national health care, abortion rights, and women's rights, with entering students maintaining a relatively liberal stance toward the environment and taxation. At the same time, students have clearly become more conservative on issues related to crime and drugs: the number of students who believed capital punishment should be abolished dropped by nearly two-thirds between the early 1970s and early 1990s, while the percentage of students who supported the legalization of marijuana dropped by one-half over the same period, with both rebounding since that time.

It is important to consider what distinct role, if any, the larger social context plays in determining student views during the college years.[21] The data in table 11.3 show that the attitude changes of students during college are remarkably consistent with trends observed across cohorts of young adults. This can be seen by comparing the 1985 and 1989 attitudes of those students who entered college in 1985 with those of a cohort of college freshmen as measured by the CIRP and those of young adult respondents (noninstitutionalized eighteen- to twenty-three-year-olds) to the General Social Survey. For example, the change during college on the political identification item for those students who entered in 1985 is toward increased polarization (a 9% drop in the middle-of-the-road category, with these respondents moving about equally to liberal and conservative positions). The same pattern is evident for the different cohorts of CIRP and GSS respondents. The results in table 11.3 also point to the sharpest increases in liberal views toward national health and abortion rights; the social trend shows the same pattern. The degree to which these social trends are consistent with changes during college is important in that it demonstrates the webbed nature of social and collegiate influences and reminds us that change during college is not synonymous with college impact. Although some of the observed changes may well be due to college impact or maturation effects, the consistency of results across college and noncollege cohorts suggests that students are not immune to larger social and political forces.

Since these attitudes seem to reflect changing political views on the national political landscape, they also affect the issues that students choose to pursue within the campus political environment. But will today's student pursue these and other issues, or are they politically apathetic, as the common wisdom has it? The data from entering college students are complex in this area, as well. For example, the number of students who worked in political campaigns declined by about two-fifths between the late 1960s and late 1970s, while the number who reported having frequent discussions about politics declined by about one-third between the late 1960s and late 1980s and reached an all-time low of 15 percent in 1995. The 2000 survey results also show that "keeping up to date with political affairs" as an important life goal dropped to an all-time low of 28 percent, compared with 42 percent in 1990 and 58 percent in 1966. These figures clearly suggest

Table 11.3

College Student and Young Adult Opinions on Social Problems, 1985 and 1989 (%)

Social Problem	Student Attitudes During College			CIRP Freshman Survey Respondents			General Social Survey Young Adult Respondents		
	1985	1989	Δ	1985	1989	Δ	1985	1989	Δ
Political ID (Political leaning)									
Far right (extremely conservative)	1	1	0	1	2	1	1	3	+2
Conservative	22	27	+5	20	21	+1	23	26	+3
Middle of the road (moderate)	50	41	−9	57	54	−3	47	38	−9
Liberal	25	29	+4	21	22	+1	28	30	+2
Far left (extremely liberal)	2	3	+1	2	2	0	2	4	+2
Attitude toward capital punishment									
The death penalty should be abolished. (Do you favor or oppose the death penalty for persons convicted of murder?) Strongly disagree or disagree (Favor)	72	73	+1	73	79	+6	73	72	−1
Attitudes toward government's role in providing health care									
A national health care plan is needed to cover everybody's health care costs. (Favor government help to cover medical costs?) Strongly agree or agree (Yes)	56	66	+10	61	76	+15	53	63	+10
Attitudes toward abortion rights									
Abortion should be legal. (Possible to obtain a legal abortion for any reason?) Strongly agree or agree (Yes)	59	74	+15	55	65	+10	35	45	+10

Source: Eric L. Dey, Alexander W. Astin, and William S. Korn, *The American Freshman: Twenty-five Year Trends* (Los Angeles: University of California, Los Angeles, Higher Education Research Institute, 1991); James A. Davis and Tom W. Smith, *The NORC General Social Survey: A User's Guide* (Newbury Park, Calif.: Sage, 1992); F. W. Wood, *An American Profile: Opinions and Behavior, 1972–1989* (Detroit: Gale Research, 1990).

Note: Wording in parentheses was used in GSS. Δ indicates raw percentage difference.

Table 11.4

College Freshmen's High School Grades, Various Years (%)

Grade	1966	1975	1984	1994
A or A+	15	18	20	28
B− to B+	54	60	58	57
C+ or less	31	21	22	16

Source: This and the following three tables are based on data from Eric L. Dey, Alexander W. Astin, and William S. Korn, *The American Freshman: Twenty-five Year Trends* (Los Angeles: University of California, Los Angeles, Higher Education Research Institute, 1991); Alexander W. Astin, Eric L. Dey, William S. Korn, and Ellyne R. Riggs, *The American Freshman: National Norms for Fall 1991* (Los Angeles: University of California, Los Angeles, Higher Education Research Institute, 1991): Alexander W. Astin, William S. Korn, and Ellyne R. Riggs, *The American Freshman: National Norms for Fall 1993* (Los Angeles: University of California, Los Angeles, Higher Education Research Institute, 1993); Linda J. Sax, Alexander W. Astin, William S. Korn, and Kit M. Mahoney, *The American Freshman: National Norms for Fall 1995* (Los Angeles: University of California, Los Angeles, Higher Education Research Institute, 1995).

that students are not politically active in traditional ways, while other information suggests that students may simply be disillusioned with and alienated from traditional politics.[22]

Educational Plans and Preferences

In addition to the changing composition of students, there have been changes in student plans and preferences for college. Some of these patterns appear to be related to student experiences in high school and to larger economic forces, and others seem more closely related to social forces like changing views about the role of women in American society. First, we consider the issue of student academic experiences during high school and how this appears to relate to their expectations for the college experience.

The data in table 11.4 show that college students who earned A grades in high school essentially doubled between 1966 and 1994, while the percentage earning C or worse grades fell by one-half. The relatively high level of student academic success before college appears to have influenced the expectations students had for college. The CIRP data show strong increases between 1973 and 1994 in the percentage of entering students who expected to earn at least a B average in college, to graduate with honors, and to be elected to an

Table 11.5

College Freshmen's Expectations Regarding College Success, Various Years (%)

Expectation	1973	1983	1994
Make at least a B average	35	41	46
Graduate with honors	9	12	16
Be elected to an academic honor society	5	7	9
Fail at least one course	2	1	1
Get tutoring help	7[a]	9	16[b]

Source: See table 11.4.

   a. 1975
   b. 1992

Table 11.6

College Freshmen's Expectations Regarding Remedial Work, by Subject, Various Years (%)

Subject	1982	1984	1993
English	11	11	12
Reading	4	5	5
Mathematics	22	27	29
Social studies	2	3	4
Science	9	10	11
Foreign language	7	10	11

Source: See table 11.4.

academic honor society (table 11.5). Over the same period, the percentage of students expecting to fail one or more courses dropped by half. These patterns might suggest that students today are better prepared than those entering college two decades ago, but students also reported that they were in need of additional academic support services. For example, the percentage of students who believed that there was a "very good chance" that they would get tutoring help in specific courses during college more than doubled between 1975 and 1992. Similarly, the percentage of students who expected to get special tutoring or remediation in mathematics, science, and foreign language increased between 1984 and 1993 (table 11.6). What makes this interesting is that, over approximately the same period, students were likely to meet the recommended levels of preparation in many of these fields (table 11.7). For example, more than 92 percent of students who

Table 11.7

College Freshmen's High School Preparation, by Subject, Various Years (%)

Subject	1984	1988	1994
English (4 years)	93	95	96
Mathematics (3 years)	85	92	92
Foreign language (2 years)	66	79	81
Physical science (2 years)	52	50	47
Biological science (2 years)	34	35	36

Source: See table 11.4.

entered college in 1994 had at least three years of math during high school, while three out of every ten students in 1993 expected to need special tutoring or remediation in math.

Taken together, these trends suggest that there has been a redefinition of the relationship between academic course work at the high school level and skills related to those courses. This puts tremendous pressure on college and university faculty to work with students who have been academically successful in high school, who met or exceeded recommended levels of high school study, but who may, nevertheless, be underprepared for college-level work as traditionally defined.

The changing pattern of students' preference for undergraduate major when they enter college is an important consideration, since beyond all of the educational philosophy that goes into designing a curriculum, a college's ability to maintain its curricular focus is necessarily dependent upon its ability to enroll students in the courses it offers. Interest in majoring in the humanities, the fine and performing arts, and the social sciences has been declining consistently over the past three decades (table 11.8). Interest in majoring in English, for example, dropped by one-half between 1966 and 2002; interest in majoring in biological or physical sciences has remained somewhat stable since the 1960s, while interest in mathematics and statistics has experienced a large decline. Although the relatively new and developing field of computer science may have captured some of the students who otherwise might have majored in mathematics or statistics, this sharp decline in the number of students who enter college with an interest in math and statistics is alarming.

The greatest change in popularity is associated with the field of business. After a period of relative stability, the percentage of stu-

Table 11.8

Undergraduate Major Preferences, Entering College Students, Various Years (%)

College Major	1966	1972	1980	1987	1993	1997	2002
Biological sciences	4	4	4	4	6	8	7
Business	14	16	24	27	16	16	16
Education	11	7	8	9	10	10	11
Engineering	10	7	12	9	9	10	10
English	4	2	1	1	1	2	2
Health professions	5	11	9	7	16	13	11
History or political science	7	4	3	3	3	4	5
Humanities	5	4	2	3	2	3	2
Fine arts	8	9	5	5	4	5	6
Mathematics or statistics	5	2	1	1	1	1	1
Physical sciences	3	2	2	2	2	2	2
Social sciences		8	5	6	7	7	7
Undecided	2	5	5	7	7	8	8

Source: Cooperative Institutional Research Program, Higher Education Research Institute, University of California, Los Angeles.

dents interested in business majors increased sharply during the late 1970s and 1980s. During the past few years, however, interest in business has stopped its climb and is currently in steep decline, with student interest now equal to that registered in the mid-1960s. The cause for this turnaround is not clear. It may be that competition for jobs has increased or that students are disillusioned with the field of business because of scandals such as insider trading, stock fraud, and the savings and loan debacle of the 1980s. While the explanation for these trends may not be clear, one thing is clear: institutions that expanded their business programs to take advantage of growth in student interest may have too many faculty in the field of business relative to student demand. This problem may be especially troublesome for the many small liberal arts colleges that avoided closure during the 1980s by moving away from a traditional liberal arts program to incorporate business education into the curriculum.[23]

While interest in business is in steep decline, interest in the health professions has been increasing. This surge of interest may reflect a search for majors that will lead to profitable and stable careers, since business has apparently lost its attraction. But education for the health professions, which is largely based in the sciences, is more ex-

Table 11.9

Undergraduate and Graduate Degree and Major Preferences, Entering
Female College Students, Various Years (number per 100 male students)

College Degree and Major	1972	1982	1992	2002
Postgraduate degree aspiration				
Law	32	81	106	96
Medical	44	90	103	152
Doctoral	64	86	99	102
Undergraduate major field preferences				
Biological sciences	64	103	102	136
Business	80	115	91	62
Education	329	375	286	240
Engineering	3	16	16	21
English	278	167	167	162
Health professions (nursing, premed, etc.)	550	331	239	248
History and political science	54	69	83	82
Humanities	204	163	121	139
Fine arts (applied and performing)	124	102	60	121
Mathematics or statistics	100	117	71	88
Physical sciences	27	38	54	71
Social sciences	227	275	247	239

Source: Eric L. Dey, Alexander W. Astin, and William S. Korn, *The American Freshman: Twenty-five Year Trends* (Los Angeles: University of California, Los Angeles Higher Education Research Institute, 1991). Eric L. Dey, Alexander W. Astin, William S. Korn, and Ellyne R. Riggs, *The American Freshman: National Norms for Fall 1992* (Los Angeles: University of California, Los Angeles Higher Education Research Institute, 1992).

pensive than that associated with business. Moreover, it is impossible to predict how long this trend will last.

Beyond the pronounced changes in the major field choices of students generally are the changing educational preferences of women. Table 11.9 shows the ratio of women students interested in degrees and fields of study, compared with male students interested in the same option. The changes over the two decades show the effectiveness of the women's movement in changing the way women (and to a lesser extent, men) think about certain degrees and careers. For example, with respect to postgraduate degree aspirations upon entry into college, women have essentially reached a point of parity with men. Indeed, aspiration for law and medical degrees among women now slightly exceeds that of men.

In the undergraduate fields in which women were most underrepresented in 1972—engineering, history and political science, biological sciences, and the physical sciences—a pattern has emerged of progress toward parity. Engineering, for example, had the smallest representation of women in 1972, and this fact remained true two decades later. Despite a fivefold jump in interest in this field between 1972 and 1982, there have been only modest changes since that time. There may still be strong institutional barriers—such as heavy mathematical course requirements without a realistic possibility of remediation and a male-dominated climate that is unwelcoming for women—that prevent interest levels from moving beyond this plateau. The other science fields with an early underrepresentation of women have fared differently: women's interest in the biological sciences moved quickly to a position of parity, while the physical sciences still have a long way to go despite a tripling of interest between 1972 and 2002. History and political science have also made progress in attracting the interest of women but still remain far below a point of parity. Education shows a declining rate of interest among women, despite being strongly dominated by women. The health professions, which include the large, female-dominated field of nursing, now attract the interest of fewer women relative to men. In English, the humanities, and the fine arts, there has been a lessening of interest among women, with the decline so sharp in the fine arts that women are now underrepresented. Women are now also underrepresented in the field of business, after reaching and exceeding a position of parity in the 1980s.

These changes will continue to have an impact on institutions as they attempt to balance their traditional educational missions and curricula with the changing interests of students. This is especially true of the changing patterns of interest among women and members of other underrepresented groups, as such trends bring with them pressure to remove inequities and achievement barriers for these groups. In addition to influencing institutional policy and practice, these shifts in student interest are also linked to larger social and economic forces (such as the projected job market) and have direct implications for the nation's talent pool. The continued advancement of all fields of practice or inquiry is determined in good part by the pool of student talent in each field and in part by higher education's ability to meet social and economic needs.

Table 11.10

Student's College Experiences, 1966–1970 and 1987–1991 (%)

Experience	1966–1970	1987–1991
Undergraduate grade point average		
A or A+	1	6
A– or B+	5	27
B	21	36
B– or C+	35	24
C	26	7
C– or less	13	2
Activities since entering college		
Joined a fraternity or sorority	20	21
Graduated with honors	14	12
Frequent activities during student's last year of college		
Drank wine or liquor	12	22
Drank beer	30	38
Stayed up all night	8	14
Participated in an organized demonstration/protest[a]	19	18
Attended a religious service	33	25
Smoked cigarettes	27	12
Percentage of students who were satisfied with:		
Overall quality of instruction	92	90
Opportunity to discuss coursework with professors outside of class	84	88
Lab facilities	90	88
Library	83	83
Overall satisfaction	74	87

Source: Unpublished tabulations, Higher Education Research Institute, UCLA.

a. Includes students marking "frequently" or "occasionally."

College Experiences

As one might expect, given the many changes described, there have been changes in the nature of the college student experience. Table 11.10 shows changes in student academic performance, activities, and student satisfaction during college from the late 1960s to the beginning of the 1990s. Perhaps one of the most striking changes has been the shift toward high grades. This may indicate that performance and academic success in college have been redefined, creating grade inflation, or it may reflect the fact that students have become more grade conscious and may be more likely to contest their grades. However, the trend may also be fueled by external pressures, as maintaining good college grades has become more closely linked to such economic considerations as the receipt of financial aid, auto insurance discounts, and access to graduate schools and jobs after college. And while more students make high grades, fewer students graduate with honors.

Despite the changing political views of students and the persistent (and somewhat contradictory) images of the typical college student as an activist or a member of a fraternity or sorority, we find very little change in the proportion of students who have participated in either of these activities since the 1960s. This suggests that these two activities are relatively generation free, since a roughly stable proportion of students have participated. But despite the apparent constancy in the proportion of students involved in these activities, different generations of students become associated with these images due to larger social and political contexts. For example, even though a minority of students participated in demonstrations in the late 1960s, the general perception of students during this era is that most did.

In terms of health and social behavior, students of the 1990s are less likely to report frequent smoking, due in part to increased health awareness and related restrictions on smoking in school, at work, and in places of entertainment. However, a higher proportion of students in 1987–91 reported that they drank wine, liquor, or beer in college than in 1966–70. While most of the students surveyed would have met drinking-age requirements by their fourth year of college, it would be difficult to restrict their associations with other students who are under the age limit. This shift in student behavior makes it extremely problematic for colleges to monitor and comply with legislation raising the drinking age. Colleges continue to provide opportunities for alcohol-free activities, but providing alternatives for healthy social lives will remain one of the continuing challenges for student affairs staffs on campus.

Student satisfaction and retention are closely related to college impact and institutional accountability, and the data show that student satisfaction with the college experience has remained generally high over time, with only small changes in specific areas of satisfaction. Although students are somewhat less satisfied with laboratory facilities and the quality of instruction on campus, in the early 1990s they were more satisfied with opportunities to discuss course work with professors outside of class.

Table 11.11

Graduation Rates, 1966–1991 (%)

Undergraduate Cohort	Obtained Bachelor's Degree	Obtained Bachelor's Degree or Completed Four Years
1966–70	47	59
1978–82	43	56
1994–2000	36	58

Source: Alexander W. Astin, *Predicting Academic Performance in College* (New York: Free Press, 1971); Kenneth C. Green, Alexander W. Astin, William S. Korn, and Patricia McNamara, *The American College Student, 1982: National Norms for 1978 and 1980 College Freshmen* (Los Angeles: University of California, Los Angeles Higher Education Research Institute, 1983); unpublished tabulations, Higher Education Research Institute.

Overall satisfaction remains high even though student retention has dropped over the years. Table 11.11 shows the proportion of three undergraduate student cohorts that stayed at the college they originally entered, using two retention measures. A decreasing proportion of students have obtained a degree in four years, but the proportion persisting through four years has remained relatively stable, suggesting that later cohorts are taking longer to graduate than earlier cohorts. There is perhaps no single explanation for why students are taking longer to graduate. Students now face additional financial pressures; financial aid has shifted from grants to loans, and to avoid excessive debt, more students are working and attending college part-time.[24] In addition, anecdotal evidence suggests that some students are finding it difficult to enroll in required courses at many large institutions, while others may be delaying their completion by taking advantage of programs for study abroad or other opportunities that broaden their experiences but that also lengthen the amount of time it takes to earn a degree.

Student retention will remain an important area of institutional accountability, and we can expect that more institutions will begin to follow closely the progress of students and make efforts to improve their college experiences. Trends in student graduation rates have redefined *persistence* such that it must be monitored from year to year and over a longer time span. Administrators, legislators, and the general public are becoming increasingly concerned about institutional retention rates, and new federal regulations require that institutions report these rates.

Students, Colleges, and Society

Changes in the composition and nature of American undergraduates and a recognition of the interconnections between students, institutions, and society force us to reconceptualize our thinking about college students. Specifically, the trends across generations of college students encourage a more complex view of the role of students in American higher education. Educational programs are intended to influence those who participate in them. However, the reverse is also true: many institutions change their recruitment strategies, services, and curricula as the constituencies they serve change. The value of an ecological perspective is underscored by the changing demography of higher education, trends in student political preferences and academic interests, and significant changes in aspects of the college experience. Service to special populations has become a central mission of some colleges, while changes in the type of student attending traditional four-year institutions reflect new needs and create new demands for institutional change. In contrast to student protests and political action, a tremendous amount of student-led change arises as the result of natural institutional efforts to serve student needs. Although many of these changes represent responses to recognized problems and come about with pressure from external constituencies (parents, alumni, taxpayers, legislators, peer institutions), they represent an attempt on the part of institutions to improve the educational process for students.

Attempts by students to change institutions through protest and other forms of direct action tend to receive the most attention. But students can also resist attempts to be changed by institutions, and administrators may find it particularly problematic to change students' social habits at institutions with strong student cultures. For example, student drinking has increased, even though new national policies designed to decrease alcohol use have been implemented by the colleges. Institutional efforts designed to eliminate fraternities' hazing and racist or sexist games have also been met with varied success. The roots of this resistance may be based both in politics and in the youth culture, so institutional rules and regulations, regardless of student input in their formation, cannot change student behavior. Thus, students and student culture may instigate change or create resistance within institutions.

Many problematic areas for institutions are caused by students following their own preferences. Perhaps the most troubling information presented in this chapter has to do with the future talent pool in specific fields. How can institutions influence students to pursue careers that will be vital in the future? At some level, students are attuned to the job market, but their goals may not be synchronized with a changing economic future: by the time students graduate from college with specific training, the availability of jobs in their intended fields may have disappeared. The increasing rapidity with which economies change suggests that the length of an undergraduate education will plague students seeking careers in fields with an unstable pattern of job growth.

A complete view of the relationship between students, colleges, and society is both reciprocal and dynamic. Adopting this ecological perspective requires that we rethink the nature of students' role in relation to institutions and the wider society. Students have proactively and subtly induced institutional and social change throughout history and will continue to do so in the future. These changes, in turn, have altered the nature of the student experience and the impact college has on students. Those interested in higher education must recognize and acknowledge these interconnections and begin to view the role of college students in more complex ways.

NOTES

1. Burton R. Clark, *The Distinctive College* (Chicago: Aldine, 1970), 253.

2. Robert Klitgaard, *Choosing Elites* (New York: Harper and Row, 1985); Alexander W. Astin, *Achieving Educational Excellence* (San Francisco: Jossey-Bass, 1985).

3. T. Dary Erwin, *Assessing Student Learning and Development: A Guide to the Principles, Goals, and Methods of Determining Outcomes* (San Francisco: Jossey-Bass, 1991); Ernest T. Pascarella and Patrick T. Terenzini, *How College Affects Students* (San Francisco: Jossey-Bass, 1991); Maryann Jacobi, Alexander W. Astin, and Frank Ayala, Jr., *College Student Outcomes Assessment: A Talent Development Perspective* (Washington, D.C.: Association for the Study of Higher Education, 1987); Astin, *Achieving Educational Excellence.*

4. Philip G. Altbach, "Students: Interests, Culture, and Activism," in *Higher Learning in America, 1980–2000,* ed. Arthur Levine (Baltimore: Johns Hopkins University Press, 1993); Patricia Y. Gurin, Eric L. Dey, Sylvia Hurtado, and Gerald Gurin, "Diversity and Higher Education: Theory and

Impact on Educational Outcomes." *Harvard Educational Review,* 72, no. 3 (2002): 300–366; Sylvia Hurtado, Eric L. Dey, Patricia Y. Gurin, and Gerald Gurin, "College Environments, Diversity, and Student Learning," in *Higher Education: Handbook of Theory and Research,* ed., John S. Smart, vol. 18 (New York: Agathon Press).

    5. Seymour M. Lipset, *Rebellion in the University* (New York: Little, Brown, 1971), 263.

    6. Altbach, "Students"; Tony Vellela, *New Voices: Student Activism in the '80s and '90s* (Boston: South End, 1988).

    7. Duane F. Alwin, Ronald L. Cohen, and Theodore M. Newcomb, *Political Attitudes over the Life Span: The Bennington Women after Fifty Years* (Madison: University of Wisconsin Press, 1991); Urie Bronfenbrenner, *The Ecology of Human Development: Experiments by Nature and Design* (Cambridge, MA: Harvard University Press, 1979).

    8. Bronfenbrenner, *Ecology of Human Development,* 13.

    9. Ibid., 17.

    10. Jeylan T. Mortimer, Michael D. Finch, and Donald Kumka, *Work, Family, and Personality: Transition to Adulthood* (Norwood, NJ: Ablex, 1986), cited in Alwin, Cohen, and Newcomb, *Political Attitudes,* 252.

    11. Alexander W. Astin, William S. Korn, and Ellyne R. Riggs, *The American Freshman: National Norms for Fall 1993* (Los Angeles: University of California, Los Angeles, Higher Education Research Institute, 1993); Eric L. Dey, Alexander W. Astin, and William S. Korn, *The American Freshman: Twenty-five Year Trends* (Los Angeles: University of California, Los Angeles, Higher Education Research Institute, 1991).

    12. Alexander W. Astin and Robert J. Panos, *The Educational and Vocational Development of College Students* (Washington, D.C.: American Council on Education, 1969); Kenneth C. Green, Alexander W. Astin, William S. Korn, and Patricia McNamara, *The American College Student, 1982: National Norms for 1978 and 1980 College Freshmen* (Los Angeles: University of California, Los Angeles, Higher Education Research Institute, 1983); *The American College Student, 1991: National Norms for 1987 and 1989 College Freshmen* (Los Angeles: University of California, Los Angeles, Higher Education Research Institute, 1991).

    13. Martha L. Hollins, Samuel F. Barbett, Rosalind A. Korb, and Frank B. Morgan, *Enrollment in Higher Education: Fall 1986 through Fall 1994* (Washington, D.C.: National Center for Education Statistics, 1996).

    14. National Center for Education Statistics, *Digest of Education Statistics, 1996* (Washington, D.C.: NCES, 1996), table 171.

    15. *Digest of Education Statistics,* National Center for Education Statics Web site: www.nces.ed.gov/pubs2003/digest02/ch_3.asp; A. P. Carnevale and R. A. Fry. *Crossing the Great Divide: Can We Achieve Quality When Generation Y Goes to College?* (Princeton, NJ: Educational Testing Service, 2000), 8.

16. William B. Harvey, *Minorities in Higher Education, 2001–2002: Nineteenth Annual Status Report* (Washington, D.C.: American Council on Education).

17. Statistics based on calculations of college enrollment by racial/ethnic group from *Minorities in Higher Education, 2001–2002: Nineteenth Annual Status Report* (Washington, D.C.: American Council on Education).

18. Carol Pearson, Donna L. Shavlik, and Judith G. Touchton, eds., *Educating the Majority: Women Challenge Tradition in Higher Education* (New York: ACE/MacMillan, 1989); Daryl G. Smith, *The Challenge of Diversity: Involvement or Alienation in the Academy* (Washington, D.C.: Association for the Study of Higher Education, 1989). Margaret L. Andersen, "Changing the Curriculum in Higher Education," in *Reconstructing the Academy: Women's Education and Women's Studies,* ed. Elizabeth Minnich, Jean O'Barr, and Rachel Rosenfeld (Chicago: University of Chicago, 1988).

19. Sylvia Hurtado, "The Institutional Climate for Talented Latino Students," *Research in Higher Education* 35 (1994): 21–41; Susan Hardy Aiken, Karen Anderson, Myra Dinnerstein, Judy Lensink, and Patricia MacCorquodale, "Trying Transformations: Curriculum Integration and the Problem of Resistance," in *Reconstructing the Academy: Women's Education and Women's Studies,* ed. Elizabeth Minnich, Jean O'Barr, and Rachel Rosenfeld (Chicago: University of Chicago Press, 1988); Sylvia Hurtado and Christine G. Navia, "Reconciling College Access and the Affirmative Action Debate," in *Affirmative Action's Testament of Hope,* ed. Mildred Garcia (Albany: State University of New York Press, 1997).

20. Alexander W. Astin, *What Matters in College: Four Critical Years Revisited* (San Francisco: Jossey-Bass, 1993); see also Pascarella and Terenzini, *How College Affects Students.*

21. Eric L. Dey, "Undergraduate Political Attitudes: An Examination of Peer, Faculty, and Social Influences," *Research in Higher Education* 37 (1996): 535–54.

22. Linda J. Sax, Alexander W. Astin, William S. Korn, and Kit M. Mahoney, *The American Freshman: National Norms for Fall 2000* (Los Angeles: University of California, Los Angeles, Higher Education Research Institute, 1995); Paul R. Loeb, *Generation at the Crossroads* (New Brunswick: Rutgers University Press, 1994).

23. David W. Breneman, "Liberal Arts Colleges: What Price Survival?" in *Higher Learning in America, 1980–2000,* ed. Arthur Levine (Baltimore: Johns Hopkins University Press, 1993).

24. College Board, *Trends in Student Aid: 1980 to 1989* (New York: College Board, 1989); Alexander W. Astin, Eric L. Dey, William S. Korn, and Ellyne R. Riggs, *The American Freshman: National Norms for Fall 1991* (Los Angeles: University of California, Los Angeles, Higher Education Research Institute, 1991).

Chapter Twelve

The Dilemma of Presidential Leadership

Robert Birnbaum and Peter D. Eckel

If any man wishes to be humbled and mortified, let
him become president of Harvard College (plaintive
cry of Harvard president Edward Holyoke on his
deathbed in 1769).

— F. S. Horn

Every decade, about five thousand persons serve as college or university presidents. Over a term of office averaging less than seven years,
the president is expected to serve simultaneously as the chief administrator of a large and complex bureaucracy, as the convening colleague
of a professional community, as a symbolic elder in a campus culture
of shared values and symbols, and (in some institutions) as a public
official accountable to a public board and responsive to the demands of
other governmental agencies. Balancing the conflicting expectations
of these roles has always been difficult; changing demographic trends,
fiscal constraints, the complexity and diversity of tasks, university dynamics, and unrealistic public expectations make it virtually impossible for most presidents to provide the leadership that is expected.

The college presidency may not be the second oldest profession in
America, but the role has existed in this country from the time of the
founding of Harvard in 1636, a century and half before there was a
nation. From the colonial period until the Civil War, institutions were
for the most part small, simply structured, and controlled by their

lay boards of trustees, leading to a weak presidency. The president's role even in those days was a demanding one and included teaching, preaching, fund raising, record keeping, and (most especially) student discipline, but in a simpler world of certain knowledge and accepted authority most presidents were able to perform effectively the tasks expected of them.

The period between the Civil War and World War I was one of expansion and transformation in higher education. New and more complex institutions were created as research and public service were added to the traditional teaching mission. The late nineteenth and early twentieth centuries were times of the "great men," presidents who often wielded unchecked authority to create great institutions. Trustee boards were increasingly composed of businessmen who embraced the developing concepts of scientific management. Viewing the college as comparable to a business firm, faculty were considered to be employees hired to do as they were told, and the president, in Thorstein Veblen's caustic term, was the "Captain of Erudition," responsible for increasing enrollment, capital, and reputation, while controlling costs.[1]

The job was clearly becoming more difficult, and observers of that day could note that "the duties imposed upon the modern university president are so multifarious that it is becoming exceedingly difficult to find a man capable of filling the position in the larger institutions."[2] But although the role had become more complex, it was still one possible to fulfill; presidents had the power, and if they wished (and many did) they could administer following the precept attributed to Benjamin Jowett, the head of Balliol College, Oxford: "Never retract. Never explain. Get the thing done and let them howl!"

As institutions became more comprehensive and involved in scholarship, the faculty became more specialized, more professionalized, and less tolerant of administrative controls. Increasingly until World War II, and then with accelerating force during the 1950s and 1960s, faculty claimed for themselves the right not only to make decisions concerning the major educational activities of the institution but also to participate fully in setting institutional policy and to have a voice in its management. The growing power of the faculty, a change significant enough to justify referring to it as the "academic revolution,"[3] was one of the forces that led postwar presidents to claim that "the fundamental difficulty with the office of university president arises out of the current system of controlling modern universities. . . . He has vast responsibilities for all phases of the life and welfare of the university, but he has no power."[4]

Presidential discretion was increasingly limited not only by forces within the academy but by those outside as well. In particular, federal and state agencies were exerting influence over matters that had previously been considered internal institutional prerogatives. The loss of effective presidential authority, related internally to changes in organizational complexity and patterns of influence and externally to increased environmental constraints, helped to transform the role from a difficult job to an impossible one.

This claim must be accompanied by a caveat. There are more than 3,500 colleges and universities, most (but not all) headed by a chief executive officer with the title of president (or, less frequently, chancellor). The composite public image of a small number of the more visible institutions tends to obscure their great diversity in size, wealth, program level, complexity, student selectivity, faculty preparation, and public or private sponsorship—all factors that affect presidential authority and therefore the extent to which presidents can be effective. The historical generalizations that have already been made, and the analyses that follow, must therefore be applied with caution. In discussing the presidential role, this chapter focuses primarily upon institutions with at least moderate enrollments, multiple missions, and comprehensive programs. Such institutions enroll most of the students in higher education, but they probably represent less than half of the total number of the nation's colleges and universities.

The Presidential Role

There is no standard definition of the presidency nor description of the expectations placed on the performance of its incumbents. Presidents traditionally have no stated term of office but serve "at the pleasure" of a public or private board of lay trustees. Institutional statutes or bylaws commonly identify the president as the chief executive and administrative officer of the board as well as the chief academic officer of the faculty, and they delegate to the president all powers necessary to perform these functions. Statements of such sweeping authority may appear to the uninitiated to offer almost unlimited control over administrative and programmatic initiatives, but the reality of presidential influence is quite different. As one president has commented, "regardless of what may appear in the charter and bylaws, the authority of the president, his real leadership, depends on the willingness of the campus to accept him as a leader. If it will not, well there are other ways for him to earn a living."[5]

There are many ways of looking at the components of the presidential role. One typical listing identifies and describes responsibilities inside and outside the institution. Inside the institution, presidents report they spend their time planning, budgeting, making personnel decisions, addressing academic issues, and dealing with students. Outside, they find themselves raising funds, building and managing board relations, working with community groups and representing the institution to external constituents, and meeting with policy makers.[6] They spend time not only constructing buildings and recruiting and hiring the brightest faculty but also upholding and embodying core academic values.

From a more analytical perspective, presidential tasks can be seen as comprising administrative, political, and entrepreneurial components.[7] As administrator, the president carries out the policies of the trustees, supervises subordinates, allocates resources, establishes systems of accountability, and performs functions similar to those found in any complex organization. As politician, the president must be responsive to the needs of various constituencies whose support is critical to the maintenance of his or her position. The interests of groups and subgroups of faculty, students, alumni, elected officials and others whose actions may constrain presidential discretion must be considered and courted, and the president must often form coalitions and propose compromises that will permit peace with progress. As entrepreneur, the president is expected to develop and exploit markets that offer necessary resources for the institution. Fund-raising is perhaps the most visible component of this role, but communicating with legislators in the statehouse or in Washington as well as interacting with corporate leaders, facilitating technology transfer agreements, supporting research incubator projects, securing licensing agreements, patents and intellectual property rights, overseeing auxiliary services (hospitals, residence halls, athletics), and maximizing endowment returns are important and time-consuming activities.

There may be agreement on the components of the role, but there is no model of the presidency that identifies priorities between them. Presidential activities are to a great extent contingent on the characteristics of their institutions, the inexorable ebb and flow of the academic calendar, the emerging exigencies of the environment, and their own personal interests. Some presidents spend a majority of their time in fund-raising, public representation, and related resource acquisition activities. The typical president spends little time on academic matters.

The pace, intensity, and comprehensiveness of the presidency are in many ways comparable to those of managers and executives in other settings.[8] But there is a fundamental difference. On a college campus the exercise of authority in governance is not solely an administrative prerogative but, rather, a shared responsibility and joint effort that properly involves all important campus constituencies, with particular emphasis given to the participation of the faculty. The influential "Joint Statement on Government of Colleges and Universities," for example, gives to the faculty the "primary responsibility" for "curriculum, subject matter and methods of instruction, research, faculty status, and those aspects of student life which relate to the educational process." In such matters, the president is expected to "concur with the faculty judgment except in rare instances and for compelling reasons which should be stated in detail." If, as it is generally agreed, the central questions that define the essential nature of a college or university are "Who should teach?" "What should be taught?" and "Who shall be taught?" the normative precepts of the joint statement reserve these matters for the direct control of the faculty and not for either the president or the trustees.

The joint statement codified what had been true for many years at academically strong campuses and what was evolving as good practice at many others. In doing so, it highlighted the basic managerial dilemma of the president; essential questions of institutional "production" or service, which would be considered matters of managerial prerogative in other settings, were in colleges and universities to be decided by the faculty, who were "employees." In a business firm, the president or CEO is solely accountable to a board of directors. In higher education, the president functions between two layers of organizational operations—the trustees and the faculty—and is accountable to both. Conflict between constituent groups is common in many organizations, but its importance and consequences for the college president may be unique. In a business firm, presidential tenure is the sole prerogative of the board of directors. Within many colleges or universities, however, faculty (and often other groups as well) assert the right to participate in presidential selection and evaluation.

And, as many presidents have discovered, a faculty vote of no confidence often has the same power to end a presidential career as does a formal vote by the trustees to whom a president legally reports.[9]

The Impossible Job

There is no educational, social, or political consensus on exactly what higher education should be doing, what constituencies it should serve, and how it should serve them. At different times and on different campuses, emphasis has been given to transmitting values, to discovering knowledge, or to improving society. Some of the manifest purposes of higher education—the education and development of individual students, transmitting the culture and advancing society in general, providing for educational justice and social mobility, supporting intellectual and artistic creativity, and evaluating society so that it can become self-renewing[10]—enjoy general support as principles but become contentious as people attempt to describe how such vague ideals should best be implemented.

In addition to these obvious aims, colleges and universities have latent purposes as well. Among other things, they serve a custodial function by removing from parents the burden of controlling the behavior of young adults; they serve as a means of certifying to employers that graduates possess diligence and at least a modicum of intelligence; they socialize students and help them develop networks that will prove useful later in life; and they perpetuate the existing social order. These latter functions often conflict with the avowed purposes of colleges and universities, and although less often discussed, they are nonetheless important.

Goals of access, quality, and diversity, which are in conflict and which call for quite different institutional structures and responses, appear and then wane on the public policy agenda in cycles; the essential educational missions of teaching, research, and service compete for resources; and there is no rational way to assess the legitimacy of the competing and incompatible demands of many internal and external groups. Internally, faculty and administrators may disagree on appropriate levels of workload or salary, students and faculty may be in conflict about degree requirements or the academic calendar, alumni and trustees may debate the virtues of tradition and change, and students may disagree with administrative perspectives on offering "living wages" to hourly university workers, making progress on campus diversity, or purchasing athletic apparel from "sweatshops." Externally, institutions may find themselves arguing with local governments over the costs and availability of civic services and about taxes, with environmental groups about research on genetically modified foods, with neighborhood associations over off campus housing, with local businesses overselling competing services, and with local institutions overaccepting transfer courses.

Virtually all of these demands have some merit, and few can be dismissed out of hand. Yet there is no accepted criterion presidents can employ to judge the benefits of one course of action over another, and little assurance that they could implement their preferences even if they could specify them. Presidential authority is limited, complete understanding of the scope and complexity of the enterprise exceeds human cognitive capability, and unforeseen changes in demographic, political, and economic conditions often overwhelm campus plans. Presidents fortunate enough to preside during good times may reap the benefits of a munificent environment over which they have had no control, and even the incompetent may appear heroic; presidents during times of depression or social ferment may reap a whirlwind they did not sow.

The following sections consider five of the factors that limit presidential leadership: the constraints on presidential discretion; the unique characteristics of academic organizations; the problems of assessing effectiveness; privatization, market pressures, and competition; and the limitations of the presidential role.

Constraints on Presidential Discretion

Many factors increasingly limit presidential leadership.[11] Some of these result from interactions with other organizations, others arise within the institutions themselves. Environmental constraints include, among others, more federal and state controls; involvement by the courts in academic decision making; layers of governance and oversight, particularly in institutions that are part of statewide systems; few opportunities for growth and consequently for changes accompanying growth; questions about the mission and purpose of higher education; concerns about costs; issues of accountability and quality; and a growing competitive and winner-take-all mentality throughout society. Within institutions, constraints to leadership arise due to involvement by faculties in academic and personnel decisions; faculty collective bargaining; goal ambiguity; fractionation of the campus into interest groups, leading to a lack of consensus and community; greater involvement by trustees into campus operations; and increased bureaucracy and specialization among campus administrators.

Statewide coordinating or governing boards in almost all states exercise increasing influence over matters reserved in the past for the campus, including such critical issues as faculty personnel policies, the creation of new academic degree programs, and the review of academic programs. They monitor institutions for program duplication, cost containment and tuition pricing, admissions policies, and transfer policies.

In addition, federal and state regulation and the courts limit presidential discretion. For instance, many state governments set the tuition levels of their public institutions, limiting ways in which institutions can generate revenue. Some states are exchanging one set of constraints for another by giving institutions freedom from certain state regulations in return for more and different performance measures. They are then tying public support to institutions' abilities to deliver on these accountability measures. Public officials, not academics, are deciding the essential performance indices, thus effectively setting institutional priorities. Other state executive or legislative agencies have become involved in facility review, administrative operations, technology purchasing, budgeting, and planning. The courts are involved in decisions such as allocating student activity fees and determining admission practice, particularly in light of affirmative action. The federal government threatens to get involved with institution policies regarding teacher preparation, early admission decisions, and college costs, to name a few hot federal topics. Although these intrusions focus mostly on public institutions, they may also, directly or indirectly, affect private institutions. As the locus of influence moves from the campus to the state, public sector presidents may find themselves becoming like middle managers in public agencies rather then campus leaders.

Accreditation—both regional, which reviews institutions, and specialized, which reviews particular academic programs and schools—influences institutional behavior, policies, and priorities. It places requirements on colleges and universities in the name of quality but, as acknowledged by some observers, may also be motivated by status, privilege, or turf. Although accreditation is voluntary, most institutions cannot choose to go without it because federal funding, prestige, and the ability of campus graduates to work in some fields are often linked to positive reviews. It is not unheard of for a single college or university to be undertaking reviews for multiple accrediting organizations concurrently or consecutively. Institutions must respond to the often narrow and frequently competing demands of each to remain in good standing. For instance, accreditation can ask institutions to hire more full-time faculty in a particular area, alter curricula, or request more resources to support a particular discipline or service. One former university president called the plethora of accreditation "a straightjacket of many colors."[12] Even the head of the Council for Higher Education Accreditation (CHEA), the oversight organization for higher education accreditation, recognizes that college and university leaders "want accreditation to cost less, take less time, and be more useful."[13]

In addition to these constraints, presidential influence is severly limited by both the paucity of resources available and the short-term difficulties in internally reallocating those resources that exist. Some intangible campus resources, such as institutional prestige and attractiveness to students and potential donors, are tied into a network of external relationships that are virtually impossible to change in the short run and difficult to change even over long periods of time. Internally, on most campuses the personnel complement is largely fixed through tenure and contractual provisions, program change is constrained by faculty interests and structures as well as by facility limitations, and yearly planning begins with the largest share of the budget precommitted.

Unique Organizational Factors

The administration of colleges and universities presents "a unique dualism in organizational structure,"[14] with two structures existing in parallel. One is the conventional bureaucratic hierarchy responsive to the will of the trustees; the other is the structure through which faculty make decisions regarding those aspects of the institution over which they have professional jurisdiction. Trustees, who hold all legal authority, are primarily business executives who are more likely than the faculty to see the organization as comparable to a business firm in its structure and authority pattern and to support top-down management. The president, viewed as their CEO, is expected to carry out their wishes and to be accountable for faculty performance. The faculty, on the other hand, expect to exercise primary authority over educational processes, and trustee or presidential intrusion into academic affairs is likely to be viewed as illegitimate.

The problems caused by dual control are exacerbated by the conflicting nature of administrative and professional authority. In most organizations, major goals and activities are subject to the bureaucratic authority of administrators, which arises from their position within the hierarchy and their legal right to give directives. The professional authority of faculty members, on the other hand, comes from their expertise and training.[15] Administrative and professional authority are not only different but also mutually inconsistent, driven by incompatible systems of authority. The president is imbedded in both authority systems, and therefore is continually subject to incompatible demands and behavioral expectations.[16] As the leader of a bureaucracy, the president is expected to establish goals, decide how they are to be achieved, scientifically organize the work of subordinates, plan, and monitor organizational functioning. As the head of a professional and collegial body, the president is expected to be the first among equals and to move the group toward consensus by listening, proposing, mediating, persuading, and influencing through information sharing and appeals to reason. The use of legal authority or status differentials, which is an important means of gaining influence in one system, is illegitimate and unacceptable in the other.

This dual system of authority is even further confused in larger and more complex institutions as schools or departments, and sometimes even certain within-department or cross-department research institutes and centers become the locus of decision making. These units may have little or no managerial culture[17] or, for the most part, any interest in university management. Thus, presidential influence over their activities decreases still further. The institution may become an academic holding company for a federation of quasi-autonomous subunits. Unable to influence the larger institution, faculty may retreat into the small subunit for which they feel affinity and from which they can defend their influence and status, and presidential influence over their activities decreases still further.

Problems of Assessing Effectiveness

The particular organizational complexities of colleges and universities, exacerbated by the conflicting demands of their environments and the difficulty of understanding exactly how they function, has led to their identification as "organized anarchies."[18] An organized anarchy exhibits three characteristics: problematic goals, an unclear technology, and fluid participation in decision-making processes.

The concept of organized anarchy suggests that colleges and universities often make choices through a process of "garbage-can decision making."[19] Problems, solutions, and participants form steady streams, flowing through the organization as if they were poured into a large can. When one participant tries to make a decision, others in the can may become attached to it because they are contemporaneous, even though they may not appear to be logically connected. For example, a presidential decision to build a faculty parking lot on some unused campus land would appear to be easily made if there were enough data on parking needs and available resources to perform a cost/benefit analysis. But such apparently simple decisions become incredibly complex as elements seen by the decision maker as extraneous (that is, "garbage") become attached to it. The biology department may argue that the lot will destroy adjacent trees and use the incident to press its continuing proposal for an institutional environmental master plan; a candidate for student government office may use the lot as a symbol of administration indifference to student needs and ask for student membership on the board of trustees; and a faculty member may link the cost to recent cuts in library budgets and use the incident as a forum for discussing educational priorities. Since "garbage" is in the eye of the beholder, it is possible for almost any two issues to be seen by someone on campus as connected and for any problem to become coupled to any decision. Making a decision on the parking lot may be impossible unless some way can be found of severing its connection to environmental plans, student trustees, and educational priorities.

Institutional outcomes may be a result of only modestly interdependent activities and are often neither planned nor predictable. For example, a campus may receive a federal research grant because a president gave additional resources to a department, because a grant proposal by chance was assigned to one reviewer rather than another, or because the granting agency was obliged to seek a geographic distribution in its awards. People in different parts of the organization may have access to information making any of these or other explanations plausible. Such ambiguity inhibits the making of valid inferences about cause and effect, and presidential learning becomes exceptionally difficult. Presidents may spend more time in sense making[20] and in engaging in activities that verify or enhance their status, than in decision making. The decoupling of choices and outcomes makes symbolic behavior particularly important.

The ambiguities of institutional life are intensified by the absence in colleges and universities of accepted and valid indicators of effectiveness. There are different definitions of effectiveness, all of which are difficult to measure; different audiences use different criteria to make the assessment; and achievement of effectiveness in one area of institutional functioning may inhibit or prevent it in another.[21] Without measures of organizational effectiveness, it becomes difficult for presidents—or others—to objectively assess presidential effectiveness. As a consequence, institutional outcomes in general, and perceptions of presidential success or failure in particular, may be "largely a matter of luck. . . . The president is always in a war, and whether he wins or loses bears only a marginal relation to his foresight, his wisdom, his charm, his blood pressure."[22] In the final analysis, "the effects that presidents can have on their campuses are confounded by the actions of other institutional leaders, changes in the environment, and internal organizational processes such as culture and history that are difficult to change. Presidents are major participants in institutional events that have important organizational consequences . . . but in many ways they follow common scripts and play roles that are independent of their own personal characteristics."[23]

Privatization, Market Pressures, and Competition

Trends in the privatization of higher education and the pull of the competitive marketplace add new challenges and exacerbate ongoing dilemmas for university presidents. Privatization, resulting from a shift in relying heavily on public or governmental funds to a greater dependence on private sources, is characterized in academe by the shift of academic research to marketable knowledge, growth of entrepreneurial goals for institutions, the outsourcing of services, and an increase in the students' burden to pay for more of their education through loans than grants. The result is a close relationship with a marketplace that favors and encourages, as well as rewards, activities and research in certain market-sensitive fields, such as engineering, applied natural science, and agricultural science over other programs, such as humanities disciplines. It also promotes activities that have a market value resulting in more students—particularly those that can afford to pay the high tuition prices—new contracts and partnership agreements and enhanced research programs.[24]

Administrators may have little option except to respond to the marketplace, for if their institution does not react effectively others—both traditional universities as well as nontraditional providers—are poised to do so. As a result of privatization and market pressures, the ability to compete—for students, resources, faculty, and prestige—in turn, becomes a strong priority. Institutions unable to be competitive may face increasingly difficult circumstances as public support does not keep pace with institutional need, students become more educated consumers, and technology and new entrants into higher education widen the field of competitors. Colleges and universities may pursue certain revenue-generating strategies over other types of activities. The downside of pursuing market goals without appropriately balancing the public good is that institutions face the threat of losing their privileged place in American society as they come to resemble other organizations. Birnbaum notes, "Our narratives once told of education for democracy, for social justice, for the whole person, for the perpetuation of civilization. That is what people came to believe colleges and universities did, and that is why we enjoyed such support and admiration. Our narratives now increasingly talk about being engines of the economy. We are, of course, but I don't believe that a utilitarian narrative alone excites the imagination of the public, or commits faculty, staff or administrators to their institutions and its success, or connects the university to our deepest human needs."[25] Privatization and the rise of the market also have the potential to change internal institutional dynamics. Power may shift even further away from the administrative center to departments, centers, and units able to generate revenue. Because of their newfound economic clout, these units in turn may demand greater autonomy from central oversight, decide to contribute less to university-wide activities and priorities, and even relocate themselves physically in their own new buildings or a separate campus. Look at the behavior of some business schools for examples.

Limitations of the Presidential Role

Much of the literature on the presidential role comes from presidents themselves. There is a tendency by some to celebrate their own accomplishments, but there is often a strong undercurrent of despair or anger along with resignation to the fact that, in the long run, their success or failure may be due more to the vagaries of luck and history than to their own dedication and skill. Presidents are subject to role overload and role ambiguity, as they respond both to their own personal interpretations of their roles and to the legitimate demands of many groups.

One consequence of multiple and conflicting roles is that any actions by a president are likely to be criticized by someone. For former University of Michigan James Duderstadt, the ongoing attacks conjured images of the ruthlessness of the Wild West: "The president is expected to be the defender of the faith, both of the institution itself and the academic values so important to the university. I sometimes thought of this latter role as roughly akin to that of a tired, old sheriff in a frontier western town. Every day I would have to drag my bruised, wounded carcass out of bed, strap on my guns, and go out into the main street to face whatever gunslingers had ridden in to shoot up the town that day. Sometimes these were politicians; other times the media; still other times various special interest groups on campus; even occasionally other university leaders such as deans or regents."[26] The pace, the unrelenting pressure, and the marginal membership of presidents in conflicting groups affect their health, both physical and mental. Every decision will have its personal costs. And private time for family or recreation will be scarce.

The popular view of the role may identify the president as a larger-than-life, heroic leader, whose wise decisions and forceful administration solve problems and advance the institution's fortunes. But in fact, presidential decisions may have little effect on disparate organizational subsystems; changes in the environment may often overpower any internal changes; and administrative structures and processes of organization and control are relatively weak vis-à-vis the autonomy of professional participants. A president can attend to only a small number of matters, but there is no way of knowing beforehand (or often even afterward, for that matter) whether these are the most important matters. These problems led Michael Cohen and James March to call the presidency an illusion: "Important aspects of the role seem to disappear on close examination. Compared to the heroic expectations he and others might have, the president has modest control over the events of college life. The contributions he makes can easily be swamped by outside events or the diffuse quality of university decision making."[27] These limits on influence and the ambiguities of purpose, power, experience, and success make it difficult for presidents to learn what works.

If the institution has ambiguous and multiple purposes and lacks a sense of shared direction, how can presidents justify their actions or know if they have been successful? If influence is dispersed throughout the institution and decentralized, how can presidents know how much power they have or what they can or cannot do? If what happens on a campus depends as much on the actions of others and on environmental pressures as it does on presidential behavior, what can presidents accurately learn from their experiences? And if presidents have confirmed their success earlier in their careers because they have been promoted, how can they assess their present success when promotion is no longer possible?

Behavioral and Cognitive Strategies

Survival requires the development of coping mechanisms that help the organization and the people within it make sense of the ambiguities of their daily lives. Colleges and universities have evolved ways of responding to the difficulties caused by their complex environmental relationships, inchoate influence patterns, and inability to rationalize their technology. For example, institutions meet the conflicting demands of interest groups by decentralizing and permitting subunits to operate in a quasi-autonomous fashion. Subunits can then meet specific needs, but the cost is high: presidential authority is diminished, it becomes almost impossible to coordinate activities, and maintaining a sense of coherence and common purpose is extremely difficult.

Institutions may attempt to cope with the difficulty of assessing effectiveness by publicly focusing attention on inputs (such as percentage of faculty with doctorates) and activities (such as the number of students studying aboard) rather than outputs (how much a student has learned). Even with calls for public accountability, increased rigor of accreditation reviews, and the assessment movement, institutions, for the most part, discourage inspection. Instead they rely on institutional reputation and tradition or, when pressed, use measures that portray them most positively rather than offer objective evaluation. Within this organizational ambiguity, with conflicting authority structures, multiple social systems, and contested goals, presidents are expected to provide leadership, direction, coherence, and progress in an organization.

Many suggestions have been offered to make the presidential job more doable. One common proposal is to strenghten the presidency through selecting better presidents. It assumes (although without supporting data) that today's presidents do not have the same characteristics of courage and decisiveness as presidents of the past. For instance, the title of a report from the Association of Governing Boards (AGB) of Colleges and Universities' Commission on the Academic Presidency boldly calls for "stronger leadership for tougher times."[28] The inference is that institutions need strong presidential leaders. This wish, however, can be a slippery slope as expectations for leaders reach new heights to which few can attain. Management scholar Henry Mintzberg wrote: "We seem to be moving beyond leaders who merely lead; today heroes save. Soon heroes will only save; then gods will redeem. We keep upping the ante. . . ."[29] The obvious solution is for presidential search committees to seek stronger and more decisive candidates. Alternatively, it has been suggested that the presidency could be strengthened by increasing the legal authority of the position as well as curtailing the influence of other stakeholders and clarifying and delimiting their roles in shared governance. If one of the causes of presidential weakness is the anarchical nature of the organization, then a possible solution is to increase the use of rational processes—rather than political or symbolic processes—in institutional decision making. But the many attempts to do so through imposing management systems, budgeting and planning processes, restructuring and re-engineering initiatives, and performance measures have by and large not had the desired and expected effects.[30] In many cases, the processes set up to respond to the problems have only exacerbated them.

It has also been suggested that presidential effectiveness might be improved if trustee boards provided more support to their presidents, giving them leadership positions on the board, encouraging faculty support for them, resisting attempts to involve boards in administration, and using presidents as their sole conduit into the administrative structure.[31] The frantic pace of presidential life has also been identified as a major constraint upon presidential effectiveness, and it has been suggested that providing presidents with more personal assistance would free their time for contemplation and long-term planning. This suggestion almost always overlooks the likelihood that presidents do not become busy people but rather that busy people become presidents. Presidents complain about lack of time for contemplation, but there is no reason to believe that if they had more free time they would use it for that purpose.

There is no dearth of advice about how to be a successful president. Some authorities suggest that presidents remain distant, others that they be intimately involved with constituents; that they focus on resource acquisition or that they focus on academic matters; that they stress accountability or that they foster creativity; that they set goals or that they help others achieve their own goals. The proposals are inconsistent, and their behavioral implications are unclear. Nevertheless, the following section suggests some presidential administrative strategies that might increase their effectiveness and improve their institutions.[32] It also examines some of the cognitive and symbolic strategies that permit presidents and institutions to cope with the discrepancies between authority and responsibility, expectations and achievement. Finally, it considers the possibility that, because of certain characteristics of colleges and universities, a weak presidency may have an important organizational function.

Successful Administrative Strategies

Successful presidents are likely to be realists rather than idealists. They accept a decentralized structure, conflicting authority systems, and loose coupling as inherent organizational characteristics and try to work within these constraints. They know that essential institutional functions are likely to continue to operate, even in the absence of presidential direction, because of ongoing administrative systems and the largely autonomous activities of professional faculties. In many ways, the organization works as a cybernetic system in which negative feedback serves to activate processes that maintain the institution's current level of functioning.[33] Presidents appreciate that some of their energy will be occupied with the day-to-day activities of monitoring these processes and with identifying and attending to institutional weaknesses and problems.

However, presidents also recognize that they can have an impact on the institution if they focus on a few limited objectives or programs and devote extraordinary energy to them. Presidents can be effective even in areas such as curriculum in which administrative influence is traditionally weak if they are willing to accept the inevitable cost of other opportunities forgone. Presidents understand that all change is not their personal responsibility as many new efforts and modifications will occur because of the leadership and initiative of faculty and staff throughout the institution, often through ongoing processes. Presidents who try to do too many things, either on their own initiative or in response to perceived environmental demands, mostly end up accomplishing none of them.

Effective presidents understand the culture of their institution and the symbolic aspects of their positions. Recognizing that their effectiveness as leaders depends upon the willingness of highly trained professionals to be followers, they avoid actions that would violate cultural and academic norms and thereby diminish their own status. Effective presidents spend a great deal of time in understanding their institutional culture. They go out of their way to walk around their campuses to see and be seen, to confer with other formal and informal campus leaders for opinions and advice, to learn institutional histories, and to understand the expectations others have of presidential behavior. They also recognize that as a symbolic leader they must consistently articulate the core values of the institution and relate them to all aspects of institutional life in order to sustain and reinvigorate the myths that create a common reality. Management skills may be a necessary, but usually not a sufficient, concomitant of presidential success. For example, Ellen Chaffee has suggested that presidents who focus on resource acquisition strategies alone to resolve fiscal crises are not as successful as those who combine them with interpretative strategies that change campus perceptions and attitudes.[34]

Since centralized control cannot be achieved in complex, nonlinear, social systems, effective presidents realize that prevention of error is not possible. They therefore emphasize the design of systems to detect error and to make institutional processes self-correcting. They support the collection, analysis, and public dissemination of data on aspects of institutional functioning, data that permit interest groups to monitor the institution. Organizational stability is increased as institutional components pay attention to different aspects of the environment and serve as controls and checks on each other's activities.

The effectiveness of a free flow of information is increased when presidents support and publicly articulate the value of open communication and a will to tolerate and encourage, rather than to punish, disagreement.

Effective presidents recognize that the inherent specialization and fractionation essential to the maintenance of quality and responsiveness must be coordinated unobtrusively in order to avoid alienation. They do this in part by establishing formal opportunities for interaction, and they emphasize forums such as senates, cabinets, retreats, and task forces that bring together persons representing different constituencies and different institutional levels. Senate presidents who sit on administrative councils, deans who attend senate meetings, and students, faculty, and administrators who serve on joint committees interact in ways that make their perceptions and interests more consistent.

Presidential effectiveness is based as much upon influence as upon authority, and influence in an academic institution depends upon mutual and reciprocal processes of social exchange. Effective presidents influence others by allowing themselves to be influenced. This requires that presidents listen carefully, which might be difficult for presidents who believe that the proper role of leaders is to tell others what to do. Academic management is not, as Mintzberg suggests, "management by barking around."[35]

Cognitive and Symbolic Strategies

Individuals typically become presidents after successful performance in a series of related positions of increasing responsibility. One reason for considering the presidency an impossible job is the extensive criticism by reputable sources directed at the presumably failing efforts of people so previously accomplished. Presidents rely upon unconscious cognitive strategies to reconcile this discrepancy between past achievement and present criticism. They see themselves as successful even as others see them as failing.

Presidents talk easily about the deficiencies of their confreres, but when asked about their own performance, self-assessments are almost uniformly positive. In one study, presidents rated the quality of their own "institutional leadership" as seventy-seven on a hundred-point scale, while they rated that of the "average president" as sixty-six and their predecessor as only fifty-two.[36] They also indicated that the quality of their own campus had improved on each of seven dimensions since they became president, a finding contradicted by a host of recent reports critical of American higher education. Presidents build schemas of effectiveness based upon previous career success; when they encounter ambiguous situations, they are likely to anticipate, and therefore to observe, successful outcomes and to attribute these to their own efforts. When presidents were asked to identify a recent event that had positive outcomes on their campus, for example, 74 percent indicated that they had initiated it. But when asked to identify an event with a negative outcome, only 14 percent accepted responsibility. There seems to be evidence of a success bias that leads these successful people to believe that they have been responsible for successful outcomes, and that permits them to disassociate themselves from failure. In a recent study of the performance of thirty-two college presidents, all but one considered themselves successful, even though a quarter of them had lost sufficient constituent support to be identified by the researcher as having been a failure at the job.[37]

Academic presidents occupy a prestigious position in American life. They are major figures in their communities, sought after as speakers for local functions, and interviewed by the media. They are at the core of impressive academic ceremonies, they have the highest salaries and most significant perquisites a campus has to offer (certain athletic coaches excluded), and they are surrounded by respectful aides and by associates with vested interests in maintaining a successful presidency.

The Latent Organizational Functions of Impossibility

It may be so vital for symbolic reasons for organizational members to believe that their leaders are important that both leaders and followers may cope with the reality of weak presidential influence by constructing an illusion of their power. We have developed highly romanticized, heroic views of leadership—what leaders do, what they are able to accomplish, and the general effects they have upon our lives. It amounts to what might be considered a faith in the potential if not in the actual efficacy of those individuals.[38]

In many situations, presidential leadership may not be real but, rather, a social attribution, a result of the tendency of campus constituents to assign to a president the responsibility for unusual institutional outcomes because the president fills a role identified as a leader, because presidents are visible and prominent, because presidents spend a great deal of time doing leaderlike things (such as engaging in ceremonial and symbolic activities), and because we all have the need to believe in the effectiveness of individual control. Leaders are people believed by followers to have caused events. "Successful leaders," says Jeffrey Pfeffer, "are those who can separate themselves from organizational failures and associate themselves with organizational successes."[39]

In organizations with clear goals, understood technologies, and hierarchical power structures, illusionary leadership may be dysfunctional. In such institutions, increasing the authority of competent leaders would reduce the extent to which their job might be thought of as impossible and would thereby increase organizational effectiveness. But when these organizational characteristics are not present, it is highly questionable whether increasing presidential power would yield positive outcomes. It may even be that the very factors responsible for the impossibility of the presidential role are also important components of organizational effectiveness and that action taken to strengthen the one would weaken the other. Higher education may be effective not despite its arational characteristics but because of them.

While presidents may rail against the frustrations of their job, they assumed their positions aware of the constraints they would face. Some may have had egocentric motives, but for most a natural interest in power, money, and prestige is strongly tempered by a dedication to the enduring values of education and a commitment to serve the interests of their institutions. If the presidency had greater authority than it does, it might attract to it a different kind of person, one perhaps less committed to the concept of leader as institutional servant and more to the concept of leader as institutional master. It might be that if presidents had greater authority they might enjoy it more, but in Harold Stoke's thoughtful aphorism, "those who enjoy it are not very successful, and those who are successful are not very happy. . . . Those who enjoy exercising power shouldn't have it, and those who should exercise it are not likely to enjoy it."[40]

The collegial traditions of higher education suggest that presidential vacancies are filled by faculty who are selected by their colleagues, serve them in leadership roles for limited terms, and then return to their first love—teaching and research. While this may be more a fond fantasy than an established fact, it reflects the normative sense among many academics that, while college teaching may be a profession, high administrative office is only one of several temporary roles within it. The critical difference is between seeing the presidency as a profession and seeing it as a role. Incumbents who view the presidency as a profession are likely to see the maintenance of their position as a major objective. Such presidents "simplify their task by making only one calculation — calculating what is contributory to the welfare of the president, given the incentives to do so in the presence of job insecurity on the one hand and the impossibility of a precise definition of the institution's general welfare on the other."[41] In contrast, incumbents who see the presidency as a role can give primary attention to the needs of the institution rather than of themselves. This makes it possible for them to accept that, sometimes, the greatest service a president can perform is to leave office, because "the survival of the president is not the goal. The leader is temporary and, if necessary, expendable in service to the potential value of the institution."[42] Presidents who view their obligations as part of a role are able to enjoy the roller coaster of the presidency during its initial phases and then leave without regret. They are able to see themselves as an important but replaceable component in a large, cybernetic organization, and they are able to "cope by perceiving exit as a symbolic, political act of a pluralistic democratic organization, not as a threat to managerial competence."[43]

Some presidents never come to terms with the impossible nature of their jobs. Frustrated in their attempts to have the influence they desire, they may eventually find solace in cognitive distortions that lead them to see what they wish to see. Others may follow the route of the zealot, redoubling their efforts as they lose sight of their goals. One consequence of these behaviors is to create self-fulfilling prophesies: aggressive administrative action leads to resistance, which in turn becomes the justification for still more assertive presidential behavior. Other presidents make peace with their positions by bringing to it an understanding of the peculiar nature of their organizations and of their roles within them. Their goal is a peaceful balance of institutional interests within which they can make marginal improvements in a limited number of areas. They reconcile themselves to the possibility of future failure by acknowledging the role played by uncontrollable external sources, recognizing that some of what happens to them — both good and bad — may be a product of luck. Presidential roles may be as much a product of social attributions as a set of desirable behaviors. By creating a role that we declare will provide leadership to an organization, we construct the attribution that organizational effects are due to the leader's behavior. This allows us to simplify and make sense of complex organizational processes that would otherwise be impossible to comprehend.[44] It is perhaps as sensible to say that successful organizational events cause effective presidents as it is to say that effective presidents cause successful events.

One of the reasons that colleges and universities have been so successful is that, as their environments have become more complex, they have created decentralized, flexible, and only moderately interdependent structures, which have been effective in responding to environmental change. This may make coordination by the president exceptionally difficult, but the same forces that limit presidential authority may also make these organizations exceptionally adaptable and stable. The paradox of an institution that gives precedence to professional, rather than administrative, authority is that management weakness may be a significant source of organizational strength.

Calls for strengthening the presidency abound, but they are commonly grounded in a view of presidential power based more on hope than on experience. The report of a comprehensive five-year study of academic leadership reached a conclusion about the importance of presidents that, if less heroic than the views of many, may be more realistic:

> Presidents may be important in some situations, but the performance of colleges may usually be less dependent upon presidential leadership than most of us care to believe. Most college presidents do the right things, and do things right most of the time. It is possible that college leaders can become marginally more effective. But those who seek major changes in the ways presidents behave, or believe that such changes will make major differences on our campuses, are likely to be disappointed. . . . Good presidents come to their positions with useful competencies, integrity, faith in their colleagues, and a firm belief that by listening carefully and working together they can all do well. In a turbulent and uncertain world, what happens after that is as much in the laps of the gods as in the hands of the president.[45]

NOTES

This chapter is a revised version of Robert Birnbaum, "Responsibility without Authority: The Impossible Job of the College President," in *Higher Education: Handbook of Theory and Research,* ed. John C. Smart, vol. 5 (New York: Agathon, 1989).

1. Thorstein Veblen, *The Higher Learning in America* (New York: Sagamore, 1957 [1918]).

2. Edwin E. Slosson, "Universities, American Endowed" in *Cyclopedia of Education,* ed. P. Monroe, vol. 5 (New York: Macmillan, 1913).

3. Christopher Jencks and David Riesman, *The Academic Revolution* (New York: Doubleday, 1968).

4. Homer P. Rainey, "How Shall We Control Our Universities? Why College Presidents Leave Their Jobs," *Journal of Higher Education* 31 (1960): 376–83.

5. Frederick F. Ness, *An Uncertain Glory* (San Francisco: Jossey-Bass, 1971).

6. Melanie Corrigan, *The American College President* (Washington, D.C.: American Council on Education, 2002).

7. Michael D. Cohen and James D. March, *Leadership and Ambiguity: The American College President* (New York: McGraw-Hill, 1974).

8. Henry Mintzberg, *The Nature of Managerial Work* (New York: Harper and Row, 1973).

9. American Association of University Professors, "Joint Statement on Government of Colleges and Universities," in *Policy Documents and Reports* (Washington, D.C.: AAUP, 1984 [1966]).

10. Carnegie Commission, *The Purposes and Performance of Higher Education in the United States* (New York: McGraw-Hill, 1973).

11. Commission on Strengthening Presidential Leadership, *Presidents Make a Difference: Strengthening Leadership in Colleges and Universities* (Washington, D.C.: Association of Governing Boards of Colleges and Universities, 1984).

12. William R. Dill, "Specialized Accreditation: An Idea Whose Time Has Come? Or Gone?" *Change* (July/August, 1998): 18–25.

13. Judith S. Eaton, "Regional Accreditation Reform: Who is Served?" *Change* (March/April, 2001): 39–45.

14. John J. Corson, *Governance of Colleges and Universities* (New York: McGraw-Hill, 1960), 43.

15. Peter M. Blau, *The Organization of Academic Work* (New York: Wiley, 1973).

16. J. Victor Baldridge, David V. Curtis, George P. Ecker, and Gary L. Riley, *Policy Making and Effective Leadership: A National Study of Academic Management* (San Francisco: Jossey-Bass, 1978); Robert Birnbaum, *How Col-*

364   Robert Birnbaum and Peter D. Eckel

leges Work: Patterns of Organization, Management, and Leadership in Higher Education (San Francisco: Jossey-Bass, 1988).

17. Derek Bok, *Universities in the Marketplace* (Princeton, NJ: Princeton University Press, 2003).

18. Cohen and March, *Leadership and Ambiguity.*

19. Michael D. Cohen, James D. March, and Johan P. Olsen, "Garbage Can Model of Organizational Choice," *Administrative Science Quarterly* 17 (1972): 1–25.

20. Karl E. Weick, *Sensemaking in Organizations* (Thousand Oaks, CA: Sage, 1995).

21. See Kim S. Cameron, "The Effectiveness of Ineffectiveness," in *Research in Organizational Behavior,* ed. Barry M. Staw and L. L. Cummings, vol. 6 (Greenwich, CT: JAI, 1984); Kim S. Cameron and David A. Whetten, *Organizational Effectiveness* (New York: Academic, 1983); Kim S. Cameron, "Measuring Organizational Effectiveness in Institutions of Higher Education," *Administrative Science Quarterly* 23 (1978): 604–32.

22. Ness, *Uncertain Glory,* 8.

23. Robert Birnbaum, *How Academic Leadership Works: Understanding Success and Failure in the College Presidency* (San Francisco: Jossey-Bass, 1992), 166.

24. Sheila Slaughter and Larry Leslie, *Academic Capitalism* (Baltimore: Johns Hopkins University Press, 1997).

25. Robert Birnbaum, "The President as Storyteller: Restoring the Narrative of Higher Education," *The Presidency* (Fall, 2003): 33–39.

26. James J. Duderstadt, *A University for the 21st Century* (Ann Arbor: University of Michigan Press, 2000).

27. Cohen and March, *Leadership and Ambiguity,* 2.

28. Association of Governing Boards of Colleges and Universities, *Renewing the Academic Presidency: Stronger Leadership for Tougher Times* (Washington, D.C.: Association of Governing Boards of Universities and Colleges, 1996).

29. Henry Mintzberg, "Managing Quietly," *Leader to Leader* 12 (1999, Spring): 24–30.

30. Robert Birnbaum, *Management Fads in Higher Education* (San Francisco: Jossey-Bass, 2000).

31. Commission on Strengthening Presidential Leadership, *Presidents Make a Difference,* xii.

32. Support for these strategies can be found in the several reports of the Institutional Leadership Project, a five-year longitudinal study of presidential, administrative, faculty, and trustee leaders at thirty-two colleges and universities. A list of these reports can be found in Birnbaum, *How Academic Leadership Works,* 231–35.

33. Birnbaum, *How Colleges Work.*

34. Ellen E. Chaffee, "Successful Strategic Management in Small Private Colleges," *Journal of Higher Education* 55 (1984): 212–41.

35. Mintzberg, "Managing Quietly."

36. Robert Birnbaum, "Leadership and Learning: The College President as Intuitive Scientist," *Review of Higher Education* 9 (1986): 381–95.

37. Birnbaum, *How Academic Leadership Works.*

38. James R. Meindl, Sanford B. Ehrlich, and Janet M. Dukerich, "The Romance of Leadership," *Administrative Science Quarterly* 30 (1985): 78–102.

39. Jeffrey Pfeffer, "The Ambiguity of Leadership," *Academy of Management Review* 2 (1977): 104–19.

40. Harold W. Stoke, *The American College President* (New York: Harper and Row, 1959).

41. Clark Kerr and Marian L. Gade, *The Many Lives of the Academic President* (Washington, D.C.: Association of Governing Boards of Universities and Colleges, 1986).

42. Joseph F. Kauffman, *At the Pleasure of the Board* (Washington, D.C.: American Council on Education, 1980), 14.

43. Donald E. Walker, "Goodbye, Mr. President, and Good Luck!" *Educational Record* (Winter 1977): 57.

44. Pfeffer, *Ambiguity of Leadership;* Meindl, Ehrlich, and Dukerich, *Romance of Leadership.*

45. Birnbaum, *How Academic Leadership Works,* 196.

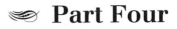 **Part Four**

Central Issues for the Twenty-First Century

Chapter Thirteen

Financing Higher Education
Who Should Pay?

D. Bruce Johnstone

The funding of higher education is a large and complex topic. It is complex in part because of its multiple sources of revenue and its multiple outputs, or products, which are only loosely connected to these different revenue sources. Furthermore, these revenue and expenditure patterns vary significantly by type of institution (university, four-year college, two-year college), mode of governance (public or private), and state. Within the private sector, expenditure levels as well as patterns of pricing and price discounting vary greatly according to institutional wealth and the depth, demographics, and family affluence of the applicant pool. In the public sector, these patterns also vary according to state funding levels, tuition policies, and enrollment limits set by state governments or public multicampus governing boards.

The topic is large because finance underlies much of the three overarching themes of contemporary higher education policy: *quality,* and the relationship between funding and quality in any of its several dimensions; *access,* or the search for social equity in who benefits from, and who pays for, higher education; and *efficiency,* or the search for a cost-effective relationship between revenues (particularly those that come from students, parents, and taxpayers) and outputs (whether measured in enrollments, graduates, student learning, or the scholarly activity of the faculty).

Within these broad themes lie public and institutional policy questions that are informed, if not answered, by economic and financial perspectives. How, if at all, can costs—especially to the taxpayer and the student—be lowered without damage to academic quality or to principles of access and participation? What are appropriate ratios of students to faculty and to professional and administrative staff at various kinds of institutions? What are reasonable conceptions and expectations of higher educational productivity? How can institutional aid, or price discounting, be used either to attract students with qualities or characteristics sought by the institution to maximize net tuition revenue? Are taxpayer dollars in the public sector best used to hold down tuition, or should they go toward expanding need-based aid, with public tuitions raised closer to the full average costs of undergraduate instruction? Are public aid dollars best used for grants or for loan subsidies? What of public aid based on academic promise and performance rather than family need? And what is the appropriate response by institutions and governments to the pervasive condition of austerity in higher education, whether brought on by declining enrollments, declining state tax assistance, or allegations of runaway costs?[1]

Although this chapter concentrates on American higher education, the financial principles and problems are much the same worldwide.[2] Our understanding of the particular financial conditions and problems of American higher education can be sharpened by noting what is peculiar to the financing of the American university: the sheer size, and consequent accessibility, or what the Europeans call "massification"; the large private sector, which includes the most and the least prestigious institutions; and the great reliance on nongovernmental revenue—mainly tuition but also private gifts and return on endowments.

Who pays and who should pay? Students and parents? Taxpayers? Philanthropists? How much higher education? At what cost or level of efficiency? These questions can be adequately addressed only within the broader context of American society in the late 1990s.

The Economic, Social, and Political Context

Higher education is recognized both as an engine of economic growth and as a gatekeeper to individual positions of high remuneration and status. Advanced education—particularly in high technology, information processing, and sophisticated management and analysis—is thought to be essential to maintaining America's economic position in the increasingly competitive global economy. It follows that most jobs of high remuneration and status will require an advanced degree, probably beyond the baccalaureate, and it further follows that the lack of postsecondary education creates a likelihood of marginal income and status. These propositions, however, do not mean that advanced education necessarily makes individuals more productive or that all recipients of advanced education will find remunerative, high-status employment. Higher education can make individuals more productive; but it can also simply screen, or select, for the kinds of intellectual, social, and personal characteristics required for the high-remuneration, high-status jobs that may be available. In short, higher education is essential for most good jobs, and the absence of education beyond high school will be an increasingly formidable barrier to obtaining them; but the mere possession of an advanced degree will guarantee neither good, nor lasting, employment.

American society is being increasingly polarized by class, race, and ethnicity. More and more children grow up in poverty, both rural and urban. The dilemma presented by higher education's gatekeeper function is that access to, and especially success in, college and university remains highly correlated with socioeconomic class. This correlation has not significantly diminished in recent years, even though American higher education is more accessible than the higher education systems of other countries. Thus, with the increasing polarization of income in the 1980s and 1990s, and with the increasing relationship of economic success in life to success in college, there is reason to be alarmed at the degree to which our colleges and universities perpetuate, and even accelerate, the intergenerational transmission of wealth and status.

As to the political context, American society, or at least a voting electorate, has become increasingly conservative. Key elements of this conservatism include resistance to the notion of a benign government, to social welfare programs, and to transfer payments from the rich to the poor. Insofar as there is to be a public agenda for education, it is to be advanced through private, or at least market-oriented, mechanisms: charter schools and vouchers for education reform and tuition tax credits and portable need-based aid to increase accessibility to higher education. A third element of this resurgent conservatism is increasing concern over crime and moral laxity, coupled with a diminishing inclination to view social deprivation or racism as an acceptable excuse for "deviant" (i.e., non-middle-class) behavior.

These themes are intertwined, of course. For example, the political inclination to seek private solutions to what used to be viewed as public problems is given impetus by declining public revenues—which, in turn, is a function, at least in part, of the globalization of the economy and the increasing propensity of wealthy individuals to flee to low-tax havens and to move their enterprises to low-wage economies. There are also internal inconsistencies among these themes: for example, increasing dissatisfaction with governmental intrusion contradicts not only the demand for more costly and intrusive accountability but also direct political intervention into matters of curriculum and programs. But these economic, social, and political themes, for all their complexity, provide a context for consideration of the three broad issues of higher education finance:

—*The size of the nation's higher educational enterprise.* How much publicly supported higher education does the nation need, or will it choose to afford, measured either in total expenditures or as a percentage of the nation's gross domestic product?
—*The efficiency and productivity of this enterprise.* What should higher education (particularly public) cost per unit, whether the unit is students enrolled, degrees granted, scholarship produced, service rendered, or combinations thereof?
—*The sources of revenue to support this enterprise.* Who pays for the costs of higher education? Students and parents? Government and taxpayers? Philanthropists?

Size of the Enterprise

The American higher education enterprise is enormous, even when controlling for our great wealth and population. For example:

— Total current-fund expenditures for all public and private nonprofit institutions of higher education in fiscal year 2000 were nearly $234 billion—of which total education and general expenditures (that is, excluding institutionally provided room and board, other auxiliary enterprises, university hospitals, Pell grants, and certain other expenditures) were almost $181.4 billion.[3]

— Total public and private expenditure on higher education, in 1998 was about 2.3 percent—the highest of the major industrialized countries.[4]

— A total of 15.9 million undergraduate, graduate, and first professional students were enrolled in the fall of 2001. Of the 13.7 million undergraduates, 56 percent were female, 60 percent full-time, and 54 percent enrolled in four-year institutions.[5] This full- and part-time enrollment constituted 63.3 percent of the preceding year's high school completers (down somewhat from a 1997 high of 67% but about the same as the early years of the 1990s), including 77.1 percent of students in the top quintile of family income, 59.4 percent in the middle quintile, and 47.8 percent of the three-year average of the lowest family income quintile. Those entering college immediately after high school also included 64.2 percent of whites, 56.1 percent of blacks (three-year average), and 48.25 percent of Hispanics (three-year average).[6]

— These students were enrolled in 4,197 colleges and universities (counting branch campuses and institutions outside of the fifty states), including 1,713 public and 2,484 private institutions, enrolling 11.8 million and 3.6 million students, respectively.[7] In addition, at least 1 million students were enrolled in 2001–02 in 5,059 nondegree-granting institutions of postsecondary education, 3,540 of which were private for-profit.

By these and other measures, it is clear that America has chosen to support a large, accessible (both in cost and in admission standards), and highly diverse system (some would say a "nonsystem") of higher education. These "choices" are made in the form of literally millions of decisions by parents and students to pay the costs of college, thereby giving expression to the value they place on higher education for themselves or for their children, and by even more citizens and elected officials, mainly at the state level, who spend tax funds to maintain public colleges and universities, to provide assistance, mostly via student aid, to private colleges and universities, and finally, to support an academic research enterprise that is far and away the largest and most productive in the world.

In the twenty-first century, four forces will expand this already large enterprise. The first is an expansion of the eighteen-to-twenty-four-year-old age cohort. Between 1996 and the year 2006, this traditional college-going age cohort will increase by about 16 percent.

The middle-age cohort will continue to decline as the low birth rates of the 1960s and 1970s work their way through, resulting in a possible decline in nontraditional enrollments. The National Center for Education Statistics projects an enrollment growth for the decade 2002–12 of 15 percent, to 17.7 million.[8] This growth will occur unevenly, concentrated mainly in the high-growth states of the West, Southwest, and South. Probably nowhere is there such anxiety over a state's ability to accommodate a projected explosion of student enrollments as in California, where experts have been forecasting "tidal wave II," during which the colleges and universities of California will need to accommodate at least 450,000 additional students by the mid 2000s if California is to maintain its historic accessibility to publicly supported higher education.[9]

A second force for more higher education is an expansion of participation and completion due to a perception of higher private rates of return and the perceived need for at least some higher education for positions of remuneration and status. If efforts to reduce the current high attrition rates in U.S. colleges prove successful, there will be a significant increase in enrollment even without any expansion of first-time participation.

A third force, related to the above, is the accretion of degree level sought by the average student. This phenomenon is probably a function of the increasing amount and complexity of knowledge, the increasing educational demands of the productive economy (whether for actual skills, or simply for higher education's screening function), and the tendency of most professions to enhance their status by requiring ever more education prior to entry and perhaps more continuing education to maintain current licensure.

A fourth force, identified more through conjecture than hard evidence, is the incentive for enhancement that seems to be built into the traditions of the academy. William Massy and Robert Zemsky identify this force as "the ratchet."[10] It manifests in a perpetual dissatisfaction on the part of professors, staff, and administrators with the status quo and in a determination to do more and better: to teach new materials, to advise students more effectively, to perform more sophisticated (and usually more costly) research, and generally to advance in the highly competitive pecking order of individual and institutional scholarly prestige, without regard to whether more and better is either cost-effective or demanded by those who must pay the bills.

The Efficiency and Productivity of the Enterprise

Another issue within the financing of higher education is the efficiency with which all of these resources are employed in the higher educational enterprise and their productivity. Productivity and efficiency look at both costs, or expenditures, and at benefits, or outputs. These concepts deal with costs *per:* whether per student (which, of course, is not really an output but which has the advantage of being easily and unambiguously measured), or per unit of research, or per unit of learning (however measured), or per learning added by the institution. Because the real outputs of the university (the discovery, transmission, and promulgation of knowledge) are both multiple and difficult to measure, and because revenue, at least for the support of instructional expenditures, follows student enrollment in both the public and the private sectors, the cost per student inevitably and overwhelmingly dominates approaches to questions of productivity and efficiency. But we ought never to forget that enrollment, however measured—and however sensitive to fields of study, levels of education, or methods of instruction—is still merely a proxy for the hard-to-measure real output, which is student learning.

Variation in Unit Costs

In the production of goods, there are usually multiple ways of combining productive inputs—mainly different combinations of labor, capital, materials, and managerial effectiveness—to produce a unit of output. The most efficient combination of inputs is determined by the alternative manufacturing technologies and the relative costs of the inputs. Given a set of input costs and a set of technologies for combining inputs into desired outputs, there is an unambiguous most efficient way: that is, a lowest cost per unit. The efficiency, then, of any alternative producer or production process can be measured by how that producer or that process compares to that most efficient way.

Higher education is not as fortunate as these goods-producing enterprises. The technology of university production (of learning and scholarship) is unclear and highly idiosyncratic to the institution, the department, and the individual professor. We do know that per student costs vary greatly. Thus, higher education is generally assumed to be more costly at research universities than at undergraduate colleges due to the higher salaries, lower teaching loads, and more extensive academic support (e.g., libraries and computer facilities) accorded the faculty of the research university. However, the direct instructional costs (especially at the margin) of at least freshmen and sophomores at a typical public research university can be rather low due to the prevalence of low-cost teaching assistants and very large lecture courses—in contrast to the typical public four-year college, where most instruction is carried out by regular faculty in moderate-sized classes, albeit with heavier average teaching loads. In the end, it is probably appropriate to claim that per student costs at a research university are higher than at a four-year college; but it must not be forgotten that this is so at least partly because of certain assumptions and cost allocations that, while reasonable, are nonetheless judgmental and sometimes questionable.

Among like institutions, most interinstitutional variation in per student costs can be attributed to differences either in the amenities provided to the students (recreational and cultural facilities, for example, or academic and student services support staff) or in the costs of faculty. Differential faculty costs, in turn, reflect differences not only in salary (which are low for part-time faculty, who provide much of the teaching at low-cost colleges, and high for the full-time senior professoriate at prestigious private colleges) but also in that other major faculty expense, time (which translates into light teaching loads at wealthy colleges and heavy teaching loads at low-cost "access" colleges).

Howard Bowen, in his classic 1980 study of higher education costs, found great variation in costs among seemingly similar institutions with seemingly similar outcomes. Among a sample of research and doctoral-granting universities arranged from lowest to highest in per student expenditures, the average university in the third quartile spent twice as much per student as the average in the second quartile, and the highest-spending university in the sample spent almost seven and one-half times as much as the first quartile average. Variation among colleges was less, but the colleges in the third quartile of per student costs still spent about 50 percent more than the colleges in the second quartile.[11] Fiscal year 2000 data on current-fund expenditures on instruction show per student spending as high as $20,815 at elite private research universities, but only $8,417 at all public universities, $4,617 at public masters colleges, and $3,912 at public two-year colleges.[12]

This great spread in unit costs is seen by some as profligacy on the part of the highest-cost institutions. Bowen accounts for such variation with his revenue theory of costs, which states that institutions raise all the money they can (which, in the case of highly endowed institutions with wealthy alumni that continue to attract children of affluent families, is a very large amount indeed), and spend all that they raise, purposefully and honorably, even though the amounts spent do not emerge from any discernible production function, as such, as in the industrial manufacture of goods.[13]

But even if the "cost" we use to calculate the cost per student at Harvard were to mean the same thing as the "cost" in per student costs at, say, neighboring Wheelock College or at UMass, Boston, we still cannot say unambiguously that Wheelock and UMass, Boston, are more efficient or more productive than Harvard. They may be cheaper per student, to be sure, but whether they are more efficient requires a measure of output that we do not have and that we probably could not agree upon. And if Harvard were to contest its possible characterization as "inefficient" or "unproductive," it would point to the extraordinary knowledge and competence of its graduates, or to the lifetime of added benefits that Harvard presumably helped to produce, or the value to the society (uncaptured by private lifetime income streams) that Harvard "created".

In short, without better agreement on the proper outputs of higher education, not to mention how to weigh and how to measure them, we are left with cost per full-time equivalent student, as best as we can measure it, as an index of productivity—and as something that should presumably get lower (or cheaper) in response to the demands of students, parents, and taxpayers that higher education become less costly.

Inflation in Unit Costs

Actually, the problem of unit costs and efficiency (or inefficiency) in higher education is less a function of unit costs, per se, and more a function of the seemingly inexorable increase of such costs and of the resulting tuition increases at rates considerably in excess of the rate of inflation. This is the "cost disease" described by William Baumol as characteristic of the so-called productivity-immune sectors of the economy, which are generally labor-intensive, with few opportunities for substitution of capital or new production technologies for labor (live theater, symphony orchestras, social welfare agencies, and education).[14] Unit costs in such enterprises track their increases in compensation. Because workers in such enterprises (e.g., faculty) typically get the same wage and salary increases as those in the productivity-sensitive, goods-producing sectors of the economy, in which constant infusions of capital and technology produce real productivity gains and allow unit cost increases to be less than compensation increases, the unit costs in productivity-immune sectors will inevitably exceed those in goods-producing sectors. Thus, unit-cost increases in higher education will be "above average." And since the rate of inflation is nothing more than a weighted average of many price increases, it is inevitable that unit costs—and thus tuitions—in higher education will rise in normal years faster than the rate of inflation.

This is the normal, or default, condition in higher education: unit costs increase slightly in excess of the prevailing rate of inflation and tuition increases even more, substantially exceeding the prevailing rate of inflation, resulting in the following:

—State governments shift the cost burden from taxpayers to students and families through very high percentage tuition increases in the public sector.
—Private colleges put more of their marginal tuition dollar back into student aid, thus requiring even larger tuition increases to keep up with rising costs.
—Faculty compensation increases exceed compensation increases generally prevailing in the economy.
—Higher education becomes "input rich" in the form, say, of more technology per student, higher faculty and staff to student ratios, or more costly physical plant per student.

All of these factors have been at work for the past decade and more, resulting in very substantial tuition increases in both the private and the public sectors. From 1990 to 2000, tuitions rose at private universities by 77 percent, at private colleges by 70 percent, at public universities by 84 percent, and at public two-year colleges by 62 percent (table 13.1). The very high rates of tuition increase in the priciest private colleges are the result of an enrichment of the amenities, a lowering of faculty/student and staff/student ratios, and the increase in institutionally provided financial aid (i.e., a lowering of the net revenue yield from a dollar of tuition increase). Rising tuitions in the public

Table 13.1

Annual Tuition and Required Fees, Private and Public College, 1980–81 and 2000–01

	Private Institutions		Public Institutions	
Year	University	Four-Year College	University	Two-Year
1980/81	$4,275	$3,390	$915	$391
1985/86	7,374	5,641	1,536	641
1990/91	11,379	8,389	2,159	824
1995/96	15,605	11,297	3,151	1,239
2000/01	20,106	14,233	3,979	1,333
% increase 1995–2000	29	26	26	8
% increase 1990–2000	77	70	84	62

Source: National Center for Education Statistics, *Digest of Education Statistics, 2002* (Washington, D.C.: U.S. Department of Education), table 312.

Note: Data have not been adjusted for changes in the purchasing power of the dollar over time.

sector are overwhelmingly caused by the withdrawal of state tax revenue and a shift in relative cost burden from the taxpayer to students and parents.[15]

Diverging Trajectories of Costs and Revenues

The natural trajectory of unit costs in higher education, as described above, is steeply upward, at rates in excess of prevailing rates of inflation. The corresponding rate of increase of anticipated revenues is substantially flatter, being dampened by the following:

— Price resistance from upper-middle-class parents, manifested both in a shift in demand to selective public universities and in "bargain hunting" for increased financial aid (lowering *net* tuition revenues).
— Price resistance from older students and from graduate and advanced professional students facing mounting debt loads.
— Decreasing support from governors and state legislatures faced with other compelling public needs, decreasing federal financial assistance, and restive or angry state taxpayers.
— Increasing costs of "big science" without concomitant increases in federal research support.

—Decreasing support for academic health centers, caught between cost-cutting insurers and low-cost alternative providers.

The resulting scenario is frightening: for high-priced private institutions feeling price resistance as well as for public colleges and universities facing declining state tax revenues without the benefit of substantial endowments, wealthy alumni, internationally eminent scientists, or deep and affluent applicant pools. Some institutions have turned their fortunes around through vigorous cost cutting, restructuring, and moving into a narrow market niche, but the future will continue to hold great uncertainty and continuing financial stress for most colleges and universities.

Sources of Revenue for the Enterprise

The financing of higher education poses the question of how the costs should be apportioned among four parties: parents, students, taxpayers, and philanthropists.[16] Parents would finance their children's education from current income, savings, or future income via increased indebtedness. Students would finance their own education from savings, summer earnings, term-time earnings, and future earnings via loans or graduate tax obligations. Taxpayers at the federal, state, and local levels would finance students' education through taxes on income, sales, property, assets, business or manufacturing taxes (via the higher prices of the goods or services so taxed) or through the indirect "tax" of inflation brought about by public deficit spending. And philanthropists would finance students' education either through endowments or current giving.

The sharing and shifting of the costs among these parties is a zero-sum game, in which a lessening of the burden upon, or revenue from, one party must be compensated either by a reduction of underlying costs or by a shift of the burden to another party. Thus, if state taxpayers' share of higher education costs is to be lessened, that reduced share must either lead to reduced institutional costs or be shifted, probably to students and parents via higher tuition. But if parents cannot pay or have enough political power to limit, by statute or regulation, a higher parental contribution (as happened when voter pressure forced Congress to eliminate home equity from the assets considered in determining "need" for awarding federal

Pell grants), the burden would shift to students, principally through higher debt loads. This scenario—lower taxpayer contributions, reduced institutional budgets, higher tuitions, level parental contributions, and much higher debt burdens—is exactly what has happened in the last decade or two.

The policy questions sharpened by the cost-sharing perspective are as follows:

—What is the appropriate amount that should be expected from parents to cover the higher educational costs of their children? Is this share to be a function only of current income, to be met by family belt tightening? Or are parents also expected to have saved from the past or to borrow against the future? Are assets to be figured in the calculation of need? How long should parental financial responsibility continue: through undergraduate years only, or until the age of, say, twenty-four or twenty-five? And what is the expected contribution from a noncustodial parent?

—With regard to student share, are there any limits to the hours of term-time work compatible with full-time study? Are there any limits to the amount of indebtedness that students should be allowed to incur in pursuit of their education? Should this limit be a function of likely completion of studies or of the anticipated earning power of the intended occupation or profession? Would this deferred payment obligation be best handled via a conventional mortgage-type loan, an income-contingent obligation, or a graduate tax obligation (assuming that the present value of the repayment stream under all options would yield the same repayments, at least over a cohort of borrowers)?

—Should public (taxpayer) financial support be linked to governmental ownership and ultimate control, as in the support of public higher education? Or should taxpayers support certain costs divorced from control, such as vouchers (e.g., Pell grants), which support both public and private—and even proprietary—sectors of higher education? Should taxpayer support per student continue to be a function mainly of family income and sector costs (e.g., public research universities as opposed to public community colleges)? Or should the government, through the financial aid system, differentiate among students by their academic potential or attempt to influence their choice of academic field or intended occupation?

Table 13.2

Increase in Average Total Costs (Tuition, Room, and Board) 1991–2002 to 2001–2002 by Sector in Current and Constant (2002) Dollars and as a Percentage of Mean Family Income by Quintile (constant 2002 $)

	Average Total Cost Private University	Average Total Cost Private Other 4-Year	Average Total Cost Public University	Average Total Cost Public 2-Year
Total cost 2001–2 (current dollars)	$29,120	$21,285	$9,953	$5,137
Total cost 1991–92 (current dollars)	17,572	13,201	6,650	3,623
Total cost 1991–92 (constant 2002 $)	22,530	16,921	7,757	4,645
% increase (current [unadjusted] dollars)	66	61	50	42
% increase (constant 2002 $)	29	26	28	11
Total cost as % of mean family income by quintile (2001–2):				
High quintile	20	15	7	4
Third quintile	68	50	23	12
Low quintile	291	213	100	51
Total cost as % of mean family income by quintile (1991–92):				
High quintile	20	15	7	4
Third quintile	59	44	20	12
Low quintile	225	185	85	51

Source: Total costs from National Center for Education Statistics, *Digest of Education Statistics, 2002,* table 312, pp. 354–55. Mean family income by quintiles from U.S. Census Bureau, *Income in the U.S., 2002,* table A-4, p. 26.

There has been a considerable increase in education costs borne by students and parents, mainly through higher tuitions, especially in the 1980s for private institutions and in the 1990s for public institutions (table 13.1). However, before drawing conclusions about either the relative shares borne by students, parents, and taxpayers or the impact of these increasing costs, we need to adjust for the impact of inflation and for increases in family incomes. Table 13.2 shows the total cost of attendance and the percentage taken from family incomes at selected income quintiles. Finally, adjusting for financial assistance—both grants and loans—further reduces the impact of these total cost increases. For example, subtracting the impact of all grants from all sources nearly eliminates the net real increase in total cost of attendance between 1992 and 1993 and between 1999 and 2000 for low-income–high-need students. Adding the increased availability of student loans, while admittedly not the same as grants, substantially meets the increased costs of attendance for middle-income, high- and moderate-need students.[17]

Tables 13.3 and 13.4 show how the expenses of private and public institutions, both high cost and low cost, are met through combinations of family contributions, federal and state aid, loans, and institutional (philanthropic) grants for high-, middle-, and low-income families.

Some observations from tables 13.3 and 13.4:

— The costs of college borne by the student and parent are high but are very high only for relatively affluent families at high-cost private institutions.
— Meeting the high costs at expensive private colleges and universities without substantial parental contributions requires both very high institutional, or philanthropic, support as well as very substantial student indebtedness.
— The key to financial accessibility lies less in level of tuition, or even in expected parental contribution, than in students' willingness to incur substantial indebtedness. Total student debt for four or more years of undergraduate education, plus three or more years of graduate or advanced professional school, can easily reach $50,000 to $100,000 or more, presenting the student with a repayment obligation that can either discourage advanced higher education altogether or distort career and other life choices.
— High-cost public institutions (high tuition plus residency) require substantial indebtedness, considerably diminishing the price advantage over high-cost private institutions.

From time to time, a proposal is made that direct public funding of state colleges and universities, at least for the support of instruction, be drastically reduced or eliminated altogether, with tuitions raised to full or near full cost, eliminating or greatly reducing what the proponents of this view call the "subsidy" to the students and families of students attending public colleges and universities. In place of direct state revenue, which currently supports from 60 to 90 percent of

Table 13.3

Student Budgets at Private Institutions, Sources of Support, by Family Income ($)

Sources of Support	High-Cost Institution ($30,000)			Low-Cost Institution ($21,000)		
	Low-Income Family	Middle-Income Family	High-Income Family	Low-Income Family	Middle-Income Family	High-Income Family
Parental contribution	$0	$6,500	$24,000	$0	$6,500	$15,000
Federal grants[a]	6,000	0	0	5,000	0	0
State grants[b]	3,000	1,000	1,000	3,000	1,000	1,000
Institutional grants	11,500	12,000	0	3,500	3,000	0
Summer savings	2,500	2,500	1,500	2,500	2,500	1,500
Student term-time earnings	3,000	3,000	1,500	3,000	3,000	1,500
Student loans	4,000	5,000	2,000	4,000	5,000	2,000
Total from taxpayer[c]	9,540	1,675	1,270	8,540	1,675	1,270
Total from parents[d]	0	6,500	24,000	0	6,500	15,000
Total from student[e]	8,960	9,825	4,730	8,960	9,825	4,730
Total from philanthropists[f]	11,500	12,000	0	3,500	3,000	0
Total	30,000	30,000	30,000	21,000	21,000	21,000

Notes: Low family income is the point below which family qualifies for maximum grants and has no expected financial contribution. Middle-income family is household earnings of $50,000; high-income family is household earnings of $100,000.

a. Assume maximum Pell plus Supplemental Educational Opportunity Grants.

b. Assume need-based plus modest nonneed-based state grants.

c. Sum of federal and state grants plus the present value of loan subsidy (assuming two and one-half years of deferment plus grace at 6 percent interest, discounted at same rate for a total of $135 per $1,000 of initial lending).

d. Expected family contribution minus assumed summer savings from the student.

e. Sum of expected term-time earnings plus summer savings plus present value of loan repayments (assuming market rate in the repayments period minus present value of in-school and grace period subsidies for a present discounted value of expected loan repayments of $865 per $1,000 of initial borrowing).

f. Total from philanthropists includes all institutional grants; assume zero for public institutions.

public four-year undergraduate instructional costs, proponents of the high-tuition, high-aid model would substitute a much expanded program of need-based grants, which would diminish as parental or student incomes rose. The grants would phase out entirely for families and students whose income was deemed sufficient to pay the full cost of tuition in addition to other expenses.[18]

Table 13.4

Student Budgets at Public Institutions, Sources of Support, by Family Income ($)

Sources of Support	High-Cost Institution ($14,000)			Low-Cost Institution ($6,000)		
	Low-Income Family	Middle-Income Family	High-Income Family	Low-Income Family	Middle-Income Family	High-Income Family
Parental contribution	$0	$6,000	$12,500	$0	$2,500	$4,500
Federal grants[a]	5,000	0	0	3,000	0	0
State grants[b]	3,000	1,000	0	1,000	500	0
Institutional grants	0	0	0	0	0	0
Summer savings	2,500	2,000	1,500	1,000	2,000	1,500
Student term-time earnings	2,500	2,000	0	1,000	0	0
Student loans	1,000	3,000	0	0	1,000	0
Total from taxpayer[c]	8,135	1,405	0	4,000	635	0
Total from parents[d]	0	6,000	12,500	0	2,500	4,500
Total from student[e]	5,865	6,595	1,500	2,000	2,865	1,500
Total from philanthropists[f]	0	0	0	0	0	
Total	14,000	14,000	14,000	6,000	6,000	6,000

Note: See table 13.3 for footnote.

The high-tuition, high-aid model is based on claims of efficiency and equity. The efficiency claim begins with the tenet of public finance theory that any public subsidy of a good or a service that consumers are likely to purchase anyway, in the absence or diminution of the subsidy, is an inefficient use of public tax dollars. The tax dollars released, if public sector tuitions were allowed to rise, would supposedly go toward public needs of greater priority: more need-based student aid, health care, public infrastructure, tax cuts, or public deficit reduction. And if the demand for public higher education should decline as a result of lower subsidies and higher prices, this too might be a move in the direction of a more efficient use of the nation's resources. Subsidies can generate overproduction of a good or service, and a higher priced public higher education might discourage ambivalent, ill-prepared students whom advocates of high tuition and high aid assume are taking up space and wasting precious resources in our public colleges and universities.

A corollary of the efficiency claim is that there exists, at least in some states, underutilized capacity in the private higher education sector that could be filled at relatively low marginal cost. A shift of tax dollars from the direct support of public colleges and universities to need-based student aid, portable to the private sector, would presumably shift enrollments there and enable the socially optimal level of enrollments to be supported more in the private sector but at a lower additional net cost to the taxpayer.

The equity argument in favor of high tuition, high aid is based on two assumptions: first, that public higher education is actually partaken of disproportionately by students from upper-middle-income and affluent families; and second, that the state taxes used to support public higher education tend to be proportionate or even regressive and thus are paid by many lower-middle-income and poor families, who are unlikely to benefit. Thus, the high-tuition, high-aid model of public higher education finance is claimed to be more equitable than across-the-board low tuition because it targets all public subsidy only on the needy and imposes full costs on students or families affluent enough to pay.

The case against the high-tuition, high-aid model rests partly on the oversimplification and political naïveté of the case made on its behalf, summarized above, and partly on the case to be made for the very existence of a public higher education sector. The case against high tuition, high aid may be summarized by four points.

First, a "sticker price" of $15,000 to $25,000 for a full-time year at a public college or university would almost certainly discourage many from aspiring to higher education, even with the prospect of financial aid or a lower tuition for those in need. The total costs to students and parents of a year of full-time study at a public four-year college or university, as shown in table 13.3, make even public higher education today a relatively heavy financial burden for most families and for nearly all independent students. This fact alone does not fully negate the more theoretical arguments of efficiency and equity presented on behalf of full-cost or near-full-cost pricing for public higher education, as summarized above. But even with financial aid, costs at a public college might seem daunting to many students and their parents, especially to students from disadvantaged and nonwhite families.

Second, a high-tuition, high-aid policy would lessen the quality of public colleges and universities. The purpose of high-tuition, high-aid plans is to reduce state tax revenues currently going to public colleges and universities, even though some proponents claim that this revenue loss would be made up by increased revenue from the much higher tuitions paid by the more well-to-do. Private sector proponents of high tuition, high aid, however, make no secret of their aim to shift enrollments and tuition dollars of middle- and upper-middle-income students (or at least the most attractive and able ones) from the public sector to the private sector. With little or no price advantage left in the public sector; with the resource advantage of large endowments, wealthy alumni, and the tradition of philanthropic support in the private sector; with the patina of elitism and selectivity associated with private colleges and universities (especially in the Northeast); and with greater constraints and burdens remaining on the public sector, many of the nation's 1,600 public colleges and universities would become places for students whom the private colleges, now priced the same as public colleges, do not accept. Such an erosion in the relative status and quality of public colleges and universities does not seem to be in the nation's public interest.

Third, high tuition does not guarantee high aid. Governors, legislators, and voters, continually pressed by public needs exceeding available resources, are likely to support that part of the public sector in which they perceive that they or their children have a stake. They are much less likely to maintain the financial aid, or "tuition discount," portion of the public higher educational budget when it is devoted almost exclusively to the poor. The not unlikely consequences of a policy of high tuition, high aid, rather than the purported enhancements of efficiency and equity, are higher tuition, lower taxes, inadequate aid, diminished access, and deteriorating public colleges and universities.

Fourth and fundamentally, the high-tuition, high-aid model is a denial of the appropriateness of higher education as a public good. The nation's public colleges and universities have been built and supported over the last century and a half not merely to provide a subsidized education to those who might not otherwise have an opportunity for higher education. Rather, voters and elected officials wanted public colleges and universities that would attract and hold the best and brightest students and scholars, serve society, aid the economy, and be a signal of the state's culture. The high-tuition, high-aid model essentially denies most of these public purposes to public higher education and substitutes only a public subsidy for those who are too poor to afford what would become an otherwise unsubsidized, expensive, and essentially privatized product. States need to consider whether these continue to be important reasons for supporting public higher education or whether they mainly want to get needy students into some college, in which case high tuition, high aid is almost certainly, as public finance theory correctly states, less expensive to the tax-payer.

Summary and Conclusions

The financial fortunes of American colleges and universities vary greatly by institution. Those relatively few private institutions with large endowments, traditions of generous alumni giving, and deep and affluent student applicant pools will experience continuing cost pressures but will be able to increase revenues commensurably and continue to prosper. Some public institutions similarly situated with deep and affluent applicant pools, with established traditions of phil-anthropic support, and with research strengths in areas of continuing public investment (e.g., biomedical and applied sciences) will prosper. Some less-well-endowed private institutions will seize a specialized market niche, either vocational (e.g., health-related professions) or cultural/ideological (e.g., conservative Christian) and, with good man-agement and low faculty costs, will also prosper. Most private colleges and universities, however, will feel a fierce revenue squeeze, primarily driven by the lack of growth in the number of upper-middle-class par-ents able or willing to pay the high tuitions and in the number of stu-dents willing to take on increasing levels of indebtedness. And most public colleges and universities will continue to experience flat or de-clining state tax support, forcing even higher tuition, more program closures, and an increasing reliance on part-time and adjunct faculty.

As more and more colleges and universities exhaust the available cost-side measures for increasing productivity, interest is turning to increasing productivity by enhancing higher education's output, or learning.[19] Expressed another way, the major remaining productivity problem in higher education may not lie in excessive costs but in in-sufficient learning—a function of such features as redundant learn-ing; aimless academic exploration; the unavailability of courses at the right time; excessive nonlearning time in the academic day, week, and year; insufficient use of self-paced learning; and insufficient realiza-tion of the potential of collegiate-level learning during the high school years. Enhancing the productivity of learning, then, would reduce vacation time and other time spent in other-than-learning activities; provide better advising and other incentives to lessen aimless curricular exploration; enhance opportunities for self-paced learning, perhaps through the aid of instructional technology; minimize curricular redundancy; and maximize the potential of college-level learning during the high school years.

Technology in the form of personal computers, new instructional software, the Internet, and instructional videocassettes, will profoundly affect the way faculty and advanced students conduct research, and it will enrich some teaching. However—aside from some pockets of distance learning and users of a virtual university, generally limited to nontraditional and technologically inclined students— technology will mainly enable more and better, not cheaper, learning.

The shift in burden from parents and taxpayers to students, paid for with more part-time (and even more full-time) work and much more debt, will continue, but there is reason to believe that the long-expected price resistance is happening. Marketing will become even more frenzied, and so will governmental efforts to "solve the problem" without spending any taxpayer revenue: tuition prepayment, tax-exempt savings plans, non-need-based price discounting, income-contingent repayment plans, and the like.

State higher education budgets will be smaller, but this reduction will be accompanied by greater flexibility and performance criteria, such as premiums to institutions that improve retention and completion rates. Most institutions have been shaping their missions for years to adjust to more low-income, minority, older, part-time, and place-bound students; greater applied and vocational interest among most students; and less revenue and the need to trim or eliminate that which is neither excellent nor popular nor central to the institution. In short, much of the vaunted restructuring that management consultants and many observers and analysts of higher education have been calling for as a solution to the financial dilemma of U.S. colleges and universities is probably not a solution at all, for the simple reason that it has been going on for years. Most of the smaller and comprehensive colleges have reallocated resources and altered their programs and faculty profiles dramatically; many have changed mission altogether. Many of those that have not are either rich or private or both and have no need to change dramatically (at least no need that can be called a public policy issue).

The largest class of institution for which this is not necessarily the case are those universities, largely regional and with minimal or uneven scholarly reputations, that continue to pursue the research university model but that are unlikely to penetrate the top ranks, measured by the scholarly prestige of their faculty or their graduate programs. Here, pressures to control costs are likely to focus on an increasing separation of funding for instruction and research, much as has occurred in the United Kingdom. If these measures are successful, the result could be less indirect public subsidization of faculty scholarship, a widening difference in faculty workloads, and a reduced administration overhead on competitive research grants.

Although American higher education does more than the systems of any other nation to provide postsecondary opportunities to those from low socioeconomic backgrounds, the larger American society is becoming not only more unequal but also more predictable in intergenerational transmission of higher educational attainment. In other words, the children of well-educated, well-off parents generally achieve and persist in college, and those of the very poor, unless they are very bright and very lucky, generally do not. The likely continuation of sharply rising public tuitions, political attacks against remedial courses, elimination of affirmative action considerations in admissions and financial aid, and the conservative assault against curricula acknowledging multicultural values will likely accentuate this pattern.

NOTES

1. The prevailing condition of austerity in higher education is described in such works as David W. Breneman, *Liberal Arts Colleges: Thriving, Surviving, or Endangered?* (Washington, D.C.: The Brookings Institution, 1994); and Bruce Johnstone, "Higher Education and Those 'Out of control Costs' " in Philip G. Altbach, Patricia J. Gumport, and D. Bruce Johnstone, *In Defense of American Higher Education* (Baltimore: Johns Hopkins University Press, 2001), 144–80.

2. For a perspective on the overwhelming condition of austerity in higher education in developing countries, and the similarity with the United States and Europe in both the analyses and policy solutions, see World Bank, *Higher Education: The Lessons of Experience* (Washington, D.C.: World Bank, 1994); Adrian Ziderman and Douglas Albrecht, *Financing Universities in Developing Countries* (Washington, D.C.: Falmer Press, 1995); Task Force on Higher Education and Society, *Higher Education in Developing Countries: Peril and Promise* (Washington, D.C.: The World Bank and UNESCO); World Bank, *Constructing Knowledge Societies: New Challenges for Tertiary Education*

(Washington, D.C.: World Bank, 2002); and Maureen Woodhall, guest editor, *Paying for Learning: The Debate on Student Fees, Grants and Loans in International Perspective.* A Special International Issue of the *Welsh Journal of Education,* vol. 11, no. 1, 2002.

3. National Center for Education Statistics (NCES), *Enrollment in Postsecondary Institutions, Fall 2000 and Financial Statistics, Fiscal Year 2000* (Washington, D.C.: U.S. Department of Education, September 2002), table 26, p. 49.

4. NCES, *Comparative Indicators of Education in the US and Other G-8 Countries, 2000* (Washington, D.C.: U.S. Department of Education), indicator 27, 75.

5. NCES, *The Condition of Education 2004* (Washington, D.C.: U.S. Department of Education, 2004), indicators 6, 7, pp. 103, 115.

6. NCES, *Digest of Education Statistics 2002,* table 184, p. 223.

7. NCES, *Digest of Education Statistics 2002* (Washington, D.C.: U.S. Department of Education, 2003), tables 244, 172, 362, pp. 296, 210, 212, 407.

8. NCES, *Digest of Education Statistics 2002,* table 174, p. 212.

9. *The Challenge of the Century* (Sacramento: California Postsecondary Education Commission, April 1995). The privately financed California Policy Center sets the number at 488,000; see *Shared Responsibility: Strategies to Enhance Quality and Opportunity in California Higher Education* (San Jose: California Higher Education Policy Center, 1996).

10. William F. Massy and Robert Zemsky, "The Lattice and the Ratchet," *Policy Perspectives,* no. 3 (Philadelphia: PEW Higher Education Research Program, 1990). Also, Zemsky and Massy, "Toward an Understanding of Our Current Predicaments," *Change,* (November/December 1995): 41–49.

11. Howard R. Bowen, *The Costs of Higher Education* (San Francisco: Jossey-Bass, 1980), 116–19.

12. NCES, *Digest of Education Statistics 2002,* tables 343, 345, 386, p. 389.

13. H. Bowen, *The Costs of Higher Education,* 19–26.

14. William J. Baumol and William G. Bowen, *Performing Arts: The Economic Dilemma* (New York: Twentieth Century Fund, 1966); also, William G. Bowen, *The Economics of the Major Private Universities* (Berkeley, CA: Carnegie Commission on the Future of Higher Education, 1968).

15. For accounts of recent tuition increases, see: Arthur Hauptman, *The College Tuition Spiral* (Washington, D.C.: College Board and American Council on Education, 1990); Carol Francis, *What Factors Affect College Tuition?* (Washington, D.C.: American Association of State Colleges and Universities, 1990); Charles T. Clotfelter, *Buying the Best: Cost Escalation in Elite Higher Education* (Princeton, NJ: Princeton University Press, 1996); Ronald G. Ehrenberg, *Tuition Rising: Why College Costs So Much* (Cambridge, MA: Harvard University Press, 2000); and Bruce Johnstone, "Higher Education

and Those 'Out of control Costs', " in Philip G. Altbach, Patricia J. Gumport, and D. Bruce Johnstone, *In Defense of American Higher Education* (Baltimore: Johns Hopkins University Press, 2001), 144–80. For time series, see College Board, *Trends in College Pricing 2003* (Washington, D.C.: College Board), available at www.collegeboard.com.

16. Some consider "business" a possible fifth party to bear a share of higher education costs. However, grants from business to higher education can be viewed in one of three ways: (1) as the purchase of a service, whether research or specialized training, in which case the grant should cover the costs of the added service but is not expected to bear a share of the core instructional costs of the college or university; (2) as voluntary contributions coming out of owner profits, in which case they would fall under "philanthropy"; or (3) as contributions considered part of the cost of doing business, included in the price of the products and paid for by the general consumer, like a sales or consumption tax, in which case the incidence, or burden, is indistinguishable from that of other taxes and may be considered to be included, at least conceptually, in the "taxpayer" party. See D. Bruce Johnstone, *Sharing the Costs of Education* (New York: College Board, 1986).

17. National Center for Education Statistics, *What Students Pay for College: Changes in Net Price of Attendance Between 1992–93 and 1999–2000.* Washington, D.C.: U.S. Department of Education, 2002, Tables 7A, 7B, pp. 33, 34.

18. The case for high tuition, high aid was popularized in W. Lee Hansen and Burton A Weisbrod, *Benefits, Costs, and Finance of Public Higher Education* (Chicago: Markham, 1969). See also Carnegie Commission on Higher Education, *Higher Education: Who Pays? Who Benefits? Who Should Pay?* (New York: McGraw-Hill, 1973); Frederick J. Fischer, "State Financing of Higher Education: A New Look at an Old Problem," *Change* (Jan./Feb., 1990); and McPherson, Shapiro, and Winston, *Paying the Piper.* The case against draws heavily on D. Bruce Johnstone, *The High-Tuition–High-Aid Model of Public Higher Education Finance: The Case Against* (Albany: State University of New York, for National Association of System Heads, 1993).

19. D. Bruce Johnstone, *Learning Productivity: A New Imperative for American Higher Education* (Albany: State University of New York Press, 1992).

Chapter Fourteen

Technology and Higher Education

Opportunities and Challenges for the New Era

Patricia J. Gumport and Marc Chun

The influence of technology on the everyday life of higher education can hardly be overestimated.[1] Its extensive effect can be suggested, for example, by briefly recounting the process of creating this chapter. Despite the fact that we two authors were both at the same institution when this chapter was written in 1997, we were both traveling, and therefore communicated with each other and with the editor via phone, voice mail, and e-mail. References and background information were located through computerized searches of library holdings, by reviewing online journals, and via the Web. Chapter drafts were beamed through phone lines electronically and as faxes. When it came time to revise this chapter for the book's most recent edition, we were working on opposite coasts. Our co-authorship again entailed electronic transmittals, this time with text colored blue and red to indicate our respective changes and deletions. Technology not only provided access to the information we used, but it shaped (as well as made possible) the techniques we used to collaborate. Indeed, despite the many ways technology facilitated our process, we were often only aware of its influence when technological difficulties arose: problems with converting files, access to e-mail, or network servers going down.

This chapter's process also serves to remind us of technology's limits—and some related effects. Despite our general reliance on the possible leverage to be gained from advances in technology, this chapter is written not to be distributed on CD-ROM or posted on a Web page, but as a chapter in a book—a medium now considered a low-tech means of disseminating knowledge. However, a Google search found the original chapter had many times been converted into a PDF file and posted as a reading on various course Web sites. Thus, some readers may see this article only in electronic form, out of context from the rest of the chapters in this book. In other words, as a largely unanticipated result, technology has afforded the authors an insight into how the original chapter was being used, something we would likely have been unaware of if the chapter had been photocopied to include in a course reader. (Although here we mainly comment on how technology shapes the process and product of knowledge creation, we recognize that technology also affects knowledge dissemination.) As a starting point for our discussion, then, although many of us take for granted the ways in which technology has altered academic work, recounting this experience suggests not only some features of this transformation but also implications stemming from our reflections on these changes.

Advancements in information technology and communications technology have made possible new approaches to teaching, learning, and research that were previously unimagined. While some developments have been wholeheartedly embraced as valuable educational innovations, others have been less enthusiastically received. The goal of this chapter is to discuss the potential effect of technology on higher education, while acknowledging its interdependence with a complex array of opportunities and pressures, both within the higher education system and in the wider society. We focus our analysis on five areas: (1) higher education and technology in modern society, (2) the historical impact of technology on education, (3) arenas of impact for contemporary advancements in higher education, (4) wider policy pressures and legitimacy considerations, and (5) resistance to widespread technological change within higher education.

Higher Education and Technology in Modern Society

Modern society calls on the educational system to engage in teaching, learning, and research, all in the name of "progress." Toward this end, in the United States, the federal and state governments have taken an interest in education at all levels, though with dramatically different arrangements for oversight. While government assumes primary responsibility for elementary and secondary education — to the extent that K–12 education is both mandatory and publicly funded—postsecondary education is characterized by more decentralized control at the state, campus, and classroom levels. The government provides financial support for tuition and research through various funding mechanisms to states, campuses, and students and legislates policies, such as Title IX and health and safety regulations. Yet government imposes few constraints on higher education's core academic processes: curriculum, teaching, learning, and classroom practices.

Given this context, traditional higher education institutions have historically been accredited as legitimate "providers," centrally positioned within teaching and research markets. At the same time, higher education has long been susceptible to a wide range of market forces and dynamics, as new providers vie to supply educational services to the postsecondary population. In a market economy, myriad institutional resources enable students to avail themselves of many sources and combinations of information and knowledge.[2] With advancements in technology, especially post–World War II, the strong market position of traditional higher education providers has faced challenges from new providers with potentially farther reaches—for example, corporations, proprietary schools, and other for-profit ventures. As an example, in the three-year period between 1997 and 2000, enrollment in for-credit distance-education courses more than doubled.[3]

Some observers claim that recent advances in technology will revolutionize teaching and learning practices and delivery systems for higher education. The current spate of technology in higher education has been branded a panacea for efficiency, access, and quality, among other ongoing demands on systems design and campus operations. However, like many shifts positioned somewhere between revolution and merely fashionable trend, technology may in the end drastically disappoint such unrealistic expectations.

Applications of technology for higher education must be seen in light of broader societal transformations in the past three decades. Not only are more applications of technology—specifically, information and telecommunications technology—designed to be part of everyday life, but lower costs, greater availability, and changes in perceived need have seen such technology adopted by greater percentages of the population. Some technology is already well entrenched and routinized, so much so that we overlook the range of functions served. In the home, telephone answering machines and portable "roam" phones now seem quaint, having been supplanted by voice mail, cellular phones, text messaging, and wireless Web browsing. Moreover, the percentage of the U.S. population that uses such telecommunication technology continues to grow; where mobile phones were once the province of the privileged, they are now used by upward of two-thirds of the population.[4] Videocassette recorders have given way to TiVo, which has recently radically redefined "remote control" by enabling users to set programs to be recorded at home from anywhere in the world via the Internet. Similarly, in the workplace it is common to see networking for local work groups, computer work stations, virtual conferences, streaming video presentations, and access to the Internet for communication and expanded markets. Of all these advancements, the personal computer has perhaps the greatest effect because it has achieved a significant presence in the daily lives of increasing numbers of Americans.[5] The range of applications for computers continues to grow: although in the larger scope such technology is relatively new, one doesn't think twice about using computers for word processing, e-mail, digital imaging, downloading music and video, and accessing the Internet. Such technological breakthroughs for home and office are typically celebrated for the ways in which they make life easier.

Technology is equally reshaping the world of higher education. Consider some examples at Stanford University. An aeronautical engineering professor lectures to her class on wing design with interactive video, which enables a classmate from one of several remote company sites to interrupt and explain that his company's wing design practice is now different. Interactive video links students in a music class from three locations simultaneously—with one-third of the class at Stanford University, one-third at San Jose State University, and one-third at Princeton University—and together they critique a classical performance. In another classroom, a course on Shakespeare is taught jointly by faculty at Stanford University and the Massachusetts Institute of Technology. In a mechanical engineering classroom, students work in teams of three to design products; yet, the team members are not located in the same place. Students linked from Stanford University, Tokyo, and New York collaborate on product design through e-mail, desktop videoconferencing—complete with a shared workspace—and overnight package-delivery services. Students in a French class use computers to complete their homework and a voice emulator allows them to listen to lessons. Across campus in the main library computer cluster, one student logs on to check her grades for her courses last quarter, while her friend does a search through biology journals on the World Wide Web. An anthropology professor demonstrates for his students a CD-ROM he developed that provides a virtual reality walk through an archaeological excavation site. A doctoral oral exam is underway through videoconferencing, connecting the main exam group with two faculty examiners located off campus—one in Boston and the other in London. Few faculty and students are aware of the full range of these initiatives. And nationwide, even fewer can afford them. In effect, differences in access to and adoption of technology create a new dimension of higher education haves and have-nots.

The information age has arguably brought about a transformation of society, dramatically changing communication, the workplace, science, and entertainment. It has also affected education, but the nature and scope of such changes are still contested. Many have trumpeted technology as an educational cure-all—sure to transform the delivery and nature of educational processes. Others remain more skeptical, claiming that systemic educational problems cannot be solved simply by technology alone because technologies are merely tools, the successful use of which may entail a paradigmatic shift in the orientation of all involved in teaching and learning. Within higher education, technology provides pressures and opportunities that make transformations possible, but such change is not a given. This point can be exemplified by taking a historical perspective.

A Historical Perspective on Technology's Effect on Education

"I believe that (it) is destined to revolutionize our educational system and that in a few years it will supplant largely, if not entirely, the use of textbooks."[6] Although this could easily be a current quote from an Apple or Microsoft executive about the future of computers, it is, in fact, Thomas Edison speaking more than eighty years ago about the motion picture. History demonstrates two certainties with respect to the effect of technology on education: first, prognosticators will herald the radical rebirth or inevitable demise of the educational system; and second, more often than not, their predictions are wrong. The educational timeline for adoption of technology is dotted with unexpected failures and unanticipated successes.

Americans seem enamored with the idea that any new technology can, in and of itself, remedy all of their troubles. In response to the overwhelming multiplicity of problems facing education, many seek the latest gizmo as the "technical fix" that the system requires. The arrival of new technologies for education has often been accompanied by bold predictions for its transformation. Recent claims about the power of "high technology" to revitalize education are therefore likely to conjure up a collective sense of social déjà vu. The introduction of the blackboard was expected to turn education on its ear. Some predicted that the spread of television would eliminate illiteracy in America;[7] a 1957 Ford Foundation report foresaw television as "the greatest opportunity for the advancement of education since the introduction of printing by movable type."[8]

By the same token, many experts sound the tocsin of doom, predicting the new technology will bring forth the downfall of the educational system. In the fifth century B.C., tremendous controversy surrounded the implementation of written records in teaching, which was considered to be the first technological innovation. Stanford University philosopher Patrick Suppes notes that at the time, many believed that adopting written materials would undermine the learning process and diminish the quality of the personal relationship between tutor and student. Plato observed the shift from oral to written tradition by recording Socrates' concerns that putting words on paper undercuts the "art of dialectic." In the dialogue "Phaedrus," Socrates predicts that using written materials "will create forgetfulness in the learners' souls, because they will not use their memories; they will trust to the external written characters and not remember of themselves. . . . They will appear to be omniscient and will generally know nothing."[9] It was also feared that the printed word would undermine the authority of the scholar because students would have new access to another source of knowledge. Observers were further concerned that this shift toward written text and standardized knowledge would lead to impersonal and repetitive action, precluding opportunities for creativity, such as when scribes would amend the manuscripts they were copying. A more recent example of doomsday prediction comes from the early 1960s, when instructional television disappointed proponents and users alike. Initial high hopes were accompanied by grave fears; some predicted that classrooms would be staffed primarily by teaching assistants whose sole role would be to keep students quiet.[10]

We now know that the predictions attached both to extreme hopes for massive improvement and to dire warnings of the unavoidable collapse of the educational system never came to pass. This is not to say that the effects of the technologies are not felt on college and university campuses; rather it is to suggest that the actual effect by no means lived up to the overinflated expectations. Nevertheless, prominent historical examples of technology and their subsequent effect on education can shed light on the current proliferation.

In some cases, introducing technology into educational settings had initially been met with lukewarm support and mixed results, but its slow adoption eventually had far-reaching impact. In the above example, written materials eventually gained popularity and found widespread use, contrary to the chorus of warnings. Moreover, not only was this technology adopted, but it also brought about other significant and profound changes in teaching and learning. The accumulation of written documents led to the development of libraries as well as to centralized and organized bodies of knowledge that were expanded as scholars developed intellectual networks. These occurred in tandem with growth in the academic profession and the proliferation of academic disciplines that so prominently carved up the academic landscape in the twentieth century.

In some cases, the lag between the development of technology and its adoption can last centuries. The historical record shows instances of some innovations spreading slowly and gaining momentum only long after their initiation. In the case of written materials, the technology of mass printing, developed by the mid-1400s, permitted educational documents to be distributed both widely and inexpensively. However, Suppes notes that, surprisingly, textbooks did not catch on until the end of the eighteenth century. Another example is formalized testing, widely used in the United States to remove bias in evaluation, as well by researchers to establish standards and to measure achievement and skills. Suppes reports that testing had been used centuries before in China for the selection of mandarins.[11]

In some cases, the impact of a technology will not be realized until it has an opportunity to spread, much in the same way that the revolutionary influence of the telephone was not felt until a critical mass became users.[12] When the technology radically alters the basic structures of the educational process or challenges long-held, taken-for-granted assumptions, it is likely to face such opposition. By contrast, when the technology fits within the basic paradigm, its adoption is often less controversial. For example, the photocopying machine—which in essence replaced the mimeograph machine—was integrated into educational settings immediately.

Of course the adoption of technology has not necessarily led to actual changes in the educational process. Many bemoan the long stream of misbegotten fads, each with its bevy of advocates and cult of enthusiasts and each of which eventually fell by the wayside. The promise held for radio and filmstrips never materialized. Tremendous initial investments were made in computer systems that have become outdated. Huge cadres of students learned computer languages that are now obsolete. Moreover, there is to date very little evidence of sustained improvements in student performance as a result of new information technology—at neither the K–12 nor the postsecondary level. Despite decades of research and wave after wave of reform, not much has changed in the classroom or, at least, not much since the implementation of written materials. The book still remains the primary classroom tool and the coming together of teachers and students still remains the essential means of teaching and learning.

Yet the current wave of technological advances may mark a new chapter in the history of higher education. The primary differences between this technology and those of the past are its extreme flexibility and its relative pervasiveness. Today's technologies are extremely malleable and do not come with an obvious targeted application or audience; it is entirely possible that some technologies may have an unlimited number of applications. In contrast, for example, to the printing press, a single technology with the explicit purpose of mass-producing books, three-dimensional (3D) modeling has many potentials in educational settings: in biochemistry to examine, build, and manipulate molecular structures; in archaeology, to map with great precision the features of a distant site so that students can examine it in labs; in art history, to model the architectural details of an ancient cathedral such that a student can "virtually" enter it and study it from any number of vantage points. In each case, the student can manipulate the model so as to access information beyond the primary purpose intended by the 3D modeler. In some important educational ways, the model may be considered "better" than the real site because it provides more complete access to more information that can be retrieved and reviewed without constraints of place or time.

In addition to its flexibility, new technology has become omnipresent throughout the system, although its adoption is not uniform because cost limits an organization's ability both to obtain it and to upgrade it. The vast mélange of applications of technology to higher education settings are still being identified. Yet the effects on higher education are already evident: all levels of the national system of higher education and its participants are affected—including external agencies that fund, regulate, and articulate with campuses, entire state systems, campus operations, faculty work roles, library services, and student life. More specifically, for example, prospective students and parents routinely get information about colleges and universities online, and increasingly they apply for admission and financial aid electronically. Course registration now occurs online; gone are the days of students standing in long lines in gymnasiums. Students and faculty search through scholarly citations and electronic databases and in some cases obtain the full text of library documents from either on campus or off campus computers as opposed to wandering through library stacks, then photocopying information. Academic support staff use computers rather than carbon paper and typewriters, order supplies and process reimbursements online, and regularly use e-mail to communicate with faculty, students, and other staff members. At the same time, academic departments have eliminated secretarial positions and encouraged their faculty members to be more self-sufficient and to handle their own scheduling, correspondence, and preparation of course materials and manuscripts. Students use videocassette players: in the event they miss a class lecture, they can now check out a video of the lecture from a departmental library in much the same way they borrow a book. To many of today's college students, these practices are taken for granted; what were previously deemed "high tech" novelties are regarded as "no big deal anymore."

These are just a few examples of how technological advancements have already altered the rhythms of higher education settings and of their potential to surpass previously taken-for-granted constraints of time, place, and participants in the process. Technology circulates so pervasively through modern society that traditional higher education is unlikely to be insulated; as new educational providers that rely on technology enter the market, they reshape the landscape of higher education. Although history has shown that the effect of technology is impossible to predict and that the most outspoken advocates and naysayers have often been inaccurate in their prognostications, it al- ready seems certain that some effects will be profound.

Arenas of Technology's Effect on Higher Education

Contemporary advancements in technology can be characterized as having potential influence on three broad arenas of higher education: (1) the nature of knowledge, (2) the process of teaching and learning, and (3) the social organization of teaching and learning in higher education.

The Nature of Knowledge

At the most basic level, technology has affected the nature of knowledge. It shapes what counts as knowledge, how knowledge is produced, how people are involved in the production of knowledge, and how academic knowledge is valued and disseminated.

One burgeoning assumption holds that legitimate knowledge must be capable of being computerized. Knowledge is increasingly created, processed, manipulated, and stored with technology. In addition, the way in which knowledge is produced in academic settings has been greatly expanded; new ways to conduct research are now possible only because of technological advances. Computers make feasible complex statistical analyses and mathematical modeling, laboratory equipment enables the study of subatomic matter and distant galaxies, and x-ray technology allows the examination of images hidden beneath the paint on artistic masterpieces.

Changes in the nature of knowledge also affect the relationships between people and knowledge in higher education. For example, the nature of what it means to be "educated" has shifted. One now must be able to demonstrate computer literacy—with rapid changes occurring in what constitutes that literacy. In the Internet era, access to many forms of knowledge is restricted to those who have the requisite skills and equipment. Even the daily lives of knowledge producers have changed; for instance, faculty who in the past gave dictation to their secretaries to type, now use computers to create their own work. Computers allow easier revisions, compared with the past when changes would require retyping an entire document; easier collaboration with both local and distant colleagues, such as exchanging documents online; and new forms of knowledge dissemination, such as electronic journals that can be read online and access to documents from World Wide Web sites.

More generally, however, advances in technology have occurred in tandem with an increased awareness of the knowledge industry in which higher education participates.[13] New markets for knowledge have ushered in new and complicated issues of intellectual property, as faculty and their employing institutions have internalized notions of the "production" and "consumption" of knowledge. This orientation has profound implications for conceptualizations of higher education's social functions: principally, a shift of the primary emphasis from the development of the individual to the transmission, production, and dissemination of knowledge. Thus students and faculty are more often seen as knowledge consumers and knowledge producers functioning within market forces. As new technology has opened up new possibilities for exchanging and packaging information, a proprietary orientation has gained prominence in higher education, given new markets for research and teaching products. New policies and personnel are required to mediate between individuals and higher education institutions in relation to the ownership and management of academic knowledge.

The Process of Teaching and Learning

Technology has also affected teaching and learning processes in higher education. In traditional higher education settings, the dominant ideal for teaching and learning has presupposed that faculty and students come together in the same place at the same time, principally communicating with the spoken word and using basic technology such as chalk, blackboard, and textbooks. The faculty member has been viewed as the "sage on the stage," and this mode of instruction gives students credit-for-contact, or *seat time,* whether they are in a lecture, a seminar, a discussion, or a laboratory.[14]

Some uses of new technologies have effected essentially *first-order* changes: efforts to make such traditional teaching and learning activities more efficient or expedient without altering the basic premises.

Technology might alter the media of information exchange without significantly affecting the basic model, including the content.

First-order changes in higher education classes are common. Several technological advancements have provided faculty with a wider range of ways to present and to represent information, including slides, filmstrips, motion pictures, and overhead projectors. Several other technological advancements have enabled faculty to capitalize on economies of scale in the classroom—the introduction of the microphone, computerized scanners for scoring tests, and copying machines to duplicate course materials. Communication outside of class hours and across distances has been strengthened through the postal service and the telephone. E-mail exchanges can dramatically increase the frequency and alter the nature of student/faculty interaction into "anytime, anywhere" contact. Numerous reports by faculty indicate that students who have not been inclined to speak in face-to-face class discussions use e-mail to communicate.[15]

Some other uses of technology extend traditional teaching and learning processes, exponentially expanding their scope without altering the underlying educational model. For example, whereas in the past students have used data sets available to them on their own campuses, computers provide access to databases around the world. This has also changed the nature of research—expanding access to new forms of information as well as the range of areas for investigation. For the most part, such technological adaptations are simply "bolted" onto old instructional methods.[16]

Computers are a prime example of technology's creating first-order change where the basic activities of education remain the same. Computerized equipment allows students to be more precise in their work, and word-processing applications make revising drafts of a paper more convenient, just as pocket calculators made mathematical computations easier. Computers have also been widely adopted, although campus approaches to implementation vary. Some colleges and universities require all students to purchase a computer, whereas others supply equipment for the campus community to share. Although estimates of computer ownership and usage differ, it is now common for students to own personal computers with CD-ROM and DVD drives, multimedia software, and Internet access.[17] Although computers offer students the possibility of doing desktop publishing, computer-aided design, and high-level modeling, some observers have claimed that despite this tremendous power, computers are often used primarily for the most pedestrian functions—word processing and e-mail. Computers also permit a first-order change on a previous second-order revolution. Just as the postal service made correspondence courses available, distance learning via the computer renders the extension of this enterprise more efficient and far-reaching—first-class mail sent through the postal service is now referred to as *snail mail*. All of this, of course, does not alter the traditional teaching and learning paradigm; technology has been used essentially to overcome some limitations of large lecture classes as well as to enhance classroom interaction and communication outside of class.

The introduction of technology can potentially bring about transformations on another level—*second-order* change. Requiring more money and redesigning courses to incorporate specific technological applications, this level of change potentially alters core educational processes and even the nature of teaching and learning. As technology deeply alters how knowledge is obtained, classified, used, and represented, such changes may reshape both the content and the delivery of education, shifting some of the most basic assumptions about educational processes.

With respect to content, technology can enable teachers to shift the focus and orientation of their courses. By relinquishing the drudgery of technical work to computer models and simulations, faculty no longer need to devote large proportions of class time to routine work—for example, calculating analysis of variance (ANOVA) by hand—and can instead consider additional principles or higher-order concepts. Technology can change the nature of the "laboratory," a pedagogical device viewed as exclusive to the natural sciences. Increasingly, faculty in the social sciences are using laboratories for students to gain hands-on experience with course material in much the same way as they have in biology, chemistry, physics, or astronomy. For example, a professor teaching a course in social stratification might ask students to manipulate census data to gain more direct experience with statistical patterns of discrimination, rather than having them just reading about the topic in a text. Students can then come to their own conclusions about social patterns based on their laboratory work. In this way, technology facilitates a shift from passive to more active learning. This is a profound transformation, from a classroom as faculty centered to a process that is student centered, and from giving academic credit for time spent on subject matter coverage to crediting students for their learning outcomes and demonstrated competence.

Faculty across the disciplines may potentially incorporate such technologies as they gain access to resources that encourage or entail redesigning courses and teaching activities. Faculty can consider how to enhance the display of information in the classroom. In the art history class, they can zoom in on details of paintings; in the literary criticism class, they can show a scene from a play. Computers are no longer seen solely as "number crunchers" but are conceived of more broadly as "symbol crunchers," with the ability to manipulate numbers, words, concepts, and images, as well as to extend communication and ultimately enrich teaching and learning relationships. The technology of the Internet and new breakthroughs in software that can evaluate open-ended responses have also made possible new means of large-scale educational assessment, such as direct assessments of student learning and measures of demonstrated ability.[18]

For every benefit technology introduces, it seems to usher in a new liability. Making library holdings available via the Internet has allowed students greater access to these materials but has also led to their overreliance on such resources (compared with books or older texts not in electronic form). It is common for students to write research papers without setting foot in a library. Students must now also be trained to differentiate between more and less reliable sources of information on the Internet because Internet sources carry no tradition of consistent and accurate documentation. The technology has additionally created new opportunities for digital plagiarism because academic papers can be so easily located and downloaded. A recent survey found that 38 percent of undergraduate students reported that they had engaged in some form of "cut-and-paste" Internet plagiarism; moreover, nearly half these students said that they did not consider this to be cheating.[19] Technology also provides a means to counter such academic dishonesty: a new mini-industry of Web sites such as Turnitin.com have emerged that compare a student's submitted work to a database of related written material and published works to determine whether a research paper has similar content; 20 percent of surveyed faculty members reported using such technology to detect plagiarism

These are just a few examples of how some of the basic building blocks of teaching and learning have been transformed. New technology alters the roles of the *participants;* students become active rather than passive learners, and faculty become "guides on the side" rather than "sages on the stage." Other actors, such as software developers, become increasingly important. Technology alters the *time* dimension: students use educational software packages at their own pace and at their convenience rather than be subjected to regimented classroom schedules. And technologies change the nature of the *content* which exacerbates the trend toward discrete knowledge units, as all-important artifacts such as syllabi, lectures, course readings, and class notes are located online. Such changes put more responsibility on students to integrate knowledge bundles, and faculty assume a primary role of assisting them through this process.

The Social Organization of Teaching and Learning

Finally, technology has affected the social organization of teaching and learning through expanding the delivery of higher education. Technology opens up the possibility to rethink the fundamentals of the higher education setting: the dimensions of roles, time, place, and organizational participants.

First, technology can alter the nature of participants' roles. As discussed, the shift in higher education may be toward a more learner-centered mode; as students turn to more individualized learning, teachers are called on to guide students through the information resources rather than to distribute content. Faculty help students learn *how to learn:* for example, faculty may now help students decide which computerized module will best suit their educational needs or how to take greatest advantage of the package. It also changes the participants, offering access to people heretofore unable to participate, including both those without the resources to attend, as well as "adult learners" for whom distance learning is more convenient. In addition, the information networks permit contact and interchanges across all conventional bounds of geography, for example, a student can use e-mail to consult with people and resources anywhere in the world.

Second, technology can alter the temporality of education. Simulations and computer modules can accommodate individual needs through self-pacing. A vivid illustration is the simulation of dissecting a virtual cadaver; unlike plunging into a real one with scalpel and rib spreaders, a student can begin anew and practice until the skills are perfected. Such practices enable the professor to monitor student progress like a coach, even within a computerized lecture hall.

Third, technology may alter the geography of education. Transcending time and place, developments in distance education, or distance learning, provide alternatives to traditional face-to-face education. Technology permits students in traditional educational settings to shift where they engage in the learning process, such as watching a "live" simulcast from a satellite classroom, listening to a presentation in the lecture hall, or watching a videotape in their residence hall room. Distance education allows students to participate in educational programs without setting foot on campus. One U.S. Department of Education report indicates that more than 3 million students pursue online degrees; those who do "college-by-computer" may never set foot on campus.[20] Nearly 10 percent of all U.S. college students fulfill at least part of their degree requirements online, and more than half of all colleges and universities offer online courses. Communication can be enhanced through e-mail, Listservs, and online discussions — blurring the boundary between in and out of class. Perhaps a more profound shift is to incorporate into a "live" class as regular students, individuals who are "place bound" at geographically remote sites. Downlink locations may be set up at other campuses, companies, community learning centers, or even high schools. Given the cycles of resource constraint in higher education — especially for public colleges and universities — virtual higher education can facilitate shared educational resources when comprehensive field coverage is deemed too costly. For example, if the University of California, Berkeley, has an expert in ancient Greek, a course can be "exported" to students on other University of California campuses. Similarly, Berkeley can be a receiving site for the courses in history or linguistics specialization at University of California, Los Angeles, if the local faculty does not include such specialists. Virtual higher education networks can facilitate cooperation within a state. North Dakota and Maine have each developed extensive interactive video networks that extend across public campuses and even to more remote sites. Such virtual higher education commonly uses a range of communications technologies — including telephone, television by satellite, videotapes, modems, and fiber-optic networks.

Fourth, dramatic shifts in the organizational landscape have resulted from this fundamental upheaval in the taken-for-granted assumptions of higher education. Most notably, computer and software companies and technical training institutes have each come to play a prominent role in education. They challenge the market share of traditional colleges and universities, recasting themselves as providers of teaching resources as well as undergraduate and graduate degrees in high-demand professional fields such as business and computer science. The University of Phoenix has achieved iconic status as a for-profit provider. While it refers to itself as "the nation's leading online university" and prides itself on a student-centered philosophy, the University of Phoenix is considered a "for-profit behemoth" by many higher education institutions.[21] It was founded in 1976 to provide educational programs for working adults. From its founding through 2000, the university has granted more than seventy thousand degrees and certificates, over half of which are bachelor's degrees.[22] The university reports that approximately 65 percent of its students obtain a degree. Approximately 70 percent of its students are enrolled in undergraduate programs, and 25 percent are enrolled in graduate programs, with twenty-five degree programs in sixteen fields. Its most popular programs are the bachelor of science degrees in management and in information technology and a general master of business administration. University of Phoenix operates out of more than one hundred sites across twenty U.S. states, Canada, and Puerto Rico, with applications in five additional states pending. The continued expansion of what is now referred to as the country's largest private university seems both rapid and limitless. By 2003, it enrolled one hundred twenty-five thousand students, of which 40 percent took online courses from more than three hundred Internet service providers. As of June 2004, the university reported a total enrollment exceeding two hundred thirteen thousand students and attributed much of this growth to its online courses. In addition to becoming more aggressive in marketing, the university intends to begin admitting students as young as eighteen.

In spite of lingering skepticism among educators that for-profit companies are no more than diploma mills, for-profits have gained legitimacy with both accreditors and employers and have become popular among the growing adult student populations seeking courses that are both convenient and of good quality.[23] Expanding options for working adults are driven by adults' and employers' aspirations. Adults who work full time want intellectual enrichment. Since the late 1980s, one company—which advertises that just because "you are not in school anymore doesn't mean you want your mind to turn to mush"—has annually enrolled five thousand students in its cable channel classes.[24] From the perspective of the employers, workers need to update their knowledge and skills to adapt to rapid technological changes in the workplace. In addition to competition, the advent of computer interactive digital technology also opens up possibilities for collaboration between people on traditional campuses and in forprofit settings. Some envision multisite learning communities replacing the classroom, the faculty, and the campus. Communications technology can allow for either synchronous or asynchronous communication, enhanced by applications such as CourseWork, Blackboard, and Whiteboard. Synchronous communication, for example, could be an online discussion about the development of a new engineering design that simulates "live" interaction. In an asynchronous communication, the participants may review work completed to date or enter modifications on a developing project.

Another visible change in higher education's organizational landscape is unprecedented collaborative ventures. Perhaps the most visible initiative across state lines is the proposal to establish a Western Governors University (WGU). Endorsed by the Western Governors Association in 1995, the cyber-university has two aims: (1) to broaden access to technologically delivered educational programming for "anytime, anywhere access" and (2) to provide certification of competency; that is, learning achieved regardless of source. WGU, which was accredited in 2003, strives to provide a free flow of high-quality educational materials across institutional, state, and other boundaries, yet maintain access at in-state tuition rates. According to the implementation plan, the new entity will broker the distribution of services, foster the development of new educational materials, and help connect "users" with "providers" through student support services. WGU was founded and is supported by nineteen states and governors; they have each agreed to assist with efforts to obtain the financial resources required to develop the virtual catalog and management systems and have promised to remove barriers that would prevent the initiative from functioning effectively. At the state level, such barriers may include, simply stated, "regulation, bureaucracy, tradition, and turf."[25] WGU's first degree and certificate programs were opened in 1998, and the first ten graduates of WGU were awarded degrees in the fall of 2002.

Proponents of WGU touted substantial potential benefits for several constituencies. Students would have greater access; employers would be able to assess skills of new employees and enable present employees to upgrade skills; colleges and universities, in addition to other providers of "educational modules," would have an expanded market; and states could better meet the demands emanating from changing demographics and labor force needs. At the same time, however, several concerns have been voiced about quality, that is, how to ensure standards, and the possible loss of public funds for existing colleges and universities. It is noteworthy that Pete Wilson, California's governor at the time, decided not to participate in the WGU and instead launched a plan for a California Virtual University (CVU). Reflecting confidence in California's established and accredited colleges and universities, the California plan proposed to develop its own virtual university that combined online courses already offered throughout the public system. When CVU opened its Web site in August 1998, it listed more than 1,600 courses from ninety-five accredited California colleges and included more than one hundred certificate and degree programs. In April 1999, however, CVU abruptly ended most of its operations due to lack of funds; the three public segments had balked at providing $1 million per year for three years to cover operating shortfalls.

Financing such virtual ventures, along with other virtual universities, concerns participants and observers alike. On the one hand, tremendous cost savings may be possible because no buildings, faculty, nor printed catalogs are required. Personnel costs are still incurred but are limited because only a few faculty need to be hired.

Many questions remain. Who will underwrite the cost of the technology? Many hardware, software, and teaching video companies are jockeying for position, in hopes of securing big profits. How will learning outcomes be assessed? Critics point to the inappropriateness of competency-based assessment, noting that higher education provides an all-important credentialing function rather than knowledge acquisition or skill building. From this perspective, a college degree may also demonstrate the ability and willingness to persevere in pursuit of a long-term goal rather than subject-matter competency. A focus on learning outcomes and competency-based testing is criticized by still others for missing crucial socialization functions. Even at its best, critics argue, virtual higher education would provide a suboptimal educational experience—the antithesis of Goffman's conception of "total institution," where socialization is most readily achieved in the bounded, residential nature of classical colleges. Of course, with increasing part-time enrollments and the expanding reach of community college courses, that classical model may end up serving a smaller and smaller proportion of the postsecondary student population, raising challenges for finding socialization alternatives such as in community-based organizations.

To summarize, technology has affected or is likely to affect many dimensions of higher education, including the nature of knowledge, the nature of teaching and learning, and the organization of teaching and learning. The phenomenon of virtual higher education incorporates issues from all three arenas and raises many difficult questions. In the previous two sections of this chapter, we have discussed the effect of technology on education in the past, at present, and potentially in the future. We have noted how some technologies have brought about revolutionary change, while others have had little if any impact. As noted at the outset, we view such variability in effect as the result neither of chance, nor of a Darwinian survival of the fittest. Because change is directly affected by social, political, and economic factors, it is essential to consider the wider policy pressures and emerging opportunities that accompany the discourse about technology. Not only is technology carried forward by individuals who negotiate the policy pressures but also by those who, at times, resist the extent to which technology takes hold in higher education.

Educational Policy Pressures and Sources of Legitimacy

Scholars have argued that ambiguity about the overall functions of higher education, which is characterized by multiple goals and unclear core technology, according to organizational theorists, makes the enterprise susceptible to policy pressures as well as institutional imperatives for legitimacy. That is, colleges and universities justify their activities—and are thereby seen as "modern," legitimate, and integral to society—by appealing to culturally approved assumptions. Improvements to higher education activities are therefore often presented as appropriate responses to distinct policy pressures. Given pervasive demands to gain efficiency, increase access, and improve quality, it is not surprising that campuses are anxiously considering technological breakthroughs and their potential applications to help fulfill these criteria. The cumulative pressure on colleges and universities to "do more with less" is a powerful catalyst for their explicit reconsideration of delivery systems, curricula, organizational structures, and the mix of technology and personnel.[26] Many hope that technology will be the key to more affordable, accessible, and effective teaching and learning.

Improvements tend to be constructed through one of three legitimizing frames: efficiency, access, or quality, each of which is cast as advancing societal aims. Notions of *efficiency* invoke the metaphors of neoclassical economics, which aim to optimize delivery of education to individuals, and to maximize individuals' subsequent contributions to society. *Access* is constructed as emancipation and social justice, wherein educational opportunities are extended to those who, for numerous reasons, have been excluded from the system of higher education. *Quality* includes shades of the previous two but with a range of supporting rationales. Each is considered below.

Technology is often framed as a means for efficiency. Higher education has traditionally been a labor-intensive industry. Strategies for cutting costs in higher education focus on personnel, which has historically accounted for approximately 80 percent of campus expenditures. Common sense indicates that fixed costs can be reduced by substitutions for more expensive labor and that economies of scale may be achieved by having instructors handle larger enrollments in their classes. From this perspective, the potential for educational technology to reduce costs by replacing faculty becomes an even more attractive policy option, especially given anticipated higher increases in enrollment in many states over the next two decades. However, while changing the mix of technology and personnel may result in long-run cost savings, the effects on educational quality are unknown. Moreover, developing and delivering technology incur considerable costs, not only to invest in hardware, software, and networking infrastructures but also to hire new personnel to maintain and support usage, as well as to retrain and upgrade the skills of existing personnel. It is worth noting that even proponents of such investments acknowledge that substituting technology for labor is unlikely to reduce costs.[27] In addition, given the outstanding social and economic returns that accrue to the overall society on the higher education investment, it is worrisome to think that the burden of capitalizing technology may be shifting to the consumer—the student.

A second way to consider how technology is constructed is to focus on the pressures for higher education to expand access to students in geographically distant areas and to students who might not otherwise have opportunities to engage in higher education. The United States has moved from elite to mass higher education; but now there is pressure to provide universal higher education. This means that colleges and universities are increasingly called on to provide educational opportunities to those who have been excluded from the system by virtue of demographic and geographic factors. Moreover, with the social value placed on "lifelong learning," increasing numbers of "adult learners" seek access to higher education as learning opportunities that overcome the boundaries of time and place become available. The question becomes, Access to what? If the answer is access to academic programs at one of the 3,600 accredited colleges and universities, then a set of logistical challenges can be identified and resolved. If, however, the answer is access to a wider range of learning opportunities in virtual classrooms and virtual universities offered by a wider range of providers, the challenges for quality assurance are enormous.

Third, the application of technology has been framed as a way to improve the quality of teaching and learning. Technology has enhanced and expanded research aspects of higher education; information technology and communications technology enhance student/faculty relationships, as well as student/student and faculty/student interactions. The aim is also to provide more tailored educational services to a more diverse student population, which is increasingly characterized by a wider range of cognitive learning styles and varying degrees of academic preparation. Such outcomes are not assured. In fact, several skeptics are concerned that technological applications may have effects opposite to those intended and may undermine the quality of teaching and learning. It is possible that e-mail will replace office hours, videos will replace active participation in class, and students at remote sites will miss out on some crucial aspects of the "hands-on, in-class" experiences. Also of concern are the viability of conducting an educational operation without faculty, the ultimate value of a credential from such an experience, the validity and utility of competency-based credentials, and whether such students will be — or will be perceived to be—less competitive in the job market and perhaps less well socialized as citizens and leaders than their counterparts who graduated from traditional colleges and universities.

Although issues of efficiency, access, and quality are often addressed separately in policy arenas, they are interdependent considerations in what constitutes legitimate higher education. For example, the argument that technology makes "continuing education" and "lifelong learning" available relies on both the rationale of efficiency —producing a workhorse that can be retrained to contend with the changing requirements of the workplace—and of access—ensuring that adult learners can participate in the system where direct contact with teachers is replaced by machines, content no longer flows directly from teacher to student, and students are increasingly learning on their own, at their own pace, and in their own space. A range of legitimizing frames can thus be used to justify this emphasis on "lifelong" and "continuing" learning for the higher education enterprise. Some may claim that this purpose increases access, while others may claim that the underlying goal of such an intention is to increase efficiency; however, its legitimacy is framed as increasing access. Lyotard cautions that we should be mindful and critical of such rhetorical games, knowing which Trojan horse belongs to which political agenda.[28]

Policy pressures for efficiency, access, and quality are longstanding and complex. However, despite some proponents' and hopeful observers' claims that the current wave of technological advancements is a magic wand to resolve these policy issues, we contend that history has shown that vigilance is advisable. The degree to which a technological change is embraced in part depends on how it is constructed and the social legitimacy it can marshal. While information technology and new networking capabilities may enhance communications environments, learning infrastructures, and information infrastructures, this new landscape of opportunities must not be embraced without caution. Adopting such technological advances is not automatic and may have unforeseen consequences.

Resistance and Uneven Impact

As technological advancements are accompanied by underlying pressures and opportunities for higher education transformation, their impact will nonetheless depend on institutional willingness, financial resources, professional interests, individual actors, and their specific locations.

Historically, higher education has been slow to adopt changes. The university emerged during medieval times, it has not changed dramatically since then; in many ways, it reflects the past. The scientific revolution took place for the most part outside of academe, and many academics shunned the industrial revolution.[29] The university's tremendous inertia is the result of a longstanding, well-established system.

Despite the tremendous public attention given to technology, to date, the majority of academic professionals across the country have not dramatically transformed their teaching methods or redesigned their courses.[30] To do so is time consuming, as is developing innovations in courseware. Such activities have not yet been significantly rewarded in promotion and tenure review the way scholarly publications have been. Perhaps disincentives within the current academic reward structure are one factor accounting for the notable absence of a burgeoning educational technology industry for higher education, in contrast to the K–12 level. It is important to note, also, that even willing faculty members may be unprepared to take on such projects. On some campuses, new positions for information resource specialists and academic technology consultants have been established to work one-on-one with faculty who want to learn. In recent years, we have seen increased interest among instructors to develop Web pages, to develop and present online course materials, to distribute and evaluate assignments, and to manage schedules and grades through institutionally sanctioned course management and "learning content management" systems. As the market for "e-learning" expands, instructional innovations may proliferate, albeit within powerful structural constraints of the academic reward structure and organizational inertia.[31]

Advancements in instructional technology are not likely to spread uniformly across the many types of higher education institutions in the United States. Differences in mission and financial resources between public systems and private campuses—as well as among community colleges, liberal arts, and research universities—may shape the decision making about alternative investments.[32] A liberal arts college, for instance, may find it preferable to link all classrooms to the Internet but cannot afford to build huge computer labs, while a community college trying to sustain expanded access may decide that it must find a way to do both. In fact, in the past several decades, community colleges have positioned themselves as one of the most visible, frequent, and enthusiastic users of several mechanisms for learning from off campus—transforming their capacity for correspondence courses and broadcasting TV courses to employing state-of-the-art video and digital communications.

All higher education institutions face the clear reality that what is now considered cutting-edge equipment and skills have a relatively short life cycle, becoming obsolete at an increasingly fast pace. While the problem of obsolescence is not unique to higher education's workplaces and educational settings, what is arguably new is the enormous cost and risk involved in making technological investments—and in failing to do so. Even Harvard did not immediately adopt computer technology early on; according to one observer, "They have the financial resources to let everyone else make the mistakes and then buy their way to the forefront when the dust has settled."[33]

It is interesting to note that much of the opposition to technological applications in education has been waged against widely touted "efficiency" imperatives by the many critics concerned about the "quality" of education delivered by new media. Statewide interactive video networks illuminate this tension. Whether such networks should simply export programs to those whose geography precludes access or whether the networks themselves should become degree-granting electronic campuses, has emerged as a topic of great controversy. University of Maine's chancellor resigned after faculty protests and a vote of "no confidence" from all seven Maine campuses. Among the most vocal critics of the Educational Network of Maine, reports stated, faculty feared distance education would "empty their classrooms and rob them of their livelihoods."[34] Yet the most evident concerns focused on matters of quality overriding potential gains in efficiency and access: effective teaching and learning delivered over such networks require different pedagogical skills than those traditionally used in face-to-face classroom interaction. Thus, while the use of technology may indeed make more information available by addressing access and efficiency, the question remains whether such "advancements" are desirable for higher education's educational quality.

Conclusion

In this chapter, we identified a number of technological applications for higher education in addition to some foreseeable opportunities and challenges. With the potential to enrich traditional classroom settings and to extend the boundaries for teaching and learning in higher education, the possible applications prompt us to rethink some fundamental beliefs about the nature of colleges and universities as places, communities, storehouses of knowledge, and sites of learning. They also prompt us to consider the respective roles of teachers and learners and the optimal conditions for learning. Unlikely to solve higher education's problems of costs or quality, technological advances do have the potential to expand access and to adapt learning venues to different cognitive styles and levels of preparation. As they do, aspects of academic organizations may be seen in a new light. For example, the library service model shifts from providing walk-in access to stored collections, to off-site accessing of information and collections that have been saved digitally for retrieval. At Stanford in 2003, a robotic page-turning and scanning device enables mass digitization of bound print materials and vast collections of unbound materials. Supported by a comprehensive hardware and software system, the imaging device allows for the manual creation and automated capture of metadata, simultaneously achieving previously unimagined capabilities for preservation and access. Such applications also reconceptualize academic knowledge, courses, and programs, which were once presumed to be the sole province of higher education, can be offered by a multitude of service providers. This will require existing colleges and universities to rethink delivery systems and devise strategies to protect and to extend their selected market niches. Thus, the implications for rethinking the "what," "where," "how," "who," and "when" of higher education are limitless.

How will the current wave of information and communication technologies affect the future of higher education? Will technological advances allow universities to provide a higher quality education to more people? Or will advances result in a net decrease in educational quality and accentuate the divide between the educational haves and have-nots? Will they make possible cost savings and productivity increases that will rescue colleges and universities from steadily tightening budgets? Or will they place additional pressure on those budgets as colleges and universities are forced to keep up technologically, without any compensatory reduction in costs or growth in revenues? Will the advances, as some have claimed, spell the eventual demise of higher education as we know it?[35]

The only prediction that can be made with real confidence is that technology will have an effect on higher education and that the impact will be far reaching. In this arena, to pretend to predict the future is simple hubris. The role that any specific technology will play in higher education cannot be forecast with any accuracy. Consider the very different histories of two recent technologies: multimedia software and the World Wide Web. Both of these developments simply allow us to bring a range of existing base technologies together into easily useable packages. However, multimedia software, an industry darling, has been consistently overpromoted and has just as consistently underperformed. In contrast, the World Wide Web, which exploded from a European physics lab and a Midwestern supercomputing center, came from out of nowhere, in the opinion of the commercial computer industry, but has changed much of the world. These examples illustrate an important point: in the arena of technology, the event horizon, beyond which accurate predictions cannot be made, is roughly six months. This is partly due to the unpredictability of technological development, but mostly due to the complex social, behavioral, and economic contexts into which new technologies are embedded. Predicting which entertainment technologies will work and which will not, which will appeal and which will not, which will sell and which will not is extremely difficult. Predicting the future of educational technology—embedded, as it is, in a far more complex and poorly understood endeavor—is next to impossible.

When considering how technology will affect higher education, we must also keep in mind that there is no single answer. Since differentiation has long been the hallmark of higher education in the United States, technological investments and applications are likely to show great variation across campuses, with dramatically different opportunities available across different populations of students and faculty. Although we advocate proceeding with caution, we also believe that it is not useful to react defensively. The massive technological changes of the new era cannot be resisted; if they are going to happen, they will happen in spite of defenses. A prudent course may be for higher education to position itself in order to survive. Others may decide that a prudent course of action is to be in front, determined to embrace and, where possible, shape the impact. In either case, technological advancements need to be seen as the means to several potential ends, not as the ends themselves. This distinction can determine whether a technological investment results in success or failure.

Finally, as we have discussed, change in the processes and products of higher education results from a complex interplay of wider societal forces. The technology discussed here is in one sense a catalyst that requires another renegotiation of the relationship between higher education and the wider society. It provides a means for society to place new demands on colleges and universities, even as it asks them to redefine their functions and roles. Technology presents opportunities but also intensifies pressure on higher education institutions to adapt. At a minimum, an increasingly technology-savvy public has a straightforward expectation that campuses acquire, maintain, and update their information and telecommunications technologies. The imperative to respond to the public's expectations is all the more acute, given the proliferation of nontraditional providers of teaching and research services that marshal these new technologies in an attempt to provide educational programs without the same "problems" of finance and relevance that face traditional colleges and universities. Yet the pressure to respond is accompanied by a high degree of ambiguity and uncertainty.

This ambiguity resides in whether, and how, colleges and universities should modify their core processes and infrastructure. Teaching and learning processes merit reconsideration in light of new technologies. Beyond that, there are complex questions of financing. As new technology becomes a more entrenched and taken-for-granted pedagogical fixture, is it the university's responsibility to provide the technology for students, or does the responsibility remain with the individual students to purchase the technology for themselves? What sorts of technology should society fairly expect colleges and universities to provide to students?[36] What level of technological services should campuses provide to update and to repair students' equipment, and who should bear the cost? Technology has also forced campuses to ask new questions about ownership, particularly as it relates to faculty, prompting campuses to develop policies on intellectual property. Does the university or do individual faculty own the technology they develop, and how does such proprietary work fit in with the processes of tenure and promotion? In thinking about supporting faculty work, the line is blurred between those activities that are organizational and work related and those that are individual and personal. How colleges and universities adapt their practices and allocate resources to support their students and faculty (particularly when this support does not directly affect teaching, learning, or research) are high-cost and high-stakes decisions.

In this sense, technological change can be seen as emblematic of other social changes facing higher education, in addition to being a yardstick for marking how well higher education is keeping up with changing societal expectations. It prompts reconsideration of core processes, and it adds to the mix of contradictory prescriptions that already challenge today's colleges and universities and the campus actors who are responsible for shepherding the enterprise through turbulent times and for making best-guess financial forecasts. Inasmuch as technology is not a magic wand but merely a set of tools, its ultimate challenge to higher education may involve not only positioning and investing amid various social, political, and economic considerations but also nurturing the imagination for harnessing its power, its as-of-yet unimagined educational potential.

ACKNOWLEDGMENTS

The writing of this chapter was, in part, supported by the Educational Research and Development Center program, agreement number R309A60001, CFDA 84.309A, as administered by the Office of Educational Research and Improvement (OERI), U.S. Department of Education. The findings and opinions expressed herein do not reflect the position or policies of OERI or the Department of Education. The chapter's preparation benefited considerably from Patricia Gumport's conversations with Stanford University Professor John Etchemendy, an innovator and astute observer who provided generous advice and insight into several examples of contemporary technological applications, in addition to articulating the wisdom of adopting a cautious yet open stance. Marc Chun acknowledges and appreciates the helpful comments of Elizabeth McEneaney and Mary Rauner.

NOTES

1. Although *technology* has many different meanings, in this chapter, we are talking more narrowly about the fungible categories of information and communications technology, including devices used to collect, to transmit, and to process information. We begin with the assumption that technological change is a *social process* — not only does technology influence society, but it is also a cultural product subject to larger social structures and social trends.

2. R. Usher and R. Edwards, *Postmodernism and Education* (London: Routledge, 1994).

3. U.S. Department of Education, National Center for Education Statistics, *Integrated Postsecondary Education Data Systems.*

4. The increases are so rapid that this figure is continually being revised.

5. A report by the National Telecommunications and Information Administration indicated that based on the 2000 U.S. census, 54 percent of the population is online.

6. S. Lohr, "When the Alma Mater Ends with '.edu'," *New York Times,* July 7, 1996, sec. 4, p. 2, col. 1.

7. In fact, new technology has changed and expanded the definition of literacy; "media literacy" is now an expectation.

8. R. Snider, "The Machine in the Classroom," *Phi Delta Kappan* 74, no. 4 (December 1992).

9. E. Fiske, "Computers in the Groves of Academe," *New York Times,* May 13, 1984, 40; Snider, "The Machine in the Classroom."

10. Lohr, "When the Alma Mater Ends with '.edu'."

11. For this and other examples, see W. Massy, *Leveraged Learning: Technology's Role in Restructuring Higher Education* (Stanford, CA: Stanford Forum for Higher Education Futures, 1995).

12. Fiske, "Computers in the Groves of Academe"; C. Fischer, " 'Touch Someone': The Telephone Industry Discovers Sociability," *Technology and Culture* 29 (1988): 32–61.

13. J. Lyotard, *The Postmodern Condition: A Report on Knowledge* (Manchester, UK: Manchester University Press, 1984). At the same time, the academic study of the knowledge industry is gaining visibility. While previously the domain of sociologists of knowledge and science, the endowment of a new chair for a "distinguished professor of knowledge" in the business school of the University of California at Berkeley signals broader interest in the phenomena. See J. Sterngold, "Welcome to Berkeley: Professor Knowledge Is Not an Oxymoron," *New York Times,* June 1, 1997, sec. 4, p. 5.

14. The role of faculty as coach or "guide on the side" has become a shorthand for describing the shift away from a belief that the faculty member should be the focus of attention and authority.

15. S. Gilbert, "Making the Most of a Slow Revolution," *Change* 28 (March/April 1996): 12.

16. C. Twigg, "Navigating the Transition," *Educom Review* 29 (November/December 1994).

17. For attempts to gauge usage and ownership, see Gilbert, "Making the Most of a Slow Revolution"; K. Green, "The Coming Ubiquity of Information Technology," *Change* 28 (March/April 1996): 25–31; and K. Green and S. Gilbert, "Great Expectations: Content, Communications, Productivity, and the Role of Information Technology in Higher Education," *Change* (March/April 1995): 8–18.

18. See M. Chun, "Looking Where the Light is Better," *Peer Review* 4 (Winter/Spring 2002): 16–25 and R. Benjamin and M. Chun, "A New Field of Dreams," *Peer Review* 5 (Summer 2003): 26–29.

19. A description of the study by Rutgers University management professor Donald L. McCabe was reported in S. Rimer, "A Campus Fad That's Being Copied: Internet Plagiarism Seems on the Rise," *New York Times,* September 3, 2003, B7.

20. E. D. Tabs, *Distance Education at Degree-Granting Postsecondary Institutions: 2000–2001* (Washington, D.C.: National Center for Educational Statistics, 2003).

21. See the *Chronicle of Higher Education,* February 14, 2003; November 1, 2002; and June 25, 2004.

22. According to the National Science Foundation's WebCASPAR data on degrees and certificates granted by institution, no degrees are listed for the University of Phoenix from 1976 through 1979. From 1980 through 2000, the University of Phoenix granted 71,011 degrees and certificates: 1,841 certificates, 4 doctorates, 0 first professional degrees, 30,131 master's, 38,875 bachelor's, and 160 associate's degrees; and total enrollment (headcount) from 1976–1998 was about 240,000. However in 2003, the University of Phoenix Web site states: "Since, 1976, more than 171,600 working professionals have earned their degree from University of Phoenix." The basis for the discrepancy is not clear, including whether an additional 100,000 degrees could have been granted from 2001 to 2003, the recent period for which data are not yet reported. Other discrepancies exist between the numbers reported by the university on the Web site and those reported in the *Chronicle of Higher Education.* For example, the former states that it has more than 17,100 instructors, while the latter reports 7,000. The two sources coincide in their characterizations of the curriculum as centrally designed by expert developers rather than by the instructors, many of whom are part time.

23. See P. Gumport and S. Snydman, "Higher Education: Evolving Forms, Emerging Markets," in *The Non-Profit Sector: A Research Handbook,* 2nd ed., ed. Walter W. Powell and Richard Steinberg (Hartford, CT: Yale University Press, forthcoming).

24. See R. Cushman's excellent article, "From a Distance: Who Needs a Campus When You Have a Downlink," *Lingua Franca* 6, no. 7 (November, 1996): 53–63, in reference to the Mind Extension University.

25. Reference by M. Leavitt, governor of Utah, "Western Governors University: A Learning Enterprise for the CyberCentury" in "Technology and the Academy," special issue, *Journal of Higher Education Outreach and Engagement* 2, no. 2 (Summer 1997).

26. For a discussion of changing environmental demands and emerging restructuring initiatives, see P. Gumport and B. Pusser, "Restructuring the Academic Environment," in *Planning and Management for a Changing Environment,* ed. M. Peterson, D. Dill, L. Mets, and Associates (San Francisco: Jossey-Bass, 1997), 453–78. For analysis of resource allocation trade offs, see Massy, *Leveraged Learning,* and W. Massy, "Life on the Wired Campus," in

The Learning Revolution, ed. D. Oblinger and S. Rush (Bolton, MA: Anker, 1997).

27. W. Massy and R. Zemsky, *Using Information Technology to Enhance Academic Productivity* (Washington, D.C.: EDUCOM, 1995).

28. R. Usher and R. Edwards, *Postmodernism and Education* (London: Routledge, 1994).

29. Snider, "The Machine in the Classroom."

30. See Green, "The Coming Ubiquity of Information Technology," for reports on the pattern of diffusion, specifically the slow adoption by the majority of the faculty.

31. Researchers are just beginning to examine what has been happening with e-learning and why. See, for example, R. Zemsky and W. Massy, *Thwarted Innovation: What Happened to eLearning and Why* (Philadelphia: Learning Alliance, University of Pennsylvania).

32. For attempts to characterize differences in technological applications by institutional type, see Green, "The Coming Ubiquity of Information Technology," as well as R. Heterick, Jr., ed., "Reengineering Teaching and Learning in Higher Education: Sheltered Groves, Camelot, Windmills, and Malls," CAUSE Professional Paper Series 10 (Boulder, CO: CAUSE, 1993).

33. Fiske, "Computers in the Groves of Academe."

34. Cushman, "From a Distance," 56.

35. For a thoughtful perspective on some of these questions, see G. Casper, "Come the Millennium, Where the University?" (paper presented at the annual meeting of the American Educational Research Association, San Francisco, April 18, 1995).

36. In large part as a response to student demand and expectation, Pennsylvania State University agreed to cover the costs for students to download music from online music service Napster. See Amy Harmon, "Penn State Will Pay to Allow Students to Download Music," *New York Times,* November 7, 2003, A1. In such precedent-setting moves, universities are supporting technology that has, at best, remote bearing on teaching and learning.

Chapter Fifteen

Graduate Education and Research

Interdependence and Strain

Patricia J. Gumport

Signs of strain are evident in American graduate education and are reflected in the national media. Student loan debt climbs to record highs, more than doubling during the 1990s. Graduate students from across the United States converge on Washington to ask Congress to overturn a 1986 policy that taxes their assistantship stipends. Graduate students orchestrate a "showdown" at the Modern Language Association national conference, seeking proportional representation in the association's governance and urging the association to advocate more forcefully for the humanities and against institutional hiring practices that replace full-time positions with part-timers and adjuncts. Pushing for recognition that teaching and research assistants are employees, more than forty thousand graduate students at more than thirty-three universities are involved in organizing drives or already have formal collective bargaining representation. A bleak national report documents dissatisfaction with doctoral programs and a dismal job market that lures the "best and brightest" students to abandon academic ambitions and explore industry alternatives.[1]

How are these events to be interpreted? Although some may be inclined to dismiss these news items as selective or dramatic representations of anomalies, the coverage has spotlighted signs of strain within the structural and normative foundations of graduate education. Several axes of tension are evident: shortsighted mechanisms for financing graduate education, inconsistent expectations for research and teaching assistantships, differential consequences of organizational restructuring across fields of study, activism linked to social movements and labor, and projections for an unfavorable academic labor market. Viewed historically, these tremors provide a general illustration of how changes in higher education's wider social, political, and economic contexts reshape the content and operation of graduate programs. Indeed, the intersection of graduate education and research is a key institutional arena where powerful forces converge—financial aid policies, exigencies of sponsored research, or economic cycles—to name a few evidenced in the aforementioned examples.

Stakeholders in the conduct of graduate education must take seriously these signs of strain and the contextual influences that exacerbate them. As a step in that direction, this chapter examines the forces reshaping graduate education in American research universities. Specifically, I focus on the intersection between doctoral education, academic research, and the federal government. The interdependence of these activities has strong historical roots in the expansion of research universities and the increased specialization of faculty across the disciplines. Although the past century reflects much continuity—especially in the structural foundations of graduate education programs—changes in political and economic contexts during the last three decades of the twentieth century also altered the operation of graduate programs, both directly, in research training practices, and indirectly, through changes in academic research.[2] As universities transformed into modern research complexes,[3] the organizational character and rhythm of academic work changed to accommodate the increased centrality of sponsored research. Research training of graduate students became reoriented to the needs of external sponsors and obtaining further funding.[4] Prioritizing the research function and its attendant imperatives over the ideals for graduate education directly challenged the presumption that faculty were engaged in the disinterested pursuit of knowledge. It also challenged the organizing principle that academic authority resides in decentralized, departmentally based graduate programs where faculty determine programmatic requirements based on intellectual grounds.

This transformation exacerbated internal tensions on campus between diverse actors protecting their various interests. University officials, faculty, and even graduate students each sought greater control in the conduct of academic affairs. Yet each became well aware of their interdependence with one another: universities rely on faculty success at obtaining grants and producing valuable research results, faculty rely on grants to support their research and training of doctoral students, faculty depend on graduate students to work on their research grants, graduate students need faculty mentoring and research training in their chosen professional specializations, students need jobs upon completion of their Ph.D.s to pay back their loans, university reputations are bolstered by successfully competing for talented graduate students and high-profile faculty, and so on. Although more visible in the sciences, these complex interdependencies apply to the social sciences and humanities as well. As a prominent common denominator across these academic fields, the expansion of undergraduate education came to depend on graduate students to serve as teaching assistants. Given these inextricable links, changes in any one area have inevitably affected the entire complex.

Historical Overview

The major transformations occurring in American higher education over the past century have their effects in graduate education as they do in other areas. Among the many external forces, funding from the federal government, substantively and symbolically, represents society's changing expectations for graduate education. In the evolving relationship between universities and the federal government, graduate education expanded to become intertwined in complex organizational arrangements with academic research, research funding, and undergraduate education. This chapter's historical overview traces a paradox of continuity alongside change: expansion in structural foundations on the one hand, amid important qualitative changes in the academic work conducted by faculty and graduate students on the other.

Although graduate education as an educational enterprise in the United States has neither been unified nor standardized, the expansion retained a fundamental structural consistency, especially at the doctoral level. By cross-national standards, this country has the largest, most decentralized, and most highly differentiated set of arrangements for advanced education—spanning more than nine hundred campuses, enrolling about 2 million students in graduate degree programs, and granting more than four hundred fifty thousand master's degrees and nearly forty-five thousand doctorates annually.[5] This tremendous breadth of activity notwithstanding, decentralized organization with faculty authority at the department level has held consistently as a structural model. The basic model for doctoral education has been similarly sustained: a few years of prescribed courses, followed by examinations for advancement to degree candidacy, culminating in a dissertation that reflects original research conducted by the student under the guidance of a faculty committee. The ideal, dating back to Humboldt, has been for students to engage in advanced study along with research training.[6] Arrangements for research training have reflected distinct disciplinary patterns: in the sciences, where research is laboratory-intensive, a graduate student may work under faculty supervision, with the dissertation as a piece of a faculty member's research project, while in the humanities, where research is library-intensive, a student may work independently, with little or no faculty or peer contact unless they initiate it, often for months at a time. These distinct patterns of social relations are, in part, intrinsic to the disciplines and tied to professional norms, the nature of disciplinary inquiry, and the type of research technology,[7] although I will argue they have been sharpened given external demands for academic science.

In contrast with such structural continuities, the historical arc simultaneously reveals profound changes in the nature of graduate study's social and intellectual relations, especially among students and faculty. As Nevitt Sanford assessed with critical concern back in 1976:

> The structure of graduate education seems to have changed hardly at all since the 1930s. . . . What has changed are the purposes for which the structure is used and the spirit with which it is managed. The motives of professors and graduate students are less purely intellectual and more professional. . . . The general climate of today is one of competitiveness among universities, between departments in a given university, and between subgroups and individuals within the same department. Students are regarded less as potential intellectual leaders and more as resources to be used in the struggle for a place in the sun.[8]

To the extent that Sanford's characterization may be considered apt today, the research foundations of graduate education need to be central to an analysis of how this shift came about and what the consequences have been. Specifically, changes in the funding patterns for graduate education and university research can be pinpointed as a critical mediating force in this transformation.

Historically, the financing of graduate education has relied primarily on the sponsorship of university research, and secondarily on a variety of loan programs as well as state-funded and institutionally funded teaching assistantships. Federal support of academic research has been concentrated in the top one hundred research universities, which comprise less than 3 percent of American higher education institutions. These top one hundred universities were awarded 80 percent of federal research and development (R&D) expenditures in 2000, and they produced nearly 50 percent of all doctoral degrees and nearly 25 percent of all master's degrees in that year.[9] Sponsored university research thus clearly has had its greatest effect on this sector of universities and the heavily funded sciences within them, but it also has salience for others throughout the system—if only by denying them funds.

Federal involvement in graduate education and research can be traced back to the late nineteenth century, when the modern research university emerged as a function of adapting campus organizational structures to accommodate graduate programs and scientific research. As these activities expanded in scale, and as faculty and campus administrators sought more external sponsors, the funding base for both activities became a source and a condition for further organizational changes on campuses and throughout the higher education system. Since the federal government has been a principal source of funds, it has played a pivotal role in these and other more subtle changes in graduate education. Three changes have been most apparent: increasing specialization in faculty and administrative positions and procedures; greater stratification together with heightened within-sector competition for fiscal and human resources; and a proliferation of organizational subunits for academic research to reflect the instrumental and increasingly economic agenda of external sponsors. How these changes came about is described below.

Nineteenth-Century Beginnings

Graduate education achieved a stable American presence during the last two decades of the nineteenth century, when awarding the Ph.D.

became a laudable academic goal. The founding of Johns Hopkins University in 1876 is often thought of as marking the establishment of graduate education. Johns Hopkins became known as the "prototype and propagator" of research as a major university function.[10] Coupled with its commitment to scientific research, Johns Hopkins offered merit-based graduate fellowships for full-time study that included state-of-the-art research training.

Both within and immediately surrounding higher education, interest in scientific research had burgeoned since the mid-nineteenth century. With great frequency, scientists and those seeking advanced study traveled to Germany for the requisite exposure. Work in chemistry, even into the 1870s, required a trip to Germany. On the American front, after initial resistance to the German idea of studying science for its own sake—and after conflicts between self-identified pure and applied scientists—scientific research gradually gained more acceptance. It took on a distinctive meaning in the American context: American science would be "a collective enterprise like those in business. Modern science needed labor, capital and management."[11] Proclamations at Johns Hopkins reflected this change in scientific research from "a rare and peculiar opportunity for study and research, eagerly seized by men who had been hungering and thirsting for such a possibility" to an increasingly more prestigious endeavor, proclaimed by Clark University's president as "the very highest vocation of man—research."[12] Science became an increasingly specialized activity that professors could pursue autonomously, yet with the security of support, personal advancement, and even prominence within an academic institution.

Following Johns Hopkins's ideal of linking scientific research and graduate education, other graduate schools emerged in the 1890s within larger universities whose undergraduate missions and size offered a broad and stable base of support in endowment funds and tuition. Some were established at the founding of a new university to offer both undergraduate and graduate instruction, as at Stanford University (1891) and the University of Chicago (1892). Others added the graduate school onto an older established private college, as in the case of Harvard University and Columbia University. Some existing state universities—Wisconsin, Michigan, and Illinois—evolved out of origins as land-grant colleges, established with government funds for agriculture and mechanical arts through the Morrill acts of 1862 and 1890, and for experimental agricultural stations fueled through the

Hatch Act of 1887. By 1900, the number of Ph.D.-granting institutions had grown to fourteen, awarding a total of three hundred doctorates.[13]

In addition to taking on scientific research commitments, Ph.D. programs came to be viewed as attractive for expanding and advancing an institution's competitive position in the growing higher education system. Desiring to confer prestige on their institutions, an increasing number of organizations sought out faculty with research interests and actively sought sponsored research funds to build laboratories that would attract eminent scientists. Since faculty increasingly wanted to pursue basic research and to train selectively chosen graduate students, institutions were compelled to provide them with opportunities for research and advanced training, and hence, graduate programs across disciplines.

Organizing Principles: Departmentalization and Disciplinary Specialization

The widespread adoption of graduate programs within higher education institutions was enhanced by the departmental organization that developed in the last quarter of the nineteenth century. Departments provided a flexible organizational structure for decentralizing and compartmentalizing graduate instruction. While Ph.D. programs were organizationally integrated as a separate level from the liberal education of undergraduate colleges, they were also made part of departments responsible for undergraduate instruction in a discipline— a linking arrangement that has been remarkably stable and uniform over time and across campuses. The drive to conform to this structure was so strong that Johns Hopkins expanded its organizational structure to offer undergraduate as well as graduate programs.

This organizational arrangement allowed for the same faculty to exercise authority over both undergraduate and graduate programs.[14] Course work and research training appropriate to each discipline could be designed and coordinated by each department's faculty. One functional by-product of this arrangement was that graduate programs maintained both faculty and institutional continuity and cohesion: faculty propagated themselves by training their professional successors; and responsibility for their graduate students kept faculty attentive to their departments. Graduate programs kept research and teaching activities interlocked and the institution functionally integrated, at least at the department level, in spite of increased disciplinary specialization.

This interdependence was crucial to the success of graduate study, perhaps most specifically in facilitating the student's transition from course work to the dissertation: among the many hurdles encountered by doctoral students across the disciplines, one that emerged as paramount and has persisted to this day. The research training experience is clearly central to a student's shift from being a consumer to a producer of research, and thus, also an integral component of successful program completion across the departments. Corresponding to established areas of knowledge, departments could design different kinds of research apprenticeships appropriate to specialized training in each of the disciplines.

The specialization of disciplines that departments mirrored represented professors' vocational interests and aspirations. In this historical period, this was especially apparent in the newly established natural and social science departments, whose very existence was justified on the basis of specialized research. Beyond the campus level, as disciplines crystallized into national professional associations, they came to serve as visible external referent groups that would give a semblance of standardization across graduate programs: "disciplines and departments had powerful reciprocal effects upon one another" in reinforcing the authority of departments on campus and the professional judgments of faculty nationally.[15] Thus, the emergence of disciplinary associations further facilitated the growth of Ph.D. programs.

Especially during the 1890s, the size and complexity of the graduate education and research enterprise encouraged coordination and control that were reflected in the emergent bureaucratic administration in universities. Although departments served faculty interests for autonomy in research and instruction, the hierarchies of rank within departments and competition across departments served administrative interests for "productive work" as measured by research activity. One observer notes, "Clearly it had become a necessity, from the administrator's point of view, to foster the prestigeful evidences of original inquiry."[16]

The dual tasks of graduate education and research were institutionalized most easily in organizations that had greater resources, both financial and reputational. Those that succeeded in the competitive drive for advancement became a peer group of leading institutions. The prominence of this tier in the American system was reflected in their founding the Association of American Universities (AAU) in 1900, marking the culmination of nineteenth-century efforts to establish graduate education and research activities. Ostensibly the AAU was founded to ensure uniformity of standards, yet it simultaneously functioned as an exclusive club.[17] The AAU signifies an implicit systemwide division of labor in the United States, where the elite institutions have differentiated themselves at the top of the hierarchy engaged in graduate education and research. Although institutions have competed for faculty, graduate students, and philanthropic support, the persistent concentration of fiscal and status resources in this sector is a distinctive feature of the American system, an institutional version of Merton's Matthew Effect.[18]

Characterized as "a new epoch of institutional empire-building," this period of American higher education reflected university concerns for status in an increasingly stratified system. Such concerns were evident in the dynamics of academic rivalry such as bidding for faculty and emulating highly regarded academic departments. While the American system is not unique in its inclination toward stratification, the institutional drive for competitive advancement within the research university sector has been characterized by one American scholar as "almost an obsession."[19]

Thus, the end of the nineteenth century saw the research university emerge as a new kind of social institution devoted to scientific research as well as to graduate education. The extent of institutional ambition was so pervasive that developing universities imitated one another in departments, programs, and faculties that they sought to develop. Across the country, homogeneity in the proliferation of graduate programs and faculty positions suggests that universities sought to acquire not only intellectual legitimacy but a new kind of economic and political legitimacy as well.

Twentieth-Century Rise of Sponsored Academic Research

The expansion of graduate education in the modern university developed hand in hand with the expanding national system of sponsored research. Initially, external resources for academic science were amassed principally from philanthropic foundations, while industry played a minimal role. After World War II, foundations and industry were eclipsed by a surge in federal government sponsorship.

The earliest sources of research sponsorship were wealthy benefactors and their philanthropic foundations. In the 1870s, philanthropic contributions to higher education averaged $6 million per year—mainly to individual scientists. By 1890, philanthropic support reflected a more widespread and instrumental orientation, directing funds to emerging universities for their potential contributions to industrial growth, employment, and commercial endeavors. Philanthropic funds supported a wide array of institutional activities, especially in the applied sciences—including equipment, overall plant expansion, and new professional schools. In some cases, the support provided large sums of money, like John D. Rockefeller's $35 million endowment to the University of Chicago. On a national scale, Rockefeller and Andrew Carnegie established the two largest foundations supporting research: the Rockefeller Foundation, established in 1913 with $182 million, and the Carnegie Corporation, created in 1911 with $125 million. In the early 1920s these foundations favored donations to separate research institutes, such as the Rockefeller Institute of Medicine and the Carnegie Institute of Washington.[20]

By the 1930s, universities could no longer depend completely on foundations as a stable external sponsor for academic science. Foundations reoriented their giving toward an integral funding base for university research, by allocating project grants and postdoctoral fellowships (for example, the Guggenheim Foundation) especially in medical research, the natural sciences, and to a lesser extent, the social sciences. For example, in 1934 the Rockefeller Foundation's funding constituted 35 percent of foundation giving, 64 percent of that to the social sciences, and 72 percent of gifts to the natural sciences.[21]

Such voluntary contributions provided universities with the resources essential to institutionalizing graduate education and scientific research as two interdependent functions. Universities and their faculties built their own rationales and adapted organizational structures to expand the scope of their research activities, while training the next generation of knowledge producers. Upholding university autonomy and academic freedom became important not only for the institution but also for individual faculty. In claiming expert authority, faculty established some distance from the agendas of campus governing boards and increasingly prominent philanthropists. Thus the professionalization efforts of faculty during this era were, in part, an effort to buffer themselves from an array of powerful external mandates, not merely an outgrowth of the knowledge explosion as is commonly cited.[22]

Private industry entered the academic scene as an unpredictable supplement.[23] As industry R&D expenditures rose in the 1920s, corporations conducted both applied and basic research in their own industrial laboratories, in communications and chemical technologies. Two prestigious research universities—the Massachusetts Institute of Technology and the California Institute of Technology—exemplified successful industrial sponsorship of university research during this era. Overall, however, corporate R&D funds stayed in their industrial laboratories through the 1930s to remain an unpredictable resource for academic science.

By the late 1930s, university research was genuinely flourishing, primarily in the nation's most visible universities. This concentration of research activity was paralleled by a similar concentration of research training activity: in 1937, sixteen universities accounted for half the total expenditures on university research and granted 58 percent of all doctorates.[24] This consolidation of research resources with doctoral-granting activity was a pattern that would persist even after this era of privately financed university research.

Surge of Federal Investment

The national government's sponsorship of research and research training evolved incrementally, rather than through a coordinated policy on science or on graduate education. Beginning with federal and state governments playing a role in land-grant campuses through agricultural research, universities increasingly were seen as a national resource for basic research and training that could assist economic growth, national security, and health care. Over time, including the two world wars, the government became the major sponsor of scientific research and higher education.

Federal involvement in academic science began with organizational efforts to designate advisory boards for scientific research. Acknowledging both the value of modern science and a perceived need to oversee the country's research intentions, the first national organization, the National Academy of Sciences (NAS), was founded in 1863.[25] In

1919, the National Research Council (NRC) was established by the NAS essentially to carry out the earlier congressional mandate. As the principal operating agency of both the NAS and—after 1964—the National Academy of Engineering, the NRC was intended to bridge the federal government, the public, and the community of scientists and engineers. Over time, the NRC has become a principal organizational vehicle for overseeing national research efforts and for monitoring how federal funds are channeled into university research.

The NRC, along with the American Council of Learned Societies (founded in 1919) and the Social Sciences Research Council (founded in 1923) depended on the resources of philanthropic foundations to assume the prominent role in facilitating and promoting university research. As channels for foundation funds, these organizations provided interested sponsors with access to scientists and scholars, as well as administrative assistance in selecting recipients of small research grants and postdoctoral fellowships in the areas of mathematics, physics, and chemistry. By the 1920s, American science was mobilized under "the guidance of the private elites" who "came together for the purpose of furthering science." The memberships of the NRC and the NAS were constituted by "the same group of individuals [who] encountered one another, in slightly different combinations."[26]

The national government's expansion of a large-scale, multiagency funding system to support academic science developed incrementally during and after each world war. In the late 1930s, annual federal expenditures for American science were estimated at $100 million; most of these funds went to applied research in federal bureaus— especially agriculture, meteorology, geology, and conservation. The shift to university-based research occurred when the expertise of academic researchers became valuable for national defense efforts.[27] In World War I, for example, the federal government financed psychologists to construct intelligence tests and encouraged scientists to follow up on diagnostic physical examinations of close to 4 million draftees. For such work, universities granted leaves to full-time life and physical scientists as well as to social scientists and historians. The government also allocated funds for researchers to work on their campuses. By World War II, government support was more extensive: in 1940, federal funds for university research totaled $31 million. During the 1940s, the Office of Naval Research contracted with more than two hundred universities to conduct about 1,200 research projects involving some three thousand scientists and 2,500 graduate students.

Between 1941 and 1945, the United States spent a total of $3 billion on R&D—one-third of which was allocated for university-based research aimed at winning the war and devising "new instruments of destruction and defense."[28]

The expansion of sponsored research in universities was coupled with expanding doctoral training. Between World War I and World War II, the number of institutions awarding doctoral degrees rose from fifty in 1920 to one hundred in 1940; and the number of doctorates awarded increased fivefold from 620 in 1920 to 3,300 in 1940.[29] In addition to such growth, a qualitative shift occurred, enhancing the caliber of doctoral students; whereas, in the 1920s, the majority of graduate students had been "undistinguished," reflecting "uneven preparation, uncertain motivation and unproven ability."[30]

By the end of World War II, the federal government came to view research universities as a precious public resource for research and research training, worthy of the government's investment and partnership—even during peacetime. The establishment of the National Science Foundation (NSF) reflected an overt federal agenda that science would indeed offer "an endless frontier," and that universities could be ideal settings for such research, as Vannevar Bush states in his 1945 report to President Roosevelt. In the 1950s, the federal research budget grew steadily and the academic research enterprise expanded in the top tier of institutions. In 1953–54, the top twenty spent 66 percent of federally sponsored research funds for academic science and awarded 52 percent of the doctorates—the bulk of them in the life sciences, physical sciences, and engineering, the same fields that received most of the federal research funds.[31]

Postwar Expansion of Funds for University Research and Doctoral Education

Spurred by the launching of Sputnik in 1957, the government provided even more funds for basic research. Federal sponsorship of research increased every year from 1958 to 1968. In that decade alone, annual federal contributions to academic research increased fivefold. As the federal investment increased, so did universities' share of total basic research, from one-third to one-half during that decade.[32] Thus, the post–World War II period clearly established research as a separate function and operation, largely paid for by the federal government, which supported universities at performing a large share of the nation's research effort.

While higher education was perceived as having an increasingly legitimate research role, enrollments rose from 3 million to 7 million students overall, and enrollments doubled within doctorate-granting universities—up from 1.24 million to 2.5 million for undergraduate and graduate levels combined. Annual Ph.D. production in science and engineering grew from 5,800 in 1958 to 14,300 in 1968.[33]

The allocation of federal research funds followed two basic imperatives that have been consistent from the outset: multiagency support, and competition among individual proposals. Federal sponsorship entailed a clear presidential directive—Executive Order 10521, in 1954—for multiagency support such that no single agency within the government was to be given sole responsibility to distribute research funds. Rather, each agency should sponsor research related to its mission, such as health, defense, and energy. In 1959, 96 percent of federal sponsorship came from five agencies: the Department of Defense; the Department of Health Education and Welfare—largely the National Institutes of Health (NIH); the Atomic Energy Commission; the National Science Foundation; and the Department of Agriculture. In the same year, more than 96 percent of the $1.4 billion allocated for research was diverted to the life sciences, physical sciences, and engineering, leaving the social sciences and particularly the humanities neglected.[34]

Lacking a unified policy with specific purposes, funding arrangements were coordinated through a mechanism of peer review by researchers in the scientific community beyond the federal government. This competitive system was the primary way the federal government sought to insure that the best research would be performed. For the most part, the federal agencies' priority was to nurture excellence; although some effort was made to disperse resources across geographic locations and to smaller institutions. The resulting pattern of funding university research has reinforced the leading tier of research universities and the science fields—with life sciences and physical sciences accounting for over half of the basic research budget.

Similar to expanding basic research funding, federal support for doctoral education intensified, mostly to train science and engineering personnel. Aside from short-term interests to advance science and technology, the federal government was mindful of improving its research capacity and developing a longer-term pipeline of trained scientists and engineers. A variety of mechanisms attracted and retained talented students in the pipeline: direct student aid, as fellowships; student aid channeled through institutions—traineeships; and project grants to individual faculty that included salaries for graduate student research assistants. The precedent for this explicit twofold agenda was set in the National Cancer Act of 1937, which set up grants-in-aid to nongovernment scientists and direct student aid in the form of fellowships. By the 1950s, the NSF offered more than five hundred prestigious portable fellowships to students.

The National Defense Education Act of 1958 conveyed a commitment to rebuild the nation's research capability through "manpower training"; specifically, to support science education through a host of fellowship and traineeship programs to be launched by a variety of federal agencies—NIH, NSF, and NASA (National Aeronautics and Space Administration). Another program was the National Research Service awards, administered through three federal agencies in the 1960s. These training programs were a deliberate effort to attract talented students with stipends for predoctoral and postdoctoral support, as well as to improve training on campuses with institutional allowances. In the decade between 1961 and 1972, these particular programs assisted more than 30,000 graduate students and 27,000 postdoctoral scholars, according to one estimate.[35]

While direct support of doctoral education—fellowships and traineeships—was done on a competitive basis, the talent and support remained concentrated at leading research universities where federally sponsored research was conducted. This resulted in a consolidation of resources for both research and doctoral education, giving these institutions a double competitive edge in attracting high-quality students and faculty.[36]

Post–World War II federal initiatives were even more instrumental in cementing the legitimacy of this interdependence: sponsored university research had short-term R&D value, and sponsored graduate education promoted "manpower training." Between the end of World War II and 1972, the federal government spent $200 billion cumulatively on R&D. Academic institutions' share of total R&D expenditures rose from 5 percent to 10 percent, while their share of basic research expenditures went from one-quarter in 1953 to one-half in the early 1970s. By the end of this era, the surge of federal sponsorship resulted in a persistent pattern: about half of the country's basic research was done in universities; about two-thirds of university research expenditures came from the federal government; and about half the federal funds for basic academic research went to the top twenty-five research universities.

Postwar Expansion of Graduate Education

Within the context of expanded sponsored research opportunities and a shifting funding base, the graduate education system continued to grow at a constant rate during each decade.[37] The end of World War II marked a turning point, as more doctorates were granted in the 1950s than in all preceding years, while the number of doctorates granted increasing from six thousand in 1950 to ten thousand in 1960. The 1960s experienced an even more dramatic expansion: a threefold increase in one decade alone—from ten thousand to nearly thirty thousand. The increase in master's degrees granted followed a similar pattern, the number awarded annually growing from about twenty-five thousand granted in 1940, and flourishing in the decades following World War II—to about sixty thousand in 1950, seventy-five thousand in 1960, and nearly three hundred thousand two decades later.

This proliferation of doctorates and master's degrees reflects both overall growth and an expansion into more fields of study, especially in the sciences and professional fields. Physical sciences, life sciences, and engineering accounted for close to half the doctorates awarded in 1965; two decades later they still predominated, although life sciences Ph.D.s edged out the other two fields. Social science and psychology remained fairly constant at about 20 percent; humanities dropped from 20 to 10 percent; and education increased from about 15 percent to 25 percent, thus reflecting an increased professional orientation of graduate study. The overall diversification of doctoral fields is marked—more than 550 fields in 1960 compared with 149 fields in 1916–18. Moreover, beyond fields of concentration, forty-seven types of doctoral degrees have been conferred besides the Ph.D., including doctors of education, social work, business administration, theology, and art. A similar orientation to the demands of the marketplace is evident in the growth of master's degrees since 1965, especially in practitioner-oriented fields. By 1982–83, only 16 percent of master's degrees were conferred in research-oriented M.A. programs; and new types of master's degrees emerged: business master's degrees increased from 7 percent to 23 percent, engineering accounted for 10 percent, and the health professions about 6 percent. Education still held the largest share, although dropping from 40 percent to 30 percent.[38]

On the whole, since World War II, graduate education at the master's and doctoral levels has grown into a vast enterprise in which the leading tier of research universities has become the model for aspiring institutions to emulate. Since less elite institutions had less of a resource base in facilities, departmental funds, and critical masses of faculty and students, they invested their resources in selected fields, although it was not until the 1970s that asserting a distinctive institutional mission become a strategy for gaining a competitive edge in specialized areas. At the leading institutions the dynamic was different: able to cover all fields, their strategy was to undertake more sponsored research and to expand Ph.D. production. This is the modern research imperative—the vehicle whereby universities protect, if not advance, their institutional mobility, for "the institution which is not steadily advancing is certainly falling behind."[39]

Thus up to the contemporary period, graduate education and research in the leading modern universities were guided by opportunities from major changes at the national level: scientific research for national defense and economic priorities; the federal government's rising research budget for both overall R&D allocations and basic research funds; multiple funding agencies helping to stabilize university autonomy; and a peer review system ideally to insure distribution of resources to the best science. With their abundance of funds unconnected to their instructional budgets, universities became the main conductors of basic research, and the federal government became the predominant external source of funds. However, at the end of the twentieth century, shifts in organization and sponsorship suggested a context of greater uncertainty, for changing funding sources, mechanisms, and allocations posed new challenges for the research foundations of graduate education.

The Contemporary Era: Signs of Strain

While the patterns that crystallized in the post–World War II period have remained prominent, university-government relations showed signs of strain. The early 1970s witnessed an economic crisis that threatened even the strong research-training link within the sciences, and even the solid resource base of the most prominent research universities. An era of retrenchment, roughly between 1969 and 1975, began with a tightening academic labor market and inflation in the wider economy. The events of this era signaled that the government could be an unstable base of economic and political support for university research and graduate education.

The dramatic expansion fueled by the post–World War II surge of federal support for university research and graduate education had appeared limitless. By the beginning of the 1970s, research universities had greatly extended their capital-intensive research infrastructure, thereby securing their position as international centers of excellence for research and research training. This expansion had generated a need for more research assistants to aid faculty, who were engaged in sponsored research projects, and this demand became a major determinant of the size and types of graduate programs. On the teaching side, surging enrollments meant that more graduate students could serve as teaching assistants for undergraduate classes. So, even while students applied to graduate school to engage in advanced study and obtain credentials, their roles as research and teaching assistants were foundational for universities to expand their institutional capacities for research and undergraduate education. As a supplement to this instrumental orientation, during this period, government agencies and foundations supported not only traineeships but also fellowships that graduate students could use to cover educational and living expenses.

The 1970s changes in the funding climate meant sharp declines in direct federal support of fellowships, and federal basic research funds were reoriented to applied projects that prioritized economic competitiveness, amid hopes that industry would become more involved in funding academic research. These shifts posed formidable challenges for the research and research training activities of universities. As Joseph Ben-David observed in 1977, a reduction of the massive federal support was "inevitable, but . . . the system was entirely unprepared for it when it came."[40] How universities managed to achieve stability, let alone thrive, in the national context of declining support is an ongoing analytical concern, as is how the higher education system as a whole succeeded at nurturing excellence in both research and research training. Enrollment and degree completion did level off in the early and mid-1970s, another indicator that expansion was not limitless. Yet the ongoing viability of graduate programs on over several hundred campuses across the United States is remarkable, given wide discrepancies in funding and the instability of support at the national and state levels.

Between 1968 and 1971 the basic research budget fell more than 10 percent in real terms.[41] Annual academic research expenditures contributed by the federal government declined from $5 billion in 1968 to $4.7 billion in 1974. The government's attention turned to short-term research that would make scientific knowledge technologically relevant. As a result, physical resources—such as equipment and campus buildings—were neglected. In addition to declining funds for academic science, support for graduate students declined; thus both research and research training became "victims of federal benign neglect."[42] The government abruptly withdrew the bulk of its direct fellowship support to graduate students, especially some of the larger programs funded by the National Institutes of Health. By one count, the 57,000 federal fellowships and traineeships funded in 1968 shrank to 41,000 in 1970; another account estimates that federal fellowships fell from 51,000 in 1968 to 6,000 by 1981. As graduate fellowships were "cut back too fast and too far," a series of national reports looked at graduate education financing. They cited the destabilizing effects of "stop-and-go" federal funds, the disadvantages of smaller-scale fellowships, with reduced support levels for four thousand new merit-based awards for gifted students each year. In place of the former support base, the government left the bulk of doctoral students to seek direct support from loans. To make up for the reduction in fellowship support, loans increased substantially during one decade alone: from 15 percent of the total graduate student enrollment in 1974, to 44 percent in 1984. It is estimated that by 1984, more than six hundred thousand students working toward graduate degrees had borrowed $2 billion from the federal government in Guaranteed Student Loans (later known as Stafford Loans).

In the 1980s, the federal government continued its indirect support of doctoral education through assistantships embedded in $13 billion of federal academic R&D. However, besides the cuts in fellowships and traineeships in the early 1970s, stipends for assistantships were also lowered subsequently when they became reconfigured as taxable pay for work rather than tax-exempt educational subsidies, in the Tax Reform Act of 1986. This initiative intended to reduce the federal deficit by taxing stipends associated with research assistantships and state-funded teaching assistantships, previously excluded from income tax.

Universities and their national representatives moved to have this legislation amended, but they were only able to get fellowship and tuition awards exempted from taxation. Assistantship stipends, a large portion of federal support for graduate students, still became taxable income. The policy change, which required technical changes in the administration of graduate student financial assistance, signaled a shift in attitudes toward graduate students: they were valued instrumentally, rather than viewed as inherently worthy of direct support.

In doctoral outputs, by the late 1980s, universities had regained the numerical losses that had occurred in the mid-1970s; annual production stabilized above thirty-five thousand, surpassing the 1973 peak.[43] Disaggregated by field of study, however, the data are mixed: indicating an increase in the number of life sciences and engineering doctorates, a marked decline of doctorates in the humanities, and slightly less of a decline in the social sciences. During the decade of the 1990s, doctoral degree production increased strongly from 1990 to 1998, and then declined by almost 4 percent to 41,140 in 1999. The century's final three decades saw a 60 percent increase in doctoral degrees awarded from 1969 to 1999, with brief periods of decline in degree production. Across the disciplines, the three-decade trend in doctoral degree production shows large increases in the life sciences (93%), social sciences (77%), and engineering (64%), relative to the smaller gain of the humanities (44%) and the physical sciences (26%).

In spite of changes in financing graduate education, in the 1990s, universities continued to perform about half of the country's basic research—a significant proportion of the overall national R&D effort. Of the total 1995 $171 billion national R&D effort, $60.7 billion was provided by the federal government and $101.7 billion by industry.[44] Most R&D funds go to development. In 1995, of the federal R&D funds, $17.1 billion were allocated for basic research, making the federal government the largest sponsor—at 58 percent—of basic research. Industry was the second largest sponsor of basic research at about $7.5 billion. Higher education institutions were third, at $3.4 billion.

The distribution of basic research funds among academic institutions indicates the persistent concentration of research activity and sponsored research resources. In the mid-1990s, the top 100 institutions accounted for more than 80 percent—$15.6 billion—of all academic R&D expenditures; the top fifty, nearly 60 percent—$11.0 billion; the top ten, approximately 17 percent—$3.4 billion. In addition,

the top-tier institutions—receiving four-fifths of all federal obligations, in which R&D funds are embedded—have remained remarkably stable; of the top one hundred from 1967, eighty-one have remained in that category for two decades.[45] The concentration had
shifted slightly since the early 1980s: in 1983, the top ten institutions
claimed only 20 percent of the research funds. The subsequent ten-
year drop reflected a slight dispersion of resources, paralleled by a
slight increase—from 17 percent to 20 percent—of funding to those
institutions below the top one hundred. The distribution of academic
R&D across fields remained essentially the same the last two decades
of the century: more than 80 percent of federal funds went to life
sciences (54%), engineering (16%), and physical sciences (11%). Although research allocations to the behavioral and social sciences increased from $0.55 billion in 1983 to $1.01 billion in 1993, these two
areas accounted for only 6 percent of the total throughout that period.

Institutions have responded to this funding base, which essentially
persists today, with their own initiatives: for example, by establishing their own teaching assistantships and research assistantships or
by drawing on institutional funds from endowments, from tuition,
or—for public institutions—from state revenues. These changes in
sources of support have been experienced by successive cohorts of doctoral students since the mid-1970s, as their graduate education became more labor-intensive (working in assistantships) and more reliant on self-support (instead of fellowships). Several elite research
universities announced they substantially increased graduate student
financial support to offer more competitive stipends and fellowships
across the disciplines.[46] Institutions have also used their own funds
to support research activities—including facilities and equipment improvement—in addition to accelerating efforts to collaborate with industry, prompting concern among some observers and participants
over a potential blurring of boundaries, if not purposes, between academic researchers and external sponsors.

Organized Research Units

In their effort to broaden their funding base, universities have elaborated their organizational structures in the form of extradepart-
mental research units that reflect increasingly specialized areas of
interdisciplinary and applied research. In the traditional historical

organization of the departmental structure, departmental faculty work as both individual investigators and mentors to their advanced graduate students in the department's degree programs. The modern period has given rise to the major exception to this mode of organization, the organized research unit (ORU). Before the twentieth century, ORUs were primarily observatories and museums, but in the post–World War II expansion of academic research, ORUs proliferated to meet new societal demands for research that did not correspond to instructional areas outlined by departments, or that were disproportionate to departments in magnitude and expense. Funded by the national government, state governments, industry, and foundations, ORUs have extended university research into interdisciplinary, applied, and capital-intensive endeavors. Estimates of the number of ORUs by the end of the 1980s ranged from a total of two thousand to more than ten thousand on American university campuses; they continue to emerge in new fields of biotechnology, microelectronics, material sciences, and artificial intelligence.[47]

While the presence of external funds from a sponsor is often the impetus for a proposed ORU, other criteria have included the presence of a critical mass of faculty and the availability of administrative support. Some ORUs even have explicit commitments to graduate education, such as graduate fellowships offered by the Stanford Humanities Center. However, as academic units outside departments, they typically lack degree-granting status. Nonetheless, ORUs have offered important advantages for graduate education. Intellectually, they can mediate between the world of disciplinary training and "real world needs and problems."[48] Practically, they may provide dissertation support and stipends for graduate students. Often they make available better research equipment. Finally, as an indirect benefit, they employ specialists—postdoctoral or nonfaculty researchers—in a temporary home akin to the departmental home in which graduate students can participate as well.

The administration of research and research training in ORUs evokes a new set of challenges when it works at cross-purposes with departmental organization. Full-time nonfaculty research personnel may supervise graduate student research assistants but do not have faculty status.[49] In general, students and younger faculty want the opportunity to work with trained researchers and up-to-date equipment in this setting. It is possible that these centers draw intellectual, organizational, and economic vitality away from department-based graduate programs and thereby jeopardize the continued viability of various departments. Not only may faculty loyalties become divided between organizational units but also budgets for research are overseen by different managers than departmental instructional budgets. Thus, a significant component of research training may end up being staffed and financed by complex administrative arrangements in which faculty allocations and budget allocations are no longer fully congruent with the actual practice of department-based graduate education. In short, the research training component of graduate education may become organizationally less visible, as it falls between the lines of departmental organization.

ORUs have become a highly visible and controversial receptacle for forthcoming industrial funds, especially as federal initiatives have been launched to encourage industrial contributions for campus-based, larger-scale operations. Beginning with the mid-1970s, the NSF established the Industry-University Cooperative Research Projects. Again in the late 1980s, the NSF promoted proposals for university-based Engineering Research Centers as well as Science and Technology Centers. These programs were to be funded initially by congressional appropriations and then to be gradually weaned from NSF funds through industrial contributions. In some locations the explicit expectation for universities to aid in the nation's economic competitiveness has provoked major controversy, while in other locations this aim has been embraced.

Graduate education and research are affected in mixed ways by initiatives that combine—or seek to replace—federal support with industrial sponsorship. Not only do resources become more concentrated, but they also become less flexible; for once a center is established, it demands to be fed. Moreover, industrial sponsorship—whether formally arranged in these kinds of ORUs, as formal research agreements, or as informal collaboration—carries some potential constraints in terms of the research process (for example, secrecy), the product (for example, negotiation over intellectual property), and exclusivity clauses against the formation of other alliances. Forming strategic alliances may catalyze conflict on campus, not only about pursuing the commercial potential of academic research, but also about a company's work, as seen in protests over a 1998 agreement established between Berkeley's College of Natural Resources and Novartis, a company that advanced work on genetically engineered crops. However, in favoring new interdisciplinary and applied sciences, and in bringing to campuses research personnel to staff those facilities, industrial sponsors may provide graduate students with exposure to timely problems, state-of-the-art research and techniques, and internships with job placement opportunities in industry, and may provide faculty with supplemental income. In fact, university leaders have recently asserted that strategic alliances with industry are even necessary for offering a top-notch graduate program in some fields because industry has an increasing monopoly of intellectual capital.[50]

While various benefits continue to galvanize university interest in collaborating with industry, funding from industry does not provide dependable long-term support that is essential for sustaining the academic research infrastructure. Given years of prior public investment in university infrastructures and the promise of continued public benefit from them, universities have made direct appeals to the federal government for sustained support of the material conditions required to pursue first-class, capital-intensive science. With much lobbying on the part of university representatives, the federal government has reluctantly agreed to sponsor some of the rebuilding and replacement of campus research facilities and equipment that was neglected throughout the 1970s and that proved insufficient as science became more capital-intensive in the 1980s. Both the NIH and the NSF have participated in this revitalization through research grants and center grants during the 1980s and 1990s, although the future flow of funding and the spirit underlying it are by no means assured.

Indirect Costs

In addition to establishing ORUs, another strategy for universities to recover the enormous costs incurred in campus research has been to renegotiate the indirect cost rate for overhead on research grants, although university administrators, campus-based researchers, and the federal agencies have been struggling to reconcile their conflicting interests. The indirect cost rate is a mechanism for distributing among sponsors and research projects the indirect costs that the institution incurs through lighting, heat, libraries, and general maintenance of the campus. Since a university wants to recoup the maximum amount possible and the researcher wants as much funding as possible for the research process itself, administrators and researchers may find themselves on opposite sides of a university's proposed increase. At the same time, the federal government wants more adequate justification of university expenses. This places university officials out in front, trying to reconcile the needs of their own campus infrastructure with reluctance from the federal funding agencies as well as from their own faculty researchers. Each university negotiates its indirect cost rate with the government; as a result, the rates vary from one campus to the next. For 2003 indirect cost rates show Columbia University at 63.5 percent, the University of Pennsylvania at 58.5 percent, and Stanford University at 60.0 percent; while the indirect cost rate is 45 percent at the University of Wisconsin, 48.5 percent at the University of Minnesota, 52 percent at the University of California, Berkeley, 53 percent at the University of Michigan, and 57 percent at the State University of New York at Buffalo.[51] Historically, private universities have set a slightly higher rate than publics, but this gap appears to be smaller in recent years.

Underlying discussions over indirect cost recovery is a widespread perception that instrumentation in university laboratories fares poorly when compared to government or commercial laboratories and the conviction that a decline in the quality of instrumentation at research universities may cause a decline in the research productivity of academic scientists, as well as in first-rate training opportunities for graduate students. The concern is whether universities are able to provide interdisciplinary research and research training without reducing the strength of traditional, disciplinary graduate education. The fear is that if universities do not make "some realistic accommodation . . . an increasingly large portion of basic research and academic activity which is necessary to the quality of [graduate] education . . . will move outside the university structure." In spite of universities' performing over half of American basic research, an increase in industry's proportional share may occur; and it is unclear whether industries will decide to collaborate with university researchers or to keep funds for their own laboratories. The long range concern is that academic departments would not be on the frontiers of research and that the best researchers would move away from graduate students, thereby jeopardizing a premise of the system—that "the best and the brightest" produce the best science and scientists at centers of excellence.[52]

Consequences for Graduate Students

In addition to the 1970s decline in direct fellowships, the changing nature of federal funds for research has had dramatic consequences for graduate students. This has been most evident for Ph.D. students in the sciences, where it has deeply affected their research training experiences, and it also continues to affect Ph.D. students in the humanities, where there has been no real federal support. Over the past two decades, graduate education has become more expensive, yet it continues to be supported in an ad hoc way. The largest potential funding base is the federal government and it is essentially unstable, resulting in increased pressure on universities to come up with funding for graduate students and increased pressure on professors to develop leaner research budgets with tighter time constraints.

Another trend that observers have directly linked to declining federal support is the lengthening of time to degree. From the early 1970s through the 1990s, the average length of time to complete a doctorate increased. Substantial differences across fields of study were also evident as of 1999, with the humanities taking the longest (a median of 8.9 years of enrollment between attaining the baccalaureate and the doctorate) and physical sciences the least time (6.8 years).

Beyond factors intrinsic to differences in disciplinary research, patterns of research training were intensified as a result of their underlying funding base, reflecting the priorities of government funding agencies and industry. In the sciences, research funding clearly has facilitated research training. In disciplines without research funds, like the humanities, the question becomes whether a research training component can be adequately provided without the substantive and symbolic support that funding provides. With no collective research agenda nor the reinforcing social structure of a laboratory setting, students in these fields function as free agents, who either develop independently or not at all.

Through recent decades, assistantships have therefore become a major source of financial aid for graduate students, along with grants and loans. The number of graduate assistants increased dramatically from 160,000 in 1975 to 216,000 in 1995. By 1999–2000, of those pursuing master's degrees, 16 percent had assistantships, up from 9 percent in 1990; and of those pursuing doctoral degrees, 47 percent had assistantships, up from 29 percent in 1990.[53] In other words, more graduate students have been working at their institutions concurrently with their graduate study. Not surprisingly, one result of this burgeoning work world has been for graduate students to unionize.

Changes in the academic workplace and momentum from faculty collective bargaining activities have strengthened the willingness and ability of graduate students to unionize. In the 1970s, dismal labor market prospects for emerging Ph.D.s exacerbated graduate students' concerns about a longer time to degree completion. Into the 1980s and 1990s, those concerns became amplified due to students' higher levels of financial indebtedness, perceptions of inadequate faculty advising, and the stark realization that benefits accrued to the universities by their leveraging faculty time through the "cheap labor" of graduate assistants, in particular teaching assistants. By the end of the 1990s, these factors contributed to a growing awareness of discrepancies between ideals and realities, and, at the national level, fostered widespread discussions about the quality of doctoral education.[54]

Only graduate students who hold positions as teaching or research assistants, or similar titles, are eligible to unionize; other graduate students are not suited to making the case that they are employees. In 2002, more than forty thousand graduate students at more than thirty-three universities were involved in organizing drives or already had formal collective bargaining representation, more than sixteen thousand of whom are members of the United Auto Workers.[55]

High loan indebtedness for graduate students has become a serious concern. Students acquire more loan indebtedness the longer they defer employment and become discouraged from the loss of momentum. In an effort to speed up the process, several programs across the country have reduced requirements for course work so that students begin working on their dissertations earlier. The University of Chicago, for example, instituted a reduced course work policy in 1982 to encourage students "to engage in their doctoral research as quickly, as clearly, and as self-consciously as possible," which would lead to "a healthier emphasis on the research stage of graduate student work."[56] The need for such a change is especially apt in the humanities where the tendency has always been to handle knowledge changes cumulatively with more and more material to incorporate into graduate course work, while in the sciences, for example, physics and biological sciences, the faculty revamp the curricula every few years. Along similar lines, the expectations for the dissertation may be revised, especially in the sciences, as well as economics, where shorter publishable articles are more valuable currency for launching a career than a long treatise.

And at the same time, recent studies documenting an overproduction of doctorates in science and engineering add to the already bleak picture for new Ph.D.s in the humanities and social sciences who are disheartened by an unfavorable academic labor market.[57] In the absence of projections for an academic hiring boom, faculty across the disciplines have begun working with doctoral students early in their programs to prepare for alternatives to an academic career. In addition, across the country, departmental admissions committees have been considering whether they should limit the number of new doctoral students admitted, or alternatively, provide prospective students with precise placement information that tracks a department's graduates.

A less visible and yet potentially more profound transformation resulting from changes in federal sponsorship of research and graduate education has occurred in the nature of student-faculty relationships during research training, especially for students in the sciences. While the historical ideal entailed a student working "at the bench" with a mentor, sponsored research is now the central medium for supervision and potential collaboration. Concerns have been raised that faculty have become more like project managers and administrators than mentor-professors, and that students are being supervised in a more directive manner—treated like employees and technicians rather than as apprentices. As one observer suggests, "the roles of faculty member (mentor) and principal investigator (employer) are becoming inconsistent, straining the incumbents. Principles and practices that the mentor would prefer are inconsistent with the needs of the scientist as employer."[58]

Conclusion: Changing Conduct in Changing Contexts

The trajectory of historical development is clear: graduate education in the United States has become so intertwined with sponsored research that graduate education and research have emerged as the foremost raison d'être for universities in the top tier, as an increasingly noble aim for lower tiers to emulate, and as an implicit professional imperative for university faculty. Historical scholarship reveals that obtaining research funds from the federal government and other patrons has been a requirement for university expansion and competitive advancement. As universities have aggressively competed for talented faculty and graduate students, they have sought to preserve their autonomy through stabilizing a support base from a plurality of sources—including external sponsors and internal revenues. At times by their own initiatives, they have attempted to create the organizational structures and amass the discretionary resources that would minimize the skewing of institutional priorities toward the economic incentives of short-term R&D sponsors.

Nonetheless, recent decades reveal that universities have been continually challenged by an inherently unstable federal funding base that left direct support for doctoral education concentrated in the physical and life sciences, even less in the social sciences, and virtually nonexistent in humanities. Over the past three decades, tension has heightened as the federal government has replaced a large proportion of fellowships and traineeships with loans incurred by individual students, leaving the bulk of support as indirect—through research assistantships on short-term R&D projects that strain the ideal mentor-apprentice relationship. Former ideals have been overshadowed by research training activities that are elaborated into finer status distinctions for students to connect with "the right" principal investigator on a "cutting-edge" and consistently funded research project. To the extent that graduate education functions as professional socialization, the professional work now modeled for students is often defined by productivity criteria and external mandates tied to other-than-scholarly agendas. Hence the question, For what kind of profession are graduate students being prepared?

The tone of this analysis has not been optimistic, in spite of the remarkable resilience demonstrated by students, faculty, and universities in the face of fluctuating resources and uncertain futures. I invoke this tone primarily because the future organization and sponsorship of graduate education requires more collective deliberation. A host of issues require further discussion beyond what graduate degree programs a campus should offer. These include the nature of research training, the adequacy of financial aid mechanisms, expectations for research and teaching assistantships across the disciplines, factors lengthening time to degree completion, the neglect of humanities and nonscience fields by external funders, the appropriateness of industrial sponsorship, and the ownership of intellectual property.

The issues are not strictly about efficient means but also about desirable ends.

Graduate student research assistants face the exigencies of an increasingly competitive arena of research support: time schedules of short-term project grants mean less leeway for mistakes; less available grant money means more competition and pressure to produce better results; sharing capital-intensive instrumentation means long hours of work, often in other cities; increased size of research teams entails perfecting a technique on one part of a project rather than completing an entire project from beginning to end; and time spent in research is valued over time spent in the "burden" of teaching younger graduate students or undergraduates. The arrangements emphasize efficiency and productivity, which promote an organizational climate of a factory floor—or a "quasi-firm"—rather than a center of learning.[59] Further evidence to support this assessment lies in the organizing efforts of graduate students to gain bargaining status as employees.[60] Also, in 1989 graduate students founded the National Association of Graduate-Professional Students to advocate for improved living and working conditions. In addition, disputes have arisen over academic authorship and ownership of intellectual property. Tensions are heightened under some arrangements for university-industry collaboration: while the exploitation of students for a faculty member's academic advancement is historically grounded in the university research system, it is another matter for a professor to profit financially from a student's work on a commercial venture.[61]

Admittedly, to identify graduate education as paying a price for its linkage to the university research enterprise marks a distinctive shift in scholarly attention. Usually undergraduate education is characterized as diminished, since undergraduate education subsidizes faculty research and graduate assistantships.[62] In truth, an argument can be made that both suffer. With greater frequency, scholars are critically examining other costs and potential trade offs in academic science with critical consequences for the vitality of the academic profession.[63] Efforts to pursue these and related lines of inquiry in graduate education have been hampered by incomplete and often inconsistent historical data. At present, the most valuable data are gathered at the national level,[64] but many of those databases have substantial limitations for addressing qualitative concerns, let alone for longitudinal analyses.

Moreover, perhaps a more formidable obstacle than data availability, collective deliberation on these issues has been undermined by unduly narrow definitions of the pressing issues in graduate education, usually as local organizational or administrative problems, rather than as symptomatic of a problematic interdependence with sponsored research or as fundamental questions of higher education policy for state and national levels. Analytical leverage can be gained by recognizing how the wider society's demands on the social functions of higher education are changing. From that vantage point, we can see graduate education as immersed in a complex institutional enterprise that produces goods and services, determines expertise, distributes resources; and regulates the uses of and access to power. At the center of this enterprise, faculty and their universities carry out their multiple roles while preparing the next generation of the academic profession and conveying to them either explicitly or implicitly what is problematic and what may be feasible solutions. Without a concerted reexamination of the ongoing interdependence between graduate education and the national R&D enterprise, underlying political and economic challenges will continue to fuel internal tensions in universities, and may even risk dismantling the historical social and human ideals of knowledge advancement in favor of purposes that, at their worst, resemble a shortsighted opportunism. Too much is at stake— the trajectory of faculty careers, the advancement of knowledge, the infrastructure of universities—for us to forego that discussion.

NOTES

1. See the *Chronicle of Higher Education,* December 14, 2001; February 25, 2003; December 18, 1998; January 17, 2003; and April 28, 2000.

2. The historical record offers different interpretations of the evolving interdependence between graduate education and research, as well as varying accounts of how well universities have adapted to external sponsors or have maintained their academic autonomy. As to the question of universities' retaining autonomy from a plurality of sponsors: for celebratory and critical interpretations, respectively, see R. Geiger, *To Advance Knowledge: The Growth of American Research Universities, 1900–1940* (New York: Oxford University Press, 1986) and D. Noble, *America by Design: Science, Technology and the Rise of Corporate Capitalism* (New York: Alfred Knopf, 1977). Scholars have separately documented the rise of modern American science— R. Bruce, *The Launching of Modern American Science: 1846–1876* (New

York: Alfred Knopf, 1987); the emergence of the American research university—Geiger, *To Advance Knowledge* and L. Veysey, *The Emergence of the American University* (Chicago: University of Chicago Press, 1965); the emergence of graduate education—R. Storr, *The Beginnings of Graduate Education in America* (Chicago: University of Chicago Press, 1953) and B. Berelson, *Graduate Education in the United States* (New York: McGraw-Hill, 1960); and postwar changes in federal support of academic science—J. Wilson, *Academic Science, Higher Education and the Federal Government, 1950–1983* (Chicago: University of Chicago Press, 1983). However, little scholarly work has been done at the intersection of these arenas to examine the factors that account for their interrelationship, with the major exception of J. Ben-David, *Centers of Learning: Britain, France, Germany, United States* (New York: McGraw-Hill, 1977). To date, most research on graduate education has been on graduate students: G. Malaney, "Graduate Education as an Area of Research in the Field of Higher Education," in *Higher Education: Handbook of Theory and Research,* vol. 4, ed. J. Smart (New York: Agathon Press, 1988). The graduate education–research nexus remains understudied and undertheorized in the higher education literature.

3. For an interesting study of "research drift" within comprehensive universities, see F. Queval, "The Evolution toward Research Orientation and Capability in Comprehensive Universities" (Ph.D. diss., University of California, Los Angeles, 1990).

4. P. Gumport, "Learning Academic Labor," *Comparative Social Research.* 19 (2000): 1–23.

5. The Integrated Postsecondary Education Data System (IPEDS) Completions Survey for 1999–2000, conducted by the Department of Education's National Center for Education Statistics (NCES), data provided by WebCASPAR.

6. B. Clark, *Places of Inquiry: Research and Advanced Education in Modern Universities* (Berkeley: University of California Press, 1995).

7. C. P. Snow, *The Two Cultures* (Cambridge and New York: Cambridge University Press, 1959); T. Becher, "The Cultural View," in *Perspectives on Higher Education: Eight Disciplinary and Comparative Views,* ed. B. Clark (Berkeley: University of California Press, 1984), 165–98. W. P. Metzger, "The Academic Profession in the United States," in *The Academic Profession: National, Disciplinary, and Institutional Settings,* ed. B. Clark (Berkeley: University of California Press, 1987), 123–208.

8. N. Sanford, "Graduate Education: Then and Now," in *Scholars in the Making,* ed. J. Katz and R. Harnett (Lexington, Mass.: Ballinger, 1976), 250–51.

9. The National Science Foundation (NSF) Survey of Research and Development Expenditures at Universities and Colleges, 2000, conducted by the NSF Division of Science Resources Statistics, data provided by WebCASPAR.

10. The earliest signs of doctoral education in the United States were the granting of the first Ph.D. in 1861 by Yale's Sheffield Scientific School, the second Ph.D. by the University of Pennsylvania in 1871, and the third by Harvard a year later. Perhaps more significant was the explicit organizational mission of graduate education in the founding of Johns Hopkins University in 1876, and Clark University in 1889. See Bruce, *Launching of Modern American Science,* 335–37.

11. D. Wolfle, *The Home of Science: The Role of the University* (New York: McGraw-Hill, 1972), 4.

12. Veysey, *Emergence of the American University,* 149, 168, 318–19.

13. R. Hofstadter and G. Hardy, *The Development and Scope of Higher Education in the United States* (New York: Columbia University Press, 1952), 44–45; and Berelson, *Graduate Education,* 33.

14. L. Mayhew, *Reform in Graduate Education,* SREB Research Monograph no. 18 (Atlanta, GA: Southern Regional Education Board, 1972), 6; and Ben-David, *Centers of Learning,* 61. See also B. Clark, *The Higher Education System* (Berkeley: University of California Press, 1983).

15. Geiger, *To Advance Knowledge,* 37; Ben-David, *Centers of Learning,* 61.

16. Veysey, *Emergence of the American University,* 177.

17. Geiger, *To Advance Knowledge,* 19.

18. R. Merton, "The Matthew Effect in Science," *Science* 159 (January 1968): 56–63.

19. M. Trow, "The Analysis of Status," in *Perspectives on Higher Education: Eight Disciplinary and Comparative Views,* ed. B. Clark (Berkeley: University of California Press, 1984), 134; and Veysey, *Emergence of the American University,* 312.

20. Bruce, *Launching of Modern American Science,* 329–34; and F. Rudolph, *The American College and University: A History* (New York: Vintage/Random House, 1962), 425–27.

21. Berelson, *Graduate Education;* and Geiger, *To Advance Knowledge,* esp. 166.

22. Much of this adapting to undertake applied research became incorporated into the ideal of service, especially for public universities. See Noble, *America by Design;* and G. Rhoades and S. Slaughter, "The Public Interest and Professional Labor," in *Culture and Ideology in Higher Education,* ed. W. Tierney (New York: Praeger, 1991).

23. Geiger, *To Advance Knowledge,* 174–225.

24. Ibid., 262.

25. Over the next decade, the NAS became the site of severe conflicts over membership—which was limited to fifty—and mission, as American scientists from different fields vied for control of the scientific community. Bruce, *Launching of Modern American Science,* 301–5, 315–17.

458 Patricia J. Gumport

26. Geiger, *To Advance Knowledge,* 13, 100, 165, 256.

27. P. Starr, *The Social Transformation of American Medicine* (New York: Basic Books, 1982), 193.

28. Wolfle, *Home of Science,* 110; D. Dickson, *The New Politics of Science* (Chicago: University of Chicago Press, 1984); and A. Rivlin, *The Role of The Federal Government in Financing Higher Education* (Washington, D.C.: Brookings Institution, 1961), 31.

29. M. Finkelstein, *The American Academic Profession* (Columbus: Ohio State University Press, 1984), 24.

30. Geiger, *To Advance Knowledge,* 220.

31. Rivlin, *The Role of the Federal Government,* 47.

32. Dickson, *New Politics of Science;* and Government-University-Industry Research Roundtable, *Science and Technology in the Academic Enterprise* (Washington, D.C.: National Academy Press, 1989).

33. Government-University-Industry Research Roundtable, *Science and Technology;* and Ben-David, *Centers of Learning,* 119.

34. D. Knight et al., *The Federal Government and Higher Education* (Englewood Cliffs, NJ: Prentice Hall, 1960), 135–37.

35. P. Coggeshall and P. Brown, *The Career Achievements of NIH Postdoctoral Trainees and Fellows,* NIH program evaluation report by Commission on National Needs for Biomedical and Behavioral Research Personnel and Institute of Medicine (Washington, D.C.: National Academy Press, 1984).

36. The concentration of doctoral degree–granting and sponsored research activity in the same universities is noteworthy. In 1993, the top thirty universities in doctoral degree production were also among the top fifty receiving federal funds for science and engineering R&D. All but four of those thirty were also listed in the top forty-two universities in terms of R&D expenditures. (Data adapted from National Science Foundation 1993 sources.)

37. Berelson, *Graduate Education;* National Research Council, *Summary Report—1986: Doctorate Recipients from United States Universities* (Washington, D.C.: National Academy Press, 1987); Department of Education, *Digest of Education Statistics—1989* (Washington, D.C.: National Center for Education Statistics, 1989); and J. Glazer, *The Master's Degree: Tradition, Diversity, Innovation,* ASHE-ERIC Higher Education Report no. 6 (Washington, D.C.: Association for the Study of Higher Education, 1986).

38. National Research Council, *Summary Report—1986;* Berelson, *Graduate Education,* 35; and Glazer, *Master's Degree.*

39. Rudolph, *The American College and University,* 239; see also P. Gumport, "The Research Imperative," in *Culture and Ideology,* ed. Tierney, 87–106.

40. Ben-David, *Centers of Learning,* 124.

41. Government-University-Industry Research Roundtable, *Science and Technology.*

42. C. Kidd, "Graduate Education: The New Debate," *Change* (May 1974):
43. See also D. Wolfle, *Home of Science,* 256; F. Balderston, "Organization, Funding, Incentives and Initiatives for University Research," in *The Economics of American Universities,* ed. S. Hoenack and E. Collins (Albany: State University of New York Press, 1990), 40; A. Hauptman, *Students in Graduate and Professional Education: What We Know and Need to Know* (Washington, D.C.: Association of American Universities, 1986); and S. Slaughter, "The Official Ideology of Higher Education," in Tierney, *Culture and Ideology,* 59–86.

43. Data are drawn from the National Research Council's reports, specifically *Doctorate Recipients from U.S. Universities: Summary Report* 1999 and 1986.

44. National Science Board, *Science and Engineering Indicators—1996* (Washington, D.C.: Government Printing Office, 1996). This reflects a major shift, with industry providing much more than the federal government. In 1986 they provided similar shares; the federal government provided $55 billion and industry provided $60 billion (National Science Board, *Science and Engineering Indicators—1987* [Washington, D.C.: Government Printing Office, 1987]).

45. Data are from National Science Board, *Science and Engineering Indicators—1996* (Washington, D.C.: Government Printing Office, 1996); and J. Sommer, "Distributional Character and Consequences of the Public Funding of Science," in *Federal Support of Higher Education,* ed. R. Meiners and R. Amacher (New York: Paragon House, 1990), 175. See also R. Geiger and I. Feller, "The Dispersion of Academic Research in the 1980s," *Journal of Higher Education* 66 (May/June 1995): 336–60.

46. See the *Chronicle of Higher Education,* September 28, 2001 and December 14, 2001.

47. R. Geiger, "Organized Research Units: The Role in the Development of University Research," *Journal of Higher Education* 61 (January/February 1990): 1–19. See also G. Stahler and W. Tash, "Centers and Institutes in the Research University," *Journal of Higher Education* 65 (September/October 1994): 540–54.

48. R. Friedman and R. C. Friedman, "Organized Research Units in Academe Revisited," in *Managing High Technology: An Interdisciplinary Perspective,* ed. B. Mar, W. Newell, and B. Saxberg (Amsterdam, The Netherlands: Elsevier Science, 1985), 75–91.

49. See C. Kerr, *The Uses of the University* (New York: Harper and Row, 1963). Estimates of the number employed in universities range from 5,000 to over 30,000. C. Kidd, "New Academic Positions: The Outlook in Europe and North America," in *The Research System in the 1980s: Public Policy Issues,* ed. J. Logsdon (Philadelphia: Franklin Institute Press, 1982), 83–96; C. Kruytbosch, "The Organization of Research in the University: The Case of

Research Personnel" (Ph.D. diss., University of California, Berkeley, 1970); A. H. Teich, "Research Centers and Non-Faculty Researchers: A New Academic Role," in *Research in the Age of the Steady-State University*, ed. D. Phillips and B. Shen, AAAS Selected Symposium Series no. 60 (Washington, D.C.: AAAS, 1982), 91–108; Government-University-Industry Research Roundtable, *Science and Technology;* and I. Feller, "University-Industry Research and Development Relationships" (paper prepared for the Woodlands Center for Growth Studies' conference on Growth Policy in the Age of High Technology: The Role of Regions and States, 1988).

50. This is in reference to the above-mentioned Berkeley-Novartis agreement. The author interviewed several university actors, including the dean who launched the initiative. See P. Gumport, "Public-Private Partnerships: Strategic Initiatives and Governance" (paper presented at the Association for the Study of Higher Education Annual Conference, Sacramento, Calif., November 21–24, 2002). See also the *Chronicle of Higher Education* coverage on December 4 and 11, 1998; June 22, 2001; and January 10, 2003.

51. Indirect cost rates for 1997 and 2003 were obtained from each university's sponsored research office. Compared with 1997, these 2003 indirect cost rates reflect a smaller gap between the public and private universities listed here. During this period, two of the three privates (Columbia and Penn) reduced their indirect cost rate, while all five of the publics increased theirs.

52. C. Frances, "1984: The Outlook for Higher Education," *AAHE Bulletin* 37, no. 6 (February 1985): 3–7; K. Hoving, "Interdisciplinary Programs, Centers and Institutes: Academic and Administrative Issues" (paper presented at the annual meeting of the Council of Graduate Schools, Washington, D.C., 1987); C. Kruytbosch, "The Future Flow of Graduate Students into Scientific Research: A Federal Policy Issue?" (paper presented at the annual meeting of the Council of Graduate Schools, Orlando, Fla., December 1979); and B. Smith, "Graduate Education in the United States," in *The State of Graduate Education,* ed. B. Smith (Washington, D.C.: Brookings Institution, 1985).

53. The best national source for such data is the National Postsecondary Student Aid Survey, which has been administered in 1987, 1990, 1993, 1996, and 2000; however, some of the survey items were modified from one administration to the next, thereby thwarting longitudinal analyses. (U.S. Department of Education, "Student Financing of Graduate and First-Professional Education, 1999–2000, Profiles of Students in Selected Degree Programs and Their Use of Assistantships, NCES 2002-166," by S. Choy and S. Geis [Washington, D.C.: National Center for Education Statistics, 2002]).

54. C. Golde and T. Dore, *At Cross Purposes: What the Experiences of Doctoral Students Reveal about Doctoral Education* (Philadelphia: Pew Charitable Trusts, 2001). Also P. Gumport, "Learning Academic Labor," *Comparative Social Research* 19 (2000): 1–23.

55. D. Julius and P. Gumport, "Graduate Student Unionization: Catalysts and Consequences," *Review of Higher Education* 26 (Winter 2002): 187–216. See also the *Chronicle of Higher Education,* January 17, 2003.

56. University of Chicago, "Report of the Commission on Graduate Education," *University of Chicago Record* 16 (May 3, 1982): 2.

57. J. Berger, "Slowing Pace to Doctorates Spurs Worry on Filling Jobs," *New York Times,* May 3, 1989, A1. For one recent study that estimated a 22 percent overproduction of science and engineering doctorates, see W. Massy and C. Goldman, *The Production and Utilization of Science and Engineering Doctorates in the United States* (Stanford: Stanford Institute for Higher Education Research, 1995).

58. E. Hackett, "Science as a Vocation in the 1990s," *Journal of Higher Education* 61 (May/June 1990): 267.

59. H. Etzkowitz, "Entrepreneurial Scientists and Entrepreneurial Universities in American Academic Science," *Minerva* 21 (1983): 198–233.

60. However, as major obstacles to these organizing efforts, structural and normative barriers impede construction of a collective identity and basis for solidarity among graduate students. See P. Gumport and J. Jennings, "Graduate Student Employees: Unresolved Challenges," *CUPA (College and University Personnel Association) Journal* 48 (Fall/Winter) 3/4: 33–37, 1997–98.

61. M. Kenney, *Biotechnology: The University-Industrial Complex* (New Haven: Yale University Press, 1986), 118–21.

62. A. Astin, "Moral Messages of the University," *Educational Record* 70 (Spring 1989): 22–25.

63. S. Slaughter, *The Higher Learning and High Technology* (Albany: State University of New York Press, 1990); Hackett, *Science as a Vocation;* and Etzkowitz, *Entrepreneurial Scientists.*

64. See the National Research Council's Survey of Earned Doctorates, which accumulates longitudinal data in the Doctorate Record File; the National Center for Education Statistics' data on enrollment and degrees awarded; and the National Science Foundation's data on Academic Science and Engineering Enrollment and Support, Federal Obligations to Colleges and Universities, and National Patterns of Science and Technology Resources. See also the Council of Graduate Schools' policy studies.

Chapter Sixteen

Curriculum in Higher Education

The Historical Roots of Contemporary Issues

Michael N. Bastedo

The curriculum in American higher education is often characterized as a pendulum swinging from one extreme to another, from religion to secular science, from prescribed study of the classics to curricular pluralism, and from tradition and conservatism to experimentation and growth. Indeed, these are some of the major tensions in the American higher education curriculum over the past three centuries, and conflict over these issues has often been intense within academic communities. The need for curriculum reform can be understood as emanating from changes in the broader society, such as scientific advancement, evolving conceptions of knowledge, changing student demographics, and more recently, labor market demands. These have often provided compelling rationales for some forms of curricular change.

We must also recognize, however, that these explanations have often been egregiously simplified. Over thirty years ago, Douglas Sloan accused historians of treating the higher education curriculum as a "morality play" where the forces of science, growth, and *Lernfreiheit* (student freedom to learn) fought the good battle against the forces of religion, stagnation, and prescription.[1] In reality, those who fought for a prescribed curriculum often struggled with how to provide some form of academic freedom to students; those who were fervent and pious followers of the Christian faith were often equal believers in the need for education in the basic sciences; those who believed that knowledge must be conserved were also committed to change and innovation. There are identifiable tensions in the curriculum, but they are not simplistic dichotomies.

In short, we must come to a more nuanced understanding of the reciprocal relationship between curriculum and society. While the curriculum can be seen as a lens for social change, it can also serve society by defining the boundaries of knowledge and thus serve as a force for social change itself, as we will see in the development of technology and the study of women and minorities. And while societal forces undoubtedly influence the curriculum, a full understanding is only possible when we understand how those changes have unfolded over time. Toward that end, we must identify the agents of change, how they organized for social action, and the dynamic relationship between actors in the university and organizations and leaders in society at large.

With these aims in mind, this chapter provides a broad overview of the historical roots of curriculum reform since the early days of the American college. Using three major tensions in curriculum reform — prescription and election, stability and growth, and conservation and innovation — these historical developments are considered analytically to understand how earlier developments have influenced contemporary debates. In the final section, we briefly consider some conceptual frameworks for understanding the dynamics of curriculum reform as well as some emerging policy issues for the coming decade.

Prescription and Election

The curriculum of the early American college was strongly influenced by the medieval English university, which trained the Calvinist ministers who immigrated to the new continent in the seventeenth century. There was one curriculum for all students, each of whom was training for a career in law or the clergy. Incoming classes were quite small; until the 1760s, all of the colonial colleges combined did not yield more than one hundred graduates per year.[2] Students themselves were generally only fourteen to eighteen years old and were often taught by the president himself. In later years, recent graduates, themselves only eighteen or nineteen years old, assisted him as tutors.[3]

Training for the Protestant ministry required learning the major languages of biblical texts—Latin, Greek, and Hebrew—so that students could understand them in the original. Study of the classical languages was also highly valued for its perceived ability to shape the human mind; the complexity of the grammatical structures of ancient languages were believed to train students to think at a more advanced level than was possible in the vernacular or other modern languages. Although basic knowledge of Latin and Greek was often required for admission, teaching in these languages comprised much of the first two years of study, with the addition of logic, grammar, and some rhetoric. As it had been in the English university, logic was highly valued for its usefulness in teaching students to think rationally and critically. In the final two years, a greater portion of the curriculum consisted of rhetoric, poetry, literature, ethics, arithmetic, and philosophy. Teaching itself consisted of lectures, verbatim recitations, and public disputations.

Emerging topics that did not fit into the ordinary curriculum were covered in weekly "extracurricular" lectures to the student body. Extracurricular topics were also occasionally taught in courses that were stated to be Latin or logic. Student literary societies served an important curricular role, promoting the reading of poetry, literature, science, and other topics that were not a priority in the standard curriculum.[4] Beyond simply reading the works, debates on these subjects were often organized by competing societies for the benefit of the campus. As is often true today, a great deal of learning in the early American college took place outside of the classroom.

As students and faculty became excited by new knowledge, they made extensive efforts to incorporate new materials into the curriculum, both formally and informally. After Timothy Dwight was hired by Yale, the senior class successfully petitioned the trustees to take lectures from him in rhetoric, history, poetry, and literature.[5] The evolution of the Scientific Revolution in European universities also could not be ignored; American faculty returned from Europe fired up to teach these new and daring subjects to eager students. Gradually, courses in physics, anatomy, chemistry and more advanced mathematics were added to the final two years of the college course.

With new topics emerging at a rapid pace, many openly considered allowing students to select the courses of their choosing. At the turn of the nineteenth century, the American college curriculum was in a state of conflict over the knowledge and skills necessary for a liberal education in contemporary society. As the interests and career goals of incoming students became more catholic, as society expected higher education to cover an increasing number of subjects, and as faculty grew restive, the curriculum came under attack from progressives for its intensive focus on ancient languages and theology. The result was unplanned growth of subjects in the curriculum without an overarching philosophy, which to some meant chaos and confusion. According to historian Frederick Rudolph, "Higher education behaved in harmony with a culture that built canals and railroads in seemingly endless number and for reasons that were often more consistent with the national psychology than with sound economic and engineering practice."[6] Students were also getting older; the age of the average college student rose throughout the nineteenth century, making the idea of an elective curriculum increasingly acceptable as students grew from boys to men.

Yet there were many opposed to such changes, for reasons both traditional and contemporary. The defense of the classical curriculum by the president and faculty of Yale College in 1828 was often seen as the last bulwark against the radical changes being proposed by students and society. The Yale Report famously defined the purpose of liberal education as providing "the *discipline* and *furniture* of the mind."[7] Intensive study of Latin and Greek, they argued, was necessary for students to expand their memory; logic and scientific experiments were required to teach students to think through complex problems. Ordinary Americans could be trained on-the-job for careers in "subordinate" positions. Yale's purpose, they argued, was to train young men from the upper classes who would serve as society's enlightened leaders and decision makers.[8]

Despite widespread acceptance of the report, Yale and the other elite colleges could not single-handedly resist the demands of a changing society, and the propulsion of increasingly rapid knowledge change. As state, community, and denominational competition drove the creation of hundreds of colleges throughout the nineteenth century, those states, communities, and denominations expected college curricula consonant with their needs and interests. Advanced education was increasingly needed for professions outside of the law and clergy, and students expected a more rational connection between their course work and future career opportunities. Faculty and students, seeing emerging knowledge being created in new academic fields such as science, economics, and sociology, expected to see that knowledge reflected in the curriculum. The complexity of these demands by college constituents made reform virtually irresistible.

Once the classical curriculum was dismantled, it happened with remarkable speed. Although Frances Wayland at Brown University had instituted an elective curriculum by 1850—and, as a result, increased enrollment by 40 percent—Harvard president Charles Eliot is usually credited with popularizing the new curriculum throughout higher education, despite being appointed nearly twenty years later.[9] By 1879, only the freshman year was prescribed for Harvard undergraduates, but there was still intense conflict over the elective reforms. Numerous public debates among high-ranking college presidents were conducted throughout the late nineteenth century. Indeed, presidents and faculty were often conflicted within themselves about the choice between prescription and election.

The changes at Brown and Harvard led to similar moves throughout higher education, part of what David Riesman has described as a "meandering snake-like procession" of ideas through colleges and universities.[10] Nevertheless, there was widespread unhappiness with the rapid decline in standards that accompanied the adoption of the elective system; students increasingly enrolled in entry-level courses and abandoned logic and languages in droves, leading to charges that the university was educating a generation of sophists and dilettantes. The appointment of A. Lawrence Lowell to the Harvard presidency in 1909 was a response to Eliot's radical overhaul of undergraduate education. Lowell's mandate was to institute a set of distribution requirements to ensure that all students received a liberal education, a plan he outlined at his inauguration with Eliot sitting next to him on the dais.

An idea that worked in theory never seemed to work well in practice. Distribution requirements forced students to select courses from particular categories, but there was still no common curriculum for all undergraduates. Proponents of a rigorous liberal education were still around to make plenty of trouble for the new system. Dissent crystallized around Robert M. Hutchins, who took over the University of Chicago in 1919 at age twenty-nine. Hutchins was driven by a desire to elevate the common man through standards of culture, thought, and morality, and thus to elevate society as well. The only way to accomplish these goals, Hutchins believed, was a prescribed program of general education.

The development of general education programs would be facilitated by institutional changes in the disciplines. Historians, who needed to introduce students to their rapidly developing discipline, developed broad courses that covered Western history from Greece to the present.[11] These courses were the basis for War Issues courses developed during World War I, whose purpose was to create solidarity between future American soldiers and their European counterparts by educating them on their common heritage.[12] These courses, in turn, led to the "Great Books" movement launched in the 1940s and 1950s and discussed later in this chapter.

The response to the concerns of Hutchins and his sympathizers within higher education was exemplified by Harvard's famous "Red Book."[13] The "Red Book" was a report written by a committee of Harvard faculty charged with evaluating the state of general education for undergraduates. The committee did not go as far as Hutchins or Adler might have hoped, but they did acknowledge that distribution requirements were inadequate and recommended that all students be exposed to the major areas of knowledge. Tension between prescription and election is evident throughout the monograph, an artifact not only of the prevailing views of the country but of the conflicting views of the faculty on the committee.[14] Once again, the Harvard plan proved to be popular, and it became a model for general education programs throughout the country.

Twenty years later, Columbia University faced concerns about its general education program, but from the opposite direction. Columbia's Contemporary Civilization program required a single course sequence in the classics for the entire first-year class, leading to attacks that it restricted the academic freedom of students and consisted of works largely irrelevant to contemporary social concerns. Daniel Bell, a prominent sociologist at the university, was asked to write a report on the subject for the consideration of the faculty. *The Reforming of General Education* (1966) was a thoughtful, pragmatic approach to the problem of general education. Bell argued that since college takes its place between the secondary school, which emphasizes facts, and the graduate school, which emphasizes specialization, "the distinctive function of the college must be to teach modes of conceptualization, explanation, and verification of knowledge."[15] The selection of canonical texts included in Columbia's program broadened the mind because the works were presented as contingent, allowing the reader to draw conclusions that differed from the professor. Material presented merely as fact or dogma, Bell argued, would lead only to specialization and vocationalism, thereby undermining the goals of general education.

Despite his defense of Columbia's core curriculum, Bell's pragmatic argument provoked those who believed that the classics were worthwhile in and of themselves. This view was most clearly expressed by Leo Strauss, a political philosopher at the University of Chicago. "Liberal education is education in culture or toward culture . . . the finished product of a liberal education is a cultured human being," Strauss wrote. "We are compelled to live with books. But life is too short to live with any but the greatest books."[16] Robert Belknap and Richard Kuhns later took an even more reactionary stance, arguing that contemporary students were ignorant, and that universities had failed to integrate the disciplines by placing a premium on specialization. "Universities and schools," they said, "have lost their common sense of what kind of ignorance is unacceptable."[17]

Allan Bloom extended this argument in *The Closing of the American Mind*. Bloom derided the culture of American college students and the curriculum of American colleges, both of which, he believed, encouraged an unhealthy cultural pluralism. Teaching students merely to be open to new cultures was wrongheaded, he said, because it is natural to prefer your own culture just as it is natural to prefer your own child over another's. Without this proprietorship of culture, students were left in a "no man's land between the goodness of knowing and the goodness of culture, where they have been placed by their teachers who no longer have the resources to guide them."[18] Students, Bloom argued, no longer had a cultural orientation with which to organize the world around them, leaving them unable to construct meaning from a stream of facts and opinions. In a society characterized by torrents of information, Bloom said, colleges have abandoned students by their ideology of openness.

Bloom's tract led to a flood of books on the state of the American college generally and liberal education specifically. Dinesh D'Souza, in *Illiberal Education,* argued that the problem was not that colleges taught non-Western culture, but that it was taught ignorantly. Instead of teaching classic non-Western texts like the *Analects* of Confucius or the *Ramayana,* he said, faculty taught politicized works like *I, Rigoberta Menchu* and *The Wretched of the Earth,* books that were written by Westerners and served merely to reflect liberal Western conceptions of non-Western peoples.[19] Thus D'Souza advocated a prescriptive but not ethnocentric curriculum that identified essential texts from both traditions. D'Souza strongly supported *50 Hours,* a similar curriculum published in 1989 under the auspices of the National Endowment of the Humanities during the Reagan administration.[20]

In the 1990s, a few scholars emerged to defend the university against these often vituperative critiques.[21] They were united in their opinion that most discussion of liberal education was oblivious to its history, and argued that curriculum has always been a contested area full of controversy and disagreement. The curriculum, even in its classical period, was never entirely static—new books gained entrance (for example, Austen, Twain, James, Freud) and old books were discarded. In this way, the curriculum has always responded to changing fashions in scholarship, taste, and the demands of an evolving society. Similarly, they argue, the new demographics of higher education mandated the inclusion of new authors in general education programs that reflected an increasingly multicultural society.

In a complementary argument, University of Chicago philosopher Martha Nussbaum argued that shaping citizens remains a vital function of higher education. Students must be prepared for a culturally diverse and international world, she said, and doing so requires understanding the perspectives of a wide variety of cultures. Nevertheless, she saw the Western tradition as remarkably consonant with emerging demands for pluralism. Books in the Western tradition can help students with the critical examination of people and cultures, including one's own, and develop the ability to think about the emotions and values of people in other cultures. This ability "to step out of your own shoes," she concluded, was key to living in a world marked by a diversity of people in race, class, gender, and sexual orientation.[22]

Thus debate over the nature and necessity of the prescribed college curriculum continues to this day. There are remarkable parallels between debates over the elective system in the 1880s and 1890s and debates over general education in the 1980s and 1990s. In both cases, the degree to which knowledge evolution and changing student demographics demand curricular reform are key points of debate. Both sides have engaged in significant debates on the utility of more traditional curricula compared to emerging subjects. The key question is always: What do college students need to learn to be educated members of society? Ultimately, general education does not exist in a vacuum, and it cannot fail to be as dynamic as the rest of the curriculum.

Stability and Growth

Persistent debates on the state of general education have occurred
amid the massive expansion of knowledge and the development of
organizational structures to support them. During the 1880s and
1890s, as the implementation of the elective system was negotiated in
colleges across the country, the modern disciplines were also beginning to emerge. In a process that Walter Metzger has called *subject
parturition,* the disciplines that we have come to understand as the
foundation of the modern university were organized into distinctive
and recognizable units.[23] As knowledge created in the university became increasingly complex and differentiated, new subjects emerged
to help define the boundaries of that knowledge. In their early days,
professors in these fields often struggled for legitimacy with professors in more established areas of knowledge. Over the years, through
a process Metzger termed *subject dignification,* these fields gradually gained legitimacy through the creation of scholarly societies, academic journals, and distinctive and rigorous methodologies.

Subject parturition was led in the nineteenth century by the sciences, which began to break out from the more general and human-
istic approach taught in the colonial and antebellum colleges under
natural philosophy. As scientific modes of investigation were incorporated and Ph.D.s returned from advanced study in Germany, the
study of science seemed increasingly differentiated from other subjects. Before the widespread adoption of the elective system, chemistry, geology, astronomy, physics, and biology were already recognized
as distinct subjects at most colleges.[24] The social sciences quickly followed, with economics emerging from political economy, and sociology
emerging from economics. These new fields were supported by scholarly societies like the American Anthropological Association, founded
in 1802, and journals such as the *American Journal of Sociology,*
founded in 1895.[25]

New forms of knowledge and methodologies for their investigation
led to new forms of classroom pedagogy. The lectures and recitations
of the early American colleges were simply ineffective methods for
science education or for advanced students at the graduate level.
Laboratory sections were added to courses to facilitate empirical investigation of scientific phenomena. While the lecture would remain
the primary mode of instruction for most of the twentieth century, the

seminar was implemented for graduate students and then gradually diffused to advanced undergraduates. Having learned the basic foundations of their field, graduate students and advanced undergraduates were deemed capable of engaging in direct dialogue with professors and colleagues.

The disciplines became increasingly specialized over the course of the twentieth century. Through the disciplines, universities helped to define what forms of knowledge were worth knowing by their placement in their curriculum, and researchers themselves established new modes of inquiry. These changes were then diffused throughout the academic field through scholarly societies and journals, and transmitted to society by graduating students and faculty who interacted with people outside the university. The curriculum was transformed further as faculty sought to teach more specialized courses, resulting in greater differentiation of courses and degrees. The professional self-identification of faculty changed concurrently. Where once a faculty member might call herself a psychologist or a biologist, later she would declare herself to be a Jungian or a neuroendocrinologist.[26]

Subjects outside of the traditional disciplines have also been accommodated, particularly in fields that are closer to the economy. Schools in medicine, law, education, social work, and public health emerged to meet the needs of an increasingly professionalized society. Academic work in these schools was often a laboratory for increasing specialization and the interdisciplinarity of knowledge. Technical and vocational subjects have become a core mission for the community colleges, ranging from automobile repair to medical technology and radiation therapy. This is not to say that vocational subjects were solely the realm of community colleges; on the contrary, students across the spectrum of colleges both public and private became increasingly vocational in their orientation and demanded curricula relevant to their needs.[27]

In recent years, the humanities have been an increasingly fertile field for the development of new programs and departments in the university. Unlike those founded in earlier periods, these programs were often explicitly connected to organized social movements led by students.[28] The civil rights movement of the 1950s and 1960s inspired student groups to demand black studies programs at more than eight hundred colleges and universities. Black faculty worked in concert with the students, making strenuous efforts to increase scholarship in the emerging field. Funding was often provided by the Ford Foundation, whose grants helped to establish many black studies programs across the country.

Over the course of the 1960s, however, black students increasingly associated themselves with the Black Power movement, a more militant attempt to force society to recognize the rights of black Americans. Students inspired by the Black Power movement often thought black faculty, tainted by their socialization in the academy, were "too white" to reflect an authentic black culture, and demanded programs that explicitly rejected the involvement of the traditional disciplines and incorporated community members into the curriculum.[29] Their goal was not simply to establish a separate curriculum, but also to transform the curriculum of the university as a whole, and to address racism in society more broadly.

Women's studies programs followed a similar path in the early 1970s.[30] Feminism was a powerful influence on young women entering the university, who demanded that the study of women and women's issues be incorporated into the curriculum. Female faculty who pursued graduate work during the 1960s often risked their careers by writing dissertations in women's studies, and once they were hired faced sharp critiques from their disciplinary colleagues that their work was methodologically weak or "too political." Women's studies faculty and students, like those in black studies, explicitly sought to change the curriculum of the university and to rectify institutionalized sexism and misogyny in society. Similar identity-based movements can be seen today in efforts to promote Chicano studies, Asian American studies, and Queer studies in the curriculum.[31]

Further growth in the higher education curriculum has resulted from interdisciplinarity, the integration of two or more disciplines to form a new content area or mode of inquiry.[32] Interdisciplinary inquiry has occurred almost since the foundation of the disciplines; recently, however, there have been movements to organize new subjects in separate departments and programs. Interdisciplinary programs are in evidence across the fields of knowledge, from biostatistics and biopsychology to area studies of Latin America, Eastern Europe, and Africa. The disciplines themselves have also become increasingly interdisciplinary, as subfields of the disciplines have grown increasingly close to their neighbors. Thus we see areas of study such as economic sociology, where sociologists have directed their energies into areas previously claimed by economists, and behavioral economics, where economists have taken on insights from psychology to paint a more realistic picture of economic behavior.

Finally, growth in the curriculum can be seen in areas that serve to segregate students and academic programs within colleges and universities.[33] In the past, differentiation of students generally occurred among colleges; increasingly, this separation also occurs *within* individual colleges. Separate admissions standards are often established for popular academic programs, especially at community colleges, forcing some students into less lucrative or less popular fields. Honors colleges, which provide special sections and other benefits to enrolled students, are a rapid growth industry in higher education; fully one-quarter of all honors programs were established at public colleges in the decade from 1989 to 1999.[34] On the other side of the academic spectrum, state officials are concerned that remedial education is increasingly provided to underprepared students, resulting in lower academic standards and persistence rates. Each of these trends has significant implications for equitable access to higher education, particularly within the public sector.

Despite all of these pressures toward growth and differentiation, with tremendous growth has also come impressive stability. Disciplines established over a century ago—some longer than that—remain the core of the academic enterprise today. If anything, there is greater consensus within the disciplines on appropriate modes of inquiry and the established domains of content. Societal demands on the university and knowledge construction have certainly become more complex over time, but the university has often adapted by accommodating those changes within its existing organizational structures. Despite seemingly unending specialization, conflict, and change, the university curriculum is a recognizably stable entity that has adapted to social, economic, and political demands.

Conservation and Innovation

One of the main forces of stability in the curriculum has been academic culture. Scholars have been trained to believe that one of the core missions of the university is to preserve the knowledge of past generations. The classical curriculum, while dynamic is some ways—through extracurricular lectures, literary societies, and the gradual adoption of new subjects—remained remarkably consistent for most of the colonial period and well into the nineteenth century. In an era when it was plausible to believe that Latin and Greek were essential to any man who considered himself liberally educated, the forces of stability were a powerful influence in the American college.

The affect of Christianity on the college curriculum cannot be underestimated. Although the central role of colleges in the preparation of ministers gradually declined, Christianity nevertheless remained infused throughout student life and the curriculum. Protestant revivalism, as expressed through the Great Awakenings of the 1740s and the early 1800s, found fertile ground in the American college. Indeed, one of the major sources of the Second Great Awakening was Yale University, and one historian has argued that colleges during this period could accurately be described as "revival camps."[35] The curriculum and Christianity were thus mutually reinforcing; faculty concern for the salvation of their students was paramount, and transmitted to students in courses such as ethics, literature, and theology.

Although science was certainly on the rise throughout the nineteenth century, there was not as sharp a divide between science and religion as is often perceived today. After the *Summa Theologica* of Thomas Aquinas, the major intellectual project of the Middle Ages was the resolution of biblical revelation with classical science and philosophy. Thus, the people who were founding new colleges as an expression of religious faith were the same people establishing science departments in those colleges, and they saw no contradiction in those two actions. The scientific method, far from undermining religion, was rather an instrument for the revelation of sacred truth.

Nonetheless, a gradual secularization of the Protestant university took hold over the course of the nineteenth and twentieth centuries. As new subjects were added to the curriculum at a rapid pace, their connection to the religious mission of the college was often increasingly tenuous. Protestant leaders, for their part, valued religious tolerance and a unified American culture, making it difficult to retain denominational separatism and distinctive religious missions.[36] As the nature of the multiversity became the secular pursuit of knowledge, religion was increasingly unimportant to the college mission, and leaders of the academy themselves were drawn from prominent academics rather than ministers. The declining influence of Christianity was quite gradual; Wellesley College, for example, did not eliminate required chapel until 1968.[37]

The secularization of the university was not entirely welcomed, and neither was the liberalization of academic requirements. Robert M. Hutchins, the University of Chicago president who led the attack on distribution requirements during the 1930s and 1940s, began to think about resurrecting more traditional curricula that would meet the standards of an earlier era. He was encouraged by John Erskine's General Honors course at Columbia University, which was an extension of the War Issues course developed by Erskine for outgoing American soldiers during World War I. Erskine designed the course in response to what he saw as the increasing specialization and vocationalism in college education, and his students read fifty-two classics from Homer to William James in a single year.[38] Hutchins soon taught a course of his own, first to high school students, and then as a Great Books course at the University of Chicago limited to twenty students by invitation.

The Great Books idea was highly influential both inside and outside of the university, leading to a small industry of book publishing and discussion groups during the 1940s and 1950s. This was initiated by the publication of Hutchins's caustic *The Higher Learning in America* in 1936, which derided the vocationalism and intellectual content of higher education and prescribed a new course centered on the classics.[39] The book was an instant bestseller despite—or perhaps because of—its rather elitist attitude toward college education. Ten years later, Hutchins left the Chicago presidency to assist the Great Books movement, which had inspired a charitable foundation, discussion groups throughout the country, and a rather lucrative company that published approved selections as *The Great Books of the Western World*.[40]

Adherents of the "Great Books" method were so pleased with the results of the courses at Columbia, Chicago, and elsewhere that they were eager to revamp an entire college based on the premise. The opportunity presented itself when 200-year-old St. John's College announced that it would close due to budget problems.[41] Stringfellow Barr and Scott Buchanan, "Great Books" adherents at the University of Virginia, decided to try and save the college by instituting a four-year prescribed course in the classics. The "New Program" curriculum that they developed based on the Chicago and Columbia models, with the addition of a substantial amount of science and mathematics, has remained largely as it was developed in 1939.[42]

St. John's College was only one of many experimental colleges founded during the post-war period, with the 1950s and 1960s being a particularly fertile period. In its willingness to upend the foundations of the college curriculum, this period is virtually unmatched in American history. Prominent examples include the University of California at Santa Cruz, whose cluster colleges tried to break down the multiversity into manageable organizational units, each with its own distinctive character. As one example, UCSC's Kresge College experimented with using t-groups in courses inspired by the 1960s encounter movement founded by Carl Rogers.[43] Another example is Black Mountain College, which attracted famous writers and artists from across the country to its utopian community in North Carolina until its collapse in 1956.[44]

The 1960s served as a period of experimentation even within traditional colleges. The emergence of national student movements and the breakdown of social conformity that characterized the post–World War II era pressured colleges to alter traditional curricular and pedagogical practices. For student activists, the curriculum had become far too abstracted from relevant political and social concerns. The best-known group was Students for a Democratic Society (SDS), which formed in 1960 to organize students around the social concerns of the period, primarily social justice issues and the Vietnam War.[45] Because the university graduated the future leaders of the country, SDS viewed reforming the university as essential to promoting social change.

Resistance to the idea of "politicizing" the university curriculum was strong, so SDS members moved to create "free universities" where any student could study or teach, and where individuals in the university community, regardless of academic qualifications, were welcome to participate. In free universities, the political neutrality of courses and instructors was explicitly rejected, because the mission was to encourage political activism to improve society. Any form of grading was often eliminated as irrelevant to the learning process. Over time, free universities were widely accepted at colleges across the country. Indeed, they were so successful that militant students, seeing that free universities were peacefully coexisting with the traditional curriculum, became disenchanted with their ability to transform the university and eventually abandoned them.[46]

As the 1960s came to a close, many students and faculty became cynical about the ability of universities to inspire social change. The persistence of the Vietnam War and the student killings at Kent State and Jackson State in 1970 coincided with an overall contraction in university growth. Student activism declined dramatically, reaching record lows in the 1980s and 1990s. The major curricular experiments in higher education had, one by one, failed to achieve their goals, leading to further cynicism and apathy. In future decades, curricular reforms would be significantly less ambitious, but would nevertheless influence the core of the educational enterprise. In an incremental manner, these changes would ultimately have more impact on the curriculum than the most ambitious experimental colleges.

The influence of technology on the modern curriculum is undeniable.[47] The information technology revolution of the 1970s and 1980s has transformed how students conduct their work and expect to obtain and transmit information. Improving student ability to use technology is often explicitly stated as part of the core educational mission of undergraduate education, and the "digital divide" is a key issue among those concerned with equity and access. The widespread adoption of the Internet by colleges and universities during the 1980s and 1990s has revolutionized our ability to obtain vast quantities of information and synthesize it in a short time. Classroom teaching itself has been changed through the use of computer laboratories, educational software, and sophisticated presentation techniques.

New forms of learning have emerged to take advantage of new technologies. Distance education, which allows instructors and students to connect visually across multiple classroom locations, has expanded access to higher education for those who live vast distances from a university or who are determined to seek out programs outside their local communities. The Internet has created innumerable opportunities for online education, where students communicate solely by discussion groups, e-mail, or in virtual chat rooms. More recently, programs have begun to experiment with combining both traditional and virtual modes of instruction as the needs of students, faculty, and the subject dictate. Although proclamations of the death of the traditional university have proved to be premature, there has been an undeniable change in the nature of academic work for many students and faculty.

Other forms of curricular experimentation are making their claims on the university as well, often with remarkable success. One prominent example is the development of experiential education and service learning programs. Service learning emerged in the experimental fervor of the 1960s from the same social movements that led to SDS and the free universities.[48] Consonant with the ideals of the time, service learning was a means for students to engage and transform society through efforts that were rewarded with academic credit by the university. At first, service learning was simply a loosely defined group of internships and volunteer activities, many with a political or non-profit bent. As notions of community service grew in society throughout the 1980s and 1990s, service learning programs grew in importance and were co-opted, becoming increasingly apolitical. Over time, service learning has emerged as an identifiable and legitimate mode of inquiry with applications across the fields of study, and serves as a demonstration of the university's commitment to public service.

Curriculum reform has also been aimed at improving student persistence and graduation rates, particularly at community colleges and public comprehensive universities. In "learning communities," groups of students enroll simultaneously in a sequence of courses, or even an entire academic program, instead of choosing those courses separately. Often these courses have a unifying theme that draws students and faculty together to study one topic intensively. Although research in this area remains embryonic, learning communities seem to promote student persistence by providing classroom experiences that are more meaningful for students, and by building support structures among students themselves.[49] Another effort to address dropout rates has been to use "supplemental instruction" in the classroom, which provides coursework in basic skills to underprepared students enrolled in traditional credit-bearing courses, rather than segregating them into separate remedial courses. Data on these programs suggests that students in supplemental instruction earn higher grades and are more likely to persist than their peers.[50]

Conclusion: Understanding Curriculum Change

For many observers, the curriculum is an "academic graveyard" where ideas for educational reform go to die. It is widely believed that the curriculum simply does not change, and that reforms never move forward, merely swinging from one extreme to the other over the course of time. On the contrary, significant changes in the curriculum have occurred in American higher education throughout its history. Although revolutionary change in the curriculum has been rare, incremental changes have often accumulated over time to create significant and lasting impacts.[51] By using the curriculum as a lens for social change, we can see the effect of society's demands on higher education, and how universities have sought to define the boundaries of knowledge and thereby influence how the public views social issues.

Knowledge differentiation is certainly a key factor in curricular change. For some, knowledge is the key unit of analysis, putting constant pressure on the university organization to adapt to its increasing complexity.[52] To cope with these unrelenting pressures, the curriculum must accommodate them by altering the content and form of courses, as well as the requirements and organization of programs and departments. Unending differentiation thus yields an organization that is remarkably adaptable to the range of demands placed upon it, but faces increasing problems of integration as students and faculty have less in common when they move further and further apart. In this perspective, general education for all students can never be resurrected, because it is impossible to build a consensus across the university on which types of knowledge are most valuable to undergraduates.[53]

Curricular change can also be understood as inhabiting within an organizational culture that supports it.[54] In this view, the curriculum is socially constructed among the constituents of the university, who interact with one another to create meaning. The curriculum itself signifies changes in the faculty's underlying assumptions about what counts as knowledge, what knowledge is most worthy of transmitting, and what organizational forms are most appropriate. The curriculum also serves as a form of organizational culture for students, by socializing them into the content and skills needed to navigate the world of the university. From this perspective, to understand curricular change we must understand the organizational culture of the university, and identify the mechanisms by which faculty and students interact within the curriculum to construct the meaning of knowledge.

Social movements can also be a key mechanism for curricular change.[55] Traditional accounts of curricular change have often identified changing student demographics—increasing numbers of minorities, women, and sexual minorities in the university—as the main causal factor behind change in the curriculum. With this explanation, there has been little understanding of how these demographics have led to actual change in the curriculum. One answer is social movements, which have organized students and faculty around political and identity-based causes to make demands for new programs and departments in the curriculum. Earlier, we saw how the Black Power movement, SDS, and feminists have organized to create new content and produce new organizational structures in the curriculum.

The construction of the curriculum can also be connected to powerful political and economic actors in society.[56] As the government and profit-seeking corporations have become increasingly involved in the funding of university research activities, their influence on the curriculum in departments and programs closely connected to those agencies has become apparent. For-profit corporations make grants to science departments and business schools; the government pours substantial funds into medical schools, science departments, and schools of education; nonprofit foundations are often significant providers of funds in the humanities and the social sciences. Although it is not yet clear how these connections yield specific changes in coursework or organizational structures, these actors are undoubtedly powerful resource providers with significant influence on research-oriented faculty.

Finally, we must consider efforts to influence undergraduate education through state policy. Nonpartisan organizations, including the Education Commission of the States and the National Center for Public Policy and Higher Education, have been sharply critical of the inability of states and colleges to improve teaching or monitor progress on student learning.[57] State policy makers in Ohio and Massachusetts have been equally critical of faculty productivity and time spent on research and service over teaching.[58] Increasingly, states are considering the use of measures such as Graduate Record Exam (GRE) scores, critical thinking inventories, and even high-stakes graduation exams to improve and assess undergraduate instruction. Although these ideas are still in their early stages, policy makers expect this to be a major policy issue for the next decade.

NOTES

1. Douglas Sloan, "Harmony, Chaos, and Consensus: The American College Curriculum," *Teachers College Record* 73 (1971): 221–51.

2. Frederick Rudolph, *Curriculum: A History of the Undergraduate Course of Study since 1636* (San Francisco: Jossey-Bass, 1977). Rudolph's work is still the standard for historical examination of the college curriculum, and his influence can be seen throughout this essay.

3. John D. Burton, "The Harvard Tutors: The Beginning of the Academic Profession, 1690–1825," *History of Higher Education Annual* 16 (1996): 1–17.

4. James McLachlan, "The *Choice of Hercules:* American Student Societies in the Early 19th Century," in *The University in Society,* vol. 2, ed. Lawrence Stone (Princeton, NJ: Princeton University Press, 1974), 449–94; Rudolph, *Curriculum,* 95–98.

5. Although the effort was successful, the lectures were not incorporated into the standard curriculum and attending students were required to get permission from their parents. Rudolph, *Curriculum,* 39.

6. Rudolph, *Curriculum,* 55.

7. "The Yale Report of 1828," in *American Higher Education: A Documentary History,* ed. Richard Hofstadter and Wilson Smith (Chicago: University of Chicago Press, 1961), 275–91. Emphasis in the original.

8. For extensive discussion of the Yale Report, see Jack C. Lane, "The Yale Report of 1828 and Liberal Education: A Neorepublican Manifesto," *History of Education Quarterly* 27 (1987): 325–38; Melvin I. Usofsky, "Reforms and Response: The Yale Report of 1828," *History of Education Quarterly* 5 (1965): 53–67; Rudolph, *Curriculum.* Rudolph has been strongly criticized for overestimating the effect of the Yale Report. See David B. Potts, "Curriculum and Enrollments: Some Thoughts on Assessing the Popularity of Antebellum Colleges," in *The American College in the Nineteenth Century,* ed. Roger Geiger (Nashville: Vanderbilt University Press, 2000).

9. Hugh Hawkins, *Between Harvard and America: The Educational Leadership of Charles W. Eliot* (New York: Oxford University Press, 1972); Phyllis Keller, *Getting at the Core: Curricular Reform at Harvard* (Cambridge: Harvard University Press, 1982).

10. David Riesman, *Constraint and Variety in American Education* (Garden City, NY: Doubleday, 1958).

11. Gilbert Allardyce, "The Rise and Fall of the Western Civilization Course," *American Historical Review* 87 (1982): 695–725.

12. Carol S. Gruber, *Mars and Minerva: World War I and the Uses of the Higher Learning in America* (Baton Rouge: Louisiana State University Press, 1975).

13. Paul H. Buck et al., *General Education in a Free Society: A Report of the Harvard Committee* (Cambridge, MA: Harvard University Press, 1945).

14. Ironically, the Harvard faculty never formally adopted the report, and it had far more influence outside of Harvard than within it. See Bruce A. Kimball, *Orators and Philosophers: A History of the Idea of Liberal Education* (New York: College Entrance Examination Board, 1995).

15. Daniel Bell, *The Reforming of General Education* (New York: Columbia University Press, 1966), 8.

16. Leo Strauss, *Liberalism Ancient and Modern* (New York: Basic Books, 1968), 3, 7.

17. Robert L. Belknap and Richard Kuhns, *Tradition and Innovation* (New York: Columbia University Press, 1977), 23.

18. Allan Bloom, *The Closing of the American Mind* (New York: Simon and Schuster, 1987), 37.

19. Dinesh D'Souza, *Illiberal Education* (New York: Free Press, 1991).

20. Lynne V. Cheney, *50 Hours: A Core Curriculum for College Students* (Washington, D.C.: National Endowment for the Humanities, 1989).

21. W. B. Carnochan, *The Battleground of the Curriculum: Liberal Education and the American Experience* (Stanford: Stanford University Press, 1993); Lawrence W. Levine, *The Opening of the American Mind* (Boston: Beacon Press, 1996); John K. Wilson, *The Myth of Political Correctness: The Conservative Attack on Higher Education* (Durham, NC: Duke University Press, 1995).

22. Martha Nussbaum, *Cultivating Humanity: A Classical Defense of Reform in Liberal Education* (Cambridge: Harvard University Press, 1997).

23. Walter P. Metzger, "The Academic Profession in the United States," in *The Academic Profession,* ed. Burton R. Clark (Berkeley: University of California Press, 1987), 123–208. See also Laurence R. Veysey, *The Emergence of the American University* (Chicago: University of Chicago Press, 1965), 121–70.

24. Metzger, "The Academic Profession in the United States," 128.

25. On the beginnings of the social sciences, see Dorothy Ross, *The Origins of American Social Science* (Cambridge, UK: Cambridge University Press, 1991); and Thomas Haskell, *The Emergence of Professional Social Science* (Urbana: University of Illinois Press, 1977).

26. For more on the differentiation of knowledge, see Burton R. Clark, *The Higher Education System* (Berkeley: University of California Press, 1983); and Patricia J. Gumport and Stuart K. Snydman, "The Formal Organization of Knowledge: An Analysis of Academic Structure," *Journal of Higher Education* 73 (2002): 375–408.

27. Steven Brint, "The Rise of the Practical Arts," in *The Future of the City of Intellect,* ed. Steven Brint (Stanford: Stanford University Press, 2002), 231–59. On the increasing vocational orientation of traditional liberal arts colleges, see Matthew S. Kraatz and Edward J. Zajac, "Exploring the Limits of the New Institutionalism: The Causes and Consequences of Illegitimate Organizational Change," *American Sociological Review* 61 (1996): 812–836.

28. Philip G. Altbach, *Student Politics in America: A Historical Analysis* (New York: McGraw-Hill, 1974); Sheila Slaughter, "Class, Race, and Gender and the Construction of Post-Secondary Curricula in the United States," *Journal of Curriculum Studies* 29 (1997): 1–30; Julie A. Reuben, "Reforming the University: Student Protests and the Demand for a Relevant Curriculum," in *Student Protest: The Sixties and After,* ed. Gerard De Groot (New York: Longman, 1998), 153–68.

29. On the Black Power movement in higher education, see Joy Ann Williamson, *Black Power on Campus* (Urbana: University of Illinois Press, 2003).

30. Marilyn J. Boxer, *When Women Ask the Questions: Creating Women's Studies in America* (Baltimore: Johns Hopkins University Press, 1998); Patricia J. Gumport, *Academic Pathfinders: Knowledge Creation and Feminist Scholarship* (Westport, CT: Greenwood Press, 2002).

31. Thomas J. La Belle and Christopher R. Ward, *Ethnic Studies and Multiculturalism* (Albany: State University of New York Press, 1996); Janice L. Ristock and Catherine G. Taylor, *Inside the Academy and Out: Queer Studies and Social Action* (Toronto: University of Toronto Press, 1998).

32. Lisa R. Lattuca, *Creating Interdisciplinarity* (Nashville: Vanderbilt University Press, 2001).

33. Michael N. Bastedo and Patricia J. Gumport, "Access to What? Mission Differentiation and Academic Stratification in U.S. Public Higher Education," *Higher Education* 46 (2003): 341–59; Patricia J. Gumport and Michael N. Bastedo, "Academic Stratification and Endemic Conflict: Remedial Education Policy at the City University of New York," *Review of Higher Education* 24 (2001): 333–349.

34. At private colleges, the figure is 39 percent. See Bridget Terry Long, "Attracting the Best: The Use of Honors Programs and Colleges to Compete for Students" (unpublished working paper, Harvard University, March 2002).

35. Sloan, "Harmony, Chaos, and Consensus," 227–32.

36. George M. Marsden, "The Soul of the American University: A Historical Overview," in *The Secularization of the Academy,* ed. George M. Marsden and Bradley J. Longfield (New York: Oxford University Press, 1992).

37. Ibid.

38. James Sloan Allen, *The Romance of Commerce and Culture* (Chicago: University of Chicago Press, 1983); and Joan Shelley Rubin, *The Making of Middlebrow Culture* (Chapel Hill: University of North Carolina Press, 1992).

39. Robert M. Hutchins, *The Higher Learning in America* (New Haven, CT: Yale University Press, 1936).

40. Allen, *The Romance of Commerce and Culture;* Robert M. Hutchins, ed., *The Great Books of the Western World* (Chicago: Encyclopedia Britannica, 1952).

41. Gerald Grant and David Riesman, *The Perpetual Dream: Reform and Experiment in the American College* (Chicago: University of Chicago Press, 1978).

42. Grant and Riesman, *The Perpetual Dream,* 40–76. Outside of St. John's, very few Great Books programs exist today. Prominent holdouts are the general education programs at Columbia University and the University of Chicago, and Stanford's Structured Liberal Education option.

43. Grant and Riesman, *The Perpetual Dream,* 77–134.

44. Martin Duberman, *Black Mountain: An Exploration in Community* (New York: E. P. Dutton, 1972).

45. Altbach, *Student Politics in America,* 221–6; and Reuben, "Reforming the University."

46. Reuben, "Reforming the University," 156. Few of the free universities exist today. At Oberlin, the Experimental College (ExCo) sponsors dozens of student-taught courses every year, and students may earn up to five ExCo credits toward graduation by either teaching or enrolling in courses.

47. Robert C. Heterick, Jr., *Reengineering Teaching and Learning in Higher Education: Sheltered Groves, Camelot, Windmills, and Malls* (Boulder: CAUSE, 1993); Martin J. Finkelstein, *Dollars, Distance, and Online Education: The New Economics of College Teaching and Learning* (Phoenix: Oryx Press, 2000). For a more critical perspective, see David F. Noble, *Digital Diploma Mills: The Automation of Higher Education* (New York: Monthly Review Press, 2001).

48. Timothy K. Stanton, Dwight E. Giles, Jr., and Nadine I. Cruz, *Service-Learning: A Movement's Pioneers Reflect on Its Origins, Practices, and Future* (San Francisco: Jossey-Bass, 1999); Janet Eyler and Dwight E. Giles, Jr., *Where's the Learning in Service Learning?* (San Francisco: Jossey-Bass, 1999).

49. Vincent Tinto, "Classrooms as Communities: Exploring the Educational Character of Student Persistence," *Journal of Higher Education* 68 (1997): 599–623; Faith Gabelnick, et al., *Learning Communities: Creating Connections among Students, Faculty, and Disciplines* (San Francisco: Jossey-Bass, 1990).

50. Deanna C. Martin and David R. Arendale, *Supplemental Instruction: Increasing Achievement and Retention* (San Francisco: Jossey-Bass, 1994).

51. For a framework for understanding incremental change in the curriculum, see Larry Cuban, *How Scholars Trumped Teachers: Change Without Reform in University Curriculum, Teaching, and Research, 1890–1990* (New York: Teachers College Press, 1999); see also David Tyack and Larry Cuban, *Tinkering Toward Utopia: A Century of Public School Reform* (Cambridge: Harvard University Press, 1995), esp. 60–109.

52. Burton R. Clark, *The Higher Education System: Academic Organization in Cross-National Perspective* (Berkeley: University of California Press, 1983).

53. Burton R. Clark, "The Problem of Complexity in Modern Higher Education," in *The European and American University since 1800,* ed. Sheldon Rothblatt and Björn Wittrock (Cambridge, UK: Cambridge University Press, 1993), 263–79.

54. William G. Tierney, *Curricular Landscapes, Democratic Vistas* (New York: Praeger, 1989); Patricia J. Gumport, "Curricula as Signposts of Cultural Change," *Review of Higher Education* 12 (1988): 49–62.

55. Sheila Slaughter, "The Political Economy of Curriculum-Making in the United States," in *The Future of the City of Intellect,* ed. Steven Brint (Stanford, CA: Stanford University Press, 2002); Slaughter, "Race, Class, and Gender and the Construction of Post-Secondary Curricula in the United States."

56. Ibid.

57. Dennis P. Jones and Peter Ewell, *The Effect of State Policy on Undergraduate Education* (Denver: National Center for Higher Education Management Systems, 1993); National Center for Public Policy and Higher Education, *Measuring Up 2002* (San Jose, Calif.: NCPPHE, 2002).

58. Michael N. Bastedo, "The Making of an Activist Governing Board," forthcoming; Carol L. Colbeck, "State Policies to Improve Undergraduate Teaching: Administrator and Faculty Responses," *Journal of Higher Education* 73 (2002): 3–25.

Chapter Seventeen

Markets in Higher Education

Students in the Seventies, Patents in the Eighties, Copyrights in the Nineties

Sheila Slaughter and Gary Rhoades

An academic capitalist knowledge/learning regime is characterized by increased commercialization of colleges and universities.[1] On the administrative side, commercialism pervades growing numbers of offices and services, ranging from enrollment management offices in student personnel services which "market" institutions to student consumers to creative products offices that manage faculty copyrights in intellectual property departments. On the academic side, commercialization spreads across the curriculum from science and engineering, where discoveries are patented and marketed, to a variety of other fields that market courseware and other instructional materials. The entrepreneurial initiatives do not benefit all students equally, nor do they necessarily generate large amounts of external revenue for all institutions, although they sometimes cause institutions to incur serious costs. Commercialization is instituted by many actors, internal and external to colleges and universities, who seek to take advantages of the new opportunities created by the neo-liberal state.

There are three major federal and state initiatives that provide a policy framework for what we call an academic capitalist knowledge/learning regime. The initiatives are: federal student financial aid policy that gives money to students rather than institutions (student as consumer); patent law and policies that marketize segments of the sciences and engineering; copyright law and policies along with information technology law and policies that provide opportunities to market curricula across colleges and universities. The period in which the academic capitalist knowledge/learning regime developed is approximately 1980–2000.

In this chapter, we describe federal and state initiatives that support academic capitalism, then examine the way institutions intersect these initiatives. The presentation of laws and policies is followed by selected examples that symbolize the academic capitalist knowledge/learning regime. We conclude each section by looking at various data sets that allow us to use financial indicators (tuition, income from patents, income from distance education) to track changes.

Although we begin with the federal government, we do not see the federal government as the sole policy driver for the academic capitalist knowledge/learning regime. Federal, state, and institutional laws and policies interact in complex ways to produce knowledge/learning regimes.[2] States have an array of initiatives that promote economic development. Many of these initiatives, ranging from workforce preparation of students to fostering industries that contribute to the states' economic base, feature participation of colleges and universities.[3] Indeed, several states frequently devise innovative solutions to pressing national problems before the federal government.[4] Colleges and universities are not simply acted upon, or "corporatized." There are actors within colleges and universities who participate in creating new knowledge/learning regimes by networking and partnering with an array of external actors. Segments of the administration and segments of the faculty work to shape the politico-legal climate that fosters an academic capitalist knowledge/learning regime, and segments of the faculty and administration actively and ardently engage in commercialization. They are reinforced by judicial decisions, administrative law, executive orders, bureaucratic procedures, and institutional policies at both the state and federal level.

Because this chapter focuses on policy, we want to clarify the theory of the state that informs our work. We see the academic capitalist knowledge/learning regime and the three policy sets on which we focus as tied to the rise of the neo-liberal state. The neo-liberal state focuses not on social welfare for the citizenry as a whole but on enabling individuals and corporations, which in the United States are legally considered as individual persons who are economic actors. The neo-liberal state concentrates funding in state agencies that contribute to economic growth, for example, research funding for corporations and academe. The neo-liberal state works to build the "new" economy, which is a knowledge or information economy. The neo-liberal state attempts to articulate national economies with global economies. To provide funds to re-shape the economy, the neo-liberal state often institutes processes of deregulation, commercialization, and privatization, re-regulating to create a state that no longer provides "entitlements" such as welfare, or that restructures and reduces general services such as health care and social security. The benefits of the neo-liberal state tend be distributed somewhat differently than those of the welfare state. They do not accrue to the citizenry as a whole; instead, they are acquired unevenly by various groups, often by the upper middle class closely associated with the growth of the new economy and by the rich. Because higher education is simultaneously a welfare function of the state and a contributor to economic growth, the policy process often plays out in ironic, contradictory and perhaps unintended ways, which we describe below.

Student Financial Aid

Despite the rhetoric of student as consumer, which implies that all students are able to make informed choices among the many U.S. institutions of higher education, federal student financial aid legislation segments student markets in higher education, directing different types of aid to very different kinds of students.[5] Some programs and appropriation patterns encourage upper middle class as well as knowledgeable, able students from other social strata to attend costly elite, (increasingly) private institutions. Other programs and appropriation patterns encourage large numbers of adult learners to upgrade their education to master skills appropriate to the new economy through two-year and four-year programs, sometimes with substantial distance education components, and often through for-profit higher education.

In the early seventies, federal legislation shifted from institutional to student aid, making students consumers.[6] The Committee on Economic Development, together with a number of foundations, particularly the Carnegie, worked assiduously for marketization of higher education. The mechanism of marketization was federal financial aid placed in the hands of students. When students were able to spend their grants at the institution of their choice, proponents of what was perhaps the first educational voucher program argued that they were introducing market discipline to institutions of higher education, forcing colleges and universities to provide better services at lower costs to attract students. The Committee on Economic Development and Carnegie also pushed strongly for all postsecondary students, whether enrolled in public or private institutions, to pay for one-third to one-half of the costs of their education, a not unrealistic expectation in what was then a low-tuition era.[7]

However, student choice in this context preferred private colleges and universities because the (public) grants for students attending private nonprofit schools were larger than to students attending publics. In other words, students received government assistance to attend more costly private institutions, while students who attended public institutions had to pay more as the cost of tuition gradually rose to one-third to one-half the cost of education. The market model of higher education encouraged competition, but did not reduce costs, a phenomenon that was in keeping with the philosophy of the neoliberal state, which sought to reduce programs for all citizens and shift costs to users. Of course, increasing tuition so that students bore a greater share of the cost of public higher education reduced the cost to the state, always an interest of taxpaying businesses. By the eighties and nineties, higher education was construed less as a necessary public or social good and more as an individual or private good, justifying "user pays" policies.[8]

Federal policy supported quasi-market competition for students among institutions of higher education on the grounds of greater efficiencies that would lead to cost reductions. Ironically, as the market model became entrenched, costs escalated.[9] Although costs went up in all market segments, niche markets developed in which a small number of (largely upper- and upper-middle-class) students competed nationally for ever more expensive places at a relatively small number of (elite and increasingly private) institutions. Federal loan programs enabled middle- and upper-middle-class students, especially those attending high cost elite private institutions, to meet higher tuition costs. In effect, federal loans subsidized markets for students by providing some students the funds to choose high tuition institutions.[10]

As the shift from grants to loans benefited those families and students with the ability to repay, so some programs in the Taxpayer

Relief Act of 1997 benefited families with money to protect. The Tax-payer Relief Act included several programs: Hope scholarships, the tax credit for lifelong learning, tax-sheltered college savings accounts, and penalty free IRA withdrawals for college expenses. The Hope scholarship provided a $1,500 nonrefundable tax credit for the first two years of college that phases out for individuals earning $40,000–$50,000 per year or couples earning $80,000–$100,000 per year. The penalty-free IRA withdrawals do not count withdrawals from IRA accounts as gross income so long as they pay for college expenses. Additionally, families may shelter up to $500 per year for each child in the same way as an IRA; these savings are taxed as an IRA, so long as the funds are spent on college expenses. This program was capped for families earning $150,000–$160,000 per year. The subsidies provided by tax credits are not trivial. "The package of tax credits and tax deductions has been estimated to cost $39 billion in the first five years, making it slightly larger than the Pell Grant program, the primary federal grant program for low income youth." [11] The increased ability of these well-to-do and/or market knowledgeable and academically able students to pay makes them preferred customers for elite institutions.

The 1997 Taxpayer Relief Act applied primarily to nonprofit institutions of higher education, whether public or private. However, some programs within the Taxpayer Relief Act benefited working adults seeking further education to better compete in the new economy. The tax credit for lifelong learning offered a nonrefundable tax credit for undergraduate and graduate education that was worth up to 29 percent of up to $5,000 per year spent on tuition and fees through 2002, and 20 percent of up to $10,000 per year after that, with the same caps as the Hope. The tax credit for lifelong learning expanded markets for for-profits, like the University of Phoenix, which for a number of years required attending students to have jobs. The tax credit created opportunities for increasing numbers of public institutions, such as the University of Maryland University College, that emulated for-profits by serving working adults retooling for the new economy. As all students paid a greater share of the cost of their tuition and fees, the costs to working adults who returned to school to improve their position in the new economy were normalized, even though those students paid a greater share of their income for tuition than did well-to-do traditional age students. [12]

The 1998 Higher Education Act further contributed to marketization through new provisions that encouraged profit taking in higher education by creating a number of special provisions to aid for-profit higher education. The law made it easier for for-profit higher education to appeal federal penalties stemming from their students' defaults on loans. Given that for-profits have an excessively high default rate, this was an important provision. Additionally, the law no longer required unannounced accreditation visits, allowing for-profit postsecondary education to prepare for inspections, making sure students were in class. Most importantly, the law no longer treated for-profits as a separate category; they were redefined as institutions of higher education. This allowed for-profits to share in federal aid. Their students were twice as likely to receive federal aid as students at nonprofits, and at the two-year level, their students received more federal aid than comparable students in public institutions. The 1998 Higher Education Act further signaled federal government support for for-profits by creating a special liaison within the Department of Education for proprietary schools, a privilege previously held only by historically black tertiary education institutions and community colleges.[13]

Currently, for-profits are lobbying to change financial aid requirements that call for institutions to register their students for at least twelve hours of instruction, offer less than 50 percent of their courses via distance education, and prohibit bonuses or incentives to admissions officers for enrolling students.[14] For-profits are also asking the Department of Education to revise rules that require 10 percent of for-profits' revenues to be other than federal aid; in other words, for-profits envision themselves as able to run on students' Pell grants and loans alone.

Changes in student aid legislation over the past thirty years contributed to the academic capitalist knowledge/learning regime by marketizing higher education. The legislation made students (partially) state subsidized consumers in quasi-markets for higher education. According to the rhetoric surrounding marketization, markets empowered students by making them consumers through allowing them to use their grant or loan to discipline markets to better serve them. However, markets in higher education seem to work like all other markets. Far from being perfectly competitive,[15] offering goods and services at the lowest price to any buyer, (deregulated and reregulated) markets tend to favor the middle and upper middle class. Just as housing markets prefer middle-class customers with high credit

ratings who are unlikely to be loan risks, and then indirectly subsidize them through mortgage tax deductions, so markets in higher
education prefer students (and families) who are confident they can
repay loans and are indirectly subsidized through parental tax relief
and higher grant/loan aid attached to private institutions. Ironically,
market legislation, which defined higher education as a private benefit captured by individuals, prefers the middle and upper middle class.

Student aid legislation also contributed to market segmentation.
While middle- and upper-middle-class students became preferred customers, lower-middle-class students and working adults entered two-
year colleges, four-year college programs with substantial distance
education components, and for-profit institutions of higher education. Given that many do not complete at two-year colleges, they receive just-in-time education that channels them into entry-level jobs
in the new economy with a modicum of skills. Working adults in four-
year programs often receive college degrees for what amounts to re-
training or professional development, allowing them to upgrade skills
to better serve the needs of the new economy corporations where they
are already employed. Although these students do not receive dramatic returns on their investment in human capital, they are often
satisfied with their education because they do better than if they had
not acquired some college education or a degree.

Since the early eighties, the cost of college has been rising steadily.
In constant (1996) dollars, the average tuition of U.S. four-year public institutions has increased by nearly 128 percent between 1980
and 2002. Private four-year institutions' tuitions have increased even
more, more than 130 percent in constant dollars over the twenty-two-
year period.[16] In 2002, at four-year private institutions, tuition and
fees averaged $18,273 and room and board averaged $6,779: when tuition and fees and room and board are combined, the average cost of
attending a private college or university was $25,052. For a four-year
public college or university the average 2002 costs were $4,081 for tu-
ition and fees and $5,327 for room and board: combined, the average
cost was $9,408.[17]

As the costs of higher education increased, federal financial aid in
the form of grants lagged behind and the share of family income required to pay for college and tuition has increased for most families.
However, federal grants to pay students' tuition decreased over the
period, while loans increased. In 1981, loans accounted for 45 percent of student federal financial aid and grants for 52 percent. In

2000, loans represented 58 percent of federal student financial aid and grants 41 percent.[18] This change, which accelerated dramatically in the nineties, shifted costs from the state to the student.

At the same time that nonprofit higher education institutions raised their tuition, targeting student niche markets, for-profit institutions multiplied. Enrollment in for-profit degree-granting institutions increased 52 percent between 1995 and 2000.[19] Students at for-profit postsecondary institutions receive federal student financial aid and loans. The majority of students enrolled in for-profits attend short-term vocational training or certificate programs. Even though the majority of for-profits do not compete directly with two- and four-year nonprofit institutions of higher education for the "market" in students, the rapid increase in for-profit higher education is a marker of the commercialization of higher education.

Market practices are increasingly incorporated in recruitment of students in four-year, nonprofit institutions. It is not just highly able students that colleges and universities are targeting, but well-to-do students whose parents can afford to pay full tuition with no financial aid. As McPherson and Shapiro put it with regard to private colleges and universities: "The simplest way to describe the change over the past decade in the way private colleges and universities approach student aid is to say that, rather than viewing student aid as a kind of charitable operation the college runs on the side, most private colleges and universities — and increasing numbers of public institutions — now regard student aid as a vital revenue management and enrollment management tool."[20]

As one commentator has suggested, "In some ways, American colleges and universities have become like airlines and hotels, practicing 'yield management' to try to maximize the revenue generated by every seat or bed. But in most cases, unlike hotels and airlines, colleges also care about who is in those seats and beds."[21] To that end, institutions develop early decision admissions policies, no-test admission policies, and on-site admissions policies, all of which are aimed at increasing their "yield" rates. Yield rates are the ratio of students who apply to those that accept. The higher the acceptance rate, the higher the rating in publications, such as *U.S. News and World Report,* that raise the market value of institutions.

Early decision admissions processes are employed by highly selective private colleges and universities. Students commit to enrolling in an institution if they are accepted in return for which they are notified earlier than those who apply to the regular process. Such a practice increases the institution's yield rate, ensuring an almost one-to-one ratio of admitted students to those who will enroll. That enables the institution to increase its yield, and thereby enhance its market position. Yet, early decision programs may not serve the interests of prospective students, or of society. In forcing earlier and earlier decisions that may not be freely informed by a range of options, they represent a case of inherent market inefficiency, of what Roth and Xiaolin[22] have referred to as "unraveling." Such a system may tend to disadvantage students who have less access to good counseling and less knowledge of the admissions process, characteristics that disproportionately describe students from lower socioeconomic backgrounds. Indeed, these programs tend to undermine efforts to enhance the demographic diversity of entering classes, a fact that led the University of North Carolina, Chapel Hill, to eliminate its program, and Richard Levin, president of Yale, to call in 2001 for the collective abandonment of such programs among selective institutions. This call has yet gone unheeded, including at Yale.[23]

A second example of institutions seeking to manipulate their selectivity scores in ways that do not serve consumer interests is the recent practice of several selective colleges to make SAT scores optional for applicants. The strategy's effectiveness has been documented by Yablon in an article entitled, "Test Flight: The Scam behind SAT Bashing."[24] The aim is to enhance a school's acceptance rate and average SAT score by making the scores optional. Less qualified students are encouraged apply, but only high scoring students are likely to submit their test scores to institutions, raising the overall selectivity profile of the institution.

"Snap apps" are another marketing tool of enrollment management offices seeking to achieve high yields. On-site admissions is an in-person, instant admissions decision program, often made during the prospective students' campus visit. In contrast to the early decision process, the decisions are not binding; the student may decide not to attend the institution. Advocates of the process see it as "a service to students and a savvy marketing tool."[25] Instant admissions benefits students, reducing the paperwork, time, and anxiety of the admissions process, and humanizing it. However, this admissions program is more typically found at less selective institutions (for example, at California State Universities versus Universities of California, at Virginia Tech and Radford University versus the University of Virginia, and at many community colleges). By employing this process such institutions are more likely to gain access to higher achieving students, who are more likely to apply for instant admissions. Therein lies part of the problem, say critics of "snap apps." Institutions accelerate admissions, leading students to make decisions on the spur of the moment. Making the choice easier and more immediate for prospective students in some sense restricts their choice (though not in a legal sense). It reduces the likelihood of prospective students shopping for colleges and exploring options that might prove to be a better fit. On-site admissions can be seen as a "hard sell" approach to recruiting students, leading students to make their decisions during their campus visit, rather than encouraging them to reflect on and deliberate about their options over time.

The federal student aid legislation was the first federal legislation to explicitly use market discourse. In some ways the market rhetoric was a trope for partial privatization in that the neo-liberal state moved to a high-tuition, low-aid position.[26] In other ways, the market rhetoric masked the continued and rising contribution by the state. Although federal financial aid has shifted from grants to loans, the amount of grant money available (although not the amount of the grant per individual) has risen every year and the loans are publicly subsidized. At the state level, support for higher education increased 13 percent (in constant dollars) from 1980 to 1998, but tuition increased faster. In other words, both the student markets for nonprofits and for-profits are heavily subsidized at both the state and federal level.

Federal and state student financial aid policy followed the general direction of neo-liberal policy, moving away from treating public benefits as social goods for the citizenry as a whole and toward making the user pay more. Public funds were shifted toward production functions by making aid available for working adults re-educating themselves for knowledge economy jobs. That well-to-do users paid (relatively) less than other users also reflected trends characteristic of the new economy and the neo-liberal state.

Patents

Before the Bayh-Dole Act (1980), federal policy placed discoveries made with federal grant funds in the public domain. Universities were able to secure patents on federally funded research only when the federal government, through a long and cumbersome application process, granted special approval. Only a small number of universities engaged in patenting before 1980.[27] The Bayh-Dole Act directly signaled the inclusion of universities in profit taking. It allowed universities and small businesses to retain title to inventions made with federal research and development monies. In the words of the Congress, "It is the policy and objective of the Congress . . . to promote collaboration between commercial concerns and nonprofit organizations, including universities."[28] Bayh-Dole "explicitly recognized technology transfer to the private sector as a desirable outcome of federally financed research, and endorsed the principle that exclusive licensing of publicly funded technology was sometimes necessary to achieve that objective."[29]

Bayh-Dole shifted the relationship between university managers and faculty in several important ways. As potential patent holders, university trustees and administrators could see all research generated by faculty as relatively easily protected intellectual property. Faculty too could better conceptualize their discoveries as products or processes, private, valuable, licensable, not necessarily as knowledge to share publicly with a community of scholars.[30] The Bayh-Dole Act gave new and concrete meaning to the phrase "commodification of knowledge." The act streamlined universities' participation in the marketplace.

The main objective of Bayh-Dole was support for small businesses, which the Reagan administration had deemed engines of economic growth. In 1983, however, Reagan extended Bayh-Dole's coverage to large corporations through executive order. After 1983, any entity performing federal R&D could patent and own discoveries made in the course of research, a shift that contributed to the privatization and commercialization of research across all categories of performers, including large corporations.

The Federal Courts Improvements Act (1982) created a new court of appeals for the federal circuit (CAFC), which handled patent appeals from district courts, thereby ending "forum shopping" in intellectual property cases, creating a more uniform approach to patents. The new court led the way for a greatly strengthened approach to intellectual property. "Before 1980, a district court finding that a patent was valid and infringed was upheld on appeal 62% of the time; between 1982 and 1990 this percentage rose to 90%."[31] The CAFC led the patent office to offer broader protections through patents. "There are now patents for genetically engineered bacteria, genetically altered mice, particular gene sequences, surgical methods, computer software, financial products, and methods for conducting auctions on the World Wide Web. For each of these, there would have been before 1980 at least serious doubt as to whether or not they would be deemed by the PTO and the courts to fall within the realm of patentable subject matter."[32]

University administrators and faculty members were well aware that strengthened intellectual property protection made patentable knowledge more valuable. The Small Business Innovation Development Act (1982) mandated that federal agencies with annual expenditures of more than $100 million devote 1.25 percent of their budgets to research performed by small businesses, on the grounds that they were critical to economic recovery. Universities strongly opposed this legislation, making the case that it diverted the mission agencies from funding university research.[33] Ironically, as universities became more deeply involved in academic capitalism, they increasingly took equity positions in small enterprises started by their faculty, often with funding provided by the Small Business Innovation Development Act.[34]

Equity deals did not occur frequently among research universities until the eighties. The number of equity deals spread among research universities, slowly at first, then, starting in the nineties, quite rapidly. Taking equity positions rather than licensing intellectual property and receiving royalties became a market strategy for research universities. According to Feldman, Feller, Bercovitz, and Burton,[35] equity provides three advantages over licensing: first, equity gives universities options or financial claims on companies' future income; second, equity deals align interests of university and firm with regard to rapid commercialization of technology; third, equity signals interested investors about the worth of the technology. These scholars attribute the rapid growth of universities taking equity positions to organizational learning through technology transfer offices.

In 2002, Feldman, Feller, Bercovitz, and Burton surveyed sixty-seven Carnegie I and II research universities that had active technology transfer operations. Of these institutions, 76 percent had taken equity in a company, and altogether had participated in 679 equity deals. Public universities appeared to make greater use of equity when compared to their private research university cohorts. Public universities took more equity in companies than private universities even though thirteen of the public universities (19% of the total sample) were prohibited by state laws from holding equity in companies. Ten of these public universities were able to circumvent state statutes by forming independent entities (501[c]3s), usually research foundations or other intermediary institutions, that were able to take equity in corporations based on faculty intellectual property. Although the study does not deal with which set of universities, public or private, initiated the first equity deals, this market strategy spread rapidly between both sets of universities, even more rapidly among the public than the private, despite the barriers to public institutions taking equity. However, both sets of institutions adopted the same strategies geared to increasing external revenue streams.

During the eighties, as universities' intellectual property activity and potential grew, state systems and/or universities and colleges initiated or began to develop and change their patent property policies. They moved from minimal policies to more expansive policies, some of which dramatically changed the way intellectual property is handled. The following data, which illustrates current practices, is drawn from a study of eighteen colleges and universities, both public and private, in six states, and addresses royalty splits, categories of persons covered by policies, exceptions to the policies, and conflict of interest.[36]

Royalties

The various patent policies offered a wide range of royalty splits among faculty, department and/or college, and university. All were sufficient to provide strong incentives to patent. The greatest incentives were for the faculty, who were able to put the income in their bank accounts, as compared to all others, who had to use the revenue stream generated by patents for institutional purposes. The policies most generous to faculty split royalties with faculty fifty-fifty. At the bottom of the range of royalty splits, faculty received one-third of the royalty income. Private universities tended to be less generous than public, with many offering faculty one-third of the income from their licenses. When policies were changed over time, they usually gave faculty a lower percentage of royalties.

Personnel Coverage

Categories of persons covered by patent policies were elaborated by many state system or college and university policies over the years. In the seventies and eighties, a number of patent policies covered only "inventors." By the mid-nineties, they included faculty, staff, graduate students, post-doctoral fellows, non-employees who participate in university research projects, visiting faculty and, in a very few policies, undergraduates.

Exceptions

Universities had long claimed ownership of discoveries made by faculty; the decisive court cases were heard in the fifties. However, initially, there were exceptions to universities' ownership claims to intellectual property patented by faculty. If faculty made the discoveries on their own time, using their own resources, and not availing themselves of university facilities, they could claim a patent for themselves — for example, if they invented something in the summer, in their garage workroom. As the academic capitalist knowledge/learning regime developed, definitions of time, resources and facilities uses were specified to the point where it was very difficult for faculty to assert any claims. For example, several policies had guidelines that indicated that if researchers depended on anything other than routinely available office equipment and commercially available software or library materials generally available in non-university locations, they were making substantial use of university resources.

Initially, state system and institutional policies addressed only patents. Over the years, forms of intellectual property covered multiplied. Among those included were licensing income, milestone payments, equity interest, mask work (which charted the topography of a semiconductor chip product), material transfer agreements, tangible property (cell lines, software, compositions of matter), and trade secrets.

Managerial Capacity

System and institutional patent policies delineated academic capitalism practices that greatly expanded market managerial capacity in colleges and universities. The new functions were many: surveilling institutional employees' intellectual property activity to ensure capture by the system or institution; reviewing and evaluating faculty disclosures; technology licensing; supervision of royalty flows, including distribution of funds within institutions; reinvestment of funds in new market activities; litigation to defend intellectual prop-

erty; evaluation of intellectual property for institutional equity investments; monitoring and occasionally administering corporations
in which the institution held equity; overseeing initial public offerings (IPOs); developing and monitoring market activity for conflict of
interest issues. As colleges and universities become more involved in
academic capitalism, they hired more managerial professional staff.
Expanded managerial capacity institutionalized business activity in
colleges and universities by allowing segments to directly engage the
market.

The multiple forms of market activity pursued by universities together with faculty's close involvement in them created many opportunities for conflict of interest. Factors that increased the possibilities
of conflict of interest for faculty were: increased magnitude of personal compensation; growing numbers of financial relationships between a creator and a company; greater commitment of a faculty's
time to a company; faculty or administrators holding equity in a company; involvement of trainees or students in a company; and involvement of patients or human subjects in company research trials. In
other words, the risk of conflict of interest increased the more closely
faculty members or creators were involved with market activity. Yet
intellectual property policies continue to aggressively promote close
involvement of faculty with the market.

A dramatic example of university patenting and licensing is provided by OncoMouse, a genetically engineered animal that reliably
reproduces characteristics of various human cancers. It was created
in Harvard Medical School laboratories in the early eighties through
manipulation of cancer causing genes. OncoMouse was patented by
Harvard and licensed by DuPont for sale as a research tool. The patent was contested by a number of groups opposed to the patenting
of living organisms, but the patent was upheld by the U.S. Supreme
Court.[37]

The mouse/research tool quickly became the standard in global
cancer research that focused on the ways in which cancers develop
and tested new treatments for breast, prostate and other forms of
cancer. The cost of the mouse created access problems for some researchers. In 2001, DuPont, Harvard, and the National Institutes of
Health signed an agreement that made the mouse more readily available to university researchers. However, DuPont will not allow the
mouse/research tool to breed nor to be used in industry supported research. Many groups, for example breast cancer activists, think these

restraints retard the development of broad understanding of cancers and treatments for them. They argue that the mouse/tool was developed in large part with public research funds and should not be privately owned. Rather, it should be freely available to all researchers.[38]

Although patents are concentrated in biology and engineering fields, they are increasingly being granted in other areas. For example, Carnegie Mellon University developed a series of Cognitive Tutor products that were licensed to Carnegie Learning, a company which spun out of the university in 1998. The instructional math software is based on artificial intelligence, integrating technology and print curricula into realistic problem situations. The company claims that minority and nonminority students using the program perform at a much higher level in classes as well as improve SAT scores.[39]

Before 1981, fewer than 250 patents were issued to universities per year. Between fiscal year 1991 and fiscal year 1999, annual college and university invention disclosures increased 63 percent (to 12,324). New patents filed increased 77 percent (to 5,545) and new licenses and options executed by universities increased by 129 percent (to 3,914).[40] Since 1980, at least 3,807 new companies have been formed based on a license from an academic institution, including the 494 established in fiscal year 2001. At the end of 2001, 159 institutions reported 2,514 start-ups were still operating. Colleges and universities received an equity interest in 70 percent of their start-ups in fiscal year 2001, compared to 56 percent in fiscal year 2000. In FY 2001, adjusted gross license income was $1.071 billion, and running royalties on product sales were $845 million.[41]

While technology transfer brings external revenue to colleges and universities, it also takes funds from them. Colleges and universities or state systems had to pay for legal fees and for technology transfer offices. In 2001, legal fees were $161 million. The magnitude of nonreimbursed legal fees has increased about 250 percent over the eleven years that ATUM has surveyed technology transfer activities. ATUM makes the case that about 40 percent of these costs are reimbursed through the legal process. However, these costs could be substantially higher, since ATUM explicitly modified its definition of legal fees in 1999, omitting major litigation to better focus on benchmarking patent prosecution costs.

In the eighties, many smaller universities and colleges received patents; the 100 largest universities had only 82 percent of all patents. However, that trend was reversed in the nineties, and the one hundred largest universities received more than 90 percent of all patents awarded. Income from patents was also concentrated in the top one hundred.[42]

Patents dramatically illustrate the growth of the academic capitalist knowledge/learning regime. Patents, licensing and running royalties, start-up companies and universities' holding of equity positions in corporations built on faculty patents are not marketlike behaviors: they are market behaviors that involve nonprofit institutions in profit taking. Yet colleges and universities are not market entities because they are chartered differently than corporations and they do not disburse profits to shareholders. Instead, funds from external market revenues are put back into the institutions. In some ways, colleges and universities that patent are able to cross the traditional borders between public and private, engaging in practices that best meet their needs for generating external revenues. If patenting, which is expensive, fails to lead to licenses and royalties, the state bears the cost in the case of public institutions. Similarly, the start-up corporations initiated by universities are in many ways a form of state subsidized capitalism, although there are few penalties for failure. Income from royalties and licenses are tax free, so long as the profits are returned to the university, and even if the profits are earmarked for further development of technology transfer. Public universities try to defend their patents by invoking the Eleventh Amendment. Although patenting and technology transfer is generally portrayed as a win-win endeavor, a relatively small number of large research universities are the only ones to generate substantial external revenues. For many smaller colleges and universities, the cost of maintaining a technology transfer office exceeds any revenues.[43]

Copyrights

In the eighties, many universities became involved in patenting. In the late eighties and nineties, many universities developed copyright policies. In the nineties, new copyright legislation was enacted as digital technologies and telecommunications grew rapidly. The new laws strongly emphasized protection of digital forms of creative expression, including new forms of intellectual property such as courseware, multimedia, electronic databases, and tele-immersion. Changes in the copyright law opened up opportunities for academic capitalism in areas other than physical and life sciences, which had been the primary fields involved in the patent phase of the academic capitalism knowledge regime. Faculty from all fields were involved with copyright because copyright applied to student instructional materials, making academic capitalism not just a knowledge regime but also a knowledge/learning regime.

The Telecommunications Act of 1996 dramatically altered the industry regulatory framework. Before 1996, the 1934 Communications Act, as implemented through the Federal Communications Commission, authorized separate monopolies: broadcast, cable, wire, wireless, and satellite. The 1996 Telecommunications Act deregulated these various industries, creating a competitive climate that favored growth of the Internet, World Wide Web, and e-business, all of which utilized previously separated communications media in new patterns. Deregulation of telecommunications created numerous possibilities for an academic capitalism knowledge/learning regime, ranging from software to distance education.

The Digital Millennium Copyright Act (DMCA) of 1998 protects digital property by prohibiting unauthorized access to a copyrighted work as well as unauthorized copying of a copyrighted work. The DMCA is far-reaching and covers an array of technologies, from web casting to hyperlinks, online directories, search engines, and the content of the materials made available by these technologies. Not only are citizens (and students) penalized for unauthorized access, devices and services that circumvent copyright are also prohibited. The law very deliberately seeks to develop electronic commerce and associated technologies by strengthening protections of all forms of digital property. There are some exceptions, the broadest being for law enforcement and intelligence. The other exceptions are quite narrow.

The DMCA has a special section on distance education. Generally, the DMCA seems to take the position that purchasing or licensing digital materials should be a cost born by distance educators, as is the case with hardware and software. Currently, exemptions for educational use of digital products are only for traditional classrooms that offer "systematic instructional activity by a nonprofit educational institution or governmental body" or for students who are in situations that make them unable to access such classrooms (Copyright Office 1999). In other words, there is no exemption for distance education networks not tied into conventional instruction. Fair use offers an exemption that might apply to distance education, but there is not yet a body of case law that clarifies how this would work. Moreover, if a U.S. educational institution transmits courses to students in other countries, the law is not clear as to which will apply, U.S. law or the law of the country receiving the transmission.

As it currently stands, the DMCA offers traditional colleges and universities an advantage in developing distance education. For the time being, they are best able to make use of such educational exemptions as exist because of the physical classroom requirement. They also benefit because for-profit distance education organizations are currently unable to access federal financial aid for their students. (However, the Department of Education has provisionally agreed to a change in these regulations, which will provide federal aid for students taking for-profit distance education courses.) Traditional colleges and universities have every incentive to try to capture a sizable market share of distance education before for-profit competition explodes.

The Technology, Education and Copyright Harmonization (TEACH) Act was passed in 2002. TEACH attempted to modify provisions of the DMCA that constrained the delivery of distance education. TEACH allows educators greater freedom than that provided by the DMCA with regard to copyrighted materials. For example, the new law allows display and performance of most works, unlike the DMCA, which limited broad classes of work, particularly those that had entertainment as well as instructional value. DMCA confined free use of copyrighted materials to classrooms; TEACH allows institutions to reach students through distance education at any location. Unlike DMCA, TEACH also lets students retain material for a short time. Further, TEACH permits digitization of analog works, but only if the work is not available in digital form.[44]

However, TEACH also has many restrictions. Copyrighted material used in distance education must: be part of "systematic mediated instructional activity"; be supervised by an instructor; be directly related to the teaching plan; be technologically limited (protected) to enrolled students; provide information about copyright protections attached to the works. The works may not be retained by students and dissemination cannot interfere with technological protections embedded in the works.[45] TEACH assigns responsibility for monitoring and policing copyright to universities, steering universities in the direction of developing copyright policies, disseminating them, and staffing copyright offices. The Act applies only to accredited nonprofit institutions, which must institute copyright policies that provide informational materials about copyright to faculty, students, and staff. Generally, the TEACH provisions are designed to permit use of digitized products and processes in distance education, but protect the material and property of copyright holders, especially for commercial developers of educational materials.

As was the case with patent policies, copyright policies moved from minimal policies to more expansive policies, some of which dramatically changed the way intellectual property is handled. The following data, which illustrates current copyright practices, is drawn from the same study of eighteen colleges and universities, both public and private, in the same six states that we used for the patent policies. As with patents, we look at the way copyright policies address royalty splits, categories of persons covered by policies, and exceptions to the policies.[46]

Institutional claims to faculty's copyrighted materials are different than institutional claims to patents. Historically, many faculty published and held copyright to scholarly and artistic materials, including instructional materials, which they created in the course of their employment at colleges and universities. They contracted with a variety of commercial publishing houses to produce and distribute their works. However, the stakes in scholarly publishing, with the exception of textbooks, were relatively small, and institutions were not interested in them. As our analysis of copyright policies demonstrates, this seems to be changing as increased use of information technology mediates instruction. Institutions are aggressively advancing claims to shares of faculty intellectual property in copyright, beginning with technology-mediated products. This is a sharp break with the past and potentially affects all faculty, regardless of field or institutional type.

Generally, our argument is that universities and colleges have initiated aggressive pursuit of external revenues based on instruction and curriculum, and a number of faculty have cooperated, participating in the commercialization of instructional materials. State system and institutional copyright policies were very often introduced after patent policies, and are substantively different than patent policies, following their own legal and product trajectories. We make the argument that knowledge in the public domain is increasingly being treated as raw material, which can be transformed into products sold for (potential) private profit or generate external revenues for colleges and universities. Over time, there is no case in which the intellectual products covered in the policies become less restrictive. Instead, the most comprehensive coverage is found in the most recent policies, providing evidence of institutions' increasingly expansive claims to copyrightable works.

Royalties

There is substantial variation among institutions on copyright royalties, with faculty's share of royalties ranging from a high of 75 percent to a low of 33 percent. Still, the shares accorded to faculty at all institutions are generous. In contrast, none of the institutions give the growing numbers of non-faculty employees involved in creating educational materials—for example, academic professionals who create web pages or course materials—any shares in royalties.

Personnel Coverage

As with patent policies, the categories of coverage in copyright policies also expanded over time. Copyright policies cover not only faculty and part-time faculty, but also a wide range of other categories of people: full-time and part-time faculty, classified staff, student employees, appointed personnel, graduate assistants and teaching associates, persons with "no salary" appointments, and visiting faculty and academic professionals. Even faculty who are employed at other institutions who work on research projects at institutions with aggressive patent policies are included in the coverage. However, there are a few cases in which coverage has not expanded. For example, only faculty are covered by the copyright and computer software policy at several institutions. There are also cases in which the expansiveness of policies is extraordinary in regard to students. For example, one institution's policy stated that not only were students using substantial university resources or those employed by the university covered by the policy but also any student not employed by the university who created copyrightable intellectual property was covered. Faculty using such volunteer, non-employed students in their scholarly work projects were requested to have students sign a form that gave ownership of the property to this university.

Exceptions

Historically, universities and colleges excepted faculty creative works from institutional ownership, and advanced claims to faculty's copyrightable intellectual products only under certain conditions. One condition was when a work produced by faculty was specified as "work for hire." The other was when faculty work that was copyrighted was specified as "within the scope of employment." This language reversed universities' traditional position with regard to faculty's copyrightable intellectual property, and enables colleges and universities to claim the material created by faculty. In their study of research universities, Lape[47] and Packard[48] noted the greatly increased number of college and university intellectual property policies have "work for hire" and "within the scope of employment" language, giving institutions a broader claim to property.

Examples of introducing and expanding "work for hire" and "within the scope of employment" language is provided by some universities in our sample. Perhaps the most extreme example is provided by the University of Utah. In 1970, Utah policy held that faculty owned almost all of their copyrighted material, with one important exception: "Notwithstanding any other university policy provision, unless other arrangements are made in writing, all rights to copyrightable material (except material which is placed on video tape using university facilities, supplies and/or equipment) and all financial and other benefits accruing by reason of said copyrightable material shall be reserved to the author, even though employed by the university." The university only claimed rights to ownership when there was a specific contract between the university and a third party, or when the author was specifically hired to do the work. (In the case of videotapes, the university also claimed ownership when its facilities, supplies, and/or equipment had been used, a point we will subsequently explore in discussing "substantial use" language.) In the 2001 revised policy, all faculty intellectual work is declared work for hire: "Works created by University staff and student employees within the scope of their University employment are considered to be works made for hire, and thus are Works as to which the University is the Owner and controls all legal rights in the work." The University agrees to transfer rights to faculty in some cases, such as in the case of "traditional scholarly work," but it claims ownership if materials are produced with the "substantial use" of university resources.

However, in many cases faculty "work for hire" is generally defined fairly narrowly. For example, at the University of Miami it refers only to "a project assigned to members of the faculty" which will be owned by the institution "only if so specified at the time of assignment by an instrument of specific detail and agreement." Similarly, in SUNY's policy, "[faculty] Work for Hire shall mean work done . . . under campus consulting, extra service or technical assistance arrangements either through contract, consultancy or purchase order, but not within the Scope of Employment."

Although work for hire is sometimes defined narrowly for faculty, this is generally not the case for academic professionals. As greater numbers of academic professionals are employed within colleges and universities, and as they become more involved in "production" activities such as the development of copyrightable educational products, institutions not only expand the personnel covered by their policies, they also define these personnel's intellectual products as works for hire. For example, the policy of the University of North Texas reads: "Electronically published course materials created jointly by faculty authors and others, whose contributions would be works for hire, will be jointly owned by the faculty author and the University." In short, managerial professionals have no property rights, and by virtue of their involvement in the educational production processes, universities expand their ownership claims.

While many faculty may be excepted from college and university copyright polices with regard to their creative work, they frequently lose that exception if they make significant use of institutional resources in the creative process. Most policies in the eighteen institutions we studied had language about "use of institutional resources" or "substantial use of institutional resources." As with patents, universities and colleges made the case that faculty use of institutional resources entitled institutional claims to intellectual property. Ironically, the institutional resources used by copyrighting faculty were often information technologies which patenting faculty may have developed and which the institution owned.

Expanded Managerial Capacity

Most of the college and university policies we studied did not develop the equivalent managerial capacity for copyrighted materials as they had for patented discoveries, for example, taking an equity position in corporations based on faculty intellectual property. However, some universities were moving in that direction with regard to copyright. The case of Brigham Young University points to growing internal capacity to commodify education on the part of universities. At Brigham Young, "the Technology Transfer and Creative Works Offices have the responsibility to license or sell the technology or work; or they may sell university developed products to end users when sales and support do not interfere with the normal activities of campus personnel, and when the sale is consistent with the educational mission of the university." If they "deem" the action "consistent with the educational mission and academic purposes of the university" they can approve the creation of an "enterprise center" that will pursue such activity. Brigham Young has a Center for Instructional Design for producing copyrightable works, a Creative Works Office to oversee "the business aspects of commercializing intellectual properties and [managing] copyright issues," and the potential of enterprise centers that will further develop and market copyrightable educational materials.

The policies of other institutions are not so elaborated, but point to some development of managerial capacity for the pursuit of academic capitalism in the realm of educational materials. Overall, it is evident that universities are developing internal, managerial capacity to create and commodify copyrightable educational materials. Such capacity and investment has not only been used to justify more aggressive ownership claims of institutions to such products, it also enables organizational production of materials independent of faculty. In contrast to patenting and technology transfer, colleges and universities can develop and produce copyrightable educational materials without the direct involvement of full-time faculty. Staff who are hired to participate in these production and commercialization activities, whether they are full-time managerial professionals or part-time faculty, generally have no claims to the proceeds of their labors, for their directed labor is regarded as work for hire, entirely within the scope of their employment.

Under many of the copyright policies we have considered, colleges and universities could hire academic professionals to develop curricular materials and part-time faculty to deliver them, and the institution would own the courses. These policies often cover distance education efforts on the part of colleges and universities. Copyright became a significant source of possible institutional revenues as colleges and universities pursued distance education. An example of the success that colleges and universities look to achieve through the management of copyrights is provided by WEB-CT. A computer science professor at the University of British Columbia developed WEB-CT, educational website software that serves as a platform for colleges and universities. The University of British Columbia spun it off as a private corporation, which "entered into production and distribution relationships with Silicon Graphics and Prentice-Hall and fast became a major player in the American as well as Canadian higher education market. By the beginning fall term of 1997, WEB-CT licensees included, in addition to UCLA and California State University, the universities of Georgia, Minnesota, Illinois, North Carolina, and Indiana, and such private institutions as Syracuse, Brandeis, and Duquesne."[49]

The University of Maryland's University College (UMUC) provides a distance education story with an interesting twist in regard to the source of profits from academic capitalism. Although UMUC was designed as a for-profit venture based on private monies, it has succeeded by tapping into state monies from Maryland and federal contracts with the military. UMUC was created with private sector investment, although in recent years it has received tens of millions of dollars in state appropriations—about $10 million in both 1999 and 2000, $15 million in 2001, and $20 million in 2002.[50] Its greatest success has been in securing military funding, to provide education to service men and women around the globe. Most recently, UMUC was awarded a Tri-Services Education contract from the U.S. Army, at a value of $350 million over 10 years. By its own accounts, members of the military accounted for 47,000 enrollments in 2002, of a total of 87,000 for all of UMUC.[51]

UMUC was initially conceived as a profit center for the University of Maryland. It was expected to bring in external revenues for the system as a whole by expanding enrollments, saving through economies of scale and through reduced instructional costs made possible by using digitized materials rather than live faculty. When costs remained high, the state of Maryland increased its contributions, perhaps because clicks and mortar were cheaper than bricks and mortar. However, the largest external revenue stream has been from the federal government, in the form of funding for the education for military services. As in several other examples we have considered, the state, at the level of the several states and the federal government, supplies the lion's share of external revenue for a system designed to tap private external revenue streams.

The networks involved in academic capitalism are extraordinarily complex. In exploring business/higher education connections, most scholars have focused on research activities and on universities.[52] Yet the commodification of education involves a wider range of higher education institutions and activities other than patenting. Copyrighting occurs not only in the sciences and engineering but across all fields in higher education, and holds out the possibility of generation of new sources and forms of higher education.

Conclusion

Over the past twenty-five years, the academic capitalist knowledge/ learning regime was instantiated in higher education. It is not the only knowledge/learning regime. It co-exists uneasily with, for example, both the military/industrial/academic knowledge regime and liberal education learning regime. While the academic capitalist knowledge/learning regime did not replace these other regimes, considerable space was created for it within colleges and universities.

The academic capitalist knowledge/learning regime was not unilaterally imposed on universities by external forces. Actors within colleges and universities worked to intersect opportunities created by the new economy. For example, the states have created an array of new opportunities. In the past five years (1997–2002), approximately half of the states have adjusted their conflict of interest laws so that universities, as represented by administrators, and faculty, as inventors and advisers, can hold equity positions in private corporations even when those corporations do business with universities. Again, these laws were not imposed on passive institutions. Universities often lobbied their state legislators to ensure the conflict of interest laws were changed, as did, for example, Texas A&M.[53] The changing politico-legal climate provided new opportunities for faculty and administrators in an uncertain resource environment.

Federal and state policies enabled colleges and universities to treat students as consumers, stimulated civilian technology policy, and created and (re)regulated the telecommunication infrastructure and product development. Only the 1972 amendments to the Higher Education Act, which created what came to be known as Pell grants, were directed toward postsecondary education. The other legislative initiatives were developed primarily to transform the industrial economy to an information economy, and to articulate the national economy with global markets. Nonetheless, actors and segments of postsecondary institutions, ranging from research universities to community colleges, worked to articulate their departments, programs, and offices with the new economy. Generally, the research and educational products, processes, and programs that they created did not contribute to the welfare of their institutions as a whole but expanded opportunities for the actors and segments of institutions able and willing to intersect with the new economy. As a result, some segments of the colleges and universities—enrollment management offices within student personnel services, programs within the life sciences and engineering that patent, and departments and programs throughout the university that manage copyrights that intersect telecommunication educational initiatives—are prospering, while many others are not. Large numbers of students served or enrolled in departments or colleges and schools do not necessarily relate to how units fare within postsecondary institutions.

NOTES

1. Sheila Slaughter and Gary Rhoades, *Academic Capitalism and the New Economy* (Baltimore: Johns Hopkins University Press, 2004).

2. Sheila Slaughter and Gary Rhoades, "Changes in Intellectual Property Statutes and Policies at a Public University: Revising the Terms of Professional Labor," *Higher Education* 26 (1993): 287–312; Sheila Slaughter and Gary Rhoades, "The Emergence of a Competitiveness Research and Development Policy Coalition and the Commercialization of Academic Science and Technology," *Science, Technology, and Human Value* 21, no. 3 (Summer): 303–39.

3. Andrew M. Isserman, "State Economic Development Policy and Practice in the United States: A Durvey Article," *International Regional Science Review* 16, nos. 1, 2 (1994): 49–110; Peter K Esinger, *The Rise of the Entrepreneurial State: State and Local Economic Development Policy in the United States* (Madison: University of Wisconsin Press, 1988).

4. David E. Osborne, *Laboratories of Democracy* (Boston: Harvard Business School Press, 1988).

5. Generally, the states that have greatly increased their student aid programs, have increased merit scholarships, which tend to benefit the well-to-do. In other words, state policies have generally followed much the same direction as federal. See Donald E. Heller, *The States and Public Higher Edu-*

cation Policy: Affordability, Access and Accountability (Baltimore: Johns Hopkins University Press, 2000).

6. Lawrence E. Gladieux and Thomas R. Wolanin, *Congress and the Colleges: The National Politics of Higher Education* (Lexington, MA: Lexington Books, 1976).

7. Committee for Economic Development, "A Strategy for Better-Targeted and Increased Financial Support," in *ASHE Reader in Finance in Higher Education*, ed. David W. Breneman, Larry L. Leslie, and Richard E. Anderson (Needham, MA: Simon and Schuster, 1996), 61–68.

8. Larry L. Leslie and Paul Brinkman, *The Economic Value of Higher Education* (New York: ACE/Macmillan, 1988).

9. Ronald G. Ehrenberg, *Tuition Rising: Why College Costs So Much* (Cambridge, MA: Harvard University Press, 2000).

10. The Middle Income Assistance Act of 1978 provided grant aid to a greater number of middle-income students and took the $25,000 limit off the Guaranteed Student Loan. The Middle Income Assistance Act was an anomalous moment in student financial aid's movement toward a greater reliance on loans, and by the eighties it proved too broad a welfare benefit for the neoliberal state. For details see James C. Hearn, "The Growing Loan Orientation in Federal Financial Aid Policy," in *ASHE Reader on Finance in Higher Education*, ed. J. Yeager, G. Nelson, E. Potter, J. Weidman, and T. Zullo (Boston: Pearson, 1998).

11. Thomas Kane, 1999, *How We Pay for College in the Price of Admission* (Washington, D.C.: Brookings Institution Press), 11.

12. Donald E. Heller, *The States and Public Higher Education Policy: Affordability, Access and Accountability* (Baltimore: Johns Hopkins University Press, 2000).

13. Michael S. McPherson and Morton O. Shapiro, *The Student Aid Game: Meeting Need and Rewarding Talent in American Higher Education* (Princeton, NJ: Princeton University Press, 1998).

14. Ibid.

15. Larry L. Leslie and Gary Johnson, "The Market Model and Higher Education," *Journal of Higher Education* 45 (1974): 1–20.

16. DePaul University, *National and Regional Trends in College Tuition*, www.oipr.depaul.edu/scripts/sir/pricing/2001/report.asp.

17. College Board, "$90 Billion Available in Student Financial Aid, with Scholarship Growth Outpacing Loan Growth," *College Board News*, 2002, www.collegeboard.com/press/article/0,3183,18420,00.html.

18. National Center for Public Policy and Higher Education, *Losing Ground: A National Status Report on the Affordability of American Higher Education, 2002,* www.highereducation.org/.

19. IPEDS Postsecondary Institutions in the United States: Fall 2001 and

Degrees and Other Awards Conferred: 2000–2001, Enrollment Survey, Vocational Education, www.nces.ed.gov/ipeds/.

20. Michael S. McPherson and Morton O. Shapiro, *The Student Aid Game: Meeting Need and Rewarding Talent in American Higher Education* (Princeton, NJ: Princeton University Press, 1998), 15–16.

21. A. B. Crenshaw, "Price Wars on Campus: Colleges Use Discounts to Draw Best Mix of Top Students, Paying Customers," *Washington Post,* October 5, 2002, A1.

22. A. E. Roth and X. Xiaolin, "Jumping the Gun: Imperfections and Institutions Relating to the Timing of Market Transactions," *American Economic Review,* 84 (1994): 992–1044.

23. C. Flores, "U. of North Carolina at Chapel Hill Drops Early-Decision Admissions," *Chronicle of Higher Education,* May 3, 2002, A38.

24. M. Yablon, "Test Flight: The Scam Behind SAT bashing," *New Republic,* October 30, 2001, 24–25.

25. E. Hoover, "Instant Gratification: On-site Admissions Programs Let Applicants Know Immediately Whether They Have Been Accepted," *Chronicle of Higher Education,* April 12, 2002, A39.

26. Carolyn P. Griswold and Ginger M. Marine, "Political Influences on State Policy: Higher-Tuition, Higher-Aid and the Real World," *Review of Higher Education* 19, no. 4 (1996): 361–89.

27. David C. Mowery and A. Ziedonis, "Academic Patent Quality and Quantity Before and After the Bayh-Dole Act in the United States," *Research Policy,* 31 (2002): 399–418.

28. *Bayh-Dole Act 1980,* Public Law 96–517, 94 Stat. 3019.

29. Adam B. Jaffe, "The U. S. Patent System in Transition: Policy Innovation and the Innovation Process," *Research Policy* 29, no. 4–5 (2000): 5331–557.

30. Gary Rhoades and Sheila Slaughter, "Professors, Administrators, and Patents: The Negotiation of Technology Transfer," *Sociology of Education* 64, no. 2 (1991) 65–77; Gary Rhoades and Sheila Slaughter, "The Public Interest and Professional Labor: Research Universities," in *Culture and Ideology in Higher Education: Advancing a Critical Agenda,* ed. W. Tierney (New York: Praeger, 1991), 187–211.

31. Adam B. Jaffe, "The U. S. Patent System in Transition: Policy Innovation and the Innovation Process. *Research Policy* 29, no. 4–5 (2000): 5331–557.

32. Ibid.

33. Sheila Slaughter, *Higher Learning and High Technology: Dynamics of Higher Education Policy Formation* (Albany: State University of New York Press, 1990).

34. Henry Etzkowitz and M. Gulbrandsen, "Public Entrepreneur: The

Trajectory of United States Science, Technology and Industrial Policy," *Science and Public Policy* 26, no. 1 (1999): 53–62.

35. M. Feldman, I. Feller, J. Bercovitz, and R. Burton, "Equity and the Technology Transfer Strategies of American Research Universities," *Management Science* 48, no. 1 (2002): 105–21.

36. Sheila Slaughter and Gary Rhoades, *Academic Capitalism and the New Economy* (Baltimore: Johns Hopkins University Press, 2004).

37. Harvard Medical School, "Statement Regarding Canadian Supreme Court Decision December 5, 2002," www.harvard.edu/news/releases/125onco mouse.html.

38. Dorsey Griffith, "Researchers Roar over Oncomouse Restrictions," *Sacramento Bee,* November 2, 2003.

39. Association of University Technology Managers (AUTM), *AUTM Licensing Survey: FY 2001* (AUTM, 2003).

40. Council on Governmental Relations, "A Tutorial on Technology Transfer in U.S. Colleges and Universities," 1999, www.cogr.edu/techtransfer tutorial.htm.

41. *ATUM Licensing Survey,* 11–12.

42. National Science Board, *Science and Engineering Indicators—2002* (Arlington, VA: National Science Foundation [NSB-02-1], 2002).

43. Sheila Slaughter and Gary Rhodes, *Academic Capitalism and the New Economy* (Baltimore: Johns Hopkins University Press, 2004).

44. K. D. Crew, "New Copyright Law for Distance Education: The Meaning and Importance of the TEACH Act," 2002, www.copyright.iupui.edu/dist_ learning.htm (accessed March 1, 2003); University of Texas System, "Management and Marketing of Copyrighted Works," 1998, www.utsystem.edu/ bor/regentalpolicies/copyrightedworks.htm (accessed March 1, 2003).

45. University of Texas System.

46. Sheila Slaughter and Gary Rhoades, *Academic Capitalism and the New Economy* (Baltimore: Johns Hopkins University Press, 2004).

47. L. Lape, "Ownership of Copyrightable Works of University Professors: The Interplay between the Copyright Act and University Copyright Policies," *Villanova Law Review* 37 (1992): 223–71.

48. A. Packard, "Copyright or Copy Wrong: An Analysis of University Claims to Faculty Work," *Communication Law and Policy* 7 (2002): 275–315.

49. David F. Noble, *Digital Diploma Mills: The Automation of Higher Education* (New York: Monthly Review Press, 2001), 31.

50. G. A. Heeger, "President's Testimony to the Maryland General Assembly, February 8–9, 2001." Online archives of presidential addresses, www.umuc.edu/president/testimony/2001/testimony.html (accessed March 1, 2003).

51. University of Maryland University College (UMUC), "The UMUC

News Page: UMUC Awarded Tri-services Education Contract for Europe," 2003a, www.umuc.edu/events/press/news143.html (accessed February 28, 2003); UMUC, "About Us," University of Maryland University College home page, 2003b, www.umuc.edu/gen/about.html (accessed February 28, 2003).

52. N. E. Bowie, *University-Industry Partnerships: An Assessment* (Lanham, MD: Rowman and Littlefield, 1994); H. Etzkowitz, A. Webster, and P. Healey, *Capitalizing Knowledge: New Interactions of Industry and Academe* (Albany: State University of New York Press, 1998).

53. Peter Schmidt, "States Push Public Universities to Commercialize Research," *Chronicle of Higher Education*, March 29, 2002, A26–27.

Chapter Eighteen

Race in Higher Education

Making Meaning of an Elusive Moving Target

Mitchell J. Chang, Philip G. Altbach, and Kofi Lomotey

Racially charged issues continue to pose enormous challenges for U.S. higher education. Race manifests itself in many ways, from intolerant incidents on campus, to policy decisions concerning affirmative action, to debates on the infusion of multicultural content into the curriculum. In this chapter, we focus on the multifaceted, complex, and contentious elements of the present racial dynamics on campus. Certainly higher education is deeply affected by broader societal trends and policies. At the same time, the nature of higher education creates a set of circumstances, as discussed in other chapters in this volume, that enables racially charged issues to develop in ways that are unique to this context. Examining racially charged campus issues may in turn improve understanding about both contemporary higher education and broader U.S. race relations.

In the last decade, the campus issues that were widely viewed as being racially charged have become increasingly more complex and politicized. This is in part due to positive progress made on campus and also the tremendous shifts in the racial landscape particularly in terms of student body composition. Struggles inspired by the modern civil rights movement can be credited with those positive changes in higher education. At the same time, the progress made contributes to greater confusion in interpreting some of the most visible racial issues in higher education: enrollment gaps, the viability of historically black colleges and universities, curricular struggles, campus balkanization, and affirmative action.

On the one hand, gone are the days when only a handful of African American students protest alone to combat expressions of racial antipathy. When a racially hostile act is observed on campus (that is, use of racial slurs, threats to specific groups of students, promotion of negative racial images, etc.), for example, active calls for attention and redress now nearly always come from a large multiracial campus contingency of faculty, administrators, staff, and students.

On the other hand, gone also are the days when issues can be understood in only racial terms. Addressing the "achievement gap" between African Americans and their white and Asian Pacific American counterparts requires more than a discussion about intractable racial barriers, but must also consider other related factors such as chronic underemployment, malnutrition, environmental hazards, inner city crime, inadequate health care, economic downgrading of labor, and so on. The persistent educational gaps between racial groups, whether measured by test scores, grades, graduation rates, or degree aspiration, are now being considered and theorized in more complex ways that seek solutions that account for racial discrimination and other related factors.

One thing that has not changed, however, is that campus race relations are of concern not only to the underrepresented groups but also to everyone involved in the academic enterprise. For one thing, racial issues still have great potential for precipitating campus disruption. More important, racial issues pervade the entire university, from debates about the curriculum to relations in residence halls, from intercollegiate sports to key decisions on admissions. Yet these discussions and observations have also become more complicated. As explanations for how race structures educational opportunities and experiences grow increasingly more complex, making sense of racial dynamics becomes highly contested and more politically charged.

What we are currently experiencing as the climate in higher education evolves toward greater diversity and a more complete eradication of the most blatant forms of racism, is an increasingly more intense struggle to define the meaning of race. For the context of higher education, this struggle can be best observed by examining how scholars, journalists, policy makers, and pundits interpret the most visible and fiercely contested race-related issues. This struggle basically boils down to whether or not race structures life experiences and opportunities, and if so, to what extent. The often contradictory and competing interpretations contribute to the construction of racial meaning in U.S. society. This is not simply an academic exercise but this struggle has and will continue to have serious implications for higher education policy, as most recently evidenced by the U.S. Supreme Court ruling regarding the use of race conscious admissions practices. Before discussing this and other significant challenges in the last decade over defining racial meaning, it is important to highlight a key shift that complicates racial dynamics on campus.

Demographics

Adding to the complexity of racial dynamics in higher education is the continued rise in the number of students and faculty of color in U.S. colleges and universities. The changing demographics of the U.S. population as well as growing demands for four-year degrees have contributed to the growth in numbers of underrepresented students. These trends placed growing pressure on U.S. colleges and universities to commit themselves to increasing racial diversity and to improving services for underrepresented students. The pressure is especially strong on the public institutions because their well being is sensitive to ever-shifting taxpayer and state demands. Even though many programs that were initially established to increase the number of underrepresented students have been around since the 1970s, they are still clouded by controversy. Still, these efforts have managed to branch out to consider, for example, the recruitment and retention of underrepresented faculty, and have generally met with little success over the past several decades.

Although the enrollment of underrepresented groups has slowly begun to increase, there is still a significant gap between their enrollment rates and that of their white and Asian Pacific American (APA) counterparts. The trends have fluctuated in the last three decades. During the 1970s, the numbers of underrepresented students enrolled in four-year institutions increased significantly due largely to political and judicial pressure following a wave of civil rights legislation. By the 1980s, however, the growth rate for most groups had slowed but picked up again in the 1990s. According to U.S. Department of

Table 18.1

College Enrollment of Underrepresented Racial Groups, 2000

	African Americans	Latinos	American Indians
Share of 18- to 24-year-olds in U.S. population (%)	14.5	17.5	1.2
Share of overall college enrollment (%)	11.3	9.5	1.0
Share of two-year college enrollment (%)	12.4	14.2	1.3
Share of four-year college enrollment (%)	10.6	6.6	0.8
Share of graduate school enrollment (%)	8.5	5.2	0.6
Share of professional school enrollment (%)	7.7	5.0	0.8

Source: U.S. Census Bureau and U.S. Department of Education.

Education figures, the number of racial minority students in all four-year institutions increased from about 931,000 (approximately 13% of the total) in 1976 to nearly 1,866,000 (approximately 21.5%) in 1995. All racial minority groups showed some increase in proportion to the enrollment distribution during that period. By 1995, of all students enrolled in four-year institutions, more than 75 percent were white, 9.7 percent were African American, 5.5 percent were Latino, 5.5 percent were APA, and less than 1 percent were American Indian. As shown in table 18.1, as of 2000, the rates of enrollment for African Americans, Latinos, and American Indians are still lower than that of each group's eligible pool, with the exception of two-year colleges for American Indians.

In the foreseeable future, higher education will still need to contend with many of the unresolved enrollment-related issues identified in previous decades. Even though there have generally been gains made in college enrollment, the trajectory of progress for underrepresented populations seems to have reached a plateau even as their general representation in the U.S. population keeps increasing. African Americans, Native Americans, and Latinos are still dramatically underrepresented in basic and applied scientific fields (that is, mathematics, chemistry, medicine, engineering, etc.). These groups also have a relatively high dropout rate, and fewer go on to graduate or professional education. These trends contribute to their underrepresentation and in some fields their alarming absence in the academic profession.

While the above snapshot provides some general insight into enrollment gaps, it does not highlight many important related issues.

Surely, racial disparities in K–12 schooling, which intersect with other forces such as economic, social, and political disempowerment, are critical aspects of understanding enrollment gaps. Those gaps, however, can also appear wider or leaner, depending on the consideration of other factors in interpreting this problem. Below we will illustrate this by providing two examples of factors that matter for interpreting enrollment disparities. We highlight this rather than issues related to college access, retention, graduate studies, and entry into the academic profession, for which there is a great deal of literature, to stress the importance of interpretation, which contributes to constructing racial meaning.

One factor that is not discussed seriously enough is the distribution of students within the educational system. Some, like Brint and Karabel,[1] reasoned that the system of higher education is highly stratified and subsequently reproduces economic and social inequities. Using Carnegie classification categories to sort out 1996 enrollment figures, Trent et al.[2] found that African Americans, Native Americans, and— to a slightly lesser extent—Latinos are underrepresented in the research I sector compared with white and APA students. APAs are nearly three times more likely than their African American counterparts to be enrolled in the research I sector. These findings raise the level of concern about racial disparities in enrollment because those institutions classified in the research I category tend to produce a disproportionate share of the nation's leaders and have the most accomplished faculties and best facilities. This evidently has implications for life opportunities, particularly the pursuit of graduate and professional studies, and overall well being.[3] Viewed in light of enrollment differences by Carnegie classification, the disparities between groups appear to be wider and more serious.

Even though there are some glaring gaps between groups, demographic changes complicate their explanation. Such changes can significantly increase heterogeneity within the group, as is the case for Asian Pacific Americans (APAs). This population has more than doubled in absolute numbers since 1980, numbering about 10 million and comprising 3.5 percent of the total U.S. population in 2000. The growth has dramatically diversified the ethnic composition of the APA population. This within-group heterogeneity creates enormous difficulties in assessing their overall educational achievement, particularly as compared to other groups.

On the surface, APAs appear to be enrolling in higher education at above–national average rates; 55.1 percent of all APAs between ages eighteen and twenty-four were enrolled in college during 1990, compared with 34.4 percent for the total population. This gross figure, however, obscures critical ethnic disparities. Chinese, Japanese, Asian Indian, and Korean Americans were twice as likely as Hmong, Guamanian, Samoan, Hawaiian, and Laotian Americans to be enrolled in college. The 1990 college enrollment rates ranged from a high of 66.5 percent for Chinese Americans to a low of 26.3 percent for Laotian Americans.[4] Treating APAs monolithically by overlooking important ethnic differences and other important historical facts such as immigration policies, exaggerates the educational achievement of APAs and can result in discriminatory policies. For example, some of the most selective and prestigious institutions in the nation were charged in the late 1980s with intentionally capping APA enrollment to address their "overrepresentation."[5] This is significant, as clearly, several APA groups were underrepresented.

We raise these issues not to provide a full discussion of enrollment but to stress two important points about interpreting racial disparities in enrollment. First, differences between groups can be exacerbated by a number of other factors such as sector. When those factors are not considered, the seriousness of enrollment gaps may be underestimated. Second, differences between groups can also be overstated when within-group variability is ignored, as is the case for APAs. The issue of within-group heterogeneity, not only by ethnicity but also by immigration status, English language proficiency, class, and so on, should be considered when interpreting enrollment figures. Apparently, a recent study by sociologist John Logan shows that Latinos who classified themselves as "black," as compared with those who classified themselves as "white" or "other," have a lower median income, higher unemployment rate, and a higher poverty rate.[6] If this is the case, educational opportunities within the Latino population are likely to vary considerably based on those racial identifiers.

The above illustrates the complex realities of present-day racial dynamics in U.S. higher education. The increasing complexity does not only affect how we understand student-level outcomes such as enrollment and graduation rates but also how we understand institutional culture and climate. The inclusion of a significant number of underrepresented students on campus has also had implications for academic institutions that are not fully understood. In the early period of active recruitment for diversity, academic institutions failed to provide adequate support services for these new students; not surprisingly, dropout rates were extraordinarily high. Later, it was recognized that these students often required enhanced assistance to overcome the disadvantages of inadequate secondary-school preparation and to cope with an unfamiliar and frequently hostile environment. The subsequent provision of such services has proved costly in terms of financial and staff resources, engendering resentment from some white students.

The combination of increasing diversity on campus at all levels (students, faculty, administrators, etc.), institutional efforts to retain and engage students, conservative backlash, and the willingness of individuals of previously excluded groups to participate in transforming institutions on behalf of social justice elevates the visibility of race on campus. The struggles, negative incidents, and outcomes that emerge from this combination of factors can be understood in a number of ways that are at times contradictory. What we wish to discuss further is not all of the various interpretations or critical moments related to what we might broadly call diversity, but how the growing confusion and uncertainty about the racial landscape intensify the struggle over defining racial meaning. We view this struggle as a key factor influencing how racial antipathy, discrimination, and inequities are invariably addressed, if at all. To examine this, we will highlight a few issues that were at the forefront of racial discourse in higher education over the past decade. Each one of these has not yet been fully understood or resolved but has the potential for shaping racial meaning in the twenty-first century.

Increasing Challenges for Historically Black Colleges and Universities

Related to the discussion about enrollment distribution by sector is the continued importance of historically black colleges and universities (HBCUs). There are currently 103 HBCUs in twenty-two states and the U.S. Virgin Islands. Those institutions had a combined total enrollment of more than three hundred thousand students in 1998, where approximately 90 percent of those students were African American. Although HBCUs no longer account for the majority of black

B.A. degree recipients, as was the case in 1944 where more than 95 percent had attended and graduated from an HBCU, they still account for approximately 27 percent as of 1992.[7]

Despite the contributions of HBCUs toward the educational self-determination of African Americans, their future is uncertain because they have been persistently underfinanced. Their uncertainty is illustrated well through the dragged out settlement of the landmark case *U.S. v. Fordice*. This case has its roots in a 1975 suit filed by Jake Ayers in federal court, on behalf of his son and other students who attended historically black Jackson State University in Mississippi. He and others demanded that the state provide equal education at HBCUs by increasing their state resources and by improving their academic quality. When the U.S. Supreme Court ruled on this case in 1992, they charged that the Mississippi higher education system was still segregated but objected to providing more public funds solely to create "more equal" institutions that function as "black enclaves by private choice."[8]

The Court suggested closing and merging institutions since, in several southern cities—including Jackson, Mississippi, and Baton Rouge, Louisiana—predominantly white and historically black colleges and universities operate side by side. Mississippi state officials found this suggestion to be politically unfeasible. The controversy and pitfalls were made clear in 1994 when two thousand students marched from Jackson State University to the state capital, protesting a plan to close one historically black school in the state and make it a part of a predominantly white school. To desegregate the state's colleges and universities as part of the settlement plan, Mississippi proposed to enroll more black students at historically white institutions and add more programs and improve facilities at HBCUs to raise their quality and subsequently attract more white students. After many more years of litigation, a seventeen-year settlement plan was approved in February 2002, which would provide $503 million to upgrade academic programs, buildings, and endowments at three HBCUs in Mississippi, but appeals were still pending in 2003.[9] This case, like other situations where efforts have been made to make HBCUs attractive to whites, have consistently failed.

The *Fordice* example illustrates the difficulty many HBCUs now face. With only a few exceptions, nearly all of these institutions rely heavily on state and federal funding, largely because of the disadvantaged economic circumstances of the population that they traditionally serve. To receive the adequate funding, some HBCUs must comply with court-ordered desegregation plans, whose goals are to diversify the student body at those institutions. Having to operate within this context raises several pressing questions about the future of HBCUs. How will the upgrading of HBCUs affect historically white institutions' commitment to enrolling larger numbers of African American students? Will greater investment in HBCUs lead to a more diverse student population at those institutions? If so, how will the proportional decline of black enrollment affect the historic mission of HBCUs? Will changes in their mission affect the overall enrollment and degree attainment of African American students?

Despite the uncertainties that face HBCUs, it seems clear that they will remain a unique sector of the higher education system well into the twenty-first century. The federal government seems willing to ensure this. In 2002, President George W. Bush issued Executive Order 13256, which established a presidential advisory committee on HBCUs and urged all executive departments and agencies to support the continuance and development of HBCUs. In addition, because the facilities on many of these campuses have been eroding, the federal government introduced two Senate bills (S2613 and HR 1606) in June 2002 to restore and preserve facilities. Nevertheless, how the challenges facing HBCUs are interpreted and contested stand to shape racial meaning because HBCUs are viewed by some as antiquated with outdated missions.

Self-Segregation and Campus Balkanization

Not surprisingly, as the proportional enrollment of students of color increases, so do their social and co-curricular options. Institutions with more diverse student bodies tend to also offer a wider range of options for academic, social, cultural, and political integration and expression on campus. Increased options empower those marginalized students by enabling them to play a more significant role in campus life, which historically did not come altogether easily but frequently resulted from active persuasion, if not protest. What is interesting is that on more racially diverse campuses, a significant number of student clubs and organizations are organized by both race (for example, an organization for Asian students) and ethnicity (for example, organizations for Chinese, Korean, Taiwanese, and Indonesian students).

As the number of those student organizations increases, they are further differentiated by political, religious, career, and other interests (for example, organizations for Korean Christians, Asian feminists, Vietnamese entrepreneurs, etc.).

Some observers have expressed serious concerns about the strain and tension related to the proliferation of student organizations that are differentiated by racial and ethnic lines. The fear is that as the student body becomes more racially diverse, the campus necessarily becomes more racially divided or balkanized. Many charge that student clubs, as well as curriculum, organized around racial or ethnic groups foster students' tendency to self-segregate. Existing research, however, does not seem to support this charge, particularly the extent to which this occurs.[10] Moreover, Daryl Smith and her colleagues,[11] in their review of the literature, reported that there are educational benefits to organizing student groups and curricula with attention to race and ethnicity. For example, student organizations that are specifically designed to support students of color appear to contribute to those students' retention, adjustment, and attachment to their institution.

Although the degree of campus racial balkanization is often overstated and the source of racial tension can be attributed to a small percentage of students, how this phenomenon is invariably understood often guides the allocation of limited institutional resources and energy. There is a tendency, particularly among white students, to blame and charge those students of color who prefer to socialize within their own racial group of self-segregating themselves. This interpretation often fails to consider the broader historical, cultural, and social forces that shape those tendencies, as well as lingering vestiges of institutional racism that are rarely ever fully addressed but compound campus racial tension.[12] It also fails to call into question the same tendencies of members of historically white social Greek organizations. Their membership, particularly in the most sought after organizations, continues to include disproportionally more white students than is reflected in the student body.

Despite the many problems with such an interpretation of campus racial dynamics, it has gained currency in constructing racial meaning, and subsequently, has led to highly problematic decision making. If racially and ethnically organized student clubs are viewed as a problem for campus race relations, then administrators will be motivated to dissolve existing organizations or limit their funding. Ironically, such action will more likely increase rather than decrease racial tension on campus.

Curriculum

Another flashpoint of controversy that will likely persist well into the next decade are calls for multicultural and ethnic studies in the curriculum. Students have actively pressed for such educational offerings on two fronts, demanding the expansion of ethnic studies programs, such as African American studies and Chicano studies, and calling for a meaningful integration of those perspectives into the entire curriculum. The fundamental purpose of these demands is basically to transform academic culture by redefining and reshaping general education, the nature of scholarship, the practice and methods of research, expectations for pedagogy, the empowerment of diverse students, and the engagement with communities. These curricular demands have aroused a good deal of opposition from faculty, who oppose tampering with the traditional curriculum, and from administrators, who fear increased costs from the creation of new specializations and courses.

Nevertheless, through political pressure and activist movements that date back to the late 1960s, these course offerings and programs continue to flourish. For example, before 1990, nineteen institutions of higher education offered programs in Asian American studies, but by 1998, there were at least thirty-seven such programs or academic units according to a directory compiled by the Association for Asian American Studies. Whereas Chicano/Latino studies is also experiencing growth, the number of African American/black studies programs and departments that grew dramatically during the 1960s and early 1970s, has stabilized. Yet comparatively, African American studies is generally much more firmly established and visible, especially at the oldest and most prestigious institutions.

Even with their recent growth, documented impact, and enhanced reputation, ethnic studies have not fully escaped from controversies that are all too similar to those experienced in the early years of their development. The most prominent and firmly established programs are by no means free from administrative meddling and challenges that undermine program stability. At Harvard University, for example, a clash in fall 2001 between Cornel West, university professor of Afro-American studies and newly appointed Harvard Presi-

528   Mitchell J. Chang, Philip G. Altbach, and Kofi Lomotey

dent Lawrence Summers made academic headlines. Some observers viewed their private meeting to discuss Professor West's scholarly work and grading practices, as a sign that the president viewed the Afro-American Studies Department as lacking high academic standards and integrity. Eventually, Professor West and another well-known colleague from the department left to take positions at Princeton University.

Gaining the necessary financial and administrative support still seems to be a struggle for other top programs. In May 1993 at the University of California, Los Angeles, for example, demonstrators smashed large plate-glass windows in the Faculty Center, where they also damaged furniture and a painting during a two-hour occupation after the university refused to grant the interdepartmental program departmental status. The police arrested ninety-nine protesters at the scene after breaking up the sit-in. A few weeks later, students, community members, and a faculty member went on a hunger strike to demand the creation of a Chicano studies department. In June of the same year, the university agreed to create the Cesar Chavez Center for Interdisciplinary Instruction but did not agree to grant departmental status, ending the hunger strike.

As more programs mature in a context of shrinking resources and white backlash fueled during the Reagan and Bush I administrations, such struggles observed at Harvard and UCLA will likely become more widespread. Yet, despite persistent opposition by conservative critics, it is clear that ethnic studies and the infusion of what Lawrence Levine[13] calls "a more eclectic, open, culturally diverse, and relevant curriculum" will become an even more prevalent feature of U.S. higher education. After overcoming difficult obstacles, those efforts are now fairly well institutionalized and are perhaps the most important legacy of the campus unrest of the 1960s and the rise of racial consciousness.[14]

Although advocates continue to fear that the substance and sustainability of those curricular efforts will be undermined by inadequate funding, white backlash, and hostile administrative maneuverings, attention should also be given to other important issues related to the success of this movement. For example, as programs become more institutionalized and mainstreamed, some fear that they may lose their "edge" in critiquing and challenging prevailing notions of power, privilege, and authority. Additionally, academic success can potentially turn attention away from those communities that inspired these fields of study, toward more inaccessible scholarship that is removed from community interests and involvement.[15] Unlike the earlier years of ethnic studies, faculty members are now more likely to have their roots in traditional academic scholarship rather than in community-minded activism. How these program and curricular shifts are interpreted will have implications for not only how they will invariably be addressed but also how race is understood in higher education.

Affirmative Action

Perhaps the single issue in recent years that most dominated racial discourse in higher education concerns the high-stakes controversy surrounding affirmative action. African Americans in particular had an enormous amount at stake because if colleges and universities were forced to admit students based solely on grades and test scores, their enrollment at the nation's most selective colleges would likely plummet from about 6 percent to less than 2 percent. Given the real or perceived stakes, this poorly defined policy captivated the attention of race experts across the nation and eventually required intervention by the U.S. Supreme Court.

The application of affirmative action has always been a topic of fierce debate since the Nixon administration pushed through the "Philadelphia Plan" in 1969.[16] This plan called for specific percentage targets of minority employees in several construction-related trades to be set forth in Philadelphia and incorporated these targets into the bid specification in all government contracts issued in that area. Two years after the Philadelphia Plan was implemented, the U.S. Supreme Court legitimized a race-conscious affirmative action model to address racial imbalance in their decision of *Griggs v. Duke Power Company*. These decisions and policies set in motion a backlash of bitter challenges to race-conscious models of affirmative action that would in the most critical moments involve higher education.

In 1978, the U.S. Supreme Court would narrow the application of affirmative action in its ruling of *Regents of the University of California v. Bakke*. This case was filed by Alan Bakke who was denied admission in 1973 and 1974 to the medical school at the University of California, Davis, and pointed to the university's voluntary affirmative action program as the main reason for the denials. The university had set aside sixteen of the one hundred spots in the first-year class for "economically and/or educationally disadvantaged" applicants. For these sixteen spots, applicants were not subjected to the same 2.5 GPA cutoff and not compared against applicants in the regular process. Bakke argued that he was better qualified according to traditional criteria than many of the minorities admitted under the special program. He claimed that the school denied him admission because of his race and thus violated his rights under Title VI and the Fourteenth Amendment.

The Supreme Court was deeply splintered over this landmark case, and issued six separate opinions. Because Justice Lewis Powell played a pivotal and decisive role, his opinion is now regularly cited to explain the resulting decision. In their defense, the University of California, Davis, medical school offered four reasons for pursuing their race conscious admissions practices. Justice Powell rejected three of those reasons. He rejected the medical school's interest in using race to reduce the lack of minorities because he believed that the state could not grant benefits solely on racial or ethnic identity. Likewise, he rejected their interest in countering the effects of societal discrimination because this interest, he believed, was not legitimate unless there were formal findings of violations from that institution. Lastly, because there was no compelling empirical evidence, he rejected the medical school's interest in increasing the number of physicians who practice in communities that lack adequate medical services.

Powell, however, accepted the medical school's argument for using race as one of many factors to achieve the benefits that flow from a diverse student body. Explaining this decision, Powell argued that the attainment of a diverse student body broadens the range of viewpoints held by the student body and subsequently allows a university to provide for students an atmosphere that is "conducive to speculation, experiment and creation." This type of atmosphere, he argued, enhances the training of the student body and better equips the institution's graduates. Because Powell believed that such goals are essential to the quality of higher education, he concluded that race-conscious admissions practices when narrowly tailored serve a compelling educational interest.

Although the Supreme Court banned the use of quotas in *Bakke,* they still made available to colleges and universities the consideration of race in more limited ways when making admissions decisions. Even after this ruling by the highest court in the nation, efforts to dismantle altogether race-conscious practices continued and intensified in the mid-1990s. In 1994, the Fourth Circuit Court of Appeals ruled in *Podberesky v. Kirwan* that a special scholarship (Banneker Scholarship Program) for African American students at the University of Maryland, College Park, was unconstitutional. Although this did not directly affect admissions practices, it still weakened race-conscious considerations in higher education. The Fifth Circuit Court of Appeals in 1996 was the first to send a strong negative message about the *Bakke* ruling, specifically Justice Powell's diversity rationale. In the *Hopwood* case, the court ruled in favor of four white plaintiffs who claimed "reverse discrimination," when they were denied admissions to the law school at the University of Texas, Austin.

Later that same year, Californian voters passed by a slim margin (54% to 46%) Proposition 209, which prohibited "preferential treatment" based on sex, color, ethnicity, or national origin. Two years later in 1998, Washington State passed Initiative Measure 200 (I200). Other cases similar to *Hopwood* also reached federal appeals court. In 2000, the Ninth Circuit Court of Appeals ruled on *Smith v. University of Washington Law School* and upheld the law school's race-conscious admissions policy, but the claim and decision were moot because the state had already passed I200. In 2001, the Eleventh Circuit Court of Appeals ruled in *Johnson v. Board of Regents of the University of Georgia* that the University's race-conscious admissions practices were unlawful. Such mixed decisions in the appeals courts put pressure on the Supreme Court to provide greater clarity of such practices.

In 2002, the Supreme Court decided to hear simultaneously two lawsuits alleging that the University of Michigan through its race-conscious admissions practices, violated both Title VI of the 1964 Civil Rights Act and equal protection under the Fourteenth Amendment. On June 23, 2003, the court ruled on both the undergraduate (*Gratz v. Bollinger*) and the law school (*Grutter v. Bollinger*) cases. In their decision, the court upheld the law school's practice of considering race by a margin of five to four but struck down the formulaic appraisal system for admitting freshmen by a margin of six to three. Even though the court narrowed the use of race by rejecting mechanical scoring systems that assign bonus points to underrepresented students, they basically left the door open for colleges and universities to continue to consider race as one factor in admissions. This marked the first time since the 1978 *Bakke* decision that the Supreme Court has ruled on the application of affirmative action in higher education.

The court's decision regarding the University of Michigan basically reaffirms much of Justice Lewis Powell's opinion in *Bakke,* namely that race can be applied appropriately as a "plus" factor in a narrowly tailored fashion when admitting students. Thus, proponents of affirmative action view the Michigan decisions as an important victory.

Most likely, the decisions will not end the controversy and the litigation. Justice Antonin Scalia, who wrote a dissenting opinion in *Grutter,* exposed a long list of problems associated with this ruling, which can potentially bring on similar lawsuits in the future. Moreover, just two weeks after the Supreme Court decision, Ward Connerly, one of the main architects behind California's Proposition 209, announced a campaign to put a similar initiative on the Michigan ballot. Given that the struggle over race-conscious models of affirmative action is far from over, the *Grutter* decision should not lull colleges and universities into complacency, but instead should invigorate serious attempts to address racial disparities and to realize the educational benefits that flow from diversity. After all, the Supreme Court expects institutions to cease diversity-enhancing race-conscious affirmative action by the year 2028.

In regards to the construction of racial meaning, there are simply too many implications that emerge from the affirmative action debates in higher education to address adequately here. The debates and developments have profoundly disrupted campus racial dynamics, especially at those institutions where the student body composition would be most affected by the abolishment of race-conscious admissions practices. The increased demonstrations and protest on behalf of affirmative action has not helped to mitigate existing resentment about perceived "special advantages" given to underrepresented students and faculty who are viewed by some as being less qualified. Certainly, how these campus-related issues are understood contributes to racial meaning.

We will highlight at least one of the many issues related to the Michigan cases, which has broader implications for racial meaning. As the cases made their way toward the Supreme Court, underrepresented students sought to serve as intervening defendants so as to offer the courts an alternative justification for race-conscious admissions policies. They essentially argued that the university needs such policies because it has repeatedly engaged in racially discriminatory and exclusionary practices, the effects of which continue to be seen on the campus. They charged, for example, that the university operated racially segregated campus housing and allowed black students to be excluded from fraternities and sororities until the 1960s, and that many of its subsequent efforts to recruit and retain minority students came about only in response to student unrest. They claimed that the vestiges of these actions continue to be felt by black and Latino students who generally remain racially isolated on the campus and are still subjected to racially hostile actions. They also charged that white applicants are systematically given unearned benefits and privileges that keep the deck stacked against minority applicants. For example, children of alumni, who are overwhelmingly white, receive four extra points on the former University of Michigan's 150-point undergraduate applicant-rating scale.

These and other remedial justification arguments that sought to draw attention to persistent societal discrimination did not have much leverage with the Supreme Court, which has consistently rejected the use of affirmative action as a remedy for anything other than proven acts of discrimination by specific institutions. The student intervenors were denied an opportunity to present oral arguments to the justices. In the end, no justice embraced the view that societal discrimination justifies race-conscious admissions, although some acknowledged that inequalities are structured by race. Curiously, twenty-five years earlier, four justices embraced remedial justification arguments in *Bakke*. So, although race-conscious affirmative action survived recent attacks, the ruling further weakened reparative justice rationales for policies that seek to assist historically disadvantaged racial minorities. Because remedial arguments initially propelled those policies, this insistent weakening will likely further limit the scope and duration of more systematic efforts to rectify past and present racism.

Conclusion

Race in higher education is a complicated issue and a moving target. Perhaps for this reason, there has been no major breakthrough in resolving what was characterized over a decade ago as a "racial crisis" in U.S. higher education.[17] We are, however, beginning to understand better the modern forms of racial discrimination,[18] how compositional shifts in the student body affect campus climate,[19] how societal and psychological forces interplay to depress academic performance,[20] and whether there are educational benefits associated with diversity,[21] to name a few.

In this chapter, we elected to highlight the complexities of racial dynamics rather than offer a comprehensive description of how race operates in colleges and universities. In doing this, we described a few key developments and issues that have recently dominated racial discourse. Although our approach does not offer any hard answers or solutions, it shows that there is an intense struggle being waged over establishing racial meaning, and this struggle has very real consequences for how racial antipathy, discrimination, and inequities are subsequently addressed, if at all.

The meaning of race in higher education is very much up for grabs as observations regarding race shift in ways that become increasingly more complex and ambiguous, yet more highly politicized. For this reason, we believe that there has to be more serious attention to the construction and refutation of racial meaning in efforts to repair what Randall Kennedy[22] calls "the gaping wounds caused by innumerable racist actions and inactions that have fundamentally betrayed America's most noble aspirations." The challenge for the next twenty-five years will not be just to make a few modest gains or avert potentially serious rollback of civil rights inspired policies. As put forth by the Supreme Court in *Grutter,* the challenge will essentially be to resolve the race problem in education, as the sun may well fully set on race conscious policies. When that time comes, will it really mean that race no longer matters? And, will this established meaning emerge from an ideological and political victory or from thoughtful consideration of empirical evidence?

NOTES

1. Steven Brint and Jerome Karabel, *The Diverted Dream: Community Colleges and the Promise of Educational Opportunity in America, 1900–1985* (New York: Oxford University Press, 1989).

2. William Trent, et al., "Justice, Equality of Educational Opportunity and Affirmative Action in Higher Education," in *Compelling Interests: Examining the Evidence on Racial Dynamics in Colleges and Universities,* eds. Mitchell J. Chang, et al. (Stanford, CA: Stanford University Press, 2003), 22–48.

3. William G. Bowen and Derek Bok, *The Shape of the River: Long-term*

Consequences of Considering Race in College and University Admissions (Princeton, NJ: Princeton University Press, 1998).

4. Shirley Hune and Kenyon S. Chan, "Special Focus: Asian Pacific American Demographic and Educational Trends," in *Minorities in Higher Education,* eds. Deborah J. Carter and Reginald Wilson (Washington, D.C.: American Council on Education, 1997), 39–107.

5. Dana Y. Takagi, *Retreat from Race: Asian-American Admissions and Racial Politics* (New Brunswick, NJ: Rutgers University Press, 1992).

6. Daniel Hernandez, "Report Shows How Racial Identities Affect Latinos," *Los Angeles Times,* July 15, 2003, A-16.

7. Walter R. Allen and Joseph O. Jewell, "African American Education Since An American Dilemma," *Daedalus* 124, no. 1 (1995): 77–100.

8. Sara Hebel, "A Pivotal Moment for Desegregation," *Chronicle of Higher Education,* October 27, 2000, A26.

9. Sara Hebel, "Desegregation Lawsuits Wind Down, but to What Effect?" *Chronicle of Higher Education,* April 12, 2002, A28.

10. Anthony Lising Antonio, "Diversity and the Influence of Friendship Groups in College," *Review of Higher Education* 25, no. 1 (2001): 63–89.

11. Daryl G. Smith, et al., *Diversity Works: The Emerging Picture of How Students Benefit* (Washington, D.C.: Association of American Colleges and Universities, 1997).

12. Mitchell J. Chang, "Racial Dynamics on Campus: What Student Organizations Can Tell Us," *About Campus* 7, no. 1 (2002): 2–8.

13. Lawrence W. Levine, *The Opening of the American Mind* (Boston: Beacon, 1996).

14. Thomas J. La Belle and Christopher R. Ward, *Ethnic Studies and Multiculturalism* (Albany, NY: SUNY Press, 1996).

15. Glenn Omatsu, "The 'Four Prisons' and the Movements of Liberation: Asian American Activism from the 1960s to the 1990s," in *The State of Asian America: Activism and Resistance in the 1990s,* ed. Karen Aguilar-San Juan (Boston: South End Press, 1994), 19–69.

16. John D. Skrentny, *The Ironies of Affirmative Action: Politics, Culture, and Justice in America* (Chicago: University of Chicago Press, 1996).

17. Philip G. Altbach and Kofi Lomotey, eds., *The Racial Crisis in American Higher Education* (Albany, NY: SUNY Press, 1991).

18. Shana Levin, "Social Psychological Evidence on Race and Racism," in *Compelling Interest: Examining the Evidence on Racial Dynamics in Colleges and Universities,* ed. Mitchell J. Chang, et al. (Stanford, CA: Stanford University Press, 2003), 97–125.

19. Sylvia Hurtado, et al., *Enacting Diverse Learning Environments: Improving the Climate for Racial/Ethnic Diversity in Higher Education Institutions* (Washington, D.C.: ASHE-ERIC Higher Education Report Series: George Washington University Graduate School of Education, 1999).

20. Claude M. Steele and Joshua Aronson, "Stereotype Threat and the Intellectual Test Performance of African Americans," *Journal of Personality and Social Psychology* 69 (1995): 797–811.

21. Jeffrey F. Milem and Kenji Hakuta, "The Benefits of Racial and Ethnic Diversity in Higher Education," in *Minorities in Higher Education: Seventeenth Annual Status Report,* ed. Deborah J. Wilds (Washington, D.C.: American Council on Education, 2000), 39–67.

22. Randall Kennedy, "Affirmative Reaction: The Courts, the Right and the Race Question," *American Prospect,* March 2003.

≫ Contributors

PHILIP G. ALTBACH is J. Donald Monan, SJ, Professor of higher education and director of the Center for International Higher Education at Boston College. He served as editor of the *Review of Higher Education.* He has written widely on higher education and is author of *Comparative Higher Education, The Knowledge Context, Student Politics in America,* and other books. He edited *International Higher Education: An Encyclopedia.*

MICHAEL N. BASTEDO is an assistant professor of higher education at the University of Michigan. His work has been published in the *Review of Higher Education, Higher Education,* and *Higher Education in the United States: An Encyclopedia.*

ROBERT O. BERDAHL is a professor emeritus of higher education in the College of Education, University of Maryland, College Park. He has written extensively on governance issues and on statewide coordination in higher education.

ROBERT BIRNBAUM is a professor emeritus of higher education at the University of Maryland, College Park. He has served as chancellor of the University of Wisconsin-Oshkosh. He is author of *How Colleges Work: The Cybernetics of Academic Organization and Leadership* and other books.

MITCHELL J. CHANG is an associate professor of higher education and organizational change at the University of California, Los Angeles, and a faculty adviser for the Asian American Studies program. He served as the lead editor of *Compelling Interest: Examining the Evidence on Racial Dynamics in Higher Education.* This book was cited in the U.S. Supreme Court ruling of *Grutter v. Bollinger,* one of two cases involving the use of race-sensitive admissions practices at the University of Michigan.

MARC CHUN is a research scientist at the RAND Corporation's Council for Aid to Education. He is a graduate of Stanford University, held a postdoctoral fellowship in sociology and education at Columbia University's Teachers College, and has taught sociology at The New School University and Manhattan College. His research focuses on social epistemology, organizational ideology, and the construction of knowledge.

MELANIE E. CORRIGAN is an assistant director of the Center for Policy Analysis at the American Council on Education. Before joining ACE, she conducted federal policy analysis and research for the National Association of Independent College and Universities.

ERIC L. DEY is an associate professor of higher education in the Center for the Study of Higher and Postsecondary Education at the University of Michigan and is associate dean of the School of Education. He was one of the chief architects of the social science research that supported the University of Michigan's legal position on the use of affirmative action in college admissions recently reviewed by the U.S. Supreme Court. He previously directed the Cooperative Institutional Research Program at the Higher Education Research Institute at the University of California, Los Angeles.

JUDITH S. EATON is president of the Council for Higher Education Accreditation (CHEA), an institutional membership organization of degree-granting colleges and universities based in Washington, D.C. Before joining CHEA, she served as chancellor of the Minnesota State Colleges and Universities, president of Community College of Philadelphia, and president of the Community College of Southern Nevada.

PETER D. ECKEL is associate director for institutional initiatives at the American Council on Education. He is the author of *Changing Course: Making the Hard Decisions to Eliminate Academic Programs* and co-author of *Taking the Reins: Institutional Transformation in Higher Education* (with Adrianna Kezar).

ROGER L. GEIGER is distinguished professor of higher education at Pennsylvania State University. He is author of *Research and Relevant*

Knowledge: American Research Universities Since World War II and is editor of the *History of Higher Education Annual.*

LAWRENCE E. GLADIEUX is an independent consultant whose clients have included the Century Foundation, EdFund of California, the National Center for Public Policy and Higher Education, the College Board, and the U.S. Department of Education. From 1981 to 2000, he served as Washington representative and policy director for the College Board.

PATRICIA J. GUMPORT is professor of education and director of the doctoral program in higher education at Stanford University. She serves concurrently as director of the Stanford Institute for Higher Education Research (SIHER) and the National Center for Postsecondary Improvement (NCPI).

FRED F. HARCLEROAD is professor emeritus of higher education at the University of Arizona and founding director of the Center for the Study of Higher Education there. Previously he served as founding president of the California State University at Hayward and as president of the American College Testing Program.

SYLVIA HURTADO is an associate professor of higher education at the University of California, Los Angeles. She previously served as a University of California President's Postdoctoral Scholar in Sociology at the University of California, Los Angeles.

D. BRUCE JOHNSTONE is a university professor of higher and comparative education at the State University of New York at Buffalo. He has served as president of the State University College at Buffalo and as chancellor of the State University of New York. He has written extensively on the economics and finances of higher education and related policy issues, particularly student financial assistance, state and federal financial support, and related topics.

JACQUELINE E. KING is founding director of the Center for Policy Analysis at the American Council on Education (ACE). Before assuming this role in October 2000, she served for four years as director of federal policy in the ACE division of government and public affairs and for two years as associate director for policy analysis at the College Board. She is editor of *Financing a College Education: How It Works, How It's Changing.*

KOFI LOMOTEY is president of Fort Valley State University in Georgia. He was provost of Medgar Evers College of the City University of New York and has taught at the State University of New York at Buffalo. He has published several books, articles, and chapters dealing with African American education and is co-editor, with Philip G. Altbach, of *The Racial Crisis in American Higher Education.* He is editor of *Urban Education.*

AIMS C. MCGUINNESS, JR., is a senior associate with the National Center for Higher Education Management Systems, Boulder, Colorado. He was previously at the Education Commission of the States (ECS). He has advised many states on major higher education reforms and also has been involved in international projects of the World Bank and the Organization for Economic Cooperation and Development.

MICHAEL A. OLIVAS is William B. Bates Distinguished Chair in Law and director of the Center for Higher Education Law and Governance at the University of Houston Law Center. Among his books are *The Law and Higher Education; Prepaid College Tuition Plans;* and the forthcoming *Dollars, Scholars, and Public Policy.*

ROBERT M. O'NEIL is professor of law and director of the Thomas Jefferson Center for the Protection of Free Expression at the University of Virginia. He served as president of the University of Wisconsin System from 1980 to 1985 and of the University of Virginia from 1985 to 1990. He has served as a trustee of several corporations and non-profit agencies, including the Carnegie Foundation for the Advancement of Teaching and the Educational Testing Service.

GARY RHOADES is a professor of higher education and director of the Center for the Study of Higher Education at the University of Arizona. He is president of the Association for the Study of Higher Education.

FRANK A. SCHMIDTLEIN is an associate professor emeritus in the Department of Education Policy and Leadership at the University of

Maryland, College Park. He serves as an associate editor of the *Higher Education Planning* and on the editorial board of *Tertiary Education and Management.*

SHEILA SLAUGHTER is a professor of higher education at the University of Arizona. She is co-author, with Larry L. Leslie, of *Academic Capitalism: Politics, Policies, and the Entrepreneurial University* and of *Higher Learning and High Technology.*

AMI ZUSMAN is coordinator of graduate education planning and analysis for the nine-campus University of California System, where she is responsible for graduate enrollment planning, workforce analysis, and assessment of graduate student outcomes. She has authored reports and articles on public and institutional policy issues in higher education, particularly on graduate education, state policy, system-level governance and policy, and higher education's relationships with K–12 education.

policies and, 108–9, 113; technology and, 404

research/teaching balance. *See* teaching/research balance

retention, student, 334–35

retrenchment, 122–23, 302–3

Rhode Island, College of, 41

Rice University, 227

Rockefeller, John D., 434

Rockefeller Foundation, 60, 256, 434

Rockefeller Institute of Medicine, 434

Roosevelt Theodore, 437

Ross v. Creighton University, 236

Rudolph, Frederick, 465

Rutgers University, 97

Sanford, Nevitt, 428

San Jose State University, 396

SAT. *See* Scholastic Aptitude Test

Scallet v. Rosenblum, 233

Scholastic Aptitude Test, 494, 501

Scott v. University of Delaware, 232–33

Scripps College, 271

Second Great Awakening, 44–45, 474

September 11, 108–13

service learning, 477–78

Servicemen Readjustment Act. *See* GI Bill

SEVIS. *See* Student and Exchange Visitor Information System

sexual harassment, 100–103, 245–46

Shapiro v. Columbia University National Bank and Trust Co., 227

Silva v. University of New Hampshire, 241–42

Sixteenth Amendment, 256

Slaughter, Sheila, 122–23

Sloan, Douglas, 462

Small Business Innovation Development Act, 497

Smith, Sophia, 53

Smithsonian Institution, 168

Smith v. University of Washington Law School, 531

Social Sciences Research Council, 436

South Carolina, College of, 45, 50

Southeast Asia, 16, 20

Southern Association of Colleges and Schools, 263, 281

Southern California, University of, 58, 103

Southern Regional Education Board, 275–77, 280

South Florida, University of, 111

South Korea, 21

Spain, 16–17

Spelman College, 271

SPREs. *See* state postsecondary review entities

Spuler v. Pickar, 232

Sputnik, 63, 164, 174, 293, 437

Stafford Loans, 443

Stanford Humanities Center, 446

Stanford University, 53, 292, 430; controversy over indirect costs at, 173, 194; indirect cost rates at, 449; technology at, 396–97, 418

state coordinating boards, 146, 148–49 208–10, 220–21, 347

State Data Exchange, 276

State ex rel. McLendon v. Clarksville School of Theology, 232

state governing boards, 146, 148–49, 207–11, 220; accountability to, 78–79, 88; autonomy and, 73; categories of, 207–9; constitutional status for, 77–78; governors and, 79; increasing influence by, 79; presidential discretion and, 347; statutory status of, 78

state government/higher education relations, 73–75, 77–82, 87–88, 116–24, 142–49, 164–67, 198–222, 254, 203–5, 347; differences in, 206–14; public agenda and, 217–22; structural and governance reorganizations, 149, 214–20

"Statement of Principles on Academic Freedom and Tenure," 93

State Policy and Community College-Baccalaureate Transfer, 258

state postsecondary review entities (SPREs), 187, 270

State Prepaid Tuition Plans, 191

State Student Incentive Grant, 175

DATE DUE

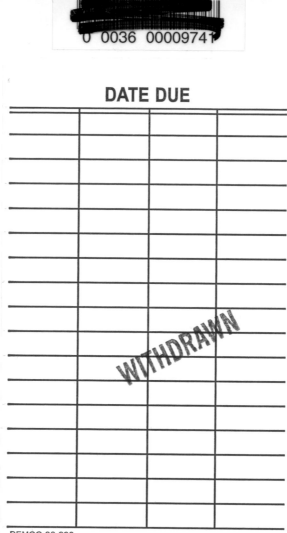

DEMCO 38-296